Windows Shortcut Keys

Press	To
F1	Display general help screens or context-sens
Alt+F4	Exit a program or shut down Windows (if n⌐
Shift+F10	Display the context menu for the selected object.
Ctrl+Esc	Activate the taskbar and open the Start menu.
Alt+Tab	Switch to the program window that was previously active.
Ctrl+X	Cut the selected object.
Ctrl+C	Copy the selected object.
Ctrl+V	Insert the cut or copied object.
Ctrl+Z	Undo the previous action.
Delete	Delete the selected object.
Shift+Delete	Delete the selected file or folder permanently without moving it to the Recycle Bin.
Ctrl+A	Select all objects (in My Computer or Windows Explorer).
F5	Refresh the My Computer or Windows Explorer window.
Backspace	View the folder one level up from the current folder.
F2	Rename the selected icon.
F3	Find a folder or file.
Shift	Disable AutoPlay for the CD-ROM you are inserting.
	Open the Start menu.
+Tab	Cycle through open application windows.
+F	Search for a file or folder on your PC.
Ctrl++F	Search for a computer on your network.
+F1	Display Windows help.
+R	Display the Run dialog box.
+Break	Display the System Properties dialog box.
+E	Run Windows Explorer.
+D	Minimize or restore all open application windows to return to the desktop.
Shift++M	Undo maximize all windows.

CW00706390

Internet Explorer Toolbar Buttons

Click	To
Back	Move back to the previous page.
Forward	Display the next page (if you backed up).
Stop	Stop loading the current page.
Refresh	Reload the current page.
Home	Return to the opening page.
Search	Find information, resources, and people on the Internet.
Favorites	Display a list of Web sites you added to the Favorites list.
History	Display a list of recently opened Web pages.
Channels	Display the Channel Bar to quickly load premium-quality Web content.
Fullscreen	Hide everything except the current Web page and the toolbar.
Mail	Run Outlook Express to check for incoming email messages.

Using and Upgrading PCs

Windows Explorer Toolbar Buttons

Click	To
Back	Display the previous screen.
Forward	Display the next screen (if you backed up).
Up	Display the contents of the folder one level up from the current folder.
Cut	Cut the currently selected file(s) or folder(s) to move them.
Copy	Copy the currently selected file(s) or folder(s).
Paste	Paste the cut or copied file(s) or folder(s).
Undo	Undo the previous action.
Delete	Delete the selected file(s) or folder(s).
Properties	Display the properties of the selected disk, file, folder, or shortcut.
Views	Change the way Windows Explorer lists files and folders.

Windows Control Panel Icons

Click	To
	Access options for users with disabilities.
	Install the software required for using a new hardware device.
	Install or remove a Windows program.
	Change the date or time on your PC.
	Adjust the display properties for your video card and monitor.
	Add or remove type styles on your PC.
	Calibrate your joystick.
	Set up an Internet connection.
	Change the key repeat delay and repeat rate for your keyboard.
	Enter settings for your modem.
	Change the mouse pointer speed, double-click interval, and mouse pointers.
	Adjust the settings for your audio and video players.
	Enter settings for connecting two or more computers on a network.
	Configure Windows for multiple users.
	Conserve power on a desktop or notebook PC.
	Set up a printer in Windows.
	Choose a time zone and enter preferences for how the time, date, numbers, and currency are displayed in your Windows programs.
	Assign different audio clips to various events in Windows.
	Display settings for optimizing your PC and controlling your system's hardware.
	Enter settings to tell your modem how to dial out.
	Run a wizard to set up your PC for multiple users.

Using

and

Upgrading

PCs

Joe Kraynak

que

A Division of Macmillan Computer Publishing, USA
201 W. 103rd Street
Indianapolis, Indiana 46290

Contents at a Glance

Using and Upgrading PCs

International Standard Book Number: 0-7897-1607-0

Library of Congress Catalog Card Number: 97-81179

Printed in the United States of America

First Printing: October 1998

00   99   98   4   3   2   1

Trademarks

Executive Editor
Angela Wethington

Acquisitions Editor
Stephanie McComb

Development Editor
John Gosney

Managing Editor
Thomas F. Hayes

Project Editor
Lori A. Lyons

Copy Editor
Julie McNamee

Technical Editor
Kyle Bryant

Indexer
Joy Dean Lee

Layout Technician
Marcia Deboy
Susan Geiselman

Proofreader
Elizabeth Deeter-Smith

Contents

Dedication

To my wife, Cecie.

About the Author

Joe Kraynak has been writing and editing computer books and other technical material for over 10 years. His long list of computer books include *The Complete Idiot's Guide to PCs*, *The Big Basics Book of Windows 98*, *10 Minute Guide to Excel*, *Easy Internet*, and *Windows 95 Cheat Sheet*. Joe graduated from Purdue University in 1984 with a Master's degree in English, a Bachelor's degree in Philosophy and Creative Writing, and a strong commitment to making computers and software easily accessible to the average user.

Acknowledgments

Several people contributed their talent and hard work into making this a successful book. Special thanks to Stephanie McComb, acquisitions editor, for choosing me to write this book and to John Gosney, development editor, for guiding the content of this book and keeping it focused on new users. Thanks to Kyle Bryant, technical reviewer, for making sure the information in this book is accurate and up-to-date. Thanks also to Julie McNamee, copy editor, for her attention to detail and to Lori Lyons, project editor, for seeing this book through the production process. The Macmillan design and production team merits a round of applause for transforming a collection of electronic files into such an attractive, bound book.

Tell Us What You Think!

As the reader of this book, *you* are our most important critic and commentator. We value your opinion and want to know what we're doing right, what we could do better, what areas you'd like to see us publish in, and any other words of wisdom you're willing to pass our way.

As the Executive Editor for the General Desktop Applications team at Macmillan Computer Publishing, I welcome your comments. You can fax, email, or write me directly to let me know what you did or didn't like about this book—as well as what we can do to make our books stronger.

Please note that I cannot help you with technical problems related to the topic of this book, and that due to the high volume of mail I receive, I might not be able to reply to every message.

When you write, please be sure to include this book's title and author as well as your name and phone or fax number. I will carefully review your comments and share them with the author and editors who worked on the book.

Fax: 317-581-4663

E-mail: office@mcp.com

Mail: Executive Editor
         General Desktop Applications
         Macmillan Computer Publishing
         201 West 103rd Street
         Indianapolis, IN 46290 USA

INTRODUCTION

THE PERSONAL COMPUTING revolution is in full swing. We are buying new PCs at a record pace, upgrading our old PCs to take advantage of the latest technologies, using powerful applications to publish documents and manage our finances, and turning to the Internet for information, entertainment, and communications.

Although this PC revolution has undoubtedly improved our lives, it has complicated our lives, as well. Now we must learn about technology even if we have no interest in it. We must know what to look for in a new PC, how to set it up, and how to run and use a wide array of programs to perform specific tasks. And, as our computers become old and obsolete, we need to know how to upgrade them to keep up with the ever-changing standards.

Using, maintaining, and upgrading your PC while trying to manage the other aspects of your life poses a difficult challenge and can make you feel as though you're falling behind in this techno-rat-race. You need a guide to lead you through the basics and bring you up to speed with the not-so-basic tasks, a mentor who will help you make the right upgrade decisions and enable you to confidently tinker with your own PC.

Welcome to *Using and Upgrading PCs*

Using and Upgrading PCs is your guide to the complex world of PCs. Here, you will learn everything you need to know to purchase the right computer for your needs, set it up, and put it to work. Your guide will lead you through the basics of using Windows and Windows programs, step you through the process of connecting to and navigating the Internet, show you how to optimize your system, help you make the right upgrade decisions, and lead you step-by-step through the process of installing your upgrades.

When you encounter a problem, *Using and Upgrading PCs* will help you track down the cause, fix the problem, and get your computer up and running in a hurry. You'll find a list of the 10 most common problems and their solutions, along with instructions that show you how to troubleshoot problems on your own.

In addition, *Using and Upgrading PCs* is packed with tips, notes, and cautions to help you make the most of your PC and avoid the most common pitfalls.

How to Use This Book

When you're busy holding down a full-time job, starting your own business, raising kids, and trying to establish a social life, you don't have time to read *any* book from cover to cover, let alone a computer book. With that in mind, we designed *Using and Upgrading PCs* to help you quickly find the information and instructions *you* need and skip the material that doesn't address your current needs.

Each chapter shows you how to perform a specific computing task: buying a new PC, setting up your PC, maintaining your PC, using Windows, printing documents, installing a new hard drive, and so on. You flip to the chapter you need, when you need it, and skip everything between. Each chapter is broken down into bite-sized sections that make the information easy to find, read, and digest.

With terse background information and a generous supply of step-by-step, illustrated instructions, *Using and Upgrading PCs* doesn't make you search through long paragraphs to figure out what to do. With this hands-on approach, you can perform the task and then return later when you have time for the details.

Using and Upgrading PCs also offers a collection of tools to help you zero in on specific information:

- *Find It the First Time Index*. The comprehensive index lists not only technically correct versions of key terms and tasks, but also the plain English versions of these terms. For instance, if your sound card isn't working, you'll find the problem listed in the index under *audio, sounds, sound card,* and *speakers*. You won't have to guess where the index may have listed the problem.

- *Running Heads*. At the top of each left-hand page is the part number and title and the chapter number and title. At the top of each right-hand page, you'll find the name of the current section. Use these entries as bookmarks to quickly skim a chapter and pinpoint topics of interest.

- *Cross-References*. Each chapter provides cross-references to other pages where you'll find related information.

Conventions Used in This Book

If you need instructions on how to use the conventions used in a book, either the book uses too many conventions or the conventions are too confusing. *Using and Upgrading PCs* uses a few simple conventions:

- Text you type appears in a monospaced font. For example, type `windows` and press Enter.

- If you need to press two or more keys to enter a command, the keys are separated by plus signs. For example, "Press Ctrl+Alt+Del to restart your computer." Hold down the first key(s) while pressing the last key and then release the keys.

- Options you select appear **bold**. If you can select the option more quickly by pressing a key that corresponds to the option's selection letter, the selection letter appears underlined, as in "Open the **File** menu and click **Save**."

- Tips, notes, and warnings are delegated to the page margins, where they'll stay out of your way until you need them.

Buying and Setting Up Your PC

Savvy PC Buyer's Guide

Choose between a desktop or notebook PC

Read and understand a computer advertisement

List the components that contribute most to a
PC's performance

Determine the amount and types of disk storage
you need

Purchase a computer that has plenty of room
for upgrades

Desktop or Notebook PC?

When you're looking at computer ads in a magazine or checking out PCs at your local computer store, you'll realize that the first PC purchasing decision you need to make is whether to buy a desktop or notebook PC. The question boils down to one consideration: Are you willing to pay double the money so you can travel with your PC? That's approximately how much extra you will pay for a comparably equipped notebook PC.

Of course, there are a few other considerations when making this first decision. The following sections list the most important considerations.

Why Not Buy a Notebook PC?

When I purchased my first notebook PC, I had high hopes of taking it with me on road trips, so I could travel more. When I started using it, however, I realized that I just didn't like it. Here's why:

- The keyboard is small and flat, making it tough to find the home keys and easy to press two keys by mistake.
- If you spill something on the keyboard, you risk ruining the entire system. On a desktop PC, you can replace the keyboard for under $40.
- The screen is small, even on "big screen" notebooks.
- The screen is slow. (Your mouse pointer will disappear as you move it.)
- The CD-ROM drive is fragile, and if you want to use a floppy disk drive, you may have to disconnect the CD-ROM drive or plug one of the drives into the printer port.
- The speakers and microphone can't compete with the audio input and output options on a desktop PC.
- Most notebook PCs are equipped with a touchpad or trackball instead of a mouse, making pointing, clicking, and dragging difficult.
- Upgrading the hard drive, RAM, or processor is difficult, if not impossible.

- It's hot. The Pentium processor, which puts out a lot of heat, can make it uncomfortable when you're typing.

- It's easy to steal. You don't want to leave a $4,000 notebook PC with your life's work on it in a hotel room.

Why Buy a Notebook PC?

If notebook PCs have so many drawbacks, why would anyone consider purchasing a notebook PC (see Figure 1.1)? Here are a few reasons :

- The new breed of notebooks are light, compact, and powerful enough to handle the most common computing tasks.

- If you frequently travel or shuffle work between your office and home, a notebook PC lets you take everything with you. You don't have to copy files back and forth between two computers.

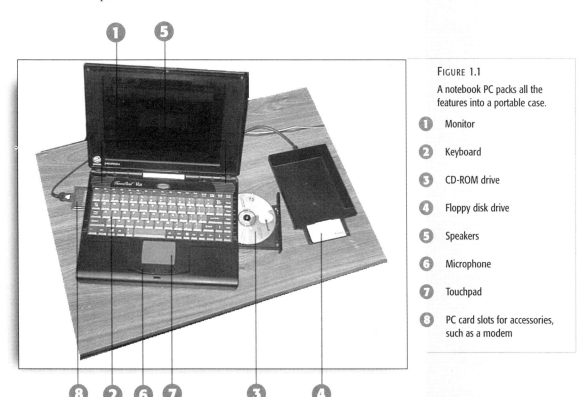

FIGURE 1.1

A notebook PC packs all the features into a portable case.

1   Monitor

2   Keyboard

3   CD-ROM drive

4   Floppy disk drive

5   Speakers

6   Microphone

7   Touchpad

8   PC card slots for accessories, such as a modem

No docking station?

Some manufacturers do not offer docking stations for their notebook PCs. If no docking station is available, make absolutely sure that the notebook has ports for connecting a standard monitor, keyboard, mouse, and speakers.

- If you have limited space on your desk, a notebook PC can usually fit.

- The PC card slots make it easy to add devices, such as a modem and network card. (Although adding a hard drive or memory is tough.)

- You can connect the notebook PC to a *docking station* (also called a *port replicator*) to connect it to a full-size keyboard, a standard monitor, a mouse, and other desktop devices.

SEE ALSO

➤ *Learn what to look for in a notebook PC, page 31*

➤ *Learn how to set up a notebook PC, page 69*

➤ *Learn how to use a notebook PC, page 269*

Performance First: What's Inside?

When people shop for a PC, they commonly focus on the hard disk size, amount of memory, the operating system, and the accompanying software. That's like buying a car because you like the paint job and the CD player.

When shopping for a PC, what's inside the PC matters most—the components that you probably understand the least, such as the system bus, the BIOS, the cache, and the processing chip. These components contribute the most to the PC's performance and are typically what manufacturers cut back on to make their prices more competitive. The following sections tell you what to look for.

Microprocessors (Processing Chip)

The *microprocessor* (CPU, or central processing unit) is the brain inside your computer, the chip that processes the complex set of instructions that makes your computer tick. When looking at microprocessors, it's tempting to focus on *clock speed*, a measure of how many millions of times the chip can process a set of instructions per second. In print, a 300MHz processor looks faster than a 200MHz processor. However, a chip with a slower clock speed can actually outperform a chip with a faster clock speed. The following factors contribute to the overall performance of the microprocessor:

- *Internal clock speed.* This is the clock speed we've been discussing, the speed that you'll find in computer ads.

- *Data bus.* The highways along which data travels inside the processor and between the processor and the motherboard (the main circuit board inside the computer). Most processors have a 32-bit *internal bus* and a 64-bit *external bus*. A wider bus can carry more data, just as a wider highway can accommodate more traffic. The external data bus is typically wider, so the fast processor can transfer data to the relatively slow motherboard without having to wait for the motherboard to catch up.

- *L1 cache.* A temporary storage area inside the processor. A *cache* stores frequently used instructions, so the processor doesn't have to wait for them. A Cyrix processor, which typically runs at a slower clock speed than a Pentium, uses a larger L1 cache to bring it up to speed with a "faster" Pentium processor.

- *L2 cache.* A temporary storage area that sits between the processor and the motherboard. Because the processor communicates with the rest of the system at one half to one third of the speed at which it communicates internally, a large, fast cache can prevent bottlenecks between the processor and the rest of your system.

- *MMX.* MMX doesn't stand for anything. It's a relatively new multimedia technology, developed by Intel, that allows your computer's processor to take on more of the workload for handling multimedia files. This enables your computer to play media files (designed for MMX) faster and more smoothly.

- *RISC/CISC Architecture. RISC*, short for Reduced Instruction Set Computing, uses a streamlined set of instructions to increase performance with less work from the processor. *CISC*, short for Complex Instruction Set Computing, uses a more comprehensive set of instructions. Most new processors use the RISC architecture.

Plummeting prices

With the increased competition between microprocessor manufacturers, you can expect the prices of microprocessors to drop significantly.

To choose a microprocessor, consider its overall performance and cost as compared with other comparable microprocessors. For example, an AMD K6-2/300 microprocessor turns in a performance rating nearly equivalent to that of the Intel Pentium II 400MHz processor and costs vendors 25% less. If you budgeted $2500 for a computer, you can apply your savings on the processor to more memory or a faster hard drive. However, because most hardware manufacturers and software developers design their products for Intel processors, sticking with a Pentium processor minimizes compatibility issues.

Table 1.1 provides a list of common microprocessors to help you with your comparison shopping. However, because manufacturers are constantly improving their chips, the latest microprocessors may not be listed.

TABLE 1.1 **Comparison shopping for microprocessors**

Microprocessor	Description
The Bargain Basement	
Pentium Classic	A big step up from the old, obsolete 486 processor, the Pentium Classic offers faster clock speeds than the 486, 16K (kilobytes) of L1 cache, and an improved architecture (design) for processing instructions.
Cyrix 6x86	Slower clock speeds than Pentium, but its 16K, unified L1 cache and superior design more than makes up for the slower clock speed.
AMD K5	Similar to the Cyrix 6x86, the AMD K5 runs more slowly than a Pentium, but the improvements in the overall design of the chip may outperform the Pentium. An inexpensive alternative to the Pentium.
High-Quality, Reasonably Priced	
Pentium MMX	MMX technology primarily improves performance for games, multimedia applications, and graphics.
Pentium Pro	A step up from the obsolete Pentium Classic, Pentium Pro provides enhanced performance for business systems and network servers, but lacks MMX technology, making it a poor choice if you plan on playing advanced computer games.
Cyrix 6x86 MX	A strong competitor to the Pentium MMX processor, the Cyrix 6x86MX turns in performance ratings only slightly lower than that of the Pentium MMX. If price is an issue, you might not notice the slight difference in overall performance.

Microprocessor	Description

High-Quality, Reasonably Priced

| AMD K6 | A challenger to the Pentium MMX and Pentium Pro that even scared Intel. Although its clock speeds lag behind those of the Pentium MMX, it has double the internal (L1) cache to help make up the difference. |

Top of the Line

Pentium II	A Pentium Pro with MMX. The Pentium II introduces 512K of L2 cache built into the chip, taking performance to the next level. As Intel pushes the clock speeds to the limit, competitors may have trouble keeping up (see Figure 1.2).
Cyrix MII	A step up from the Cyrix 6x86 MX, this chip was designed to go head-to-head with the Pentium II. Again, Cyrix's clock speeds are slower than those of the Pentium II, but the oversized L1 cache and other design enhancements bring the chip's overall performance rating in line with that of the Pentium II.
AMD K6-2	The K6-2 with 3DNow! outperforms both the Pentium II 300MHz and 350MHz and only slightly underperforms the Pentium II 400MHz chip. Offering improved performance for multimedia and games, the AMD K6-2 is an inexpensive alternative for the Pentium II.

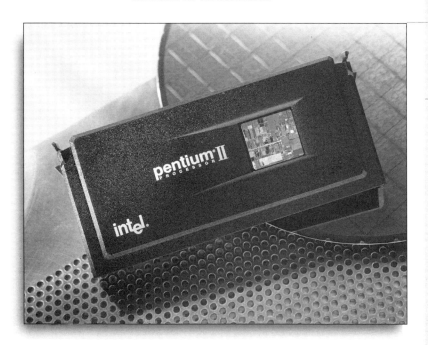

FIGURE 1.2

The Pentium II microprocessor is a powerhouse. (Courtesy of Intel Corporation.)

SEE ALSO

➤ *Learn how to upgrade your microprocessor, page 607*

System BIOS

The *BIOS* (Basic Input/Output System) is the first set of instructions your computer loads on startup. It controls the overall operation of your computer, telling your computer how to access RAM and communicate with your disk drives and the ports (outlets) for your keyboard, mouse, monitor, and printer.

Although the BIOS is fairly standard, make sure the BIOS was developed by a reputable company, such as Phoenix or AMI, and check on the date of the BIOS. An old BIOS may not be able to recognize newer devices, such as *USB* (Universal Serial Bus) ports.

Most importantly, make sure the PC is equipped with a *flash* BIOS. With a flash BIOS, you can update the BIOS by running a program rather than by replacing the chip on which the BIOS is stored. Most computers manufactured in the last three years use a flash BIOS.

SEE ALSO

➤ *Learn how to check and change your PC's BIOS settings, page 567*

➤ *Learn more about USB, page 785*

RAM (Memory) Amount and Speed

With microprocessor speeds pushing into the 400MHz range and programs requiring more and more memory, you should make sure that your system has quick RAM and plenty of it. Here's what you should look for in a new system:

- *Minimum of 32MB RAM.* Many low-cost systems come with 16MB, which is the least amount you need to run Windows 98. When you're running the latest programs, working with graphics and video, or playing games, 16MB means trouble. 32MB is the least you need; 64MB is strongly recommended.

- *EDO or SDRAM.* Until just recently, EDO DRAM (Extended Data Out Dynamic Random Access Memory) was standard

---

BIOS type and date

When a PC starts up, before it loads Windows, it displays the name of the BIOS manufacturer and the date the BIOS was revised. However, the information disappears quickly.

fare for most computers because the motherboard wasn't designed to keep up with the faster SDRAM (Synchronized DRAM) chips. On newer systems, especially those equipped with Pentium II processors, don't settle for EDO. SDRAM offers a 10 percent performance boost.

- *Expandability.* At some point in your computer's life, you will want to add memory. Make sure the RAM sockets are not all occupied with low-capacity *SIMMs* (single in-line memory modules) as shown in Figure 1.3. To save money, some manufacturers insert four 8MB SIMMs into the RAM sockets instead of installing two 16MB SIMMs and leaving two sockets open. On such a system, you would have to remove two 8MB SIMMs to install additional SIMMs. Also, make sure you can install RAM directly on the motherboard instead of having to install a special memory board.

FIGURE 1.3
RAM chips are commonly packaged on SIMMs that plug into sockets on the motherboard.

SEE ALSO
➤ *Learn more about RAM, page 578*
➤ *Learn how to install additional RAM, page 583*

Disk Drives

Every PC should have at least three disk drives: a hard disk drive, a floppy drive, and a CD-ROM or DVD/CD-ROM combination drive. You should also consider purchasing a backup drive, to make it easier to back up files from your hard drive and restore those files in the event that the hard drive becomes damaged or you accidentally delete a file. The following sections show you what to look for when comparing disk drives and describe alternative storage devices.

Buyer beware: proprietary memory

Watch out for *proprietary* memory, which requires you to purchase RAM from the same company you purchased the computer. Obtaining proprietary memory upgrades later may be difficult and costly.

Hard Drive Size and Speed

A hard drive is the PC's main, permanent storage device (see Figure 1.4). The drive sits inside the system unit, usually near the floppy and CD-ROM drives, but is not visible from the outside of the PC. The disk on which data is stored is sealed inside the drive's case, so you never remove the disk.

FIGURE 1.4

A typical hard disk drive. (Courtesy of Western Digital.)

When shopping for a PC, it's easy to focus on the size of the hard drive. If you flip through computer ads, you can tell that a 2 gigabyte (GB) hard drive is pretty much obsolete, that a 4GB drive is standard, and that an 8GB drive will last you well into the 21st Century. It's easy to skip over the acronyms and technical details, such as ATA, EIDE, and 9.5ms.

Although the storage capacity of the drive is important, you should shop for speed, as well. A slow hard drive can significantly drag down the overall performance of your PC. When comparing hard drives, look for the following:

- *Size.* Should be 4GB or larger.

- *Average seek time.* 8–12ms (milliseconds). This standard measures the time it takes the drive to move the read/write mechanism to a specific point on the disk. The smaller the number, the faster the drive.

- *Transfer rate.* 12–16 MBps (megabytes per second). This rate represents the amount of data the drive can send to the PC per second. The higher the number, the faster the drive.

- *Disk cache.* 512K is standard, the more the better. The disk cache is a temporary storage area on the drive that quickly supplies data to the PC without having to access the disk itself.

- *EIDE.* Short for Enhanced Intelligent Drive Electronics, a step up from the obsolete IDE drives. Because they are fast, inexpensive, and reliable, EIDE drives are the most popular drives. The drive plugs into an EIDE controller card inside the PC, and you can string two drives together using a single cable that connects to the controller.

- *ATA.* Short for AT Attachment, a common standard for IDE and EIDE drives. ATA is actually another name for IDE drives. Fast ATA is the same as EIDE. You'll see newer computers that come with an Ultra ATA drive, which is a step up from EIDE drives, offering a 33MBps transfer rate. In the not-so-distant future, you'll see ATA/66 drives that offer transfer rates of 66MBps.

- *SCSI.* Pronounced "Scuzzy" and short for Small Computer System Interface, SCSI provides speedier data transfer rates than are available through standard serial or parallel ports and allows you to connect up to seven devices to the same port or adapter. SCSI drives typically cost more than comparable EIDE drives and may not achieve maximum performance on desktop PCs. SCSI drives are more common on network servers (powerful PCs designed for sharing).

SEE ALSO

➤ *Learn how to optimize your hard drive in Windows, page 254*
➤ *Learn more about different types of hard drives, page 589*
➤ *Learn how to install a new hard drive, page 587*

CD-ROM or DVD Combo?

For years, CD-ROM drives (see Figure 1.5) were standard equipment on new PCs. Without a CD-ROM drive, you couldn't install or use the most popular applications, games, or educational software.

Although that's still the case, DVD (*digital versatile disk* or *digital video disk*) is fast becoming the new standard. A DVD disk can store over seven times as much data as a CD, making them useful for storing full-length movies. DVD is perfect for playing high-tech games, interactive presentations, and multimedia resources, such as encyclopedias. Fortunately, most DVD drives can play CDs, as well.

FIGURE 1.5

A CD-ROM or DVD/CD-ROM combination drive is an essential part of any PC. (Courtesy of Creative.).

In short, when purchasing a new computer, make sure it has a drive that can handle both CDs and DVDs.

Floppy Disk Drive

Even with the advanced storage devices available, the floppy disk drive won't go away. Nearly every PC sold in the last 20 years has come with some sort of floppy disk drive, and the newest breed of PCs has held to this tradition. There's really not much to consider here.

Backup Drive

To back up 1GB of data from your hard drive onto 3½-inch floppy disks would take over 300 disks, and you would have to sit in front of your PC and feed the disks to the computer on request. That's no way to live your life, so when you purchase a PC, make sure it comes with a backup drive or some sort of high-capacity removable storage device.

If money is no object, opt for a device that can store at least half as much data as your hard disk drive on a single tape or cartridge. Most backup programs can compress the files so they require half as much storage space, meaning you could fit the contents of your entire hard drive onto a single disk or tape. With such a system, you can schedule unattended backups or start the backup just before you leave work or head to bed.

If money is an object, get the highest capacity backup drive you can afford, but plan on swapping disks during the backup. Here are some other considerations:

- *Tape backups.* Typically inexpensive, but loud and slow. Because the tape has to run past the read/write head, it can take a long time for your backup utility to find a file you want to recover.

- *Low-capacity, removable disks.* Many new systems with large hard disks (4GB or larger) are equipped with drives that use 100MB disks. That means you'll need 4 or 5 disks for each gigabyte you want to back up. These drives are fine for selective backups or transferring files from one computer to another, but they're not practical for regular, full-system backups.

- *High-capacity, removable disks.* Expensive, but over the long run, the added convenience pays off. Many manufacturers offer drives that can back up 1GB or more onto a single disk or cartridge quickly and quietly. Some drives, such as the Iomega Ditto Max Professional, can store up to 10GB on a single disk! Figure 1.6 shows an external, 1GB Iomega Jaz drive with disk.

FIGURE 1.6

The Iomega Jaz drive uses high-capacity removable disks.

SEE ALSO

➤ *Learn how to back up files from your hard disk to a backup tape or disk, page 341*

➤ *Learn how to choose a backup device and install it on your PC, page 659*

Display Adapters and Monitors

Although a monitor looks like a small TV, the purchasing decisions are a little more complicated. The monitor plugs into a display adapter inside the system unit that controls the way the display image is generated. When shopping for a PC, you need to look at both the display adapter and the monitor.

The display adapter (graphics accelerator) is most important. A high-quality display adapter shifts the workload for rendering the display from the microprocessor to the display adapter, improving the system's overall performance. Here's what you should look for in a display adapter:

- *AGP.* Short for *Accelerated Graphics Port*, AGP is an improved port that the display adapter plugs into. It can transfer data between the system unit and monitor twice as fast as the old PCI port. Make sure the card features AGP texturing (*direct memory execution* or *execute mode*) for enhanced performance display 3D graphics.

- *3D Acceleration.* This is a must for the latest computer games, advanced graphics programs, and for rendering 3D, virtual worlds.

- *Video RAM.* 4–8MB. The video RAM allows the adapter to store more instructions, freeing your primary RAM for other tasks and allowing instructions to pass more quickly from the adapter to the monitor.

- *Additional features.* Some display adapters, such as ATI's All-in-Wonder, offer additional features, including the ability to view TV on your monitor and play video clips from a camcorder.

Of course, the monitor itself is important. When comparing monitors, display size and quality are most important. Here's what you should look for:

- *Size.* 15-inch is on its way out, 17-inch is standard, 19-inch is great if you can afford it.

- *Flat-panel displays.* If you need to conserve space on your desk, get a flat-panel display. These thin, light-weight monitors are about four times thinner than a standard monitor. You can set the monitor on a stand or even hang it on a wall (see Figure 1.7). However, flat-panel displays for desktop PCs are expensive and relatively new, so compare the display quality to that of a standard CRT display before you buy. Also, make sure the monitor comes with a solid warranty and is backed by an established company.

- *Dot pitch.* .28 for a 15-inch monitor, .26 for a 17-inch monitor, .21 for a 19-inch monitor. Dot pitch represents the size of the dots that make up the display. In general, the smaller the dot pitch, the sharper the image.

- *Refresh rate.* 75Hz or higher. A monitor generates a display by blasting an electron beam at the pixels inside the monitor to make them light up. The gun zips by each row of pixels from top to bottom and then repeats the process to keep the pixels glowing. If the refresh rate is lower than 75MHz, the monitor may have an imperceptible flicker that can harm your vision and give you headaches (or a perceptible flicker that can drive you crazy).

FIGURE 1.7

If your desk is already cluttered, consider purchasing a flat-panel monitor.

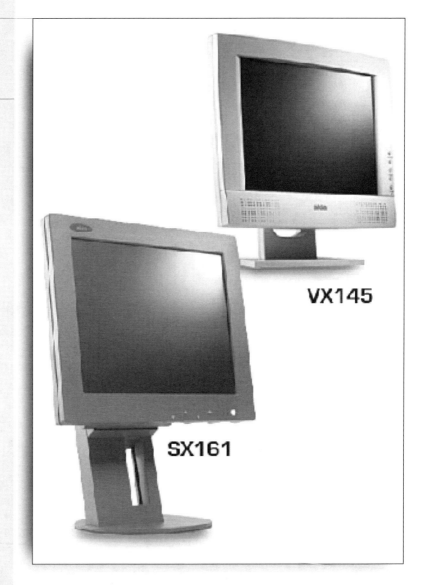

VX145

SX161

Speakers and microphone?

Some monitors come with built-in speakers and a microphone, which look pretty cool and save you some space. However, the sound quality is usually sub-standard and makes it difficult to upgrade.

SEE ALSO

➤ *Learn more about shopping for graphics accelerators, page 643*

➤ *Learn how to upgrade your display adapter, page 648*

➤ *Learn more about choosing a monitor, page 652*

Audio Capabilities

If you go to the movies, you know that a good sound system can make or break a movie, especially an action flick. Likewise, a computer's sound system can significantly enhance a computer game, business presentation, or multimedia application. In addition, if you play audio CDs, DVD movies, or musical instruments on your PC, a good audio system is essential.

When comparing audio systems, you should consider several factors:

- *Compatibility.* To use your sound card with the widest range of available programs, including DOS games, make sure the sound card is compatible with Sound Blaster.

- *Fidelity.* 16-bit 44.1kHz. This matches the standards used for audio CDs.

- *Wavetable audio.* Wavetable technology allows developers to digitize real-world sounds, so a PC can play them. Although these files are large and difficult to manage without some compression scheme, they are popular, so make sure your sound card can handle them.

- *Speakers.* 10 Watts or higher. Sound produced by the best sound card on the market will sound lousy when played through low-quality speakers.

- *Subwoofer.* If you plan on playing combat games or viewing DVD movies, make sure the sound system includes a sub-woofer to blast out those deep, bass booms (see Figure 1.8).

- *MIDI port.* Short for *Musical Instrument Digital Interface*, MIDI allows you to connect a musical instrument, such as a digital piano keyboard, to the sound card so that you can play and record your own music.

- *Game port.* Most sound cards include a game port into which you can plug a joystick. If your PC has a separate game port, you don't need an extra one on the sound card.

- *Full-duplex.* This allows sounds to pass in and out of the sound card at the same time. If you plan on placing phone calls over the Internet, full-duplex audio is a must. Otherwise, you and the person you call will have to take turns talking, which makes for a very choppy conversation.

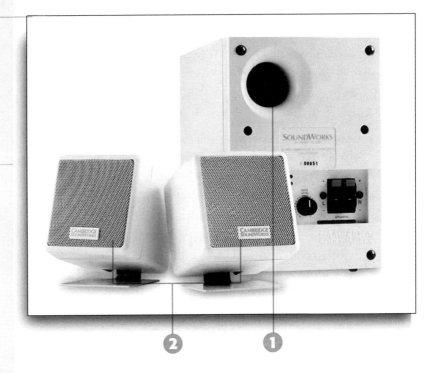

FIGURE 1.8

The subwoofer handles low-level bass, while the satellite speakers handle the rest. (Courtesy of Creative.)

1 Subwoofer

2 Satellites

SEE ALSO

➤ *Learn more about different sound cards, page 770*

➤ *Learn how to upgrade your PC's sound system, page 777*

➤ *Learn how a CD-ROM or DVD drive can enhance your system, page 621*

Fax Modem

To wander the Web, send and receive email messages, and use your computer as a fax machine, you need a good fax modem. A modem (short for MOdulator/DEModulator) converts digital signals from your PC into analog signals that can travel over standard phone lines, and converts incoming analog signals into digital signals that your PC can process (see Figure 1.9). The main consideration when comparing modems is speed.

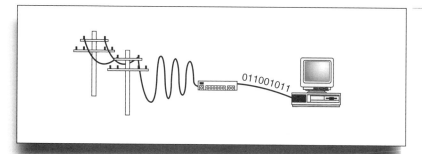

FIGURE 1.9

A modem converts analog signals into digital signals that the PC can process.

33.6K and 56K Modems

Modem speeds are measured in kilobytes per second (Kbps, commonly shortened to K). The most popular fax modems transfer data at rates of 28.8K, 33.6K, and 56K. If you decide to go with a standard modem, here's what you should look for:

- *Internal*. Although external modems have indicator lights that can help you troubleshoot modem problems, the modem connects to the serial port, leaving you with one less serial port to use. They also take up space on your desk and give you another power cable to tangle.

- *33.6K or faster*. Most Internet service providers and commercial online services support 33.6K transfers. 56K is close to the maximum speed supported by standard phone lines. (The 56K speed applies only to incoming data; the speed limit for outgoing data stands at about 33.6K.)

- *Flash ROM*. This allows you to upgrade the device by running a program that updates the modem's internal instructions. Without flash ROM, you must replace the ROM chip on the modem or the entire modem.

- *Voice support*. With voice support, you can use your computer as an answering machine—people can leave voice messages when you're away from your computer.

- *Fax support*. With a fax modem, you can use a special fax program (typically included with the modem) to send and receive

External modems

Although I recommend an internal modem, just to keep your desktop tidy, external modems offer several benefits. The indicator lights can help you track down common problems, and the modem doesn't take up another expansion slot in your PC.

Modem speed limits

Several factors contribute to the speed of your modem connection, including the quality of the phone lines in your home or office and the quality of your phone service. Don't expect a 56K connection just because you have a 56K modem.

faxes. Of course, you can't feed a printed page through the fax modem, but you can fax documents you create in other applications. (Some all-in-one printers that can print, copy, fax, and scan use the fax modem to send and receive faxes.)

ISDN

Short for Integrated Services Digital Network, *ISDN* is a system that allows your computer, using a special ISDN modem, to perform digital data transfers over special phone lines. Non-ISDN modems use analog signals, which are designed to carry voices. ISDN connections can transfer data at a rate of up to 128K, compared to about 56K for the fastest analog modems.

ISDN uses two 64K channels allowing you to use one channel for voice calls and the other for your PC communications. For example, you can talk on the phone while using the Internet. When you're not talking on the phone, the two channels combine to provide the 128K data transfer rate.

Before you purchase an ISDN modem, check with your phone company to determine if ISDN service is available in your area and ask about the installation and service costs. Also make sure that your Internet service provider supports ISDN connections and find out how much extra they charge for an ISDN connection. Many services charge for each 64K line.

SEE ALSO
➤ *Learn more about modem types and standards, page 674*
➤ *Learn how to install an internal modem, page 682*

Modem Alternatives

Although modems provide an inexpensive way to connect to the Internet, they are relatively slow when compared to network Internet connections. For increased speed, consider the following options:

- *Satellite dish.* A satellite connection pulls data into your PC at about four times the speed of an ISDN modem. Because the satellite dish receives signals from the airwaves, you can use a satellite dish almost anywhere. The drawbacks of satellite dishes are that the equipment and service is expensive, and the dish can carry data only one way—into your system. You'll still need a modem for outgoing signals.

- *Cable modem*. A cable modem can transfer data to your computer at an amazing rate—4MBps! However, the service is expensive and may not be available in your area. In addition, like a satellite dish, cable modems can only receive data, requiring a standard modem for carrying outgoing signals. However, cable companies are working on systems that can carry signals two ways.

Planning for Expansion

When you're handing over $2,000 or $3,000 for a PC, the last thing you want to think about is installing additional equipment. However, this should be one of your primary concerns. For instance, if you purchase a PC that uses a PCI expansion slot for the graphics adapter, you can rule out upgrading to an AGP graphics adapter in the future.

The All Important Ports

The easiest way to upgrade a PC is to install an external device, such as a printer, joystick, MIDI instrument, or external drive. With external devices, you don't have to flip the hood on your system unit or mess with the inner workings of your PC. When purchasing a PC, make sure it has the ports you need:

- *Parallel port*. ECP (Extended Capabilities Port) is standard on new PCs, allowing you to connect a bidirectional printer to the PC and perform faster data transfers for external drives and scanners.

- *Mouse port*. Serial or PS/2 mouse. Make sure the system comes with two serial ports or one serial port and a separate mouse port. Otherwise, you'll have to disconnect your mouse to use a different serial device.

- *Keyboard port*. PS/2 keyboard port is standard.

Daisy-chain

Daisy-chain means you can plug one device into the system unit, another device into the first device, and so on. You can do this with a SCSI adapter, as well, but SCSI standards vary, making compatibility a big issue.

- *Serial port*. A serial port is useful for connecting two computers directly with a data cable or connecting an external modem or disk drive. However, the parallel port offers faster data transfers for external disk drives.

- *Game port*. To add a joystick to your PC, the PC must have a game port. The game port is typically built in to the PC or sound card.

- *MIDI port*. To attach a MIDI device, such as a digital piano keyboard, your system needs a MIDI port, typically integrated with the sound card.

- *USB port*. The ultimate in Plug and Play technology, USB allows you to install devices without turning off your computer or using a screwdriver. You plug the component into the USB port, and it works. USB allows you to connect up to 127 devices to a single port. You can daisy-chain the devices with cables up to 5 meters long or connect a USB *hub*, which contains several USB ports (see Figure 1.10). Many systems come with two USB ports.

- *FireWire*. FireWire is an older technology that originated with Apple computers. Like USB, FireWire allows you to connect equipment without turning off the PC and daisy-chain devices. It is especially useful in connecting camcorders, TVs, and stereo equipment to PCs. FireWire is already being used to connect some camcorders to VCRs and TVs. However, FireWire support is not yet built in to Windows.

- *IrDA (infrared) port*. Infrared technology enables wireless connections between the PC and peripherals, including mice, printers, keyboards, and networks. Infrared works like a TV remote control. To function properly, the peripheral must support infrared communications and there must be a direct line of site between the PC and the peripheral. You won't find many infrared devices on the market, and infrared technology isn't perfected yet, so don't worry too much about buying a PC with an infrared port. On a combination PC/TV, an infrared port is essential for the remote keyboard and mouse.

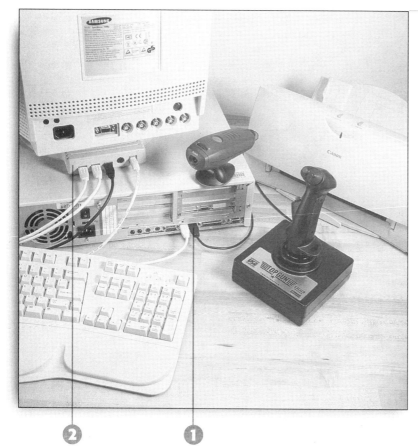

FIGURE 1.10

With USB, you can connect several devices to a single port. (Courtesy of Intel Corporation.)

1 USB port on system unit

2 USB hub

SEE ALSO

➤ *Learn more about the ports on your computer, page 782*

➤ *Learn how to install additional ports, page 787*

Expansion Slots

Nearly every device you connect to your PC plugs into an *adapter card* (a printed circuit board) that's inserted into an *expansion slot* on the motherboard (see Figure 1.11). If you want to add a sound card, SCSI interface, scanner, modem, or other device to your computer, you may have to add an expansion board, so make sure the computer has a few *open* expansion slots. Here are the types and numbers of open expansion slots you should look for:

- *Two ISA slots.* Some expansion boards still follow the old ISA standard, so make sure you have at least two ISA slots to handle the older boards.
- *Three PCI slots.* Most PC expansion boards are designed for PCI slots. You can use the PCI slots to add a SCSI or USB adapter later.

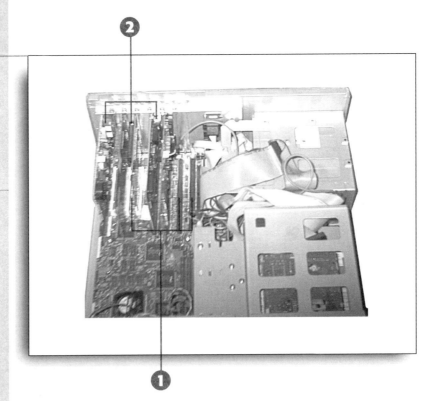

FIGURE 1.11

Expansion slots allow you to plug additional devices into the system unit.

1 Expansion slots

2 Expansion boards

SEE ALSO

➤ *Learn how to install an expansion board, page 560*

Open Drive Bays

New computers are typically equipped with a hard drive, floppy drive, CD-ROM drive, and backup drive, leaving little room for expansion. Make sure the computer comes with at least two open drive bays for installing an additional hard drive or a removable disk drive or tape backup unit.

Power Supply

Although the PC's power supply is probably sufficient to run the devices that the manufacturer installed on the computer, it may not produce the wattage required for future upgrades. PC manufacturers have been known to trim costs by using power supplies that have lower ratings, so make sure your power supply is designed to meet your future needs. Table 1.2 lists the power supply requirements for typical desktop PCs.

TABLE 1.2   **Power supply ratings for desktop PCs**

PC Type	Power Rating
Standard desktop	200 Watts
Minitower	250 Watts
Full tower	300 Watts

SEE ALSO

➤ *Learn how to determine if a power supply is sufficient for your system, page 573*

Finding the Right Notebook PC

If you decide to purchase a notebook PC, lower your standards. A typical notebook PC typically doesn't offer the powerful microprocessor, RAM, drive space, or expandability you'll find in a desktop model. When shopping for a notebook PC, you need to shift your focus a little and consider a few additional features, as explained in the following sections.

Weight

In the notebook arena, the lightweights win. When you're toting your notebook PC around the airport, you don't want an additional ten pounds hanging on your arm. Look for a notebook that weighs in at 4–8 pounds—expect to pay more for lighter notebooks.

Display

If you plan to do much work on the notebook, make sure the display doesn't cause you to squint. Don't settle for less than a 12.1-inch TFT (active matrix) 800×600 display, 75Hz or faster. TFT (short for thin film transistor) is a technology used to improve the resolution on flat-panel displays. On a TFT screen, each pixel (screen dot) is controlled by up to four transistors. Active matrix screens have a higher refresh rate and are much more responsive. Avoid cheaper notebooks that use passive matrix displays.

Compare displays before you buy. Some displays rival the quality you'll find on a standard desktop monitor, although other displays look like something you'd see on your calculator.

Check for glare

Don't let the salesperson lead you into a dark room to check out displays. Face the display toward an open window or next to a bright light when comparing displays. They all look good in the dark.

Hard Drive

Don't settle for less than a 2GB hard drive; 4GB is better. Other than that, follow the same recommendations I gave for desktop PCs.

RAM (Memory)

As with a desktop PC, don't settle for less than 32MB of RAM, preferably SDRAM. Find out the total amount of RAM the notebook PC can hold (at least 64MB) and what's involved in installing additional RAM. Many notebook PC manufacturers require that you send the PC to them for RAM upgrades.

Battery

You have three choices here: nickel cadmium (NiCad), nickel metal hydride (NiMH), or lithium-ion. Although lithium-ion batteries are more expensive, they're lighter and run longer between charges. Find out how long it takes to charge the battery, how many hours you can operate the notebook between charges, and how many times you can charge the battery.

Keyboard

Make sure the keyboard is roomy, that the keys aren't scrunched too close together and that you like the feel of the keyboard. Although most notebook PCs have a PS/2 keyboard port for connecting a full-size keyboard, you don't want to have to lug another keyboard around with you.

Pointing Device

Pointing devices on notebook PCs are a necessary evil. Touchpads are too touchy, the little red button on IBM notebooks is a nuisance, and a trackball makes it tough to drag the pointer. In my opinion, the touchpad is the best of the three. Just make sure the notebook PC has a PS/2 mouse port or an open serial port, so you can add a mouse later.

CD-ROM and Floppy Drive

A floppy drive and CD-ROM drive are standard equipment on notebook PCs, but how they're handled can make a big difference. The drive might be permanently installed in the notebook PC, may connect to the PC with a parallel cable, or may be *swappable* with the CD-ROM drive. The swappable (also called *modular*) configuration is best. You can install the floppy disk drive only when you need it, and leave the CD-ROM drive installed for most other tasks.

DVD on a Notebook PC?

Many newer notebook PCs offer a CD-ROM/DVD combo drive. If you are planning to use the notebook PC as a desktop replacement, consider purchasing the combo drive.

Audio System

The audio system on notebook PCs is anemic, generally due to the poor quality of the speakers and microphone. Make sure the notebook PC has audio input and output jacks for connecting more powerful speakers and a real microphone. If you plan on placing phone calls over the Internet, make sure the audio system supports full-duplex communications.

PCMCIA (PC Card) Slots

Most newer notebook computers make it much easier to upgrade memory, drives, modems, and so on, by using PCMCIA cards (or PC cards). (PCMCIA is short for *Personal Computer Memory Card International Association*). PC cards are small devices that plug directly into expansion slots on the *outside* of the computer. These cards are about the size of credit cards, and you can insert them when the power is on. It's sort of like inserting a disk in a floppy disk drive (see Figure 1.12).

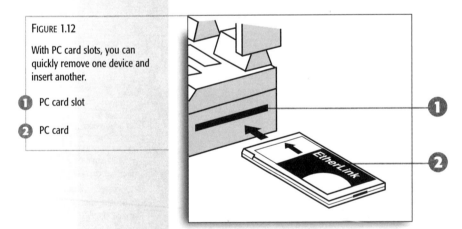

FIGURE 1.12

With PC card slots, you can quickly remove one device and insert another.

1 PC card slot

2 PC card

When you are shopping for a PCMCIA card, you should keep in mind that there are three types of cards. They are all the same length and width, but their thickness varies:

- Type I cards (up to 3.3 mm thick) are used primarily for adding memory to a computer.

- Type II cards (up to 5.5 mm thick) are typically used to add a fax modem, network adapter, or CD-ROM drive (the drive is connected to the PCMCIA card with a cable).

- Type III cards (up to 10.5 mm thick) are usually used for adding a hard disk drive.

Your notebook computer should have one or more PCMCIA slots. These slots also come in three types:

- Type I slots can use only one Type I card.

- Type II slots can use one Type I card or two Type II cards.

- Type III slots can use one Type III card or one Type I card and a Type II card.

SEE ALSO

➤ *Learn how to safely insert and remove PC cards, page 270*

Ports

As with desktop PCs, notebook PCs use ports for connecting the PC to peripheral devices, such as printers. Make sure the notebook PC offers a docking station add-on, as explained in the following section, or that it comes equipped with the following ports:

- *Parallel port.* Required for connecting to a printer or an external disk drive.

- *Serial port.* This comes in handy for installing an external modem or a mouse.

- *PS/2 keyboard port.* When you're tired of dealing with a dinky keyboard, you need a port for connecting a full-size keyboard.

- *Display adapter.* This is useful for connecting your notebook PC to a standard monitor.

- *Infrared port.* Although not required on a desktop PC, the infrared port is useful on a notebook PC for establishing network connections and printing to a portable printer that supports infrared communications.

- *USB port.* For future expansion, a USB port is essential.

Playing the slot machine

The PCMCIA slots are typically numbered 0 and 1. Insert your first card in the 0 slot and the second one in the 1 slot; otherwise the cards may not work properly. Check your computer's documentation to determine which slot is which.

Modem

Most notebook PCs come with a PC card modem. Look for a 33.6K or 56K modem. Alternatively, you can connect an external modem to the notebook PC's serial port and use the PCMCIA slots for other add-ons.

Docking Station

Although you may not need a docking station right now, make sure you can get one later. You can't just go out and purchase a generic docking station and plug in your notebook PC; you must purchase a docking station specifically designed for your notebook.

A docking station commonly includes expansion slots for installing additional devices, extra ports for connecting to a standard monitor and keyboard, and additional drive bays for storage devices. When you plug the notebook PC into the docking station, you essentially transform it into a desktop PC, giving yourself the best of both worlds (see Figure 1.13).

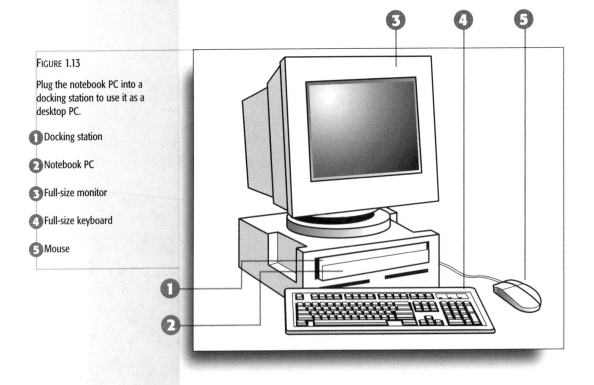

FIGURE 1.13

Plug the notebook PC into a docking station to use it as a desktop PC.

1 Docking station

2 Notebook PC

3 Full-size monitor

4 Full-size keyboard

5 Mouse

PC Buyer's Checklists

This chapter addressed most of what you should consider when shopping for a desktop or notebook PC. However, remembering all the details when you're out shopping can be tough, so use Tables 1.3 and 1.4 as quick reference checklists.

TABLE 1.3   **Desktop PC shopper's checklist**

Component	Minimum Requirements
Processor (CPU)	Pentium II or better, 300MHz or faster.
Cache	512K L2 pipeline burst cache.
RAM	32MB (preferably 64MB) SDRAM or EDO RAM.
Hard drive	4GB drive with access times ranging from 8–12ms (milliseconds); the lower the number the better.
USB ports	Two USB ports.
Monitor	SVGA, non-interlaced, 15-inch or 17-inch monitor with a dot pitch of .28 or less, 1024C768 resolution.
Display card	AGP graphics card with 4MB RAM.
Floppy drive	3½" floppy disk drive.
CD-ROM/DVD	CD-ROM/DVD combo drive.
Backup drive	At least half the capacity of your hard disk drive.
Audio	32-bit, wavetable sound card, 10-watt speakers, and a good microphone. 64-bit sound cards are better.
Game port	Yes.
Modem	33.6K data transfer, 14.4kbps fax transfer, plus voice support.

TABLE 1.4   **Notebook PC buyer's checklist**

Feature	Minimum Requirements
Processor (CPU)	Pentium MMX, 166MHz.
Cache	512K L2 pipeline burst cache.
RAM	32MB SDRAM or EDO RAM.

continues…

TABLE 1.4   **Continued**

Feature	Minimum Requirements
Weight	4–8 pounds.
Display	12.1-inch Active matrix TFT 800×600 resolution or better, 75Hz or faster.
Hard drive	2GB or larger.
Battery	Lithium-ion or better.
Keyboard	Roomy.
Touchpad	Yes, but make sure there's a free serial port for connecting a mouse.
Floppy drive	Integrated or swappable with CD-ROM drive.
CD-ROM/DVD	CD-ROM drive with option to upgrade to DVD later.
Audio	16-bit stereo or better plus audio input and output jacks.
Game port	Only if you think you might want to play video games on your notebook.
PCMCIA slots	Two PCMCIA slots.
USB ports	Two USB ports.
Infrared port	Overhyped, but nice to have for future options.
Modem	33.6K or faster with fax.
Docking station	Strongly recommended, but if no docking station is available, make sure the notebook has external ports for a mouse, keyboard, and standard monitor.

Setting Up and Starting Your PC

Find an appropriate place for your PC

Safely unpack your PC and its accessories

Connect the keyboard, mouse, monitor, printer, speakers, and other accessories to your PC

Set up a notebook PC

Boot (start) your PC for the first time

Setting Up Your Work Area

Before you unpack your computer and start connecting the various components, spend a little time arranging your computer's future home. Moving the computer after everything is connected can be quite a chore. Following is a list of considerations:

- Choose a place that is conducive to the PC's intended purpose. If you intend to use the PC as a tool for the family, place it in a room that's convenient for everyone and where you can supervise your kids. If the PC is for work, place it in a quiet den or a separate room.

- House the computer next to a grounded outlet that's *not* on the same circuit as a clothes dryer, air conditioner, or other power-hungry appliance. Power fluctuations can damage your computer and destroy files. If you're in an old house and you're not sure whether the outlet is grounded, go to the hardware store and buy an outlet tester; it has indicator lights that show if the outlet is properly grounded.

- Keep the computer away from magnetic fields created by fans, radios, large speakers, air conditioners, microwave ovens, and other appliances.

- Choose an area near a phone jack or install an additional jack. You'll need the jack for connecting your modem. Most modems have an in and out jack, so you can connect a phone to it and share the line, although your modem will tie up the phone when you're connected.

- Place your computer in an environment that is clean, dry, cool, and out of direct sunlight. If you have no choice, cover the computer after turning it off to keep it clean. (Don't cover it when the power is on; it needs to breathe.)

- To reduce glare from the monitor, position your desk so the monitor doesn't directly face a window or other source of bright light. Otherwise, the glare will make the screen difficult to see.

- Give the computer room to breathe. The computer has fans and vents to keep it cool. If you block the vents, the computer might overheat.

In addition to making your computer comfortable, consider your own comfort, and think about ergonomics. You want your monitor at eye level and your keyboard and mouse at about elbow-level as you sit at your desk. Purchase a comfortable chair that features lower-back support.

Safety Precautions

When you bring your PC home (or when it's delivered), you will be tempted to tear into the boxes and unpack everything. Before you do, read the following list of precautions for unpacking and connecting your equipment:

- Take your time. It's easy to get flustered and make mistakes when you're not relaxed.
- Clear all drinks from the work area. You don't want to spill anything on your new computer.
- Don't force anything. Plugs should slide easily into outlets. If you have to force something, the prongs are probably not aligned with the holes they're supposed to go in. Forcing the plug will break the prongs.
- Don't turn on *anything* until *everything* is connected.

SEE ALSO

➤ Learn more about safety precautions when working on your PC, page 557

Unpacking Your PC and Accessories

Everyone knows how to open a box, so you don't need detailed instructions on how to unpack your PC and other toys. However, there are a few cautions and tips you should be aware of:

- When unpacking your equipment, keep the boxes on the floor to avoid dropping any equipment.
- Don't cut the boxes. Carefully peel off the packing tape. This serves two purposes: It reduces the risk of hacking through a cable or scratching a device, and it keeps the boxes in good condition in the event that you have to return a device to the manufacturer.

Get a bookcase

Your PC arrives with a lot of luggage, including documentation, CDs, and other supplies. You should keep all this material right next to your computer.

- If you have trouble pulling a device, such as a monitor, out of the box, turn the box on its side and slide the device out onto the floor. Don't try to flip the box over and pull the box off of the device.

- Save all the packing material, including the Styrofoam and plastic bags. Many manufacturers accept returns only if you return the device as it was originally packed. The packing material is also useful if you move to a different house.

- Read the packing list(s) thoroughly to make sure you received everything you ordered.

- Find all the cables. The cables are often stored in a separate compartment at the bottom of the box. They're easy to overlook.

- Inspect the cables. Look for cuts in the cables and check for bent pins on the connectors. Although you can straighten the pins using tweezers or needle-nose pliers, you can easily snap off a pin, voiding the warranty. If you find a bent or damaged pin, call the manufacturer.

- If your computer arrived on a cold day, give the components time to adjust to the temperature and humidity in the room. Any condensation needs to dissipate before you turn on the power.

Arranging Your PC and Accessories

Setting up a notebook PC

If you purchased a notebook PC, the steps for setting it up are quite different. See "Setting Up a Notebook (Portable) PC" later in this chapter.

When everything is unpacked, arrange all the devices on your desk before connecting anything. If you connect the devices and then rearrange them, you'll tangle the cables.

If you have a standard desktop unit, you can place the monitor on top of it. If you have a mini-tower or full tower system unit, you can set the tower on the floor. (If the floor is carpeted, set the unit on an anti-static pad to prevent static build-up that could damage the sensitive components inside the system unit.)

Arranging your system unit and accessories

1. Place your system unit on your desk or below your desk (for mini-tower or full tower models) as shown in Figure 2.1.

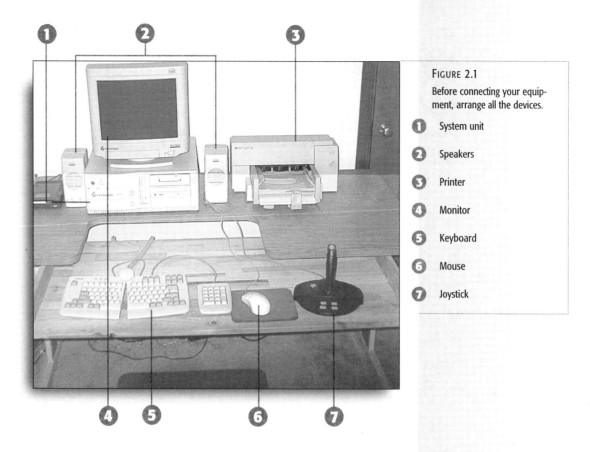

FIGURE 2.1

Before connecting your equipment, arrange all the devices.

① System unit

② Speakers

③ Printer

④ Monitor

⑤ Keyboard

⑥ Mouse

⑦ Joystick

2. Gently set your monitor on the desk or on top of the system unit, so the center of the screen is at eye level.

3. Place your keyboard at a comfortable level where you intend to do your typing.

4. Place your mouse to the right of the keyboard (or to the left, if you're left-handed).

5. Place the printer in a convenient location next to the system unit. You'll want the printer pretty close, so you can feed it paper and remove your printed documents.

6. Place the speakers about six feet apart and at least four feet away from you. Any closer and you minimize the effect of stereo output.

7. If your sound system came with a subwoofer, place it at least three feet from the system unit and any disks.

8. Arrange any additional devices in positions where you will most likely use them.

Easy Connections with USB and SCSI Ports

If you had the foresight to purchase a system with *USB (Universal Serial Bus)* and/or *SCSI (Small Computer System Interface)* ports and accessories designed to use these ports, setting up your PC will be much easier than the standard setup. Both of these technologies allow you to link devices together in a chain. After you've connected one device, you connect other devices in the same way.

Connecting USB Devices

USB is a relatively new technology that allows you to connect up to 127 devices to a single port. In addition to performing its usual job, such as printing, a USB device acts as a *hub* (a common connection point) for other USB devices. For example, you plug your USB printer into a USB port on the back of the system unit and then plug another device, such as a USB scanner, into the printer (see Figure 2.2). Using this *daisy-chain* configuration, USB allows you to connect several devices to a single port. It also allows you to safely connect devices while your computer is on.

You can connect nearly any type of device that supports USB into a USB port, including a keyboard, mouse, printer, scanner, monitor, or disk drive. The USB connectors are typically flat and narrow and shaped to match the port. In addition, most USB devices do not require a separate power cable, because the USB cable carries the power. This cuts down on the number of cables you need to connect (and untangle).

Another benefit of USB is that the connections are *self-terminating*. That is, your computer "knows" which device is the last in the chain. With SCSI devices, discussed in the next section, you must flip a switch or physically plug a terminator into the open SCSI port on the last device.

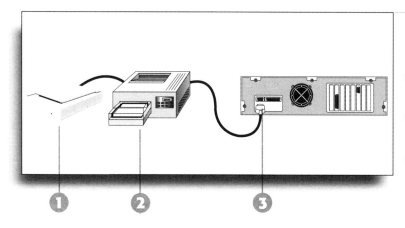

FIGURE 2.2

USB offers the ultimate port for connecting multiple devices.

1 USB scanner connected to USB printer

2 USB printer connected to USB port

3 USB port on system unit

SEE ALSO

➤ *Learn more about USB ports, page 785*

➤ *Learn how to add a USB port to a PC, page 788*

Connecting SCSI Devices

SCSI is an older technology that was first popular on Macintosh computers. Although similar to USB in that it allows you to connect several devices to a single port, a standard SCSI port supports only seven devices. In addition, SCSI comes in several flavors, so you must be careful when shopping for SCSI devices and connection cables. A SCSI device is not compatible with all SCSI ports.

When connecting SCSI devices, you connect one device to the SCSI port, connect the next SCSI device to the first, and so on, as shown in Figure 2.3. You must then flip a switch on the last device or plug a terminator into its second SCSI port to indicate that this is the last device in the chain.

SEE ALSO

➤ *Learn more about SCSI ports, page 783*

➤ *Learn how to add SCSI to your PC, page 788*

➤ *Learn about SCSI hard drives, page 599*

Internal SCSI connections

Most SCSI adapters have a single SCSI port that pokes out the back of the system unit. However, the adapter may also have a connector on the card that connects an internal hard drive or other device. When counting the number of devices attached to your SCSI adapter, include any internal devices.

FIGURE 2.3

You can connect up to seven devices to a standard SCSI port.

1 An external drive connected to a SCSI port

2 You can connect another SCSI device to the SCSI port on the first device.

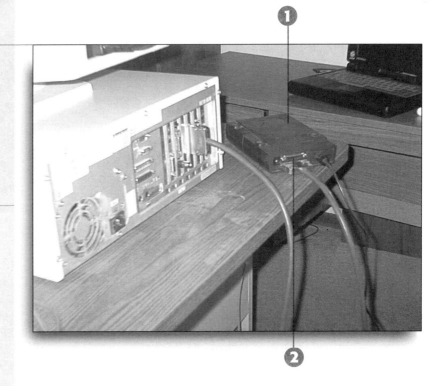

Connecting the Monitor

Most monitors have two cables: a standard 15-pin VGA cable and a power cable. The 15-pin VGA connector has the shape of the letter D and plugs into a video port of the same shape—the connector fits only one way. However, you should be careful not to confuse the video port with other ports on the back of the system unit:

- The serial port resembles the video port. Make sure you use the video port, which is typically marked with a monitor icon.

- If the manufacturer added a graphics accelerator card to the PC, you may have two video ports: one that's built-in to the system (typically near the keyboard, mouse, and printer ports) and another where the expansion slots are located. Connect to the video port in the expansion slot. That's the graphics accelerator card that the manufacturer added to boost the display performance.

- If your monitor has a USB or VESA (Video Electronics Standards Association) cable, plug it into the matching port. USB and VESA monitors may have built-in speakers. These advanced cables are capable of carrying both video and audio signals, allowing you to skip the steps for connecting your speakers.

Gently insert the video connector into the video port. If the connector has screws on it, tighten the screws to secure the connector to the port (see Figure 2.4). This prevents the connector from jiggling loose.

Some system units have two power outlets: one for the system unit's power cable and the other for plugging in the monitor. The outlet for the monitor should be marked A/C Output. Plug the monitor's power cable into this outlet. If the system unit has only one outlet, plug the monitor into your surge suppresser, as explained in "Connecting the Power Cables," later in this chapter.

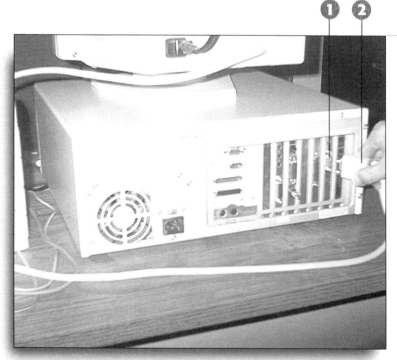

FIGURE 2.4

Gently insert the video connector into the video port.

1 If the system has two video ports, connect to the video port in the expansion slot.

2 Tighten the screws.

Fewer than 15 pins?

If the VGA plug has fewer than 15 pins, don't worry—some monitors use fewer pins.

Some high-performance monitors use a separate *coaxial cable* to carry each signal. These monitors typically use five BNC connectors, similar to the connectors used on a TV set. The five-connector system provides a clearer line of communication between the system unit and the monitor, reducing effects such as color bleeds, fuzziness, and ghost images.

To connect a monitor that uses this configuration, use a cable that has a standard 15-pin connector on one end and five separate BNC connectors on the other. Follow the color-coding scheme to connect the BNC connectors to the monitor and then plug the standard 15-pin connector into the video port on the system unit. Use Table 2.1 to match the cable colors with the labels on the monitor.

TABLE 2.1   Color codes and functions of monitor BNC cables

BNC Cable Color	Carries	Label on Monitor
Red	Red video	R
Green	Green video	G
Blue	Blue video	B
Black	Horizontal sync	H or H/V
Gray	Vertical sync	V

SEE ALSO

➤ *Learn what to look for in a graphics adapter, page 643*

➤ *Learn how to install a graphics adapter, page 648*

➤ *Learn more about different monitor types, page 652*

Connecting a Mouse or Other Pointing Device

With today's graphical user interfaces (such as Windows), a mouse or other pointing device (touchpad, trackball, and so on) is an essential piece of equipment. Although connecting a pointing device is easy, the connectors vary from system to system. Following is a list of common connection types:

- *PS/2 style*. Most mice use a PS/2 connector, a round, 6-pin connector that plugs into a PS/2 mouse port. A PS/2 connector typically has a line or arrow molded into the outside of the plug to indicate the top of the plug. Some mice come with a serial-PS/2 adapter that allows you to connect a PS/2 mouse to a serial port, in the rare case that your PC has no PS/2 port.

- *Serial*. Many mice use a nine-hole, D-shaped, serial connector that plugs into a serial port of the same shape. The serial port may be marked COM1 or COM2 (*COM* is short for *communications*). Use the COM1 port for your mouse. Serial ports may also be labeled 1010, which indicates that the port is capable of sending a string of digital signals.

- *USB*. As discussed earlier in this chapter, USB allows you to string together up to 127 devices. If you have a USB port and keyboard, connect the mouse to the USB port on the keyboard. You can connect the mouse to a different USB device, but because you will use your keyboard and mouse in close proximity, the keyboard connection is the most logical.

- *Infrared*. Most infrared mice come with an infrared connector that plugs into a PS/2 mouse or serial port. Plug the infrared connector into the port and position the infrared receptor so you can point your mouse directly at it. For best results, you should position the mouse 1–5 feet from the receptor.

- *Keyboard/mouse combination*. On some systems, the mouse is attached to the keyboard, in which case, you don't have to connect anything.

To connect your mouse or other pointing device, carefully insert the mouse plug into the PS/2 mouse port or the serial port, as shown in Figure 2.5. Because the PS/2 mouse port and the PS/2 keyboard port are nearly identical, make sure you're connecting to the mouse port. On most systems, a mouse icon marks the mouse port. Newer systems may color-code the mouse and keyboard plugs and outlets.

9- and 25-pin serial ports

Your computer may have a 9-pin serial port and a 25-pin serial port (which resembles the printer port). You can connect a serial device (for instance, a mouse or modem) to either port.

The pins on a PS/2 mouse bend easily, so don't force the plug. If it doesn't slide easily into the port, line up the pins on the plug with the holes in the port and try again.

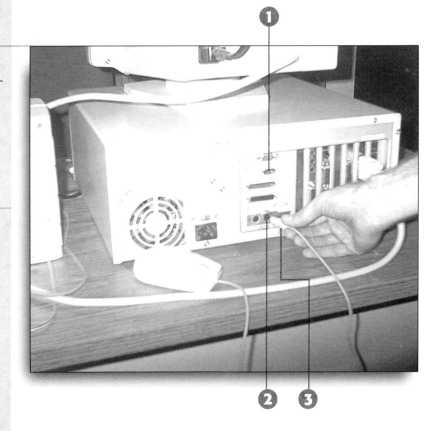

FIGURE 2.5

On most systems, the mouse connects to the PS/2 mouse port or to the serial port.

1 9-pin serial port

2 PS/2 mouse port

3 PS/2 mouse connector

SEE ALSO

➤ *Learn more about pointing devices, page 717*

➤ *Learn what to look for in a mouse, page 718*

Connecting the Keyboard

Assuming you already connected your mouse to the PS/2 mouse port, there should be only one open PS/2 port for the keyboard. Look on the system unit for a port that's marked with a small keyboard icon. If the system comes with a PS/2 keyboard *and* a PS/2 mouse, the keyboard and mouse ports look almost identical—they're both round and have six holes. Although you won't damage the keyboard by plugging it into the mouse port, the keyboard will work only if it is connected to the correct port (see Figure 2.6).

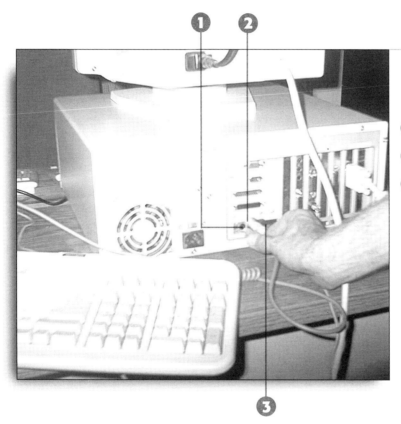

FIGURE 2.6

To connect a PS/2 style keyboard, plug it into the PS/2 keyboard port.

1 PS/2 keyboard port

2 PS/2 style keyboard connector

3 PS/2 mouse port

Some newer keyboards are designed for USB ports. Instead of using a round connector (such as a PS/2 style keyboard), the connector is oblong. You insert the connector into the port (it fits only one way), and then you can connect other devices to USB ports on the keyboard.

Infrared keyboards are popular for big-screen TVs. The USB port is located on the front of the system unit, and you use the keyboard as you would use a TV remote control. In some cases, the keyboard comes with its own infrared connector that you must plug into the serial port on the back of the PC. In either case, you need not physically connect the keyboard to the system unit. An infrared beam acts as the connection between the system unit and the keyboard.

SEE ALSO

➤ *Learn what to look for in a keyboard, see page 718*

Connecting Speakers and a Microphone

Nearly all new PCs have built-in audio support and come equipped with speakers and a microphone for inputting and outputting audio signals. The procedure for connecting the speakers and microphone is more similar to setting up a stereo system than it is to connecting other PC accessories. However, due to recent advances in PC audio technology, the procedures vary depending on the system. The following sections explain the most common PC audio configurations.

Standard, Two-Speaker Setup

Most systems come with two speakers that plug into the audio output jacks on the sound card. On standard 16-bit sound cards, you will find only one audio output jack. You plug the connector on the left speaker into the audio output jack on the sound card. (Don't confuse it with the audio in jack, which allows you to connect your PC to a stereo system and record sounds.) You connect the right speaker to the left speaker, as shown in Figure 2.7. The speakers must also be connected to a power source. See "Connecting the Power Cables," later in this chapter for details.

Connecting your audio equipment

1. Plug the left speaker into the audio out jack.

2. Plug the right speaker into the audio out jack on the left speaker.

3. Plug the microphone into the microphone in jack.

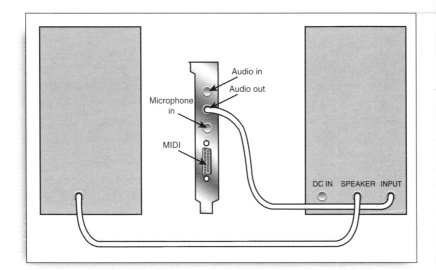

With the latest advances in PC audio, you may encounter a couple variations in the way your speakers connect to the sound card:

- If your sound card has two audio out jacks, one is an amplified jack and the other (usually marked Line Out) carries a non-amplified signal. Use the line output (non-amplified) jack. Low quality amplifiers used in sound cards may lower the sound quality.

- 32-bit sound cards typically have two audio output jacks like those used on stereo systems or VCRs. Plug the left speaker into the jack marked Left RCA (the white jack) and plug the right speaker into the jack marked Right RCA (the red jack).

SEE ALSO

➤ *Learn what to look for in a sound system, page 770*
➤ *Learn how to install a new sound card, page 777*
➤ *Learn how to adjust the volume and balance in Windows, page 779*

Can I use regular stereo speakers?

Speakers have strong magnets that can cause interference with your monitor and may damage data. You can use regular speakers, but place them at least three feet away from your monitor, system unit, and disks. Computer speakers are *shielded* to weaken the magnetic fields.

Two Speakers and a Subwoofer

The latest PC audio systems come as three-piece units: two speakers and a subwoofer. The subwoofer is a speaker that increases the low-end bass output, which provides more realistic sounds for games, audio CDs, and any DVD movies you play on your PC. A logic circuit inside the sound card directs the low-end bass signals to the subwoofer. Your other speakers—called *satellites*—handle the high-end audio output.

The most important consideration when you are connecting a subwoofer is its location. Because the subwoofer is not shielded, the magnetic field it creates can distort your display and damage data. Position the subwoofer at least three feet from your monitor and any storage disks (on the floor, under your desk is as good a place as any).

To connect the subwoofer and speakers, connect the two speakers to the sound card as explained in the previous section. At the back of one of the speakers is a jack for the subwoofer. Connect the specified cable from this jack to the subwoofer, as shown in Figure 2.8.

More power!

For enhanced audio, consider connecting the audio out jack on your sound card to the audio in jack on your stereo system's amplifier. Your stereo system's amplifier and speakers should provide superior sound quality. Just keep those standard speakers away from your system—they're not shielded.

FIGURE 2.8

Connect the subwoofer to the subwoofer output jack on the back of one of the speakers.

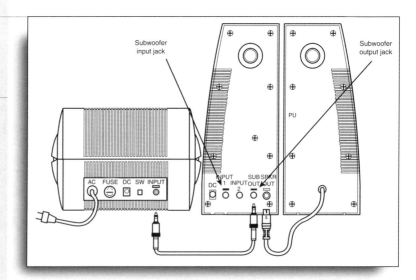

Speakers on the Monitor

If your monitor contains built-in speakers, the speaker connections might be built-in to the monitor cable or may require separate connections. The following list describes the most common configurations:

- *Separate audio cables*. The speakers have their own cables that connect to the sound card, as explained earlier in "Standard, Two-Speaker Setup."

- *Built-in connection*. The monitor cable contains the wires for the speakers. This is common on VESA and USB monitors.

- *Y-connector*. This configuration is similar to using separate audio cables. The monitor has a single cable, but at the end of the cable are two or three connectors: the standard 15-pin video connector that plugs into the video port, and one or two audio jacks that plug into the audio output jack(s).

SEE ALSO

➤ *Learn   more   about   audio   features   on   monitors,   page   23*

Connecting the Microphone

Microphones come in all shapes and sizes. You can use a standard microphone, which is pretty bulky, a headset, one that clips on your lapel or hangs from the monitor, or a small, freestanding unit that you can place next to your keyboard. Whichever type you have, the connection is the same: You plug the microphone into the microphone (MIC) jack on the sound card, as shown in Figure 2.9.

What About CD-ROM and DVD Audio?

To play sounds from an internal CD-ROM or DVD drive through your sound card, you need not make additional connections. A small cable inside the system unit connects the drive directly to the sound card. You can use the headphone jack on the front of the drive to listen to audio CDs, but you usually experience greater sound quality by playing audio CDs through your sound card and speakers.

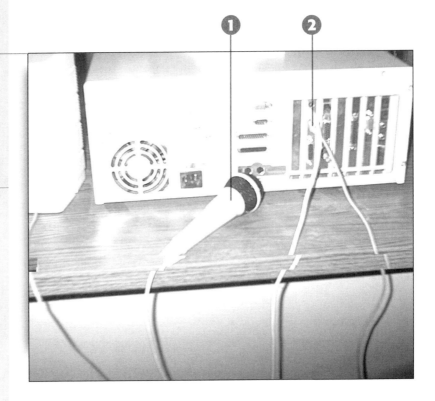

FIGURE 2.9

Plug the microphone into the microphone jack on the sound card.

 Microphone

 Microphone in jack

If you have an external CD-ROM or DVD drive, plug the drive into the specified port and connect the audio output jack to the audio in jack on the sound card. You must also plug the drive into a power outlet.

SEE ALSO

➤ *Learn what to look for in a CD-ROM drive, page 626*

➤ *Learn how to install a CD-ROM or DVD drive, page 633*

Connecting Your Modem

Connecting a standard internal modem to a phone jack is as easy as hooking up a telephone, but the modem has two jacks: line (or Telco, for "telephone company") and phone (or Tel Set, for "telephone set"). Connect a standard telephone cable from the line jack to the phone jack (on your wall), as shown in Figure 2.10. If desired, you can plug a phone into the phone jack, so you can use your phone to place calls as you normally do.

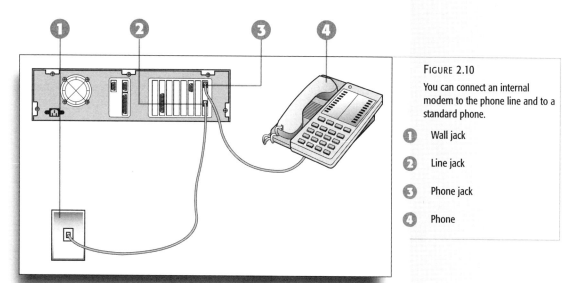

FIGURE 2.10

You can connect an internal modem to the phone line and to a standard phone.

1 Wall jack

2 Line jack

3 Phone jack

4 Phone

An external modem requires three connections: phone jack, serial port, and power supply. The phone jack connections are identical to those used for an internal modem. Connect a standard RJ11 phone cable from the wall jack to line (or Telco) jack on the modem. Connect a standard serial communications cable from the serial port on the modem to the serial port on the system unit. Then, plug the modem's power cord into one of the outlets on the surge suppresser or UPS.

SEE ALSO

➤ *Learn more about different modem types, page 674*

➤ *Learn more details about connecting an external modem, page 681*

➤ *Learn how to set up your modem in Windows, page 683*

➤ *Learn how to use your modem to connect to the Internet, page 391*

➤ *Learn how to disable call waiting, page 407*

Consider using a separate phone line

If you use the same phone line for your modem and voice calls, picking up the phone can disconnect your modem, as can call waiting. Consider having a second phone line installed or have your current phone line converted to an ISDN line, which essentially provides you with two phone lines.

Connecting an ISDN Modem

ISDN (short for *Integrated Services Digital Network*) enables digital transfers over phone lines, supporting data transfer rates of up to 128Kbps (four times faster than 28.8KB modems). In addition, an ISDN line provides two channels: one 64KB channel for voice communications and one for digital data transfers, so you can talk on the phone while working on the Internet. When you're not talking on the phone, the two channels join forces to provide a 128Kbps data connection.

Connecting an ISDN modem is as easy as setting up a standard modem, although you must choose the desired cable type—RJ11 (standard 4-pin phone cable) or RJ45 (8-pin network cable). Both types of cable work, and you don't have to rewire the telephone cables in your home. However, if you use an RJ45 cable, you must replace the standard RJ11 phone jack on your wall with an RJ45 jack. Follow the same installation instructions provided in the previous section.

SEE ALSO

➤ *Learn what how to install and set up an ISDN modem, page 681*

Connecting a Cable Modem

Although relatively expensive and not readily available, cable Internet service is a great innovation, allowing you to copy data to your computer at a rate of over 4MB/sec! The only drawback is that most cable modems only receive data—you need a separate, standard modem to handle outgoing signals.

Does this slow down communications? Not that much. When you're on the Internet, you typically send very little data—small bits of data to request Web pages and other resources. The Web pages, audio and video clips, animations, and other data you receive accounts for most of the traffic, so speeding up the transfer rate for incoming data significantly increases the speed at which you can skip around on the Web.

Two-way cable?

Cable companies are working on ways to establish two-way communications over cable connections, but their work is in its early stages.

Connecting the cable modem is as easy as connecting cable TV. You connect a standard cable from the cable modem to the cable outlet (installed by the friendly cable guy). However, because cable PC service carries signals only one way (into your computer), you must connect a standard modem to the phone line to carry outgoing signals. To install a standard modem, follow the instructions given earlier in "Connecting Your Modem."

SEE ALSO
➤ *Learn how to install and set up a cable modem, page 686*

Connecting a PC Satellite Dish

Several PC dealers offer a satellite option when you purchase a system. The initial cost is fairly high ($300–$800) for the satellite package plus installation. In addition, you'll need to install a standard modem and set up an account with a separate Internet service provider to carry outgoing data. In addition to the initial cost and $50 activation fee, you can expect hourly connect time charges of $.50–$2.00, depending on the option (the more hours you pay for in advance, the cheaper the rate). Yeah, speed costs.

The installation procedure is fairly complicated, even if the adapter is already installed in the system unit. You must install the satellite dish on the outside of your home or office and point it at the correct angle (to the south), so it can receive the satellite signals. You must also connect a standard modem to the phone line, as explained earlier.

SEE ALSO
➤ *Learn how to install a PC satellite dish, page 687*

DirecPC and DirecDuo

Two of the most popular satellite services are DirecPC and DirecDuo (for both TV and Internet service) from Hughes Network Systems. Contact any large computer retailer for details, or visit **www.direcpc.com**.

Connecting Your Printer

The printer connection should be the easiest of all your connections, assuming you received a printer cable with your system. Many printers come without a cable, so you must purchase the cable separately. The type of cable you need depends on the printer type:

- *Standard printer*. You can use a standard Centronics printer cable or IEEE 1284 bidirectional printer cable. This standard cable has a 25-pin D-shaped connector to connect to the PC's parallel printer port and a Centronics 36 (flat) plug that connects to the printer.

- *Bi-directional printer*. You should use an IEEE 1284 bi-directional printer cable to avoid problems. The cable looks like a standard Centronics cable, but it supports bidirectional printing, which is featured on all new printers through the ECP parallel port standard.

- *Serial printer*. You should use a standard serial cable with a 9-pin connector on each end. Serial printers are much slower than parallel printers, so they're not very popular. However, a serial cable is capable of carrying data over longer distances, so if the printer needs to be more than 20 feet from the system unit, consider using a serial printer.

- *USB printer*. Newer printers may support USB, which allows for even faster printing than bidirectional printers. To connect a USB printer, you must have a USB cable with the proper connectors on each end.

Connecting a parallel printer

1. Plug the 25-pin D connector into the 25-hole parallel port on the back of the system unit, and tighten any screws (see Figure 2.11).

2. Plug the Centronics 36 connector into the Centronics port on the printer.

3. If the Centronics 36 port has bail wires, push them in toward the plug until they snap in place.

SEE ALSO

➤ *Learn what to look for in a new printer, page 730*

➤ *Learn how to set up Windows to use your printer, page 737*

➤ *Learn how to print documents, page 233*

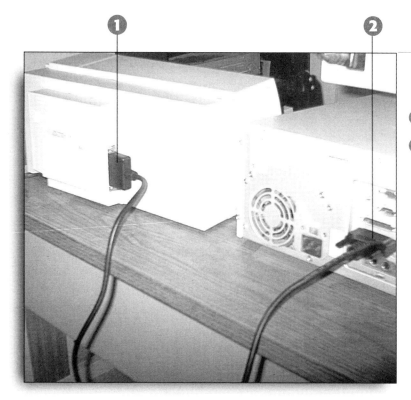

FIGURE 2.11

A parallel printer cable connects the system unit to the printer.

1. Centronics 36 port

2. 25-pin parallel port

Connecting Additional Peripherals

Your PC may have come with additional devices, such as a joystick or scanner, that you must connect to the system unit. To connect these accessories (peripheral devices), you follow the same steps you followed for connecting other devices: Match the plug to the outlet, plug in the device, and secure it to the system with the screws on the plug.

The following sections provide additional details for specific devices, telling you where to look for the outlets and how to plug two devices into the same port.

SEE ALSO

➤ *Learn what to look for in a notebook PC, page 31*

➤ *Learn how to set up a notebook PC, page 691*

➤ *Learn how to use a notebook PC, page 269*

Connecting a Joystick or Game Pad

The game port is on the back of the system unit. Your PC may have a built-in game port or use the MIDI/game port on the sound card. Plug the joystick or game pad connector into the game port, as shown in Figure 2.12. (Some PCs come with a special game port adapter that allows you to connect two game controllers for multi-player games.)

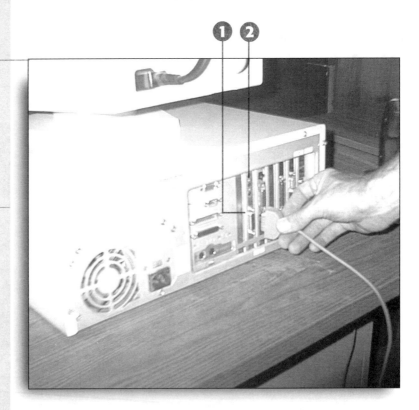

FIGURE 2.12

If your system does not have a dedicated game port, use the MIDI/game port on the sound card.

 MIDI/game port

Sound card

If you have a relatively new, digital game controller, you won't have to do much to set up the joystick, because digital controllers automatically calibrate themselves. Older, analog joysticks require manual calibration.

SEE ALSO
➤ *Learn how to install and calibrate your joystick in Windows, page 726*

Connecting a Scanner

Most scanners connect to a SCSI or parallel port, although some newer scanners support USB connections. If your system has a separate SCSI port or two parallel ports, you won't have any trouble plugging in the scanner. You insert the SCSI or 25-pin parallel connector into the SCSI or parallel port, and you're ready to roll. To connect a USB scanner, plug it into the USB port on the system unit or on another USB device, such as the printer.

However, if your system unit has only one SCSI or parallel port, and a printer or other device is already connected to that port, you must purchase an adapter that allows you to connect two or more devices into the same port. See "Connecting Two or More Devices to One Port," later in this chapter.

SEE ALSO

➤ *Learn what to look for in a scanner, page 743*

➤ *Learn how to install a scanner, page 748*

Connecting a Digital Camera

The digital camera category encompasses a wide range of products, including cameras that permanently attach to your PC for video phone calls and cameras that you can use to take snapshots and then connect to your PC to copy the images to your hard disk.

Digital cameras commonly connect to a serial, parallel, or SCSI port, although newer digital cameras may support USB connections. As with scanners, the connection is easy, assuming you have an open port for the camera. If no port is open, you'll need an adapter to connect two devices to a single port, as explained in "Connecting Two or More Devices to One Port," later in this chapter.

SEE ALSO

➤ *Learn how to buy, set up, and use a digital camera, page 757*

Connecting to Another Computer (Networking)

As PCs become more powerful and inexpensive, many families and small-business owners are purchasing new PCs, passing their old PCs down to other family members, and trying to figure out how to connect the two PCs to take advantage of networking features, such as hardware and data sharing and communications.

If you purchased a network-ready computer, it already has a network adapter installed. You must install a network card on the other computer and then choose the type of network cables you want to use. This is a much more complicated procedure than plugging in a printer, and it requires you to plan ahead.

You can also set up a simple two-computer network by connecting the serial or parallel ports on the two computers with a special data cable and using the Windows Direct Cable Connection utility. Or, you can network over the phone using Dial-Up Networking.

SEE ALSO

➤ *Learn how to set up and use a simple network in Windows, page 291*

Connecting Two or More Devices to One Port

The number of PC accessories is mind boggling: printers, audio systems, modems, game controllers, scanners, digital cameras, backup drives, and so on. When you spin your system unit around and realize that the number of plugs exceeds the number of ports, you face the question that most PC enthusiasts eventually must confront: "Where am I going to plug in all this stuff?"

You have two options. The expensive, somewhat complicated option is to install more ports, as explained in Chapter 38, "Adding Ports for Connecting Additional External Devices." The inexpensive, easy alternative is to use a Y-connector or port splitter that allows you to connect two devices to a single port. When shopping for such an adapter, keep the following in mind:

- To connect two devices to a parallel port, you need a pass-through adapter or Y-connector that allows the printer to stay connected while you're using the other device (for instance, a scanner). However, you can't use both devices at the same time; the pass-through adapter prevents the need to disconnect one device while using the other.

- To connect two devices to a SCSI port, you connect the devices in a *daisy-chain* configuration. For example, if you have a SCSI scanner and an external drive, you connect the drive to the SCSI port and then plug the scanner into the open SCSI port on the external drive. You may have to flip a switch or attach a terminator to the last device in the chain.

- USB devices are similar to SCSI devices, requiring a daisy-chain configuration. You plug one device, such as a keyboard, into the USB port, and the next USB device, such as a mouse, into the first.

SEE ALSO
➤ *Learn how to install additional ports, page 787*

Connecting the Power Cables

After you've connected all the accessories to your system unit, you can plug the system unit and accessories into a power outlet.

To prevent power surges (typically caused by lightning) from damaging your equipment, you should make sure the outlet is grounded. If your home or apartment was built in the past 10 years, you can be fairly certain that all the power outlets in your home are three-pronged, grounded outlets, but you should test the outlet you intend to use for your PC to make sure. Obtain an outlet tester from the local hardware or electronics store and plug it in. Lights on the tester indicate if the negative and positive terminals are hooked up properly and if the outlet is grounded.

If the test shows that the outlet is not grounded, you have two choices: hire a certified electrician to install a grounded outlet or plug in a three-pronged adapter that has a grounding tab or wire. If you choose the second option, secure the grounding tab or green grounding wire to the cover plate, using the screw that holds the cover plate in place. Test the outlet again.

No protection with a power strip

A basic power strip offers no protection against power surges. It acts as an extension cord, allowing you to connect several devices to a single outlet. I strongly advise against using unprotected outlets.

When you are sure the outlet is grounded, plug a power strip, surge suppresser, or uninterruptible power supply (UPS) into the outlet, and then plug your system unit and all external accessories into the power strip, surge suppresser, or UPS. The following sections explain the benefits of using a surge suppresser or UPS and show you how to arrange your cables.

Using a Surge Suppresser

A power surge can easily damage or destroy the sensitive electrical components inside your PC. To protect your PC completely, you should unplug it during electrical storms. Be sure to unplug the modem, too.

To further protect your computer (and to protect it when you're not there to unplug it), you should connect the system unit and any other devices (including your modem) to a *surge suppresser* (or *surge protector*). A surge suppresser prevents high voltage current from passing through it and absorbs excess energy to prevent it from passing through to your equipment.

When shopping for a surge suppresser, here's what you should look for:

- *A reliable manufacturer.* If you get your surge protector from the bargain rack at Wal-Mart, don't expect it to protect your system. APC and Tripp Lite are two manufacturers with solid reputations.

- *A UL rating of 400 or less.* The UL rating represents the maximum voltage that the surge suppresser will let pass through it.

- *An energy-absorption rating of 400 or more.* The energy-absorption rating represents the amount of energy the suppresser can absorb before it's toasted.

- *A sufficient number of outlets for both power cords and phone lines (RJ11 jacks).* A surge from a lightning bolt passing through your phone lines and modem to your system unit's motherboard can fry your entire system.

- *A guarantee.* Many companies offer not only a money-back guarantee, but also a guarantee that covers the cost of any devices damaged by a power surge if the power suppresser fails to do its job.

To connect your equipment to a surge suppresser, plug the surge suppresser into a grounded outlet and plug your system unit and all accessories into the outlets on the surge suppresser. Most surge suppressers have a switch that you must turn on; the switch lights when the unit is on.

Using an Uninterruptible Power Supply (UPS)

Superior to a power strip and more powerful than a surge suppresser, a UPS is a device that not only protects against power surges but also supplies power to your system during power outages.

You connect your system unit and accessories to the UPS the same way you connect to a surge suppresser. Plug the UPS into a grounded outlet and then plug your system unit and accessories into the UPS.

The UPS draws power from the outlet to charge a battery and then feeds power to your system from the battery. During a power outage, a typical UPS battery can keep your PC running for 10 to 30 minutes, long enough for you to save your work, and usually long enough to keep your computer running until the lights come back on.

When shopping for a UPS, look for the following features:

- *Maximum volt-ampere output of 300–400VA.* This indicates the number of devices the UPS can power. Most Pentium systems require a UPS with a rating of 300VA to keep the power supply running. If you plug in a 17-inch monitor and a few additional devices, you'll need a UPS with a higher VA rating. Multiply the amperage of each device by the voltage (usually 120V) and add the results.

- *Sufficient outlets.* You'll need an outlet for each device you intend to plug in plus two phone jacks—one from the wall jack to the UPS and another from the UPS to the modem.

- *Reliability during a power outage.* Four types of UPSs are available: standby or offline, online, line interactive, and

Powering up your system from the suppresser

Although you can turn your computer on and off from the surge suppresser and save wear and tear on individual buttons, some devices (especially printers) don't shut down properly unless you use the power button on the printer. Check your documentation.

Ferroresonant. With both the offline and line interactive UPS, there is a slight dip in power when the UPS changes from direct power to battery power during an outage. An online UPS provides a constant, steady source of power from the battery at all times, preventing power dips and other fluctuations. The Ferroresonant UPS switches between direct and battery power, like a standby or line interactive UPS, but it regulates the voltage to prevent power dips, fluctuations, and line noise while working in standby mode.

- *User-replaced batteries.* Make sure you can replace the batteries yourself. Some units come with batteries that must be replaced by the manufacturer. Check on battery life and on the price of replacement batteries. High-end units allow you to replace batteries while the UPS is in use.

- *Indicator lights.* High-end units provide lights that indicate whether the unit is using direct power or battery power, when the batteries are running low and when they need to be replaced, and if the power outlet is properly wired.

- *Automatic system shutdown utilities.* Some high-end units come with software utilities that can automatically shut your system down in the event that the duration of the power outage exceeds the available time the batteries can supply power.

- *Guarantee.* The manufacturer should not only guarantee the UPS, but also offer reimbursement for any devices that suffer damage from a power surge while connected to the UPS.

Arranging Your Cables

After you've connected everything, the back of your PC looks like a bowl of Ramen noodle soup. Although the mess may not cause major problems, you should try to move any modem or phone cables away from the other cables to prevent interference. In addition, you should arrange the cables to prevent them from getting tangled around your feet and to make it easier to work on your PC later.

Money-saving tip

Purchase a UPS that has a power rating high enough to run only the system unit. Plug your other devices into a high-quality surge suppresser. You need the UPS primarily to protect you from losing any work you haven't saved to disk. The other devices, including your printer and scanner, don't need a continuous power supply.

The easiest way to arrange your cables is to fold up any excess cable and secure it with a plastic tie (the kind commonly packaged with trash bags). You can also purchase special cable hangers at your local electronics store. You affix the hanger to your desk or wall and then snap the cables into clips. Duct tape works fine, but removing it later can damage your desk or wall and leave a sticky residue on the cables.

Setting Up a Notebook (Portable) PC

You might think that setting up a notebook PC is a no-brainer—you plug it in and start using it. Although it's true that the system unit, monitor, and pointing device are all integrated, additional devices, such as a CD-ROM drive, floppy disk drive, and modem, are not built in to the system unit as they are on a desktop PC. Before you can use these devices, you must connect them, as explained in the following sections.

SEE ALSO

➤ *Learn how to connect a notebook PC to a docking station, page 273*

➤ *Learn how to use the infrared port on a notebook PC, page 279*

➤ *Learn how to attach a mouse to your notebook PC, page 285*

Loading the Battery

Your notebook PC should include a battery that normally comes packaged in an anti-static bag. Remove the battery from its bag, being careful not to touch the contacts. Turn the computer off and slide the battery into the battery compartment (typically on the underside of the notebook PC). The battery should snap in place (see Figure 2.13).

Connect the power cord to the DC-in port and plug it into a grounded power outlet. Most notebook PCs have a built-in battery charger that charges the battery whenever the battery power runs low, regardless of whether the PC is in use or not. The battery you receive usually needs a charge.

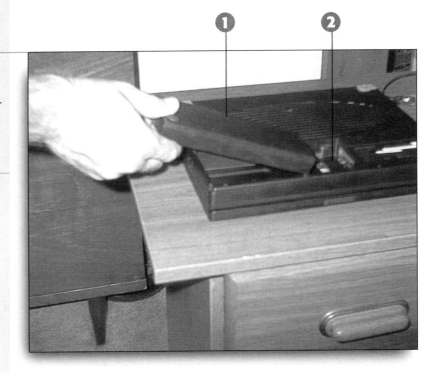

FIGURE 2.13

Insert the battery into the battery compartment and snap it in place.

1 Battery

2 Battery compartment

SEE ALSO

➤ *Learn how to conserve battery power on a notebook PC, page 281*

Installing PC Cards

Most notebook PCs have two PC card slots that allow you to install additional devices, such as a modem, network card, or joystick. The cards are about the size of a credit card, but thicker.

Check the documentation to determine whether it is safe to insert a card while the power is on. Also find out which slot to use for the first card you install and for the second card. Slots are usually designated 0 and 1. Use slot 0 for the first card and slot 1 for the second.

To insert a card, hold the card by its edges with the label facing up and insert it into one of the PC card slots. Push the card in all the way, so it's flush with the edge of the PC. With most cards, you must also connect a cable to the card. For example, most PC card modems have a narrow port into which you plug a connector that has the required phone jacks (see Figure 2.14).

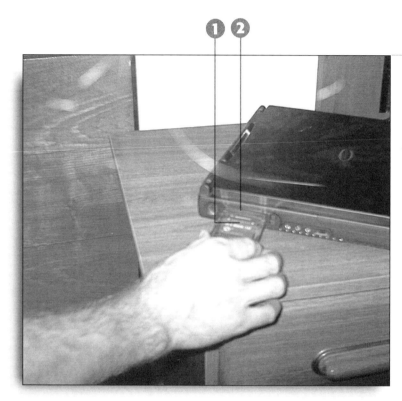

FIGURE 2.14

Insert the PC card into the PC card slot and push it in.

1 PC card

2 PC card slot

After inserting the card, you must install a device driver that tells your computer how to communicate with the card. See Chapter 11, "Using Windows on a Notebook PC," for details. Chapter 11 also shows you how to safely eject a PC card.

SEE ALSO
➤ *Learn how to safely insert and remove PC cards, page 270*

Connecting a Disk Drive

Most notebook PCs offer a modular CD-ROM, DVD, and floppy disk configuration that features a swappable drive bay. You insert the drive into the built-in drive bay on the notebook PC.

You'll commonly insert the CD-ROM drive into this bay, but you can insert a floppy disk drive, instead.

To connect another disk drive, you must connect to an open port or to a PC card. Many notebook PCs allow you to connect a second drive to the parallel port. If given a choice, connect the floppy disk drive to the parallel port and install the CD-ROM drive in the internal port—it's faster (see Figure 2.15).

If you must connect the drive to a PC card, insert the PC card and connect the cable from the drive to the PC card, as explained in the previous section.

FIGURE 2.15

A typical notebook PC with a CD-ROM drive and a floppy disk drive.

❶ CD-ROM drive connected to internal drive bay

❷ Floppy drive connected to parallel port

Pre-Flight Checklist

Before you flip the power switch or press the power button on your PC and accessories, you should check your cable connections to make sure you've connected everything to the proper ports and to the power outlets and ensure that the connections are secure. The following pre-flight checklist leads you through the necessary checks.

Checking your cable connections

1. Make sure your surge suppresser or UPS is securely plugged into a grounded power outlet.

2. Make sure your system unit, monitor, printer, and any other accessories that require a separate power supply are plugged into outlets on the surge suppresser or UPS.

3. Check your printer and mouse connections to make sure you haven't plugged the keyboard into the mouse port and vice versa.

4. Make sure all cables are securely attached to the proper ports on the system unit. Gently tug or jiggle the cables to test the connections. If any screws are loose, tighten them now.

5. Follow each cable from the system unit to the corresponding device to ensure that the other end of the cable is securely connected to the device. If the port on the accessory has clips or bale wires for securing the plug, make sure they're in place.

6. Follow the cables from any accessories back to the system unit (or, in the case of USB and SCSI devices, back to the other device the cable is supposed to connect to) to ensure that the device is connected properly.

Starting Your PC

Turning on a PC isn't quite as easy as turning on a TV set, especially the first time you turn on your PC. When you first turn on your PC, Windows runs and checks to see which hardware is installed on your computer. If a device is not on, Windows cannot detect it and will not prompt you to install the software required for using the device. So, turn on your equipment in the proper sequence.

On all systems, the PC manufacturer installs Windows so it can start and test the PC before shipping it. However, the

Hold that button!

Power buttons differ. On some systems, you press and release the button to turn on the power. You'll feel the button click when you press it. On most notebook PCs and some desktop models, you must press and hold the button for a couple seconds.

manufacturer typically tests the PC without the printer and other accessories connected, so the first time you run your PC with everything connected, Windows runs the Add New Hardware Wizard. (A *wizard* is a series of dialog boxes that leads you step-by-step through the process of performing a task.)

The Add New Hardware Wizard steps you through the process of installing the software (called a *device driver*) that tells Windows how to communicate with the device. If a device came with its own device driver (on a floppy disk or CD), use that driver instead of the driver included with Windows. The Add New Hardware driver displays an option named **Have Disk** that allows you to install a driver from a disk. Otherwise, you must install the driver from the Windows CD.

Turning on your computer

1. Turn on your monitor. The monitor takes some time to warm up and displays startup messages when you turn on the system unit.

2. Turn on the printer.

3. Turn on any external drives or other devices, including the speakers.

4. Turn on the system unit.

5. If Windows detects any devices that were not installed by the manufacturer, it automatically installs the software (drivers) for the devices or runs the Add New Hardware Wizard. Follow the wizard's instructions (see Figure 2.16).

What You'll See on Startup

When you start your PC, the system performs a series of internal checks and loads the basic instructions it needs to operate and use devices such as the hard drive. These instructions are called the *Basic Input Output System* or *BIOS*, and are stored on a chip inside the system unit.

Integrated monitor?

On notebook PCs and some desktop models, the monitor is integrated with the system unit. You press one power button or flip one switch on the system unit to start both the monitor and system unit.

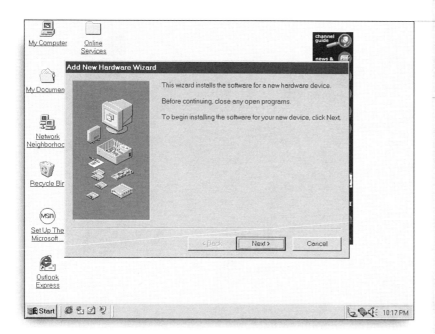

FIGURE 2.16
Use the Add New Hardware Wizard to install drivers for your PC accessories.

As the system starts, it displays the name and date of the BIOS along with details about the amount of RAM (memory) installed, the disk drives, and other hardware. It may also display a message telling you which key to press to enter the BIOS setup. You'll learn how to do this in Chapter 24, "General Installation Precautions and Procedures."

After loading the BIOS, the system checks your floppy disk drive and hard disk drive for the operating system, Windows, which provides the bulk of the instructions your computer needs to operate. If you have a disk in the floppy drive, your computer will display an error message saying that the disk is not a system disk. Eject the disk and press any key to resume startup.

The system then loads Windows from the hard disk and displays the Windows desktop, shown in Figure 2.17.

SEE ALSO

➤ *Learn how to check and change the BIOS settings on startup, page 567*

FIGURE 2.17

When your PC has finished booting itself, it displays the Windows desktop.

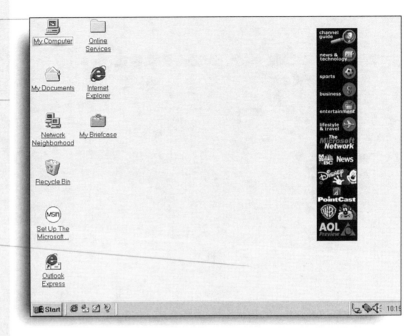

Leaving the Power On

Faster startup

To increase the speed at which your computer starts, you can change the BIOS settings to tell your computer to look to the hard drive for startup instructions and to bypass some internal checks.

At this point, you may be wondering if it's better to leave your PC on or turn it off when you're not using it. In most cases, leaving the PC on is a good idea. Newer system units and monitors have built-in power-saving features that automatically shut down the devices that use the most power: disk drives and monitors, or place them in standby mode.

Turning your PC on and off places additional strain on the power switches and sensitive electrical components. Each time you turn the computer off and back on, the components cool down and heat up, which, over a long period of time, can cause components or solder joints to crack.

SEE ALSO

➤ *Learn how to adjust the power settings in Windows, page 224*

Maintaining Your Equipment

Obtain the proper tools for cleaning your system

Preventive maintenance

Clean your mouse to prevent erratic mouse pointer movement

Clean your disks, drives, and printer

Annual maintenance checklist

Janitorial Tools

Before you start cleaning your equipment, gather the following cleaning supplies:

- *Screwdriver or socket wrench for taking the cover off of your system unit.* (If you don't feel qualified to go inside the system unit, take your computer to a qualified technician for a thorough annual cleaning. It really does get dusty in there.)

- *Computer vacuum.* Yes, they have vacuum cleaners especially designed for computers.

- *Can of compressed air.* You can get this at a computer or electronics store. If you decide to forego the vacuum cleaner, you can use the compressed air to blow dust out of the system unit.

- *Soft brush* (a clean paintbrush with soft bristles will do). Use the brush to dislodge any stubborn dust that the vacuum won't pick up.

- *Toothpicks.* The only tool you need to clean your mouse.

- *Cotton swabs.*

- *Paper towel.*

- *Rubbing alcohol.*

- *Distilled water.* (You can get special wipes for your monitor, but paper towels and water will do the trick.)

- *CD wipes.* You can use window cleaner and a soft cotton cloth when you're in a pinch, but CD wipes are softer and more effective.

Safety Precautions and Preventive Maintenance

You don't want to ruin your computer in the process of cleaning and maintaining it, so follow a few simple precautions:

- Before you work inside the system unit, shut down your system and unplug it.

Disk cleaning kit?

Don't run out and buy a disk or CD-ROM cleaning kit. If your drive is having trouble reading disks, then get the kit and clean the drive.

- When working inside the system unit, hold onto the metal case with one hand to prevent static electricity from building up. Or, purchase a grounding strap from your local electronics store and wear it as you clean.

- Don't touch any components or soldered areas on the circuit boards.

- When vacuuming inside the system unit, avoid flipping any switches or knocking components or jumpers off of the printed circuit boards.

- Always check the documentation that came with a device for specific instructions on which parts you should clean and which parts you should never even touch. The documentation should also list the preferred cleaning solution(s) to use.

- Avoid using ammonia-based cleaning solutions. Use only rubbing alcohol and distilled water.

- In general, use rubbing alcohol for cleaning metal and glass parts of your computer. It works well and dries fast, making it an excellent cleaning solution for electronic devices. Water is best for cleaning plastic and rubber—the monitor case, printer, mouse ball, print rollers, and so on. Rubbing alcohol tends to dry out rubber and can harm the finish on some plastics.

Of course, the best option for cleaning your system is to keep it clean. Here are some tips to help you keep your system clean so you won't have to clean it as often:

- Vacuum around the system unit every time you vacuum the room. The system unit has one or more fans that suck air through the system unit to cool the electrical components. They also suck in dust.

- Use a mouse pad and wipe it off every couple days. The mouse ball will pick up hair, dust, crumbs, and any other debris and deposit it on rollers inside the mouse. If you don't clean up around the mouse, you'll be cleaning the mouse every month.

- Don't smoke around your system. Smoke can leave a permanent residue on the electrical components.

Use approved cleaning solutions

Refer to your PC's documentation to determine the approved cleaning solution for a device. ArmorAll may make your car look nice and shiny, but using it on your PC could cause damage and void the warranty.

- Wash your hands before you work. If you don't keep your hands clean, the keys on your keyboard will go gray prematurely (fortunately, the gray keys don't show the dirt). You can purchase a keyboard cover, but nobody really likes typing through a rubber sheath.

- Cover your computer with a sheet when you're vacuuming or dusting the room. A vacuum cleaner stirs up a lot of dust. Be sure to remove the sheet when you're done, so it doesn't restrict air flow around your PC.

- Change the air filters on your furnace every month to reduce the amount of dust from the air ducts.

SEE ALSO

➤ *Learn more about safety precautions for working inside a PC, page 557*

Vacuuming and Dusting Your Equipment

Cheap system unit air filter

If you can determine where the air is coming into the system unit, cut a square of sheer hosiery fabric, stretch it over the openings, and tape it in place. (Keep the tape away from the openings.) Check the filter regularly and replace it whenever dust builds up. Don't tape over any fan that's pumping air OUT or you'll trap the dust in.

Work from the top down and from the outside in. Start with the monitor. (You can use your regular vacuum cleaner for this part; if you have a brush attachment, use it.) Run the vacuum up and down all the slots at the top and sides of the monitor. This is where most of the dust settles. Work down to the tilt-swivel base and vacuum that (you may need a narrow hose extension to reach in there). Now vacuum speakers, around the outside of the printer (don't go inside), and any other devices. If the dust is stuck to a device, wipe it off with a damp (not soaking wet) paper towel.

Next, vacuum the system unit. When vacuuming, make sure you vacuum the ventilation holes. Any other openings in the case act as additional ventilation holes: the floppy disk drive, power button, CD-ROM drive, open drive bays, and so on. Vacuum these openings.

Finally, vacuum the dust from the cables behind your computer. Dust accumulates on the cables and the surge suppresser or UPS. Many surge suppressers have outlets that face up; these outlets can quickly become filled with dust.

Every year or so, you should vacuum inside the system unit,

using a special vacuum cleaner designed for this. Take the following steps.

Vacuuming inside the system unit

1. Carefully remove the system unit cover.

2. Keeping the tip of the vacuum away from all electrical components, vacuum any low-lying areas, including the motherboard and expansion boards, and the areas near the bottom of the case (see Figure 3.1).

3. Vacuum the fan blades, the area around the fan, and the ventilation holes.

4. Vacuum around the disk drives.

5. If you cannot reach a dusty area with the vacuum cleaner, wipe the dust out with a dry cotton swab or blow it out with compressed air.

6. Replace the system unit cover.

Do not use a household vacuum on your PC

Use only a PC vacuum to clean inside the system unit. The suction and air flow on any standard vacuum cleaner is too strong and could suck chips off the circuit boards.

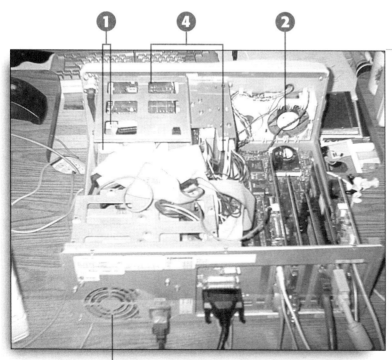

FIGURE 3.1

Clean inside the system unit at least once every year.

① Vacuum horizontal surfaces and low-lying areas.

② Vacuum the fan blades and the area around the fan(s).

③ Vacuum around the ventilation holes.

④ Vacuum around the disk drives.

Cleaning Your Monitor

Like a TV, a monitor's electrostatic charge attracts dust, and you have to clean it every couple weeks. Check the documentation that came with your computer or monitor to see if it's okay to use window cleaner on the monitor—the monitor may have an anti-glare coating that can be damaged by alcohol- or ammonia-based cleaning solutions. (If window cleaner is not okay, use water.) Spray the window cleaner (or water) on a paper towel, just enough to make it damp, and then wipe the screen. *Don't* spray window cleaner or any other liquid directly on the monitor; you don't want moisture to seep in.

You can purchase special anti-static wipes for your monitor. These not only clean your monitor safely, but they also discharge the static electricity to prevent future dust build-up.

Cleaning Your Mouse

Cheap trick

Don't waste your money on anti-static wipes. Wipe your monitor with a used dryer sheet. (A new dryer sheet might smudge the screen with fabric softener.)

If you can't get your mouse pointer to move where you want it to, you can usually fix the problem by cleaning the mouse. Flip the mouse over and look for a hair or other debris on the mouse ball or on your desk or mouse pad. It that doesn't work, give the mouse a thorough cleaning, as explained in the following steps.

Mouse cleaning

1. Turn the mouse over and remove the mouse ball cover (typically, you press down on the cover and turn counterclockwise).

2. Remove the mouse ball and wipe it thoroughly with a moistened paper towel (no alcohol).

3. Inside the mouse, gently scrape the rings off the three mouse rollers using a cotton swab or the side of a toothpick. Turn the rollers while you scrape, to remove the entire ring (see Figure 3.2).

4. Turn the mouse back over and shake it to remove any dirt you dislodged from the rollers.

5. When the mouse ball is dry, insert it and replace the cover.

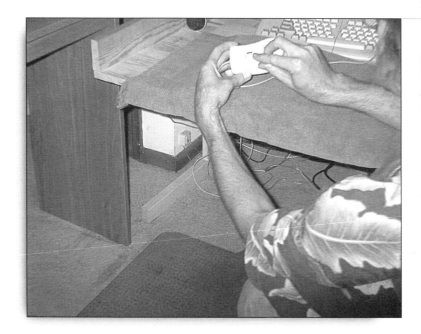

FIGURE 3.2

Gently scrape the rings from around the rollers inside the mouse.

Cleaning Your Keyboard

Your keyboard is like a three-dimensional place mat, catching any dust and debris that falls from above. The easiest way I've found to clean a keyboard is to turn it upside-down and shake it gently. Repeat two or three times to get any particles that fall behind the backs of the keys when you flip it over. If a gentle shake is not enough to dislodge the debris, turn the keyboard upside-down and blow compressed air between the keys.

For a more thorough cleaning, shut down your computer, and disconnect the keyboard. Dampen a cotton swab with rubbing alcohol and gently scrub the keys. Wait for the alcohol to evaporate before reconnecting the keyboard and turning on the juice.

If you spill a drink on your keyboard, try to save your work and shut down the computer using your mouse. Flip the keyboard over. If you spilled water, let the keyboard dry out thoroughly. If you spilled something sticky, give your keyboard a bath or shower with lukewarm water. Take the back off of the keyboard, but *Don't* flip the keyboard over with the back off or parts will scurry across your desktop. Let it dry for a couple days (don't use a blow-dryer), and put it back together. If some of the keys are still sticky, clean around them with a cotton swab dipped in rubbing alcohol. If you still have problems, buy a new keyboard; they're relatively inexpensive.

SEE ALSO

➤ *Learn how to replace your keyboard when it is damaged, page 718*

Cleaning Your Disk Drives

Damaged disk drive

Although disk drives are fairly reliable, the read/write head inside the drive may go out of alignment or the spin mechanism may wear out. If the drive has trouble reading all disks, try cleaning the drive. If cleaning doesn't help, replace the drive.

Disk drives are almost maintenance free. The internal hard disk is permanently sealed inside the drive, and as long as you vacuum around the openings of external drives on a regular basis, they should remain clean and trouble-free inside. However, if you have a CD-ROM drive or a DVD drive, you should wipe the drive tray with a moist towel whenever you see dust or dirt on it.

You may have seen cleaning kits for floppy disk drives and CD-ROM drives. The kit comes with a disk (or disc) and some cleaning solution. You squirt the cleaning solution on the disk, insert it in the drive, and then eject the disk after it has spun a few revolutions. My advice is to avoid these cleaning kits unless the drive is having trouble reading every disk you insert. In most cases, the drive is fine, but the disk is damaged or dirty. The following section explains how to inspect and clean CDs.

SEE ALSO

➤ *Learn how to scan for and repair disk problems, page 259*

Cleaning Your CDs

If your CD-ROM drive is having trouble reading a disc, the disc is usually the cause of the problem. CD-ROM drives read from the bottom of the disc (the side without print), check for dirt, fingerprints, and scratches. Even a small piece of lint can render a disc unreadable.

To clean the disc, use a special wipe for CDs and wipe from the center of the disc to the outer edges, as shown in Figure 3.3. If you don't have special wipes, spray a little window cleaner on the bottom of the disc and use a soft, cotton cloth to wipe the disc. Make sure the disc is completely dry before inserting it in the drive.

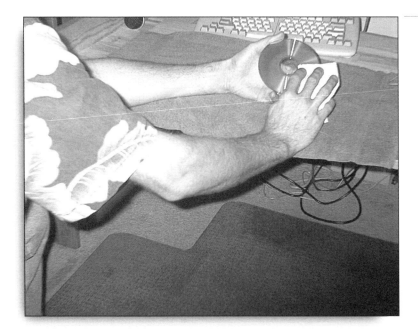

FIGURE 3.3
To clean a CD, wipe the bottom of the CD from the center to the outside edges.

On some systems, the reading mechanism inside the drive is visible when you open the drive; it looks like a small glass eye. If you can see the mechanism, check for dust and wipe it off with a dry cotton swab.

Maintaining Your Printer

Printer maintenance varies widely from one printer to another. If you have a laser printer, you'll need to vacuum or wipe up toner dust and clean the little print wires with cotton swabs dipped in rubbing alcohol. For an inkjet printer, you may have to remove the print cartridge and wipe the print heads with a damp cotton swab. If you have a combination scanner/printer, you may have to wipe the glass on which you place your original.

You also need to be careful about the cleaning solution you use. Most printer manufacturers tell you to use only water on any of the inside parts: print rollers, print heads, and so on. In other cases, you can use a mild cleaning solution. Some manufacturers recommend rubbing alcohol on some, but not all, parts.

Even with all of these variables, there are a few things you can do to keep the printer in peak condition and ensure high-quality output:

- When turning off the printer, always use the power button on the printer (don't use the power button on your power strip). This ensures that the print head is moved to its resting position. On inkjet printers, this prevents the print head from drying out.

- Vacuum inside the printer. Open any doors or covers to get inside.

- If the ink starts to streak on your printouts (or you have frequent paper jams in a laser printer), get special printer-cleaner paper from an office supply store and follow the instructions to run the sheet through your printer a few times.

- Using a damp cotton ball, wipe paper dust and any ink off of the paper feed rollers. *Don't* use alcohol. *Don't* use paper towel; fibers from the paper towel could stick to the wheels.

PC Maintenance Schedule

You probably have a maintenance schedule for your home. You clean the gutters every spring and fall, change the filters on your furnace every month, and treat a few stubborn drains every couple months. You should follow a similar schedule for cleaning and maintaining your PC. Use Table 3.1 as a guide.

TABLE 3.1   **PC maintenance schedule**

Frequency	Task
Weekly	Wipe monitor
	Vacuum all equipment
	Wipe off mouse pad
Monthly	Clean mouse ball and rollers
	Vacuum thoroughly around and under system unit
	Blow dust from under keyboard keys
Annually	Vacuum inside system unit
	Wipe dirt off keyboard keys
As needed	Clean disk drives
	Clean CDs or DVDs
	Run cleaning paper through printer

Maintaining Your System, Disks, and Files

System maintenance requires more than keeping your computer clean. You should back up your files regularly, remove unnecessary files from your hard disk, update device drivers, and update your software. To perform these maintenance tasks, you use special programs, called *utilities*. Windows comes with the system utilities you need.

SEE ALSO

➤ *Learn how to use the Windows system utilities, page 247*

➤ *Learn how to back up files from your hard disk, page 341*

➤ *Learn how to manage your disks, folders, and files in Windows, page 177*

Using Windows

Windows Basics

Navigate the Windows desktop

Run Windows and DOS programs

Resize and rearrange program windows

Enter commands using menus and toolbar buttons

Install and uninstall programs

Starting Windows

There's nothing to starting Windows. It starts automatically when you turn on your computer. On startup, Windows displays a *splash* screen as it loads its startup files. The length of time this splash screen appears depends on the speed of your computer and on the complexity of the startup files. As you install programs and add devices, the startup files become larger, adding time to the Windows startup.

If your system is set up to use passwords, you may be prompted to enter your username and password (see Figure 4.1). Type your name in the **User name** text box. You don't have to type a password; you can enter a password later, if you choose to use one. Passwords allow you to customize Windows for different users; they don't protect your computer against unauthorized use. For example, if several people share the same computer, each person can customize Windows as desired.

FIGURE 4.1

When Windows starts, it may prompt you to enter your name and password.

1 Type your name.

2 Password is optional.

3 Click **OK**.

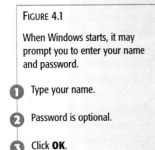
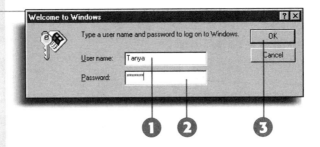

When the Windows startup is complete, the Windows desktop appears. The desktop is a *graphical user interface* that allows you to run programs by clicking icons (small pictures that represent programs) or by selecting programs from the **Start** menu. The following section takes you on a tour of the Windows desktop.

SEE ALSO

➤ *Learn how to start your computer properly, page 73*

➤ *Learn how to set up Windows for multiple users, page 322*

➤ *Learn how to log on to a network, page 305*

Windows Desktop Tour

The Windows desktop (see Figure 4.2) is modeled after your desktop. It is a work area that contains the tools required to perform your computing tasks and that allows you to spread out any documents you are creating or editing. Although your Windows desktop may differ from the desktop shown in Figure 4.2, depending on which Windows components and programs are installed on your computer, your desktop should have the following items:

- *Windows icons.* Typically located on the left side of the desktop, the Windows icons include My Computer, Recycle Bin, and Online Services. You will learn how to add icons to the desktop in Chapter 8, "Customizing Windows."

- *Start button.* In the lower-left corner of the screen is the **Start** button. You click the **Start** button to open a menu listing the programs and features installed on your PC.

- *Taskbar.* The taskbar displays buttons for any programs that are currently running. To switch to a program, click its button. The taskbar may also include the Quick Launch toolbar (to the right of the **Start** button), which contains buttons for running Internet programs and quickly returning to the desktop.

- *System tray.* On the right end of the taskbar is an area that displays the current time along with icons for accessing the audio controls and for programs that are running in the background.

- *Channel bar.* If you have Windows 98 or Windows 95 with Internet Explorer 4, the Channel bar appears on the desktop. You can use this bar as a channel changer for the Web and add your own buttons to it.

Getting to Know the Windows Icons

The Windows icons allow you to quickly run programs, delete and restore files, explore your system resources, access the Internet, and more. Table 4.1 lists the most common Windows icons you'll find on the desktop.

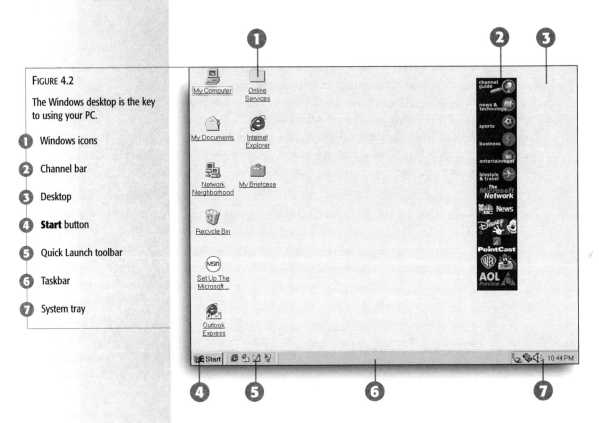

FIGURE 4.2

The Windows desktop is the key to using your PC.

1 Windows icons

2 Channel bar

3 Desktop

4 **Start** button

5 Quick Launch toolbar

6 Taskbar

7 System tray

TABLE 4.1   **Windows desktop icons**

Icon	Name	What It Does
	My Computer	Displays a window that allows you to view the contents of your disks and folders, set up printers, and configure Windows.
	My Documents	Provides quick access to any folders or files you store in the My Documents folder.
	Internet Explorer	Runs Internet Explorer, the Web browser that is included with Windows 98. The first time you select this icon, the Internet Connection Wizard appears, prompting you to set up your Internet account.

Icon	Name	What It Does
	Network Neighborhood	Appears only if you installed network or Dial-Up Networking support for Windows. This icon opens a window that allows you to access other computers and resources on your company's network, assuming your computer is connected to a network.
	Outlook Express	Runs the Windows email and news program, which allows you to send and receive typed messages over the Internet and to connect to electronic message boards to read and post messages.
	Recycle Bin	Acts as a safety net for files that you choose to delete. When you delete a file, it is placed in the Recycle Bin and remains there until you choose to empty the Recycle Bin or the bin becomes full and starts automatically deleting the oldest trash.
	My Briefcase	Appears only if you chose to install the Windows notebook tools during the Windows installation. You can use Briefcase to quickly transfer data from your desktop computer to your notebook or vice versa.
	Online Services	Provides tools for subscribing to most of the major commercial online services, including America Online, Prodigy, CompuServe, and The Microsoft Network.
	Set Up the Microsoft...	Leads you through the process of subscribing to The Microsoft Network. This is the same icon you find in the Online Services folder.

SEE ALSO

➤ *Learn how to manage disks, folders, and files with My Computer, page* 177

➤ *Learn how to navigate the Web with Internet Explorer, page* 411

My desktop background is different

The figures in this book show a standard Windows background with a solid color. The manufacturer may have installed a special background on your system or Windows may be set up to use a Web page as the background. To change the background, see Chapter 8.

➤ *Learn how to use the Network Neighborhood, page 310*

➤ *Learn how to use Outlook Express, page 435*

➤ *Learn how to delete and recover files using the Recycle Bin, page 192*

➤ *Learn how to safely transfer document files between two computers, page 276*

➤ *Learn how to set up an account with a commercial online service, such as America Online, page 364*

The Many Faces (Versions) of Windows

During its illustrious career, Windows has undergone many transformations. The very popular Windows 3.1 (not covered in this book) was the first version to succeed in making PCs easier to use. It consisted of a simple desktop with program group icons. You double-clicked a program group to open a window that contained icons for running specific programs. You then double-clicked a program's icon to run the program.

With Windows 95, Microsoft completely revamped the desktop, placing icons for the programs you use most right on the desktop and transforming program groups into submenus on the **Start**, **Programs** menu. Windows 95 also introduced the taskbar for quickly switching from program to program. However, Microsoft has developed several versions of Windows 95, so your version may look and behave a little differently than other versions you may encounter.

To determine which version of Windows 95 you have, right-click My Computer and click **Properties**. This opens the System Properties dialog box, which displays the Windows 95 version number. Table 4.2 lists and describes the different versions of Windows 95. Note that some versions are marked OSR, which stands for OEM (Original Equipment Manufacturer) Service Release. This means that the version was never sold directly to consumers, so you could get the version only by purchasing a new computer.

TABLE 4.2 **Windows 95 versions**

Version Number	Version Name	Enhancements
4.00.950	Windows 95	None. This is the original version of Windows 95.
4.00.950A	Service Release 1	Bug fixes. Microsoft posted a service release upgrade on its Web site and made it available to both OEMs and the general public. Also known as OSR1.
4.00.950B	OSR2 and 2.1	Fat32 to increase hard disk storage, enhanced support for PCMCIA, power management improvements, Web integration with Internet Explorer 4.0, and DirectX 2.0 (for multimedia and games). OSR2.1 includes USB support.
4.00.950C	OSR2.5	Upgrade to Internet Explorer 4.01, USB support, DirectX 5 support, updated Online Services folder, and minor fixes.

On its surface, Windows 98 doesn't look or act much differently from Windows 95 OSR2. However, Windows 98 makes all the improvements to Windows 95 accessible to the general public through an upgrade. In addition, it contains additional support for newer hardware technologies and a collection of useful utilities for maintaining, optimizing, and automating your system. Following is a list of the major improvements in Windows 98:

- The Active Desktop provides single-click access to programs and documents on your computer.

- The taskbar includes a new toolbar called *Quick Launch*, which allows you to quickly run programs for accessing the Internet. You can turn on additional toolbars and drag icons to the Quick Launch toolbar to configure it.

- The **Start**, **Find** submenu (which you may have used to search for files on your computer) now helps you search for people and resources on the Internet.

- Windows 98 comes with Internet Explorer 4, a set of programs for accessing the Internet. The Internet Explorer suite includes Internet Explorer (for viewing Web pages),

Outlook Express (for email and newsgroups), NetMeeting (for placing phone calls across the Internet), FrontPage Express (for creating your own Web pages), and a few additional Internet tools.

- The **Start**, **Favorites** submenu allows you to quickly access Web pages and other objects that you have marked as Favorites.

- Windows 98 supports FAT32 for enhanced data storage. The FAT32 Converter lets you divide a large hard drive into smaller sectors, so small files don't take up so much space. This can help you reclaim hundreds of megabytes of wasted space (*slack space*) on a large hard drive.

- Automatic updates allow you to upgrade to the latest release of Windows by downloading updates from Microsoft's Web site (on the Internet). This ensures that you are working with the latest release.

- Enhanced power saving features allow Windows to automatically power down the monitor and disk drives when you're not using your computer. You can leave your computer running without wasting energy.

- The Windows 98 Maintenance Wizard optimizes your system for you to increase performance.

- Windows has built-in support for the latest technologies, allowing properly equipped PCs to tune in to TV stations and control electronic devices, such as stereos, VCRs, and DVD players. Windows 98 also includes support for USB devices.

- A new Effects tab in the Display Properties dialog box provides additional control over the appearance of desktop icons.

- The new Backup applet supports additional backup devices, making it less likely that you'll need a special backup program.

- Task Scheduler allows you to automate your computer by having Windows run programs or open documents at a scheduled time or when a particular event occurs (such as when you start your computer).

This book covers Windows 98. If you are using Windows 95, purchase and install the Windows 98 upgrade. To take advantage of many of the hardware upgrades discussed in Part IV, "Upgrading Your PC: Installing New Hardware," you need Windows 98.

Running Programs

Windows is designed to make it easy to run programs. Instead of typing a command to run the program, you select the name of the program from the **Start**, **Programs** menu or one of its submenus or click its icon on the desktop or in the My Computer window. The following sections show you various ways to run programs.

Using the Windows Start Menu

The **Start** menu contains the names of most programs installed on your PC. You run a program by selecting it from the **Programs** submenu or one of its submenus (see Figure 4.3).

Running a program from the Start menu

1. Click the **Start** button.

2. Point to **Programs**.

3. If the program is on a submenu, point to the name of the submenu.

4. Click the name of the program.

SEE ALSO

➤ *Learn how to rearrange programs and program groups on the Start menu, page 214*

Launching Programs from the Desktop

The Windows desktop offers the most convenient access to programs. Initially, the desktop contains icons for running Windows programs, such as My Computer, but you can place additional icons, called *shortcuts*, on the Windows desktop.

Programs, applications, and utilities

A *program* is any set of instructions that tell your computer how to perform a task. An *application* is a program that allows you to perform a task, such as creating and printing a document or managing your checkbook. A *utility* is a program that helps manage or protect your PC or the files on it; for example, an antivirus disk scanning program is a utility.

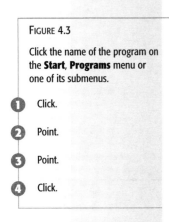

FIGURE 4.3

Click the name of the program on the **Start**, **Programs** menu or one of its submenus.

1 Click.

2 Point.

3 Point.

4 Click.

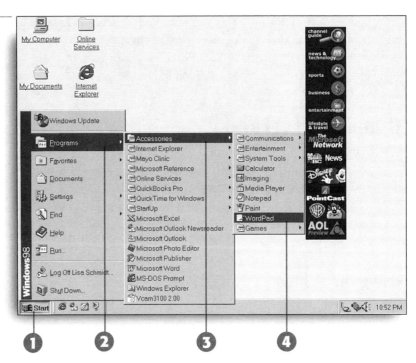

If the names of the icons on the Windows desktop are underlined (see Figure 4.4), *Web Style* is on—you can run a program by single-clicking its icon. (Web Style is a Web integration feature introduced in Windows 95 OSR2 and carried over to Windows 98.) If the names are not underlined, you must double-click the program's icon when instructed to click it. See Chapter 5, "Working on the Windows Active Desktop," for details about Web Style.

SEE ALSO

➤ *Learn how to place shortcut icons on the Windows desktop, see page 213*

➤ *Learn how to turn Web Style on and off, see page 128*

Switching Between Running Programs

Windows allows you to have several programs running at the same time. You can play a game of Solitaire in one window while typing a letter in another window, and calculate your checkbook balance in a third Window. You can even have Windows print a document displayed in one window while you work in another. This is called *multitasking*, and is one of the biggest improvements Windows introduced to the PC.

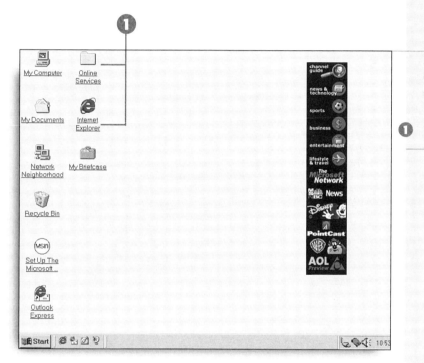

FIGURE 4.4

With Web Style on, Windows gives you single-click access to running programs.

❶ Icon names are underlined.

As you run programs, the program windows overlap and sometimes hide one another. You must be able to quickly bring a specific window to the top of the stack. Windows provides several ways to move a Window to the top:

- Click the program's button in the taskbar (see Figure 4.5). The taskbar contains a button for each currently running program.

- Click any part of the program's window (assuming some part of the window is visible).

■ Hold down the Alt key while pressing the Tab key repeatedly. The first time you press Alt+Tab, a dialog box appears, displaying buttons for all the currently running programs. As you continue to hold down the Alt key while pressing Tab, Windows moves the highlight from one program to the next. When the desired program is highlighted, release both keys.

SEE ALSO

➤ *Learn how to configure the taskbar, see page 217*

FIGURE 4.5

To quickly switch to a program that is currently running, click its button on the taskbar.

 Taskbar

❷ Buttons for currently running programs

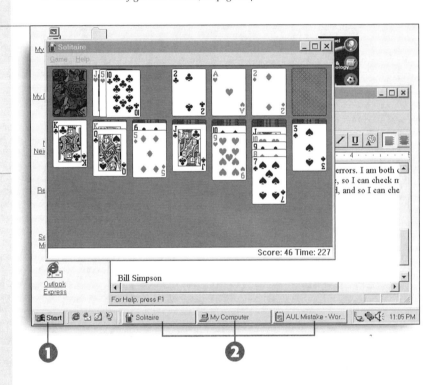

Exiting Programs

Before you exit a program, you should save any work you have done as a file (see Chapter 6, "Creating and Saving Documents"). This moves your work from memory, where the program stores it as you are working on it, to your hard disk, a permanent storage medium. You can then exit the program by taking one of the following steps:

- Click the Close button $\boxed{\times}$ in the upper-right corner of the program's window.
- Click **File** in the menu bar near the top of the program's window and click **Exit**.
- Right-click the program's button in the taskbar and click **Close**.

Running the Windows Accessories

If you purchased a new computer, it probably came bundled with a fine collection of programs for creating documents, playing games, researching topics, and much more. Windows also comes equipped with a collection of less sophisticated programs that can fill in the gaps and keep you entertained in the event that your PC didn't include much software.

Windows calls these small programs *accessories* and places icons for them on the **Start**, **Programs**, **Accessories** submenu. Table 4.3 lists the common accessories and provides a brief description of each accessory. You might notice that the table omits some advanced programs that you might have on your **Accessories** menu (or a submenu). These advanced programs are covered in later chapters.

If you can't find an accessory on your **Accessories** menu (or on one of its submenus), it may not be installed on your system. See Chapter 8 for instructions on how to install Windows components from the Windows CD.

TABLE 4.3   **Windows accessories**

Icon	Accessory	Description
Accessories Menu		
🖩	Calculator	A computerized version of a hand-held calculator.
🖼	Imaging	A graphics program that's useful for displaying and editing images you find on the Internet, digitized photos, and scanned images.

continues…

TABLE 4.3   **Continued**

Icon	Accessory	Description
Accessories Menu		
	Notepad	A text editor that's useful for creating and editing small text-only files (without fancy type). Text-only files are useful for sharing documents and for creating batch files (files that contain a series of commands).
	Paint	A graphics program that allows you to create your own pictures by drawing shapes and painting colors on the screen.
	WordPad	A low-end word processing program for creating typed documents, such as letters. Unlike Notepad, WordPad has text formatting tools to change the type style and text size.
Communications Submenu		
	Phone Dialer	Converts your computer and modem into a programmable phone. You can use it to dial the phone for you.
Entertainment Submenu		
	CD Player	Plays audio CDs, so you can listen to music while you work.
	Media Player	A program for playing audio and video clips, animations, and audio CDs. Useful for playing media files on the Web.
	Sound Recorder	An audio program that allows you to record your voice or record from an audio CD, store your recording as a file, modify it, and play it back.
	Volume Control	A utility for adjusting the volume and balance for audio input and output devices. You can also display Volume Control by right-clicking the speaker icon in the system tray and clicking **Show Volume Controls**.
Games Submenu		
	FreeCell	A sort of reverse Solitaire. You start with all the cards face up and have four free cells to use for moving the cards around. You can win any game, but it's tough.

Icon	Accessory	Description
	Hearts	A four-player game in which you try to stick the other players with the high-point cards. You can play against other people over a network or play against the computer.
	Minesweeper	A game in which you flip tiles to reveal where the mines are not located. If you flip a tile that conceals a mine, the mine blows up and you lose.
	Solitaire	A computer version of the classic card game. Great for mouse practice.

System Tools Submenu

Icon	Accessory	Description
	Disk Cleanup	Deletes unnecessary files from your hard disk to free up storage space.
	Disk Defragmenter	Rearranges files on your hard disk to make the disk work faster and more efficiently.
	Drive Converter	Converts a large hard drive to Fat32, so files are stored more efficiently on smaller storage units.
	Maintenance Wizard	Runs several utilities to optimize your system. You can set it up to run on schedule.
	ScanDisk	Checks for errors on your computer's hard disk and fixes them.
	Scheduled Tasks	Allows you to run programs automatically at a scheduled time or whenever you start your computer.
	System Information	Displays information about your system, including the amount of memory installed and the amount of disk space available. Also allows you to run other troubleshooting programs.

SEE ALSO

➤ *Learn how to use the Windows Maintenance Wizard, page 248*

➤ *Learn how to clear unnecessary files from your hard disk, page 252*

➤ *Learn how to make a large hard disk store files more efficiently, page 254*

➤ *Learn how to speed up your hard disk drive, page 258*

➤ *Learn how to search for and repair disk problems, page 259*

➤ *Learn how to find out more about your PC, page 261*

The DOS prompt

Before Windows, when you started your computer, the first thing you saw was the DOS prompt, which looked like **C:\>**. You typed commands at the prompt to run programs and perform other tasks, such as deleting and copying files. (Microsoft's version of DOS is called MS-DOS.)

Running DOS Games and Programs

DOS (pronounced "DAWSS," and short for Disk Operating System) is the guy that Windows placed on the unemployment list. However, you'll still find some DOS programs, especially games, and you should know how to run them. Fortunately, most DOS programs run under Windows even better. Unfortunately, installing and running DOS programs is a little more difficult.

Installing a DOS program

1. Insert the program's first floppy disk or the CD.
2. Click or double-click My Computer on the Windows desktop.
3. Click or double-click the icon for the drive that contains the disk or CD.
4. Click the Setup or Install icon.
5. Follow the installation instructions.

The easiest way to run a DOS program is to place an icon for the program on the desktop and then click or double-click the icon to run the program.

Making an icon for running a DOS program

1. Click or double-click the My Computer icon.
2. Click or double-click the icon for your hard disk drive.
3. Click or double-click the folder in which you installed the DOS program.
4. Using the right mouse button, drag the icon for running the DOS program to the desktop and release the mouse button. (If the My Computer window is full-screen, resize it so you can see the desktop, as explained in the next section.)
5. Click **Create Shortcut Here**.

After you have created an icon for running the DOS program, click or double-click the icon to run the program. If the program doesn't run or doesn't perform as expected, try the following:

- Click **Start**, point to **Programs**, and click **MS-DOS Prompt**. Change to the folder in which you installed the program by typing cd *foldername* and pressing Enter. Type the command for running the program as specified in the program's documentation and press Enter.

- Restart Windows in MS-DOS Mode, as explained in "Shutting Down Windows," at the end of this chapter. Then, try running the program from the DOS prompt, as explained previously.

- Right-click the DOS program's icon, click **Properties**, and adjust the program's properties to give it additional memory and resources. Check the program's documentation for details on how to run it effectively in Windows.

When you run a DOS program, it opens in a window, as do Windows programs, although the window looks different. A DOS window has some standard buttons for controlling the window and using the DOS program along with your Windows programs. Table 4.4 lists and describes these buttons. To exit a DOS program, use the program's **Exit** command. If the DOS window remains open, type exit and press Enter to close the program and return to Windows.

TABLE 4.4 **DOS Window buttons and controls**

Button	Name	Description
Auto	Font	Enables you to select the font size for displayed text. The Auto setting automatically adjusts the font size when you resize the window.
	Mark	Turns on Mark mode, which allows you to use your mouse to select text you want to copy or move to another document.
	Copy	Copies the selected text to the Windows Clipboard, so you can paste it into other documents.
	Paste	Inserts the contents of the Windows Clipboard into the currently displayed document.
	Full Screen	Displays the program in Full-Screen mode instead of in a window. This button is not available in some programs.
	Properties	Displays the Properties dialog box for this program.

continues...

TABLE 4.4   **Continued**

Button	Name	Description
🖫	Background	By default, this button is active, preventing the program from doing anything when you are working in other programs. If you want the program to be able to perform tasks in the background, click this button to turn it off.
A	Font	Displays a dialog box for changing the font size for displayed text. This button performs the same function as the Font drop-down list on the left end of the toolbar.

Moving and Resizing Windows

It's common practice to have several windows on the desktop at the same time. You may be writing a letter to your insurance company in one window, using the Windows Calculator in another window, and playing a game of Solitaire in still another window. As you open more windows, your desktop can become cluttered, making it difficult to access other programs or copy data from one document to another.

The solution is to move and resize your windows to arrange them in convenient areas on the desktop. Windows offers several options for resizing and arranging windows on the desktop.

Arranging and resizing Windows

1. To quickly clear a window from the desktop without exiting the program, click the Minimize button ▬.
2. To make a window appear full-screen, click its Maximize button ☐. The Maximize button is replaced by the Restore button.
3. To return a maximized window to its previous size, click the Restore button 🗗.
4. If a window is neither maximized nor minimized, you can resize it by dragging one of its borders or a corner of the window (see Figure 4.6).
5. To move a non-maximized window, drag the window's title bar.

6. To rearrange all the open windows, right-click a blank area of the taskbar and select the desired arrangement: **Cascade Windows** (overlapping windows), **Tile Windows Horizontally** (side-by-side), **Tile Windows Vertically** (stacked), or **Minimize All Windows**.

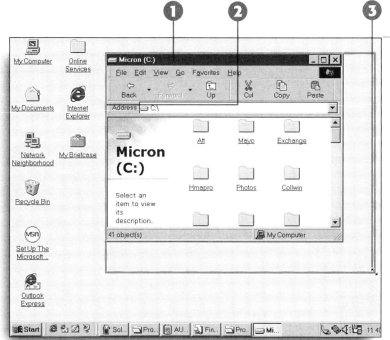

FIGURE 4.6

Drag the corner or edge of a window to resize it.

1 Drag the top or bottom to make the window shorter or taller.

2 Drag the left or right edge to make the window wider or narrower.

3 Drag the corner to change the window's height and width.

In some programs, you can open two or more documents, each in its own window. The windows behave like program windows—you can maximize, minimize, or restore the document windows *inside* the program window. To switch from one document window to another in most programs, you choose the desired window from the **Windows** menu in the program's menu bar.

Scrolling Inside a Window

Program and document windows are like windows in your house or car. If you peer through a window, you see only a portion of the landscape. Program and document windows limit your view

Quick maximize/restore/minimize

To quickly maximize or restore a window, double-click its title bar (the blue bar at the top of the window). You can right-click a button in the taskbar to view options for controlling a minimized window (such as closing the window). In addition, you can quickly minimize or restore a program window by clicking its button in the taskbar.

in a similar way. If the window contains more data than it can display, some of the data is outside your view.

To overcome this limitation, Windows uses scrollbars. If the contents of a window exceed the window's height or width, scrollbars appear along the right side or bottom of the window. You can use the scrollbars to bring data into the window's display area (see Figure 4.7):

- Click the arrow at the end of a scrollbar to scroll incrementally up, down, left, or right. Hold down the mouse button to scroll continuously. In a text document, this typically scrolls one line up or down or one space left or right.

- Drag the scroll box inside the scrollbar to slide the contents up, down, left, or right.

- Click inside the scrollbar on either side of the scroll box to scroll one screen up, down, left, or right.

FIGURE 4.7

Use scrollbars to display the contents of a window.

1 Drag the scroll box to scroll continuously.

2 Click in the scrollbar to scroll one screen.

3 Click an arrow to scroll in small increments

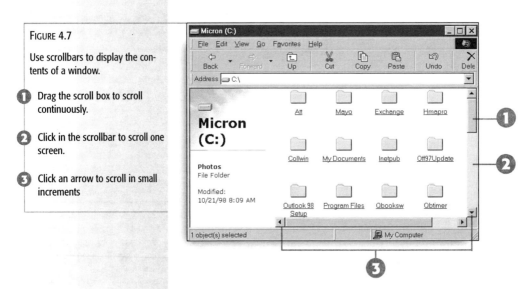

Scrolling with Your Keyboard

As you are working on a document, your fingers spend more time on the keyboard than on the mouse. You might find it more convenient to use your keyboard to scroll. Use the following keystrokes to scroll in most windows containing text:

- *Arrow keys* move up, down, left, or right in small increments.
- *Page Up* displays the previous screen.
- *Page Down* displays the next screen.
- *Home* moves to the beginning of the current line.
- *End* moves to the end of the current line.
- *Ctrl+Arrow key* moves one word to the left or right or one paragraph up or down.
- *Ctrl+Page Up* moves to the top of the previous page.
- *Ctrl+Page Down* moves to the top of the next page.
- *Ctrl+Home* moves to the beginning of the document.
- *Ctrl+End* moves to the end of the document.

Scrolling with a Microsoft IntelliMouse

Microsoft recently developed a new mouse, called the IntelliMouse, that has a wheel between the left and right mouse buttons. You can quickly scroll with the IntelliMouse by rotating the wheel. Spin the wheel toward you to scroll down or away from you to scroll up. The wheel performs different functions depending on the program you are using it with.

Entering Commands

Windows provides several ways to enter commands. The most common method is to click a menu's name to open it and then click the desired option on the menu. You can also click program or document icons to run programs or open documents. To save you some time, Windows offers keyboard shortcuts that allow you to bypass the menu system for common commands, such as saving and printing documents. For example, you can press Ctrl+S in most programs instead of opening the **File** menu and selecting **Save**. Windows also allows you to bypass the menu system by clicking buttons in your programs' toolbars. The following sections show you various ways to enter commands in Windows.

IntelliMouse support

Although the Microsoft IntelliMouse buttons are compatible with most programs, the wheel may not be supported in some programs. The IntelliMouse is supported in all the Windows 98 accessories, including Internet Explorer.

Entering Menu Commands

The easiest way to enter commands in Windows and Windows programs is to select commands from menus. You have already selected commands from the **Start** menu at the bottom of the Windows desktop. Most programs contain a menu bar near the top of the program window that displays the names of several menus. You open a menu by clicking its name or by holding down the Alt key while pressing the underlined letter in the menu's name (for instance, you press Alt+F to open the **File** menu), as shown in Figure 4.8.

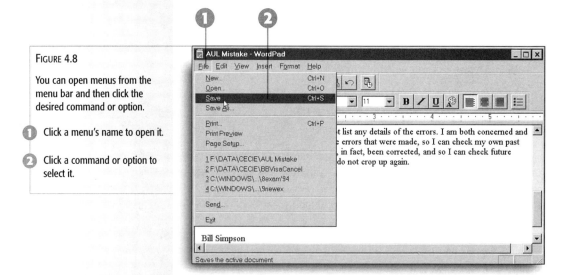

FIGURE 4.8

You can open menus from the menu bar and then click the desired command or option.

❶ Click a menu's name to open it.

❷ Click a command or option to select it.

As you work with menus, you will notice that menu commands may not all look the same. The appearance of each command provides a clue as to what will happen if you select the command:

- A standard command with no arrow or ellipsis (...) executes immediately when you select it. For instance, if you select **Edit**, **Paste**, the program immediately pastes the object you just copied into your document at the insertion point, no questions asked.

- A command followed by an ellipsis (…) displays a dialog box that prompts you to enter additional preferences or give your confirmation. You must respond to the dialog box and click a button or press a key to complete the command. See "Responding to Dialog Boxes" later in this chapter.

- A command followed by an arrow opens a submenu that provides a list of additional commands. For example, if you click the Windows **Start** button and point to **Programs**, a submenu appears displaying a list of installed programs you can select. Rest the mouse pointer on the option to open the submenu.

- A checked option allows you to turn the option on or off. If the option has a check mark next to it, the option is on. You select the option to turn it off (removing the check mark). For example, a program may have several toolbars you can turn on or off.

- A grayed or dimmed command is disabled; you cannot select it. For example, if you run My Computer and open the **Go** menu, the **Back** option appears gray because you haven't moved forward yet.

Using Toolbars

Many Windows programs display a toolbar near the top of the window (typically just below the menu bar) that allows you to bypass the menu system and quickly enter commands. To enter a command, click the appropriate button on the toolbar (see Figure 4.9).

Right-Clicking for Context Menus

Before Windows, your right mouse button was fairly useless. In Windows and in most Windows programs, you can use the right mouse button to display *context menus*. For instance, if you right-click the Windows desktop, a context menu pops up offering commands for controlling the Windows desktop (see Figure 4.10). Context menus are useful because they display the most common commands for the selected object.

ScreenTips

In many programs, when you rest the mouse pointer on a toolbar button, a box or balloon pops up displaying the name or function of the selected button. In Microsoft programs, these are called *ToolTips* or *ScreenTips*.

FIGURE 4.9

Toolbars provide buttons for bypassing the menu system.

1 Toolbar

2 Click a button to enter the desired command.

3 ScreenTip

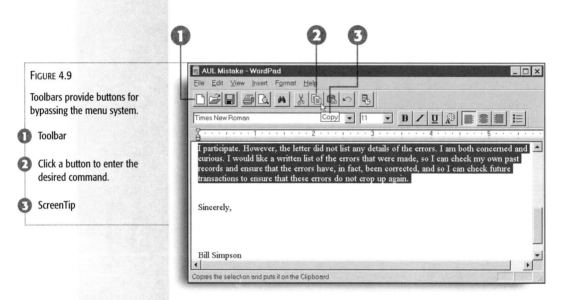

FIGURE 4.10

Context menus contain the most common commands for the selected object.

1 Right-click the object.

2 Point to the submenu name, if required.

3 Click the desired command.

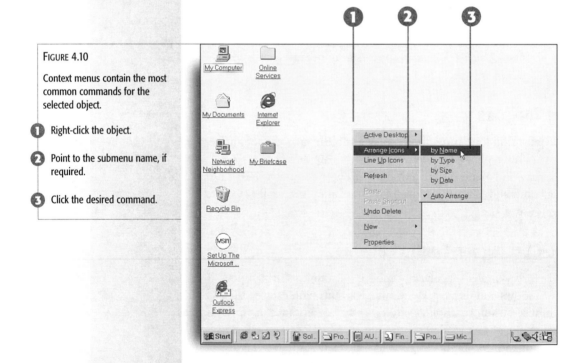

Bypassing Menus with Shortcut Keys

Although menus are the most intuitive tools for entering commands, they are also one of the slowest. To streamline the process, Windows and most Windows programs allow you to press key combinations to bypass the menu system. For example, you can press F1 to get help or press Alt+F4 to exit a program. Table 4.5 lists the most common keyboard shortcuts for Windows. Check the documentation that came with your other programs for additional keyboard shortcuts.

TABLE 4.5   Windows keyboard shortcuts

Press	To
F1	Display general help screens or context-sensitive help for the current dialog box
Alt+F4	Exit a program or shut down Windows (if no program is active)
Shift+F10	Display the context menu for the selected object or the current position of the insertion point
Ctrl+Esc	Activate the taskbar and open the **Start** menu
Alt+Tab	Switch to the program window that was previously active
Ctrl+X	Cut the selected object
Ctrl+C	Copy the selected object
Ctrl+V	Paste the cut or copied object
Ctrl+Z	Undo the previous action
Delete	Delete the selected object or the character to the right of the insertion point
Ctrl+A	Select all objects (in My Computer or Windows Explorer)
F5	Refresh the My Computer or Windows Explorer window
Backspace	View the folder one level up from the current folder
F2	Rename the selected icon
F3	Find a folder or file
Shift+Delete	Delete the selected file(s) or folder(s) without using the Recycle Bin
Shift (CD Player)	Disable AutoPlay for the CD-ROM you are inserting

If your keyboard has a key with the Windows logo on it (typically positioned near the lower-left corner of the keyboard), you can use this key to save additional keystrokes (see Table 4.6).

TABLE 4.6   **Windows logo key shortcuts**

Press	To
Windows	Open the **Start** menu
Windows+Tab	Cycle through open program windows
Windows+F	Find files or folders
Ctrl+Windows+F	Find a computer on your company's network
Windows+F1	Display help for Windows
Windows+R	Display the Run dialog box, which you can use to type the command for running a program
Windows+Break	Open the System Properties dialog box
Windows+E	Run Windows Explorer
Windows+D	Minimize or restore all open program Windows (same as clicking Show/Hide Desktop in the Quick Launch toolbar)
Shift+Windows+M	Undo Minimize All Windows

You'll need them later

Although these shortcut keys may not be of much use to you when you're first learning Windows, they can come in handy later. Mark this page with a Post-It, so you can quickly return to it.

Responding to Dialog Boxes

Whenever you select a command that is followed by an ellipsis (...), Windows displays a dialog box prompting you to enter additional information or confirm the action. Although dialog boxes vary in appearance, the following items are common to most dialog boxes (see Figure 4.11):

- *Tabs* contain groups of related options. To switch to a page of options, click the tab for that page. (Use Ctrl+Tab (the Tab key) to cycle through the tabs with your keyboard.)

- *Text boxes* allow you to fill in the blanks. You click in a text box and type the desired setting or information. In most text boxes, you can double-click to highlight the selected entry and then start typing to replace it.

- *Option buttons* allow you to select only one option in a group of options. When you select a different option, the currently selected option is turned off.

- *Check boxes* allow you to select any of several options in the group. Unlike option buttons, you can select as many check box options as desired. To turn an option on or off, click its check box. A check mark indicates that the option is on.

- *List boxes* allow you to select from two or more options. If the list is long, a scrollbar appears to the right of the list. Use the scrollbar to bring additional options into view.

- *Drop-down lists* are similar to list boxes, but the list initially displays only the currently selected option. To open the list, click the down arrow to the right of the list. You can then select the desired option.

- *Spin boxes* typically double as text boxes. You can click in the text box and type the desired setting or click the up- and down-arrows to the right of the list to change the setting incrementally.

- *Sliders* are like levers. You drag the slider up, down, left, or right to increase or decrease a setting, such as the speaker volume.

- *Command buttons* allow you to execute or cancel a command. Most dialog boxes have three command buttons: OK or Yes (to execute the command), Cancel (to abort), and Help (to display additional information about the listed options).

You can use your mouse or keyboard to navigate dialog boxes. To use the mouse, click the desired option or command button. To navigate with the keyboard, use the following keystrokes:

- Press Ctrl+Tab to flip from one tab to the next or Ctrl+Shift+Tab to flip back.

- Press Tab to move from one option to the next or Shift+Tab to skip back.

- Press the Spacebar to select the option button or place a check mark in a check box.

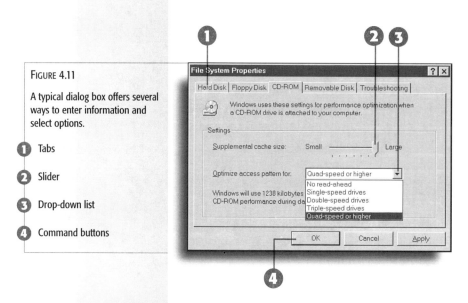

FIGURE 4.11

A typical dialog box offers several ways to enter information and select options.

1 Tabs

2 Slider

3 Drop-down list

4 Command buttons

Getting help in a dialog box

Many dialog boxes have their own built-in help system. If a question mark button appears in the upper-right corner of the dialog box, click it, and then click the option for which you need help. In some cases, you can right-click the option and select **What's This** to display context-sensitive help.

- Press Alt+Down Arrow to open a drop-down list.
- Use the arrow keys to highlight an entry in a list box or drop-down list.
- Type an entry in a text box.
- Press Enter to activate the selected command button.

Installing Programs

During the Windows installation, the installation utility added any Windows programs to the **Start**, **Programs** menu. If you installed Windows 98 over a previous edition of Windows, the installation utility added any programs that you installed in your previous Windows version to the **Start**, **Programs** menu.

If those programs do not appear on the menu, or if you have a new program you want to install, you can run the installation routine from Windows 98, as explained in the following sections.

Checking Available Disk Space Before Installing

Before you install any new program, you should make sure you have enough free space on your hard disk. The program's package should specify the required disk space. In addition, you should have 30MB or more of free disk space that Windows and your programs can use as *virtual memory*. Virtual memory is disk space that Windows uses as additional memory.

To check your disk space, Alt+click My Computer. My Computer displays the total size of the disk and the amount of free space remaining. If your disk does not have sufficient space, you must remove other programs and clear unnecessary files from your disk.

SEE ALSO

➤ *Learn how to clear unnecessary files from your hard disk, page 252*

➤ *Learn how to remove programs from your system, page 120*

➤ *Learn how to remove Windows components you don't use, page 204*

Automated CD-ROM Installations

Many newer programs are packaged on a CD-ROM and support the Windows AutoPlay feature. To install the program, you just load the disc into the CD-ROM drive. Windows runs the AutoPlay utility, which typically displays a welcome screen and a button for installing the program. Follow the onscreen instructions.

Installing a Program with Add/Remove Programs

The standard way to install a new program is to use the Windows Add/Remove Programs utility.

Install a new program

1. Click the **Start** button, point to **Settings**, and click **Control Panel**.

2. Click or double-click **Add/Remove Programs**.

3. Click the **Install** button (see Figure 4.12).

4. Insert the program's CD or the first floppy disk and click the **Next** button. Windows searches any disks in your floppy drive and CD-ROM drive for the Setup or Install file, and displays its name.

Program installation routines vary

The steps for installing programs vary from one program to another. However, all Windows programs come with an Install or Setup file that you can run to start the installation. After you run the file, it typically displays a series of dialog boxes that lead you through the installation process.

FIGURE 4.12

Use Add/Remove Programs to install new programs.

1 Click the **Install** button.

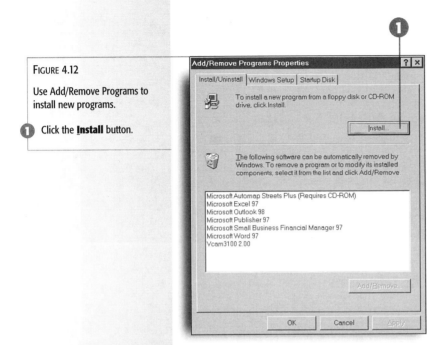

Bypassing Add/Remove Programs

You can run a program's installation from My Computer. Insert the program's disk or CD, click My Computer, and click the icon for the floppy drive or CD-ROM drive. Click the file named Setup or Install.

5. Click the **Finish** button.

6. Follow the program's installation instructions.

Removing Programs

When you buy a new computer, it seems as though it has an endless supply of hard disk space. A 2GB hard drive seems big until you install Windows and a few programs that take up 80MB each. It's easy to install programs on your hard drive. You install the program, use it for a few months, lose interest, and find a new program to install. Pretty soon, your disk is full.

It's tempting to just delete the folder that contains the program's files. That gets rid of the program, right? Not entirely, especially if the program you're trying to get rid of is a Windows program. When you install a Windows program, it commonly installs files not only to the program's folder, but also to the \Windows,

Windows\System and other folders. It also adds settings to the Windows Registry, which are not removed unless you follow the proper routine. To remove the program completely, you must use the Windows Add/Remove Programs utility.

Removing Windows Programs

When you install a program that's designed to work under Windows, it typically adds its name to a list of programs you can remove. This list is displayed in the Add/Remove Programs dialog box, making it easy to safely remove the program.

Uninstalling a program

1. Click the **Start** button, point to **Settings**, and click **Control Panel**.

2. Click the **Add/Remove Programs** icon.

3. Click the **Install/Uninstall** tab, if it is not already selected.

4. Click the name of the program you want to remove (see Figure 4.13).

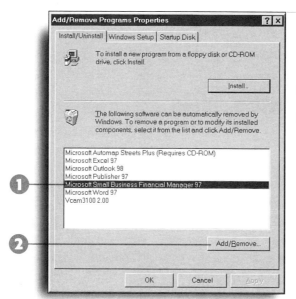

FIGURE 4.13

Add/Remove Programs displays a list of installed programs you can remove.

1️⃣ Click the program's name.

2️⃣ Click the **Add/Remove** button.

5. Click the **Add/Remove** button.

6. Follow the onscreen instructions to remove the program.

Running the Program's Setup Utility

If the name of the program you want to remove does not appear in the Add/Remove Programs list, you may be able to use the program's own setup utility to remove the program. Take one of the following steps:

- Use My Computer to display the contents of the folder for the program you want to remove. If you see a **Setup** or **Install** icon, double-click it, and follow the onscreen instructions to remove the program.

- Click the **Start** button, point to **Programs**, and point to the program's menu name. Look on the submenu that appears for a **Setup**, **Install**, or **Uninstall** option. If the menu has such an option, select it and then follow the onscreen instructions to remove the program.

In many cases, the program's setup utility allows you to remove the entire program or only selected components. If you use the program but do not use its advanced features, you can save disk space by removing only the components you do not use.

Getting Help

Windows contains its own online help system that can answer most of your Windows questions and provide additional background information about Windows features. It offers a table of contents and an index to help you find specific information.

To access online help, click the **Start** button and click **Help**. The Windows Help window appears (see Figure 4.14), offering the following three kinds of help:

- *Contents* works like an online user's manual. You click a book icon or name to view a list of related topics and then click the desired topic to display information in the right pane.

No uninstall option?

If you don't see a Setup or Install button, the best thing to do is to obtain a program that's designed especially to help you remove other programs from your hard drive. Remove-It and Clean Sweep are two of the more popular programs. However, these programs are most useful if you install them *before* installing other programs, so the uninstall program can record all changes to your system.

- _Index_ displays a comprehensive list of topics. You type the desired topic in the text box above the index, and Windows scrolls down to display a list of topics that match your entry.

- _Search_ provides a tool that searches through the entire contents of the help system to find references to the word or phrase you specify.

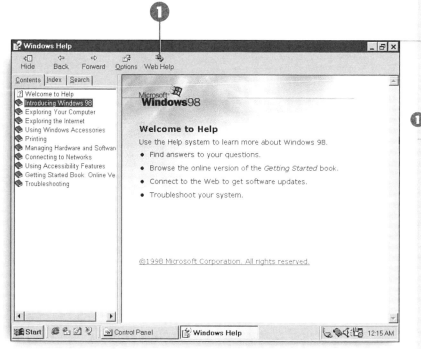

FIGURE 4.14

The Windows Help system offers a table of contents, index, and search tool.

1 Web Help button

If you have an Internet connection, click the **Web Help** button to connect to Microsoft's Web site and obtain technical assistance.

SEE ALSO

➤ _Learn how to connect to the Internet, page 391_

➤ _Learn how to find technical assistance on the Web, page 851_

Shutting Down Windows

You are probably aware that you do not simply turn off your computer when you are finished working. Windows and your programs store data electronically in memory while you work, and you must follow the proper shutdown procedure to ensure that anything you have been working on is saved to your hard disk. Using the Windows **Sh̲ut Down** command ensures that you have saved your work before exiting.

When shutting down, you should be aware of the following options:

- When you choose **Start**, **Sh̲ut Down**, a dialog box appears, allowing you to restart your computer. This is useful if you make changes to Windows or install a new program that requires you to restart.
- The Shut Down Windows dialog box also allows you to restart in MS-DOS mode, so you can enter commands at the DOS prompt.
- The Shut Down Windows dialog box may offer Stand By mode, which allows you to keep the computer on and conserve energy. In Stand By mode, your work is not saved to disk, so before you shut down in Stand By mode, save your work.

Shutting down Windows

1. Click the **Start** button and click **Sh̲ut Down**.
2. Click the desired shutdown option: **Sh̲ut Down**, **R̲estart**, **Restart in M̲S-DOS Mode**, or **Standby**.
3. Click **OK**.
4. If you chose **Shut Down**, wait until Windows displays a message indicating it is safe to shut down your computer.
5. Turn off the system unit, the monitor, and any other external accessories, such as the printer and speakers.

Some computers support *hibernation mode*, which can turn on this feature in Windows, so that when you press the PC's power button (or close the lid on a notebook PC), Windows saves your work and places your PC in standby mode. The next time you turn on your PC, it will jump into action and be ready to use. (If your PC does not support hibernation mode, this option will be unavailable in Windows.)

Turning on hibernation mode

1. Click the **Start** button, point to **Settings**, and click **Control Panel**.

2. Scroll down to and click the **Power Management** icon.

3. Click the **Hibernate** tab and click the option for turning on hibernation mode to place a check in its box.

4. Click the **Advanced** tab.

5. Click **When I press the power button on my computer** and click **Hibernate**. (If you are using a notebook PC, you can click **When I close the lid of my computer** and then click **Hibernate**.)

6. Click **OK** to save your settings.

SEE ALSO

➤ *Learn more about conserving energy on a notebook PC, page 281*

➤ *Learn how to adjust the power management settings for any computer, page 224*

Working on the Windows Active Desktop

Turning on the Active Desktop

One of the biggest improvements introduced in later versions of Windows 95 and in Windows 98 is the Active Desktop, a feature that transforms your Windows desktop into an automated information center.

The Active Desktop also offers a new, improved interface for accessing your programs and documents. With the Active Desktop, the Windows desktop functions as a Web page, allowing you to run programs and open documents with a single click of the mouse.

The idea behind the Active Desktop is that it provides a seamless connection between the Web, your company's network, and your local PC. This makes the desktop more interactive and gives you greater control over its appearance and functionality.

One of the best features of the Active Desktop is that it allows you to place components (*Active Desktop Components*) of any size and dimensions on your desktop. In other words, you can go beyond desktop icons and place objects such as stock tickers and scrolling news headlines right on your desktop. With Active Desktop Components, you have complete control of their size and position. You can even set up desktop components to receive automatic updates from the Web during the day.

Turning on Web Style in My Computer

Internet connection not required

You can use many of the Web integration features without being connected to the Internet. And although the Active Desktop is designed for use with Internet Explorer, you can use other Web browsers, such as Netscape Navigator, to manage the tasks of downloading Web content for updating your Active Desktop components.

My Computer allows you to work in Web Style or Classic Style. In Web Style, you no longer click an icon to select it. Instead, you simply point to the icon. To access a drive, open a folder or file, or run a program, you no longer need to double-click; instead, you point to the desired icon and click once.

If this is your first encounter with Windows, you should pick up these techniques fairly quickly. However, if you are accustomed to working in previous versions of Windows, you may have to shed your old habits and learn some new moves.

Because the remaining chapters in this book assume you have Web Style turned on, make sure it's on.

Turning on Web Style

1. Click or double-click **My Computer** on the Windows desktop.

2. Open the **View** menu and click **Folder Options**.

3. Click **Web Style** and click **OK** (see Figure 5.1).

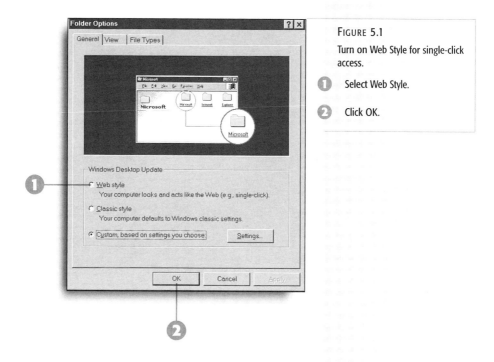

FIGURE 5.1

Turn on Web Style for single-click access.

❶ Select Web Style.

❷ Click OK.

SEE ALSO

➤ *Learn what to look for in a notebook PC, page 31*

➤ *Learn how to set up a notebook PC, page 69*

➤ *Learn how to use a notebook PC, page 269*

Turning on View As Web Page

In addition to providing single-click access, Web Style converts your desktop and folder windows into a two-layer work area: an icon layer and an HTML (Web page) layer. (HTML, short for Hypertext Markup Language, is a set of codes used to format Web pages.) The icon layer controls the appearance and behavior of the icons, and the HTML layer controls the background.

In My Computer, the HTML layer is responsible for displaying the graphic bar on the left side of the window that displays information about the selected object. For example, if you point to a disk icon, the bar displays a pie chart showing the amount of disk space in use and the amount of free space available (see Figure 5.2). On the desktop, the HTML layer is responsible for displaying the Windows background, the Channel bar, and any other *Active Desktop Components* you choose to place on the desktop. (An Active Desktop Component is a framed object that can automatically download updated content, such as sports scores or stock prices, from the Web.)

FIGURE 5.2

The HTML layer in My Computer displays an information bar.

1 Web Style controls the appearance of the icons.

2 View As Web Page controls the HTML layer.

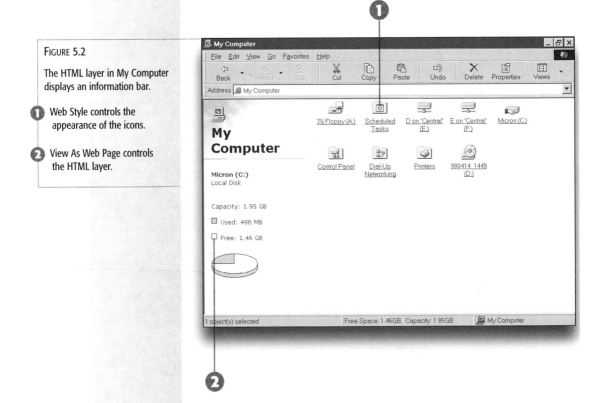

You can leave Web Style on (for single-click access) and turn the HTML layer on or off in My Computer or on the desktop by performing one of the following steps:

- In My Computer, display the contents of the desired folder. Open the **View** menu and click **As Web Page**.

- Right-click a blank area of the Windows desktop, point to **Active Desktop**, and click **View as Web Page**.

Customizing Web Style

Maybe you don't like single-click access, but you do like the way My Computer displays information about selected objects. Windows gives you the option of using only those Active Desktop features you like. You can enter your preferences for the following options (see Figure 5.3):

- **Active Desktop.** You can choose to enable Web content on the desktop or use the classic desktop, which does not display Web content. (You can change this option more easily by right-clicking the desktop and choosing **Active Desktop**, **View As Web Page**.)

- **Browse folders as follows.** You can choose to use one My Computer window to display the contents of selected disks and folders. If you choose to have each folder opened in a separate window, when you click a folder icon, My Computer opens a new window; this can quickly clutter your desktop.

- **View Web content in folders.** You can have My Computer display the HTML layer behind the contents of all your folders or only in those folders you choose to view as Web pages.

- **Click items as follows.** You can turn single-click access on or switch back to double-clicking to open an item. You can also choose to have icon names underlined or have the underline appear only when you point to (select) an icon.

FIGURE 5.3

The Custom Settings dialog box allows you to mix and match Classic and Web Style features.

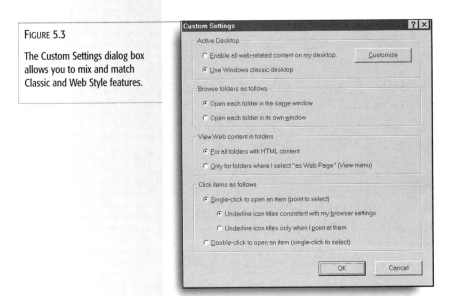

Entering Web Style preferences

1. In My Computer, open the **View** menu and click **Folder Options**.

2. Click **Custom, Based on Settings You Choose**.

3. Click the **Settings** button.

4. Enter your preferences, as explained previously.

5. Click **OK** to return to the Folder Options dialog box.

6. Click **OK** to save your settings.

Working with Single-Click Access

Single-click access provides a much faster way to navigate your computer and its resources...once you get used to it. If you've been working with previous versions of Windows, however, the transition can be a little tough. The following tips will help you make a successful transition:

- To select (highlight) an icon, point to it (rest the mouse pointer on it).

- To select additional icons, hold down the Ctrl key while pointing at the icons.
- To select a group of neighboring icons, select the first icon and then hold down the Shift key while pointing to the last icon.
- To display the contents of a disk or folder, click the disk or folder icon.
- To run a program, click its icon.
- To open a document file, click its icon. (When you install most programs, Windows creates a file association between the program and the types of files that program can open. If you click an icon for a document file that is not associated with a program, Windows prompts you to choose a program.)

Using the Quick Launch Toolbar

To the right of the Start button is the Quick Launch toolbar, which allows you to quickly run programs with a single click. Table 5.1 lists the Quick Launch buttons and briefly describes each button.

TABLE 5.1 **Quick Launch toolbar buttons**

Button	Name	What It Does
	Launch Internet Explorer Browser	Runs Internet Explorer, a program that opens multimedia pages on the Web.
	Launch Outlook	Runs Outlook Express, an Internet email/newsgroup program that displays incoming email messages and lets you send email messages. It also allows you to access newsgroups, where people read and post messages.

continues

TABLE 5.1   **Continued**

Button	Name	What It Does
	Show Desktop	Quickly returns to the Windows desktop when active program windows are obscuring or hiding the desktop. Show Desktop toggles the desktop on and off, so you can quickly return to your programs when you're done working on the desktop.
	View Channels	Runs Internet Explorer and displays the Channel bar, which allows you to flip from one Web page to another as though you were using a TV channel changer.

To use most of the buttons in the Quick Launch toolbar, you must have an Internet connection, as explained in Chapter 16, "Setting Up Your Internet Connection."

You can customize the Quick Launch toolbar by adding buttons for your favorite programs, removing buttons, and resizing the toolbar. In addition, you can turn off the toolbar, turn other toolbars on, and even create your own toolbars. See Chapter 8, "Customizing Windows," for details.

SEE ALSO

➤ *Learn how to configure the Quick Launch toolbar, page 218*

Navigating the Web with Windows Explorer

Windows Explorer has the same enhancements you find in My Computer. Windows Explorer provides single-click access to programs and files and offers the Internet Explorer toolbar, which you can use to browse the Web or your company's intranet. (An *intranet* is a network that is set up to look and act like the Web, making it easier for users to share network resources.)

In addition to improved file management tools, Windows Explorer is completely integrated with Internet Explorer through *ActiveX* (a shared programming environment), allowing you to open and view Web pages right inside the Windows Explorer window. You simply run Windows Explorer and click **Internet Explorer** in the folder list. Internet Explorer takes control of the toolbar and the right pane to display Web pages and the tools you need to navigate them. (To set up an Internet connection, see Chapter 16, "Setting Up Your Internet Connection.")

Opening Web pages with Windows Explorer

1. Right-click the **Start** button and click **Explore**.

2. If prompted to connect to the Internet, enter the phone number and required logon information for your Internet service provider and click **Connect**.

3. Windows Explorer loads the opening Web page and displays it in the pane on the right. You can click links to jump from one page to another.

4. Click the **Back** button to redisplay the contents of your computer. You can then click the **Forward** button to return to the Web page.

5. Click the plus sign next to **Internet Explorer** (in the left pane) to view a list of pages you visited. Click the name of a page to return to it (see Figure 5.4).

6. The **Address** text box allows you to enter both Web page addresses and paths to your disks and folders. In addition, you can open the **Address** drop-down list to select folder views or Web pages you have recently accessed.

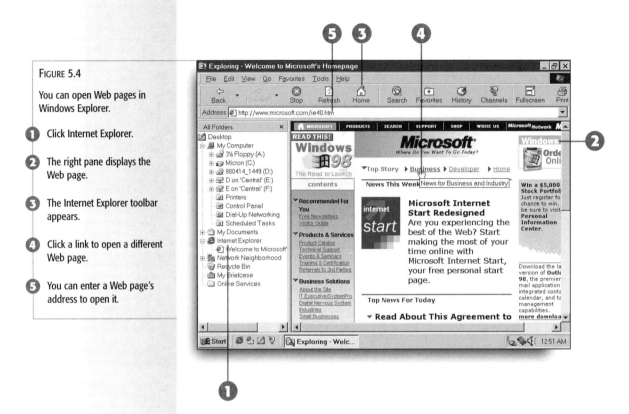

FIGURE 5.4

You can open Web pages in Windows Explorer.

1 Click Internet Explorer.

2 The right pane displays the Web page.

3 The Internet Explorer toolbar appears.

4 Click a link to open a different Web page.

5 You can enter a Web page's address to open it.

Tuning In to the Web with the Channel Bar

In a concentrated effort to transform your computer monitor into a TV set, Web developers have come up with some innovative tools. Microsoft's entry innovation is the Channel bar, displayed prominently on the Windows desktop, which acts as a channel changer for the Web.

With Channels, you can tune in to the best sites the Web has to offer. The Channel bar comes with a Channel Finder that allows you to select from popular sites and then place those sites on the channel changer. To view a site, you click a button on the channel changer; it's just like flipping channels on your TV set!

If your desktop does not display the Channel bar, right-click the desktop and click **Properties**. Click the **Web** tab, place a check mark in the **Internet Explorer Channel Bar** box, and click **OK**.

Adding channels

1. Establish your Internet connection.

2. On the Channel bar (on the Windows desktop), click the button for a site or category that interests you, such as Sports or Business. Internet Explorer starts and displays the Channel Guide page.

3. On the left side of the screen, click the link for the desired channel. The right frame displays a preview of the site (see Figure 5.5).

Under construction

The Channels feature is relatively new and might not work as smoothly as opening standard Web pages in Internet Explorer. Expect to encounter more warnings and confirmation dialog boxes than you normally see.

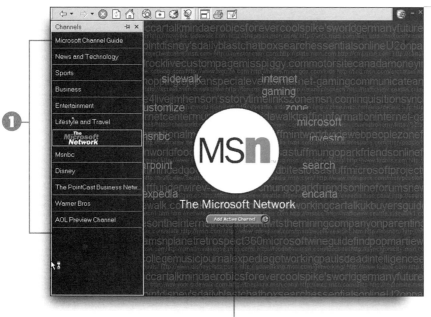

FIGURE 5.5

You can add buttons for your favorite sites to the Channel bar.

① Click the desired category and site.

② Click the link for adding the channel.

Disappearing Channel bar

Depending on how the site is set up, it might open the page in Full Screen view and hide the Channel Bar. To bring the Channel Bar back into view, roll your mouse pointer to the left side of the screen. To return to Normal view, click the **Fullscreen** button in the toolbar.

4. To add the site to your Channel Bar, click the **Subscribe** or **Add Active Channel** link or its equivalent. (Not all pages use "Subscribe" or "Add Active Channel" as the name of the link for adding a channel.) The Modify Channel Usage dialog box appears.

5. Enter your subscription preferences to have up-to-date Web pages automatically downloaded (see Figure 5.6).

FIGURE 5.6

By subscribing to a channel, you can have Internet Explorer automatically download updated Web pages.

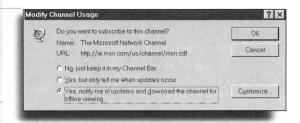

Channel or Active Desktop Component?

Some sites might offer two links: one for adding a channel and another for adding an Active Desktop Component to your Windows desktop.

6. Click **OK**.

7. A button for the selected channel is added to the Channel Bar. To tune in to a site, click its button in the Channel Bar.

SEE ALSO
➤ *For more information on Internet connection, page 391*

Adding and Removing Desktop Components

As explained earlier in this chapter, the Windows desktop consists of two layers: an *HTML layer* and an *icon layer*. This allows you to place active desktop components that are HTML-friendly right on your desktop as *frames* (windows that contain Web pages and other Web content).

Adding an Active Desktop Component

1. Right-click a blank area of the Windows desktop, point to **Active Desktop**, and click **Customize My Desktop**.

2. In the Display Properties dialog box, click the **Web** tab.

3. Click the **New** button.

Watch those online charges

Be careful when using automatically updating desktop components. If your phone company or ISP charges you by the minute or hour, these automatic updates can become costly. In addition, if you have a single phone line, Windows will keep updating these components regularly, keeping your phone line tied up.

4. When asked if you want to go to the Active Desktop Gallery, click **Yes**. Internet Explorer runs and loads the Active Desktop Gallery Web page.

5. Follow the trail of links to the desired desktop component.

6. Click the link or button to download the component and place it on your desktop (see Figure 5.7).

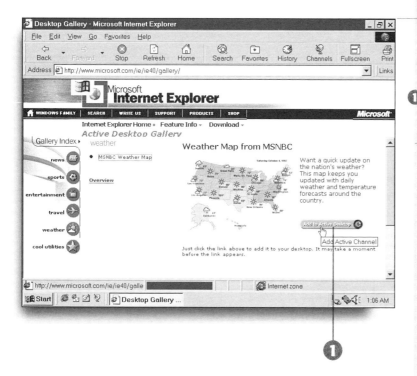

FIGURE 5.7

You can quickly add an Active Desktop Component to your desktop.

❶ Click the link for adding the Active Desktop Component to your desktop.

7. When prompted to confirm, click **Yes**.

8. Choose the desired subscription option to have updated content delivered to your desktop (see Figure 5.8).

9. Click **OK**.

10. To move a component, point to the top of the component to display the title bar and then drag the title bar (see Figure 5.9).

11. To resize a component, drag one of the corners of its frame to the size you want, and then release the mouse button.

FIGURE 5.8

Choose the desired subscription option to automatically download updated information.

FIGURE 5.9

You can move and resize an Active Desktop Component.

1 Point to the top of the component to display the title bar.

2 Drag the title bar to move the component.

3 Drag an edge or corner of the frame to resize the component.

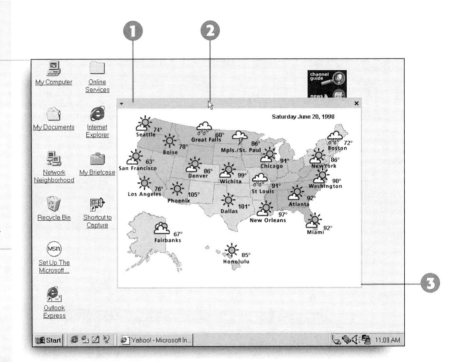

12. To shut down the component, and prevent it from automatically connecting to the Internet to download updated content, click its **Close** button.

You can add a Web page to the desktop as an Active Desktop Component. In Internet Explorer, display the link for the page you want to use and resize the Internet Explorer window so you can see a blank area on the desktop. Drag the link from the Web page over the desktop and release the mouse button. Click **Create Active Desktop Item(s) Here**.

Changing subscription settings

You can change the subscription settings for a desktop component at any time. In the Display Properties dialog box, click the **Web** tab. Click the component whose subscription settings you want to change and click the **Properties** button.

If you find that you no longer use an Active Desktop Component, you can easily turn it off or completely remove it from your system.

Removing an Active Desktop Component

1. Right-click a blank area of the desktop and click **Properties**.
2. In the Display Properties dialog box, click the **Web** tab.
3. To turn off a component, click its check box to remove the check mark.
4. To completely remove a component, select it and click the **Delete** button.
5. When prompted to confirm, click **Yes**.
6. Click **OK** to save your changes.

Creating and Saving Documents

Type letters, reports, and other documents

Create newsletters, greeting cards, signs, and other publications

Use a spreadsheet to perform calculations

Manage your personal finances

Create, save, and open files

Understanding Document Types

Unless you purchased your computer to use solely as a game machine and entertainment center, you probably want to use it to create documents, including letters, reports, greeting cards, images, spreadsheets, and graphs. In fact, most of the programs you will use in Windows are designed to help you create and print documents.

To create a document, you must use an *application* designed for the type of document you want to create. For example, if you need to type a letter, compose an essay, or create a resume, you use a word processing program. To calculate and track numbers, you type data into a spreadsheet.

The following sections explain the most common document types and the programs used to create them. Each section shows you a typical program in action, so you'll know what to expect and how to start creating your own documents.

Word Processing

A word processing program essentially transforms your computer into a typewriter that not only makes typing much easier, but can actually help you compose and perfect your work. It has an endless supply of electronic paper that scrolls past the screen as you type, and because it's electronic, you don't have to worry about making mistakes. Just go back and type over the errors— no messy correction fluid, no erasing, and no wasted paper. You print your document only after you've perfected it.

Most word processing programs come with a bundle of fancy features, including graphics support (for pictures), tables (for aligning data in columns), tools for checking your spelling and grammar, and commands for creating a table of contents and index. You can spend a good part of your adult life learning how to use these features to improve your work and save time. However, if you just want to type and print a document, such as a letter, you need to perform only a few simple tasks:

- *Type.* You need to type your documents. When you run a word processing program, it opens a document window that contains an *insertion point* (or *cursor*)—a vertical, blinking line that shows where characters will appear as you type. Just start typing (see Figure 6.1). To start a new paragraph, press Enter.

- *Edit.* After you have created a draft of your document, you can change the information onscreen until it is just the way you want it. You can use the Delete and Backspace keys to make minor changes or use the Cut, Copy, and Paste features (described later in this chapter) for major revisions.

- *Format.* At any time, you can begin working on the appearance of the document. This includes setting margins and line spacing, setting tabs, changing the way the text is aligned, and changing typestyles and type sizes. You'll learn more about formatting documents later in this chapter.

- *Print.* When you've completed your document, you'll want to print it. For details about printing documents, see Chapter 9, "Printing from Windows."

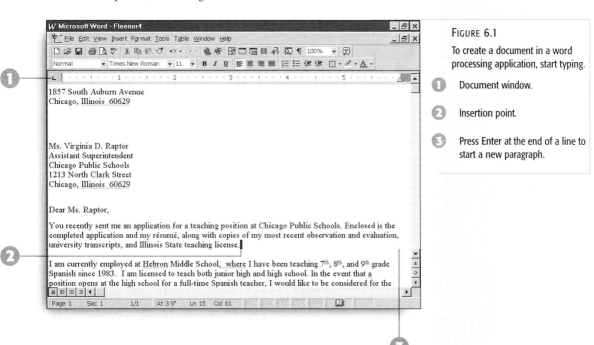

FIGURE 6.1

To create a document in a word processing application, start typing.

1. Document window.

2. Insertion point.

3. Press Enter at the end of a line to start a new paragraph.

Multiple document windows

Just as you can open two or more program windows on the Windows desktop, you can open two or more document windows in most applications. This allows you to copy and paste selected text from one document to the other. To change from one window to the other, select the desired document from the **Window** menu.

SEE ALSO

➤ *Learn how to create a new document, page 158*
➤ *Learn how to save a document, page 172*
➤ *Learn how to print a document, page 240*

Desktop Publishing

Unlike word processing programs, which allow you to type and format large blocks of running text, desktop publishing programs treat each page as a canvas on which you place various objects, including headlines, pictures, and snippets of text. Each object is contained in its own *frame*, allowing you to position the objects precisely on a page or on several pages to create your publication. In addition, you can lay one frame on top of another to layer the objects (see Figure 6.2).

A typical desktop publishing program displays a page surrounded by a "paste-up board," on which you can place objects temporarily in order to rearrange objects on the page.

FIGURE 6.2

With a desktop publishing program you layer objects on a page to create your publication.

1 Text frame

2 Picture frame

3 Headline

4 You can drag objects onto the work area and then drag them back onto the page.

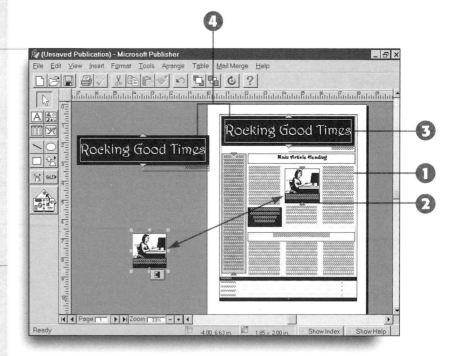

In a desktop publishing program, you can't just start typing. To add text to a page, you must first enter the command for inserting a text frame and then drag the mouse pointer on the page to create a rectangle of the desired size and dimensions. You then type your text inside the text frame. To insert a picture, you perform similar steps, first creating a picture frame and then inserting a clip art file or a file for a picture you created.

Although layering objects gives you complete control over the relative positions of objects, working with layers of objects poses a challenge. The objects act like playing cards; one object can obscure the object that's beneath it (see Figure 6.3). Desktop publishing programs have commands for moving objects forward or backward in the stack and for controlling the way text wraps around an object that is on top of it. To successfully create a publication, you must master these layering tools.

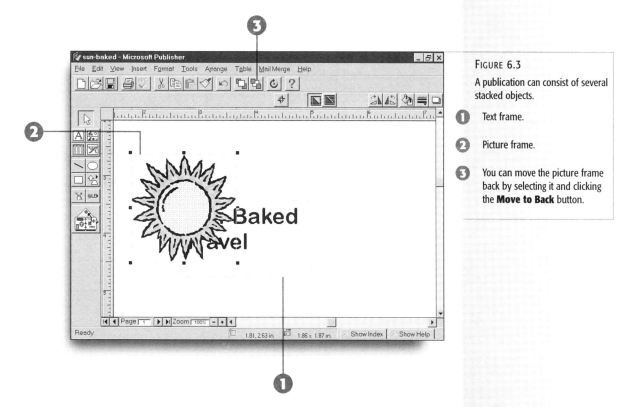

FIGURE 6.3

A publication can consist of several stacked objects.

1 Text frame.

2 Picture frame.

3 You can move the picture frame back by selecting it and clicking the **Move to Back** button.

SEE ALSO
➤ *Learn how to work with pictures, page 154*

Spreadsheets

There's no mystery to spreadsheets. A checkbook is a spreadsheet. A calendar is a spreadsheet. Your 1040 tax form is a spreadsheet. Any sheet that has boxes you can fill in is a type of spreadsheet.

What makes spreadsheets special is that they can perform mathematical calculations. For example, you can create a budget worksheet that automatically totals your utility bills for the last six months and calculates the average to show you approximately how much money you need each month to cover your utility bills. In addition, the spreadsheet can graph the budget values to show you the percentage of your budget that goes for such items as food, clothing, entertainment, housing, and utilities.

A spreadsheet is a grid, consisting of columns and rows that intersect to form thousands of small boxes called *cells*. Each column is assigned a letter, and each row is numbered. The spreadsheet uses this letter/number scheme to assign each cell an *address*. For example, the cell in the upper-left corner of the spreadsheet is cell A1. Spreadsheets use the cell addresses in formulas. For example, the formula A1+A2+A3 totals the values in cells A1–A3.

To create a spreadsheet document, type the following entries into the cells (see Figure 6.4):

- *Column and Row Headings*. The headings indicate the type of information in the column or row. For example, column headings may consist of the names of months: January, February, March, and so on. Row headings may describe categories, such as Food, Clothing, Entertainment, and Housing Expenses.

- *Values*. These are the numerical entries. For example, if you're creating a spreadsheet to use for invoicing, you might type the number of items ordered and the price of each item.

- *Formulas*. A formula performs calculations using the values you entered and displays the result in the cell that contains the formula. Formulas consist of cell addresses, values, and mathematical operators, and typically start with an equal sign (=) to tell the spreadsheet that it is a formula. Mathematical operators are + (addition), - (subtraction), * (multiplication), and / (division). For example, the formula =A1+A2+A3/3 determines the average of the values in cells A1–A3. Formulas can be much more complex.

- *Functions*. Functions are complex, ready-made formulas that perform a series of mathematical operations. For example, the function =PMT(C7,C8,C5,C11) calculates the monthly loan payment given the interest rate, number of payment periods, the amount of the loan, and the future value (0, assuming you plan on completely paying off the loan).

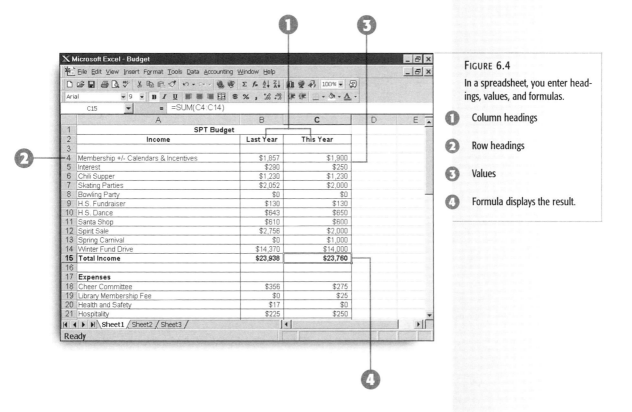

FIGURE 6.4

In a spreadsheet, you enter headings, values, and formulas.

1. Column headings

2. Row headings

3. Values

4. Formula displays the result.

SEE ALSO
➤ *Learn how to format spreadsheets, page 170*

Databases

Whether you need to create a simple Address Book, keep track of medical records, or manage inventory and human resources at a large company, you can use a database to help you manage your data. A database allows you to enter data, quickly retrieve specific data, and even combine the data from two or more database files to generate reports.

To use a database, you first create a database file and then enter your data. To enter data, you type entries on *forms* or in a table. Each form has several *fields* (text boxes), each of which contains a single entry (for example, Last Name, First Name, Address) as shown in Figure 6.5.

FIGURE 6.5

To create a database, you fill out forms.

1 Form.

2 Fields.

3 Click to save the data you entered and display a new, blank form.

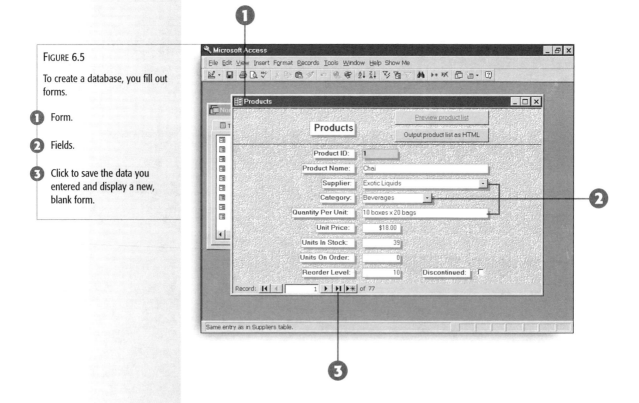

When you fill out a form and save it, you create a *record*. Each record contains data for a specific person or item. For example, you might create a record for each item in your company's inventory, including the item's order number, description, cost, the price you charge for it, and the number in stock. Creating records is the most time-consuming aspect of databases.

After you have created a database, you can use the database management tools to do the following:

- *Find records*. Most databases allow you to flip through your records page by page. To find a specific record, you can open a blank form and type an entry that's unique to the desired record (such as a part number or employee identification number).

- *Sort records*. Databases can quickly sort records based on the entries in a particular field. For example, you can sort the records in a customer database by last name, ZIP code, or phone number.

- *Filter records*. To extract a small group of records, you can filter the records. For example, you can type an entry that tells the database to display only those invoices entered between 9/1/98 and 10/15/98.

- *Create reports*. Reports extract data from one or more database files and arrange the data on a page. Reports are useful for creating documents such as membership directories, invoices, and quarterly reports.

You can also *merge* your database with another document to create a series of documents that contain different information. For example, you can create a form letter in your word processor that includes codes for inserting names and addresses from the database. You can then merge the form letter with the database to create a stack of form letters addressed to different people.

Personal Finance

If you currently manage your personal or business finances with a checkbook, ledger sheet, and calculator, you know that the process is work-heavy and prone to error. Writing checks by hand requires you to enter a lot of duplicate information. You write the date on the check, the name of the person or business, the amount of the check (both numerically and spelled out), and a memo telling what the check is for. Then you flip to your checkbook register and enter all the same information again. If you happen to make a mistake copying the amount from your check to your register, reconciling your checkbook can be an exercise in futility.

With a personal finance program, your computer enters the date automatically. You enter the name of the person or business to whom you're writing the check, the check amount (only once), and a memo telling what the check is for. The program spells out the check amount on the check, enters the required information in the checkbook register, and calculates the new balance (see Figure 6.6). This eliminates any discrepancies between what is written on the check and what appears in the register. It also eliminates any errors caused by miscalculations.

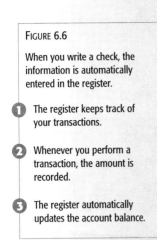

FIGURE 6.6

When you write a check, the information is automatically entered in the register.

1 The register keeps track of your transactions.

2 Whenever you perform a transaction, the amount is recorded.

3 The register automatically updates the account balance.

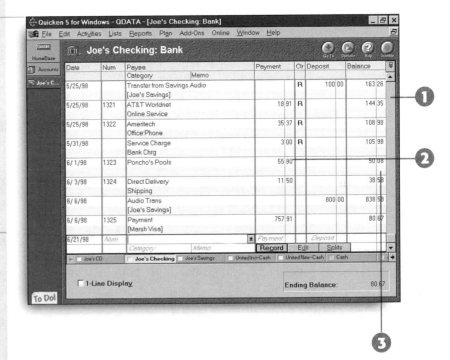

Financial programs are not merely automated checkbooks. Most financial programs offer advanced features for financial planning, budgeting, and estimating your taxes. Following is a list of useful features you'll find in most financial programs:

- *Recurring entries.* If you have a monthly bill that is the same each month (a mortgage payment, rent, or budgeted utility payment), a recurring entry feature can save you some time and prevent errors. The program issues the same payment each month.

- *Bill planning.* You enter the information for all the bills you have to pay for the month and then mark the bills you currently plan to pay. The program compares the total amount with your current checking account balance to determine whether you have enough money. You can then prioritize your bills.

- *Electronic bill paying.* If your computer has a modem, you may be able to pay your bills without writing a check. You must subscribe to a service that's wired into your mortgage company, bank, utility company, and other institutions that support automatic withdrawals and electronic bill paying. You can then use the service to manage all your accounts. If you owe money to a person who is not connected to the system, the service sends the person a paper check in the mail.

- *Reminders.* A Reminder feature automatically tells you when a bill is due. You specify the number of days in advance you want to be notified. When you start your computer, the program displays a message letting you know if any bills are due.

- *Budgeting.* Any financial advisor will tell you that the first step in achieving financial success is to determine how much money is coming in and where it's all going. With a good budget tool, you gather your records, enter the requested data, and the program displays the harsh realities. You can then start trimming your expenses in certain categories or start looking for a second job.

- *Investment manager*. After you have a budget and are saving loads of money, you may decide to invest that money. If you do, an Investment Manager feature can help you keep track of how your investments are doing.

- *Income tax estimator*. Compare how much you are actually paying in taxes to how much you should be paying to determine whether you are on track for the year.

- *Financial advisor*. Some personal finance programs offer financial advice to help you if you need life insurance or are contemplating how much you should be saving each month to send Junior to college.

- *Loan and investment calculators*. Most personal finance programs come with several specialize calculators that act as mini spreadsheets. If you're planning on purchasing a car, a loan calculator can determine your monthly payment based on the loan amount, term, and percentage rate. An investment calculator can calculate the amount of money you should set aside each month to meet your future savings goals.

- *Online services*. Most personal finance programs can now link you electronically to bank, loan, and investment services, making it easier for you to access information about your finances. Instead of matching your checkbook register to a paper bank statement, you can download the statement from the bank and have the finance program automatically reconcile your register.

Graphics

As our society becomes more visually oriented, graphics are becoming more important not only as decorative objects in publications but also as communication tools. To keep up, you need to know how to use graphics applications to insert pictures in your printed documents and add video clips and animations to the documents you publish electronically.

The term *graphics application* is one of the broadest application categories. It covers everything from clip art collections to CAD (computer-aided design) applications that can be used in conjunction with computer-aided manufacturing to program automated machines. The following list describes the most common graphics applications:

- *Clip art collections.* For those of us who cannot draw, clip art provides an easy way to insert predrawn images into our documents. Many word-processing and desktop publishing programs come with their own clip art collections. Figure 6.7 shows the clip art collection included with Microsoft Office. In most programs, you'll find the command for inserting clip art on the **Insert** menu.

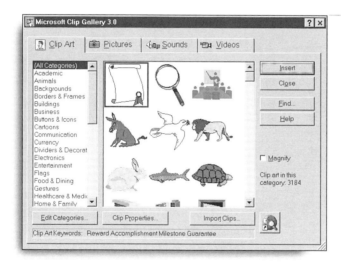

FIGURE 6.7

Clip art collections allow you to add graphics to your documents without having to draw.

- *Business presentations.* With a business presentation program, such as Microsoft PowerPoint, you can create your own slideshows. A typical slide consists of a title, a bulleted or numbered list, and a picture or graph. You choose an overall design and color scheme to apply to all the slides and then you insert the desired objects on each slide. The presentation program typically offers various ways to output the presentation: on 35mm slides, transparencies, or onscreen.

- *Drawing*. Drawing programs allow you to create illustrations by layering lines and basic shapes on a page. Although this sounds archaic, professional drawing programs, such as Corel Draw are capable of creating full-color ads like those used in magazines. Many programs have built-in drawing tools that allow you to add lines, arrows, and basic shapes to your documents.

- *Painting*. With paint programs, the page becomes a canvas on which you paint pictures. You can use a mouse or other pointing device to apply strokes of color to the page. Windows comes with a basic paint program called Paint. To experiment, click **Start**, **Programs**, **Accessories**, **Paint**.

- *Photo editing*. With a photo editing program, you can scan in a photo or retrieve photos from a digital camera. You can then adjust the contrast, color, and brightness of the image, rotate it, crop it, and modify it in other ways. You can print the image or insert it in one of your documents.

- *Video capture*. With a video capture board and application, you can play video clips from a camcorder through your PC and play them back to a recording tape. Video capture is very useful for including video clips on Web pages and in business presentations and for editing home video.

- *Interactive multimedia*. Interactive multimedia programs, such as Macromedia's Director Multimedia Studio, allow you to create your own three-dimensional, interactive presentations. For example, you can create an interactive tutorial complete with video clips, audio clips, animations, and clickable buttons for navigating the tutorial. You can place your multimedia presentation on the Web or distribute it as a program.

- *CAD*. Computer Aided Design programs, such as AutoCAD, are industrial strength applications typically used for design and modeling. However, there are trimmed down CAD applications that can help average users with specific design tasks, such as designing the floor plan for a new home, remodeling rooms, and landscaping.

SEE ALSO

➤ *Learn how to move and resize pictures in your documents, page 154*

Web Pages

Even if you haven't opened a Web page, you've probably seen Web pages on TV or in magazines. Because these pages are published electronically, they can include much more than text and pictures. Web pages commonly feature animated text and graphics, audio and video clips, and interactive programs.

To format these documents, display pictures and other objects on a page, and ensure that the pages can be opened in different Web browsers, the pages use a standard set of formatting codes called *HTML* (Hypertext Markup Language). These codes work behind the scenes, so you don't see them on a typical Web page.

To create a Web page, you use an HTML editor. Windows 98 and some later versions of Windows 95 include an HTML editor called FrontPage Express. You use an HTML editor as you would use a word processing program to type your text and insert graphics and other objects. In addition, the HTML editor allows you to mark pictures and text as links that point to other Web pages and resources on the Internet (see Figure 6.8). As you type, format, and insert objects, the HTML editor inserts the required HTML codes for you, so you don't have to type the complex codes yourself.

SEE ALSO

➤ *Learn how to open Web pages on the Internet, page 411*

➤ *Learn how to create and publish your own Web pages, page 424*

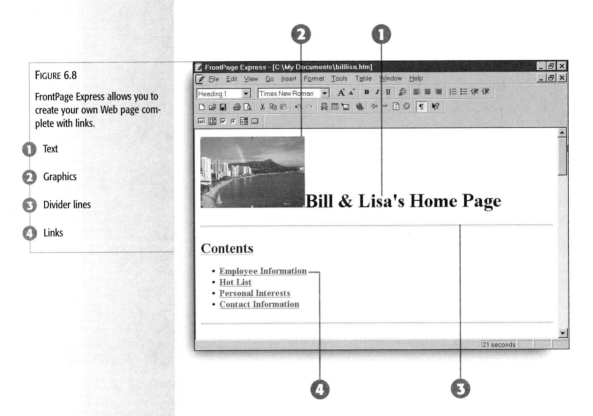

Creating a New Document

**Use your word processing
program**

Most new word processing programs, including Microsoft Word,
have HTML editing features that can
convert a standard document into
HTML format or help you create
a Web page from scratch and
publish it.

Most applications automatically create a new document when
you start the application. On startup, the application displays a
blank document window in which you can start typing, drawing,
or entering data. The document starts as a blank sheet of paper
and typically expands as you type.

As you create the document, the program stores it in RAM (your
computer's electronic memory). To preserve your data, you must
name your document and save it as a file on your computer's
hard disk.

After you save the document and close its window, the program
displays a blank screen with no document window. To continue
working on something else, you must either open a saved document or create a new document. The following sections explain

the various ways you can create a new document and introduce some tools you can use so you don't have to start from scratch.

Starting from Scratch

To create a new document in most programs, open the **File** menu and click **New**. What happens next varies from program to program. The following list describes the most common scenarios:

- A dialog box appears presenting you with a list of templates or wizards you can use to start creating typical documents. For example, in a word processing program, the dialog box may ask if you want to create a letter, resume, memo, or Web page. See the following two sections for instructions on how to proceed.

- A dialog box appears asking if you want to create a new document, open an existing document, or start with a blank page. Make your selection and click the appropriate command button to continue.

- The program automatically opens a blank document window. Start working.

Using a Template

Several years ago, software developers finally realized that people don't like to start from scratch. It's easier and less intimidating to modify an existing document than to confront a blank page. Even a simple fill-in-the blanks memo form is easier to work with than trying to lay out the memo and then type your entries.

Because of this, most applications come with a set of *templates*—pre-designed documents that typically contain a little text and placeholders for pictures and for specific entries, such as a mailing address.

Creating a new document from a template

1. Open the **File** menu and click **New**.
2. Click the name of the template you want to use and click **OK**. The application displays the template in its own window.

Quickly create a blank document

To quickly create a blank document click the **New** button in the program's toolbar. In most programs, this tells the program to open a new document window, no questions asked.

3. If the template includes instructions on how to proceed, follow the instructions (see Figure 6.9). If no instructions are displayed, modify the existing document as desired.

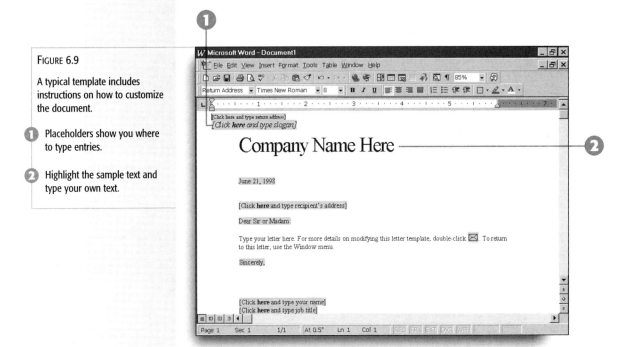

FIGURE 6.9

A typical template includes instructions on how to customize the document.

1 Placeholders show you where to type entries.

2 Highlight the sample text and type your own text.

Using Wizards

A wizard is a series of dialog boxes that leads you through the process of performing a task by asking you questions and prompting you to type entries and select options. Windows itself uses many wizards to lead you through involved tasks, such as installing new hardware and programs and setting up an Internet connection.

Many applications also use wizards to lead you through the process of creating custom documents. Unlike templates, which automatically plop a pre-created document on your screen, wizards give you more control over the document, prompting you to choose an overall design and type specific text.

Creating a document using a Wizard

1. Open the **File** menu and click **New**.

2. Click the wizard you want to use and click **OK**.

3. Follow the wizard's instructions, and click the **Next** button to proceed see Figure 6.10).

4. In the final dialog box, click **Finish**. The wizard creates the document according to your specifications and displays it in its own document window.

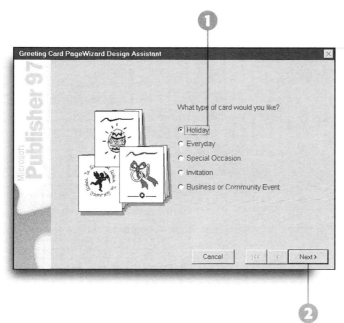

FIGURE 6.10

A wizard displays a series of dialog boxes, instructing you on how to proceed.

① Enter your preferences.

② Click **Next**.

Editing Your Document

After a document is open, you can edit it by deleting, inserting, moving, and copying text and other data. Of course, the procedures for performing such tasks vary depending on the type of document you are creating. For example, in a text document, you insert text by clicking where you want text inserted and then typing the text. In a graphics program, you use the mouse to paint or draw objects in the desired locations. In a spreadsheet, you type data into cells.

Create a document from My Computer

Many programs add their names to the **File**, **New** menu in My Computer, allowing you to quickly create a document without first running the program. In My Computer, open the **File** menu, point to **New**, and click the type of document you want to create.

Inserting and Deleting Text

Undoing mistakes

Before you delete or cut text or make any other major changes to a document, find the program's **Undo** command (usually on the **Edit** menu and in the standard toolbar). The Undo feature keeps track of your changes and allows you to undo a long list of actions. However, after you close the document, you can no longer undo your changes.

To make minor text revisions in any document, point to the text you want to edit and click to position the insertion point. Use the Delete key to delete characters to the right of the insertion point or press the Backspace key to delete characters to the left. In a text frame or box (as in a desktop publishing program), you must click the text frame or box and then click to position the insertion point. To insert text, just start typing.

To replace an entry in a spreadsheet, click its cell, type your new entry, and press Enter. To edit an entry instead of replacing it, double-click in its cell.

Selecting Text and Other Objects

In many cases, you need to do more than delete or insert a few characters or words. You may need to cut an entire paragraph, move it to a different location in your document, or rearrange the objects (lines, ovals, rectangles, and so on) that make up a drawing. To make these more significant modifications, you need to master a few techniques for selecting text and other objects.

Although selection techniques vary from program to program, there are some standard procedures you can follow:

- In a word processing program, position the insertion point at the beginning of the text and then drag to the right and down to extend the highlighting.

- In most word processing programs, the area between the left edge of the window and the text is a selection area. When you move the mouse pointer into the selection area, the pointer changes direction. Click to the left of a line to select it or drag down to select multiple lines.

- In a desktop publishing program, first click the text frame that contains the text you want to select. Then, drag over the text as you would in a word processing program.

- In a spreadsheet program, click a cell to select it. To highlight multiple cells, drag over them. You can click the column letters and row numbers (the headings just outside the spreadsheet) to select an entire column or row.

- To select a picture or other non-text object, click the object or one of its edges. Handles (small squares) appear around the object. You can then drag the object or its outline to move it.

- Press Ctrl+A to select all text in a document or all the cells in a spreadsheet. (This is a universal shortcut in Windows programs.)

Copying and Pasting Data

After you have highlighted a chunk of text or selected one or more objects, you can cut and paste the selection to move it or copy and paste the selection to duplicate it. The **Edit** menu contains all the commands you need to cut, copy, and paste. In addition, most programs also offer the following shortcuts:

Ctrl+C to copy.

Ctrl+X to cut.

Ctrl+V to paste.

Right-click the selection to display a context menu that offers the Cut, Copy, and Paste commands.

High-end Windows programs support a data-sharing technology called *OLE* (pronounced oh-LAY, short for *Object Linking and Embedding*). With OLE, you can copy data from one document and then paste it into another document to create a live connection between the pasted data and the original document. If you edit the data in the original document, the pasted data automatically reflects the changes. (To share data dynamically, both programs must support OLE.)

SEE ALSO

➤ *Learn how to add and remove components, page 204*

Linking data between documents

1. Select the data you want to copy.

2. Click the **Copy** button 🖺.

More selection techniques

Most programs offer additional techniques for selecting text and objects. In many programs, you can hold down the Shift key and use the arrow keys to extend the highlight. Other programs allow you to double-click to highlight a word, triple-click to highlight a paragraph, or Ctrl+click to highlight a sentence. Check your program's Help system to learn about additional shortcuts.

Where does it go?

When you copy or cut data, it is placed on the Windows Clipboard, where it stays until you copy or cut other data. You can view the contents of the Clipboard by choosing **Start**, **Programs**, **Accessories**, **System Tools**, **Clipboard Viewer**. If the Clipboard Viewer is not available, you can install it from the Windows CD.

3. Change to the document in which you want to paste the data. (This can be in the same program or a different program.)

4. Open the **Edit** menu and click **Paste Special**. The Paste Special dialog box appears, as shown in Figure 6.11.

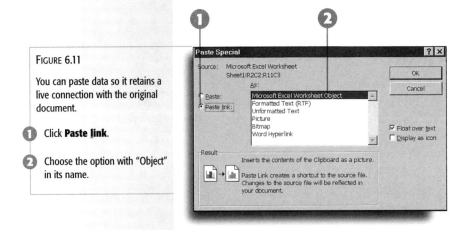

FIGURE 6.11

You can paste data so it retains a live connection with the original document.

1 Click **Paste link**.

2 Choose the option with "Object" in its name.

5. Click **Paste link** (or the equivalent command) and click **OK**.

6. In the **As** list, click the option with "Object" in its name.

Drag-and-Drop Editing

The most intuitive way to move text or other objects is to use the mouse. Position the mouse pointer over the selection and then press and hold down the left mouse button and drag the selection to the desired location. When you release the mouse button, the selection is moved to the new location.

To copy the selection instead of moving it, hold down the Ctrl key and drag. A plus sign appears next to the mouse pointer, indicating that you are copying the selection. When you release the mouse button, a duplicate copy of the selection is inserted in the document.

Working with Graphics

When you click a picture or other object in a document, handles (small squares) appear around the object. To move the object, drag it or drag its outline to the desired location. To resize the object, drag one of its handles, as shown in Figure 6.12.

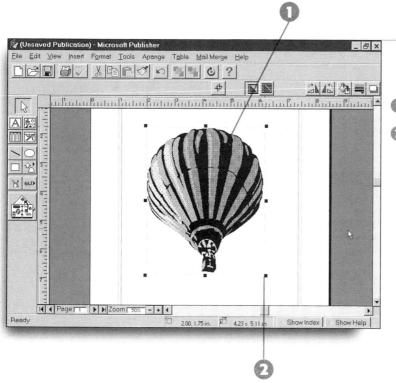

FIGURE 6.12

When a picture or similar object is selected, handles appear around it.

1 Drag the picture to move it.

2 Drag a handle to change the object's size.

You can cut, copy, and paste the object using the same steps you use with text, including dragging and dropping the object. When working with pictures and similar objects in a document, keep the following points in mind:

- With drawing objects, such as lines and circles, you must drag the object's edge to move it. If you click inside a circle, for example, the circle will no longer be selected.

- To resize an object but retain the object's relative dimensions, drag a corner handle. To change only the width or height, drag a side handle or a handle in the center top or bottom border.

- To resize an image from the center out, in some programs, hold down the Shift key while dragging the handle.

- If you cannot select an object by clicking it, it is probably behind another object. Click the object that's in front and click the Send to Back button 🖼️ . (Commands for layering objects may differ in a specific program.)

- To move or resize several objects as a group, Ctrl+click each object (in some programs, use Shift+click) and then drag any of the objects to move them or drag any handle to resize them. In some programs, you can select a command to group the objects, in which case one set of handles appears around all the objects.

Formatting Your Document

Creating a document is not simply a matter of typing text and inserting pictures. You must also *format* the document to position the text and objects on the page and to control the page layout and text appearance. In most documents, use the following three formatting options:

- *Page formatting* controls the overall layout of the page, including its margins, *headers* (text printed at the top of every page), and *footers* (text printed at the bottom of every page).

- *Paragraph formatting* controls paragraph layout, including how far the paragraphs are indented from the left and right margins, the space before and after the paragraphs, and whether the paragraphs are formatted as numbered or bulleted lists.

- *Character formatting* controls the appearance of each letter, number, or symbol in the text. You can control a character's *font* (type style and size), *position* (normal, superscript, or subscript), color, and *enhancements* (such as bold, italic, and underlining).

Changing the Margins

Documents typically use a standard 1-inch margin. However, you may want to increase the margins if you have a one page document that's running a little short or if you want to indent a paragraph to set it off from surrounding text.

To change the margins for an entire document, open the **File** menu and choose the **Page Setup** command or its equivalent. Enter the desired margin settings and click **OK**.

To change the margins for one or more paragraphs in the document, highlight the paragraphs and use the indent markers, as shown in Figure 6.13. If the ruler is not displayed, open the **View** menu and click **Ruler**. If there is no **View**, **Ruler** command, use the **Format**, **Paragraph** command to indent the paragraphs, as explained in the next section.

> **Quick formatting with a toolbar**
>
> Most programs have a formatting toolbar that contains buttons for the most common formatting options. These toolbar buttons typically allow you to change the type style and size; make text bold, italic, or underlined; align paragraphs (left, center, or right); and create bulleted or numbered lists.

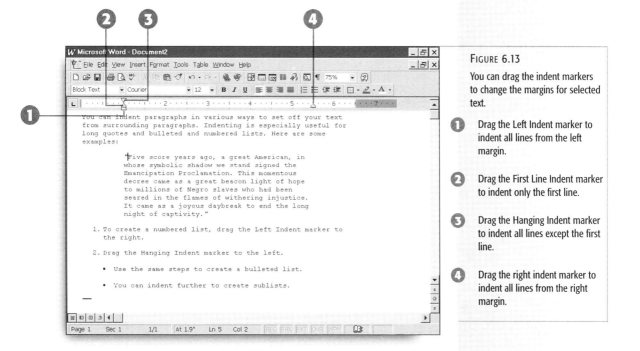

FIGURE 6.13

You can drag the indent markers to change the margins for selected text.

1. Drag the Left Indent marker to indent all lines from the left margin.

2. Drag the First Line Indent marker to indent only the first line.

3. Drag the Hanging Indent marker to indent all lines except the first line.

4. Drag the right indent marker to indent all lines from the right margin.

Change margins in Print Preview

Open the **File** menu and click **Print Preview**. In Print Preview mode, many programs display rulers along the top and left side of the preview area. You can drag the margin markers in the rulers to quickly adjust the margins.

Formatting Paragraphs

It's tempting to do most of your paragraph formatting with the two universal formatting keys: the Spacebar, and the Enter key. If you need an extra blank line between paragraphs, press the Enter key twice. If you want to indent the first line of a paragraph, press the Spacebar five times. The trouble with this approach is that it's sloppy and it makes it difficult to adjust text later.

Word processors come with special paragraph formatting commands. To format an existing paragraph, click inside the paragraph first; to format several paragraphs, select them (you need only select a portion of each paragraph that you want to format). In most programs, you choose the **Format**, **Paragraph** command to display a dialog box that allows you to enter all your preferences:

- *Line spacing.* You can single-space, double-space, or select a fraction, for example 1 1/2 for a line and a half. In addition, you can specify the amount of space between this paragraph and the next or previous paragraph. For example, you can single-space the lines within a paragraph, and double-space between paragraphs.

- *Indents.* Normally, you indent the first line of each paragraph five spaces from the left margin. However, you can also indent the right side of a paragraph, or set a long quote off by indenting both sides. In addition, you can create a *hanging indent* for bulleted or numbered lists.

- *Alignment.* You can have text left-aligned (as normal), centered, right-aligned (pushed against the right margin), or fully-justified (spread between margins as in newspaper columns).

- *Tab settings.* Tab stops are typically set at every five spaces, so whenever you press the Tab key, the cursor moves five spaces to the right. You can change both the tab stop position and its type. The tab stop type determines how the text is aligned on the tab stop, as shown in Figure 6.14.

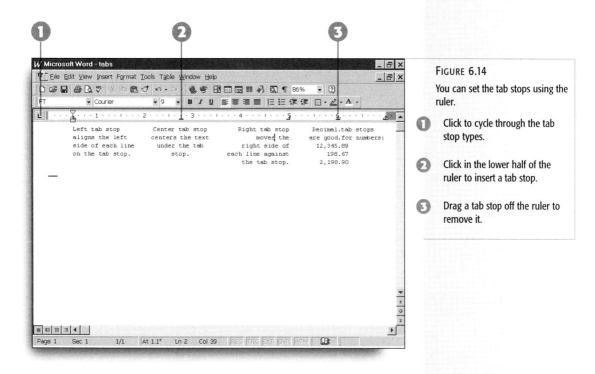

FIGURE 6.14

You can set the tab stops using the ruler.

1. Click to cycle through the tab stop types.

2. Click in the lower half of the ruler to insert a tab stop.

3. Drag a tab stop off the ruler to remove it.

Formatting Text

To emphasize key words and phrases, many word-processing programs let you select from various *fonts* (also known as *typestyles*), sizes, and enhancements.

A *font* is any set of characters that have the same design, such as Courier or Garamond. The font size is measured in points (72 points per inch). An *enhancement* is any variation that changes the appearance of the font. For example, boldface, italics, underlining, and color are all enhancements; the character's design and size stay the same, but an aspect of the type is changed.

Changing the appearance of text

1. Highlight the text.

2. Open the **Format** menu and choose **Font** or **Character** to display the dialog box shown in Figure 6.15.

3. Click the font you want to use. The preview area shows a sample of the selected font.

4. Choose the desired type size.

5. Choose any enhancements you want to apply to the text.

6. Click **OK**.

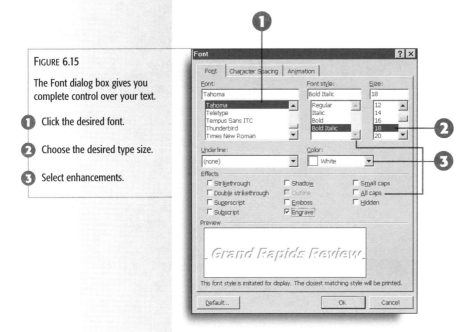

FIGURE 6.15

The Font dialog box gives you complete control over your text.

1 Click the desired font.

2 Choose the desired type size.

3 Select enhancements.

Formatting Tables and Spreadsheets

Although you can use many of the same formatting tools you use in a word processor to format a spreadsheet or table, such as fonts and text alignment, spreadsheets and tables offer some additional options:

- *Column width*. To make a column wider or narrower, click the column's heading (the letter at the top of the column) and then drag the line on the right side of the column heading to the left or right.

- *Row height*. If you use large text in a cell, the text may appear chopped off at the top. Click the row's heading (the number to the left of the row) and drag the line below the heading up or down to change the row height.

- *Values.* You may want to have some values displayed as dollar amounts, percentages, or in some other format. Instead of typing those symbols yourself, have the spreadsheet program do it for you. In most spreadsheet programs, choose **Format**, **Cells** and enter your preferences.

- *Cell borders.* When you're working in a table or spreadsheet, the program displays gridlines to indicate the cell borders. However, these lines do not print, making it difficult to follow a row or column. To add lines that do print, use borders. You can turn on borders between columns and rows or use borders around entire cells. To apply borders, highlight the cells, choose **Format**, **Cells**, click the **Border** tab, and enter your preferences, as shown in Figure 6.16.

- *Cell shading.* Another way to make rows and columns easy to follow or to call attention to important cells is to add cell shading. For example, you can highlight the net profit or loss on a spreadsheet to highlight the bottom line. To add cell shading, choose **Format**, **Cells**, click the **Shading** or **Pattern** tab and click the desired color.

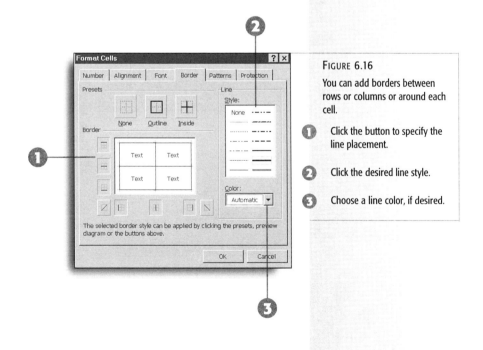

FIGURE 6.16

You can add borders between rows or columns or around each cell.

1. Click the button to specify the line placement.

2. Click the desired line style.

3. Choose a line color, if desired.

Saving Your Document as a File

As you type, draw, or enter data to create a document, your computer saves your work in RAM (random access memory). *RAM* is an electronic area that stores your work as long as your computer's power is on. If you turn your computer off or if power is interrupted for any reason, everything stored in RAM is immediately erased.

To store your work permanently, you must save it as a file on your computer's hard disk. The hard disk drive acts as a tape recorder for your data, but instead of storing your data on tapes, the hard drive stores it on an internal disk. When you turn off your computer, the data remains on the hard disk, and you can "play back" the data later.

Saving a document for the first time

1. Open the **File** menu and select **Save** or click the **Save** button 🖫.

2. Open the **Save in** drop-down list and click the name or icon for the disk on which you want to save the document (see Figure 6.17).

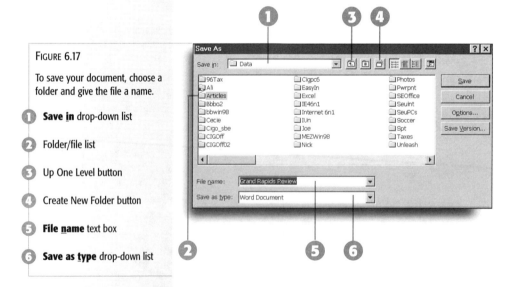

FIGURE 6.17

To save your document, choose a folder and give the file a name.

1 **Save in** drop-down list

2 Folder/file list

3 Up One Level button

4 Create New Folder button

5 **File name** text box

6 **Save as type** drop-down list

3. In the folder list, click or double-click a folder to open it. Continue double-clicking folder icons until you have opened the folder in which you want to save the document.

4. If you go too far down the folder/file list, click the Up One Level button 🔁 to move up one level in the list.

5. Drag over the entry in the **File name** text box and type the name you want to give the document.

6. To save the file for use in a different program, open the **Save as type** drop-down list and select the file format for the desired program.

7. Click the **Save** or **OK** button. Your program saves the document on the specified drive, in the currently selected folder, using the filename you entered.

You must name the file only the first time you save it. Subsequent saves are much easier; just click the Save button 💾 or press Ctrl+S. You should save your document every five to ten minutes to prevent losing data in the event of a power outage. If your computer is connected to a UPS, you can save less frequently, but you should save your document before stepping away from your computer.

To close the document, open the **File** menu and click **Close** or click the **Close** button ❌ in the upper-right corner of the document's window. If the document window is maximized, its Close button is directly below the program window's Close button. Be careful not to click the program's Close button by mistake.

SEE ALSO
➤ *Learn how to manage your files, page 177*
➤ *Learn how to create new folders for storing your files, page 186*
➤ *Learn how to delete files, page 192*

Navigating the Save As Dialog Box

When you choose to save a document for the first time, the Save As dialog box appears and displays the contents of the current disk and folder. You can use this dialog box to change to a different folder and enter a filename for your document.

Filename rules

Windows 95 and 98 place few restrictions on naming files. You can use long filenames, up to 255 characters including spaces. The only characters you cannot use are the following:

\ / ? : * " < > and |

At first this dialog box might seem a bit difficult to maneuver. Use the following controls to change to the desired disk and folder and to name your document (refer to Figure 6.17):

- **Save in** is a drop-down list that displays the available disks on your computer. Open this list and select the name or icon for the disk on which you want to save the file.

- Folder/file list displays the contents of the currently selected disk or folder. To open a folder, double-click its icon.

- Up One Level 🔼 button moves up one level in the folder list. For example, if the C:\Data\Vacation folder is open and you click Up One Level, the contents of the Data folder are displayed.

- Create New Folder button creates a new folder on the current disk or in the current folder. You can then enter a name for the new folder and double-click its icon to activate it.

- **File name** text box is where you type a name for your document. If the **File name** text box already has an entry in it, double-click the entry and type a new name to replace it.

- **Save as type** drop-down list allows you to save the document in a format that can be used by another program. For example, if you've created a report using Microsoft Word and you want to share the file with a person who uses a different word processor, such as WordPerfect, you can save your document in that word processor's format—as a WordPerfect file.

Creating a Duplicate Copy of Your Document

You can often save time creating a document by modify an existing document. However, you may want to keep the original document for your records. The solution is to create a duplicate copy of the document. You can then edit the clone without affecting the original.

Copy a document

1. Open the document.

2. Open the **File** menu and click **Save As**. This displays the Save As dialog box, the dialog box you used to save the document the first time.

3. Highlight the entry in the **File name** text box and type a new name for the file.

4. Click the **Save** or **OK** button.

SEE ALSO
➤ *Learn how to copy files, page 187*

Opening Your Document

When you save and close a document, your computer stores it safely on disk. If you decide to edit or print the document later, you must run the program used to create the document and then open the saved document file. When you open a document, the program reads it from the disk, stores it in memory, and displays it onscreen in a document window, where you can work on it or print it.

In most programs, you use the **File**, **Open** command to open a document. This displays the Open dialog box, which is very similar to the Save As dialog box you used in the previous section. It contains a **Look in** drop-down list, which allows you to select the disk where the document file is stored, and a folder/file list from which you open the folder the file is stored in and select the file. The Open dialog box might also contain the **Files of type** drop-down list that allows you to specify the file's format.

SEE ALSO
➤ *Learn how to edit file associations, page 199*

Opening a saved document

1. Open the **File** menu and click **Open** or click the Open button 📁.

2. Open the **Look in** drop-down list and select the disk on which the document is stored.

Opening documents from My Computer

You can quickly open a document from My Computer or Windows Explorer by clicking the file's name. If the file type is not associated with the application you want to use to open the file, you must associate the file to the application.

3. In the folder/file list, click or double-click a folder to open it. Continue clicking or double-clicking folder icons until you have opened the folder in which the document is stored.

4. If you go too far down the folder/file list, click the Up One Level button 🔼 to move up one level in the list.

5. If the document was created in a program other than the program you are using to open it, open the **Files of type** drop-down list and select the file format for the desired file.

6. Click the name of the document you want to open.

7. Click the **Open** button.

Shortcuts for Opening Documents

Most Windows programs allow you to bypass the **File, Open** command by pressing Ctrl+O. In addition, many Windows programs create a list of documents that you have recently opened and worked on and display that list at the bottom of the **File** menu. In those programs, you can open a document by opening the **File** menu and clicking the name of the document.

Such programs might also allow you to specify the number of recently opened documents that are listed on the **File** menu. For example, in Microsoft Word, you can select **Tools**, **Options** and click the **General** tab to display a spin box that allows you to set the number of recently opened files that Word keeps track of (from 0 to 9 documents).

Default File Locations

If you store most of the documents you create in a single folder, you might be able to tell your program to open that folder whenever you choose to save or open a document. By setting a default folder, you save yourself the trouble of always having to select the disk and folder in which you want the file stored. Check the program's documentation to determine how to set a default document folder. (Many Windows programs use the My Documents folder as the default folder for saving and opening documents.)

Managing Disks, Folders, and Files

Check out what's on your disks and in your folders

Create new folders on your hard disk

Copy, move, and delete files

Link a document file with the program you use to open it

Format floppy disks

Navigating My Computer

Windows provides two tools for managing your folders and files: My Computer and Windows Explorer. My Computer provides quick access to your disks and folders, displaying icons for all the disks, folders, files, and programs on your computer. Windows Explorer, described in "Navigating Windows Explorer" later in this chapter, is a better tool for copying and moving files and managing your folders.

To run My Computer, click the My Computer icon (on the Windows desktop). My Computer appears, displaying icons for all the disks on your computer, plus icons for system management tools you may frequently access, including the Windows Control Panel and Printers (see Figure 7.1). To view the contents of a disk, click its icon. You can then click a folder icon to display the folder's contents or click a file icon to run a program, open a document, or use a utility in the Control Panel.

FIGURE 7.1

My Computer provides quick access to your computer's resources.

① Floppy disk

② Hard disk

③ CD-ROM

④ Control Panel, for accessing system utilities

⑤ Dial-Up Networking for network and Internet access

⑥ Printers for installing and managing printers

⑦ Scheduled Tasks for automating programs

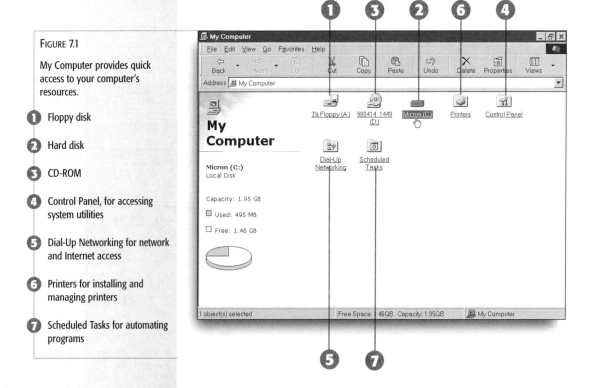

Accessing resources with My Computer

1. Click the **My Computer** icon (in the upper-left corner of the desktop, unless you moved it).

2. To view the contents of a disk, click its icon.

3. To display the contents of a folder, click its icon.

4. Click the **Back** button to back up to the previous folder or disk, or all the way back to the initial display.

5. When you back up, the **Forward** button is activated. Click **Forward** to move ahead to the next folder.

6. To quickly change to a different disk or folder, open the **Address** drop-down list and select the desired disk or folder.

7. To quickly return to a disk or folder you have previously viewed, open the **File** menu and select the disk or folder.

SEE ALSO

➤ *Learn more about Web Style, page 128*

Navigating Windows Explorer

Windows Explorer is a more sophisticated folder- and file-management tool than My Computer. It displays a window consisting of two panes. The left pane displays a list of disks and folders on your computer. The right pane displays the contents of the selected disk or folder. You can click disk and folder icons, just as you can in My Computer, to display the contents of a disk or folder. In addition, you can drag folders and files from one pane to another to quickly copy or move them to other folders or disks.

If you worked with Windows Explorer (or My Computer) in Windows 95, the biggest improvement you will notice in Windows 98 is that the toolbar is different. To make your computer as easy to navigate as the World Wide Web, Microsoft redesigned the toolbar by adding Back and Forward buttons that allow you to quickly return to a folder or disk. The toolbar also contains an **Address** text box/drop-down list into which you can type the path to a folder or the address of a Web page.

Blocked access to Windows folder?

Microsoft apparently doesn't want you to mess with the files in the Windows folder. When you click the Windows folder with **View as Web Page** on, the resulting window is blank. You must click **Show files in the Web bar** on the left to display the files. A better solution is to turn off **View as Web Page** for the Windows folder; open the **View** menu and click **As Web Page**.

Opening Web pages in Windows Explorer

You can also use Windows Explorer to open and display Web pages.

The steps you take to display the contents of disks and folders in Windows Explorer differ quite a bit from the steps you take in My Computer.

Accessing resources with Windows Explorer

1. To run Windows Explorer, right-click the **Start** button and click **Explore**.

2. To display the folders on a disk or the subfolders inside another folder, click the plus sign next to the disk's or folder's icon (see Figure 7.2).

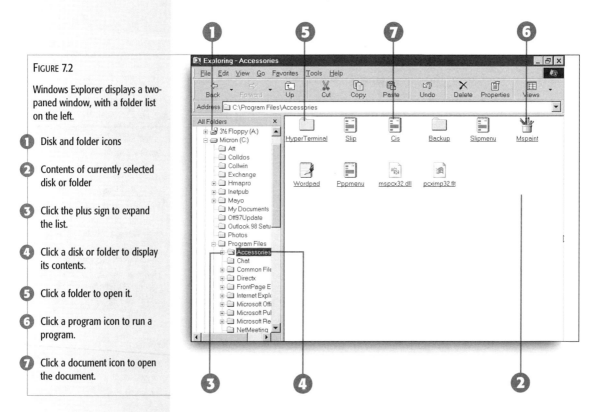

FIGURE 7.2

Windows Explorer displays a two-paned window, with a folder list on the left.

① Disk and folder icons

② Contents of currently selected disk or folder

③ Click the plus sign to expand the list.

④ Click a disk or folder to display its contents.

⑤ Click a folder to open it.

⑥ Click a program icon to run a program.

⑦ Click a document icon to open the document.

3. To display the contents of a disk or folder, click its icon. The right pane displays the contents.

4. You can click a folder icon in the right pane to display its contents.

5. You can click a file's icon to run a program or open a document.

6. To stop displaying the folders on a disk or the subfolders in a folder, click the minus sign next to the drive or folder icon.

7. As you move through folders, the **Back** button is activated. Click the **Back** button to back up to the previous folder or disk or all the way back to the initial display.

8. When you back up, the **Forward** button is activated. Click **Forward** to move ahead to the next folder.

9. To quickly change to a different disk or folder, open the **Address** drop-down list and select the desired disk or folder.

10. To quickly return to a disk or folder you have previously viewed, open the **File** menu and select the disk or folder.

SEE ALSO

➤ *Learn how to navigate the Web from Windows Explorer, page 134*

➤ *Learn more about navigating the Web, page 411*

Controlling Folder and File Views

My Computer and Windows Explorer initially list files alphabetically by name and display large icons. Although this is usually the most useful way to organize files, you can change the way files are displayed to make them more manageable. For example, you may want to list files by type, to keep program and document files separate. You may also want to display small icons to fit more filenames on the screen.

The **View** menu contains the following options for controlling the way files are displayed:

- **Large Icons** displays big icons, which are useful indicators of file types.

- **Small Icons** displays tiny icons, displaying more filenames in the window (see Figure 7.3). In this view, files are listed in several newspaper-like columns with folder icons typically displayed at the top.

- **List** displays tiny icons, but arranges the icons in tabular columns with folder icons typically displayed on the left.

FIGURE 7.3

You can see many more files and folders with Small Icons on.

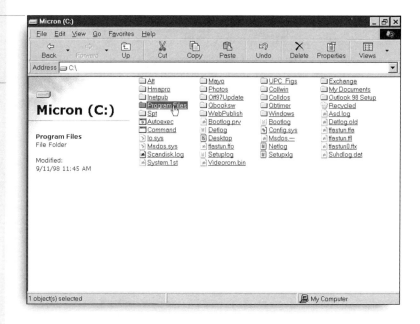

- **Details** displays tiny icons and information about each file, including its size and the date on which it was created. Details view is most useful when you need information about a file. (In Details view, a gray bar appears above the file list. You can click a column header in the gray bar to sort by the file's name, type, size, or date. Click again to reverse the sort order.)

The **View, Arrange Icons** menu contains additional options for positioning the icons:

- **By Name** arranges the file list in alphabetical order, displaying folder names first.

- **By Type** arranges the file list in alphabetical order according to filename extension. For example, a file named letter.doc appears before a file named letter.xls. Folder names appear first.

- **By Size** displays small files first followed by larger files.

- **By Date** displays the most recently modified files first.

- **Auto Arrange** is a check mark option that tells My Computer or Windows Explorer to automatically rearrange the file list whenever you insert or move a file. This option is especially useful in Large Icons view, where icons may overlap if you move one icon on top of another.

The **View**, **Line Up Icons** option arranges the icons in columns and rows without changing their relative positions in the list.

SEE ALSO

➤ *Learn how to work on the Windows desktop, page 93*

Using the Toolbar

The Standard toolbar at the top of My Computer and Windows Explorer contains several controls for changing file views, navigating your folders, and copying, moving, and deleting files. Table 7.1 lists and describes these controls.

Arranging desktop icons

To arrange icons on the Windows desktop, right-click the desktop, point to **Arrange Icons**, and click the desired arrangement.

TABLE 7.1 **Standard toolbar controls**

Icon	Control Name	Purpose
Address ⊐ C:\	**Address**	Lists all the disks and folders on your computer. Use the **Address** list to quickly change to a disk or move back up the folder list.
⇦ Back	**Back**	Displays the previously opened disk or folder. This button doubles as a drop-down list, which displays a brief history of disks and files you recently opened. (Click the downward-pointing arrow on the right side of the button to display the list.)
⇨ Forward	**Forward**	Moves ahead to a disk or folder, if you clicked the **Back** button to back up. This button also doubles as a drop-down list.
⮝ Up	**Up**	Moves up one level in the folder list. For example, if you open the \Data\Letters folder, clicking Up displays the contents of the \Data folder.

continues...

TABLE 7.1 **Continued**

Icon	Control Name	Purpose
Cut	**Cut**	Removes the selected folder or file from its current location, allowing you to paste it in a different folder.
Copy	**Copy**	Creates a copy of the selected folder or file, so you can paste it on another disk or into another folder while leaving the original in place.
Paste	**Paste**	Inserts the cut or copied file(s) or folder(s) onto the currently active disk or into the active folder.
Undo	**Undo**	Reverses the previous action. This option is useful if you delete a file or folder by mistake.
Delete	**Delete**	Moves the currently selected file(s) or folder(s) to the Recycle Bin.
Properties	**Properties**	Displays information and settings for the selected disk, file, or folder.
Views	**Views**	Opens a drop-down menu offering the same options you find on the **View** menu: **Large Icons, Small Icons, List**, and **Details**.

Configuring My Computer or Windows Explorer

In addition to changing the appearance and arrangement of the file list, you can use the **View**, **Folder Options** command to display a dialog box for additional configuration options. The Folder Options dialog box has the following three tabs:

- **General** lets you turn Web Style on or off or choose a combination of Web and Classic Style options.

- **View** provides options for making all your folders look alike, displaying or hiding system files, displaying the path to the current folder in the title bar, and for hiding filename extensions for known file types. (Filename extensions are typically the last three characters following the period in a file's name.

The extension indicates the file's type—program file, word-processing file, graphics file, and so on.) By default, filename extensions are hidden; you can tell what kind of file you are dealing with by looking at its icon.

- **File Types** displays a list of document file types that are associated with programs on your computer. When a document file type is *associated* with a program, you can open the document file by clicking on it. Windows runs the associated program, which then opens the document. See "Creating and Editing File Associations," later in this chapter for details.

Selecting Folders and Files

Before you can copy, move, rename, or delete folders and files, you must learn the various techniques for selecting files and folders. Selecting an individual item is easy—you point to it. However, there are several less intuitive techniques for selecting multiple files as shown in Table 7.2.

TABLE 7.2 **Techniques for selecting multiple files or folders**

Technique	Description
Edit, **Select All** or Ctrl+A	Selects all folders and files displayed in the window.
Shift+point	To select adjacent files or folders, point to the first item, and then hold down the Shift key while pointing to the last item in the group.
Ctrl+point	To select non-adjacent files or folders, point to the first item, and then hold down the Ctrl key while pointing to additional items. You can also Ctrl+point to deselect files.
Drag	To select adjacent files, point just above and to the left of the upper-leftmost file in the group, hold down the mouse button, and drag down and to the right. A selection box appears as you drag. Any files or folders inside the box are highlighted.

continues

TABLE 7.2   **Continued**

Technique	Description
Edit, Invert Selection	Select the files you do not want to work with, and then open the **Edit** menu and choose **Invert Selection**. The selected files are deselected and the unselected files are highlighted.

Creating a New Folder

Selecting in Classic Style

If you selected Classic Style or turned off single-click access, you must Ctrl+click or Shift+click to select multiple files or folders rather than using Ctrl+point or Shift+point.

Your hard disk already has several folders created and used by Windows 98, including \Windows, \Program Files, and \Accessories. In addition, whenever you install a program, it typically creates its own folder or collection of folders and uses those folders for storing its program files.

To organize and manage the document files you compose, you need to create and use your own folders and subfolders. These folders serve a dual purpose; they keep your documents separate from the many program files already on your disk, and they place your files in logical groups to make them easy to find later. For example, you may create a folder called \Data that contains subfolders such as \Finances, \Resumes, \Evaluations, and \Diary. These folders might contain subfolders that further subdivide your files into groups.

Creating a folder

  1. Display the contents of the disk or folder in which you want the new folder placed.

  2. Open the **File** menu, point to **New**, and click **Folder**. A new folder named New Folder appears at the end of the file list (see Figure 7.4).

  3. Type the desired name for the folder (up to 255 characters, including spaces) and press Enter.

SEE ALSO

➤ *Learn how to rename your folders, page 189*

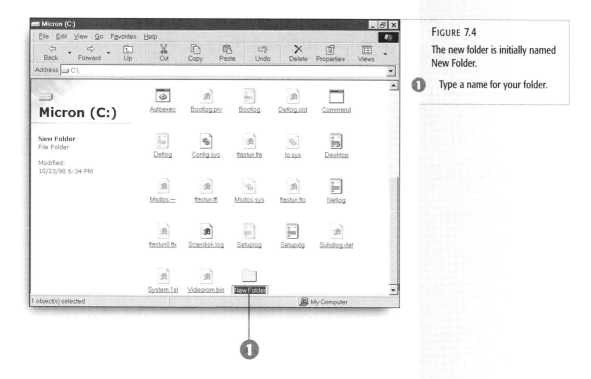

FIGURE 7.4

The new folder is initially named New Folder.

1 Type a name for your folder.

Copying and Moving Files and Folders

You frequently copy paper documents to distribute or modify the copies and perhaps to create backup copies in case the original document is lost or destroyed. You might move a document from one folder to another to reorganize your documents, or rename documents to make them easier to find and distinguish from other documents.

You can perform similar tasks with your digital files. For example, you can copy files to a floppy disk to share them with friends or colleagues, copy a file so you can modify the copy without changing the original, or move files from one folder to another to reorganize them.

You can copy or move files or folders using My Computer by cutting or copying the items and then pasting them to the desired disk or folder. Or, you can open two My Computer windows and drag the items from one window to another. However,

Right-click new folder

A quick way to create a new folder is to right-click a blank area inside the window, point to **New**, and click **Folder**.

you might find it easier to copy and move items in Windows Explorer—you drag the selected items from the right pane over a disk or folder icon in the left pane. When dragging and dropping items in My Computer or Windows Explorer, keep the following points in mind:

- When you drag items to a different folder on the same disk, Windows assumes you want to move the items. To copy the items, instead, hold the Ctrl key while dragging.

- When you drag items to a different disk or a folder on a different disk, Windows assumes you want to copy the items. To move the items, instead, hold down the Shift key while dragging.

- The Shift+drag and Click+drag moves are a little tricky. Start dragging the files and then press and hold the Ctrl or Shift key. If you hold down the key before you start dragging, Windows "thinks" you are selecting files.

- If you accidentally move or copy the wrong files, immediately open the **Edit** menu and click the **Undo** option or press Ctrl+Z.

Copying and moving with My Computer

1. Select the file(s) and/or folder(s) you want to copy or move.

2. To copy the selected items, click the **Copy** button (or press Ctrl+C). To move the items, click the **Cut** button (or press Ctrl+X).

3. Change to the disk or folder in which you want the cut or copied items placed.

4. Click the **Paste** button (or press Ctrl+V).

Copying and moving with Windows Explorer

1. In Windows Explorer's right pane, select the file(s) or folder(s) you want to copy or move.

2. In the left pane, display the icon for the disk or folder to which you want to copy the files. Do *not* click the disk or folder icon; doing so changes the contents of the right pane.

3. Point to one of the selected items in the right pane and hold down the left mouse button.

Right-drag for more options

For a list of options, including **Move** and **Copy**, use the right mouse button to drag folders or files. When you release the mouse button, Windows display a context menu of available options.

Don't replace existing files or folders

Be careful when copying or moving files. If the destination disk or folder already has a file with a name that matches a file that you are copying or moving to it, Windows displays a warning asking if you want to replace that file with the file you chose to copy or move. You may want to cancel the operation and rename one of the files before proceeding.

4. Drag the items over the icon for the destination disk or folder so the icon is highlighted and release the mouse button (see Figure 7.5).

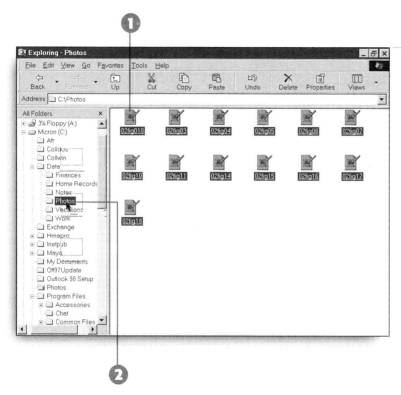

FIGURE 7.5

You can quickly copy or move selected items from the right pane to a disk or folder displayed in the left pane.

❶ Select the file(s) or folder(s).

❷ Drag the selected items over the icon for the destination disk or folder.

To quickly copy files to a floppy disk, select the files, right-click one of the selected files, point to **Send To**, and click **3½ Floppy (A)**.

SEE ALSO

➤ *Learn how to back up files on your hard disk, page 341*

Renaming Folders and Files

As you create folders and save files, you name them, but you might not always give them the most unique and descriptive

Add disks and folders to Send To

If you commonly copy files to a particular disk or folder, add it to the **Send To** menu. Right-click the **Start** button and choose **Explore**. Click the Send To folder. Right-drag a disk or folder icon to the Send To folder, release the mouse button, and click **Create Shortcut(s) Here**.

names. Later, you find that the name doesn't really indicate the contents of the folder or document or you discover that the name is just too long. Fortunately, renaming a folder or file is easy.

Changing a folder or filename

1. Right-click the icon for the folder or file you want to rename and click **Rename**.
2. Type the new name.
3. Press **Enter** or click a blank area.

Finding Folders and Files

Quick rename

To quickly rename a folder or file, point to its icon to select it, press F2, type the new name, and press Enter.

In a perfect world, people are careful about organizing their documents in folders and giving document files logical names. In the real world, most of us are too busy to arrange our files neatly in folders. We save files and quickly forget their names and where we stored them.

Fortunately, Windows has a search tool that you can use to track down your files and folders by searching for them by name or by searching for a unique word or phrase in the document. You enter a portion of the file or folder name or type some unique text that you know is in the document, and Windows presents a dialog box listing all the files and folders that match your entry. You can choose to search in a particular folder, in all the folders on a disk, or on all disks on your system.

Locating files and folders

1. Click the **Start** button, point to **Find**, and click **Files or Folders** (or press Ctrl+F in My Computer or Windows Explorer).
2. If you know the name or partial name of the folder or file, type it in the **Named** text box (see Figure 7.6).
3. To search for files that contain a unique word or phrase, type the word or phrase in the **Containing text** text box.
4. Open the **Look in** drop-down list, and select the disk where you think the file is stored or choose **My Computer** to search all disks. (You can click the **Browse** button to choose a specific folder.)

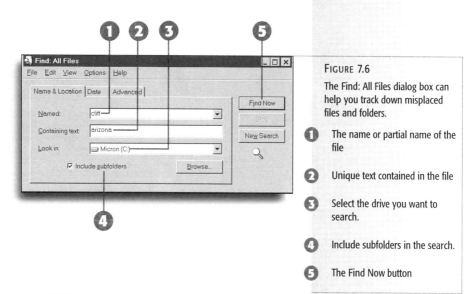

5. To search all subfolders of the currently selected disk or folder, make sure **Include subfolders** is checked.

6. Click the **Find Now** button. Windows searches the selected drive(s) and folder(s) for files or folders that match your search instructions and displays a list of all the files and folders it found at the bottom of the dialog box.

7. In the file and folder list, you can select, cut, copy, delete, or open folders and files, just as if you were working in My Computer.

If the search does not provide the desired results, edit your search instructions and click the **Find Now** button again. To start over from scratch, click the **New Search** button to delete all search instructions and any settings you entered on the **Date** or **Advanced** tabs. Then, perform the search.

SEE ALSO

➤ *Learn how to locate other computers on a network, page 310*

Searching for Partial Names

If you know the name of a file, finding the file is easy. You enter the file's complete name to find an exact match. However, if you

---

Saving your search instructions

You can save your search entries to quickly perform the same search later. Open the **File** menu and select **Save Search**. When you save a search, Windows places an icon for the search on the desktop. To perform the same search, click the icon.

give a file a long name, you may remember only a portion of the name. In such a case, you can enter the part you remember. Windows finds all the files with names that contain the specified string of characters. For example, if you search for "book," Windows finds all files with "book" in their names, including bookmark.htm, bookkeeping.xls, and bookings.doc.

In addition, you can use *wild cards* in your search. A wild card is a character that stands in for characters you cannot remember. You can use two wild cards: the asterisk (*) and the question mark (?). The asterisk represents any group of characters. The question mark stands for any single character. For example, if you're unsure of the file's name, but you know it is a word processing document that has the .doc extension, you can search for *.doc. If you know that the filename contains only four letters and you are unsure of its extension, you might search for ????.*.

Searching File Contents

If you have forgotten the name you gave one of your documents, the search tool can help you locate the file based on its contents. To find a file, you can type a portion of the file's name, or you can leave the **File Name** text box blank. You then type one or two unique words that are contained in the document. For example, to find a file that contains information about your mutual funds, you might search for "mutual fund." Windows then searches the contents of the files in the specified folder or drive for the word or phrase you typed.

Deleting and Undeleting with the Recycle Bin

Occasionally, you should do a little house cleaning on your disks to rid them of folders and files you no longer use or need. You can delete files from either Windows Explorer or My Computer by selecting the file(s) and clicking the **Delete** button.

When you choose to delete files, Windows doesn't actually remove them from the disk. Instead, Windows moves them to

Don't forget the **Documents** menu

If you've recently worked on the misplaced document, open the **Start** menu and point to **Documents**. This menu displays a list of the 15 most recently created or edited documents. Also, check the bottom of the **File** menu in the program you used to last edit the document.

the Recycle Bin, just as if you had moved the files to a different folder on your hard disk. Even if you turn off your computer, the deleted files remain safe until you empty the Recycle Bin.

SEE ALSO

➤ *Learn how to use Disk Cleanup to remove files from the Recycle Bin, page 252*

➤ *Learn how to optimize your hard disk, page 258*

Deleting Folders and Files

There are two ways to place files in the Recycle Bin: You can drag files or folders from My Computer or Windows Explorer over the Recycle Bin icon or you can select the items and perform one of the following steps:

- Click the **Delete** button.
- Press the Delete key.
- Open the **File** menu and click **Delete**.
- Right-click a selected item and click **Delete**.

When you choose to delete items, Windows displays a dialog box prompting for your confirmation. Click **Yes** to move the items to the Recycle Bin or click **No** to cancel.

Deleting items with drag and drop

1. Resize the My Computer or Windows Explorer window, so you can see the Recycle Bin icon.

2. Select the file(s) and/or folder(s) you want to delete.

3. Drag the selected item(s) over the Recycle Bin icon and release the mouse button.

4. Click **Yes** to confirm.

SEE ALSO

➤ *Learn how to remove unnecessary files from your hard disk, page 248*

Restoring Folders and Files

Because the Recycle Bin acts as a folder, you can open it and drag files and folders out of it to restore them. You can also use

---

Be careful!

Windows sets aside only a specific percentage of the space available on your hard disk for the Recycle Bin. When the Recycle Bin is full, Windows starts bumping deleted items out of the Recycle Bin to make room for the newly deleted items. So, although the Recycle Bin is a safety net, you still have to be a little careful.

Permanent deletions

To bypass the Recycle Bin and permanently delete selected files and folders, hold down the Shift key while pressing the Delete key or clicking the **Delete** button. Be careful with this option; you may not be able to recover the deleted items.

the Recycle Bin's **File**, **Restore** command to automatically undelete files and folders and restore them to their original locations on your disk. To restore an item, perform one of the following steps:

- Right-click the icon for the item you want to restore and click **Restore** (see Figure 7.7).

- Select the item(s) you want to restore and then open the **File** menu and click **Restore**.

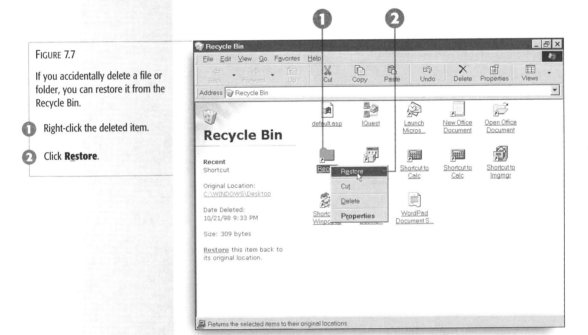

FIGURE 7.7

If you accidentally delete a file or folder, you can restore it from the Recycle Bin.

1 Right-click the deleted item.

2 Click **Restore**.

Emptying the Recycle Bin

The Recycle Bin is set up to use 10% of your hard disk space for storing deleted files. To free up some disk space, you can empty the Recycle Bin. Before you do, however, check the contents of the Recycle Bin to make sure there's nothing in it that you might need later.

Dumping the Recycle Bin

1. Click the Recycle Bin icon on the Windows desktop.

2. Open the **File** menu and click **Empty Recycle Bin**.

3. When prompted to confirm, click **Yes**.

Configuring the Recycle Bin

Although the Recycle Bin is a useful tool in helping you recover accidentally deleted items, you may want to change the way it does its job. For example, you might want it to use less disk space or stop asking for your confirmation every time you make a conscious decision to delete a file or folder.

You can control the Recycle Bin by changing its properties. Right-click the Recycle Bin icon and click **Properties** to display the Recycle Bin Properties dialog box, shown in Figure 7.8. Enter your preferences for the following:

- If your computer has more than one disk drive, you can choose **Configure drives independently** to enter different Recycle Bin properties for each disk. If you choose this option, click the tab for the disk whose settings you want to change.

- To have files and folders permanently removed from your disk when you delete them, rather than having them moved to the Recycle Bin, select **Do not move files to the Recycle Bin...** to place a check mark in its box. (This is a risky option. When you choose to delete files, they are permanently removed from your system.)

- To increase or decrease the amount of disk space allotted for temporary storage, drag the slider to specify the percentage of space you want the Recycle Bin to use.

- By default, Windows displays a Confirm dialog box whenever you choose to delete files. You can turn this option off by removing the check mark from the **Display delete confirmation dialog box** check box.

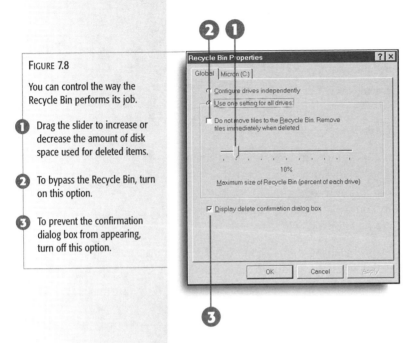

FIGURE 7.8

You can control the way the Recycle Bin performs its job.

1 Drag the slider to increase or decrease the amount of disk space used for deleted items.

2 To bypass the Recycle Bin, turn on this option.

3 To prevent the confirmation dialog box from appearing, turn off this option.

Safety first

Do not turn off *both* **Display delete confirmation dialog box** and **Do not move files to the Recycle Bin...**. Turning off both options disables all safeguards. If you turn off both options, when you choose to delete an item, Windows permanently removes it from your disk without warning.

Displaying Disk, Folder, and File Properties

Each disk, folder, and file on your computer has properties that indicate the item's name, date, settings, and attributes. The properties vary depending on the selected item, as explained in the following list:

- *Disk properties* display the disk's label (name), the total amount of storage space on the disk, and the amount of used and free space. The Properties dialog box also has a **Tools** tab that provides easy access to disk maintenance tools, including ScanDisk and Backup (see Figure 7.9).

- *Data file properties* display the file's attributes: System, Hidden, Read-Only, and Archive. The System attribute marks files that you should not alter or delete. My Computer and Windows Explorer hide system files to prevent accidental deletions, and Windows displays a special warning when you are about to delete or modify a system

file. *Hidden* keeps the file hidden to prevent accidental deletions. *Read-Only* lets you open the file, but does not allow
you to save changes to it. *Archive* is used to determine if a
file has changed since you last backed it up. If the file has
changed, the Archive attribute is turned on, indicating to the
backup program that this file needs to be backed up.

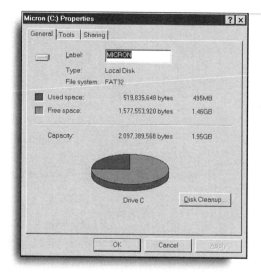

FIGURE 7.9
The Disk Properties dialog box
indicates available disk space and
provides easy access to disk maintenance tools.

- *Folder properties* are similar to data file properties and
  include the four attributes described in the previous item.
  However, the folder Properties dialog box has one additional option: **Enable Thumbnail View**. With this option on,
  My Computer and Windows Explorer can display small pictures of data files that support the Thumbnail feature in
  place of the standard icons. To view the pictures, display the
  folder's contents, open the **View** menu, and click
  Thumbnails (see Figure 7.10).

- *Program file properties* vary depending on the type of program. For DOS programs, the Properties dialog box contains several tabs full of options. For Windows programs,
  the properties include the standard file attributes along with
  information about the program's version number.

FIGURE 7.10

In Thumbnail view, My Computer displays small images of each document instead of icons.

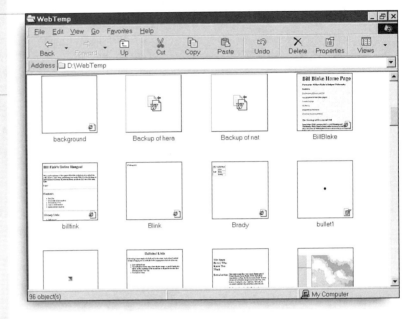

- *Shortcut properties* allow you to change the settings for a shortcut. For example, you can specify a shortcut key combination for running the associated program and specify the size of the window that appears when you first run the program.

- *Network sharing properties* are available for disks, files, and folders on a network. If you work on a network, the Properties dialog box has a **Sharing** tab which contains settings that specify whether the item is shared or requires a password for access.

SEE ALSO

➤ *Learn how to use the Disk Cleanup utility, page 252*

➤ *Learn how to make your hard disk store files more efficiently, page 254*

➤ *Learn how to speed up your hard disk drive, page 258*

➤ *Learn how to find and repair errors on your hard disk, page 259*

Creating and Editing File Associations

As explained in Chapter 6, "Creating and Saving Documents," you can click a document's icon to quickly open it in the program you used to create it. What makes this work is *file association*. Whenever you install a program, Windows associates the program with file types that the program can open. When you click a document file, Windows runs the program associated with this file type, and the program opens the document. File associations also control the following:

- *Web page links*. If you click a link on a Web page that points to a file that the Web browser itself cannot play, such as a video clip, Windows runs the required program, which then opens the file.

- *Printing*. You can right-click a document icon in My Computer or Windows Explorer and click **Print** to have Windows open the document in its associated program and print it.

If no file association exists for a file you click, Windows displays a dialog box listing installed programs. You can choose a program from the list to create a file association on-the-fly, assuming one of the installed programs is capable of opening this type of file (see Figure 7.11).

Editing file associations

1. In My Computer or Windows Explorer, open the **V**iew menu and click **Folder Options**.

2. Click the **File Types** tab.

3. Use the down arrow key to scroll through the list of registered file types. Keep your eye on the Extension entry in the **File type details** area to determine the file type (see Figure 7.12).

4. Highlight the file type you want to associate with a different program, click the **Edit** button.

5. Under **Actions**, click **Open** and then click the **Edit** button.

6. Click the **Browse** button to select a different program for opening files of this type.

Quickly viewing properties

To quickly display the properties for a particular object, hold down the Alt key while clicking the icon.

FIGURE 7.11

If the selected file is not associated with an installed program, Windows prompts you to pick a program to use.

1 Click the program's name.

2 Make sure **always use this program to open this file** is checked.

3 Click **OK**.

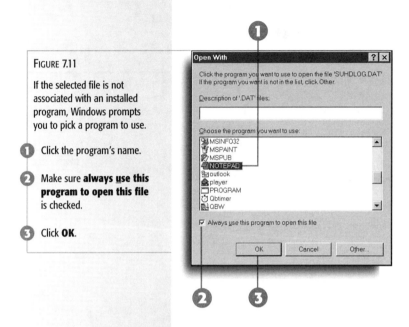

FIGURE 7.12

You can pick a different program for opening a type of file.

1 Highlight the file type you want to associate with a different program.

2 Click the **Edit** button.

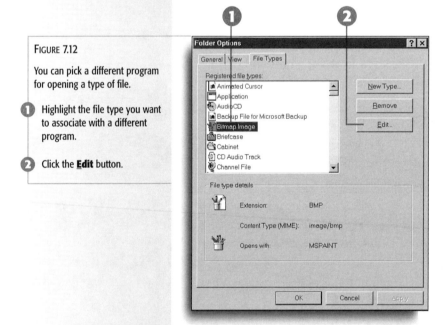

7. Change to the desired program's disk and folder, select the file that starts the program, and click **Open**. The file's location and name are inserted in the **Application used to perform action** text box.

8. Click **OK**. You are returned to the Edit File Type dialog box.

9. Click **OK** to save your change.

10. In the Folder Options dialog box, click **OK**.

SEE ALSO

➤ *Learn how to play media files on Web pages, page 422*

Formatting Floppy Disks

With the increased popularity of the Internet and email, people are relying less and less on floppy disks to exchange files. Instead of handing a floppy disk or sending files by standard mail to a friend or colleague, you can send files over the phone lines much faster and easier. However, you may still use floppy disks to store copies of important files or to exchange files if you do not yet have an Internet connection.

Before you can use a floppy disk to store files, you must *format* the disk (unless you purchased preformatted disks). You may also want to format a disk to erase any files on the disk or to ensure that an old disk is properly formatted.

Formatting a floppy disk

1. Insert the floppy disk into your computer's floppy disk drive.

2. In My Computer or Windows Explorer, right-click the drive's icon and select **Format**. The Format dialog box appears (see Figure 7.13).

3. Open the **Capacity** drop-down list and select the setting that matches the floppy disk's capacity (not the drive's capacity).

4. Select the desired format type: **Quick** (for reformatting a disk) or **Full** (for formatting a new disk or refreshing an old disk).

Deleting file associations

You can also use options on the **File Types** tab to remove file associations or to create new associations. Be careful when creating new file associations. Only one program can be assigned the task of opening a particular file type. Before creating a new type, you should remove the file type from the **Registered file types** list.

Formatting deletes data

Formatting a floppy disk erases any data the disk may contain. Format only blank disks or disks that contain files you will never again need. To check if a disk contains files, insert it in your floppy disk drive, and switch to the drive with My Computer or Windows Explorer.

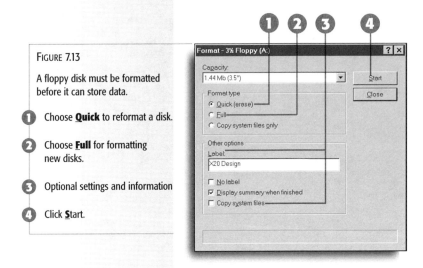

FIGURE 7.13

A floppy disk must be formatted before it can store data.

1 Choose **Quick** to reformat a disk.

2 Choose **Full** for formatting new disks.

3 Optional settings and information

4 Click **Start**.

5. Click in the **Label** text box and type a name for the disk (up to 11 characters), or select **No label**.

6. To give this disk the capability to start your computer, click **Copy system files** to place a check in its box.

7. Click the **Start** button. Windows formats the disk and displays summary information about the disk.

8. Click **Close** to close this information box.

9. Repeat these steps to format additional disks, if desired, and then click the **Close** button.

SEE ALSO

➤ *Learn how to fix a damaged floppy disk when the drive cannot read it, page 259*

Customizing
Windows

Add Windows features omitted during a standard installation

Install and remove fonts

Add shortcuts to the Windows desktop

Customize the Start menu, taskbar, and Quick Launch toolbar

Schedule programs to run automatically

Conserve energy with Windows' power-saving features

Adding and Removing Windows Components

If you performed a typical installation of Windows or you received your PC with Windows installed, the installation placed the most common Windows components on your computer. To save disk space, a typical installation does not install advanced Windows components, such as Direct Cable Connection, networking support, and additional sound schemes and wallpaper.

If you find that a component discussed in this book is not on your system, however, you can easily add it by using the Windows Setup tab in the Add/Remove Programs dialog box. In addition, if your computer is running low on disk space, you can quickly remove Windows components that you don't use.

Windows components are organized by category. When you want to add or remove a component, you must select the category (such as Internet Tools) and then click the **Details** button to view a list of components in that category. Table 8.1 lists the categories and the components you will find in each category.

SEE ALSO

➤ *Learn how to prepare a PC for use by the disabled, page 865*

➤ *Learn how to use the Web Publishing Wizard, page 431*

TABLE 8.1   **Windows 98 components**

Component	Description
Accessibility Options	
Accessibility Options	Includes special keyboard, sound, display, and mouse options for people with mobility, visual, or hearing impairments.
Accessibility Tools	Offers a screen magnifier and additional options for changing the behavior of the mouse.

Component	Description
Accessories	
Calculator	Performs mathematical calculations.
Desktop Wallpaper	A collection of background images you can use for your Windows desktop.
Document Templates	A collection of predesigned documents that can help you quickly create common documents in your Windows programs.
Games	Includes Minesweeper, Hearts, Solitaire, and FreeCell.
Imaging	A program that displays common graphic images, allows you to edit and enhance images, and provides scanner support.
Mouse Pointers	A collection of alternative mouse pointers.
Paint	Lets you create your own paintings and graphic images.
Quick View	Allows you to preview common types of document files in My Computer or Windows Explorer (or on the desktop) without having to open them.
Screen Savers	A collection of animated screens for protecting your monitor during long pauses in computer activity.
Windows Scripting Host	An advanced tool for automating tasks in Windows.
WordPad	Allows you to create and print typed documents.
Communications	
Dial-Up Networking	Connects your computer to another computer or the Internet via modem.
Dial-Up Server	Allows your computer to answer incoming phone calls and share resources with another computer via modem.
Direct Cable Connection	Allows you to connect two computers using a special cable and share resources between them.
HyperTerminal	Allows your computer to dial into another computer via modem.
Microsoft Chat	A program that allows you to enter chat rooms where groups of people hang out and type messages to each other.

continues

TABLE 8.1   **Continued**

Component	Description
Communications	
Microsoft NetMeeting	Allows you to place a voice phone call over an Internet connection.
Phone Dialer	Dials a phone number for you. You can then pick up the phone and start talking.
Virtual Private Networking	Allows you to securely connect to private networks over a public (Internet) connection.
Desktop Themes	
Various	Includes a collection of desktop themes that control the appearance of the Windows desktop, mouse pointers, screen savers, and background sounds.
Internet Tools	
FrontPage Express	Allows you to create and publish your own Web pages electronically.
VRML Viewer	Displays and helps you navigate interactive, three-dimensional worlds on the Internet.
Wallet	Allows you to securely perform electronic transactions over the Internet.
Personal Web Server	Configures your computer to act as a Web server, allowing you to test your Web pages before placing them on the Web.
Real Audio Player	Allows you to play Real Audio recordings that you might encounter on the Web. These recordings play immediately after you click a link for the clip, so there is no delay while your Web browser downloads the clip. It's sort of like listening to a radio.
Web Publishing Wizard	Leads you step-by-step through the process of transferring a page (or a collection of pages) to a Web server.
Web-Based Enterprise Management	Includes components that system administrators can use to manage and troubleshoot network servers.
Outlook Express	
Outlook Express	Microsoft's Internet email program, which is installed by default.

Component	Description
Multilanguage Support	
Multilanguage Support	Adds support for foreign languages, including Baltic, Cyrillic, and Greek.
Multimedia	
Audio Compression	Supports audio compression to help keep recorded audio files small.
CD Player	Allows you to play audio CDs in Windows.
Macromedia Shockwave	Includes Shockwave Director and Flash, two very useful programs for playing media files on the Web.
Media Player	Plays common audio and video file types.
NetShow	Plays NetShow multimedia files, which provide a TV/radio-like quality to Web page presentations.
Sound Schemes	A collection of audio clips that you can apply to Windows events, such as warning messages and Windows shutdown.
Sample Sounds	A collection of audio clips that you can use to test the audio output of your computer.
Sound Recorder	A tool for recording sounds from a microphone, audio CD, or other audio input device.
Video Compression	Supports video compression to help keep recorded video files small.
Volume Control	A convenient tool for setting the volume of speakers, microphones, and other audio input and output devices on your computer.
Online Services	
Various	Allows you to quickly connect to and set up an account for popular online services, including America Online and The Microsoft Network.
System Tools	
Backup	Copies files from your hard disk drive, compresses them, and stores them on floppy disks or a backup drive.
Character Map	Allows you to insert special characters and symbols in documents.

continues

TABLE 8.1   **Continued**

Component	Description
System Tools	
Clipboard Viewer	Displays the contents of the Windows Clipboard, which you use to copy and paste data between documents.
Disk Compression	Tools for compressing the files on your hard disk so they take up less space.
Drive Converter	Converts file storage on your computer to FAT32, so you can store more files on a disk without compressing files.
Group Policies	Provides support for workgroups on a network.
Net Watcher	Enables you to monitor your network and its connections.
System Monitor	Tracks system performance.
Resource Meter	Displays system resources so you can determine if your system is running low on resources.
WebTV for Windows	
WaveTop Data Broadcasting	Adds WaveTop capability to your TV tuner, so you can receive specialized Web content through your computer's TV tuner without having to use a separate Internet service provider.
WebTV for Windows	Supports TV tuner cards, allowing your computer to display standard TV broadcasts on your computer. Also supports Web TV broadcasts and program guides without a TV tuner card.

Adding Windows components

1. Click the **Start** button, point to **Settings**, and click **Control Panel**.

2. The Control Panel opens. Click **Add/Remove Programs**.

3. In the Add/Remove Programs Properties dialog box, click the **Windows Setup** tab.

4. In the **Components** list, click the category that contains the component you want to install or remove, and then click the **Details** button (see Figure 8.1). (To install all components in a category, click the category's check box and skip to step 7.)

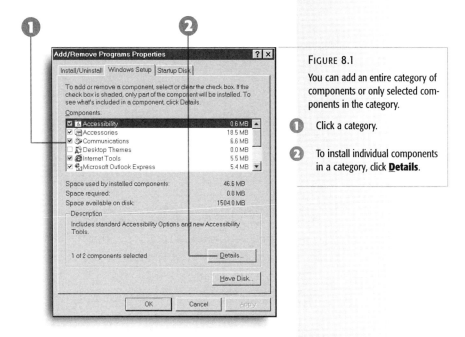

FIGURE 8.1

You can add an entire category of components or only selected components in the category.

❶ Click a category.

❷ To install individual components in a category, click **Details**.

5. Click in a component's check box to turn the check mark on (install a component) or off (remove a component).

6. Click **OK**. You are returned to the Add/Remove Programs Properties dialog box.

7. Repeat steps 4–6 if necessary to mark other components you want to add or remove.

8. When you're satisfied with your choices, click **OK**.

9. If prompted to insert the Windows CD, insert the CD in your CD-ROM drive and click **OK**. You may be prompted to restart Windows.

Removing and Adding Fonts

Windows and most Windows programs come with their own fonts that control the way text is displayed onscreen and in print. When you install a program, it dumps its fonts into the \Windows\Fonts folder. This folder can quickly become cluttered with fonts you never use.

Customizing Windows

SEE ALSO

➤ *Learn how to change the appearance of your text with fonts, page 169*

If you are running low on disk space, you should consider removing fonts that you do not use. The Windows Font Manager allows you to preview fonts and then quickly remove them from your system. It can also display a list of fonts that are similar to help you decide which fonts you can live without.

Removing fonts

1. Click the **Start** button, point to **Settings**, and click **Control Panel**.

2. In the Control Panel, click the Fonts icon (see Figure 8.2).

3. Double-click the icon for the font you might want to delete so you can preview it before removing it. Windows displays sample text in the selected font.

4. When you finish previewing the font, click the **Done** button.

5. To delete a font, click its name or icon.

6. You can select additional fonts by Ctrl+clicking their names.

7. Open the **File** menu and click **Delete**.

8. When Windows prompts you to confirm the deletion, click **Yes**.

Don't delete system fonts

Do not remove the font named MS Sans Serif. Windows uses this font, which is easy to read, to display text in its windows, menus, and dialog boxes. If you remove this font, Windows will use a different font, which might not display all onscreen text.

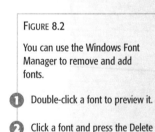

FIGURE 8.2

You can use the Windows Font Manager to remove and add fonts.

❶ Double-click a font to preview it.

❷ Click a font and press the Delete key to remove it.

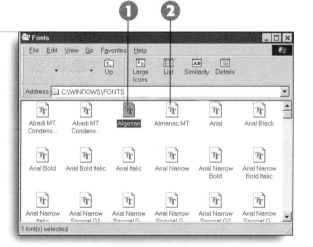

You can also use Font Manager to install additional fonts that you want to use in your documents. Some programs come with addition fonts on a CD that are not added during the installation. In addition, you can purchase font collections on CD and install them using Font Manager.

Installing fonts

1. Insert the disk or CD that contains the font you want to install.

2. Click the **Start** button, point to **Settings**, and click **Control Panel**.

3. In the Control Panel, click the Fonts icon.

4. Open the **File** menu and click **Install New Font**.

5. Open the **Drives** drop-down list and choose the disk drive where the fonts are stored.

6. In the **Folders** list, double-click the folder in which the font is stored. (You may have to double-click subfolders to access the fonts.)

7. Click the font you want to install (see Figure 8.3). To select additional fonts, Ctrl+click their names.

8. Make sure **Copy fonts to Fonts folder** is checked. Then click **OK**.

Checking out similar fonts

You can click the **Similarity** button in the toolbar to group similar fonts; this allows you to trim the number of fonts although still giving you enough different fonts to use in your documents.

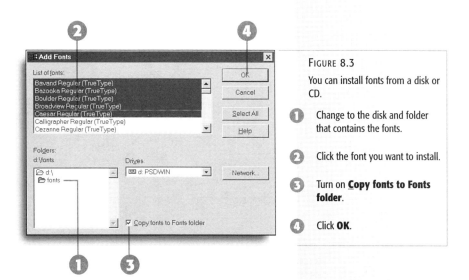

FIGURE 8.3

You can install fonts from a disk or CD.

1. Change to the disk and folder that contains the fonts.

2. Click the font you want to install.

3. Turn on **Copy fonts to Fonts folder**.

4. Click **OK**.

Changing the System Date and Time

In the system tray, Windows displays the current time according to your computer. Rest the mouse pointer on the time display to view the date. If the date and time are incorrect, you should adjust them. The date and time settings not only affect the Windows display but also carry over to your programs. For example, a personal finance program automatically inserts the current date when you record transactions, and your email program time-stamps any email messages you receive.

Changing the date and time

1. Right-click the time display and select **Adjust Date/Time** or double-click the time.

2. Click the up- or down-arrow to the right of the year spin box to set the current year.

3. Open the month drop-down list, and select the current month.

4. Click the current date in the calendar.

5. To set the time, click the hour, minute, or second, and click the up-or down-arrow to the right of the time display to change the setting (see Figure 8.4).

FIGURE 8.4

You can adjust the date and time to have your computer display them correctly.

❶ Click the hour, minute, or seconds.

❷ Click the up- or down-arrow button.

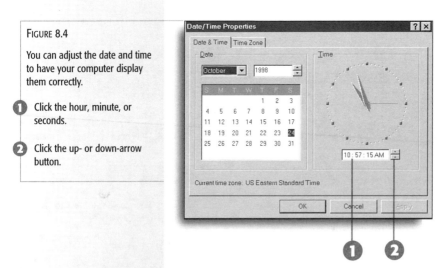

6. Repeat step 5 as needed until the correct time is shown.

7. To have Windows automatically adjust the time for daylight savings time, click the **Time Zone** tab.

8. Open the drop-down list and select the time zone in which you live.

9. Make sure **Automatically adjust clock for daylight saving changes** has a check mark next to it.

10. Click **OK**. The correct time should now appear in the taskbar.

Adding Shortcuts to the Desktop

Whenever you find yourself running Windows Explorer or My Computer to access the same disk, run the same program, or open the same folder or file, it's a good sign that you can save time by placing a shortcut for it on the Windows desktop. Instead of sifting through a long list of folders to open the folder or file or run the program, you can just click its shortcut.

SEE ALSO

➢ *Learn how to check the properties of a shortcut icon, page 196*

➢ *Learn more about the desktop icons, page 93*

➢ *Learn how to transform shortcut icons into buttons on the Quick Launch toolbar, page 218*

Create a shortcut icon

1. Display the icon for the disk, folder, or file.

2. Resize the window so you can see a blank area on the desktop.

3. Use the right mouse button to drag the icon to the Windows desktop and release the mouse button (see Figure 8.5).

4. Click **Create Shortcut(s) Here**.

My computer keeps losing time

If your PC keeps losing time, it could be a sign that the internal battery needs to be charged or changed. If you commonly turn off your computer, leave it on for a couple days to see if the battery will hold a charge. If your computer continues to lose time, replace the battery. The battery also supplies power to the CMOS chip, which stores important system settings.

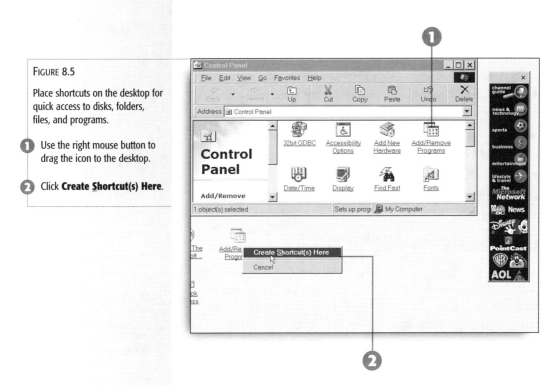

FIGURE 8.5

Place shortcuts on the desktop for quick access to disks, folders, files, and programs.

1 Use the right mouse button to drag the icon to the desktop.

2 Click **Create Shortcut(s) Here**.

In the lower-left corner of every shortcut icon is a tiny box with an arrow in it. This indicates that the shortcut icon merely points to the original file, so you can safely delete the shortcut without deleting the disk, folder, or file. To delete a shortcut, right-click it and click **Delete**.

Rearranging the Start Menu

After you install a program, you may find that you have to work your way through several layers of submenus to run programs you commonly use. To fix this problem, you can customize the **Start** menu by creating your own submenus and by moving submenus or programs. You can also move programs to the top of the **Start** menu, so you don't have to deal with submenus.

The easiest way to rearrange items on the **Start** menu is to drag and drop folders (program groups) and icons.

Rearranging the Start menu with drag and drop

1. Click **Start**, point to **Programs**, and point to the submenu or program you want to move.

2. Drag the submenu or program up or down on the menu to the desired position. A horizontal line appears, showing where the program or submenu will be moved.

3. Click the mouse button.

Adding a Program to the Start Menu

Although most commercial programs automatically add their names to the **Start** menu during the installation, you may download a shareware (try-before-you-buy) program from the Internet and have an old DOS program that isn't listed on the **Start, Programs** menu. You can add the program to the **Start** menu yourself.

Placing a program on the Start menu

1. Click **Start**, point to **Settings**, and click **T**askbar.

2. Click the **Start Menu Programs** tab, as shown in Figure 8.6.

> **Place an object at the top of the Start** menu
>
> To place a program at the top of the **Start** menu, drag its icon from the Windows desktop, My Computer, or Windows Explorer over the **Start** button. Release the mouse button.
>
> **Start** menu context menu
>
> Right-click a submenu or program name on the **Start, Programs** menu or one of its submenus to display a context menu with additional options. You can use the context menu to remove (delete) submenus and program names from the **Programs** menu. However, this does not remove the program from your system.

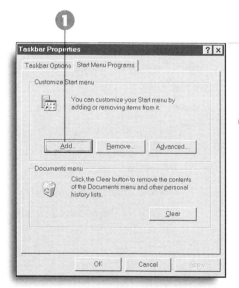

> **FIGURE 8.6**
>
> You can add programs to the **Start** menu using the Taskbar Properties dialog box.
>
> **①** Click the **Add** button.

3. Click the **Add** button.

4. Click the **Browse** button to locate the program.

5. Change to the drive and folder that contains the file that executes the program, select the file, and click **Open**.

6. Click **Next**.

7. Select the folder in which you want the program placed (the menu on which you want it to appear) and click **Next**.

8. Type the program's name as you want it to appear on the menu.

9. Click the **Finish** button. You are returned to the Taskbar Properties dialog box.

10. Click **OK** to save your changes.

SEE ALSO
➤ *Learn how to install a new program, page 118*

Drag a shortcut onto the Start menu

You can quickly place a shortcut at the top of the **Start** menu by dragging an icon from My Computer over the **Start** menu.

Removing a Program from the Start Menu

If you add enough programs to the **Start, Programs** menu, it will eventually become so tall that scroll buttons appear at the top and bottom of the menu. At this point, you should realize that it's time to downsize.

You can quickly remove an item from the **Start, Programs** menu by right-clicking the item and clicking **Delete**. If you have some heavy-duty cleanup, you can use the Taskbar Properties dialog box.

Removing a Start menu program

1. Right-click a blank area of the taskbar and click **Properties**.

2. In the Taskbar Properties dialog box, click the **Start Menu Programs** tab.

3. Click the **Remove** button.

4. To display the contents of a folder, click the plus sign (+) next to its name.

5. Click the program or folder you want to remove.

6. Click the **Remove** button.

7. Click **Close** to return to the Taskbar Properties dialog box.

8. Click **OK** to close the Taskbar Properties dialog box.

SEE ALSO
➤ *Learn how to remove programs from your hard disk, page 120*

Moving and Resizing the Taskbar

The taskbar isn't glued to the bottom of your screen. It acts more like an expandable refrigerator magnet. You can move it, resize it, and even hide it:

- To move the taskbar, drag a blank area of the taskbar to a different edge of the screen (see Figure 8.7).

- To resize the taskbar, drag the top of the taskbar up or down. (Be careful not to make the taskbar disappear by dragging too far down. If you slip, move the mouse to the edge of the screen so the pointer appears as a two-headed arrow and drag up.)

- To hide the taskbar, right-click a blank area of the taskbar, click **Properties**, and turn **Auto Hide** on. Click **OK**. When the taskbar isn't active, it ducks out of the way; to bring it out of hiding, point to the edge of the screen where the taskbar usually hangs out.

In the Taskbar Properties dialog box, you can turn off **Always on top**, so program windows can lay over the taskbar. This gives you more room for viewing documents, but it makes it tough to switch to a different program. You'll find that **Auto Hide** works much better.

SEE ALSO
➤ *Learn how to use the taskbar to switch between running programs, page 100*

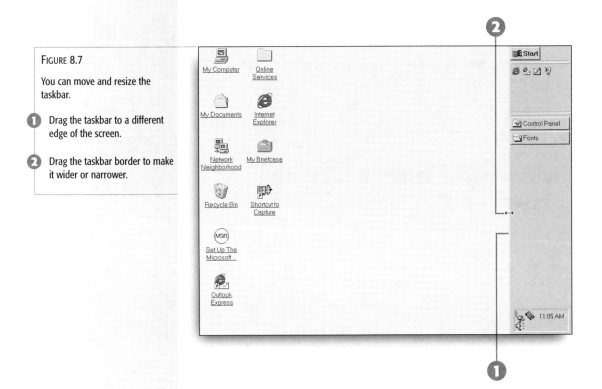

FIGURE 8.7

You can move and resize the taskbar.

1 Drag the taskbar to a different edge of the screen.

2 Drag the taskbar border to make it wider or narrower.

Creating Your Own Taskbar Toolbars

In addition to providing a means for quickly switching between running programs, the taskbar contains a Quick Launch toolbar that allows you to run programs with a single mouse click. Initially, this toolbar contains buttons for quickly returning to the Windows desktop, running Internet Explorer (the Web browser), and accessing the Channels bar. However, you can customize the toolbar (see Figure 8.8):

- Drag icons from My Computer, Windows Explorer, or the desktop over the Quick Launch toolbar to create buttons for accessing disks or folders, opening files, or running programs.

- Because the Quick Launch toolbar is so narrow, it can't display more than four buttons. When it's full, an arrow button appears at one end of the toolbar; click the arrow button to scroll buttons into view.

- To widen the toolbar, drag its right edge. (You can also resize the taskbar, as explained in the previous section, to accommodate the buttons.)

- To remove a button, right-click it and click **Delete**.

- To move the Quick Launch toolbar, drag its left edge to the right. It swaps places with the area on the taskbar that displays program buttons.

- To turn on other toolbars, right-click a blank area of the taskbar or Quick Launch toolbar, point to **Toolbars**, and click the toolbar you want to turn on. (Follow the same steps to remove toolbars.)

SEE ALSO

➤ *Learn how to use the Quick Launch toolbar to quickly run programs, page 133*

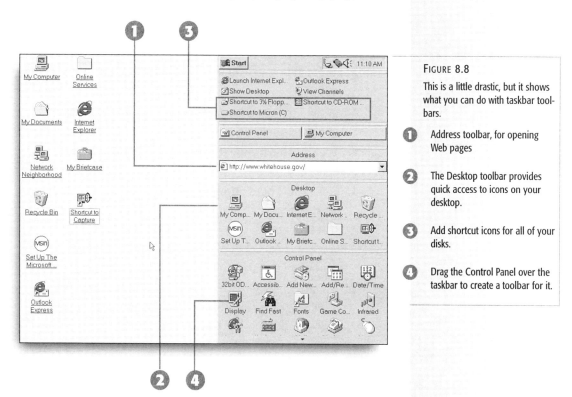

FIGURE 8.8

This is a little drastic, but it shows what you can do with taskbar toolbars.

1 Address toolbar, for opening Web pages

2 The Desktop toolbar provides quick access to icons on your desktop.

3 Add shortcut icons for all of your disks.

4 Drag the Control Panel over the taskbar to create a toolbar for it.

Using Desktop Themes

When most people start to play around in Windows, one of the first things they do is change the desktop colors and background. People enjoy having control over their work environment, and this carries over to their personal computers.

In addition to the standard display properties, which were also available in Windows 95, Windows 98 comes with a collection of desktop themes. These themes change the appearance of nearly everything on the Windows desktop, including the icons used for My Computer and the Recycle Bin, the mouse pointer, program and document windows, dialog boxes, and the screen saver. For example, if you choose the Dangerous Creatures desktop, the Network Neighborhood icon changes into a tarantula, your mouse pointer becomes a jellyfish, and sharks and stingrays swim across your monitor when the screen saver kicks in.

Turn on a Desktop Theme

1. Click the **Start** button, point to **Settings**, and click **Control Panel**.

2. In the Windows Control Panel, click the Desktop Themes icon.

3. In the Desktop Themes window, click the **Save** <u>**A**</u>**s** button to save your current desktop settings as a starting point.

4. Type a name for the theme in the **File** <u>**name**</u> text box, and then click the <u>**Save**</u> button.

5. Open the <u>**Theme**</u> drop-down list and choose the desired desktop theme. The selected theme appears in the preview area (see Figure 8.9).

6. You can click any of the **Previews** buttons to check things out before you make a commitment.

7. You can disable individual components of the desktop theme by clicking the name of each component to remove the check mark from its box.

8. Click **OK** to save your settings.

Make a folder into a toolbar

To create a toolbar containing buttons for the items in one of your folders, drag a folder icon from My Computer or Windows Explorer over a blank area of the Quick Launch toolbar and release the mouse button.

Install Desktop Themes

Desktop Themes are not added during a typical installation. You must run the Windows Setup utility again to install them. See "Adding and Removing Windows Components," earlier in this chapter.

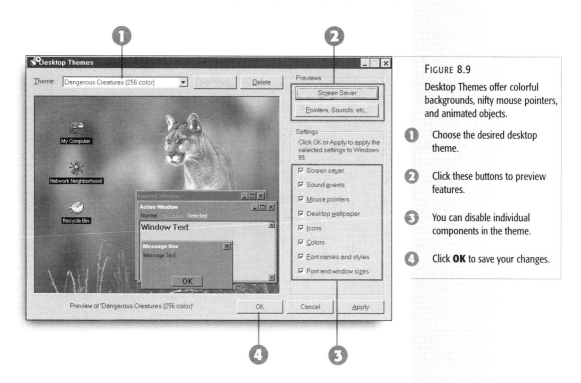

FIGURE 8.9

Desktop Themes offer colorful backgrounds, nifty mouse pointers, and animated objects.

❶ Choose the desired desktop theme.

❷ Click these buttons to preview features.

❸ You can disable individual components in the theme.

❹ Click **OK** to save your changes.

Adjusting the Display Settings

When you installed Windows, Windows automatically selected a monitor type for you and set the color of the desktop background. Unless you have stumbled across the Display icon in the Control Panel, you might think that you are stuck with the colors and appearance of your screen. The truth is that you have almost complete control over the appearance of Windows.

To change the appearance of your desktop or the resolution (quality) of the display, click the Display icon in the Control Panel or right-click a blank area of the desktop and **Properties**. In either case, the Display Properties dialog box appears, presenting the following tabs for changing your display properties:

- **Background.** Lets you choose a pattern, image, or Web page as your Windows background. This is like throwing a tablecloth over the desktop and setting your icons on it.

- **Screen Saver.** Blanks your screen or displays a moving image that prevents passers-by from seeing what you're working on when you're away from your desk. The screen saver password is easy to bypass, so don't waste your time.

- **Appearance.** This tab lets you change your screen colors. Choose a color scheme to start with and then tweak the color settings and font sizes for different Windows objects, such as title bars, menus, dialog boxes, and scrollbars.

- **Web.** See Chapter 5, "Working on the Windows Active Desktop" and specifically the section titled "Adding and Removing Desktop Components," in that chapter to learn about this tab.

- **Effects.** Provides options for changing the appearance of desktop icons and a few other minor desktop features. Great for playing pranks on coworkers, but the options aren't that significant.

- **Settings.** Here's where the real options hang out. You can change the screen colors and resolution to improve the display quality or speed. Make sure the **Colors** setting is 256 or higher and that the **Desktop Area** is 640X480 or higher (I prefer 800X600) as shown in Figure 8.10.

SEE ALSO

➤ *Learn how to add hardware to improve the display quality and speed, page 643*

➤ *Learn how to install an updated device driver for your display adapter, page 819*

The **Settings** tab really should have its own bulleted list. This tab, along with the **Advanced** button in the lower-right corner can significantly improve your computing experience or make you want to roll your computer down the stairs. Your should understand these options and be aware of common variables:

- The **Colors** setting is most important in displaying pictures. With a setting below 256 colors, most images, video clips, and games are going to look blocky.

- The **Desktop Area** setting controls the size and quality of the display. With a low setting, such as 640X480, dialog boxes may be so big that they don't even fit on the screen.

At high resolutions, icons and text may be too tiny to work with. My recommendation is to use 640X480 with small fonts (see the next bullet) or 800X600 with large fonts. If you have a larger screen and need to view pictures in higher resolutions, go with a higher setting, turn on large fonts, and turn on large icons (on the **Effects** tab).

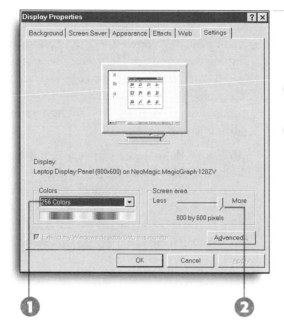

FIGURE 8.10

You can change the Window display settings to control the overall appearance of Windows.

① Make sure **Colors** is set to 256 or higher.

② A good, standard resolution is 800X600.

- To change the default font size for Windows, click the **Advanced** button. Open the **Font size** drop-down list and click the desired font size. (You'll have to restart your computer after changing the font size.)

- In the Advanced Properties dialog box, leave the **Adapter** tab alone. If you choose the wrong adapter, you can really foul up your display.

- You should usually avoid the **Monitor** tab as well, but this tab can come in handy if Windows won't allow you to lower the **Screen area** setting. Try choosing one of the standard monitor types with a lower resolution. For example, if you have a notebook PC that supports 800X600 and you want to reduce the screen area to 640X480, choose a standard 640X480 monitor.

- Click the **Performance** tab and make sure the **Hardware Acceleration** slider is at the maximum setting. If Windows crashes frequently, try lowering this setting a little at a time to see if that helps.

Adjusting the Power Saving Settings

Going for speed

All the extras you turn on—desktop themes, backgrounds, screen savers, colors, higher resolutions, shortcuts, Active Desktop, and so on—consume system resources and require more power to generate and refresh the display. To increase performance, stick with the basics.

If you return from lunch and notice that your screen is blank, don't panic. Windows has power conservation features that can automatically power down your monitor and hard disk drive when you haven't pressed a key or moved your mouse for a certain amount of time. To make Windows snap out of it, roll the mouse around or press the Shift key (you can press any key, but Shift is safest).

To disable these features or change the amount of time Windows waits before powering down your hardware, you can use the Windows Power Management utility. To run it, display the Windows Control Panel and click the Power Management icon. The Power Management Window appears, as shown in Figure 8.11. You can change the following settings:

- **Power Schemes.** You can choose a power scheme for a desktop or portable PC or choose **Always On** to prevent Windows from powering down the monitor and hard drive.

- **System Standby.** Available only on PCs that support it, this option reduces your PC's overall power consumption when it is not in use.

- **Turn off monitor.** Choose the number of minutes or hours you want Windows to wait before turning off the monitor. You can choose **Never** to keep the monitor running.

- **Turn off hard disks.** Choose the number of minutes or hours you want Windows to wait before powering down the hard disk drive(s). You can choose **Never** to keep the disk drive(s) running.

- **More options?** If you're working on a notebook PC, Power Management displays additional options for conserving power when the PC is running on batteries.

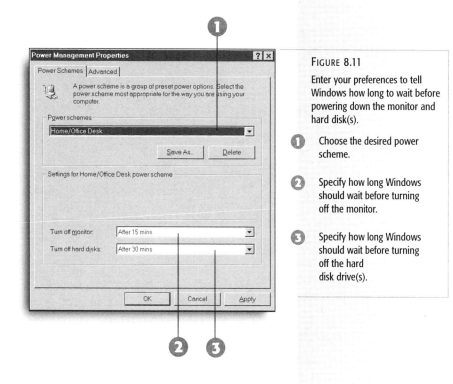

FIGURE 8.11

Enter your preferences to tell Windows how long to wait before powering down the monitor and hard disk(s).

1 Choose the desired power scheme.

2 Specify how long Windows should wait before turning off the monitor.

3 Specify how long Windows should wait before turning off the hard disk drive(s).

SEE ALSO

➤ *Learn how to make your notebook PCs battery run longer, page 281*

➤ *Learn how to change your computer's built-in power-saving options, page 567*

Setting Up Programs to Run Automatically

Task Scheduler is a new Windows tool that allows you to set up programs to run and perform tasks automatically at a specified date and time. If you use Task Scheduler, it runs whenever you start Windows and it remains in the background. When the scheduled time arrives, Task Scheduler launches the designated program, which then performs the specified task.

Task Scheduler is particularly useful for automating system management tasks, such as backing up files on your hard disk, optimizing your hard disk, and checking disks for errors.

Trouble waking up your PC?

When you move the mouse or press the Shift key to activate the monitor and disk drives, Windows takes a few seconds to display the desktop. If your PC locks up, the Windows power-saving features may be conflicting with features built into your PC. Disable the Windows power-saving features.

Scheduling a program to run

1. Click the **Start** button, point to **P**rograms, **Accessories**, **System Tools**, and click **Scheduled Tasks**.

2. Click **Add Scheduled Task**.

3. When the Add Scheduled Task Wizard appears, click the **N**ext button.

4. Click the program that you want Task Scheduler to run automatically and click **Next**.

5. Type the name of the program as you want it to appear in the task list (or accept the original program name).

6. Select the desired schedule for running the program: **Daily, Weekly, Monthly, One time only, When my computer starts**, or **When I log on**. Click **Next**.

7. Enter the desired settings to specify the time and days you want the program to run. Click **Next**.

8. To enter preferences that control the program's operation, select **Open Advanced Properties for this task when I click Finish**, and click **Finish**.

9. Enter settings unique to the selected program to specify the way you want it to run and click the button for accepting your settings. (See Figure 8.12.)

FIGURE 8.12

In this example, you can change settings for ScanDisk to have it proceed without prompting for your confirmation.

1 Make ScanDisk automatically fix disk errors.

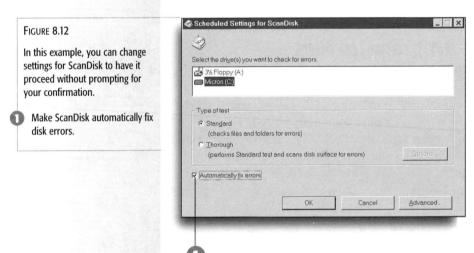

10. (Optional) To enter advanced settings, click the **Settings** tab and enter your preferences.

11. Click the **Close** (**X**) button to close Task Scheduler but keep it running in the background.

SEE ALSO

➤ *Learn how to set up several Windows utilities to optimize your system regularly, page 247*

Like most programs that run in the background, Task Scheduler displays an icon in the system tray (on the right end of the taskbar) when it is running. You can use this icon to display and control Task Scheduler in the following ways:

- To pause Task Scheduler and prevent scheduled programs from running when you are working in another program, right-click the Task Scheduler icon and click **Pause Task Scheduler**. A red X symbol appears on the Task Scheduler icon.

- To reactivate Task Scheduler after pausing it, right-click the icon and click **Continue Task Scheduler**.

- To view a list of scheduled programs, double-click the Task Scheduler icon. Icons for your scheduled tasks appear, as shown in Figure 8.13. You can click the icon for a scheduled task to change its properties.

- To remove a program from the list, point to it and click the **Delete** button.

- To turn off Task Scheduler so it will no longer run programs automatically, display the Task Scheduler window, open the **Advanced** menu, and click **Stop using Task Scheduler**.

- To turn Task Scheduler back on, first run it by choosing **Start**, **Programs**, **Accessories**, **System Tools**, **Scheduled Tasks**. Open the **Advanced** menu and choose **Start using Task Scheduler**.

All programs differ

Some programs prompt you for instructions or confirmation. If you schedule a program to run at a time when you will not be using your computer, you must make sure you set up the program to proceed without displaying prompts, if possible.

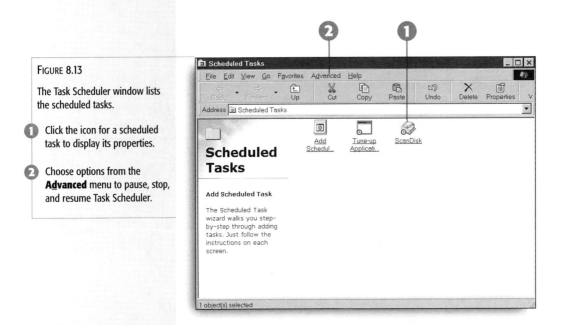

FIGURE 8.13

The Task Scheduler window lists the scheduled tasks.

1. Click the icon for a scheduled task to display its properties.

2. Choose options from the **Advanced** menu to pause, stop, and resume Task Scheduler.

Adjusting Mouse Settings

Because Windows is so point-and-click dependent, a mouse or other pointing device (such as a touchpad or trackball) is an essential tool. However, if you're left-handed trying to use a right-handed mouse, if your mouse pointer disappears as you move the mouse, or if your finger's not fast enough to double-click, the mouse can be more of a burden than a tool. To make your mouse behave, you can adjust its settings in Windows.

To adjust the mouse settings, open the Windows Control Panel and click the Mouse icon. You can then enter the following changes:

- If you are left-handed, click **Left-Handed**. This setting switches the buttons so you click with the right button and "right-click" with the left button.

- To change the speed at which you must click twice for a double-click, drag the **Double-Click Speed** slider to the left or right. You can double-click the jack-in-the-box to determine if you like the new setting.

- To change the appearance of your mouse pointer, click the **Pointers** tab and then open the **Scheme** drop-down list and select the desired mouse pointer collection.

- To change the speed at which the pointer moves across the screen, click the **Motion** tab and drag the **Pointer speed** slider to the left or right (see Figure 8.14).

- To have the mouse pointer leave a shadow as you move it, on the **Motion** tab, click **Show pointer trails** and use the slider to make the trails long or short. (This option is especially useful for notebook PCs because the mouse pointer commonly disappears if you move the mouse fast.)

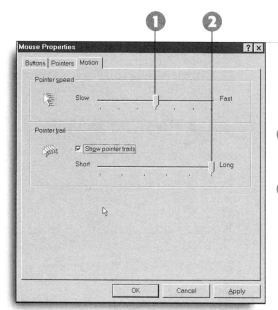

FIGURE 8.14

The Mouse Properties dialog box lets you control your mouse's behavior and change the appearance of the mouse pointers.

1 You can change the speed at which the pointer moves across the screen.

2 Mouse trails help you keep track of the position of the mouse pointer.

SEE ALSO

➤ *Learn how to install a new mouse, page 718*

➤ *Learn how to clean your mouse, page 82*

➤ *Learn how to use a Microsoft IntelliMouse, page 111*

➤ *Learn how to use a mouse on a notebook PC, page 285*

➤ *Learn how to troubleshoot mouse problems, page 817*

More options?

Your Mouse Properties dialog box might have additional tabs or settings, depending on the mouse. If you have a Microsoft IntelliPoint Mouse, for instance, the Mouse Properties dialog box contains options for automating the mouse and configuring the wheel that sits between the left and right mouse buttons.

Adjusting Keyboard Settings

Windows gives you a little control over the behavior of your keyboard and the appearance of the insertion point. To adjust the keyboard settings, open the Windows Control Panel and click the Keyboard icon. You can then enter your preferences for the following keyboard features (see Figure 8.15):

- **Repeat delay.** Controls the amount of time you have to hold down a key before it starts to repeat the keystroke. If you're typing two or three characters when you meant to type only one, you may want to increase this setting.

- **Repeat rate.** Controls the speed at which a key repeats itself when you hold it down. If you commonly type a series of dashes or periods, you may want to increase this setting to have them repeated more quickly.

- **Cursor blink rate.** Controls the rate at which the insertion point blinks.

FIGURE 8.15

Enter keyboard settings to control the repeat delay, repeat rate, and the rate at which the insertion point blinks.

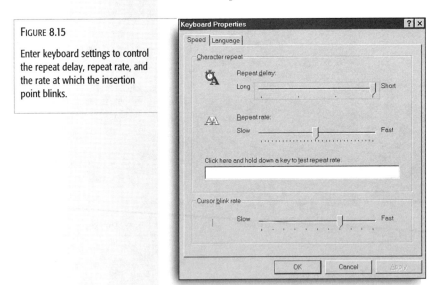

SEE ALSO

➤ *Learn how to enter disability settings for a keyboard, page 871*

➤ *Learn how to use the keyboard to move the mouse pointer, page 870*

➤ *Learn how to clean your keyboard, page 831*

➤ *Learn how to install a new keyboard, page 718*

Printing from Windows

Print fast in draft mode

Generate high-quality printouts

Print and collate multiple copies of a document

Pause, resume, and cancel printing

Save time with printing tips and shortcuts

Checking Your Printer Settings

When you installed Windows, the setup program should have automatically installed any Plug and Play devices, including your printer (or led you through the installation process). If your printer was not connected or you chose to skip the printer setup, see Chapter 34, "Installing a New Printer" for instructions on how to set up a new printer in Windows.

When you install a printer, Windows uses the printer's default settings to control the paper size and type, text and graphics quality, and other properties of the printer. Before you print, you should check and change some of these settings to increase the speed or quality at which your printer prints and to prevent problems.

You can change the settings for a single document or change the default printer settings to control the way all documents are printed. The steps may vary depending on the type of printer you're using and the printer driver you installed:

- If you installed a printer driver from the Windows CD, refer to Table 9.1 for a list of printer settings and descriptions.

- If you installed a printer driver that came with the printer, see "Dealing with Variables," later in this chapter.

SEE ALSO

➤ *Learn how to install a printer driver, page 737*
➤ *Learn how to change the settings for a single document, page 240*
➤ *Learn to work with variables, page 238*

Adjusting the default printer settings

1. Click the **Start** button, point to **Settings**, and click **Printers**.

2. Right-click the icon for the printer you use most, and make sure **Set as Default** is checked.

3. Right-click the icon for the printer whose properties you want to change and click **Properties**. The printer's Properties dialog box appears.

4. Click the tab for the settings you want to change, as listed in Table 9.1, and enter your preferences (see Figure 9.1).

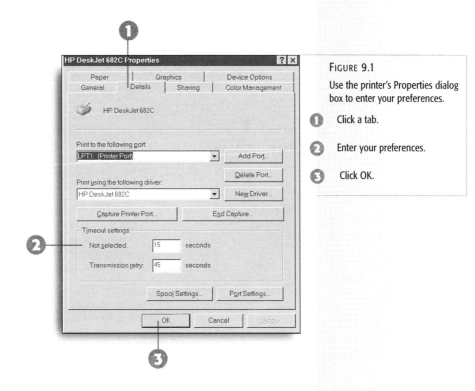

FIGURE 9.1
Use the printer's Properties dialog box to enter your preferences.

① Click a tab.

② Enter your preferences.

③ Click OK.

5. After entering the desired settings, click **OK.**

TABLE 9.1   **Standard Windows printer options**

Option Name	Description
General	
Comment	Optional entry that provides a description of the printer.
Separator Page	Inserts a page after each document you print. This is useful if you're printing several documents or are printing on a network where other people may be printing documents. The **Full** setting inserts a page with text and graphics; the **Simple** setting inserts a page with text only.

continues…

TABLE 9.1 **Continued**

Option Name	Description
Details	
Print to the Following Port	Tells Windows into which port the printer is plugged. If you receive an error message indicating that the port you are trying to print to is unavailable (but you know the printer is turned on), try printing to a different port. Most printers connect to the LPT1 port.
Print Using the Following Driver	Specifies the printer driver you want to use. The driver tells Windows how to communicate with the printer. You might need to update or change the driver if you are having severe printing problems.
Not Selected	Tells Windows how long to wait before displaying an error message when your printer is not connected or turned on. If error messages frequently pop up when you start printing, try bumping up this setting.
Transmission Retry	Tells Windows how long to wait before displaying an error message when Windows has trouble sending data to your printer. If you try to print and an error message pops up saying the printer was not selected or is not ready, increase this setting by 15-30 seconds.
Color Management	
Profiles Currently Associated with This Printer	Allows you to assign a color profile to match the displayed colors with the printed colors. If you are a graphic artist and require a better indication onscreen of how image colors will appear in print, you can choose a specific color profile.
Sharing (Network Only)	
Not Shared	Marks your printer as an unshared resource.
Shared As	Allows you to share the printer that is connected to your computer with other computers on the network. If you choose **Shared As**, you must enter a name for your printer. You can also specify a password to prevent unauthorized printing.

Error messages

Printing is responsible for a good percentage of the error messages you'll encounter. If a light on the printer is blinking, the problem is usually with the printer (no paper, paper jam, or the printer is simply not ready). If the printer does not respond or your system locks up, you can usually trace the problem back to the Windows printer driver or a printer setting.

Option Name	Description
Paper	
Paper Size	Specifies the size and type of paper you are printing on (such as standard 8 1/2- by 11-inch paper or a #10 envelope). Choose the paper size you most commonly use as the default; you can select a special paper size for printing individual documents.
Orientation	Sets the print direction. You can print in **Portrait** or **Landscape** (sideways) orientation.
Paper Source	Specifies the paper tray to use for printers that have more than one paper tray.
Media Choice	Specifies the paper type. For example, your printer might be able to print on glossy paper or transparencies.
Graphics	
Resolution	Sets the number of dots per inch that the printer uses for printing images. With higher resolution, print quality is higher, but printing takes longer and uses more ink or toner.
Dithering	Specifies how shading is handled. Fine dithering uses many small dots to render the shading to make the image appear smoother.
Intensity	Specifies how dark you want the graphics printed.
Fonts	
Cartridges	Specifies the number of print cartridges installed. Some printers allow you to add fonts and memory to the printer using cartridges. Fonts stored on cartridges typically print faster than soft fonts (fonts generated from software).
TrueType Fonts	Tells the printer how to handle TrueType fonts, an advanced type of software font that you can set to any size. The **Print TrueType as Graphics** setting generates the highest text quality. Treating TrueType fonts as outline soft fonts provides for faster printing but lower quality. Printing TrueType fonts as bitmaps provides slow, high-quality printing.

continues…

TABLE 9.1   **Continued**

Option Name	Description
Device Options	
Print Quality	Typically gives you three options: **Normal** (medium speed and quality), **Fast** (low quality, but fast), and **Presentation** (high quality, but slow).
Printer Memory	Displays the amount of memory typically installed in the printer by the manufacturer. If you add memory by installing a memory board or cartridge, you must change the **Printer Memory** setting here. Do not specify more memory than your printer has, or Windows will feed the printer more instructions than it can handle.
Page Protection	If your computer has a great deal of memory, you might be able to turn on page protection to use a portion of memory as a buffer area for large or complex documents.
Printer Memory Tracking	Specifies how conservatively or aggressively your printer driver should monitor the printer's memory usage. If you receive an error message when you try to print a large or complex document, you might want to enter a more aggressive setting. However, doing so could overload your printer's memory and result in garbled output.

SEE ALSO

➤ *Learn how to install a new printer, see page 729*

➤ *Learn how to install an updated printer driver, see page 737*

➤ *Learn how to print to a network printer, see page 313*

➤ *Learn how to troubleshoot printing problems, see page 825*

Dealing with Variables

If you used special software that came with your printer to set it up, the dialog box you use to change your printer's properties might look much different than what you see here. Figure 9.2 shows the Properties dialog box for an HP DeskJet 680C. When changing print settings, be flexible and expect some variations.

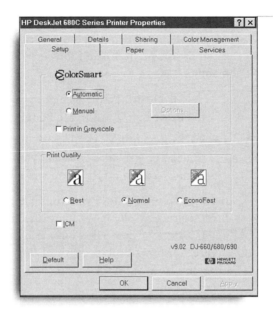

FIGURE 9.2

If you installed the printer driver that came with the printer, the options may differ from the standard Windows printer options.

Making Sure Your Printer Is Online

Before you print, you should make sure your computer has plenty of paper and is online. Most printers have an online light that stays lit when the printer is ready to print. If the light is blinking, you may have to reset the printer.

You should also check to make sure that your printer is not paused or offline in Windows. Click the icon for your printer to display the Print Manager dialog box. Check the following:

- Open the **Printer** menu and make sure **Pause Printing** is *not* checked.

- Open the **Printer** menu and make sure **Set As Default** *is* checked.

- If you are printing from a notebook PC, open the **Printer** menu and make sure **Use Printer Offline** is *not* checked. This option lets you defer printing when you're on the road and don't have access to a printer.

Printing a Document

Although it is becoming common to share documents electronically via email or by publishing them on the World Wide Web, paper is still the most popular medium. To create a paper document, you must open it in the program you used to create it (or a compatible program) and then use the program's Print command:

Preview before you print

Previewing a document before you print it can save time, effort, and supplies spent in reprinting—if it's a long document and you forgot to put in page numbers, for example. You can usually access the print preview feature by clicking a **Print Preview** button or by choosing **File**, **Print Preview**.

- To quickly print a file using the default print settings, click the **Print** button 🖶 in the Standard toolbar.

- To print additional copies, specific pages, or to change the print settings before you send your document off to the printer, open the **File** menu and click **Print**.

If you choose the **File**, **Print** command, the program displays a Print dialog box, allowing you to specify how you want the document printed. This dialog box varies from program to program. Figure 9.3 shows a typical Print dialog box for a word processing program. It provides the following controls:

- **Name.** The program assumes you want to use the printer you marked as the default. To use a different printer, select it from the drop-down list. Some desktop publishing and graphics programs include a "printer" that allows you to output the document to a file that you can send to a professional printing service for high-quality output.

- **Properties.** This displays the printer's Properties dialog box, described in the previous section. Here, you can enter preferences that affect the printing of only this document.

- **Print to file.** Prints the document to a file so you can copy the file to a different computer to print from that computer. This creates a .prn file that you can print on nearly any computer. However, this option can cause problems—if you forget to turn it off, whenever you print a document, the document is sent to a file instead of to the printer.

- **Page range.** Lets you print pages selectively. For example, you can print only the first three pages of a 20-page document. In most programs, you separate page numbers with commas (1,4,6), specify page ranges with hyphens (2–6), or use some combination of page numbers and ranges (1,4–6,8–13). In most programs, you can also print selected (highlighted) text; however, you must highlight the text before entering the **Print** command.

- **Copies.** Enables you to specify the number of copies you want printed and whether you want the copies collated. With collation, the program prints all the pages of one copy and then all the pages for the next copy, and so on. Without collation, all copies of page 1 are printed first, and then all copies of page 2, and so on.

- **Print <u>w</u>hat.** Some programs allow you to save document summaries, notes, and other information along with the document itself. The **Print <u>w</u>hat** drop-down list lets you choose what you want to print—in most cases, the document.

- **<u>O</u>ptions.** Allows you to enter additional printing options, associated with the program. For example, the program may allow you to print pages in reverse order so you don't have to shuffle the pages when you're done printing.

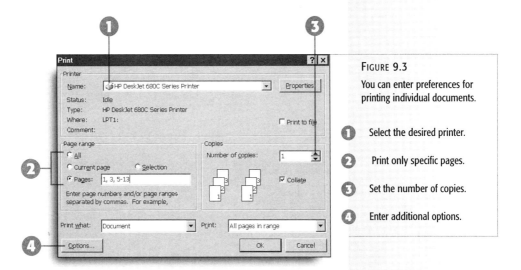

FIGURE 9.3

You can enter preferences for printing individual documents.

1. Select the desired printer.

2. Print only specific pages.

3. Set the number of copies.

4. Enter additional options.

Managing Your Print Jobs

Most printers are set up for *background printing*. When you use the **Print** command, the program saves instructions on how to print the document to a temporary file. Windows then feeds (*spools*) the instructions to the printer when the printer is ready to receive them. This allows you to continue to work in other programs as the document is printing.

However, print spooling does make it a little more difficult to manage the actual printing. Because Windows is busy feeding instructions to your printer, you can run into problems when you are printing several documents and you need to pause or cancel the printing operation.

Network control, or lack of it

If you are using a printer that is physically connected to a different computer, you may not have control of the print jobs, unless the printer is set up to give you full access to its settings. You will still be able to display Print Manager, but you may not be able to pause, cancel, or rearrange print jobs in the queue. To cancel a print job, you may need to contact the network administrator.

Fortunately, Windows has a tool called *Print Manager* that displays the names of all the documents currently being printed. You can use Print Manager to remove one or more documents from the *queue* (the waiting line), to rearrange documents in the queue, and to pause or cancel printing.

Displaying Print Manager

When you start printing, the Print Manager icon appears in the system tray (at the right end of the Windows taskbar). Double-click the Print Manager icon 🖨. Windows displays the print queue window (see Figure 9.4), which contains a list of documents currently being printed.

FIGURE 9.4

Print Manager displays a list of documents currently being printed.

① Document currently printing

② Documents waiting to be printed

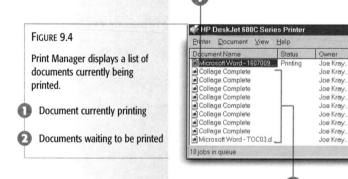

Managing the print queue

1. Double-click the Print Manager icon 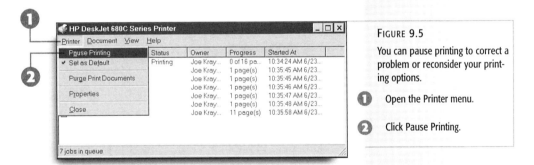 in the system tray.

2. To pause printing, open the **P**rinter menu and select **P**ause **Printing**.

3. To remove a document from the print queue, click the document's name, open the **D**ocument menu, and click **C**ancel **Printing**.

4. To cancel printing altogether, open the **P**rinter menu and click **Pur**g**e Print Documents**.

5. To move a document up or down in the print queue, drag the name of the document up or down in the list.

6. To resume printing (if you paused it), open the **P**rinter menu and click **P**ause **Printing**.

Pausing the Printer

If you start printing a document and have second thoughts about printing it or decide to check something out before you continue, you can pause the printer. Open the Print Manager's **P**rinter menu and click **P**ause **Printing** (see Figure 9.5).

Because the printer has its own memory, the printer continues printing until it has carried out the instructions stored in its memory. In many cases, the printer spits out several pages before it stops. However, Windows immediately stops sending additional instructions to the printer.

Have patience

If the printer doesn't start printing right after you enter the **Print** command, don't keep entering the command. This stuffs the print queue with additional copies of your document. When the printer finally starts printing, you'll end up with a stack of copies.

FIGURE 9.5

You can pause printing to correct a problem or reconsider your printing options.

1 Open the Printer menu.

2 Click Pause Printing.

When you are ready to resume printing, open the **P̲rinter** menu again and choose **P̲ause Printing**.

Rearranging Documents in the Print Queue

If you typically print a single document and wait until it is finished printing before printing another, you may never have to deal with the print queue. However, if you compose several documents and then print them at one time, the print queue can become packed with documents waiting to be printed. If you decide that you would like one document printed before another, you can move it up in the queue (see Figure 9.6).

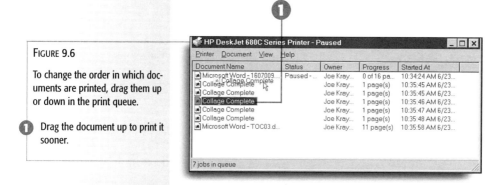

FIGURE 9.6

To change the order in which documents are printed, drag them up or down in the print queue.

❶ Drag the document up to print it sooner.

Canceling Print Jobs

If you printed a document by mistake or lost patience and clicked the Print button several times, your print queue may be backed up with documents. Sometimes the best solution is to cut your losses and cancel printing altogether. To cancel printing, open the **P̲rinter** menu and click **Purge Print Documents**. To cancel printing for a single document, open the **D̲ocument** menu and click **C̲ancel Printing**.

Tips for Quick Printing

Printing can be one of the most time-consuming aspects of personal computing, and one of the loudest. To help you cope, try the following tricks:

- To quickly print a document, right-click its icon in My Computer or Windows Explorer and click **Print**. Windows opens the document in the associated program and starts printing it. (This works only if the document is associated with a program.)

- To quickly print several documents, select them and then right-click one of the documents and click **Print**.

- Drag the document's icon over the icon for your printer and release the mouse button. If you like this tip, place a shortcut for your printer on the Windows desktop to make it easily accessible.

- If printing slows down your PC, making it difficult to work in another program, defer printing. Open the Print Manager's **P**rinter menu and click **P**ause Printing. Print your documents as you normally do, and then when you're done working in your other programs, open the **P**rinter menu and click **P**ause Printing to start printing. (This trick also helps when you have a noisy printer.)

- If you have a bi-directional printer (check the printer's documentation), you must have a bi-directional printer cable to take advantage of bi-directional printing. If the printer came with its own cable, the cable should be a bi-directional cable. Check the cable for fine print; if it's a bi-directional cable, it should be marked IEEE 1284. You should also check your PC's system BIOS to determine if your parallel printer port is set up for bi-directional printing.

SEE ALSO

➤ *Learn how to check your system BIOS settings, page 567*

➤ *Learn more about working in My Computer, page 178*

➤ *Learn how to clean your printer, page 85*

Computer lock up?

If your computer locks up or crashes while you're printing, when you restart your computer, Windows displays a prompt asking if you want to continue printing the documents, print them later, or cancel printing. In most cases, you're better off canceling your print jobs and printing the documents fresh.

Using the Windows System Maintenance Tools

Make Windows start faster

Make your programs run faster

Reclaim space on your hard disk

Scan for and repair disk errors

Make your hard disk store files more efficiently

Running the Windows Maintenance Wizard

As you install programs, wander the Web, and create documents, your system continually becomes slower and less efficient. If a program's installation utility automatically adds the program to the StartUp menu, Windows starts more slowly. When you wander the Web, Internet Explorer saves Web page files to your hard disk (without asking you), cutting down on available space. When you create and edit documents, programs often place temporary files on your disk that remain there until you delete them. And files on your hard disk continually become more and more fragmented as parts of files are stored on separate areas of the disk.

The Windows Maintenance Wizard can keep your computer in tip-top condition by performing the following tasks automatically:

- *Prevent programs from running on startup.* When you install some programs, they add their names to the Windows StartUp folder, so they run automatically when you start Windows. This slows down the Windows startup. However, if you have an antivirus program that runs on startup, keep it running to protect your system.

- *Defragment your hard disk(s).* This rearranges the parts of each file on your hard disk to place them on neighboring storage areas and moves programs to a place on the disk where the drive can quickly access them.

- *Scan your hard disk(s) for errors and correct them.* The most common fix is to remove useless parts of files and folders that your system loses track of.

- *Delete unnecessary files.* These files include temporary files (files that Windows and your programs use as they work but may "forget" to delete), Web pages and associated files that your Web browser saves to your hard disk, old ScanDisk files, and program files you may have downloaded from the Internet.

Optimize your system

1. Click the **Start** button, point to **Programs**, **Accessories**, and then **System Tools**, and click **Maintenance Wizard**. The Maintenance Wizard displays a brief description of itself.

2. Click **Custom** and click **Next**.

3. Click the time you want Maintenance Wizard to optimize your system (a time when you normally have your computer on but you are not using it). Click **Next**.

4. To prevent any program from running on startup, click its check box to remove the check mark. Click **Next**.

5. Leave **Yes, defragment my disk regularly** turned on (see Figure 10.1). Click the **Reschedule** button.

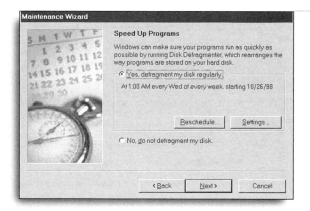

FIGURE 10.1
The Maintenance Wizard helps you set up several Windows optimization utilities to run automatically.

6. Enter settings to specify when you want program files rearranged. Click **OK**.

7. Click the **Settings** button.

8. Click the disk drive on which you normally install programs or choose **All Hard Drives**. Click **OK**.

9. Click **Next**. The wizard asks if you want ScanDisk to check your hard disk drives for errors.

10. Make sure **Yes, scan my hard disk for errors regularly** is selected.

11. Click the **Reschedule** button.

12. Choose a daily or weekly schedule to keep your disk drives running at peak performance. Click **OK**.

13. Click the **Settings** button.

14. If you have more than one hard disk drive and you want ScanDisk to check only certain drives, Ctrl+click a drive to have ScanDisk skip it.

15. In the **Type of Test** area, leave **Standard** selected so ScanDisk will not test your hard disks for physical defects. (You can perform this check manually on a monthly or semimonthly basis.)

16. Click **Automatically Fix Errors** to allow ScanDisk to perform its corrections without your intervention. Click **OK**.

17. Click **Next** when you return to the wizard. The wizard displays a list of file types it can automatically delete.

18. To prevent the wizard from deleting some of the listed file types click the **Settings** button.

19. Click a file type to mark those files for deletion, or remove the check mark to prevent those files from being deleted.

20. Click the **Reschedule** button to choose the time when you want files deleted and click **OK**.

21. Click the **Next** button. The wizard displays a list of optimization activities it will perform at the scheduled time(s).

22. To have the wizard perform those activities now, choose **When I Click Finish**.

23. Click the **Finish** button.

SEE ALSO

➤ *Learn how to scan for and fix hard disk errors, page 259*

➤ *Learn how to defragment your hard disk, page 258*

➤ *Learn how to install a faster hard drive, page 587*

➤ *Learn how to schedule programs to run on startup, page 225*

Leave your computer on

Be sure to leave your computer on at the scheduled time so that Windows can perform the optimization activities.

Updating Windows with Windows Update

Microsoft is continuously perfecting Windows, adding new device drivers, correcting known problems, and improving its performance. To use the latest version of Windows, you should check for and install updates on a regular basis (at least every couple of months).

In the past, you had to check Microsoft's Web site for updates, download the updates, and install them on your computer. In Windows 98, the process is much easier. You simply run the Windows Update utility from your computer. Windows connects you to the Microsoft Web site, checks for updates, and then downloads and installs any available updates.

Updating Windows 98

1. Click the **Start** button and click **Windows Update**. Windows runs Internet Explorer, connects you to the Internet, and loads the Microsoft Windows Update page. (If prompted to register, follow the onscreen instructions.)

2. Click the **Product Updates** link. (If you're prompted to confirm the download and installation of a control, click **Yes**.)

3. The Active Setup dialog box asks for permission to check your system (see Figure 10.2.). Click **Yes**. A list of uninstalled components and newer versions of installed components appear.

4. To install the new or updated component, click its check box (see Figure 10.3).

5. Click the **Download** button (you may have to scroll to the top of the page) and follow the onscreen instructions.

SEE ALSO

➤ *Learn how to obtain and install updated device drivers, page 251*

➤ *Learn how to connect to the Internet, page 391*

➤ *Learn how to navigate Web pages, page 411*

Steps may vary

Because Microsoft is constantly working on improving the Windows Update feature, and because Windows Update runs on the Internet (not from your copy of Windows), the steps for downloading and installing updates frequently change. Whenever you work on the Internet, remain flexible.

FIGURE 10.2

Windows Update can determine which Windows components are installed on your PC.

FIGURE 10.3

The Windows Update page displays a list of new and updated components you can download and install.

❶ Update categories are listed on the left.

❷ Click the check box for the desired component.

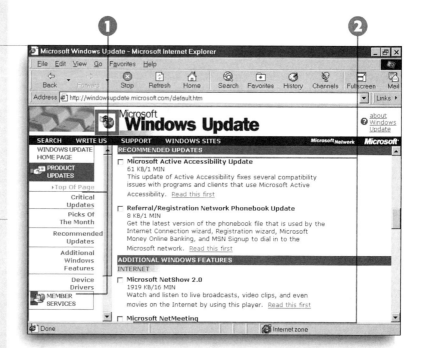

Reclaiming Disk Space with Disk Cleanup

Internet programs and other programs scatter temporary files on your hard disk during their operation. After weeks of use, these programs can clutter your hard disk with several megabytes of useless files. This not only decreases the space you have for storing the files you need, it also slows down your system. Windows has less drive space for use as *virtual memory* (drive space used as memory), and it causes other files on your disk to become more *fragmented*.

To optimize your hard disk, you should remove useless files regularly. If you use the Windows Maintenance Wizard to clean up your disks at scheduled times, you do not have to clean them up yourself. However, if you chose not to schedule the Maintenance Wizard for regular use, you can clear useless files from your hard disk manually or by using the Disk Cleanup utility.

Disk Cleanup can increase the amount of free disk space by removing the following items:

- Temporary Internet files.
- Downloaded program files (program files you downloaded from the Internet).
- The contents of the Recycle Bin.
- Old ScanDisk files (files that ScanDisk creates to allow you to recover lost data; usually these files contain nothing useful).
- Temporary files that your programs create and use during operation but do not delete when you exit.
- Programs you no longer use.
- Windows components that you do not use.

Clearing files from your hard disk

1. Click the **My Computer** icon on the Windows desktop.
2. Right-click the icon for the disk you want to clean up and click **Properties**.
3. In the Properties dialog box, click the **Disk Cleanup** button. The Disk Cleanup dialog box for the selected disk drive appears.
4. Click the check box next to each type of file you want to remove from the disk to place a check mark in its box (see Figure 10.4).
5. Click **OK** to have Disk Cleanup automatically remove the specified files.

Remove programs you don't use

To remove programs and Windows components that you no longer use, click the **More Options** tab, click the **Clean Up** button, and use the Add/Remove Programs dialog box.

FIGURE 10.4

Disk Cleanup can automatically remove marked file types from your hard disk.

1 Place a check mark next to each type of file you want deleted.

2 Click **OK**.

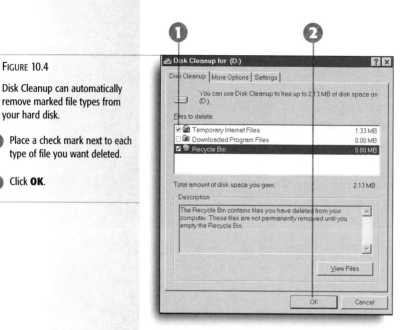

SEE ALSO

➤ *Learn how to add and remove Windows components, page 204*

➤ *Learn how to use the Windows Maintenance Wizard to schedule regular disk cleanings, page 248*

➤ *Learn how to empty the Recycle Bin yourself, page 194*

Optimizing Your Hard Drive with Fat32

As computers become more complex, program and document files are becoming larger and larger. Five years ago, a typical program would take up a couple megabytes (MB) of disk space. Today, each program can consume 10MB or more. In addition, as you explore the Internet, you will commonly encounter graphics and audio and video clips that are over 2MB.

As files become larger and as your own thirst for the latest programs and media increases, your hard disk quickly becomes packed. To help, Windows offers a utility for making your hard drive use its storage space more efficiently: Drive Converter (Fat32). (*FAT* is short for *file allocation table*, a map that your drive uses to locate storage areas on a disk.)

To understand Drive Converter, you must first understand how older hard disk drives have stored data in the past. If you have a hard drive larger than 500MB, older operating systems (using FAT16) would use 32 kilobytes (KB) of hard drive space to store every file containing 32KB or less of data. For example, a 2KB file would still take up 32KB of disk space. You could partition your hard disk drive into units smaller than 500MBs to make the operating system store files in 4KB chunks instead, saving you up to 40% of wasted space. However, partitioning the hard disk drive destroys any data the disk contains. FAT32 can perform the optimization without destroying data. (The conversion process may take well over one hour depending on the size of your hard disk.)

Converting a hard drive to Fat32

1. Click the **Start** button, point to **Programs**, **Accessories**, **System Tools**, and click **Drive Converter (FAT32)**. The Drive Converter Wizard displays a description of what it will do.

2. Click **Next**. Drive Converter analyzes your hard disk drive(s) to determine which drive(s) are currently using FAT16.

3. Click the drive you want to convert (see Figure 10.5) and click **Next**. Drive Converter displays a warning indicating that you will not be able to access the converted drive using a previous version of Windows, MS-DOS, or Windows NT.

4. If you don't plan on ever running your system under any operating system other than Windows 98 or a later version of Windows 98, click **OK**. Drive Converter checks for any running programs that might interfere with its operation and displays a list of them.

5. Close any of these programs and click **Next**. Drive Converter prompts you to back up the files on your hard disk before continuing.

Making small drives more efficient

You cannot use DriveSpace on FAT32 drives. If you have a large hard drive of 1 gigabyte (GB) or more, use FAT32. If you have a smaller hard drive, use DriveSpace, as explained in the next section.

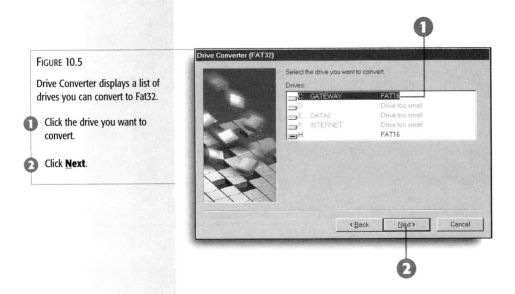

FIGURE 10.5

Drive Converter displays a list of drives you can convert to Fat32.

1 Click the drive you want to convert.

2 Click **Next**.

6. To back up your hard disk, click **Create Backup** and perform the backup.

7. When you return to Drive Converter, click **Next**. Drive Converter indicates that it must restart your computer in MS-DOS mode.

8. Close any programs you are currently running and click **Next**. Drive Converter starts the conversion process.

Compressing Disks with DriveSpace

The problem with Drive Converter is that it cannot increase disk drive space on smaller hard disks. If you have a 500MB or smaller hard disk drive, you must free up disk space using a different utility: DriveSpace. *DriveSpace* compresses the files on the hard drive so they take up less space when not in use. When you run a compressed program or open a compressed file, DriveSpace automatically decompresses it. Because DriveSpace must decompress files when you run a program or open a document, it slightly decreases overall system performance. However, if your system is running low on disk space and you don't want to install a larger drive, DriveSpace is your best option.

SEE ALSO

➤ *Learn how to install a bigger, faster hard drive, see page 587*

➤ *Learn how to perform a backup, see page 341*

Compressing a disk with DriveSpace

1. Click the **Start** button, point to **Programs**, **Accessories**, **System Tools**, and click **DriveSpace**. The DriveSpace window appears.

2. Choose the disk drive you want to compress. If you choose a floppy disk drive, insert the disk into the drive.

3. Open the **Drive** menu and click **Compress**. The Compress a Drive dialog box displays a graph of how much free space the drive currently has and how much it will have after compression (see Figure 10.6).

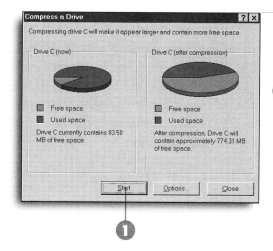

> **Back up your disk drive**
>
> Before using any disk compression utility, you should back up the files on your hard disk.

FIGURE 10.6

DriveSpace displays before and after graphs to show you how much drive space you'll have.

1 Click the **Start** button.

4. Click the **Start** button. A confirmation dialog box appears, prompting you to create or update your Windows Startup disk before proceeding.

5. Click **Yes** and follow the onscreen instructions to create a startup disk. Another confirmation dialog box appears, prompting you to back up your files before proceeding.

6. Click **Compress Now**.

7. Wait until the compression is complete. This can take from several minutes to several hours depending on the size of the disk.

Defragmenting Your Hard Drive

Whenever you delete a file from your hard disk, a storage area on the disk becomes free for use again. The next time you save a file, Windows uses this free area to store as much of the file as will fit. It then saves the rest of the file in other storage areas. As you delete and save files, the files become more and more *fragmented*, and the drive's read/write head must skip around the disk to read a file. This slows down the overall speed of your system.

To help, Windows 98 includes Disk Defragmenter. This useful utility reads files from the disk, positions important program files on the disk to make them run faster, and rearranges the parts of each file to place them in neighboring storage areas on the disk. This not only increases the speed at which programs run and files open, but it also leaves your disk with a large storage area that Windows can use as virtual memory (disk space used as memory). It also reduces future file fragmentation.

Defragmenting a disk

1. Click the **Start** button, point to **Programs**, **Accessories**, **System Tools**, and click **Disk Defragmenter**.

2. In the Select Drive dialog box, open the drop-down list and choose the disk drive you want to defragment.

3. Click the **Settings** button.

4. In the Disk Defragmenter Settings dialog box, make sure the first two options are checked.

5. Click **OK**.

6. When you return to the Select Drive dialog box, click **OK**.

7. Defragmenter starts to defragment files on the selected drive and displays its progress (see Figure 10.7). Click **Show Details** to see Defragmenter in action.

FIGURE 10.7
Defragmenter displays its progress.

❶ For more information, click **Show Details**.

SEE ALSO

➤ *Learn how to use the Maintenance Wizard to schedule defragmenting, page 248*

Scanning for and Repairing Disk Errors

Any time you turn off your computer without using the Windows **Start**, **Shut Down** command, whenever Windows locks up, and whenever your computer shuts down as the result of a power outage, files and folders can become damaged or your computer can lose track of temporary files. This can cause your computer to run more slowly and crash more frequently in the future.

In addition, an old disk (hard or floppy) can start to develop bad *sectors* (storage areas on a disk), making these sectors unreliable. If your computer saves part of a file to a bad sector or one that is going bad, you run the risk of losing that portion of the file and perhaps the entire file. And if the sector stores a system file, you might not even be able to start your computer or run Windows.

To clean up your disk, recover lost files, delete useless file fragments, and block out any bad sectors, you should run ScanDisk regularly. You can also run ScanDisk on damaged floppy disks to recover files and repair a disk that your computer is indicating is unreadable.

ScanDisk provides the following options for scanning and repairing disks:

- **Standard** quickly scans the disk for damaged files and folders and fixes any problems. Avoid using your computer during a standard check. If you save files (or your program saves backup information to the disk ScanDisk is checking), ScanDisk starts over.

- **Thorough** tests each storage area of the disk to ensure that it can reliably store data. This can take several hours on a large hard disk and is best done when you are not using your PC. Run a thorough check every three months or so, and start it just before you leave work or are about to go to bed.

- **Automatically fix errors** tells ScanDisk to do whatever it needs to do without prompting for your confirmation.

Running ScanDisk

ScanDisk runs automatically

If you start your computer after shutting it down improperly, Windows automatically runs ScanDisk on startup and repairs any disk problems. Do NOT cancel the operation before it is complete.

1. If you are using ScanDisk to check and repair a floppy disk, insert it in the disk drive.

2. Click the **Start** button, point to **Programs**, **Accessories**, **System Tools**, and click **ScanDisk**.

3. Click the disk drive that contains the files and folders you want to check and repair (see Figure 10.8).

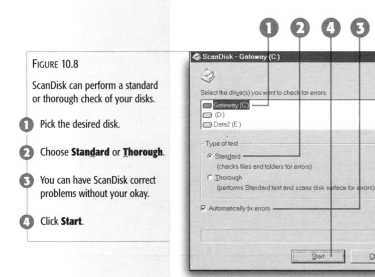

FIGURE 10.8

ScanDisk can perform a standard or thorough check of your disks.

1 Pick the desired disk.

2 Choose **Standard** or **Thorough**.

3 You can have ScanDisk correct problems without your okay.

4 Click **Start**.

4. To check files and folders for errors without checking the actual surface of the disk, click **Standard**. To repair folders and check for any defective areas on the disk, click **Thorough**.

5. To have ScanDisk proceed without prompting for your input, click **Automatically fix errors** to place a check mark in its box.

6. Click the **Start** button. ScanDisk checks for errors, fixes any problems, and displays a dialog box showing the results.

7. Click the **Close** button to return to ScanDisk's opening window.

8. You can repeat steps 2–6 to check and repair files and folders on additional disks. Click the **Close** button when you are done.

Using the System Information Utility

The System Information utility is a new feature of Windows that gives you convenient access to information about your PC and a launch site for other helpful tools. When you start the System Information utility, it initially displays the amount of RAM your system has, the type of microprocessor it uses, the version of Windows it's running, how much free space you have on your hard disk, and the percentage of system resources available for Windows and your programs. It also provides quick access to the following information (see Figure 10.9):

- *Hardware Resources* displays information about the devices installed on your PC, to help you determine if two devices are conflicting (trying to use the same resources).

- *Components* displays information about the device drivers installed in Windows. A device driver is the software that provides the instructions Windows needs to communicate with the device.

- *Software Environment* displays a list of the programs currently running in Windows. Sometimes, when you exit a program, some of the program's components remain in memory, taking up space required by other programs. The Software Environment list can help you determine which program is causing the problem.

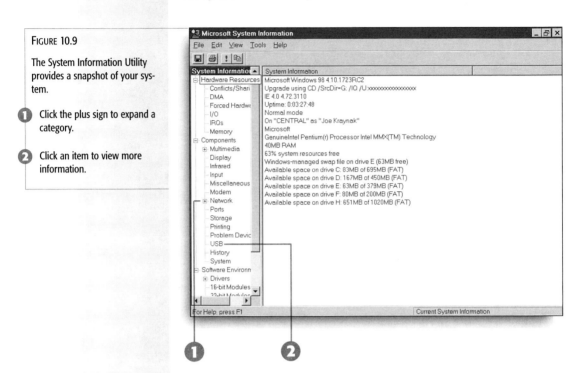

FIGURE 10.9

The System Information Utility provides a snapshot of your system.

1 Click the plus sign to expand a category.

2 Click an item to view more information.

The System Information does more than provide information about your PC. It also provides several tools to help you prepare for catastrophes, recover from unavoidable glitches, and gather the information that a technical support person needs to help you solve a problem. You can find the following tools on the **Tools** menu:

- **Windows Report** allows you to send an email message to Microsoft's technical support department to seek help with a Windows problem. This tool gathers information from your system and sends it along with your message, so the technical support person has the information required to troubleshoot the problem.

- **Update Wizard Uninstall** removes an updated device driver installed using Windows Update if the driver performs worse than the driver you were using.

- **System File Checker** scans the Windows system files for problems, restores the files from backups (if needed), and allows you to extract individual files from the Windows CD. (If a Windows file becomes corrupted or is accidentally deleted, you can reinstall the file from the Windows CD, assuming you know which file to reinstall.)

- **Signature Verification** searches for signed and unsigned files on your system and checks signed files to ensure that they have not been tampered with. (A signed file is one that Microsoft has given a digital signature.)

- **Registry Checker** checks the Windows Registry and offers to back it up. The Registry contains settings for Windows, programs, and devices installed on your PC. If this file is corrupted, all sorts of bad things can happen: Windows may not run, menu options may disappear, programs may refuse to run, and you may not be able to use a device that's connected to your PC. See the next section, "Backing Up the Windows Registry," for details.

- **Automatic Skip Driver Agent** (ASD) tells Windows to stop loading a driver if that driver has caused Windows to fail to start on the previous attempt. You can use ASD to determine which drivers have been deactivated and to reactivate a driver, so Windows will try to load it again.

- **Dr. Watson** runs in the background, keeping track of operations as you work and collecting information when a problem occurs. Dr. Watson can often display suggestions on how to correct a problem. If you run into a problem while you're working, you can call up Dr. Watson by double-clicking its icon in the system tray. You can then create a log (a file that contains information about the cause of the problem) and send the log file to a technical support person to provide that person with valuable troubleshooting information.

- **System Configuration Utility** provides a list of commands and settings that Windows automatically loads, allowing you to easily disable these commands and settings. In some cases, a technical support person leads you through troubleshooting steps by telling you to disable certain commands and options.

- **ScanDisk** is the ScanDisk utility you encountered earlier in this chapter.

- **Version Conflict Manager** helps you install the previous version of Windows or of another program when an upgrade causes problems. When you upgrade Windows or another program, Windows keeps a backup copy of any replaced files. Version Conflict Manager helps you recover these files.

Running the System Information Utility

1. Click **Start**, point to **Programs**, **Accessories**, **System Tools**, and then click **System Information**. The opening screen displays general information about your computer's processor, memory, and available disk space (see Figure 10.9).

2. To view more detailed information, click the plus sign next to the desired category.

3. Click the item for which you want to view additional details.

4. To run one of the tools described earlier, open the **Tools** menu and click the name of the desired tool.

SEE ALSO

➤ *Learn more about troubleshooting hardware problems in Windows, page 799*

➤ *Learn more about troubleshooting software problems in Windows, page 837*

➤ *Learn how to find out more about specific Registry edits that can solve Windows problems, page 851*

Backing Up the Windows Registry

Because the Registry is such an important file, Windows keeps a backup copy of it and scans the Registry for problems just before startup. If Windows detects a problem with the Registry, it automatically loads the backup Registry so Windows can start successfully.

You can use Registry Checker to create an updated backup copy of the Registry. You should do this before editing the Registry (as explained in the next section). If you make a mistake while editing the Registry, you can restore the backup copy.

Backing up the Registry

1. In the System Information window, open the **T**ools menu and click **Registry Checker**. Registry Checker scans the Registry for problems and asks if you want to back up the Registry.

2. Click **Y**es.

3. When the Backup Complete dialog box appears, click **OK**.

If you edit the Registry and encounter problems afterward, or if Windows fails to load the correct Registry during startup, you can restore a backup copy of the Registry.

Restoring a backup Registry

1. Exit any programs that are currently running.

2. Open the **Start** menu and click **Sh**u**t Down**.

3. Click **Restart in MS-DOS Mode** and click **OK**.

4. At the DOS prompt, type scanreg /restore and press **Enter**.

5. Choose the Registry backup marked with a date indicating the last time Windows successfully started (see Figure 10.10), and press **Enter**.

Editing the Registry

Sometimes, the only way to correct a problem with Windows or one of your programs is to edit the Registry. The common scenario is that you find a fix on the Internet, or a tech support person tells you to make a specific change to the Registry. Don't make any changes unless you know exactly what you're changing and why you're changing it.

You may also want to edit the Registry if there is no other way to enter a particular configuration setting. For example, say you want clean up your **Start** menu by removing the **Favorites** sub-menu. You can't delete it from the menu or from My Computer. The solution is to edit the Registry. (I'll show you how to do this later.)

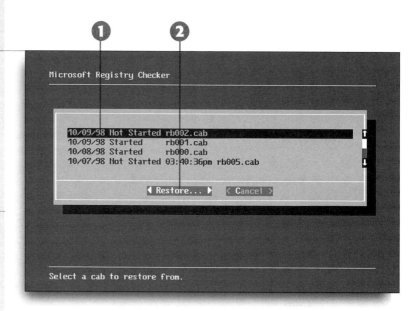

FIGURE 10.10

Pick the Registry backup that successfully started Windows most recently.

1 Click the most recent Registry backup that successfully started Windows.

2 Press Enter to choose Restore.

Before you edit the Registry, you should be aware that a minor typo in the Registry can bring Windows to its knees. You should first try to find a way to change a setting using a utility in the Control Panel.

To edit the Registry, run the Windows Registry Editor. Registry Editor displays a list of folders, each folder containing several *keys*. In some cases, you'll need to create a key, but in most cases, you edit an existing key to change its setting. (To add a key, open the **Edit** menu, point to **New**, and click **Key**.)

Editing the Registry

1. Open the **Start** menu and click **Run**.
2. Type regedit and click **OK**.
3. Click the plus sign next to the HKEY folder in which you want to enter your change.

Registry hacks

PC magazines commonly have articles explaining how to *hack* the Registry. Hacking consists of going behind the scenes with an operating system or program to reprogram it. You can purchase special programs for editing the Registry, or purchase Norton Utilities, which includes the Norton Registry Editor.

4. Continue expanding the list and then click the desired folder.

5. To change a value, double-click it in the list on the right (see Figure 10.11).

6. Enter your changes and click the **OK** button.

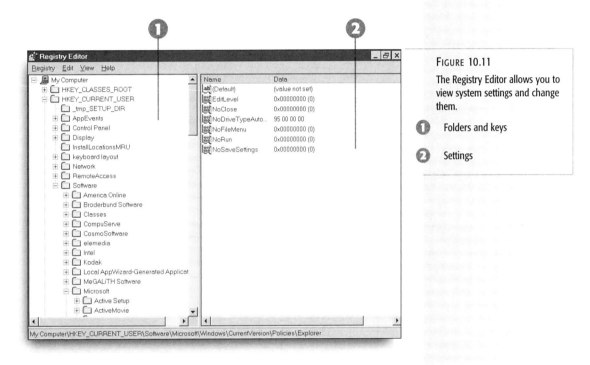

FIGURE 10.11

The Registry Editor allows you to view system settings and change them.

1 Folders and keys

2 Settings

If you enjoy reconfiguring your system, the Registry can provide hours of entertainment. Before you start playing around, however, back up your Registry. Here are a few minor changes you can make to the Registry:

■ *Remove the Favorites menu from the Start menu.* In the Registry Editor, go to HKEY_CURRENT_USER\ Software\Microsoft\Windows\CurrentVersion\Policies\ Explorer. Choose **Edit**, **New**, **DWORD Value**. Change the default name to NoFavoritesMenu. Press **Enter**. Change the Value Data setting to 1. Click **OK** and restart Windows. You can still access Favorites from Windows Explorer and Internet Explorer.

- *Remove ScreenTips for the Minimize, Maximize, and Close buttons.* When you point to a window's Minimize, Maximize, or Close button, a ScreenTip pops up. You can disable ScreenTips for these buttons. In the Registry Editor, go to HKEY_CURRENT_USER\Control Panel\desktop. Double-click UserPreferencemask. Change the first value in the Value Data entry to the following value:

    If first value is "e," replace it with "6"

    If first value is "a," replace it with "2"

    If first value is "c," replace it with "4"

    If first is value is "8," replace it with "0" (zero)

    For example, if the initial entry were "ae 00 00 00," the new entry would be "2e 00 00 00." If you set up profiles in Windows (for multiple users), you may also need to change the key under HKEY_USERS\.Default\Control Panel\desktop. Exit the Registry and restart Windows.

- *Remove the arrow from shortcut icons.* In Registry Editor, go to HKEY_CLASSES_ROOT\lnkfile and HKEY_CLASSES_ROOT\piffile and delete the IsShortcut value. When you create new shortcuts, the little box with the arrow in the lower-left corner of the shortcut icon will not be present.

- *Make a cascading Control Panel menu.* This one doesn't require using the Registry Editor. Right-click the **Start** menu and click **Open**. Choose **File**, **New**, **Folder**. Point to the folder, press F2, and give the folder the following name:

    ```
    Control Panel.{21EC2020-3AEA-1069-A2DD-08002B30309D}
    ```

More Registry hacks

For additional information on how to configure Windows using Registry Editor, search the Web for `windows registry hack`.

Using Windows on a Notebook PC

Safely insert and remove PC cards

Plug your notebook PC into a docking station or port replicator

Transfer files between your notebook and desktop PCs

Connect to an infrared printer

Make your notebook PC run longer on a single charge

Use a mouse instead of the touchpad or trackball

Adding and Removing PC (PCMCIA) Cards

If you have ever installed an expansion board in a desktop PC, you know how inconvenient it is to upgrade your PC. You must remove the cover from your system unit, remove the cover plate at the back of the PC, install the board, and then put everything back together again. And if the board conflicts with other devices on your PC, you have to flip the hood again and use jumpers or switches to change the card's settings.

Most newer notebook PCs make it much easier to upgrade by using *PCMCIA cards* (*PC cards*, for short). These cards are about the size of credit cards, and you can insert them when the power is on.

SEE ALSO

➤ *Learn about the different types of PCMCIA slots, page 34*

➤ *Learn how to set up a notebook PC, page 69*

Inserting PC Cards

Because Windows supports Plug and Play PC cards, you can swap cards in and out of the slots without turning off the PC and without having to worry about setting jumpers or DIP switches to prevent hardware conflicts.

Inserting a PC Card

Hot plugging

Ideally, you should be able to insert and remove PC cards without having to turn off your PC or restart it. This is called *hot plugging*. However, some older PC cards and notebook PCs may not support the latest PC card standards, which allow for hot plugging. To prevent damaging your notebook PC or PC card, check the manufacturer's documentation to determine if it is safe to exchange cards while your system is running.

1. Insert the PC card (label up) into one of the PC card slots on your computer (see Figure 11.1). If you have two empty slots, typically marked 0 and 1, use the number 0 (top) slot first. The card should be firmly seated in the slot, but don't force it. Windows sounds a two-tone beep (a medium tone followed by a high tone) to indicate that it has identified and activated the card. If this is the first time you've inserted the card, Windows runs the Add New Hardware Wizard.

FIGURE 11.1

Insert the PC card into the PC card slot and push it in gently but firmly.

2. Click **Next**. The wizard asks if you want to search for the best driver for the device or display the drivers on a specific disk.

3. Click **Search for the Best Driver for Your Device** and click **Next**. The wizard displays a list of all the locations it will search.

4. If the device came with an installation disk or CD, insert it into the floppy disk drive or CD-ROM drive and click **Floppy Disk Drives** and **CD-ROM Drive**.

5. Click **Next**. The wizard locates the required driver and displays its name.

6. Click **Next**.

7. The wizard displays a message indicating that it has successfully installed the driver. Click **Finish**.

8. If the card requires you to connect a cable or phone line, plug the cable or phone line into the opening on the card.

SEE ALSO

➤ *Learn how to update Windows with Windows Update, page 251*

Microsoft Windows Update

The Microsoft Windows Update option tells Windows to check Microsoft's Web site for updated drivers. If you have not yet registered your copy of Windows 98, the Microsoft Windows Update option will be unavailable (grayed out).

Removing PC Cards

Because PC cards allow you to add devices on-the-fly, you can eject one PC card and replace it with another to use a different device. However, before ejecting a PC card, you should disable it in Windows. This unloads the driver and shuts the power off to the PC card slot.

Eject a PC card

1. Click the **PC Card (PCMCIA) Status** icon in the system tray, and then click the **Stop** option for the card you want to remove (see Figure 11.2). A dialog box appears, indicating that it is safe to remove the card.

2. Click **OK**.

3. Press the Eject button next to the PC card. The card pops out of the slot, and Windows emits a two-toned beep (a high tone followed by a medium tone). Pull the card out of the slot.

FIGURE 11.2

Before you eject a PC card, you should turn it off.

1 Right-click the PC Card icon.

2 Click the desired Stop option.

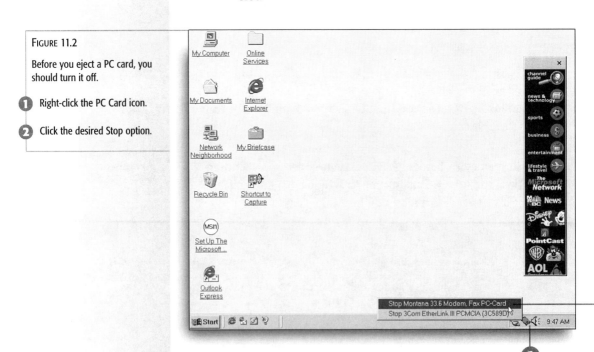

Plugging In to a Docking Station

A docking station or *port replicator* is a unit that contains ports for a monitor, printer, keyboard, mouse, speakers, and other devices. A docking port on the back of the notebook PC plugs into the docking station, which connects the notebook PC to the other devices. Before you plug your notebook PC into a docking station, check the notebook PC's documentation to determine whether the PC has a Plug and Play BIOS and if it supports hot plugging:

- *Plug and Play BIOS.* These built-in instructions allow you to plug your notebook PC into the docking station and start using the devices that are connected to the docking station. Windows automatically detects when the notebook PC is docked or undocked.

- *Hot plugging.* If your notebook PC supports hot plugging, you can safely plug the notebook PC into the docking station and remove it when the power is on. If your notebook PC does not support hot plugging, you must turn the power off before docking and undocking your PC.

If your notebook PC has a Plug and Play BIOS and supports hot plugging, your life is going to be easy. To dock the PC, simply plug it into the docking station. To undock the PC, open the **Start** menu and click **Eject PC**. This releases the notebook PC from the docking station, so you can safely remove it.

If your notebook PC does not have a Plug and Play BIOS or if the manufacturer does not offer a docking station or port replicator for the PC, you must create two *hardware profiles* in Windows: one for the docked state and one for the undocked state. A hardware profile tells Windows which device drivers to load on startup. When you start Windows, it will attempt to determine which hardware profile to load and may prompt you to select the profile.

If you don't have a docking station, check your notebook PC to determine whether it has ports for connecting a monitor, keyboard, mouse, and other devices. Connecting devices separately is much less convenient than using a docking station, but it does allow you to use your notebook PC more like a desktop model.

Did you already run Windows when docked?

If you docked your notebook PC and ran Windows, the Original Configuration contains a list of device drivers it will load whether your system is docked or not. In such a case, you'll need to work backward. Rename Original Configuration "Docked," copy it to create a new configuration called "Undocked," and then *disable* devices in the Undocked profile that are unavailable when the PC is *not* connected to the docking station.

Create a new hardware profile

1. Alt+click **My Computer**.

2. On the **Hardware Profiles** tab, click **Original Configuration**.

3. Click the **Rename** button, so you can call the Original Configuration Undocked.

4. Type Undocked and click **OK**.

5. Click the **Copy** button to create a copy of the Undocked configuration and modify it to create a new Docked configuration.

6. Type Docked as the name of your new configuration and click **OK** (see Figure 11.3).

FIGURE 11.3

You should have two hardware profiles: Docked and Undocked.

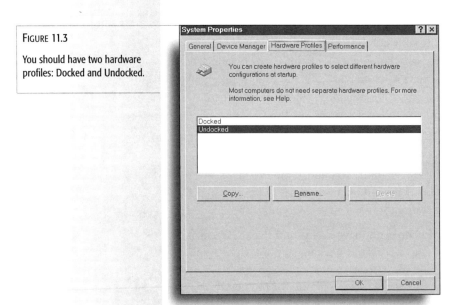

7. Open the **Start** menu and click **Shut Down**.

8. Click **Shut Down** and click **OK**.

9. Plug your notebook PC into the docking station or connect the desired peripherals (mouse, keyboard, monitor) to the designated ports on the notebook PC.

10. Turn on your notebook PC.

11. When Windows prompts you to choose a hardware profile, type the number for the Docked profile and press **Enter**.

12. Windows starts, detects the new devices, and installs the required drivers. If Windows fails to detect the new devices, open the Control Panel and click the **Add New Hardware** icon.

13. Follow the wizard's instructions to install drivers for the new devices.

Now that you have two hardware profiles, there may be some devices in a profile that you want to disable. For example, if, in the docked state, your notebook PC is connected to a mouse, you may want to disable the touchpad. Or, if there is a conflict between two similar devices, such as the notebook PC's monitor and a standard monitor, you must disable the device you don't want to use.

Disabling devices in a profile

1. Alt+click **My Computer**.

2. On the **Hardware Profiles** tab, click the profile that contains a device you want to disable.

3. Click the **Device Manager** tab.

4. Click the plus sign next to the type of device you want to disable.

5. Double-click the name of the device you want to disable.

6. Click **Disable in this hardware profile** and click **OK** (see Figure 11.4).

7. If needed, repeat step 6 to disable additional devices.

8. Click **OK**.

SEE ALSO

➤ *Learn how to find and install updated device drivers, page 819*

FIGURE 11.4

Disable any devices that are
not connected to the PC in this
hardware profile.

1 Click **Disable in this
hardware profile**.

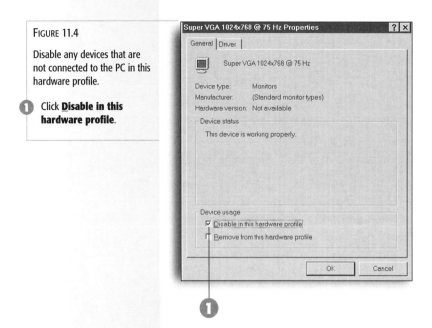

Taking Work on the Road with Briefcase

If you have both a notebook and a desktop PC, you probably
need to transfer files from your desktop PC to your notebook
PC to take work with you on trips. If you edit the files on your
notebook PC, you must then copy them back to the desktop PC
to ensure that you have the most recent versions on both PCs.

Of course, you can exchange files between your notebook and
desktop PCs by using My Computer or Windows Explorer to
transfer the files with a floppy disk. However, this is not the
most efficient or secure method. If you happen to forget which
files are the most recent, you run the risk of replacing the new
versions with older ones.

Fortunately, Windows offers a convenient tool for safely transferring files between PCs: Briefcase. With Briefcase, you open
an electronic "briefcase," copy the desired files to it, and then
drag the Briefcase icon over your floppy disk icon. Windows
copies all the files in the Briefcase to the floppy disk. Briefcase
also keeps track of file versions to help prevent you from accidentally overwriting newer files with their older versions. When
you copy files back to your desktop PC, Briefcase indicates
which files are newer.

Take files on the road

1. In Windows Explorer or My Computer, select the folder(s) or file(s) you want to place in the Briefcase.

2. Right-click one of the selected items, point to **Send** **T**o, and click **My Briefcase** (see Figure 11.5).

No My Briefcase icon?

If there is no My Briefcase icon on your Windows desktop, it may not be installed. To quickly add a new Briefcase, right-click the desktop and choose **New**, **Briefcase**.

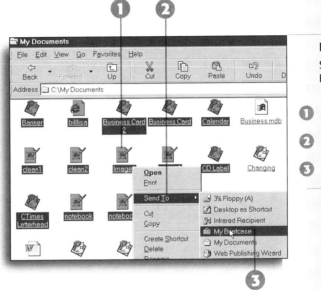

FIGURE 11.5

Send the selected files to My Briefcase.

1 Right-click a file.

2 Point to **Send** **T**o.

3 Click **My Briefcase**.

3. If the Welcome to the Windows Briefcase dialog box appears, click **Finish** to copy the selected items to your Briefcase.

4. Insert a blank disk into the floppy disk drive and then drag and drop the My Briefcase icon over the floppy disk icon. (Or, right-click **My Briefcase**, point to **Send** **T**o, and click **3½ Floppy (A)**.)

5. Remove the floppy disk.

6. Insert the floppy disk into your other PC.

7. Run My Computer and click the floppy drive icon.

8. Drag and drop the My Briefcase icon onto the Windows desktop.

9. To open a file from the Briefcase, run the program you want to use to open the file and choose its **File**, **Open** command.

10. Open the **Look In** drop-down list, click **My Briefcase**, and open the document file as you normally would.

11. When you are ready to end your trip, drag and drop the My Briefcase icon onto the icon for your floppy disk.

12. Eject the floppy disk and store it safely.

Returning files to the desktop PC

1. Insert the floppy disk into your desktop PC's floppy drive and click the floppy drive's icon in My Computer.

2. Run My Computer and click the floppy drive icon.

3. Drag and drop the My Briefcase icon onto the Windows desktop.

4. Click the My Briefcase icon to display its contents.

5. Click the **Update All** button.

6. If desired, you can prevent a file from being updated by right-clicking it and choosing **Skip** (see Figure 11.6).

7. After marking any files you want to skip, click the **Update** button.

FIGURE 11.6

Briefcase shows you which files are newer versions.

① To skip a file, right-click it and click **Skip**.

② Click **Update**.

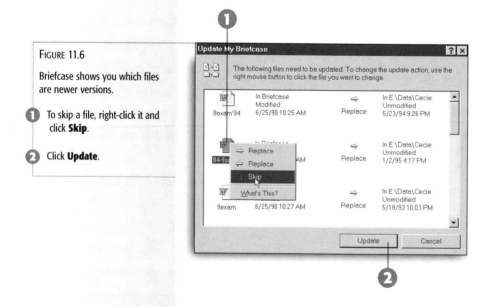

SEE ALSO

➤ *For instructions on installing Windows components, see page 204*

Linking Your Notebook and Desktop PC

Windows includes a feature called Direct Cable Connection, which allows you to connect two computers by using a serial or parallel *data* cable. (You cannot use a standard serial or parallel printer cable.) When the computers are connected, you can use one computer to link to the other computer and use its files, programs, and printer, just as if you were working on a network.

Direct Cable Connection is especially useful if you need to transfer large amounts of data from one computer to another. You simply copy a folder from one computer, switch to the other computer, and paste the folder on the desired hard disk. With Direct Cable Connection, you can connect any two PCs: two desktop PCs, two notebook PCs, or a notebook and desktop PC.

Although not difficult, the procedure requires you to install the Windows networking components, mark resources on the two computers as shared, and navigate the mini-network you create.

SEE ALSO

➤ *Learn how to install the Windows networking components, page 300*

➤ *Learn how to set up a direct cable connection, page 306*

➤ *Learn how to share files between two computers, page 307*

Using an Infrared (Wireless) Connection

Most notebook PCs have a built-in infrared (IRdA) port that supports cable-free (wireless) connections. With an infrared port, you can connect to an infrared network adapter, printer, mouse, keyboard, and any other PC accessory that supports infrared communications.

Windows has built-in support for infrared devices and includes a special device driver for the infrared port. When you enable infrared communications in Windows, Windows runs the

Direct line of site required

There must be a direct line of site between the two infrared devices. If the infrared port (marked IR on most PCs) is at the back of the PC, and you're trying to use an infrared mouse to one side of the PC, the mouse may have a little trouble communicating with the PC.

Infrared Monitor in the background and displays an icon for it in the system tray. The Monitor checks the infrared port regularly to determine if any infrared devices are within range. It then automatically establishes a connection with the device.

SEE ALSO

➤ *Learn how to install infrared ports on a PC, page 786*

➤ *Learn more about installing and using infrared ports, page 793*

Enable infrared communications

1. In the Control Panel, click the Infrared icon. The Infrared Monitor dialog box appears.

2. In the **Options** tab of the Infrared Monitor dialog, place a check mark in the **Enable infrared communication** check box (see Figure 11.7).

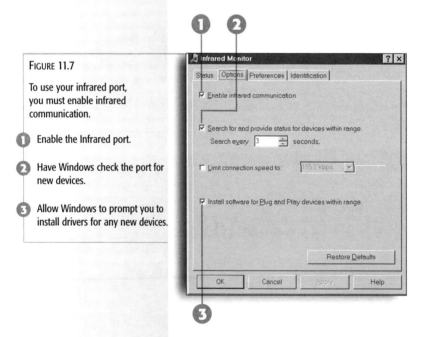

FIGURE 11.7

To use your infrared port, you must enable infrared communication.

1 Enable the Infrared port.

2 Have Windows check the port for new devices.

3 Allow Windows to prompt you to install drivers for any new devices.

3. Place a check mark in the **Search for and provide status for devices within range** check box.

4. Enter the desired number of seconds to specify how frequently you want Windows to check for new devices.

5. Make sure **Install software for <u>P</u>lug and Play devices within range** is checked.

6. Click the **Preferences** tab.

7. Place a check mark next to all three options, so Windows can notify you of the status of your infrared connections.

8. If you are using the infrared port to connect to a network, click the **Identification** tab and specify your computer and workgroup name.

9. Click **OK**.

10. Right-click the Infrared Monitor icon in the system tray to view the infrared communications options.

Conserving Battery Power

With a fully charged battery, a notebook computer can operate for about two and a half hours maximum. That's not much time if you are putting in a full day's work on the road. The Windows Power Management utility can double the life of your battery by powering down your monitor and hard disk drive after a specified amount of time. You can even turn on warnings to have Windows notify you when the battery is running down, so you can save your work and shut down Windows before the battery goes dead.

To change any of the Power Management settings in Windows, you use the Power Management utility in the Control Panel. When you click the Power Management icon, a dialog box appears, presenting you with two sets of power-saving options: options for when the computer is plugged in and options for when it is running on batteries.

Entering Power Management settings

1. Open the Control Panel and click the Power Management icon. The Power Management dialog box appears (see Figure 11.8).

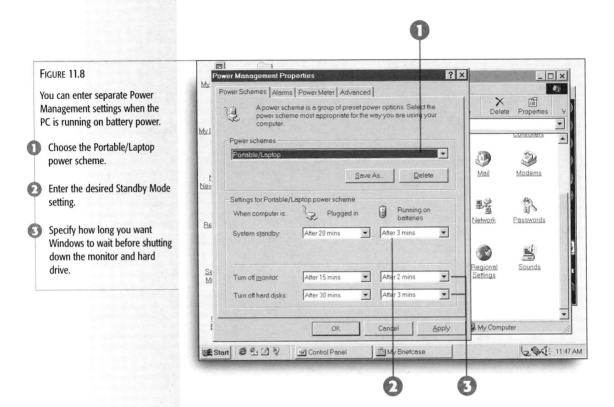

FIGURE 11.8

You can enter separate Power Management settings when the PC is running on battery power.

1 Choose the Portable/Laptop power scheme.

2 Enter the desired Standby Mode setting.

3 Specify how long you want Windows to wait before shutting down the monitor and hard drive.

2. Open the **Power schemes** drop-down list and click **Portable/Laptop**.

3. Open the **System standby, Running on Batteries** drop-down list and choose the number of minutes of inactivity you want to pass before Windows puts your PC in Standby mode (turning off the monitor and hard drive but ready to leap into action).

4. Open the **Turn off monitor** drop-down list and choose the number of minutes of inactivity you'll allow to pass before Windows turns off the monitor.

5. Open the **Turn off hard disks** drop-down list and choose the number of minutes or hours of inactivity you'll allow to pass before Windows turns off the hard disk drives.

6. Click the **Alarms** tab. By default, Windows displays a message whenever the battery power level reaches 5% and 3%. You can drag the sliders to the right to be notified sooner or to the left to be notified later.

7. To change the way Windows notifies you of low battery power, click one of the **Alarm Action** buttons.

8. In the Low Battery Alarm Actions dialog box, turn on **Sound Alarm** if you want Windows to sound an alarm when the battery power drops to the specified level.

9. Under Power Level, click **When the Alarm Goes Off, the Computer Will**, and then open the drop-down list and choose **Standby** or **Shutdown**. Standby keeps Windows running but turns off the monitor and hard disk drives.

10. To force your notebook computer to go into Standby or Shutdown mode even if a program is not responding, click **Force Standby or Shutdown Even if a Program Stops Responding.** (This can cause data loss, however, so you may want to leave this option off.)

11. Click **OK.**

12. Click the **Advanced** tab. **Show Power Meter on Taskbar** is on by default. You should leave this option on, so you can easily see the battery power level in the system tray.

13. To prevent unauthorized use of your computer when it goes off standby, choose **Prompt for Password When Computer Goes Off Standby.** Click **OK.**

SEE ALSO

➤ *Learn how to adjust Power Management settings for when the PC is plugged in, page 224*

> **Check your battery power**
>
> If you leave **Show Power Meter on Taskbar** turned on, a battery icon appears in the system tray (on the right end of the taskbar). To see how much power is left, rest the mouse pointer on the icon. If your notebook is plugged in, Windows displays a plug icon.

Deferring Printing

You can purchase light-weight, portable printers that connect to your notebook PC's parallel printer or infrared port. Some notebook PCs even have their own built-in printer. If you don't have a portable printer or chose not to pack it, you can print your documents offline and then connect to a printer later to print them out.

Printing offline

1. Open the **Start** menu, point to **Settings**, and click **Printers**.

2. Right-click the icon for the printer you normally use and click **Use Printer Offline** (see Figure 11.9).

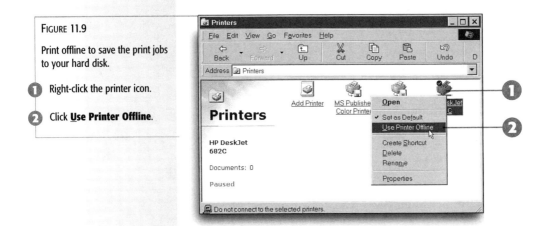

FIGURE 11.9

Print offline to save the print jobs to your hard disk.

1 Right-click the printer icon.

2 Click **Use Printer Offline**.

3. Print your documents as you normally would.

4. When you are ready to print out the documents, connect your notebook PC to your printer.

5. Open the **Start** menu, point to **Settings**, and click **Printers**.

6. Right-click the icon for the same printer you selected in Step 2 and click **Use Printer Offline**. Windows sends the documents to the printer.

SEE ALSO

➤ *Learn how to check your printer settings, page 234*

➤ *Learn how to print a document, page 240*

➤ *Learn how to manage documents that are waiting to be printed, page 242*

Attaching a Mouse to Your Notebook PC

Although touchpads are nifty devices, they can cause problems as you type. Even if you crank the sensitivity down, any slight tap from your thumb can send the mouse pointer scurrying across the screen or select an option you did not intend to select. Trackballs aren't much better, offering no convenient way to perform drag-and-drop operations.

The solution is to ditch the built-in pointing device and use a mouse. A mouse is small enough to stick inside your notebook PC's carrying case, and it will make your work on the road that much easier.

To use a mouse, you can install the mouse driver and then disable the driver for the touchpad or trackball.

Installing a mouse on your notebook PC

1. With the power off, plug your mouse into the mouse port or serial port.

2. Turn on your computer.

3. If Windows does not detect the device, open the Control Panel and click **Add New Hardware**.

4. Follow the Add New Hardware Wizard's instructions to install the mouse driver.

5. Alt+click My Computer.

6. Click the **Device Manager** tab.

7. Click the plus sign next to **Mouse**.

8. Double-click the driver for your touchpad.

9. Click <u>D</u>isable in this hardware profile and click **OK** (see Figure 11.10).

10. Click **Close** to save your settings and then restart Windows if prompted to do so.

FIGURE 11.10

Disable the driver for your built-in pointing device.

1 Click **Disable in this hardware profile**.

2 Click **OK**.

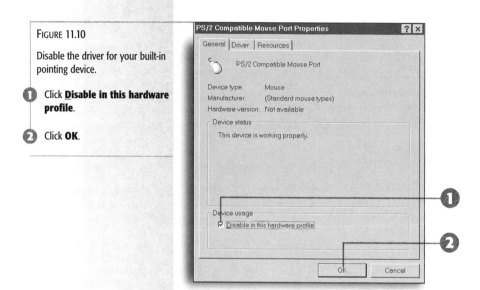

SEE ALSO

➤ *Learn how to install other devices that allow you to communicate with your PC and enter data, page 717*

➤ *Learn how to clean your mouse, page 82*

➤ *Learn how to use a Microsoft IntelliMouse, page 111*

➤ *Learn how to configure your mouse, page 228*

Using Your Notebook PC in a Corporate Setting

Notebook PCs are not only useful for taking a little work home from the office or performing some light editing on the road; their portability also makes them ideal for carrying presentations into boardrooms, connecting to the company network or intranet from remote locations, and interfacing with a client's network.

However, when I say that notebook PCs are "ideal" for these tasks, I mean that given an ideal situation, the notebook PC can handle the job. In practice, taking advantages of these notebook features requires a great deal of preparation and coordination.

Showing up at a client's company in the hopes that the sales presentation stored on your notebook PC will go off without a hitch is a bit much to expect.

The key to successfully manage your notebook PC in a corporate setting is preparation. The following sections run through a couple of the more advanced tasks you can perform with your notebook PC in a corporate environment and explain what you need to consider.

Preparing to Show Electronic Presentations

The days of 35mm slideshows and overhead transparencies are coming to an end. Salespeople, trainers, and educators commonly display their slideshows electronically, using projectors and speaker systems to display slideshows that include animated text and transitions, video clips, audio clips, and other media.

Notebook PCs make it convenient to carry your presentation with you, assuming the PC is equipped with the required output devices:

- *Projector*. The key to any presentation is the projector. To use a projector with your notebook PC, you must connect it to the video out port on your notebook PC. Before giving your presentation, make sure you have the correct driver loaded for the projector. You may have to fiddle with hardware profiles to disable the notebook's monitor. To learn how to disable devices, see "Plugging In to a Docking Station," earlier in this chapter.

- *Remote pointer*. If you're standing in front of an audience, you can't use your mouse to navigate. Here's where an infrared port comes in handy. Use an infrared pointing device to move the mouse pointer. Make sure you stand within range of the notebook PC and that your infrared pointer has a direct line of site to the infrared port on the notebook.

- *Speaker system*. For presentations that include music, narration, or other audio, make sure your sound system is up to the task. You don't want to play audio through the small

Zip disks

Zip disks or other high-capacity, removable disks are excellent for storing presentations. Instead of packing your hard drive, you can store each presentation on a separate disk and pop in the one you want to use.

speakers on your notebook PC. Connect to a stereo receiver and amplifier that produces high-quality output. Test the system before you go on stage to ensure the sound quality is good and is in sync with the slideshow.

- *Cables and power cords.* When you're walking in to an unfamiliar room to give a presentation, make sure you have a long extension cord and the cables needed to set up your projector and audio system.

Preparation is the key to success. Before giving your presentation, take the following steps to prepare:

- Rehearse your presentation thoroughly with the equipment you plan to use. If your audience must wait while you figure out how to connect your projector to your PC, they will not be impressed.

- Adjust the display resolution for maximum clarity from the projector.

- Show up an hour before the meeting, set up your equipment, and make sure it works. This is a good time to adjust the focus on your projector.

SEE ALSO

➤ *Learn to adjust display settings, page 221*

➤ *Learn more about portable disk drives, page 659*

Connecting to Your Office from a Remote Location

Never leave your home or office thinking that you can easily connect to your desktop PC or your company's network or intranet simply by dialing in with your modem. These connections require that you enter the proper connection settings, which can be tricky and require a little help from your company's network administrator.

Before you leave on a trip, set up your connection and test it using the phone line in your home or office. (If your network is at home, you might need to use the neighbor's phone.) Enter the settings for the desired connection:

■ *Desktop PC*. You can use your notebook PC to connect to your desktop PC when you're on the road. To do this, you must set up your desktop PC as a Dial-Up Networking server and create a Dial-Up Networking connection on your notebook PC.

■ *Network*. Follow the instructions in Chapter 12, "Networking with Windows," to install the Windows networking components. Set up a Dial-Up Networking connection to dial into the network. Check with your network administrator to determine which network protocol you need to install. Enter the required logon information.

■ *Intranet*. Create a Dial-Up Networking connection for connecting to the intranet. With the help of the network administrator, enter the required TCP/IP settings and logon information.

SEE ALSO

➤ *Learn how to connect to your network from a remote location, page 316*

Networking with Windows

Obtain the networking hardware you need

Install the Windows networking components

Set up a simple peer-to-peer network

Set up a direct cable connection between two PCs

Connect to other PCs on the network

Share disks, folders, files, printers, and other resources

Networking Overview

The two basic types of networks are client/server and peer-to-peer. On a *client/server network*, all PCs (the *clients*) are wired to a central PC (the *network server*). Whenever you need to access a network resource, you connect to the server, which then processes your commands and requests, links you to the other PCs, and provides access to shared equipment and other resources. Although somewhat expensive and difficult to set up, a client/server network offers two big advantages: It is easy to maintain through the network server, and it ensures reliable data transfers.

On a *peer-to-peer network*, PCs are linked directly to each other, without the use of a central PC. Each PC has a network card that is connected via a network cable to another PC or to a central *hub* (a connection box). Many small businesses use this peer-to-peer configuration because it doesn't require an expensive network server and it is relatively easy to set up. However, a peer-to-peer network does have a few drawbacks: It is more difficult to manage, is more susceptible to packet collisions (which occur when two PCs request the same data at the same time), and is not very secure because no central PC is in charge of validating user identities.

Windows 98 has built-in support for peer-to-peer networking, making it relatively easy and inexpensive to set up a small network. If you need to connect a few PCs in a relatively small work area, you'll learn how to do it in this chapter.

Inexpensively Connecting Only Two PCs

Working on a client/server network

If your PCs are already networked, skip ahead to the section called "Logging On and Off," to learn how to connect to the network. Refer to "Sharing Resources on the Network," later in this chapter, to learn how to use disks, folders, files, printers, and other network resources.

To network more than two PCs, you need to install a network adapter in each PC. The adapter is a printed circuit board that plugs into an expansion slot inside the system unit. If you have only two PCs to connect, you don't need network adapter cards. All you need is a serial or parallel data cable to connect the serial ports or parallel ports on the two PCs. You can then run Direct Cable Connection to connect the two PCs.

When shopping for and installing the data cable, keep the following points in mind:

- The cable must be a *data transfer* cable. You cannot use a standard serial modem cable or parallel printer cable. (You can purchase a null-modem adapter to convert a serial modem cable into a data transfer cable.)

- Some cables come with both serial and parallel port connectors. Do not connect the serial port on one PC to the parallel port on the other; however, you want a parallel-to-parallel or serial-to-serial port connection.

- Some desktop PCs have two serial ports: 9-pin and 25-pin. You can plug a 9-pin connector into a 25-pin outlet by using a special 9-to-25-pin adapter.

- Before connecting the cable, shut down Windows on both PCs and turn off both PCs.

Connect the data transfer cable to the serial or parallel ports on both PCs, and then skip ahead to "Installing the Windows Networking Components," later in this chapter.

Obtaining the Required Networking Hardware

The easiest way to network two or more PCs is to use a networking kit. The kit typically comes with two or three NICs (*network interface cards*), a network cable, and software (which you don't need if Windows 98 or 95 is running on both PCs). Some kits include a *network hub* that acts as a central connection box. If you would rather purchase the equipment separately, here's what you need:

- *An Ethernet network card for each PC you want to network.* (Some PCs come with a network card.) If you have a notebook PC with a PCMCIA slot, you can purchase a PCMCIA network card. When purchasing a network card, consider the type of network cable you want to use, as explained next.

Transferring files to a new PC

If you just purchased a new PC, use Direct Cable Connection to connect your new PC to your old PC and transfer your document files to the new PC.

- *Network cables.* The network cables connect the network card on one PC to the card on the other PC. You can use a *twisted-pair cable* (also called an *RJ-45 cable*), which looks like a telephone cable, or a *BNC cable* (*British Naval Connector*, also called a *thin coaxial cable*), which looks like a cable for connecting a VCR to a TV set.

Combination NICs

When shopping for a NIC, look for combination cards, which provide both a twisted pair and BNC port.

- *Network hub.* If you use twisted-pair cables to connect more than two PCs, you must connect each PC to a central hub. If you use BNC cables, you can connect the PCs directly (without a hub).

- *T-connectors and terminators.* If you use a BNC cable, you must install a *T-connector* on the BNC port of each network card. You must also cap any open leg of a T-connector with a *terminator*.

Although there are other network types (Token Ring, Fiber Distributed Data Interface, Asynchronous Transfer Mode, and so on), this chapter focuses on Ethernet, a standard defined by the Institute for Electrical and Electronic Engineers. Ethernet has three advantages over other network types: speed (transfers of up to 10Mbps), cost (relatively inexpensive to set up), and ease of setup.

Planning Your Network

At this point, you might be wondering which is the best way to network PCs—by using twisted-pair cables and a hub or by connecting directly with BNC cables, T-connectors, and terminators? To decide, you need to consider cost, reliability, the number of PCs you need to connect, and the type of connector on your network interface card (NIC). You have the following three options:

- To connect only two PCs if your NICs have twisted-pair ports (they look like enlarged phone jacks), get a *cross-over*, twisted-pair Ethernet cable. A regular twisted-pair cable will not work; you must use a cross-over cable, so you won't have to connect to a central hub.

- To connect more than two PCs that have NICs with twisted-pair ports, get regular twisted-pair cables and a network hub (starting at about $50). You must connect a twisted-pair cable from each PC to the hub (see Figure 12.1). I strongly recommend the hub configuration; just make sure you get a hub with enough ports for future expansion.

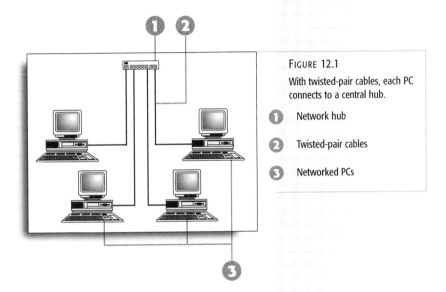

FIGURE 12.1

With twisted-pair cables, each PC connects to a central hub.

1. Network hub

2. Twisted-pair cables

3. Networked PCs

- To connect two or more PCs that have NICs with BNC ports, you need a BNC cable, a T-connector for each port, and a terminator for the two T-connectors that are connected to only one other PC. If a PC is connected to two other PCs, a cable runs from each leg of the T-connector to another PC. If the PC is connected to only one other PC, a cable runs from one leg of the T-connector to the T-connector on the other PC. You must cap any open leg of a T-connector with a terminator (see Figure 12.2).

When choosing the connector and cable type, be aware of the distance limitations of the cables. There are two types of BNC cables: thicknet, which can carry signals up to 500 meters, and thinnet, which can carry signals up to 200 meters. Twisted pair cable can carry signals up to 100 meters. (There is some debate over whether shielded twisted pair cable can carry signals more reliably over longer distances.) If twisted-pair cable seems too short for your situation, keep in mind that you're going to be connecting to a central hub; you can run each PC to the hub with a 100 meter cable for a total run of 200 meters.

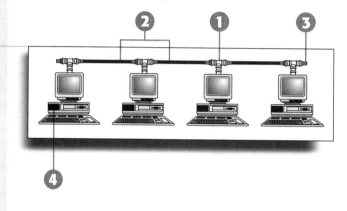

FIGURE 12.2

BNC cables allow you to string together several PCs directly.

1 T-connector

2 BNC cables

3 Terminator

4 Networked PCs

The cost difference between the two types of cable connections is minimal. An eight-port hub costs about $70, but the twisted-pair cable is less expensive than BNC cable and doesn't require a T-connector on each NIC.

Pre-Wiring Considerations

Connecting two PCs with a BNC cable

With BNC ports, you cannot directly connect the ports with a coaxial cable, as you can when connecting a VCR to a TV set. Even if you are connecting only two PCs, you must use a T-connector on each BNC port and then cap the open leg of each T-connector with a terminator.

If you're networking PCs in close proximity to one another, running the cable is easy. You can purchase precut cables with the proper connectors on each end and run the cable under carpeting or along the baseboards. Just make sure it's out of the way, so nobody will trip over it.

When connecting PCs that are some distance apart, expect some complications. Unless you can find a trained rat to pull networking cable along your heating ducts, you're going to face a long weekend setting up your network. To prepare for the daunting task, obtain the required tools and supplies:

- *A roll of BNC or RJ-45 cable*. (Measure the distance from one PC to the next and add twenty feet to the total to determine the amount of cable you'll need.)

- *BNC or RJ45 connectors*. You'll need two connectors for each segment of cable.

- *Wire cutters*. If your crimping tool isn't a combination cutter/crimper.

- *Crimping tool*. After you cut the cable, you need a crimping tool to attach a BNC or RJ-45 connector to each end of the cable. Most crimping tools come as combination wire cutter/crimping devices.

- *Drill*. You'll probably need to drill holes in the floor or walls to pass the cables through.

- *RJ-45 wall jacks*. (Only if you're setting up a hub configuration.)

If you're setting up a hub configuration, the best way to do it is to install a wall jack near each computer you want to network. RJ-45 wall jacks look like telephone jacks. You can place the hub in a central location, such as the basement, and run RJ-45 cables from the wall jacks to the hub. Purchase some precut RJ-45 cables to connect the NIC on each PC to the wall jack. This makes everything look neat and tidy. If you're not concerned about neat and tidy, you can run the RJ-45 cable right from the NIC, through the hole in the wall or floor, and connect it directly to the hub.

Connecting BNC cable is similar, but you have no central hub. Set up the connections just as you would connect a VCR player to a TV set. However, don't try to use some four-way splitter to connect the NICs. You must have a direct cable connection from one PC to the next. If you're concerned about the appearance of the cable coming through the wall, you can use wall-mounted BNC jacks, but make sure one wall-mounted BNC jack leads directly to only one other jack; don't use splitters.

Installing the NICs and Cables

Custom cables

If the idea of cutting and crimping doesn't appeal to you, and you're better at measuring distances than I am, take the measurements and contact a cable supply company to create custom cables for you. You can find several of these companies on the Web. Try Cable City at www.cablecity.com or 1-800-900-9008.

The first step in setting up your network is to install the network interface cards and connect your PCs using the required cables. To install the network interface cards, take one of the following steps:

- *Standard expansion board.* Open the system unit and insert the network interface card into one of the open expansion slots.
- *PC card.* If you're networking a notebook PC, plug the PC card into the PCMCIA slot on your notebook PC. Plug the network cable adapter (with the network port(s)) into the card (see Figure 12.3).

SEE ALSO

➤ *Learn how to install an expansion board, page 560*

➤ *Learn how to insert a PC Card, page 270*

FIGURE 12.3

Insert the PC card and connect the network cable adapter.

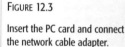 PC card

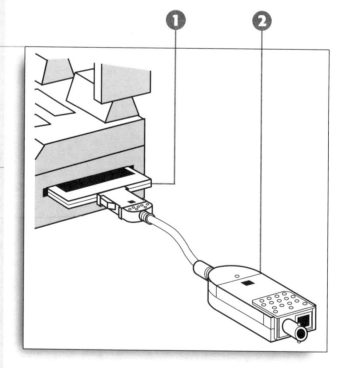 Network cable adapter

After the NICs are in place, connect the networking cables to the NICs. The connections vary depending on the NIC ports and cables you are using:

- *Network hub with twisted-pair cables.* Connect a standard twisted-pair cable from the twisted-pair port on each PC's NIC to the hub (see Figure 12.4).

- *BNC connections.* Connect a T-connector to the BNC port on each PC's NIC, and use BNC cables to connect the T-connectors. Cap any open leg of the T-connectors with a terminator (see Figure 12.5).

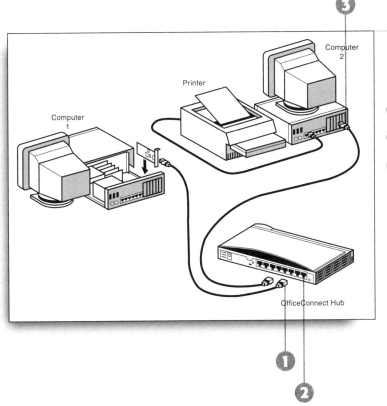

FIGURE 12.4

Connect each PC to the central networking hub with a twisted pair cable.

① RJ-45 connector

② Network hub

③ NIC

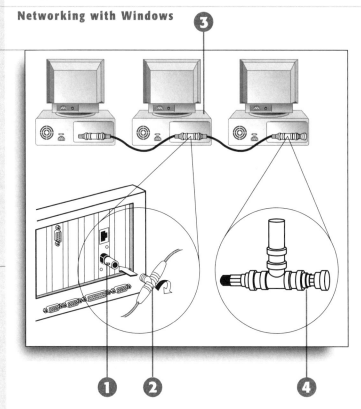

FIGURE 12.5

Connect the PCs using BNC cables.

1 BNC connector

2 T-connector

3 PC connected to two other PCs

4 If the PC is connected to only one other PC, cap the open end of the T-connector with a terminator.

After installing the NICs and cables, start each PC. If the PC supports Plug and Play and the NIC is Plug and Play compatible, when you start your PC, Windows automatically detects the NIC and installs the software required for using it. If the NIC is not Plug and Play compatible, run the Add New Hardware Wizard to install the required software.

SEE ALSO

➤ *Learn how to install device drivers, page 566*

Installing the Windows Networking Components

If you performed a standard Windows installation, the Windows networking components are not installed on your PC. To establish a connection between two or more PCs, you must install these components on every PC you want to network. Read through the following list to decide which components you should install:

■ *Dial-Up Networking, for modem, Internet, and network support.* This component is essential for connecting two or more PCs, whether you're setting up a peer-to-peer network, a direct cable connection, or an Internet connection.

■ *Dial-Up Server, for connecting to another PC from a remote location using a modem.* This component is not required for setting up a network. This component is useful if you have one PC at home and another at work; you can call your PC at work and retrieve files from it. It's also useful if you frequently travel and need to connect to your office PC when you're on the road.

■ *Direct Cable Connection, for connecting two PCs using a data cable.* This component is not required for setting up a network. Install it only if you are connecting two PCs without NICs.

Installing Windows networking components

1. In the Windows Control Panel, click the Add/Remove Programs icon.

2. Click the **Windows Setup** tab to display a list of component categories.

3. In the **C**omponents list, click **Communications**.

4. Click the **Details** button.

5. Place a check mark next to **Dial-Up Networking** and any of the other two networking components you need (see Figure 12.6).

6. Click **OK** to return to the Add/Remove Programs Properties dialog box.

7. Click **OK** to save your changes.

8. If prompted to insert the Windows 98 CD, insert the CD into your CD-ROM drive and click **OK**.

SEE ALSO

➢ *Learn how to install Windows components, page 204*

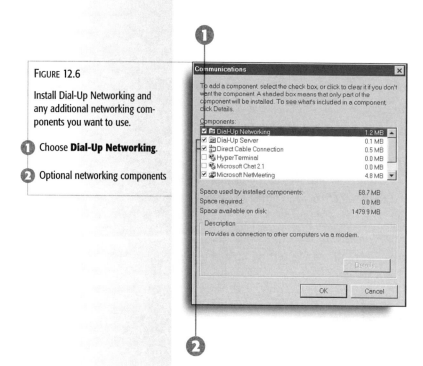

FIGURE 12.6

Install Dial-Up Networking and any additional networking components you want to use.

1 Choose **Dial-Up Networking**.

2 Optional networking components

Adding Network Protocols and Services

After the network components are installed, you must install network protocols and services. A *protocol* is a set of rules that governs the exchange of data over the network. Think of a protocol as a language that all the PCs on the network agree to speak. The following list explains the three most popular network protocols:

- *TCP/IP for Internet access.* You need to install TCP/IP for your Internet connection, so install it now.

- *NetBEUI for fast data transfers.* NetBEUI is the network protocol your networked PCs use to share files, folders, and other resources.

- *IPX/SPX for playing multi-player games over a network connection.* Protocol used for playing games with other users over a network.

Network services enable PCs to share resources on the network. You should install two services: Client for Microsoft Networks (which provides general peer-to-peer network support) and File and Printer Sharing (which enables users to share data files and hardware devices). Figure 12.7 shows the protocols and services you should install.

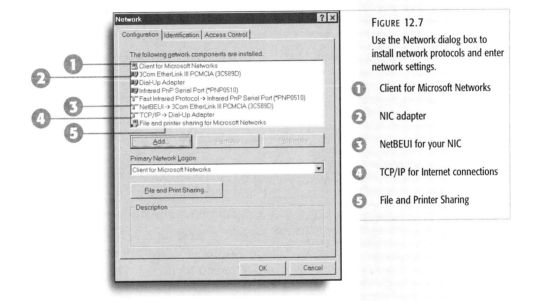

FIGURE 12.7

Use the Network dialog box to install network protocols and enter network settings.

① Client for Microsoft Networks

② NIC adapter

③ NetBEUI for your NIC

④ TCP/IP for Internet connections

⑤ File and Printer Sharing

Installing network protocols and services

1. In the Control Panel, click the Network icon. The Network dialog box appears, displaying a list of installed protocols.

2. Click the **Add** button. The Select Network Component Type dialog box appears.

3. Click **Client** and click **Add**.

4. Click **Microsoft** and click **Client for Microsoft Networking**. Click **OK**.

5. Click the **Add** button.

6. Click **Protocol** and click the **Add** button. The Select Network Protocol dialog box lists manufacturers and network protocols.

7. In the Manufacturers list, click **Microsoft**.

8. Click **IPX/SPX**, **NetBEUI**, or **TCP/IP** to add a desired protocol.

9. Click **OK**. You are returned to the Network dialog box, where the new protocol is added to the list of network components.

10. Open the **Primary Network Logon** drop-down list and choose **Client for Microsoft Networks**.

11. Click the **File and Print Sharing** button.

12. Select the desired sharing option(s) to share file(s), printer(s), or both and click **OK**. You are returned to the Network dialog box.

13. Click the **Identification** tab, and then enter a name for your PC in the **Computer Name** text box. This name identifies your PC to other PCs on the network.

14. Click in the **Workgroup** text box, and then type the name of the workgroup to which you belong. On a small network, use the same workgroup name for every PC.

15. Click the **Access Control** tab and make sure **Share-Level Access Control** is selected. This allows you to assign different access privileges to each PC on the network.

16. Click **OK**.

When you install a network protocol, it links itself to various adapters. For example, if you install TCP/IP and you have a Dial-Up adapter (for connecting to the Internet) and a network adapter (for your NIC), TCP/IP is linked to both the Dial-Up adapter and the NIC. This can cause conflicts between the network and Internet connections.

If you run into connection problems later, open the Control Panel, click the Network icon, and remove the extraneous protocol entries from the list of installed network components. For example, if the list includes entries for TCP/IP->Dial-Up Adapter and TCP/IP->*NIC* (where *NIC* is the name of your network interface card), click **TCP/IP->*NIC*** and click the **Remove** button. Likewise, if the list includes entries for NetBEUI->Dial-Up Adapter and NetBEUI->*NIC*, click **NetBEUI->Dial-Up Adapter** and click the **Remove** button.

Logging on to the Network

To connect your PC to the network, you must log on with your username and password. When you log on, Windows establishes the connection between your PC and the other PCs on the network so you can access shared files and resources. If the network has an administrator, he or she assigns the username and password. If you are on a small network, you and the other people on the network can discuss the usernames and passwords you want to use.

After logging on, you can connect to a particular server or to other PCs on the network that act as servers. A client/server network might have several servers. For example, there might be a marketing and sales server, a production server, and a human resources server. In such cases, you can log on to the network and then log on and off the various servers. On a peer-to-peer network, your PC acts as a network server whenever someone accesses a network resource through your PC. When you connect to another PC, your PC acts as the client.

Logging on to the network

1. When you start your PC, Windows displays the Enter Network Password dialog box. In the **U**ser name box, type your name (see Figure 12.8).

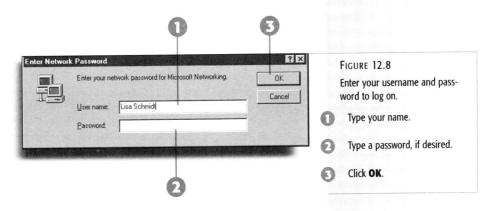

TCP/IP security risks

Enabling TCP/IP *and* file and printer sharing for your NICs allows Internet users to connect to your network PC and share files and printers. To disable file and printer sharing for TCP/IP, double-click **TCP/IP->*NIC***, click the **Bindings** tab, and remove the check mark next to **File and Printer Sharing**. You can also protect your network by installing a proxy server with firewall protection as explained in "Sharing a Modem," later in this chapter.

FIGURE 12.8

Enter your username and password to log on.

❶ Type your name.

❷ Type a password, if desired.

❸ Click **OK**.

2. In the **Password** text box, type a password (or leave it blank to log on without a password).

3. Click **OK**. If you entered a password, you are prompted to confirm. (The confirmation dialog box appears only the first time you log on.)

4. Type the password again and click **OK**.

Logging off

1. Shut down any programs that are currently running.

2. Open the **Start** menu and click **Log Off** *Yourname*. The Log Off Windows dialog box appears, asking for your confirmation.

3. Click **Yes**. Windows restarts and displays the Enter Network Password dialog box, allowing a different user to log on.

4. If you logged off to disconnect from the network, click **Cancel**. Otherwise, another person can log on or you can log on under another name.

Setting Up a Direct Cable Connection

If you're setting up a bona fide network, skip to the next section to learn how to set up resources for sharing on the network. To use a direct cable connection to transfer files between PCs, you must run Direct Cable Connection on both PCs.

Direct Cable Connection leads you through the required steps to set up one PC as the *host* and the other as the *guest*. The host is usually the more powerful of the two PCs. If you are connecting a desktop and notebook PC, the desktop PC is typically the host.

Setting up a Direct Cable Connection

1. Turn off the two PCs, connect them with the required data transfer cable, and turn them back on.

2. On the host PC, click the **Start** button, point to **Programs**, **Accessories**, and click **Direct Cable Connection**. The

Direct Cable Connection Wizard appears.

3. Click **Host** and click **Next** (see Figure 12.9). You are prompted to pick the port in which you plugged the cable.

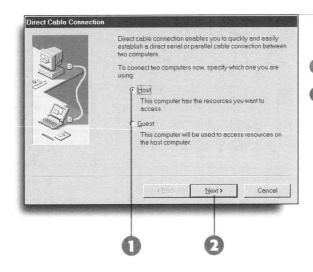

FIGURE 12.9

Set up the main PC as the host.

① Click **Host**.

② Click **Next**.

4. Select the port to which you connected the data transfer cable and click **Next**.

5. On the guest PC, click the **Start** button, point to **Programs**, **Accessories**, and click **Direct Cable Connection**.

6. Click **Guest** and click **Next**. You are prompted to pick the port in which you plugged the cable.

7. Select the port and click **Next**.

8. Go back to the host PC and click **Finish**. The host PC displays a dialog box indicating that it is waiting for the guest PC to connect.

9. On the guest PC, click **Finish**.

Sharing Resources on the Network

For one PC (the client) to access disks, folders, files, and printers on another PC (the server), the server must give the client permission to share the resource. Windows provides two ways to share network resources:

- *User-level access* allows you to assign access to users and workgroups on the network. When a user needs to access a resource, Windows checks the person's username or workgroup name to determine if the person has permission to access the resource. The user does not have to enter a password. User-level access is available only on a client/server network—a network that has a central server running special server software, such as Windows NT or NetWare. On a simple peer-to-peer network, like the one described in this chapter, user-level access is not an option.

- *Share-level access* allows you to assign a password for each resource you want to share. For example, you might use one password for a particular folder and another password for your printer. To share the resource with another person on the network, you give that person the required password.

The following sections provide instructions on how to mark resources as shared and access shared resources on the network.

Marking Resources as Shared

To allow another PC on the network to share data that's on your PC or use a printer or other device that's connected to your PC, you must mark the resource as shared. Windows provides two levels of sharing:

- *Full access* allows another PC to use resources on your PC just as if they were stored on the other PC. The user can open a file, modify it, and save it to your hard disk; copy, move, and delete files from your hard disk; and copy files from his or her PC to yours.

- *Read-only access* permits the other users to open files and copy files from your hard disk. It does not allow the other user to save a modified file, delete files from your hard disk, or copy files to your hard disk.

You can assign different share levels to disks, files, and folders on your PC. For example, you can choose to share only certain folders or files, assign full access to one folder and read-only access to another, and require other users to enter passwords to use a particular resource.

Marking a drive, folder, or printer as shared

1. Right-click the icon for the disk, folder, or printer you want to share and click **Sharing**. The Properties dialog box for the selected disk or folder appears with the Sharing tab in front (see Figure 12.10).

2. Click **Shared As**. The **Share Name** text box automatically displays the drive letter or folder or printer name.

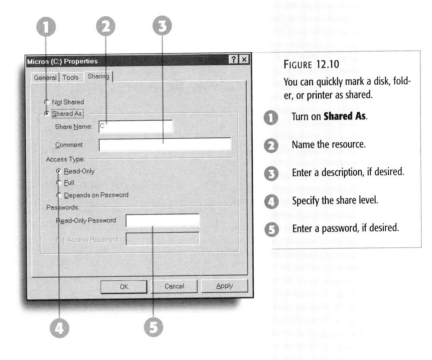

FIGURE 12.10

You can quickly mark a disk, folder, or printer as shared.

1. Turn on **Shared As**.

2. Name the resource.

3. Enter a description, if desired.

4. Specify the share level.

5. Enter a password, if desired.

4. If desired, type a different name for the drive, folder, or printer.

5. (Optional) Type a brief description of the resource in the **Comment** text box.

6. Under **Access Type**, choose the desired share option: **Read-Only, Full**, or **Depends on Password** (to use a different password for read-only or full access).

7. To require a password for accessing the resource, click in the Password text box and type the password. (If you chose Depends on Password in the previous step, enter different

passwords for the **R̲ead-Only Password** and the **Fu̲ll Access Password**.)

8. Click **OK**.

9. If you entered a password, Windows prompts you to confirm it. Type the password again and click **OK**. You are returned to My Computer or Windows Explorer, and a hand appears below the icon for the shared disk, folder, or printer.

To terminate sharing, right-click the icon for the disk, folder, or printer and choose **S̲haring**. On the **General** tab of the Properties dialog box, select **N̲ot Shared** and click **OK**.

Accessing Resources with Network Neighborhood

When you connect to the network, you can access any shared disks, folders, and printers on other PCs that are connected to the network, assuming you have the right password (if a password is required). However, locating shared resources can be difficult, especially on a large network.

Fortunately, Windows has tools to help you track down network resources and manage them. The most basic tool is the Network Neighborhood. When you click the Network Neighborhood icon on the Windows desktop, a window displays icons for all the PCs that are on the network. You can then browse the shared resources on the PCs, just as if they were on your PC.

Navigating the network

1. On the Windows desktop, click the Network Neighborhood icon. My Computer opens the Network Neighborhood and displays icons for all the PCs on the network (see Figure 12.11).

2. Click the icon for the PC you want to access. A folder is displayed for each shared drive and folder on the network PC.

3. Click the icon for the drive or folder you want to access. If accessing the resource requires a password, a dialog box appears, prompting you to enter the password.

4. Enter the required password and click **OK**. Folders and files appear as if they were on your PC.

No password required

To provide access to a disk or folder without prompting the person for a password, leave the **Password** text boxes blank. This saves time on a small network on which you fully trust the other users.

Find a computer on the network

If your network is large, you can use the **Start**, **Find**, **Computer** command to search for a specific PC on the network, assuming that you know its name.

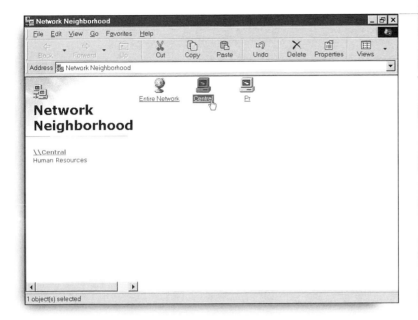

**Network
Neighborhood**

5. If you have full access to the disk and folder, you can copy files from the network PC to your PC and vice versa.

6. If you try to enter a command that you do not have permission to enter on the network PC, an error message appears, indicating that the network has denied you access. Click **OK**.

You can also access the Network Neighborhood by selecting it from the **Address** drop-down list in My Computer, from the folder list in Windows Explorer, from the **Look in** drop-down list in the Open dialog box (**File**, **Open**), and from the **Save in** drop-down list in the Save dialog box (**File**, **Save As**).

Mapping a Drive or Folder to Your Computer

If you frequently access a particular disk or folder on the network, you can *map* the disk or folder to a drive on your PC. For example, if your PC has a hard drive C and a CD-ROM drive D, you can map a network drive or folder to your PC as drive E. The drive then appears in the following windows and dialog boxes:

- *My Computer*. The drive appears in the opening My Computer window as a network drive.

- *Windows Explorer*. The drive appears in the folder list (left pane) in Windows Explorer.

- *File lists*. If you choose **File, Save** or **File, Open** in your applications, you can open the **Look in** or **Save in** drop-down lists and choose the mapped drive, just as if it were installed on your PC.

Map a network drive or folder to your PC

1. In the Network Neighborhood, right-click the network drive or folder that you want to map to your PC and click **Map Network Drive**. The Map Network Drive dialog box appears (see Figure 12.12).

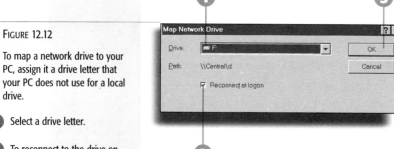

FIGURE 12.12

To map a network drive to your PC, assign it a drive letter that your PC does not use for a local drive.

① Select a drive letter.

② To reconnect to the drive on startup, turn on **Reconnect at logon**.

③ Click **OK**.

2. Open the **Drive** drop-down list and choose a drive letter to assign to the network disk or folder.

3. To have Windows automatically log on to this disk or folder on startup, click **Reconnect at logon**.

4. Click **OK**.

5. Switch back to the opening My Computer window to display the icon for the mapped drive or folder (see Figure 12.13).

SEE ALSO

➤ *Learn how to manage disks, folders, and files in Windows, page* 177

FIGURE 12.13
Icons for the mapped network dri-ves appear in My Computer.

① Mapped network drives

Installing a Network Printer

To use a network printer, you must install the printer in
Windows. Windows copies the required printer driver from the
PC on which the printer is actually installed to your PC. You can
then print documents to the network printer just as if the printer
were connected to your PC.

Install a network printer

1. Click the **Start** button, point to **Settings**, and click
   Printers. The contents of the Printers folder appears.

2. Click the Add Printer icon. The Add Printer Wizard
   appears.

3. Click **Next**. The wizard asks if you want to install a local or
   network printer.

4. Click **Network Printer** and click **Next**. The wizard
   prompts you to specify the path to the printer.

5. Click the **Browse** button. The Browse for Printer dialog
   box displays a list of all PCs on the network.

6. If necessary, click the plus sign next to the PC that is connected to the printer. The printer's icon appears as shown in
   Figure 12.14.

FIGURE 12.14

You can install a network printer to use as if it were connected to your PC.

1 Click the icon for the network printer you want to install.

2 Click **OK**.

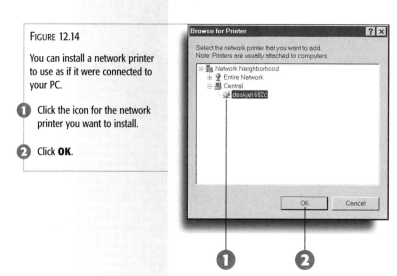

7. Click the printer's icon and click **OK**. You are returned to the wizard where the path to the network printer is displayed.

8. Click **Next**. The wizard displays the name of the printer as it appears on the network PC. You can change the name, if desired.

9. To use this printer as the default printer for all your Windows applications, click **Yes**. Click **Next**. The wizard now asks if you want to print a test page.

10. Click **Yes** or **No** and click **Finish**. If you chose to print a test page, the wizard sends the page to the network printer. Windows copies the necessary printer files from the network PC to your PC and returns you to the Printers folder. An icon for the network printer appears.

SEE ALSO

➤ *Learn more about installing printer drivers, page 737*

➤ *Learn how to print a document, page 240*

➤ *Learn how to manage documents that are currently printing, page 242*

Sharing a Modem

Installing a separate modem and phone line for every PC in your home or office can become costly, especially if you decide to speed up your Internet connection with an ISDN line or PC satellite dish. You can save the costs of redundant equipment by sharing a modem and Internet connection over the network.

You might think that sharing a modem would be as easy as sharing a printer. Unfortunately, Windows has no built-in support for modem sharing. To share a modem, you must install a utility that makes the PC with the modem act as a *proxy server*. The proxy server performs three important functions:

- *It filters out requests for unauthorized content.* This gives the network administrator (or whoever is in charge of the PC that has the shared modem) control over what passes through the proxy server.

- *It quickly fulfills requests for data.* For example, the proxy server caches the Web pages that each user on the network requests. When another user requests the same page, the proxy server can deliver it without having to download it again.

- *A proxy with firewall protection prevents unauthorized access to your network.* (Turning on file and printer sharing for your network opens the door to unauthorized network access through the TCP/IP connection.) The firewall blocks prevents intruders from breaking in.

To share a modem on a peer-to-peer network, download a modem sharing utility from the Web or purchase a commercial product and install it on the PC that has the modem you want to share. Following is a list of some of the better modem sharing utilities for Windows. Most of these programs offer a shareware version that you can use for free on a two computer network. To connect additional computers, you must purchase a version that offers support for additional PCs.

- *WinProxy* is one of the most popular modem/Internet sharing utilities. Price varies based on the number of PCs you want to connect. For more information and to download a trial version, go to www.ositis.com or call 1-888-946-7769.

- *WEBetc* by Technocratix is another popular modem/Internet sharing utility that's a bit more expensive than WinProxy. WEBetc acts as a proxy server and features firewall protection. For more information, visit www.technocratix.com/webetc.

- *Modem Share 32* by Artisoft is less expensive than WinProxy or Technocratix and offers many of the same features. To find out more, visit Artisoft's Web site at www.artisoft.com.

Installing a modem sharing program typically requires three steps. First, you install the program on the server (the PC that has the modem you want to share). You must also install the program on the clients (the PCs that are going to access the modem on the server). On each client PC, you must enter settings in your Web browser and other Internet client software to tell the client software to connect to the proxy server. The last step consists of entering the proxy server's address. Follow the instructions included with the modem sharing program.

Connecting to Your Network from a Remote Location

If you are on the road and you need to use your desktop computer or you need to log on to your network, you can use Dial-Up Networking to place the call. You can then copy files and run programs from your desktop computer or network server. Although sharing files and programs over a modem connection provides relatively slow performance, it does give you access to resources you would not otherwise be able to use.

To use your notebook computer to dial into your desktop computer from a remote location, you must first set up your desktop computer as a *Dial-Up Networking server* (or *Dial-Up Server*). This enables the desktop computer to answer incoming calls and establish communications with your notebook computer. Your notebook acts as the *Dial-Up Networking client*. You must create a new Dial-Up Networking connection, supplying Dial-Up Networking with your desktop computer's phone number.

Although this isn't a complicated task to pull off, it is tedious. The step-by-step instructions provide an overview of the process. Before you take these steps, work through Chapter 12, "Networking with Windows," to ensure that the Windows networking components are installed.

Setting up a remote connection

1. Double-click the Network icon in the Control Panel and use the **Add** button to install the following network components on *both* computers: Client for Microsoft Networks, Dial-Up Adapter, and a network protocol (TCP/IP, NetBEUI, or IPX/SPX). Stay in the Network box until step 4.

2. Open the Windows Control panel and click the Network icon.

3. Make sure **Primary Network Logon** is set as **Client for Microsoft Networks**. Do this on both computers.

4. Click **File and Print Sharing** and turn on all the options.

5. Double-click **File and Printer Sharing for Microsoft Networks**, choose **Browse Master** and make sure its Value is set to **Automatic**.

6. Click **OK**.

7. On the desktop computer, enter share settings for any disks or folders you want to be able to access.

8. On the desktop PC, open My Computer and click the Dial-Up Networking icon.

9. Open the **Connections** menu and click **Dial-Up Server**.

10. Enter your preferences, and be sure to require a password; otherwise, anyone with a PC, modem, and too much free time can break into your computer. A Dial-Up Server icon appears in the system tray.

11. On your notebook computer, run Dial-Up Networking from My Computer and double-click the **Make New Connection** icon. Follow the instructions to create an icon for dialing your desktop computer. (If your desktop PC is going to be outside of your destination's area code, keep that in mind when you're typing the phone number.)

Before you leave on your big trip, make sure you turn on your desktop PC, or it won't answer the phone. When you're on the road, plug your notebook's modem into a phone jack, click the Dial-Up Networking icon you created, and click **Connect** to dial your desktop computer. When your desktop PC answers, double-click the Network Neighborhood icon on your Windows desktop to access your desktop PC's disks and folders.

Sending Messages Across the Network

If you have used an online service, such as America Online, you know that you can send messages (called *instant messages* or IMs) to other people who are currently signed on. When you send a message to another member, it pops up on the member's screen, and the member can then choose to reply to or ignore your message.

If you work on a network, you can use a similar feature in Windows, called WinPopup, to send messages to your colleagues on the network and to read messages sent by others.

Sending messages across the network

1. In My Computer, navigate to the Windows folder and click WinPopup. Repeat this step on all the networked PCs.

2. To send a message, click the **Send** button.

3. Click **User or Computer** (to send a message to an individual) or **Workgroup** (to send a message to everyone in the workgroup) as shown in Figure 12.15.

4. Type the name of the user, PC, or workgroup in the **To** text box.

5. Type your message in the **Message** area.

6. Click **OK**. The message pops up on the screens of those people to whom you addressed the message. WinPopup notifies you whether the message was properly transmitted or not.

Run WinPopup automatically

To ensure that everyone on the network is running WinPopup, add it to the **Windows Startup** menu on each PC. You can drag the WinPopup icon from the Windows folder over **Start**, **Programs**, **Startup**, and then drop it on the **Startup** menu.

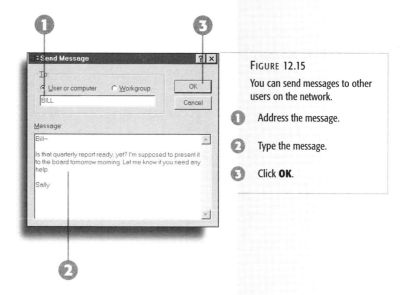

FIGURE 12.15

You can send messages to other users on the network.

① Address the message.

② Type the message.

③ Click **OK**.

Using Your PC and Windows at Home

Set up a unique Windows configuration for each family member

Turn your PC into a voice mail message center

Install and play computer games

Use your PC for educational purposes

Plan your next vacation

Renovate and automate your home

Making the Most of Your Home PC

Using a PC in an office environment is fairly obvious. You use a word processing program to type letters and other documents, a spreadsheet program for calculations and graphs, a database program for managing records and creating reports, and a business presentation program for creating slideshows and overhead transparencies.

When you bring a PC into your home, however, it takes on some new responsibilities. In addition to performing the standard chores of creating and printing documents, the PC now becomes a game and entertainment center, a library, a financial consultant, and even a travel agent. It can answer the phone, record voice mail messages, send and receive faxes, and even automate your home.

This chapter opens your eyes to the possibilities of using a PC in your home and shows you how to configure your PC for use by multiple family members.

Setting Up Windows for Multiple Users

If you share your PC with other family members, everyone needs access to it, and each person probably has a different idea on how to set up the Windows desktop and configure the work environment. This poses a problem: You don't want to have to reconfigure your system each time someone else messes with the Windows settings.

To solve this problem, Windows allows you to set up your system for more than one user. Each user is given a username and password that identifies the person. When the person configures the Windows desktop or the work environment, Windows saves the changes for that person. Each person can then configure Windows separately without affecting anyone else's settings.

Turning on Multiple User Support

1. Click the **Start** button, point to **Settings**, and click **Control Panel**.

2. In the Windows Control Panel, click the Passwords icon.

3. In the Passwords Properties dialog box, click the **User Profiles** tab.

4. Click **Users can customize their preferences and desktop settings** (see Figure 13.1).

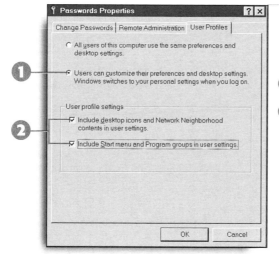

FIGURE 13.1

Use the Passwords Properties dialog box to turn on support for multiple users.

1 Select **Users can customize**...

2 Turn on both User Profile options.

5. Under **User profile settings**, turn on **Include desktop icons** and **Include Start menu and Program groups**.

6. Click **OK**. You are prompted to restart Windows.

7. Close any programs you are currently running, and then click **Yes**. When Windows restarts, it prompts you to enter your username and password.

8. Enter your name in the **User name** text box and your password in the **Password** text box. Click **OK**. (Each person using this computer should perform this step and the next one to log on.) Windows prompts you to confirm your password.

Omit the password

If you are not concerned about system security, and you want to set up your computer for multiple users, each person can leave the **Password** text box blank. To log on to Windows, the user enters his username.

9. Type the password in the **New Password** and **Confirm New Password** text boxes and click **OK**.

10. Windows indicates that you have not logged on to this computer before and asks if you would like to save any settings you enter for the next time you log on. Click **Yes**.

SEE ALSO

➤ *Learn how to log on to a network in Windows, page 305*

Logging Off

When you are finished working with the PC, you should log off to prevent the next user from changing your Windows settings. Before logging off, exit any programs you were using. Then, click the **Start** button and click **Log Off** *Yourname*. The Welcome to Windows dialog box appears, allowing the next user to log on.

Working with Passwords

Although passwords are useful for protecting each person's Windows configuration settings, they can cause problems if a user forgets his password, if the password file becomes corrupted, or if you just decide that you don't like being prompted for a password every time you start Windows. Fortunately, you can control and even remove Windows passwords:

- To change your password, open the Control Panel, click the Passwords icon, and click **Change Windows Password**. In the **Old Password** text box, type your current password. In the **New Password** and **Confirm New Password** text boxes, type your new password. Click **OK**. To remove the password, leave the **New Password** and **Confirm New Password** text boxes blank. (You'll still be prompted for a username on startup.)

- If you've forgotten your password, when the Welcome to Windows dialog box appears, click **Cancel**. Click the **Start** button, point to **Find**, and click **Files and Folders**. In the **Named** text box, type *.pwl. In the **Look in** text box, type c:\windows. Click **Find Now**. Click the password file you want to delete and press the **Delete** key (see Figure 13.2). You can then restart Windows and enter your username and a new password. (Yes, the password feature is easy to bypass, so don't rely on it to keep people from using your PC.)

- To prevent Windows from prompting for a password on startup, open the Control Panel and click the Passwords icon. Click **Change Windows Password**. In the **Old Password** text box, type your current password. Leave the **New Password** and **Confirm New Password** text boxes blank. Click the **User Profiles** tab. Click **All users of this computer use the same preferences and desktop settings**. Click **OK**.

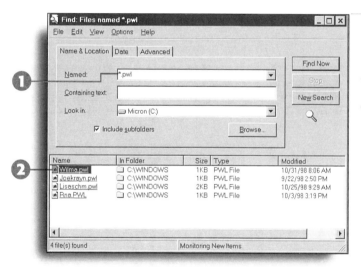

FIGURE 13.2

If you forget your password, delete your password file.

➊ Search for .pwl files.

➋ Click the password file you want to delete and press the Delete key.

Making Your PC Answer the Phone

Most modems have built-in voice support, which allows you to use the modem not only to talk to other computers, but also to receive standard phone calls and record voice messages. Modems typically contain their own software for answering incoming calls and may even allow you to set up a separate voicemail box for each member of the family. If the modem's messaging software is not installed on your PC, run the installation from the disks or CD that came with the modem.

Although the steps for activating voicemail vary depending on the program, here's what you generally have to do:

1. Turn on auto-answer so the modem will answer the phone when it rings. You can set the number of times you want the phone to ring before the modem answers.

2. Plug a microphone into your sound card's MIC jack and record your greeting. In some cases, you can record your greeting by speaking into the phone.

3. Leave your PC on and your messaging program running so it can answer the phone.

When someone calls, your messaging program automatically answers, plays your greeting, and records any message the caller leaves. You can then play back your messages, as shown in Figure 13.3.

Playing back messages via the sound card

Because voice message software communicates directly with the modem, the steps for playing recorded messages can be a little confusing. You may have to connect the Line Out jack on your modem to the Line In jack on your sound card to play voice messages through your speakers.

FIGURE 13.3

Play back your voice messages.

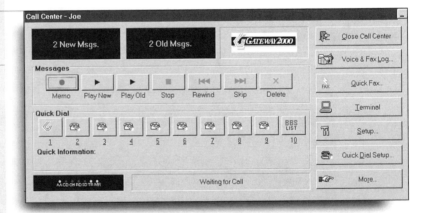

Using Your PC as a Fax Machine

With a fax modem and software, you can transform your PC into a fax machine. Of course, you won't be able to feed paper documents into it (unless you have a scanner or a combination fax/printer), but a fax modem can convert document files into faxes and receive and print faxes.

To send a fax, the fax software converts each page of your document into a graphics file. It then transmits the graphics files over the phone lines to the recipient's fax machine. WinFax Pro makes sending a fax as easy as sending an email message (see Figure 13.4).

When someone sends you a fax, the program automatically answers the phone and converts the incoming signals into a graphics file, which you can then view or print in the fax program.

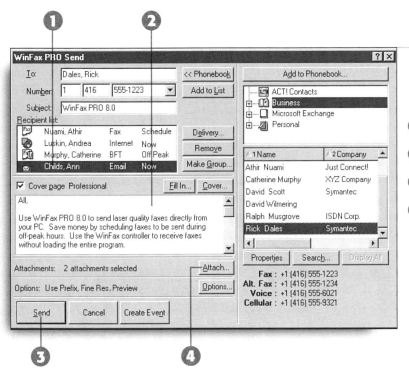

FIGURE 13.4

In WinFax Pro, you compose and send a fax just as you would send an email message.

❶ Select the recipients.

❷ Type a cover page.

❸ Click **Send**.

❹ Attach the documents you want to fax.

No fax/voicemail software?

If you have a fax modem with voice support but no fax/voice-mail software, try WinFax Pro 8.0 or later. WinFax is the leading fax/email/voicemail software package. For information about WinFax, visit Symantec's Web site at **www.symantec. com/winfax**, where you can copy a free trial version of WinFax.

If the messaging program supports both voicemail and fax, the program answers the phone, determines if the incoming call is a fax transmission or voice call and then routes the call to the required feature—the voicemail box or the fax feature.

Managing Your Investments

Chapter 6, "Creating and Saving Documents," shows how you can use a personal finance program to write checks, reconcile your checkbook register, and manage your bank and charge accounts. However, personal finance is more complicated than that. You probably have a 401K account through work, an SEP or Keogh account if you're self-employed, or mutual funds or stocks of your own.

Trying to track one of these investments by using the quarterly reports you receive in the mail and a calculator fails to give you the insight you need to make sound investment decisions. To help, most personal finance programs provide tools for creating and analyzing your investment portfolio. These tools can download stock and mutual fund prices from the Internet, list the current share price and the total value of your investment, compare the percentage returns on your investments, and even chart your investments (see Figure 13.5). For additional information about Quicken, go to Intuit's Web site at www.intuit.com or call 1-800-224-0991.

FIGURE 13.5

Quicken can help you manage your investment portfolio.

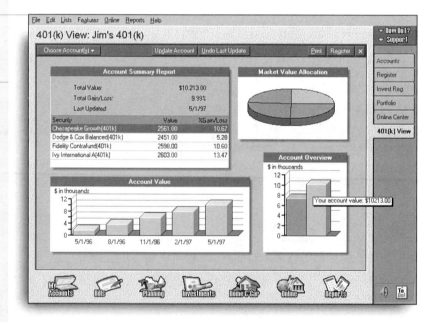

SEE ALSO

➤ *Learn how to use personal finance programs, page 151*

Starting Your Own Business

When you're starting your own business, you tend to focus on setting up your store or arranging your office space and establishing your clientele. Only after you've been in business for a while do you realize how much time and effort you must put into managing the business finances. You must track your income and expenditures, send invoices, track payments, and pay estimated quarterly taxes. If you have employees, you must also set up a payroll system and withhold taxes.

With a small-business financial program, such as QuickBooks or Peachtree Complete, you can handle the finances yourself. These programs offer features for keeping customer and employee records, tracking inventory and purchase orders, creating and printing invoices, estimating taxes, and managing payroll (see Figure 13.6). For information about QuickBooks, visit Intuit's Web site at www.intuit.com/quickbooks. To learn more about Peachtree, go to www.peachtree.com.

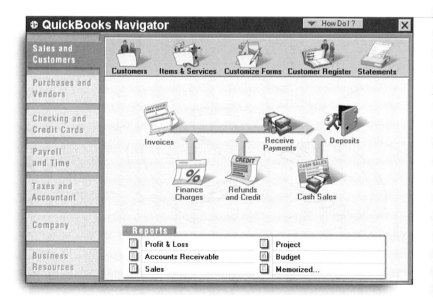

FIGURE 13.6
QuickBooks provides all the tools you need to manage your own business.

Sketching Your Family Tree

Most of us are interested in finding out where we came from. We know who our parents are, and we usually know a little about our grandparents, but beyond that, things get a little fuzzy. Of course, we had great grandparents and great-great-grandparents, but where did they come from? What did they do for a living? And how and when did they pass away? All this information can be fascinating, if you just had some way to collect it and organize it.

Fortunately, there are several programs that can help you locate information about your long lost relatives and chart it with a family tree. The most powerful and popular of these programs is Family Tree Maker (see Figure 13.7), which offers tools not only to enter data you already have but also to research your genealogy. The Deluxe edition comes on nine CDs, including two CDs packed with social security records and five CDs with actual family trees from around the world. You might be able to graft your branch onto an existing tree! You can connect to the Family Tree Maker home page on the Web (www.familytreemaker.com) for additional assistance in tracking your roots.

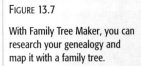

FIGURE 13.7

With Family Tree Maker, you can research your genealogy and map it with a family tree.

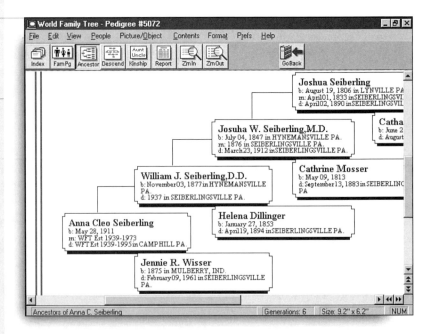

Taking Control of Your Health

Doctors and healthcare workers have been telling us for years that they are not solely responsible for our health. It's our job to live healthy lifestyles, know our limitations, and listen intelligently to what our bodies are telling us. We can't expect a quick fix. However, overworked doctors rarely have the time for preventive medicine or time to fully explain the causes of our maladies. It has become our job to gather the information we need.

One of the best programs for finding answers to your own health questions is Home Medical Advisor (see Figure 13.8). Home Medical Advisor is a multimedia CD that's packed with useful features:

- An interactive video doctor, who asks you a series of health-related questions and suggests possible causes and treatments

- A guide to preventive healthcare that explains techniques for avoiding common maladies, lowering your blood pressure, and keeping yourself fit

- A database full of common medications, so you can learn more about what your doctor prescribed, any side effects you might experience, and potential drug interactions

- A list of emergency procedures to teach you what to do in the event of an accident

- Video clips of standard medical procedures, so you'll know what to expect when you visit the hospital

- A tool for keeping track of your own medical records and the records of the rest of your family

You can obtain more information about Home Medical Advisor from The Learning Company's Web site at www.softkey.com. The Learning Company and Broderbund recently merged, so check Broderbund's Web site at www.broderbund.com, as well.

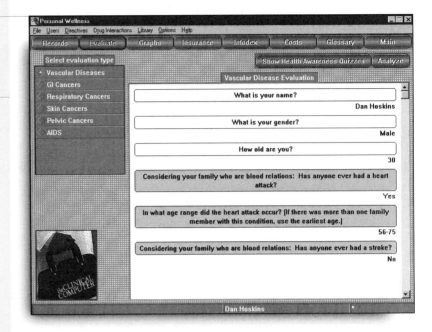

FIGURE 13.8

Home Medical Advisor can answer your most pressing medical and health-related questions.

Get Cooking with Your PC

Your PC can't beat eggs, sauté vegetables, or baste a chicken, but with the right software, it can provide you with a collection of recipes and tools for organizing your own recipes. It can also help you modify the recipes; you specify the number of people you want to serve, and the program adjusts the amount of each ingredient accordingly. Most cooking programs can even print a grocery list for you.

Your choice of cookbook CD depends on your palate. If you're looking for a simple database program to help you organize your recipes, adjust the number of servings, and generate grocery lists, Master Cook, shown in Figure 13.9, is an excellent choice. Master Cook also allows you to download recipes from the Internet and store them in the database.

The software market is also populated with celebrity cookbooks authored by the likes of Graham Kerr, Jenny Craig, and Sheila Lukins as well as great chefs from around the world.

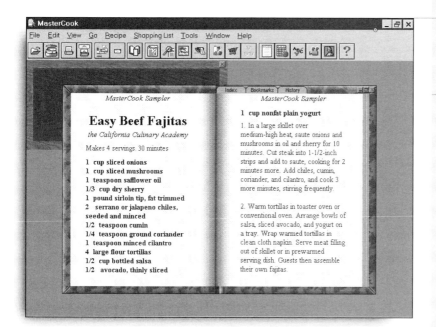

FIGURE 13.9

With Master Cook, you never have to dig through your recipe file again.

Planning Your Next Road Trip

If you're a AAA member, you can have the service put together a travel packet for you, including highlighted maps to lead you from your home to your destinations and lists of restaurants, hotels, and attractions along the way. If you're not a AAA member, or you just prefer planning your own trips, there are several trip-planner programs that can help.

The main feature of most trip planners is a routing tool that determines the shortest or fastest route between the departure and destination points. You click your point of departure, your desired destination, and the program highlights the best route. In most trip planners you can choose to take a slow, leisurely journey or the fastest trip possible, and the program suggests the appropriate route.

In addition, trip planners typically include information to help you locate motels, restaurants, historical sites, and even banks and ATMs. Figure 13.10 shows you what you can expect from

Home productivity software

If you're in the market for home-based software products, check out the following companies:
Broderbund at
www.broderbund.com
Sierra at
www.sierra.com
The Learning Company at
www.softkey.com
and At Home Software at
www.athomesoftware.com

GPS support

Most of the popular travel planners offer GPS (Global Positioning System) support. For around $150, you can purchase a GPS device to place in your car. You download the directions from the travel planner to the GPS, and the GPS (using satellite communications) informs you of upcoming turns and exits.

a trip planner. Following is a list of popular trip planners along with Web sites where you can find out more about them:

AAA Map'n'Go at www.delorme.com

Rand McNally's TripMaker Deluxe at www.randmcnally.com

Microsoft's Expedia Trip Planner at www.microsoft.com

Door-to-Door at www.travroute.com

FIGURE 13.10

You can plot the shortest route to your destination.

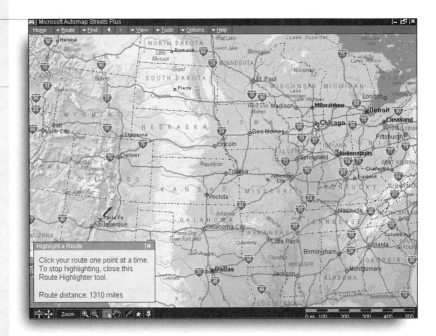

Playing Games

Your PC isn't all business. Install a joystick, and you transform your PC into a two-thousand-dollar, 32-bit game system. For another 40 bucks, you have a personal chess guru, who will not only play with you 24 hours a day, but can also teach you some tricks and strategies. Add a 3D video card with a 19-inch monitor and a 64-bit sound card with a subwoofer, and you can pretend you've been flown to another planet to blast evil aliens.

The game software category is one of the most diverse, including adventure games (such as Myst), combat games (such as

Mech Warrior), standard card games, board games, virtual sports, strategy games (such as SimCity, shown in Figure 13.11), and much more.

FIGURE 13.11
With SimCity, you're elected mayor of a virtual city.

Using Your PC for Educational Purposes

Your PC is one of the best educational tools in your home. It has an infinite amount of patience, allows you to learn at your own pace, provides an interactive interface to you for instant feedback, and provides better research tools than you'll find in most neighborhood libraries. The following list describes the most popular types of educational software:

- *Multimedia encyclopedias.* Although many of the digital encyclopedias lack the depth of their printed counterparts, digital encyclopedias are much better at helping you locate specific articles and find cross-references. They also add another dimension to learning by featuring audio and video clips (see Figure 13.12). In the near future, look for encyclopedias on DVD, which will provide the depth missing from many of the CD-ROM titles.

FIGURE 13.12

Encyclopedias on CD-ROM make it easy to find specific information and cross-references.

- *Reading*. Reading programs, such as the popular Reader Rabbit, make it fun for kids to perform demanding and repetitive drills and exercises. These programs interact with the child, providing immediate feedback and allowing the child to fully master a skill before moving on.

- *Writing*. Kids like to write. Given a little encouragement (and some free reign with the color printer), they'll write their own stories, create cards, write and illustrate letters to their friends, and even pen a few notes to their parents. Writing programs, such as Microsoft's Creative Writer, encourage children to play with language and expand their writing skills while giving them the freedom to compose on their own.

- *Math*. The secret to success in mathematics, and in most disciplines, is practice. Math programs, such as MathBlaster, use games to lead students through the necessary drills, challenging them to perform quick calculations.

- *History*. One of the most popular programs for helping students with their history lessons is *Where in Time Is Carmen*

Sandiego? With a few clues in hand, students must track down Carmen Sandiego as she travels through time and space, highlighting the most important historical events.

- *Foreign language.* Everyone would like to know another foreign language, but few of us have the determination to learn one. Foreign language programs can lead you through the necessary vocabulary drills, help you with pronunciation, and correct you when you make errors in syntax.

- *Music.* If you have a sound card with a MIDI port, you can plug in a MIDI piano keyboard and start playing tunes through your PC. A company called Jump! Music markets a product called the *Piano Discovery System* that comes with a MIDI piano keyboard and a CD that includes interactive piano lessons.

- *Testing.* A little practice can raise a student's standardized test scores, giving the student the freedom to attend the college of his choice and obtain the all-important grants and scholarships. You can find several programs to help students practice for the GRE, SAT, ACT, and LSAT, just to mention a few of the more popular tests.

Making a Digital Photo Album

Computers have revolutionized the photo industry. Now, instead of having shoe boxes and drawers packed with old, unlabeled photos, you can have your photos scanned in and placed on CDs. You can then use any CD-ROM drive that supports Kodak Photo CD (most do) to read and display the images on your monitor, print the images, and paste them into your documents (see Figure 13.13). You can even use special imaging software to adjust the brightness, contrast, and color of your digital images.

If you have a CD-ROM drive that can write to CDs, you can use a digital camera to take pictures, download them to your PC, and then store them on CDs, without having to wait for them to be developed. Each CD can store approximately 100 high-resolution photographs.

What about the Internet?

The Internet also provides a healthy selection of educational resources. On the Internet, you'll find online encyclopedias, educational games, teacher resources, a support network for home schooling, and much more. With email and chat, the Internet is also a great tool for cross-cultural studies.

FIGURE 13.13

You can pull up digital photos right on your monitor.

SEE ALSO

➤ *Learn how to shop for, install, and use a digital camera, page* 757

➤ *Learn how to shop for, install, and use a scanner, page* 741

Automating and Securing Your Home

It's tempting to think of your PC as another home appliance. However, your PC is much smarter than any other device in your home. With its built-in intelligence and some additional hardware and software, your PC can act as a control center, turning lights on and off, starting the coffee before you wake up, monitoring motion detectors inside or outside your home, and automatically adjusting the thermostat.

Most home automation systems consist of a program, a transmitter that connects to the serial or parallel port on your PC, and X10 switches, into which you plug the devices you want to control. The system either sends signals through your home's existing wiring or uses a radio frequency transmitter to turn devices on and off.

After connecting the hardware and attaching switches to the devices you want to control, you enter your preferences for turning the devices on and off.

Remodeling Your Home

If you're a homeowner, you probably have your own vision of the perfect floor plan. Maybe you'd like a larger bathroom with a Jacuzzi, a kitchen that opens out into the living room, and a deck out back. Or maybe you'd like to get rid of that low-hanging ceiling and make your home more open.

Whatever your vision, you can sketch it into reality by using a home design program. These programs are scaled-down versions of CAD (computer-aided design) programs and are typically packed with sample floor plans and basic shapes to mark entrances, windows, and stairways and even play around with the location of your furniture and appliances (see Figure 13.14). Some home design programs can even help you determine the materials you need and help you estimate the job cost.

ActiveHome

One of the most popular home automation systems is ActiveHome, which includes the software, computer connection, one transceiver (for appliances), one lamp module (for lights), a full-size remote control, and a key chain remote. To learn more about ActiveHome, visit www.x10.com or call 1-800-675-3044.

FIGURE 13.14

With Broderbund's 3D Home Architect, you can view your design in three dimensions.

Backing Up and Restoring Files

Shop for a practical backup device

Devise a backup strategy to ensure reliable recoveries

Back up your entire system

Back up the document files you create

Restore files without overwriting new files with old files

Understanding the Purpose of Backups

The most valuable part of your PC is the data stored on its hard disk. You can replace the system unit, the monitor, the printer, and all the other devices, but trying to re-create your documents and databases, remembering all the email addresses of your friends and colleagues, and restoring the configuration settings for Windows and your other programs is impossible.

Because your data and program settings are so valuable, you should back up your files regularly and store your backups somewhere away from your computer, so they will be safe in the event of a theft or fire.

Backing up consists of copying selected folders and files from your hard disk to a set of floppy disks or to a special backup drive (typically a tape drive). The backup operation compresses the files so they take up less space.

Choosing a Backup Device

One of the main reasons people refuse to back up their files regularly is that their PCs do not have a practical backup device. Nobody is going to attempt to back up 2GB of data onto over 700 floppy disks! As a result, most users back up only the document files they create, if they back up any files at all.

The first step in performing reliable backups is to obtain a device that makes it practical to back up files regularly. When shopping for a backup device, you should focus on the following features:

- *Storage capacity*. Ideally, the backup device should be able to store the entire contents of your hard disk (in a compressed state) onto a single tape or disk. For example, if you have a 4GB hard disk, look for a backup device that can store at least 3GB on a single tape or disk. Backup programs compress files at slightly less than a 2-to-1 ratio (typically about 1.7-to-1), so a 3GB backup disk can store the entire contents of a full 4GB hard disk.

- *Speed*. Removable disk drives, such as the Iomega Jaz drive, are nearly as fast and quiet as an internal hard drive. Tape backup drives are much slower and noisier, because the drive must run a tape past the read/write head. If you plan on doing unattended backups, however, speed and noise may not be an issue.

- *Cost*. In the cost category, tape backups win hands down. A typical tape backup drive costs $200–$300, and you can expect to spend about $5 per gigabyte of storage. The cost of removable disk drives vary. Large removable disk drives can cost $500 or more and may require you to install a SCSI interface for another $200. In addition, high-capacity, removable disks are much more expensive—$50–$75 per gigabyte.

If you have an Iomega Zip drive or a similar drive that stores 100MB on a single disk, the drive is more useful for transferring files between computers or storing presentations than for backups. You can use the drive for backups, but because the disk capacity is so much lower than a typical hard disk, you'll have to swap disks during the backup. This makes it inconvenient for performing unattended backups.

Another backup option that's becoming more popular is to use a CD-R (CD-Recordable) or CD-RW (CD-ReWritable) drive. The cost for CDs is about the same as tape backups, CDs take up less space, the backups proceed much more quickly, and because CDs provide random access to files on the discs (like hard drives), restoring individual files is much easier. In addition, you can use the CD-R or CD-RW device to read CDs and to *burn* your own CDs for distributing files, storing photos and video clips, and much more. The drawback is that you can store only about 1GB per CD. In the future, DVD-RW (Digital Versatile Disk, ReWritable) drives will overcome this limitation.

SEE ALSO

➤ *Learn how to select, install, and use a portable drive, page 659*

Developing a Backup Strategy

Backup files are only as good as they are recent. You don't want to back up *all* your files *every* day, but you do want daily backups of files that have changed. To accomplish this, you can perform a *full backup* each week and perform *incremental backups* daily. (A full backup backs up all files. An incremental backup backs up only new files and those files that have changed since the last backup.)

Parallel port drives

Some backup devices can connect to the parallel port, providing a much slower data transfer rate than drives that connect to the SCSI or IDE adapter. If you have a desktop and a notebook PC, however, you can use the device to perform back-ups on both of your PCs.

Weekly Backup Strategy

The safest backup strategy consists of performing a full backup once a week and daily incremental backups. This ensures that you have a complete and up-to-date backup of your system and can lose no more than one day of work.

To perform the weekly backup, you need four sets of two backup tapes (eight in all). The first backup tape of each set is used for a full backup at the beginning of the week. The second tape is used for the daily incremental backups. The following week, you repeat the process using another set of tapes. This provides you with four complete backups, in the event that you want to restore an older version of a file.

Backing up safely

1. The first day you back up your files, label one backup tape "Full 1" and use it to perform a full backup.

2. Label another tape "Incremental 1" and use it to perform an incremental backup on the remaining six days of the week.

3. On the first day of the second week, label a new backup tape "Full 2" and use it to perform a full backup.

4. Label another tape "Incremental 2" and use it to perform an incremental backup on the remaining six days of the week.

5. Continue with this procedure until you have four two-tape backup sets.

6. On the fifth week, reuse the Full 1 and Incremental 1 tapes to back up your system.

Monthly Backup Strategy

Although the weekly backup strategy is the most thorough, keeping track of four sets of tapes may seem a little excessive. If you don't install new programs regularly or create or edit files on a daily basis, try a monthly backup strategy.

This strategy requires two sets of two backup tapes. Use the first tape of a set for a full backup each month. Use the second tape for your daily incremental backups. At the start of the next month, you perform the same routine with a second set of tapes.

Backing up on a 30-day cycle

1. Label one backup tape "Full 1" and use it to perform a full backup.

2. Label a second backup tape "Incremental 1" and use it to perform daily incremental backups for the next 29 days.

3. Label your third backup tape "Full 2" and use it to perform a full backup.

4. Label your fourth backup tape "Incremental 2" and use it to perform daily incremental backups for the next 29 days.

5. For the third 30-day cycle, reuse the Full 1 and Incremental 1 tapes to back up your system.

Backing Up Your Entire System

Whenever you purchase a new PC, you should back up everything and store the backup tape or disk somewhere safe. Many new systems come with pre-installed software that is not included on CDs or floppy disks. If you were to lose any of the pre-installed files, there would be no way to recover them. In addition, you should perform a full backup regularly, as explained in the previous section.

Backing up everything

1. Exit any programs that are currently running.

2. Click the **Start** button, point to **Programs**, **Accessories**, **System Tools**, and click **Backup**. Microsoft Backup runs and displays the Microsoft Backup Wizard, which prompts you to choose the desired action (see Figure 14.1).

Data-only backups

If you back up nothing else, at least back up the document files you create and your financial records. A quick way to do this is to create a separate folder on your hard disk named Data and store all documents and financial files in this folder (or in a subfolder of the Data folder). You can then choose to back up only the files in the Data folder.

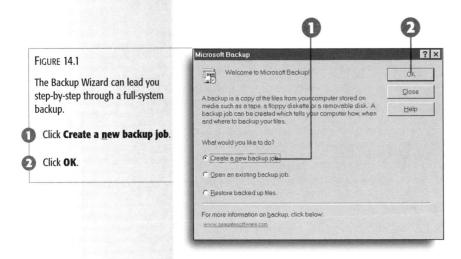

FIGURE 14.1

The Backup Wizard can lead you step-by-step through a full-system backup.

1 Click **Create a new backup job**.

2 Click **OK**.

Running the Backup Wizard

Backup is set up to run the Backup Wizard when it starts. If the Backup Wizard does not start automatically, open the **Tools** menu and click **Backup Wizard**.

No backup device?

A dialog box may appear indicating that Backup did not find a special backup drive. If you're backing up to a removable disk (such as a floppy disk or Iomega Jaz disk) or a hard disk, click **No**. If you know that a special backup drive is installed, click **Yes** to run the Add New Hardware Wizard and set it up in Windows.

3. Choose **Create a new backup job** and click **OK**.

4. Backup prompts you to specify what you want to back up. Choose **Back up my computer** and click **Next**. You are now prompted to back up all files or only those files that have changed since the last backup.

5. Choose **All selected files** and click **Next**. Backup prompts you to choose the type of backup device you want to use.

6. Open the **Where to back up** drop-down list and click the desired device type. (Choose **File** to back up to a hard disk, floppy disk, or removable disk.)

7. If you chose **File** in the previous step, click the folder button ⊞ , select the desired disk, and click **Open**.

8. Click **Next**. Backup indicates that it will compare files after the backup to verify the copies against the originals and that it will compress files to fit more on a disk or tape.

9. Make sure both options are checked and click **Next**. You are prompted to type a name for the backup.

10. Type a brief description, such as "Full System," and then click the **Start** button. Backup starts backing up the files and displays a dialog box telling you to insert a disk or tape in the selected drive.

11. Insert the disk or tape and click **OK**. (You might have to swap disks or tapes during the backup operation if the amount of data to be backed up is more than one disk or tape can store.)

Dealing with Skipped Files and Other Errors

Everyone will tell you to perform a full system backup to save each and every file on your hard disk. However, Windows Backup has a slight glitch—it doesn't back up files that are in use. This includes program files, essential Windows files, and user files that contain your configuration settings. Because these files are in use, trying to back them up would result in a file sharing violation in Windows, which could cause your system to crash. To avoid this, Windows skips the file.

There is a workaround to the problem, but it's not pretty. When Backup is finished performing a full system backup, it displays a dialog box indicating that it encountered errors during the backup. Click the button for viewing the backup report to display a list of files that were not successfully backed up (see Figure 14.2). Print the backup report.

Formatting backup tapes

If the backup tape you inserted is not formatted, Backup formats it before the backup. You can start formatting a tape yourself; open the **Tools** menu, point to **Media**, and click **Format**.

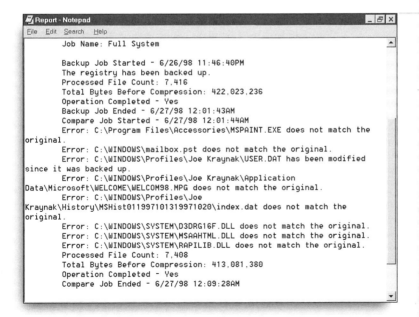

FIGURE 14.2

The backup report provides useful information about skipped files and backup errors.

Copy every file that was not successfully backed up to a separate folder on your hard disk. Back up this folder, as explained in "Backing Up Selected Folders and Files," later in this chapter. If you need to restore your system later, restore all the files on your full system backup, and then restore the files from the new folder to their original locations.

Entering Backup Preferences

Although the Backup Wizard offers the easiest way to perform full and incremental backups of entire disks, you may want to change the backup settings to change the compression ratio, exclude files from the backup, or enter additional preferences. Before entering your preferences, you should create a new backup job for storing the settings.

Create a new backup job

1. Click the **Start** button, point to **Programs**, **Accessories**, **System Tools**, and click **Backup**.

2. When the Backup Wizard appears, click the **Close** button.

3. Click the check box next to the disk you want to back up. To back up only selected folders and files, see "Backing Up Selected Folders and Files" later in this chapter.

4. Click the **Options** button.

5. Enter your preferences for the options listed in Table 14.1 and click **OK** (see Figure 14.3).

6. Open the **Job** menu and click **Save As**.

7. Type a name for the new backup job and click the **Save** button.

TABLE 14.1   **Backup options**

Option	Description
General	
Compare original and backup files...	Compares the original files to the backed up files to ensure that they were successfully backed up. This adds time to the backup but allows you to view any backup errors.

Option	Description
General	
When backing up the media	Allows you to specify the desired compression ratio. You can turn compression off, use moderate compression to save time, or use maximum compression to save space. Although the compression takes time, it saves some time, because your system transfers smaller files to the backup drive.
If the media already contains backups	If the backup disk or tape already contains a backup file, you can choose to tack on the new backup file to the disk or overwrite the old backup file with the new file.
Password	
Protect this backup with a password	To prevent unauthorized access to the data on your backup tape or disk, you can password-protect it.
Type	
All selected files	Backs up all selected files. If you are backing up all folders and files on a disk, this option specifies that you want everything backed up.
New and changed files only	Backs up only those files that have changed since the last backup.
Differential backup type	Backs up all files that are new or that have changed since the last full backup. Differential backups are more thorough than incremental backups and take more time.
Incremental backup type	Backs up all files that are new or have changed since the last full or incremental backup.
Exclude	
Do not back up these file types	Allows you to mark certain file types that you don't want to back up. For example, you may want to exclude temporary (TMP) files, Web page (HTML) files, or backup (BAK) files. Click the Add button to add file types to the list.
Report	
List all files that were backed up	Displays a list of all files that were successfully backed up. You can safely leave this option off.

continues...

TABLE 14.1 **Continued**	
Option	**Description**
Report	
List files that were <u>n</u>ot backed up	Make sure this option is on. You should view a list of any files that Backup skipped.
List <u>e</u>rrors reported while backing up files	Make sure this option is on. If Backup encounters errors that prevent it from successfully backing up a file, you want to know about it.
List <u>w</u>arnings reported while backing up files	This is another useful option to keep on. It displays warnings that could signal problems with Backup or with the files you're trying to back up.
List unattended <u>m</u>essages and prompts	If you perform unattended backups, keep this option on, so you'll know what Backup decided to do without your confirmation.
Show report <u>s</u>ummary	The Report Summary displays the information you chose to view, including a list of skipped files, errors, warnings, and unattended messages. Keep this on.
Perform an <u>u</u>nattended backup	Gives Backup the okay to proceed with a backup operation without prompting for your confirmation when it encounters problems. If you want to start the backup and then let it run while you do something else (like sleep), turn on this option.
Advanced	
Back up windows <u>r</u>egistry	Tells Backup to back up the Windows Registry file even when you're not backing up the Windows folder.

Additional preferences

To enter general preferences for all backup jobs, open the **Tools** menu and click **Preferences**. In the Preferences dialog box, you can choose to prevent the Backup Wizard from running when you start Backup, back up the Registry whenever you back up the Windows folder, and have Windows show the number and size of files before backing up.

SEE ALSO

➤ *Learn how to backup the Windows Registry without Backup, page 264*

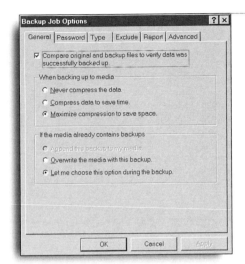

FIGURE 14.3
You can enter preferences to control the backup operation.

Performing an Incremental Backup

Whenever Backup backs up a file, it turns off the file's archive attribute, indicating that the file has been backed up. When you create or edit a file, the file's archive attribute is turned on, indicating that it has not been backed up. During an incremental backup, Backup searches for files whose archive attribute is turned on, backs up those files, and turns their archive attribute off. With a differential backup (refer to Table 14.1), Backup backs up the changed files but leaves the archive attribute on; the next time you perform a backup, these files will be backed up again.

Backing up only new and changed files

1. Exit any programs that are currently running.

2. Click the **Start** button, point to **Programs**, **Accessories**, **System Tools**, and click **Backup**. Backup runs and displays the Backup Wizard, which prompts you to choose the desired action.

3. Choose **Create a new backup job** and click **OK**.

4. Backup prompts you to specify what you want to back up. Choose **Back up my computer** and click **Next**. You are now prompted to back up all files or only those files that have changed since the last backup (see Figure 14.4).

Quick backups from My Computer

To quickly run Backup from My Computer, right-click the icon for the disk you want to back up and click **Backup**.

FIGURE 14.4

You can choose to back up only those files that have been created or changed since the last backup.

5. Choose **New and changed files** and click **Next**. Backup prompts you to choose the type of backup device you want to use.

6. Open the **Where to back up** drop-down list and click the desired device type. (Choose **File** to back up to a hard disk, floppy disk, or removable disk.)

7. If you chose **File** in the previous step, click the folder button , select the desired disk, and click **Open**.

8. Click **Next**. Backup indicates that it will compare files after the backup to verify the copies against the originals and that it will compress files to fit more on a disk or tape.

9. Make sure both options are checked and click **Next**. You are prompted to type a name for the backup.

10. Type a brief description, such as "Increment," and then click the **Start** button. Backup starts backing up the files and displays a dialog box telling you to insert a disk or tape in the selected drive.

11. Insert the disk or tape and click **OK**. (You might have to swap disks or tapes during the backup operation if the amount of data to be backed up is more than one disk or tape can store.)

Backing Up Selected Folders and Files

In most cases, you should do a full or incremental backup of your entire hard disk, so you won't miss any folders or files that have changed. If you have document files in a separate folder or special files that you want to back up more often than others, however, you can back up only those files. For example, whenever I take a trip, I back up all my document files on a single tape and pack the tape.

Backing up specific disks, folders, and files

1. Exit any programs that are currently running.

2. Click the **Start** button, point to **Programs**, **Accessories**, **System Tools**, and click **Backup**.

3. Choose **Create a new backup job** and click **OK**.

4. Backup prompts you to specify what you want to back up. Click **Back up selected files, folders, and drives** and click **Next**. Backup displays a dialog box similar to Windows Explorer.

5. To expand the list of folders on a disk or in a folder, click the plus sign next to the disk or folder.

6. To select all folders and files on a disk or in a folder, click the check box next to the disk or folder in the list on the left.

   To select specific folders and files on a disk or in a folder, click the disk or folder (not its check box) in the list on the left and click the check box next to each folder and file in the list on the right (see Figure 14.5).

7. Click **Next**. You are now prompted to back up all files or only those files that have changed since the last backup.

8. Choose **All selected files** to perform a full backup or **New and changed files** to perform an incremental backup.

9. Click **Next**. Backup prompts you to choose the type of backup device you want to use.

10. Open the **Where to back up** drop-down list and click the desired device type. (Choose **File** to back up to a hard disk, floppy disk, or removable disk.)

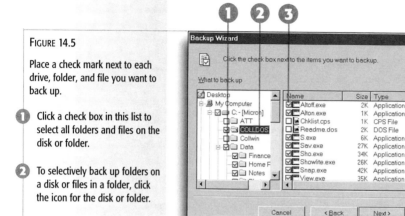

FIGURE 14.5

Place a check mark next to each drive, folder, and file you want to back up.

1 Click a check box in this list to select all folders and files on the disk or folder.

2 To selectively back up folders on a disk or files in a folder, click the icon for the disk or folder.

3 Use the file list to mark specific folders and files for backup.

11. If you chose **File** in the previous step, click the folder button ![folder icon], select the desired disk, and click **Open**.

12. Click **Next**. Backup indicates that it will compare files after the backup to verify the copies against the originals and that it will compress files to fit more on a disk or tape.

13. Make sure both options are checked and click **Next**. You are prompted to type a name for the backup.

14. Type a brief description, such as "Full Data," and then click the **Start** button. Backup starts backing up the files and displays a dialog box telling you to insert a disk or tape in the selected drive.

15. Insert the disk or tape and click **OK**. (You might have to swap disks or tapes during the backup operation if the amount of data to be backed up is more than one disk or tape can store.)

Scheduling Unattended Backups

You would think that Microsoft designed Task Scheduler and Backup to work together. That would certainly take the hassle out of daily backups. You could schedule a full backup of your entire system once a week and perform daily incremental back-ups for the remaining six days. All you would have to do is make sure the right tape or disk was in the backup drive at the sched-uled time.

Unfortunately, Task Scheduler can run Backup but it can't initi-ate a backup job, even if you turn on Backup's unattended back-up option. To have scheduled backups run automatically, you must install a more robust backup program. If your backup drive came with its own backup utility, try using it to schedule unat-tended backups. Try one of the following full-featured backup utilities:

- *Cheyenne Backup* from Computer Associates is a high-powered backup utility that supports unscheduled backups, backs up the Windows Registry, and supports a wide range of backup devices, including Jaz, Zip, and QIC tape backup drives. For more information, check out the Computer Associates Web site at www.cheyenne.com or call 1-800-243-9462.

- *Seagate Backup Exec* is the full-featured version of Microsoft Backup. If you like the look and feel of Microsoft Backup and want the additional tools of a full-featured backup pro-gram, get Seagate Backup. For more information, check out www.seagatesoftware.com.

- *HP Colorado Backup* is designed to be used with HP Colorado tape backups. Colorado tape backup drives have been around for years. If you don't yet have a system for backing up, check out HP Colorado tape backup drives at www.hp.com/tape/colorado.

SEE ALSO
➤ *Learn how to use Task Scheduler to automate other Windows programs, page 225*

Creating an Emergency Recovery Disk

After you've backed up your system, you might start to feel con-fident. You now have a complete collection of everything that's on your hard disk on a backup tape. If your hard drive goes belly up, you pop in the tape and then… Well, you can't start your PC from a backup drive, so even if you do have a full backup of your system, you need some way to get your PC up and running before you can restore files.

Making an emergency recovery disk

1. Click the **Start** button, point to **Settings**, and click **Control Panel**.

2. In Control Panel, click the **Add/Remove Programs** icon.

3. Click the **Startup Disk** tab.

4. Click the **Create Disk** button (see Figure 14.6).

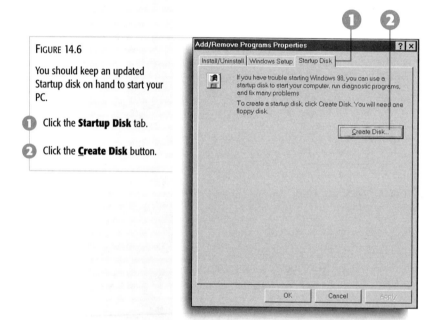

FIGURE 14.6

You should keep an updated Startup disk on hand to start your PC.

① Click the **Startup Disk** tab.

② Click the **Create Disk** button.

5. If Windows prompts you to insert the Windows 98 CD, insert it and click **OK**. Windows copies the files required for the startup disk and prompts you to insert a floppy disk.

6. Insert a blank floppy disk or one that contains files you no longer need. Click **OK**. Windows formats the disk (if needed) and copies the necessary recovery files to the disk.

7. When you are returned to the Add/Remove Programs Properties dialog box, click **OK**.

SEE ALSO

➤ *Learn how to recover control when Windows crashes, page 839*

Restoring Files

Hopefully, you will never need the backups you created. However, if your hard disk drive goes belly up or you permanently delete an important file by accident, you can use your backups to recover some or all of your files.

Before you restore a file from your backups to your hard disk, realize that you run the risk of overwriting a newer version of a file on your hard disk with an older file from your backup. If you're restoring program files, this could cause problems with Windows or one of your programs. Before restoring files, read the following tips and precautions:

- If you accidentally delete a file, try restoring the file from the Recycle Bin first.
- If you think you may have misplaced the file, use **File**, **Find**, **Files and Folders** to search My Computer for the file.
- Do *not* perform a full restore unless absolutely necessary. Restore only the files that are missing or damaged.
- If you must perform a full restore, make sure you've turned on the option telling Backup not to overwrite files of the same name or to overwrite only older files. The option for not replacing files is on by default.

Restoring files

1. Insert the backup tape or disk.

2. If Backup is not running, click the **Start** button, point to **Programs**, **Accessories**, **System Tools**, and click **Backup**.

If Backup is running, open the **Tools** menu, choose **Restore Wizard**, and go to step 3.

3. Click **Restore backed up files** and click **OK**.

4. Open the **Restore from** drop-down list and choose the type of backup device you're using. (Choose **File** to back up to a hard disk, floppy disk, or removable disk.)

5. If you chose **File** in the previous step, click the folder button 🗐 , select the desired disk, and click **Open**.

6. Click **Next**. Windows searches the specified restore device for the names of backups you performed and displays a list.

7. Click the name of the backup set from which you want to restore files and click **OK**. Restore creates a list of the folders and files stored in the selected backup set and displays a list of disks that the files were backed up from.

8. To restore all the files on a disk, click the check box next to the disk's letter.

To restore only selected folders or files, mark the folders and files you want to restore, as shown in Figure 14.7.

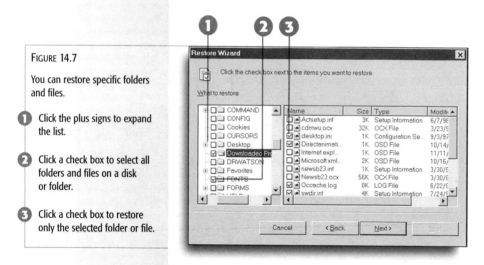

FIGURE 14.7

You can restore specific folders and files.

❶ Click the plus signs to expand the list.

❷ Click a check box to select all folders and files on a disk or folder.

❸ Click a check box to restore only the selected folder or file.

9. When you finish selecting the disks, folders, and files you want to back up, click **Next**. Restore prompts you to specify the drive and folder in which you want to restore the files. By default, Restore places the files on the disk and folder from which they were backed up.

10. Click **Next**. Restore asks if you want to replace files on your hard disk with files from the backup.

11. Choose one of the following options:—**Do not replace the file on my computer** (safest), **Replace the file on my computer only if the file is older** (pretty safe), or **Always replace the file on my computer** (risky).

12. Click the **Start** button. The Media Required dialog box appears.

13. Choose the media type on which the backup files are stored and click **OK**. Restore copies the files from the backup disk or tape and places them on the specified disk and folder.

Restoring Your System After a Crash

PCs rarely crash severely enough to require a full system restore. If your system locks up, don't assume that you have to restore everything. Try restarting your PC. In most cases, Windows restarts in Safe mode, and you can recover control of your system by changing your system settings (via the Control Panel) or by restoring a file from the Recycle Bin.

If Windows doesn't start, insert the emergency startup disk into the floppy drive and turn on your PC. If Windows starts at the DOS prompt (A:>), type `c:` and press Enter to determine if you can use your hard drive. If the DOS C:> prompt appears, type `cd\windows`, press Enter, type `win`, and press Enter again. This should start Windows.

If you cannot change to drive C or Windows still refuses to run, try to restore Windows from your system backup. To do this, you'll need your Windows startup disk, the Windows 98 CD, and your full system backup.

Restore Windows 98

1. With your computer off, insert the emergency startup disk you created into your PC's floppy disk drive.

2. Turn on your PC. Your PC should start and display the Windows 98 Startup menu.

3. Choose **Start computer with CD-ROM support**. The A:> prompt should appear.

4. Type the letter of your CD-ROM drive followed by a colon and press Enter; for example, type d: and press Enter.

5. Type cd tools\sysrec and press Enter.

6. Type pcrestor and press Enter. The Windows 98 Setup utility starts and runs the System Recovery Wizard.

7. Eject the emergency startup disk.

8. In the System Recovery Wizard, click **Next**.

9. Type your name and company name and click **Next**.

10. Click **Finish**. The Microsoft Backup Welcome dialog box appears.

11. Click **Restore backed up files** and click **OK**.

12. Follow the wizard's instructions to perform a full restore operation on your PC.

Going Online Via Modem, the Internet, and Online Services

Using America Online and Other Commercial Services

Start an account with a commercial online service

Connect to and navigate America Online

Learn your way around CompuServe

Connect to and use Prodigy Internet

Check out The Microsoft Network

Setting Up Your Online Account

Commercial online services, such as America Online, Prodigy, and CompuServe, have popularized online communications. Through these services, you can access news, weather, investment information, technical support, online businesses, the Internet, chat rooms, and much more.

To get online with one of these services or to connect to the Internet, you have two options. You can quickly set up an account with a commercial online service (America Online, AT&T WorldNet, CompuServe, Prodigy Internet, or The Microsoft Network) or use an independent *Internet service provider (ISP)*, as explained in the next chapter.

All commercial services include Internet support. In addition, they provide high-quality content that you can receive only by subscribing to the service. For example, America Online features special news and financial areas that you cannot access from a simple Internet connection. However, commercial services typically charge a little more than ISPs and may not provide quality Internet support.

The following sections show you how to set up accounts with the major commercial online services using software included on the Windows CD. Although these services offer a free trial membership, you have to enter a credit card number to sign up. You can cancel your membership before the trial period expires to avoid charges.

SEE ALSO

➢ *Learn how to set up an Internet connection with a local Internet service provider,* *page 391*

Using the Online Services Folder

The Windows desktop includes a folder named Online Services, which provides convenient access to the most popular commercial services. On the desktop, you'll also find an icon for The Microsoft Network, Microsoft's own commercial service (see Figure 15.1).

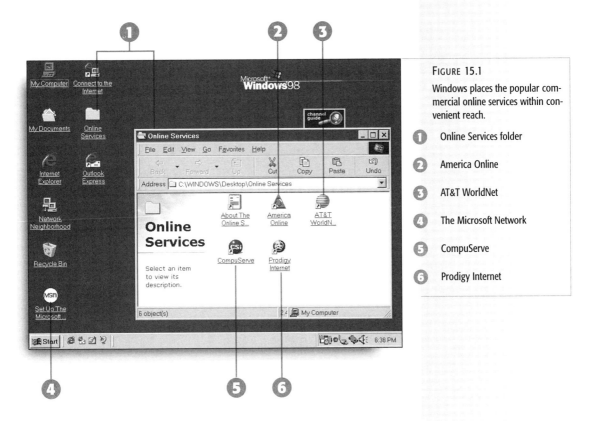

FIGURE 15.1

Windows places the popular commercial online services within convenient reach.

1. Online Services folder

2. America Online

3. AT&T WorldNet

4. The Microsoft Network

5. CompuServe

6. Prodigy Internet

These icons allow you to set up accounts with the following five services:

- *America Online*. America Online (AOL for short) is the most popular online service on the planet. It offers simple navigational tools, great services, and a friendly, hip social scene. If you want to chat with others, AOL is the place to go. However, its popularity is its major weakness, making it difficult to connect to the service at times.

- *CompuServe*. CompuServe is a more technical, business-oriented online service that's tough to navigate and offers limited chat support. If you're looking for business information, special-interest forums (bulletin boards), and Internet support, CompuServe is an excellent service. If you're a rank beginner, CompuServe isn't the best service to start with.

- *Prodigy Internet.* As its name states, Prodigy Internet is an Internet service, designed mainly for navigating the Web and sending and receiving email. Although Prodigy offers few exclusive features, it provides a fast Internet connection, excellent navigational tools, and a custom page that displays the current news headlines, weather report, stock updates, and much more.

- *AT&T WorldNet.* Like Prodigy, AT&T WorldNet is an Internet service that offers a few navigational tools for accessing specialized Internet resources. Unlike Prodigy, AT&T WorldNet provides few tools for navigating the Internet or making it more manageable.

- *The Microsoft Network.* The Microsoft Network (MSN for short) is an Internet service that's very similar to Prodigy Internet. With MSN, you use Internet Explorer to navigate the Web and Outlook Express for email. MSN is more closely integrated with the Windows desktop, allowing you to skip from one feature to another by using a context menu. It also offers some great tools for online chat.

Signing Up for a Service

To start an account with any of the commercial online services, you must first install the software. On the Windows desktop, click the Online Services folder and then click the icon for the desired service. (To install The Microsoft Network software, click Set Up The Microsoft Network icon on the Windows desktop.) Follow the onscreen instructions to install the software and sign up for the service.

The installation routine for America Online and Prodigy leads you through the process of signing up for the service. To sign up for CompuServe or The Microsoft Network, you must perform additional steps:

- *CompuServe.* Click the **Start** button, point to **Programs**, **Online Services**, **CompuServe**, and click **Sign Me Up**. Follow the onscreen instructions.

- *The Microsoft Network*. On the Windows desktop, click the Signup for a New MSN Account icon and then follow the onscreen instructions.

When you choose to start an account, the service uses the modem to dial a toll-free number that lists local numbers. By selecting a local number, you avoid long-distance charges. After you select a local number (and usually an alternate number, in case the first number is busy), the program disconnects from the toll-free connection and then reconnects you locally. Most services then ask you to supply the following information:

- Your modem settings. The installation routine for most online services can automatically detect the installed modem and enter the required settings. You may be asked to specify the speed of your modem.

- Any special dialing instructions, such as a number you must dial to connect to an outside line.

- Your name, address, and telephone number.

- A credit card number and expiration date. (Even if the service offers a free trial membership, you have to enter a credit card number.)

- The name (screen name) and password you want to use to log on to the service. (Write down the name and password you use, in case you forget it. Without this information, you will not be able to connect.)

- An acceptance of the terms of service (TOS) or rules you must follow to continue to use the service. If you break the rules, the service may terminate your account.

SEE ALSO
➤ *Learn how to select, install, and configure a modem, page 674*

Using America Online

When you install America Online, it adds icons for running itself all over your Windows desktop. You'll find an icon right on the desktop, in the Quick Launch toolbar, in the taskbar's system

Screen name/email address

Your screen name acts as your email address, which people using the same service can use to send you messages. People using other online services can send you messages by tacking on the service's *domain name* to the email address. (A domain name is the address of the service, sort of like your city, state, and ZIP code.) For example, if your screen name is blondiex123 and you use America Online, the sender would enter blondiex123@aol.com as your email address.

tray, and at the top of the **Start** menu. Click any of these icons to run America Online.

When America Online starts, it displays the Sign On dialog box (see Figure 15.2). Initially, the **Select Screen Name** drop-down list has only one name in it—the name you chose when you signed up for your account. (You can add screen names for other family members or other people with whom you share your PC.) Make sure your screen name is displayed and then click the **SIGN ON** button.

FIGURE 15.2

America Online asks for your name and password before dialing.

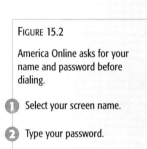

1 Select your screen name.

2 Type your password.

3 Click **SIGN ON**.

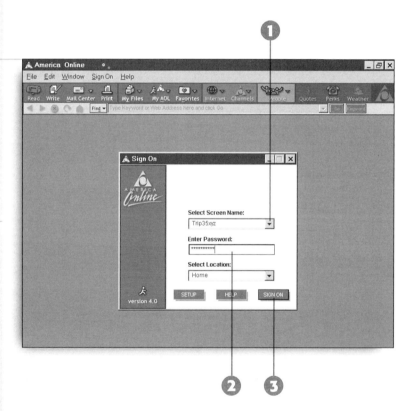

Navigating America Online

When you first connect to America Online, the service typically displays a series of advertisements. Just keep clicking **No Thanks** or **Cancel** to make the messages go away. You should finally come to a Welcome window that contains buttons or icons for the Mail Center (where you can check your email), the Internet, the People Connection (for chatting online), Channels (for popular content categories), What's New (new features of the service), and additional buttons for news and other features (see Figure 15.3).

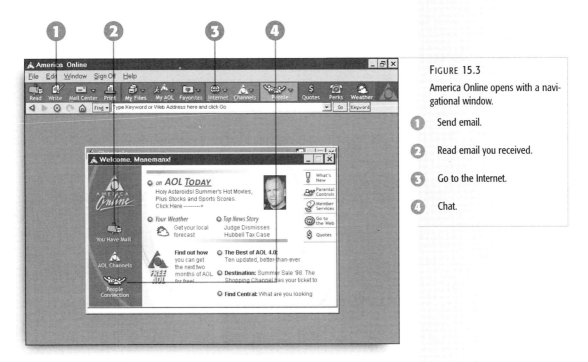

FIGURE 15.3

America Online opens with a navigational window.

1 Send email.

2 Read email you received.

3 Go to the Internet.

4 Chat.

Click the **AOL Channels** button. The Channels window appears. It acts as a kiosk, displaying buttons for various content categories, including News, Sports, Entertainment, and Games. Click a button for the area you want to explore. As you click buttons and other text and graphics, you may notice that whenever you position the mouse pointer over an object that takes you somewhere else, the mouse pointer appears as a hand. This indicates that the object under your mouse pointer is a *hyperlink* (an object that points to another resource). Keep clicking to follow the trail of links to the desired destination.

Menus and toolbars

Near the top of the AOL program window is a menu bar and two toolbars to help you navigate the service. The toolbar just below the menu bar contains buttons for AOL's most popular services. The toolbar below it is mainly for navigating Web pages (on the Internet).

Navigating with Keywords

In addition to allowing you to follow a trail of links to a specific area of interest, America Online provides a keyword feature that gives you a direct flight to your destination. Click the **Keyword** button on the toolbar or press Ctrl+K, type the name of your destination (for example, Newsweek), and click **Go**. If you don't know the keyword for the desired feature, press Ctrl+F to display the Find Central window.

Sending and Reading Email

With email, you can send messages to anyone in the world who has an email account. You address the message, type a description of it, type the message, and send it. You can even attach graphics files and other file types to your messages.

To address a message to another AOL member, just type the person's screen name. To address a message to a person who uses a different online or Internet service, you must type the person's username followed by the @ sign and the *domain name* of the person's online or Internet service. For example, if the person's username is `jimtyler` and the person uses Prodigy, the email address would be `jimtyler@prodigy.com`. The domain name is the service's Internet address.

Sending an email message

1. Start AOL and click the **Write** button.

2. In the **Send To** text box, type the email address of the person to whom you want to send the message.

3. Click in the **Subject** text box and type a brief description of your message.

4. In the message area, type your message. You can use the buttons above the message area to format your text, insert a picture, or add a link (see Figure 15.4).

5. To send a file along with your message, click the **Attachments** button to display the Attachments dialog box. Otherwise, skip to step 9.

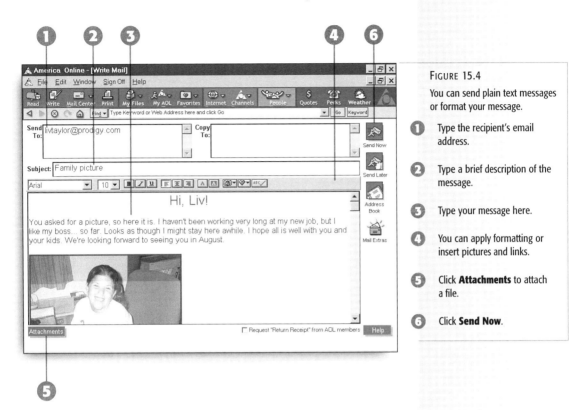

America Online - [Write Mail]

File   Edit   Window   Sign Off   Help

Read Write Mail Center Print My Files My AOL Favorites Internet Channels People Quotes Perks Weather

Type Keyword or Web Address here and click Go   Go Keyword

Send To: livtaylor@prodigy.com   Copy To: Send Now

Subject: Family picture   Send Later

Arial   10   Address Book

Hi, Liv!

You asked for a picture, so here it is. I haven't been working very long at my new job, but I like my boss... so far. Looks as though I might stay here awhile. I hope all is well with you and your kids. We're looking forward to seeing you in August.   Mail Extras

Attachments   Request "Return Receipt" from AOL members   Help

FIGURE 15.4

You can send plain text messages or format your message.

1 Type the recipient's email address.

2 Type a brief description of the message.

3 Type your message here.

4 You can apply formatting or insert pictures and links.

5 Click **Attachments** to attach a file.

6 Click **Send Now**.

6. Click the **Attach** button to display the Attach dialog box.

7. Change to the disk and folder that contains the file you want to send and click **Open**.

8. Repeat steps 6 and 7 to attach additional files and then click **OK**.

9. Click the **Send Now** button. In a matter of seconds, the message appears in your friend's mailbox.

Whenever someone sends you an email message, it is stored in your electronic mailbox on the service's computer. When you sign on, AOL plays a voice recording saying, "You've Got Mail," and activates the **Read** button in the toolbar. To display a list of messages you've received, click the **Read** button. Double-click the description of the message you want to read. The message appears in its own window. To reply to the message, click the **Reply** button (see Figure 15.5).

Formatting email messages

If the recipient uses an email program that supports only plain text messages, any formatting you apply to your message may be lost making the message unreadable.

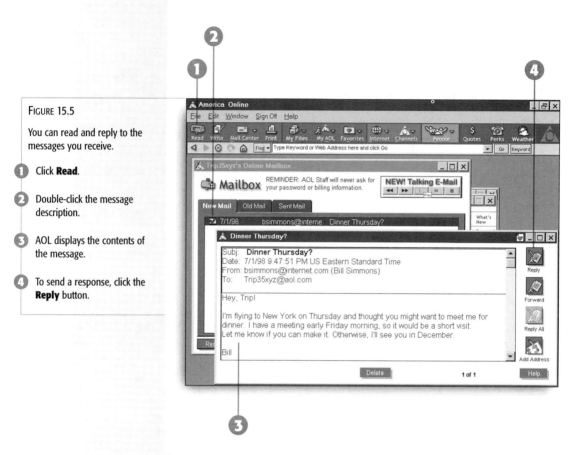

FIGURE 15.5

You can read and reply to the messages you receive.

1 Click **Read**.

2 Double-click the message description.

3 AOL displays the contents of the message.

4 To send a response, click the **Reply** button.

SEE ALSO

> *Learn more about sending and receiving email messages, page 435*

Chatting

If you don't like waiting for mail, you can converse with your friends, colleagues, and complete strangers in one of the many chat rooms on AOL. You pick a room in which up to 23 people are hanging out and then start typing and sending messages. Your messages appear on the screens of the other people in the room, and their messages appear on your screen. If you prefer to talk in private with one or more other users, you can create your own private room and invite other users to join you.

To chat on AOL, click the **People** button and click **Find a Chat**. In the **Categories** list (on the left) click the desired chat category. In the **Featured Chats** list, double-click the desired chat room. (If the room is full, AOL displays a dialog box offering to take you to a room like the one you selected.) AOL places you in the selected chat room and displays a chat window consisting of the following three areas (see Figure 15.6):

- *Ongoing discussion*. As you and others type and send messages, all the messages appear in this area. If the chat room has a talkative crowd, the messages scroll pretty quickly, so you need to stay on your toes.

- *List of chatters*. In this list, you see the screen names of everyone in the chat room. Double-click a member's name to display a dialog box with options for checking the person's profile (information the person entered about herself) or for sending the person an IM (instant message). An instant message pops up only on the screen of the person to whom you sent the message, so nobody else in the chat room can see it.

- *Message area*. Below the ongoing discussion is a text box into which you type your messages. Click in the text box, type your message, and click the **Send** button or press Enter. Your message pops up in your chat window and in the chat window of each person in the room.

Connecting to the Internet

Although AOL serves up a healthy selection of services and activities, you'll find much more on the Internet. AOL provides links to the Web (for pulling up multimedia pages) and newsgroups (electronic bulletin boards). To connect to the Web or newsgroups, click the **Internet** button on AOL's toolbar, and click the desired option:

- **Go to the Web** runs Internet Explorer, which opens and displays your home page (the starting Web page). You can click icons and highlighted text, called *links*, to skip from page to page. To open a specific page when you know its address, click in the **Address** text box, type the address, and press Enter (see Figure 15.7).

AOL's Instant Messenger

You can create a buddy list in AOL to have the service notify you when a friend is online. You can then send the person a private message and carry on a live conversation. If your friend is not an AOL member, have him download AOL Instant Messenger from AOL's Web page at www.aol.com.

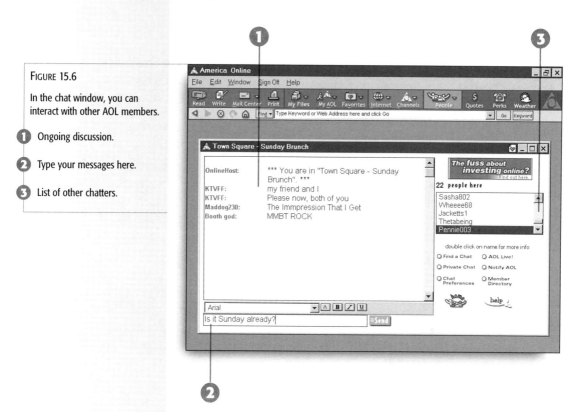

FIGURE 15.6

In the chat window, you can interact with other AOL members.

❶ Ongoing discussion.

❷ Type your messages here.

❸ List of other chatters.

- **AOL Netfind** runs Internet Explorer and opens AOL's Internet search page, a form you can fill out to search for specific information and sites on the Web.

- **Newsgroups** displays a window with options for learning more about newsgroups, displaying a list of newsgroups, adding a newsgroup to your list of favorite newsgroups, and searching for newsgroups.

- **FTP (File Transfer)** allows you to copy a file from or to an Internet site.

- **Internet White Pages** displays an online telephone directory you can search for a person's address and phone number.

- **Internet Yellow Pages** displays an online telephone business directory you can use to find companies that offer products or services you need.

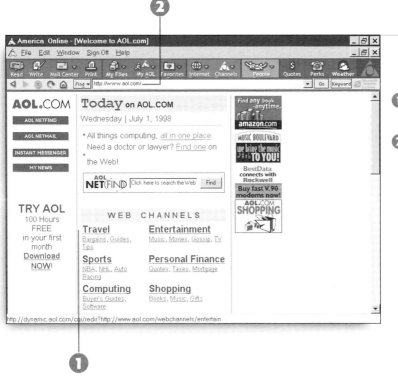

FIGURE 15.7

AOL uses Internet Explorer to open Web pages.

① Click a link to skip to a different page.

② To open a specific page, type its address and press Enter.

SEE ALSO

Getting help on AOL

For additional information on how to navigate AOL and use its many features, open the **Help** menu and click the desired type of help. You can get help offline through a standard help system or online from other members or from AOL technical support personnel.

Using CompuServe

When you install CompuServe, it does not add an icon to the Windows desktop as AOL does. You have to dig through a long series of menus to find it: Click the **Start** menu, point to **Programs**, **Online Services**, **CompuServe**, and click **CompuServe**. If, during the installation, you chose to have CompuServe save your password, CompuServe automatically dials into the service and establishes a connection. If you chose not to have your username and password saved, open the **Access** menu and click **Connect** (or press Ctrl+K). The Required Connection Information dialog box prompts you to type your password. Type your password and click **OK**.

After CompuServe establishes the connection, it displays the Home Desktop (see Figure 15.8) or CompuServe's home page on the Web. (If the Web page appears, click the **Main Menu** button just above the page to display the Home Desktop.) CompuServe uses several desktops as navigational kiosks. When you select a CompuServe feature, such as Chat, the desktop for the selected feature appears. After you've displayed two or more desktops, you can switch from one to another by selecting the desired desktop from the **Window** menu.

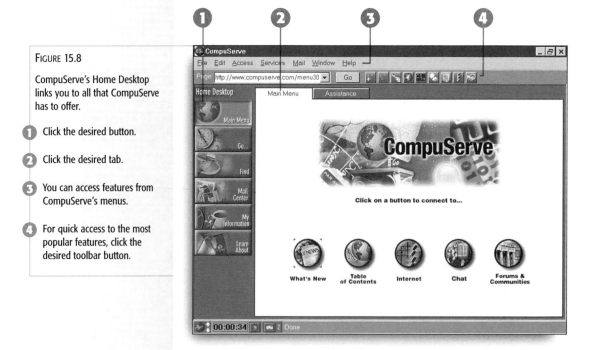

FIGURE 15.8

CompuServe's Home Desktop links you to all that CompuServe has to offer.

1 Click the desired button.

2 Click the desired tab.

3 You can access features from CompuServe's menus.

4 For quick access to the most popular features, click the desired toolbar button.

Use the following six buttons on CompuServe's Home Desktop to navigate the service:

- **Main Menu.** Displays two tabs—**Main Menu** and **Assistance.** The **Main Menu** tab allows you to view news stories, open the CompuServe table of contents (Web page), access the Internet, enter a chat room, and connect to CompuServe forums (online bulletin boards). The **Assistance** tab helps you find answers to your questions.

- **Go.** Displays three tabs—**Go** (to quickly return to a feature you recently viewed), **Favorite Places** (to return to a feature you marked as a favorite place), and **Parental Controls** (to block access to certain features and Internet content).

- **Find.** Displays three tabs—**Services** (to find a CompuServe feature), **Files** (to find a specific file), and **Members** (to locate contact information for another CompuServe member).

- **Mail Center.** Displays four tabs—**Read** (to display email messages you received), **Create** (to send email messages), **Address Book** (to create a list of people you frequently write to), and **Search** (to find messages in your mailbox).

- **My Information.** Displays two tabs—**Filing Cabinet** (listing messages you chose to save) and **To-Do List** (for performing tasks, such as sending messages, that you chose to postpone).

- **Learn About.** Allows you to access CompuServe help for topics including mail, the Internet, and navigating CompuServe.

You can access many of the same features by selecting the desired feature from one of CompuServe's menus (at the top of the screen) or by clicking a button just below the menu bar.

Sending and Reading Email

If you know a person's email address, sending the person a message using any email program is easy. You type the person's address, type a brief message description, type the message, and click the **Send** button.

Extra charges

CompuServe charges extra for many of its best features, so be sure to check for any additional costs before using a service. CompuServe displays a dollar sign next to the names of services that cost extra.

To send an email message to another CompuServe member, type the member's name and CompuServe ID number. To send a message to a person who uses a different commercial service, type the address in the following format:

INTERNET:*username@domain.com*

The address must start with INTERNET:, followed by the person's username, the @ sign, and the domain name of the server. If someone is writing to you, he must address the email message using your user ID number but replace the comma with a period. For example, if your user ID number is 123456,7890, the person needs to address the message to 123456.7890@ compuserve.com.

Sending an email message

1. On the **Main Menu**, click the **Mail Center** button.
2. Click the **Create** tab.
3. Click the **New** button.
4. In the **Name** text box, type the person's real name.
5. Click in the **Address** text box and type the person's email address.
6. Click in the **Subject** text box and type a brief description of the message.
7. Click in the message area and type your message.
8. To attach a file to your message, click the **Attach File** button, select the desired file, and click the **Open** button.
9. Click the **Send** button.

Chatting

Composing messages offline

Most online services give you a set amount of connect time for a monthly fee. To reduce the amount of time you use the service, compose messages offline (when you're not connected) and choose the option for sending the messages later. You can then connect, send all messages, and immediately disconnect.

CompuServe's chat feature isn't the best. You won't have access to chat rooms (called *CB channels*) for at least a day after you sign up for the service, because CompuServe must first verify your account information. After you do gain access, you'll have to take steps to activate parental controls, even if you don't have kids who use the service. When you finally gain access, finding a chat room that interests you and has some people in it is tough.

Chatting on CompuServe

1. On the Home Desktop, click the **Main Menu** button and click the **Main Menu** tab.

2. Click the **Chat** button. The Chat window appears, displaying links to information about CompuServe chat and buttons for accessing chat rooms and learning about special chat events and conferences.

3. Click the **General Chat** button and skip to step 5 or click the **Adult Chat** button and move on to step 4.

4. If you clicked **Adult Chat**, double-click the option for the desired type of adult chat: **Adult Key Chat** (clean and polite), **Casual Adult Chat** (clean and fast), or **Intimate Adult Chat** (a little more risqué).

5. When prompted to type a nickname, type a name you want to use to identify yourself in the chat room and click **OK**.

6. Click the **Chat** button. CompuServe displays a list of available chat rooms.

7. Double-click the name of the desired chat room. A chat window appears, displaying the ongoing discussion (see Figure 15.9).

8. To "say" something, type your message in the text area near the bottom of the window and click **Send** or press Enter.

9. To view the names of the people currently in this chat room, click the **Who's Here** button near the top of the window.

10. In the Who's Here window, you can check a member's profile, invite the person to chat privately, invite a group of people to chat privately, or add the person's name to the Friends list.

11. To leave the chat room, click the window's Close (**x**) button.

12. To leave the chat feature entirely, click the **Leave Chat** button.

SEE ALSO

➤ *Learn how to chat on the Web, page 494*

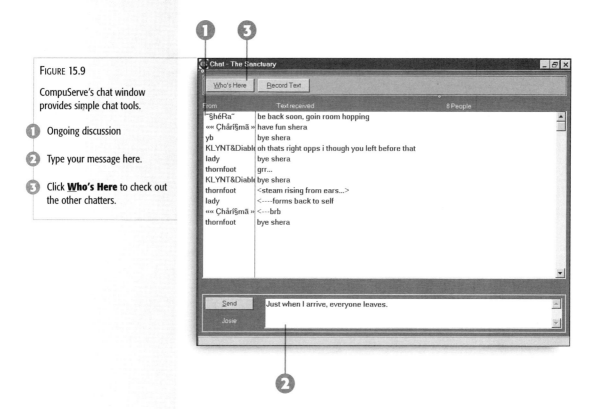

FIGURE 15.9

CompuServe's chat window provides simple chat tools.

1 Ongoing discussion

2 Type your message here.

3 Click **Who's Here** to check out the other chatters.

Connecting to the Internet

Although CompuServe's chat support is substandard, and the navigational tools for its members-only services are not very user-friendly, CompuServe's Internet support is excellent. CompuServe provides all the tools you need to access the Web, perform FTP file transfers, connect to newsgroups, and use other Internet features.

To connect to the Internet, take one of the following steps:

- On the Home Desktop, click the **Main Menu** button, click the **Main Menu** tab, and click the **Internet** button.

- Open the **Services** menu and click **Internet**.

- To open a Web page you recently visited, on the Home Desktop, click the **Go** button, click the **Go** tab, click the name of the desired page, and click the **Go** button again.

If you used one of the first two options, the Browser Desktop appears. Click the button for the desired Internet feature and then follow the trail of menus and links to the desired feature. To skip out to the Web, click the **Access the Web** button and click **OK** when prompted to type a Web page address. CompuServe's home page appears, as shown in Figure 15.10. To open a specific Web page, type its address in the **Page** text box near the top of the window and press Enter. You can use the **Page** arrow buttons below the text box to flip back and forth through pages you've already opened.

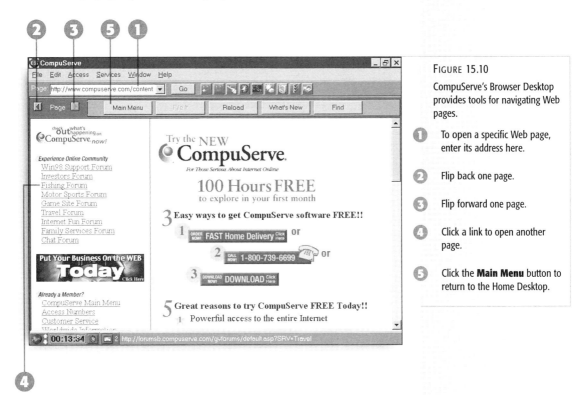

FIGURE 15.10

CompuServe's Browser Desktop provides tools for navigating Web pages.

1 To open a specific Web page, enter its address here.

2 Flip back one page.

3 Flip forward one page.

4 Click a link to open another page.

5 Click the **Main Menu** button to return to the Home Desktop.

Using Prodigy Internet

In the past, Prodigy struggled to make it as a standard online service. Its homely interface and second-rate services were no competition for a slick online service, such as America Online. However, Prodigy has reinvented itself as Prodigy Internet, replacing its clunky interface with a clean Web page and integrating itself with Internet Explorer.

When you start Prodigy (by clicking the Prodigy icon on the Windows desktop), Internet Explorer runs and loads the Welcome to Prodigy page. You can click a link to follow an online tutorial on how to use Prodigy Internet or click the **I'm Ready to Go** link to open your personal home page. (You can return to your personal home page at any time by clicking the **Home** button in Internet Explorer's toolbar.)

Your personal home page is your starting point (see Figure 15.11). Here, you'll find Prodigy tools and links for accessing other Prodigy and Internet features:

- **Shortcuts.** To quickly jump to an area or topic that interests you, open the **Shortcuts** drop-down list, click the desired item, and click the **Go** button.

- **Personal Access Center.** Provides options for checking email, customizing your personal Web page, and accessing Prodigy Internet services, such as chat and message boards.

- **Excite Search & Channels.** Here you'll find a list of links to popular categories, including News and Entertainment. To browse the Web, click a category and then follow the trail of links to display pages related to the category. You can also search for pages; click in the **Search** text box, type a brief description of the topic, and click the **Search** button.

- **Today at Prodigy Internet.** To keep you informed of updates at Prodigy Internet, Prodigy displays a list of links you can click to read about current events and updates. Prodigy changes the Topics List daily.

- **My News.** Throughout the day, Prodigy displays a list of news headlines from UPI and Reuters news services. Click a headline to display the entire story.

- **My Stocks.** This area initially displays information about the major stock indices, including Dow, Nasdaq, and S&P 500. You can create your own investment portfolio to display the ever-changing value of your investments throughout the day.

- **My Community.** This area contains links for accessing the tools you need to communicate with other people online. From this area, you can access chat and message boards, send personal messages to your friends, and check out people's Web pages.

- **My Sports.** Displays up-to-the-minute sports scores, allowing you to keep track of how your favorite teams are doing.

- **My Reminders.** This nifty feature helps you set up your Web page as a personal information manager to help remind you of important dates. Initially, the area displays only upcoming holidays, but you can click the **Change** button to add important dates to the reminders list.

- **My Horoscope.** To view your daily horoscope, just enter your birthday.

- **Tools for Living.** Here, you'll find links for all the personal reference material you need to survive on a daily basis: telephone directories, maps, driving directions, online shopping centers, and much more.

- **Featured Services.** If you're looking for deals, check out this area. You'll find special deals for airline flights, car rentals, computer hardware, and other products and services, in addition to online sweepstakes and contests.

- **My TV Listings.** If you misplaced your TV Guide, you can get the TV listings for your area. Just enter your ZIP code and specify the date and time.

SEE ALSO
➤ *Learn how to navigate the Web with Internet Explorer, page 412*
➤ *Learn how to watch TV on your PC, page 691*

Sending and Reading Email

Because Prodigy uses the Windows Internet tools, you use Outlook Express to send and receive email. To read any messages you've received, click the **Get Mail** link on your personal Web page. This runs Outlook Express, which downloads any messages from your Prodigy email account. For details about using Outlook Express to receive and send email messages on the Internet, see Chapter 18, "Sending and Receiving Email Messages."

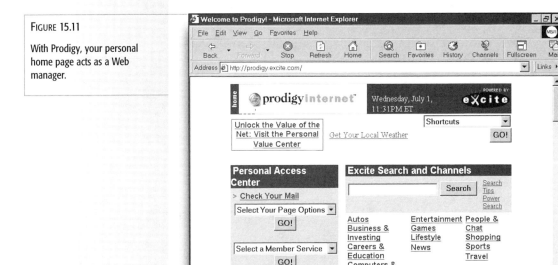

Your email address consists of your username followed by the @ sign, followed by "prodigy.com." For example, if your username were skippybowman, your Prodigy email address would be skippybowman@prodigy.com. Because Prodigy uses an Internet mail program, you address messages to Prodigy members and non-members using the same format: *username@domain.name*.

SEE ALSO

➤ *Learn how to use Outlook Express to send and receive email messages, page 435*

Chatting

Unlike AOL and CompuServe, whose chat rooms are populated mainly with their members, Prodigy uses Web chat tools that any Internet user can access. This gives you a wider selection of chat rooms with a more diverse population. The chat tools run right inside the Internet Explorer window and provide you with the controls you need to view the ongoing discussion, send messages, check out other chatters, and send private messages to individuals.

To enter a chat room, return to your personal home page and click the **People & Chat** link. Follow the trail of links to select the desired chat room. When prompted, enter the name you want to use to identify yourself in the chat room and click the **Chat Now** button.

When you first enter a room, a large gray box appears displaying a message indicating that the chat tool is loading. In a few moments, the chat window appears, as shown in Figure 15.12, and you can start chatting.

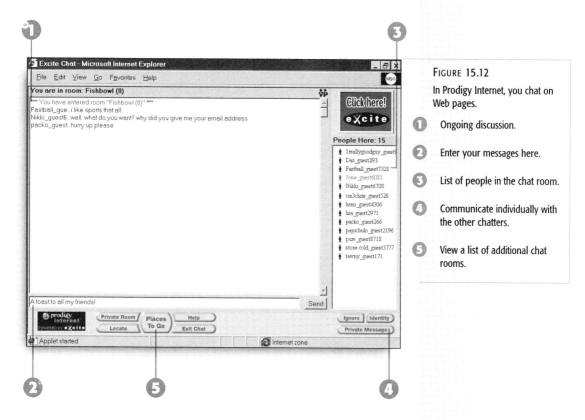

FIGURE 15.12

In Prodigy Internet, you chat on Web pages.

1. Ongoing discussion.

2. Enter your messages here.

3. List of people in the chat room.

4. Communicate individually with the other chatters.

5. View a list of additional chat rooms.

SEE ALSO

➤ *Learn other ways to chat on the Internet, page 501*

Connecting to the Internet

You don't need to connect to the Internet from Prodigy, because Prodigy is an Internet service—the Prodigy service is designed not as an alternative to the Internet but as a management tool for the Internet. As such, it provides the tools you need to successfully navigate the Internet and put it to work for you.

Using The Microsoft Network

Microsoft's entry into the online services market is The Microsoft Network (MSN), an Internet service that is more closely integrated with the Windows desktop. To connect to MSN, take one of the following steps:

- Click The Microsoft Network icon on the Windows desktop. When prompted, type your name and password.

- Click The Microsoft Network icon in the system tray and click **Connect to MSN** or use the context menu to choose a specific MSN feature. You can use this menu after you connect to quickly skip around MSN and explore its many features.

The first time you choose to connect, MSN prompts you to type your name and password and choose a local number to dial. Enter the username and password you chose when you signed up for the account. Click the **Settings** button and then click the **Phone Book** button and use the Phone Book dialog box to choose a local phone number. Save your settings. When you return to the MSN-Sign In dialog box, you can choose to have MSN remember your password and dial automatically when you choose to connect. Click the **Connect** button to establish the connection.

MSN runs Internet Explorer and leads you through a lengthy sign-on procedure. Follow the onscreen instructions to enter your preferences for using the service. Eventually, MSN displays a custom home page that you can use to check email, navigate the Web, and access special MSN services (see Figure 15.13). This page consists of five sections:

- **Email**. Notifies you if you have received any email messages. MSN automatically sends you one message to give you some practice. Click the **You have 1 new message** link to run Outlook Express and display your messages.

- **Search**. Allows you to search the Internet for specific information. Open the **Select Provider** drop-down list and click the search tool you want to use. In the **Enter Query** text box, type your search phrase and click **go!**. This displays a list of links you can click to open pages that contain relevant information.

- **Web Directory**. Displays a list of popular categories. To browse Web pages in a particular category, click the category and follow the trail of links to the desired page.

- **Microsoft Network Sites**. This drop-down list allows you to access MSN content available only for MSN members. Here, you will find links to premium content, including MSNBC News, Microsoft Investor, and Slate Magazine online.

- **MSN Update**. Displays links for checking out what's new on the MSN service. This list changes daily to keep you up on the latest developments at MSN.

Sending and Reading Email

MSN uses Outlook Express to send and receive email. You can run Outlook Express from MSN by clicking the **Mail** button in Internet Explorer's toolbar or by clicking the email notification link on your personal home page. For details about using Outlook Express to receive and send email messages on the Internet, see Chapter 18.

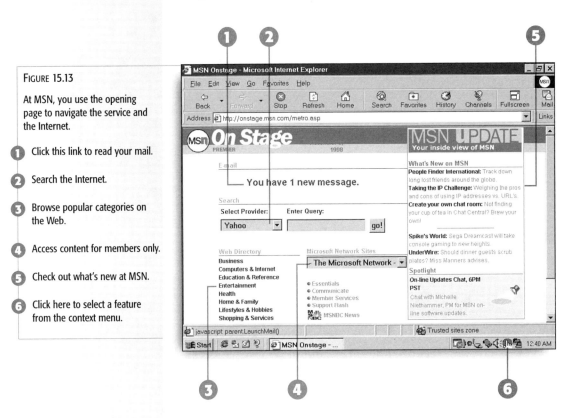

FIGURE 15.13

At MSN, you use the opening page to navigate the service and the Internet.

1 Click this link to read your mail.

2 Search the Internet.

3 Browse popular categories on the Web.

4 Access content for members only.

5 Check out what's new at MSN.

6 Click here to select a feature from the context menu.

MSN also offers a great communications feature, called Friends Online, which allows you to create a list of your MSN buddies and have MSN notify you when a friend of yours is online. You can then select the person's name from the list and send the person a message, invite the person to a chat room, or call the person with NetMeeting (an Internet Phone program included with Windows). Because Friends Online works only for MSN members, it isn't quite as cool as AOL's Instant Messenger.

To set up this feature, click The Microsoft Network icon in the system tray and click **Set Up Friends Online**. Click the **Add Friends** link, fill out the form shown in Figure 15.14, and click **Search**. To view a list of any friends who are online, click The Microsoft Network icon in the system tray.

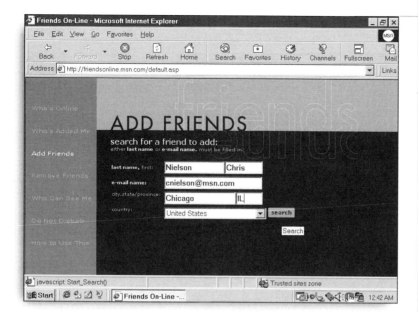

FIGURE 15.14

You can create a list of friends on MSN and have the service notify you when they're available.

Chatting

Like Prodigy, MSN allows you to chat directly on Web pages, and it doesn't make you select a chat room first. To start chatting right away, click The Microsoft Network icon in the system tray, point to **Communicate**, and click **Chat Central**. MSN immediately takes you to the chat lobby, where you'll find a room packed with talkative chatters.

The opening chat window is fairly basic, displaying the ongoing discussion, a list of people in the chat room, and a place for you to type your messages. You can't check a person's profile or use any other advanced chat features.

To use the more advanced features, click the **Browse Chats** button near the bottom of the chat page, click a chat category, and click the desired room name. MSN runs Microsoft Chat, which displays the ongoing discussion as a comic strip (see Figure 15.15). With Microsoft Chat, you can pick a comic strip character for yourself, check information about other people in the room, send private messages to other chatters, and much more. See Chapter 21, "Real-Time Chatting with Other People," for details on how to use a specialized chat program.

FIGURE 15.15

Microsoft Chat displays the ongoing discussion as a comic strip.

❶ Ongoing conversation

❷ Type your message here and press Enter.

❸ Right-click a person's name to view a context menu for the person.

❹ Change your character's expression.

Connecting to the Internet

Like Prodigy, MSN is an Internet service, so you don't need to select a special option to access the Internet from MSN. After you're connected, you're on the Web. To navigate, use Internet Explorer's navigational tools, as explained in Chapter 17, "Exploring the World Wide Web."

MSN Help

For additional information on how to use MSN, get help online. Click The Microsoft Network icon in the system tray, point to **Member Services**, and click **Help & Support**.

Setting Up Your Internet Connection

Find a reliable, affordable Internet service provider

Obtain the information you need to set up your Internet account

Use the Internet Connection Wizard to enter Internet settings

Establish your Internet connection

Troubleshoot your connection when it's not working

Getting Started

To access the Web, email, newsgroups, or other Internet services, you must first establish a connection between your computer and the Internet. You can connect by using a commercial online service, as explained in the previous chapter, or by using a local Internet service provider (ISP). For a monthly fee, the ISP provides you with a phone number to dial into and connect with the ISP's network, which is wired to the Internet.

The ISP's network acts as the *server*, processing your PC's requests for data and serving up the requested data from the Internet. Once you've established a connection with an ISP, you can run Internet programs, called *client software*, on your PC to access various Internet features, such as the Web, email, newsgroups, FTP file transfers, and chat.

To connect to and use the Internet, your PC must be properly equipped:

- *28.8Kbps or faster modem*. Web pages contain graphics, video clips, and other media objects that take a long time to travel through the phone lines. You should have a modem that can receive data at least at a rate of 28.8Kbps. If you need only email, you can get by with a slower modem.

- *SVGA monitor*. Graphics and video clips look fuzzy on anything less than an SVGA monitor.

- *Speaker and sound card*. If you want to listen to recordings or music clips on the Internet, you need a sound card and speakers.

- *TCP/IP program*. This program dials into your Internet service provider's computer using your modem and establishes the basic connection. Fortunately, Windows comes with its own TCP/IP program—Dial-Up Networking, which you'll learn how to set up later in this chapter.

- *Internet client software*. Client software allows you to access specific Internet features, including the Web, email, and newsgroups. You should have a copy of the latest version of

Internet Explorer or Netscape Communicator, which both include a Web browser, email and newsgroup support, videoconferencing software, and a Web page editor.

SEE ALSO

➤ *Learn how to buy and install a modem, page 673*

➤ *Learn how to add audio features to your PC, page 769*

Finding an Internet Service Provider

After your PC is properly equipped to handle the Internet, your next job is to find an ISP that provides a reliable, affordable local connection. Expect to pay about $20 to $25 per month for near-ly unlimited access using a standard 28.8K to 56K modem (more for ISDN, satellite, or cable modem service). You should also look for an ISP that you can connect to without dialing a long-distance number and that has a good reputation for getting users connected during the busiest times. The following list describes various resources you can use to find a reliable ISP:

- *Commercial service*. As you learned in the previous chapter, commercial online services all offer Internet support. You'll find the best Internet support through Prodigy and MSN.

- *Phone company*. Many phone companies double as ISPs. Get your latest phone bill and call customer service to determine if they offer Internet service.

- *Internet referral service*. Run the Internet Connection Wizard, as explained later in this chapter and have it recom-mend an ISP. This approach has an added advantage—after you select an ISP, the Internet Connection Wizard sets up your account automatically.

- *Phone book*. Flip through the Yellow Pages and check for ISPs under Internet or Computers.

- *Computer store*. Most computer retailers can recommend an ISP that their customers use.

- *The Internet*. If you already have an account with a commer-cial online service and want to change over to an ISP, use

Reliability is everything

When you're looking for an ISP, reliability and support should be at the top of the list. A popular ISP isn't always the best, because it may not have the equipment required to support its popularity. Changing ISPs later is a drag—you must change your email address and then notify all your contacts of the change and possibly reprint your business cards.

Living in the boonies?

If you live in the country, finding an ISP that you can connect to by dialing a local number is nearly impossible. However, some larger services, such as Sprint, offer 1-800 numbers you can use. Expect to pay about $5 per hour in addition to the $20 to $25 monthly service charge.

the commercial online service's Internet feature to search the Web for ISPs. Try `www.ispfinder.com` or `www.isps.com` to search for ISPs by area code.

When you contact an ISP for more information, ask the following questions:

- What's the monthly fee, and how many hours of connect time does the fee cover?
- If you're connected beyond the allotted time, how much extra is charged per hour?
- Is there a setup or activation fee?
- What connection types are available? 56K, ISDN?
- How much storage space do you get for your own Web pages?
- What are their billing options?
- Can you save money by paying several months in advance?
- What's the modem-to-user ratio? The ratio of 7 users to 1 modem is considered acceptable, but the lower the better. If the ratio is 10 users to 1 modem, you'll frequently receive busy signals when you try to connect.
- What are the technical support hours of operation and how accessible is technical support? When you're setting up your connection, you may need to work one-on-one with a technical support person. After your connection is up and running, you shouldn't need much additional help.
- If you think you might want to publish advanced Web pages, ask if the ISP supports FrontPage extensions, such as hit counters (that indicate how many people viewed your page) and automated email forms (to make it easy for people to send you email messages). Although this may not be important when you're first starting out, it can pose limitations later.

Information You Need

To set up your account, you will need information and settings that tell your computer how to connect to the service provider's computer. Obtain the following information from your ISP:

- *Username*. This is the name that identifies you to the ISP's computer. It is typically an abbreviation of your first and last name. For example, Sally Krieger might use salkrieger as her username. You can choose any name you like, as long as another user is not already using it.

- *Password*. The ISP may allow you to select your own password or assign you a password. Be sure to write down the password in case you forget it. Without the right password, you will not be able to connect to the service provider's computer.

- *Connection Type*. Most ISPs offer PPP (Point-to-Point Protocol), but you might encounter a service provider who uses the older SLIP (Serial Line Internet Protocol). Point-to-Point Protocol is easier to set up and provides faster data transfer. If given a choice, choose PPP.

- *Domain Name Server*. The *domain name server* locates computers on the Internet. Each computer on the Internet has a unique number that identifies it, such as 197.72.34.74. Each computer also has a domain name, such as www.whitehouse.gov, which makes it easier for people to remember the computer's address. When you enter a domain name, the domain name server looks up the computer's number and locates it.

- *Domain Name*. This is the domain name of your service provider's computer (for example, internet.com). You will use the domain name in conjunction with your username as your email address (for example, salkrieger@internet.com).

- *News Server*. The news server allows you to connect to any of thousands of newsgroups on the Internet to read and post messages. Newsgroups are electronic bulletin boards for special interest groups. The news server name typically starts with "news" and is followed by the service provider's domain name (for example, news.internet.com).

- *Mail Server*. The mail server is in charge of electronic mail. You need to specify two mail servers: POP (Post Office Protocol) for incoming mail, and SMTP (Simplified Mail Transfer Protocol) for mail you send. The POP server's

Tech support

When you're obtaining information from the ISP, get the technical support department's phone number and hours of operation. If you encounter problems, you may need to call for help.

name typically starts with "pop" followed by the service provider's domain name (for example, `pop.internet.com`). The SMTP server's name typically starts with "smtp" or "mail" followed by the service provider's domain name (for example, `smtp.internet.com`).

- *Email Address.* If you plan on receiving email messages, you need an email address. Your address typically begins with your username followed by an at sign (@) and the domain name of your service provider (for example, `salkrieger@internet.com`).

Running the Internet Connection Wizard

Windows' Internet Connection Wizard (ICW) leads you step-by-step through the process of finding an ISP (if you haven't yet found one) or entering the settings for connecting to your ISP. ICW displays a series of dialog boxes prompting you to enter each piece of information. ICW then creates a Dial-Up Networking icon you can click to establish your connection.

Locating and setting up an ISP connection

1. On the Windows desktop, click the **Connect to the Internet** shortcut, or click the **Start** button, point to **Programs** and then **Internet Explorer**, and click **Connection Wizard**.

2. Click **I Want to Sign Up and Configure My Computer for a New Internet Account**.

3. Click **Next**.

4. Exit any programs that are currently running and click **Next**. ICW dials a toll-free number to connect you to Microsoft's Internet Referral Server and downloads a list of local Internet service providers (see Figure 16.1).

5. Click the name of the service provider you want to use and click **Next**.

6. Follow the onscreen instructions, which vary from one provider to another, and enter the requested information.

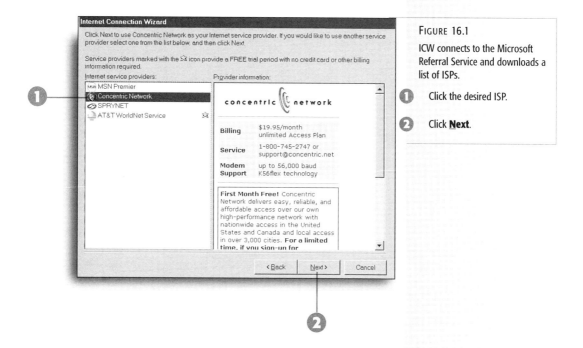

FIGURE 16.1

ICW connects to the Microsoft Referral Service and downloads a list of ISPs.

1 Click the desired ISP.

2 Click **Next**.

Entering settings for an existing account

1. On the Windows desktop, click the **Connect to the Internet** shortcut, or click the **Start** button, point to **Programs** and then **Internet Explorer**, and click **Connection Wizard**.

2. Click **I Have an Existing Internet Account...** and click **Next**. ICW now prompts you to specify the type of connection you want to set up.

3. Click **Select This Option If You Are Accessing the Internet Using an Internet Service Provider...**. Click **Next**. You are now prompted to set up a new account.

4. If you are using a modem to connect, click **Connect Using My Phone Line**. If you are using a network connection, click **Connect Using My Local Area Network (LAN)**. Click **Next**.

5. Click **Create a New Dial-Up Connection** and click **Next**.

6. If you are connecting via modem, in the **Telephone Number** text box, type the phone number for connecting to the ISP. Click **Next**. ICW prompts you to enter your username and password.

7. Type your username in the **User Name** text box and then click in the **Password** text box and type your password. Click **Next**. You are now asked if you want to change the advanced settings.

8. Click **Yes**, so you can check the settings before you continue. Click **Next**. ICW asks you to specify the type of connection: SLIP (Serial Line Internet Protocol) or PPP (Point-to-Point Protocol).

9. Choose the connection type specified by your service provider. If you're unsure, click **PPP (Point to Point Protocol)**. Click **Next**. You are now asked to specify the type of logon procedure.

10. Most service providers allow Windows Dial-Up Networking to enter your name and password for you, so leave **I Don't Need to Type Anything When Logging On** selected. If your service provider requires you to log on manually or use a special logon script (usually supplied by the service provider), select the desired option. Click **Next**. ICW prompts you to enter your IP (Internet Protocol) address. This address, which most ISPs assign automatically when you log on, identifies your computer on the Internet.

11. If your ISP assigns you an IP address when you log on (or if you're unsure), leave **My Internet Service Provider Automatically Assigns Me One** selected. If your ISP assigned you a permanent address, select **Always use the following** and type your address in the **IP Address** text box. Click **Next**.

12. If your service provider specified a DNS address, choose **Always use the following** and enter the DNS address in the **DNS server** text box (see Figure 16.2). Click **Next**. You are now prompted to enter a name for the connection.

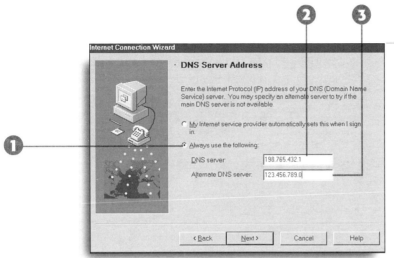

FIGURE 16.2
If your ISP provides a DNS
server address, you must enter it.

1 Choose **Always use the
following**.

2 Type the DNS server's address.

3 If your ISP has a second DNS
server, enter its address here.

13. Type a descriptive name for your ISP and click **Next**. ICW
asks if you want to set up your email account.

14. Click **Yes**, click **Next**, and follow the onscreen instructions
to set up email. ICW asks if you want to set up your news
server account.

15. Click **Yes**, click **Next,** and follow the onscreen instructions
to set up a connection to the news server. ICW asks if you
want to set up your directory service account.

16. Leave **No** selected and click **Next**. (You can set up a directory service later, if needed.) The Complete Configuration
dialog box informs you that you have entered all the
required information.

17. Click **Finish**.

SEE ALSO
➤ *Learn how to set up an email account, page 436*
➤ *Learn how to set up a news server account, page 456*
➤ *Learn how to use a directory service to find people on the Internet, page 451*

Connecting to the Internet

ICW creates an icon for your ISP and places it in the Dial-Up Networking folder. To connect to your ISP, open My Computer, click the Dial-Up Networking icon, and click the icon for your ISP. The Connect To dialog box appears (see Figure 16.3), displaying your username and password. (Your password is displayed as a series of asterisks for security purposes.)

FIGURE 16.3

When you click your ISPs Dial-Up Networking icon, you are prompted to enter your username and password.

1 Type your username.

2 Type your password.

3 Turn on **Save password**, if desired.

4 Click **Connect.**

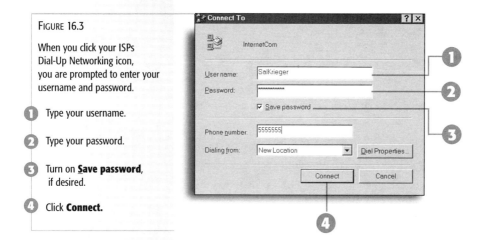

No Save password option?

If you don't have the **Save password** option, Client for Microsoft Networks is not installed. In the Control Panel, click the Network icon, click the **Add** button, and double-click **Client**. Click **Microsoft** and then double-click **Client for Microsoft Networks**. Make sure **Client for Microsoft Networks** is selected as the Primary Network Logon and click **OK**.

If your username and password are not displayed, type the entries in the **User name** and **Password** text boxes. If desired, place a check mark in the **Save password** check box. This saves your username and password, so you won't have to type it again the next time you logon. If you share your computer with someone else, and you do not want that person using your Internet connection, clear the check box. Click the **Connect** button.

After you click the **Connect** button, Dial-Up Networking dials into your service provider's computer and displays messages indicating the progress: Dialing…, Checking username and password…, and Connecting…. Assuming that Dial-Up Networking successfully logged you on, the Connection Established dialog box appears (see Figure 16.4), indicating that you are connected. You can now run Internet programs, as explained in later chapters, to navigate the World Wide Web, send and receive email, and so on.

You can click the **Close** button to close the dialog box without disconnecting. An icon for your connection appears in the system tray. Double-click the icon at any time to view your connection status. To disconnect, right-click the icon and click **Disconnect**.

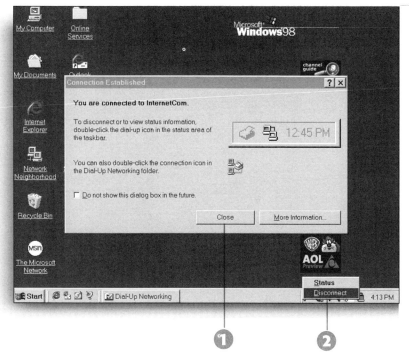

FIGURE 16.4

The Connection Established dialog box lets you know that your PC is connected to the ISP.

① Click **Close** to close the dialog box without exiting.

② Right-click this icon and click **Disconnect** to terminate the connection.

SEE ALSO

➤ *Learn how to navigate the Web after connecting to the Internet, page 411*

➤ *Learn how to send and receive email messages after connecting to the Internet, page 435*

Troubleshooting Connection Problems

Connection problems are the most difficult to troubleshoot, because there are so many variables. You may have mistyped your username, password, the ISP's phone number; the line might be busy; your modem may not be set up properly in

Windows; a Dial-Up Networking setting may be incorrect; or your call waiting service may be disconnecting you.

The following sections help you track down the causes of most connection problems and fix the problems that you have control over. If the problem is with the ISP's computer, you'll need to contact a technical support person and iron out any difficulties.

Did Windows Fail to Detect Your Modem?

If you receive a message indicating that Windows cannot detect a modem on your system, the modem is not properly installed. If you have an external modem, make sure it is plugged into the correct serial port on your PC, check the power cable, and make sure the modem is turned on.

If the external modem is properly connected or you have an internal modem, open the Control Panel, click the Modems icon, and check the modem's properties. Here's what you need to check:

- Make sure your modem is in the list of installed modems. If your modem is not listed, click the **Add** button and use the Add New Hardware Wizard to install it. If the list contains two or more modems and you use only one, click the name of any modem you don't use and click the **Remove** button.

- Click the name of your modem and click **Properties**. Make sure Windows has assigned the modem to the correct COM (communications) port. If you're not sure, write down the current setting and then pick a different COM port and try connecting again. (While you're in the Properties dialog box, make sure the modem's speaker volume is turned up so you can hear any sounds it makes as it dials and connects.)

- Make sure the modem is not conflicting with another device, such as your mouse or sound card. To check for conflicts, Alt+click **My Computer**, click the **Device Manager** tab, and click the plus sign next to Modem. If your modem has a yellow caution sign or a red warning symbol next to its name, it's conflicting with another device.

- If all else fails, remove all modems from the list, shut down and restart Windows, and let Windows detect and install your modem. If Windows does not detect your modem, run the Add New Hardware Wizard.

SEE ALSO

➤ *Learn how to install the correct device driver for your modem, page 683*

➤ *Learn how to use the Windows Modem Troubleshooter to find the cause of a problem, page 801*

➤ *Learn how to resolve device conflicts, page 802*

Did Windows Display a No Dial Tone Detected Message?

You can turn dial tone detection off, but before you do that, check your phone line. If you use the same phone line for voice calls from your home or office, make sure the phone is not currently being used. Also check the phone line from your modem to the phone jack to make sure it has not been disconnected.

A quick way to check your modem/phone line connection is to plug a phone into the modem's phone jack, pick up the phone, and listen for a dial tone. If you don't hear a dial tone, Windows won't hear it either. Check your phone lines.

If you can hear a dial tone, but Windows still doesn't detect it, try turning off dial tone detection in Windows.

Turn off Dial Tone Detection

1. Open the Control Panel and click the Modems icon.

2. Make sure your modem is selected and click the **Properties** button.

3. Click the **Connection** tab and remove the check mark from the **Wait for dial tone before dialing** check box (see Figure 16.5). Click **OK**.

4. Click **OK** to save your settings.

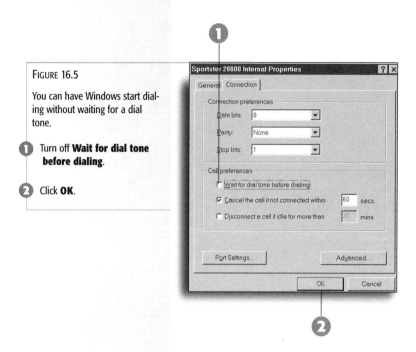

FIGURE 16.5

You can have Windows start dialing without waiting for a dial tone.

❶ Turn off **Wait for dial tone before dialing**.

❷ Click **OK**.

Is Your Modem Dialing?

Assuming you didn't mute your modem, you should be able to hear your modem dial a number. If you can't hear it, connect a phone to your modem's phone jack, pick up the receiver, and use the phone to listen in while your modem dials.

If your modem isn't dialing, Windows is not detecting the modem. Follow the troubleshooting procedure in the earlier section, "Did Windows Fail to Detect Your Modem?".

Is the ISP Answering?

If your modem is dialing, Dial-Up Networking should display messages indicating that the modem is dialing and at least attempting to establish a connection. If the connection is broken *before* your username and password are verified, the ISP isn't answering. The problem may be that you're dialing the wrong number, the line is busy, or the ISP is hanging up immediately after receiving your call.

Check the phone number in the Connect To dialog box to make sure you entered it correctly. If the phone number is correct, wait five or ten minutes and try connecting again. If the problem persists, contact your ISP's technical support department and describe the problem. The ISP's server might have been down or busy when you attempted to call. If you continue to have problems connecting, consider using a different ISP.

Is Your Username/Password Being Rejected?

As Dial-Up Networking establishes the connection, watch the dialog box carefully. If Dial-Up Networking starts to connect, indicates that it is verifying your username and password, and then immediately disconnects, check the following:

- Retype your username and password exactly as specified by your ISP.

- If this is the first time you're trying to connect, wait a few hours or try the connection tomorrow. Your ISP may not have set up your account yet.

- If the problem persists, call your ISP and verify your username and password.

Is the Connection Broken After Your Password Is Accepted?

If Dial-Up Networking dials, connects to the ISP, checks your username and password, and then disconnects you, there may be a problem with the Dial-Up Networking settings you entered. Check these settings.

Check your Dial-Up Networking settings

1. Click **My Computer** and click the **Dial-Up Networking** folder.

2. Right-click the icon for your ISP and click **Properties**.

3. Click the **Server Types** tab.

4. Open the **Type of Dial-Up Server** drop-down list and choose the correct server type (specified by your service provider): PPP or SLIP.

5. Under **Allowed Network Protocols**, make sure **TCP/IP** is the only option with a check mark next to it. If NetBEUI or IPX is listed, remove the check marks next to their names.

6. Click the **TCP/IP Settings** button.

7. If your ISP specified an IP or DNS address to use, make sure the proper addresses are entered. Click **OK**.

8. Make sure **Log On to Network** is turned off. If this option is selected, Windows looks for a Windows network before logging on, which can cause delays or aborted calls.

9. Click **OK** to save your changes.

If this does not fix the problem, open the Windows Control Panel again and click the Network icon. In the list of network components, make sure the following components are listed (see Figure 16.6):

- *Client for Microsoft Networks*. This component allows your PC to use client software to connect to an Internet server and access its resources. If Client for Microsoft Networks is missing, click the **Add** button to install it.

- *Dial-Up Adapter*. This is the component that enables your modem to dial out and connect to a remote computer or network. If Dial-Up Adapter is missing, click the **Add** button to install it.

- *TCP/IP or TCP/IP->Dial-Up Adapter*. This entry binds TCP/IP protocol to the Dial-Up Adapter. TCP/IP is the language your PC uses to communicate over the Internet. If this entry is missing, click the **Add** button to install the TCP/IP protocol. (TCP/IP->Dial-Up Adapter appears only on network-capable PCs. If your PC does not have a network card, you'll see TCP/IP. In either case, TCP/IP is installed.)

You may also experience connection problems if TCP/IP is bound to your network adapter. If you continue to have problems connecting, try removing all TCP/IP-> components except TCP/IP->Dial-Up Adapter.

SEE ALSO

➤ *Learn how to install the Windows networking components, page 300*

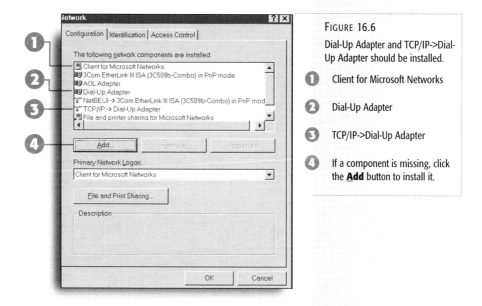

FIGURE 16.6

Dial-Up Adapter and TCP/IP->Dial-Up Adapter should be installed.

1 Client for Microsoft Networks

2 Dial-Up Adapter

3 TCP/IP->Dial-Up Adapter

4 If a component is missing, click the **Add** button to install it.

Are You Being Disconnected After Connecting Successfully?

Several factors might be at work here. If you use the same phone line for voice calls and you or someone else picks up a phone that's on the same line, you might be automatically disconnected. In addition, if you have a weak phone line connection, an old phone line, or a connection with a lot of noise, the connection may be weak. Have your phone lines checked.

If you have call waiting, any incoming calls automatically disconnect the modem. You should disable call waiting whenever you dial into your online service or Internet service provider. Windows can automatically disable call waiting for an online call. When you disconnect, call waiting is automatically turned back on.

408

Modem problem?

Some modems are more sensitive to line noise than other modems and may disconnect more frequently.

Disabling Call Waiting

1. Open the Windows Control Panel and click the Modems icon.

2. Make sure your modem is selected and click the **Properties** button.

3. Click the **D**ialing **Properties** button.

4. Choose **To Disable Call Waiting, Dial** and choose or type the number you must dial to disable the call waiting feature. This number is usually ***70**. Click **OK**.

5. When you return to the Modems Properties dialog box, click **OK** to save your changes.

Speeding Up Your Internet Connection

When Dial-Up Networking establishes a connection, it displays the speed at which data is being transferred. Expect the speed to be slightly less than your actual modem speed. For example, if you have a 28.8Kbps modem, expect an actual speed of 24–26Kbps. If you're using a 56K modem, expect speeds in the range of 40–45Kbps for incoming data transfers and less than 33Kbps for outgoing transfers. These speed dips may be the result of line noise or problems with your service provider.

If Dial-Up Networking shows that the speed is half of what your modem is capable of, then you should be concerned. For example, if your 28.8Kbps modem is chugging along at 14,400bps, you should check the following:

- *Possible line noise*. If you typically connect at a higher speed, you may have a bad connection. Try disconnecting and reconnecting. If the connection is always slow, check the phone lines in your house and call your local phone company to report line noise.

- *Check your modem setup*. In the Control Panel, double-click the Modems icon. Click the name of your modem and click the **P**roperties button. Under **Maximum Speed**, open the drop-down list and try choosing the highest setting (see Figure 16.7). Disconnect and reconnect to see if your connection speed has increased.

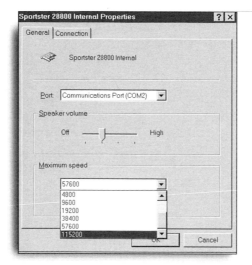

FIGURE 16.7

Try setting up your modem to connect at the highest speed.

- *Does your service provider support your modem speed?* Many service providers support only up to 33.6Kbps modems. If you have a 56Kbps modem, it will only transfer data at the rate that the service provider's modem is operating. 56Kbps modems can *send* data at speeds only up to 33.6Kbps.

- *Does your service provider know that you're using a high-speed modem?* In many cases, the service provider gives you a different phone number to use to connect at a specific speed. You may be set up to dial into a slower modem than the service provider has available. Call your service provider for more information.

Exploring the World Wide Web

Surf the Web with Internet Explorer or Netscape Navigator

Mark your favorite Web pages for quick return trips

Search the Internet for information

Accessorize your Web browser with plug-ins and ActiveX controls

Create your own Web page and publish it on the Web

Using a Web Browser

The single most exciting part of the Internet is the World Wide Web (or "Web" for short). With an Internet connection and a Web browser, you have access to billions of electronic pages stored on computers all over the world. Whatever your interest—music, movies, finances, science, literature, travel, astrology, body piercing—you'll find hundreds of pages to explore.

To cruise around the Web, you need a special program called a *Web browser*, which works through your ISP to pull up documents on your screen. You can choose from any of several Web browsers, including the two most popular browsers, Netscape Navigator and Internet Explorer. In addition to opening Web pages, these browsers contain advanced tools for navigating the Web, finding pages that interest you, and marking your favorite sites and pages.

Nickel Tour of Internet Explorer

To run Internet Explorer, go to the Windows desktop and click the Internet Explorer icon or click the **Launch Internet Explorer Browser** button in the Quick Launch toolbar. If your PC is not connected to your ISP, the Connect To dialog box appears. Type your username and password, as explained in the previous chapter, and click the **Connect** button. After Dial-Up Networking establishes your Internet connection, Internet Explorer loads the Microsoft home page (see Figure 17.1).

You can start to wander the Web by clicking links (highlighted text or pictures). Click the **Back** button to flip to a previous page, or click **Forward** to skip ahead to a page you've visited but backed up from. You'll learn more about navigating Web pages later in this chapter.

Nickel Tour of Netscape Navigator

If a friend or colleague recommended that you use Netscape Navigator, instead of Internet Explorer, you can use Internet Explorer to download Netscape Navigator from Netscape's Web site. You can download Navigator (the Web browser) or

Netscape Communicator—a suite of Internet programs that includes Messenger (for email), Collabra (for newsgroups), Composer (for creating Web pages), and Conference (for Internet phone calls).

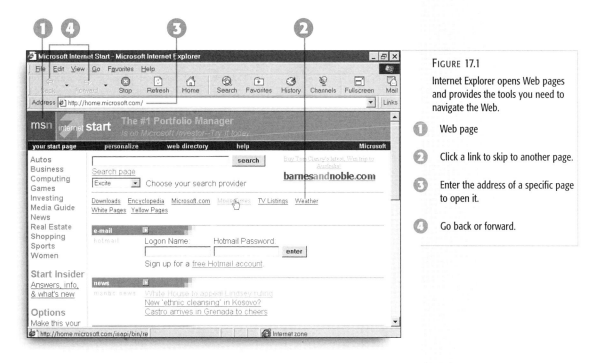

FIGURE 17.1

Internet Explorer opens Web pages and provides the tools you need to navigate the Web.

1   Web page

2   Click a link to skip to another page.

3   Enter the address of a specific page to open it.

4   Go back or forward.

To connect to Netscape's Web site, run Internet Explorer, type www.netscape.com in the **Address** text box (below the toolbar), and press Enter. Follow the trail of links to download Navigator or Communicator. After downloading the installation file, run My Computer, change to the folder in which you saved the file, and click the file's icon. Follow the onscreen installation instructions.

After you install Navigator (or Communicator), you should have an icon on your Windows desktop named Netscape Navigator or Netscape Communicator. Click the icon. Again, if your computer is not connected to the Internet, the Connect To dialog box appears. Type your username and password, as explained in the previous chapter, and click the **Connect** button. The

Netscape Navigator window appears and opens Netscape's home page (see Figure 17.2).

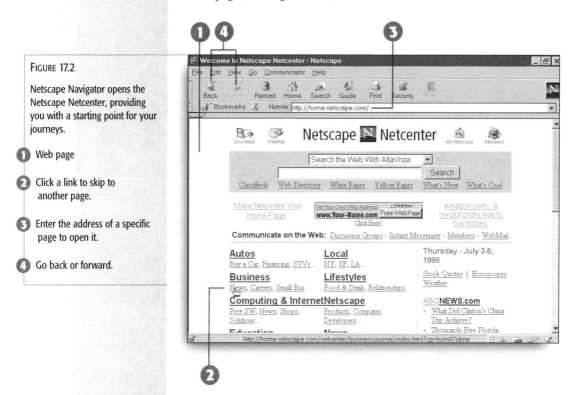

FIGURE 17.2

Netscape Navigator opens the Netscape Netcenter, providing you with a starting point for your journeys.

1 Web page

2 Click a link to skip to another page.

3 Enter the address of a specific page to open it.

4 Go back or forward.

The procedure for wandering the Web with Navigator is fairly standard; you click links to jump from one page to the next. Links typically appear as blue, underlined text or as buttons or icons. After you move from one page to another, you can click the **Back** button to return to previous pages, or click the **Forward** button to move ahead to pages you've visited but backed up from. You'll learn more about these standard navigational tools later in this chapter.

Navigating Pages with Links

The Web works like a multimedia encyclopedia on CD. You select a topic of interest, and the encyclopedia displays a page of relevant information. The page typically contains text, images, and highlighted text that points to other related articles on the CD. You click the highlighted text, and the encyclopedia opens and displays the related information.

The Web provides a similar interface and similar tools for jumping from one page to another. On most pages, you can click a *link* to skip to a different page or return to the Web site's home page (its opening page). Links typically appear as icons, pictures, or blue, underlined text. When you move your mouse pointer over a link, the pointer turns into a hand, indicating that it is hovering over a link. To activate the link and skip to its associated page, click the link.

Some Web sites use special graphics, called *imagemaps* to help you navigate. In an imagemap, several areas of the image act as links to different pages. In most cases, the map has some text that indicates where each link will take you (see Figure 17.3).

FIGURE 17.3

An imagemap contains several areas that act as links.

1   Click the link to open its page.

Opening Specific Pages with Addresses

Each Web page has a unique address that starts with http://. HTTP is short for *Hypertext Transfer Protocol*, which is the set of rules that governs data transfer on the Web. In an address, http:// is followed by the *domain name* of the computer on which the Web page is stored. For example, the address for the White House Web site is http://www.whitehouse.gov. Following the domain name is the path to the folder in which the Web page file is stored and the name of the file. For instance, the address of a specific page at the White House Web site might be http://www.whitehouse.gov/WH/glimpse/top.html.

When typing Web page addresses, you can omit the http:// at the beginning of the address; your Web browser supplies it for you. When entering the path to the folder or the filename, case is important. In the previous example, typing /wh instead of /WH would result in an error. Case is not important with the domain name, but it is important in folder names and filenames.

Domain name only

You don't need to enter a Web path to a folder or a Web page filename. Simply type the site's domain name (for example, www.abc.com) and press **Enter**. This usually opens the site's default home page and you can click links to browse pages at the site.

If you know the address of a Web page you want to open, you can enter the address in the text box just above the Web page—the **Address** text box in Internet Explorer or the **Go To** text box in Navigator.

Opening a specific Web page

1. Click in the **Address** or **Go To** text box to highlight the address of the current page (see Figure 17.4).

2. Type the address of the page you want to open.

3. Press Enter.

Returning to Pages You Visited

As you move from one page to another, the Web browser keeps track of the pages you've visited. It also stores the pages in a temporary holding area, called the *cache*, so it can quickly reopen the pages rather than retrieving them from the Web.

Internet Explorer and Netscape Navigator have several tools you can use to quickly retrace your steps on the Web and return to sites when you've forgotten their addresses.

FIGURE 17.4

You can open a specific page by entering its address.

1   Type the address here and press Enter.

Using the Back and Forward Buttons

The Back and Forward buttons are the most basic tools for reopening Web pages. You click the button to move back or forward through your trail of Web pages. These buttons also double as drop-down lists:

- In Internet Explorer, click the arrow to the right of the **Back** or **Forward** button and then click the name or address of the desired page.

- In Netscape Navigator, click the **Back** or **Forward** button, hold down the mouse button, and then click the name or address of the desired page.

The **Address** and **Go To** text boxes also function as drop-down lists. Click the arrow next to the **Address** or **Go To** text box and then click the address of the page you want to revisit.

Clear the cache

Cached files can occupy a great deal of disk space. Clear the cache regularly. In Internet Explorer, choose **View, Internet Options**, and click the **Delete Files** button. In Navigator, choose **Edit, Preferences**, click the plus sign next to **Advanced**, click **Cache**, and click the **Clear Disk Cache** button.

Using the History List

Navigate with keystrokes

Press Ctrl+← to move back to the previous page or Ctrl+→ to move forward.

Although the **Back** and **Forward** buttons eventually take you back to where you were, they don't get you there in a hurry or keep track of pages you visited yesterday or last week. For faster return trips and a more comprehensive log of your Web journeys, Web browsers feature *history lists*:

- In Internet Explorer, click the **History** button to display the History bar on the left side of the window. Click the day or week during which you visited the Web site and then click the Web site's name to view a list of pages you viewed at that site. To open a page, click its name (see Figure 17.5).

- In Navigator, open the **Window** menu and click **History** or press Ctrl+H to view the history list. Double-click the name of the page you want to revisit.

FIGURE 17.5

Internet Explorer's History bar makes it easy to revisit Web sites.

1 Click the day or week icon.

2 Click the Web site's name.

3 Click the page you want to revisit.

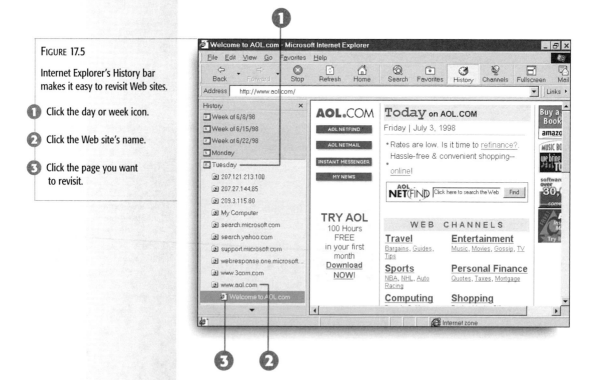

Marking Your Favorite Pages

As you wander the Web, you will pull up pages that you know you'll want to return to in the future. When you happen upon such a page, flag it by creating a *bookmark* or marking the page as a *favorite*. This adds the page's name to the **Bookmark** menu (in Navigator) or **Favorites** menu (in Internet Explorer). The next time you want to pull up the page, you select it from your customized menu. In Netscape and Internet Explorer, take the following steps to add your favorite pages to a menu:

- In Navigator, press Ctrl+D or drag the little icon that's next to the **Location** text box over the **Bookmarks** icon and release the mouse button. This places the page name on the **Bookmarks** menu. You can also drag links over the Bookmarks icon.

- Right-click a blank area on the current page or right-click a link and click **Add Bookmark** or **Add to Favorites**.

- In Internet Explorer, open the **Favorites** menu, and click **Add to Favorites**.

In Internet Explorer, when you choose to add a page to the **Favorites** menu, the Add Favorite dialog box appears, asking if you only want to add the page to your **Favorites** menu or have Internet Explorer automatically download updates (*subscribe* to the page). If you choose to subscribe, Internet Explorer connects to the Internet at the scheduled times (typically when Internet traffic is light) and downloads the latest version of the page. When you choose to open the page, Internet Explorer quickly loads it from the cache rather than from the Web.

After you have added a page to the **Bookmarks** or **Favorites** menu, you can quickly open the page by opening the menu and clicking the name of the page (see Figure 17.6).

Using Web Search Tools

The Web is the perfect example of how too much information can be as useless as too little. You can skip from one Web page to the next for hours and never discover what you originally were searching for.

Expand your history list

You can specify the number of days you want your Web browser to log in the history list. In Internet Explorer, choose **View**, **Internet Options**, and enter the desired number of days below History. In Navigator, choose **Edit**, **Preferences**, click **Navigator**, and type the desired number of days below History.

Make your own submenus

You can get fancy with Favorites and Bookmarks by creating sub-menus. In Navigator, open the **Bookmarks** menu and click **Edit Bookmarks**. In Internet Explorer, open the **Favorites** menu and select **Organize Favorites**. In either program, you get a window that lets you rearrange your bookmarks or favorites and create submenus (folders).

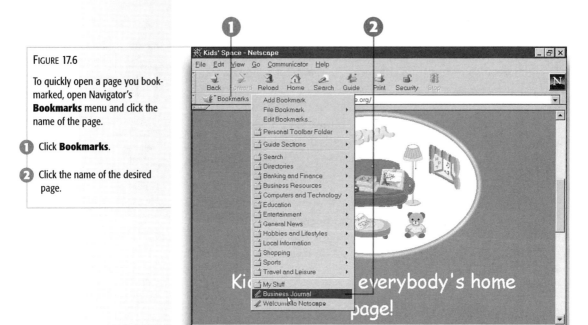

FIGURE 17.6

To quickly open a page you book-marked, open Navigator's **Bookmarks** menu and click the name of the page.

1. Click **Bookmarks**.

2. Click the name of the desired page.

Fortunately, the Web offers several search tools that filter through an index of Internet resources to help you find what you're looking for. You connect to a site that has a search tool, type a couple words that specify what you're looking for, and click the **Search** or **Find** button. Following is a list of addresses for some popular search tools on the Web:

www.yahoo.com

www.excite.com

www.lycos.com

www.infoseek.com

www.altavista.com

www.webcrawler.com

Most Web browsers now have a **Search** button that connects you to various Internet search tools. In Netscape Navigator, the **Search** button connects you to Netscape's Netcenter search page, where you'll find links to several search tools.

In Internet Explorer, the **Search** button displays a Search bar on the left side of the window. You execute your search from the Search bar, and Internet Explorer displays the results right inside the bar. You can then click links in the Search bar to open pages in the main window; you don't have to click the **Back** button to return to the search results (see Figure 17.7). To hide the Search bar, click the **Search** button in Internet Explorer's toolbar.

SEE ALSO

➤ *Learn how to find people using Web directories, page 451*

FIGURE 17.7

The Search bar lets you quickly preview the pages that the search tool found.

❶ The Search bar

❷ Click a link to preview it in the main window.

Working with Graphics

The Web is packed with pictures, illustrations, cartoons, and photographs. As you browse the Web, you may want to save the images for future reference or for use on your own Web pages (if you have the author's permission, of course). You can save images to disk or use the image as your Windows wallpaper (desktop background). To save an image or use it as your Windows wallpaper, take one of the following steps:

- *Save image*. Right-click the image and click **Save Picture As** (Internet Explorer) or **Save Image As** (Navigator). Use the resulting dialog box to save the image in the desired folder.

- *Use image as wallpaper*. Right-click the image and click **Set As Wallpaper**.

Most word processing and desktop publishing programs support the two most common graphics file types used on the Web: GIF and JPG (or JPEG). You can insert the images right into your documents. To open and print saved images, use the Imaging program included with Windows. To run the program, click the **Start** button, point to **Programs**, **Accessories**, and click **Imaging**.

Playing Media Files

Your Web browser isn't just a fancy page flipper. It has the capability to display most graphic file types, play almost any sound file, and show more video file types than just about any dedicated video player can handle. However, your Web browser cannot play all file types. To play a file type that it cannot handle, your browser needs a special program: a *plug-in* or *ActiveX control*.

Plug-ins (mainly used in Navigator) are small computer programs that add to the capabilities of the browser. When you click a link for a file that Navigator can't handle, Navigator runs the plug-in, which then opens and plays the file.

ActiveX controls (mainly used in Internet Explorer) are similar to plug-ins, in that they handle files Internet Explorer cannot

Enhance images

Although the Windows Imaging program is useful for viewing and printing images, it provides no tools for touching up and enhancing graphics. For more control over your downloaded images, try PaintShop Pro. You can download a shareware version of PaintShop Pro from www.jasc.com. See "Finding Plug-ins and ActiveX Controls," later in this chapter, for more information on finding shareware and freeware programs.

play. Unlike plug-ins, which act as separate programs, ActiveX controls are more integrated with Internet Explorer, allowing the control to play files right inside the Internet Explorer window.

Installing Plug-ins and ActiveX Controls

You usually don't need to hunt for plug-ins and ActiveX controls. If you click a link that requires a plug-in, Navigator displays the Plugin Not Loaded dialog box. Click **Get the Plugin** to download and install it. In Internet Explorer, when you click a link that requires an ActiveX control, Internet Explorer displays a security warning asking for your confirmation. If the ActiveX control has been certified as safe, click **Yes** to download and install it. If it has not been certified, click **No**. (If Internet Explorer refuses to download a required ActiveX control, check the security settings. If security is set to high, Internet Explorer will not download ActiveX controls.)

SEE ALSO

➤ *Learn how to check security settings, page 514*

Finding Plug-Ins and ActiveX Controls

If you click a file type that your browser cannot play, and the browser doesn't prompt you to install the required plug-in or ActiveX control, you may have to search for it yourself. The Web has several sites that act as plug-in and ActiveX repositories, helping you find and install the required add-on. When you need to find a plug-in or ActiveX control, try the following sites:

Stroud's: cws.internet.com

TUCOWS: www.tucows.com

DOWNLOAD.COM: www.download.com

BROWSERS.COM: www.browsers.com

Most of these sites provide a description of each add-on program and indicate whether it is an ActiveX control (for Internet Explorer) or plug-in (for Navigator). Make sure you get the version of the add-on designed for your browser. The reviews of

Which add-ons are installed?

To find out which plug-ins you already have in Navigator, open Navigator's **Help** menu and click **About Plug-ins**. If you're using Internet Explorer, use My Computer to open the Windows\Downloaded Program Files folder to view a list of installed ActiveX controls.

ActiveX risks

ActiveX controls that come from unlicensed sites do pose a security risk. Before giving your okay to download and install an ActiveX control, make sure Internet Explorer displays its certificate. If Internet Explorer shows that the control is not certified, cancel the download and contact the developer of the ActiveX control to determine why the control has not been certified.

these add-on programs typically contain links to the developer's home page, where you can obtain additional information and register the program (see Figure 17.8).

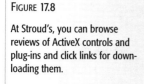

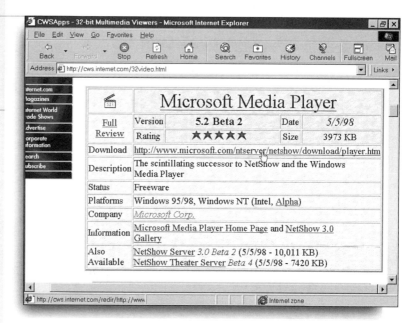

Making Your Own Web Pages

After you've pulled up a few Web pages, you may find the urge to make your presence known on the Web. You can do this by creating and *publishing* your own Web page. Both Internet Explorer and Netscape Communicator come with their own page-layout programs that make Web page creation as easy as creating a document in a word-processing or desktop publishing program. The following sections show you how to create a basic Web page, format it, and add graphics and links.

Creating a Simple Page

With FrontPage Express or Netscape Composer, you don't have to start your Web page from scratch. FrontPage Express features a Personal Home Page Wizard that leads you step-by-step through the process of creating a Web page. With Netscape Composer you can download a Web page template from Netscape's Web site and edit the template to create a custom Web page.

Making a Web page in FrontPage Express

1. Click the **Start** button, point to **Programs**, **Internet Explorer**, and click **FrontPage Express**.

2. Open the **File** menu and click **New**.

3. Click **Personal Home Page Wizard** and click **OK**. The first Personal Home Page Wizard dialog box appears, prompting you to select the contents of your home page (see Figure 17.9).

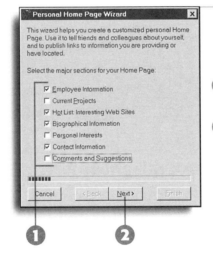

FIGURE 17.9

In FrontPage Express, the Personal Home Page Wizard helps you create a simple Web page.

① Click the content areas you want to place on your page.

② Click **Next**.

4. Select each section you want to include on your home page. Each item you select will appear as a heading on your page.

5. Click **Next**. You are now asked to name the page.

6. In the **Page URL** text box, type the name of the page (its filename). The name should have the filename extension .htm or .html.

7. In the **Page Title** text box, type the name of the page as you want it to appear in the title bar when a visitor opens the page in his Web browser.

ISP page name requirements

Many service providers require that you use a specific filename for your Web page, such as default.htm or index.htm. Check with your ISP.

8. Click **Next**. The remaining dialog boxes vary depending on the content you selected in step 4.

9. Follow the onscreen instructions to enter your preferences.

10. When the last dialog box appears, click **Finish**. The wizard creates your home page and displays it in FrontPage Express, where you can edit it.

Using a Netscape template

1. Click the **Start** button, point to **Programs**, **Netscape Communicator**, and click **Netscape Composer**.

2. Click the **New** button in Composer's toolbar.

3. Click **From Template**.

4. Click the **Netscape Templates** button. Composer runs Navigator which connects you to Netscape's Templates page.

5. Scroll down the page and click the link for the template you want to use. The page appears in Navigator.

6. Open Navigator's **File** menu and choose **Edit Page**.

7. The page appears in Composer, where you can start editing it.

Formatting Your Text

Every page is a template

If you see a page design on the Web that you like, send an email message to the author asking if you can use the overall design for your own Web page. Save the Web page as a file on your hard disk, open it in your HTML editor, and customize it.

Formatting text in an HTML document is no different from formatting text in any of your other documents. You highlight the text you want to format and then apply the desired text or paragraph format. What makes HTML formats different is that they are somewhat limited by HTML standards. These standards prescribe generic coding in an attempt to make Web pages compatible with all browsers and to give the browser more control over the way Web pages are displayed.

Figure 17.10 shows some common HTML formats applied to a sample page in FrontPage Express. Note that the buttons in the Formatting toolbar are fairly standard.

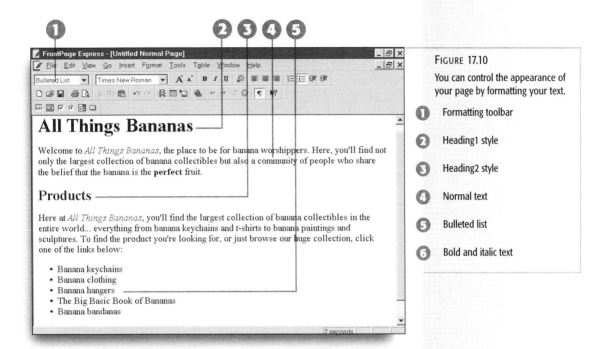

FIGURE 17.10

You can control the appearance of your page by formatting your text.

1   Formatting toolbar

2   Heading1 style

3   Heading2 style

4   Normal text

5   Bulleted list

6   Bold and italic text

Adding Graphics and Other Media

When you wander the Web, you'll notice that text-only pages are rare. Documents are dynamic, multi-dimensional, and interactive. You'll also notice that you spend much more time viewing a page that contains pictures, video clips, audio clips, and animations than you do viewing pages that contain only text. Graphics and media clips make pages more engaging.

Fortunately, adding graphics and media files to your Web page is not that difficult. You move the insertion point where you want the object placed, enter the command for inserting a picture or object and then use the resulting dialog box to insert the file.

Inserting a picture

1. Move the insertion point to where you want the image inserted.

2. In the toolbar, click the **Image** or **Insert Image** button.

3. Click the **Browse** or **Choose File** button.

4. Change to the folder that contains the graphic file and double-click the file's name. The image is added to the page at the insertion point (see Figure 17.11).

FIGURE 17.11

You can make your page more attractive and engaging by adding pictures.

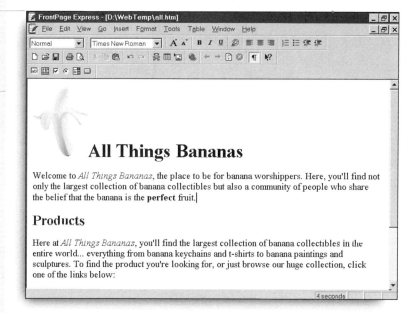

Graphic file formats

Most Web browsers can display graphics stored as GIF or JPG files. If you insert files in other formats, the people who visit your site may not be able to view the graphics.

After inserting a picture, you can move it, resize it, or control the way text wraps around it:

- To move an image, drag it.
- To resize an image, click it and drag one of its corners or edges.
- To change the way surrounding text wraps around the image in FrontPage Express, right-click the image and click **Image Properties**. Click the **Appearance** tab and enter your preferences.
- To change the way surrounding text wraps around the image in Netscape Composer, right-click the image and click **Image Properties**. Enter your preferences.

SEE ALSO
➤ *Learn how to take digital photos for placing on your Web pages, page 757*
➤ *Learn how to create your own video clips using a video capture board, page 691*

Adding Links

Most Web pages have links. These links may point to different areas on the same page, related pages at the same Web site, previous pages, completely unrelated pages, files or graphics, audio or video clips, email addresses, or any other objects on the Internet. To keep your page from being just another dead end on the Web, insert links.

Inserting a link

1. Highlight the text or click the image that you want to use as your link.

2. Click the **Link** button in Composer or the **Create or Edit Hyperlink** button in FrontPage Express.

3. Type http:// followed by the page address you want the link to point to (see Figure 17.12).

4. Click **OK**. If you used text as the link, it appears blue and underlined.

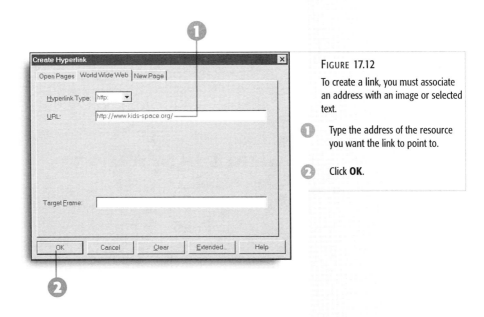

FIGURE 17.12

To create a link, you must associate an address with an image or selected text.

1 Type the address of the resource you want the link to point to.

2 Click **OK**.

If you have a long Web page, you might want to place a table of contents at the top of the page that provides links to various places on the page. This would allow the visitor to quickly navigate your Web page, without having to rely solely on the scrollbar.

To create a link that points to a specific part of a page, you must first mark the destination point as a *bookmark* or *target*. You can then create a link that points to the bookmark instead of to a URL. (I usually insert all my bookmarks first.)

Linking on the same page

1. Move the insertion point where you want the target or bookmark placed.

2. In Composer, click the **Target** button. In Internet Explorer choose **Edit**, **Bookmark**.

3. Type a name for the target or bookmark and click **OK**.

4. Insert a link, but instead of typing a page address, choose the target or bookmark from the **Target** or **Bookmarks** list.

Publishing Your Web Page

Linking to your email address

If you want people to contact you, add a link that points to your email address. When prompted to type an address for the link, type `mailto:` followed by your email address (for example, `mailto:lbritton@internet.com`).

When you finish creating your Web page, you must place it on a Web server where other people can open and view it with their Web browsers. In the past, the only way to place a page on a Web server was to use a separate FTP (File Transfer Protocol) program. However, FrontPage Express and Composer come with their own Web publishing tools that make the process much easier.

Finding a Home for Your Page

Check your page first

Before you unveil your page to the public, open it in your Web browser, proofread it thoroughly for spelling and grammatical errors, make sure all the links work, and check the graphics.

Before you start, you need to make sure you have somewhere to store your Web page. The best place to start is with your ISP. Most providers make some space available on their Web servers for subscribers to store personal Web pages. Call your service provider and find out the following information:

- Does your service provider make Web space available to subscribers? If not, maybe you should change providers.

- How much disk space do you get, and how much does it cost (if anything)? Some providers give you a limited amount of disk space, which is usually plenty for one or two Web pages, assuming you don't include large audio or video clips.

- Can you save your files directly to the Web server or do you have to upload files to an FTP server?

- What is the URL of the server to which you must upload your files? Write it down.

- What username and password do you need to enter to gain access to the server? (This is typically the same username and password you use to connect to the service.)

- In which directory must you place your files? Write it down.

- What name must you give your Web page? In many cases, the service lets you post a single Web page, and you must call it index.html or default.html.

- Are there any other specific instructions you must follow to post your Web page?

- After posting your page, what will its address (URL) be? You'll want to open it in Internet Explorer as soon as you post it.

If your service provider does not offer Web page service, fire up Internet Explorer, connect to your favorite search page, and search for places that allow you to post your Web page for free. These services vary greatly. Some services require you to fill out a form, and then the service creates a generic Web page for you (you can't use the page you created in FrontPage Express). At others, you can copy the HTML coded document (in Notepad or WordPad) and paste it in a text box at the site. A couple of other places will let you send them your HTML file and associated files. Find out what's involved.

Publishing with the Web Publishing Wizard

FrontPage Express allows you to post your page to the Web using the **File**, **Save As** command and the Web Publishing Wizard, included with Windows. If your ISP is set up to work

Store all Web page files in one folder

You will save yourself some time and trouble by placing your Web page and all graphic files in a single folder separate from other files. You can then easily transfer the entire contents of the folder to the Web server.

along with the Web Publishing Wizard, the process is fairly straightforward. The Web Publishing Wizard can upload your files via FTP or publish them directly to your Web folder, depending on the system your ISP uses.

Publishing your Web page from FrontPage Express

1. Open the page you want to place on the Web.

2. Open the **File** menu and click **Save As**.

3. Type a title for your page and click **OK**. If your Web page has graphics, FrontPage Express asks if you want the graphic files posted to the Web site.

4. Click **Yes to All**.

5. Follow the Web Publishing Wizard's instructions to enter the settings your ISP specified for publishing your Web page.

If all goes as planned, your Web page and associated files should be on your ISP's Web server. You can now open the page in Internet Explorer by entering the address your ISP assigned to the page.

However, the Web Publishing Wizard isn't the smooth, efficient tool that Microsoft claims it is. If your ISP doesn't fully support the Web Publishing Wizard, the wizard will have trouble connecting to your ISP and transferring your files. If you run into problems, contact your ISP for assistance.

Publishing from Netscape Composer

Netscape Composer's Web page publishing feature is much more reliable and easy to use than the Web Publishing Wizard. If you know the address of the Web or FTP directory in which you must place the files and your username and password, Composer can publish your page in a matter of seconds.

Publishing a Web page from Composer

1. Open the page you want to place on the Web.

2. Click the **Publish** button.

3. Enter the HTTP or FTP address that your service provider told you to use (see Figure 17.13).

4. Enter your username and password.

5. To send all the files in your folder, click **All files in page's folder**.

6. Click **OK**.

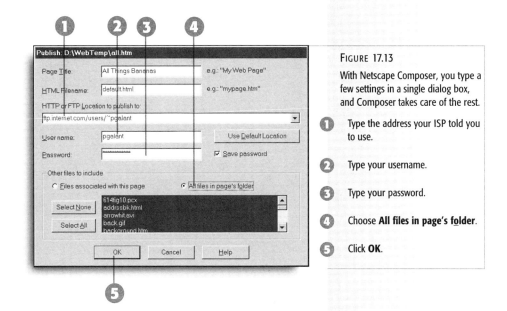

FIGURE 17.13

With Netscape Composer, you type a few settings in a single dialog box, and Composer takes care of the rest.

1 Type the address your ISP told you to use.

2 Type your username.

3 Type your password.

4 Choose **All files in page's folder**.

5 Click **OK**.

Uploading Files with FTP

Many ISPs require that you upload (copy) your Web page file and all associated files to a directory set aside for you on the ISP's FTP server. You can use the Web Publishing Wizard to perform the FTP upload or publish the files to the FTP server from Composer, as explained in the previous two sections.

Another option is to use a dedicated FTP program. Most FTP programs are structured like Windows Explorer. The program displays the contents of your disk in one pane and the contents of the FTP server in the other. To move files from your disk to the FTP server (or vice versa), you copy them from one pane to the other (see Figure 17.14).

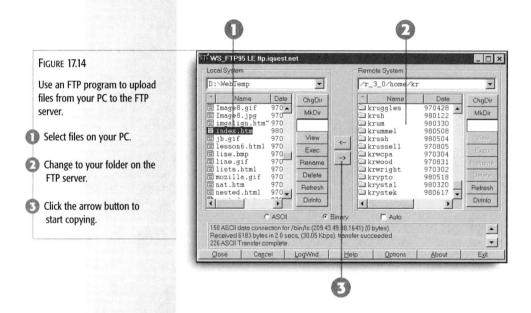

FIGURE 17.14

Use an FTP program to upload files from your PC to the FTP server.

❶ Select files on your PC.

❷ Change to your folder on the FTP server.

❸ Click the arrow button to start copying.

SEE ALSO

➢ *Learn how to obtain, install, and use a specialized FTP program, page 471*

Sending and Receiving Email Messages

Connect to an email server to check for incoming messages

Read and reply to messages you receive

Compose and send email messages anywhere in the world

Attach files to the messages you send

Create your own email Address Book

Find friends and relatives using directories on the Web

Setting Up an Email Account

The hardest part about email is getting your email program to connect to your Internet service provider's email server, which acts as an electronic post office. If you are using one of the major commercial online services, such as America Online or CompuServe, you can relax; the installation program took care of all the details for you. You just click the email button and start using it.

However, if you have a local service provider and are using a dedicated email program, such as Microsoft's Outlook Express or Netscape Messenger, then you must first enter information telling your email program how to connect to the mail server. You need to enter the following information:

- *Your name.* This is your real name as you want it to appear on the recipient's screen.

- *Your email address.* Your email address is usually all lowercase and starts with your first initial and last name (for example, jsmith@iway.com). However, if your name is John Smith (or Jill Smith), you might have to use something more unique, such as JohnHubertSmith@iway.com.

- *Outgoing mail (SMTP) server address.* Short for *Simple Mail Transfer Protocol*, the SMTP server is the mailbox into which you drop your outgoing messages. The address usually starts with "smtp" or "mail" (for example, mail.iway.com or smtp.iway.com).

- *Incoming mail (POP3) server address.* Short for Post Office Protocol, the POP server is like your local post office. It receives incoming messages and places them in your personal mailbox. The address usually starts with "pop" (for example, pop.iway.com).

- *Account.* The account name is usually your username, the name you use to log on to the service. However, your ISP may use a different system to assign email accounts.

- *Password.* Typically, you use the same password for logging on and for checking email.

The first time you run your email program, it should step you through the process of setting up your email account. (In fact, if you used the Internet Connection Wizard to set up your ISP connection, it prompted you to set up your email and news server accounts.) However, if you chose not to set up an account at first or you signed up for another email account, you can add it by performing the following steps.

Setting up an email account in Outlook Express

1. Click the Outlook Express icon on the Windows desktop or click the Launch Outlook Express icon in the Quick Launch toolbar.

2. Open the **Tools** menu and click **Accounts**.

3. Click the **Add** button and click **Mail**. The first Internet Connection Wizard dialog box appears asking for your name.

4. Type your name as you want it to appear on messages you send. (This can be your real name or a nickname.) Click **Next**.

5. Type your email address so people can reply to your messages. Click **Next**. You are now prompted to type the address of the mail server used for incoming and outgoing mail.

6. Open the **My incoming mail server is a ___ server** drop-down list and select the type of server used for incoming mail: **POP3** or **IMAP** (see Figure 18.1).

7. Type the addresses of the incoming and outgoing mail servers and click **Next**.

8. If the server requires you to log on, select one of the following logon settings:

   Log on using if your mail server requires you to enter a name and password to connect. Enter the required name and password in the appropriate text boxes.

   Log on using secure password authentication (SPA) if your mail server requires you to connect using a digital certification.

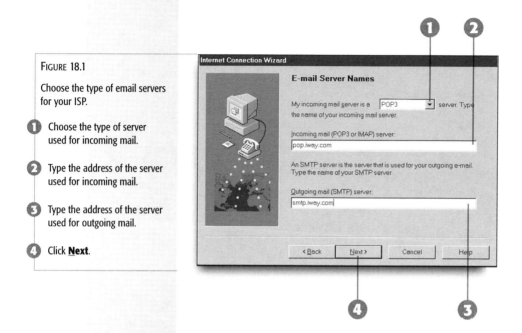

FIGURE 18.1

Choose the type of email servers for your ISP.

1 Choose the type of server used for incoming mail.

2 Type the address of the server used for incoming mail.

3 Type the address of the server used for outgoing mail.

4 Click **Next**.

9. Click **Next**. You are prompted to enter a "friendly" name for this account.

10. Type a brief name to help you recognize the account, and click **Next**. You are now prompted to specify how you connect to the Internet.

11. Click **Connect using my phone line** or **Connect using my local area network (LAN)** to specify how you connect to the Internet. Click **Next.**

12. If you chose to connect using your phone line, click **Use an existing dial-up connection** and click the Dial-Up Networking connection you use to connect to your ISP. Click **Next**.

13. Click the **Finish** button. The Internet Accounts dialog box appears, showing the name of the mail server you added (see Figure 18.2).

14. To use this account as the default (if you have more than one email account), select the account name and click **Set as Default**.

15. Click **Close** to return to the Outlook Express window.

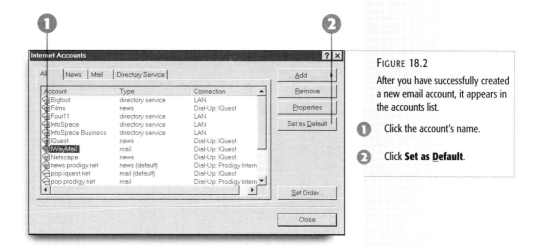

FIGURE 18.2
After you have successfully created a new email account, it appears in the accounts list.

➊ Click the account's name.

➋ Click **Set as Default**.

Setting up an email account in Netscape Messenger

1. Click the **Start** button, point to **Programs**, **Netscape Communicator**, and click **Netscape Messenger**.

2. Open the **Edit** menu and click **Preferences**.

3. Click the plus sign next to **Mail and Groups** and click **Identity**.

4. Type your name and email address in the designated text boxes.

5. Under **Mail and Groups**, click **Mail Server**.

6. In the **Mail server user name** text box, type your mail server logon name, as specified by your ISP.

7. In the **Outgoing mail (SMTP) server** text box, type the address of the mail server used for the mail you send.

8. In the **Incoming mail server** text box, type the address of the mail server used for handling the messages you receive.

9. Under **Mail Server Type**, choose **POP3** or **IMAP**, as specified by your ISP.

10. Click **OK**.

To set up an email account in a different email program, run the program and enter the Preferences or Options command. Enter the email server addresses and the required information for logging on to the servers.

SEE ALSO
➤ *Learn how to set up a Dial-Up Networking connection, page 391*

Receiving and Reading Messages

Whenever someone sends you an email message, it doesn't just pop up on your screen. The message sits on your service provider's mail server until you connect and retrieve your messages. There's no trick to connecting to the mail server, as long as you entered the connection information correctly. Most programs check for messages automatically on startup or display button you can click to fetch your mail.

Retrieving your email

1. Run your email program.

2. Click the button for retrieving your email. In Outlook Express, click the **Send and Retrieve** button. In Netscape Messenger, click the **Get Msg** button. The program retrieves your mail and then displays a list of message descriptions.

3. To display the contents of a message, click its description. Most email programs display the contents of the message in a pane below the message list.

4. To display the message in its own window, double-click its description (see Figure 18.3).

Replying to Messages

To reply to a message in most email programs, you click the **Reply** or **Respond To** button. This opens a window that automatically inserts the person's email address and a description of the message. Many email programs also quote the contents of the original message, so the recipient can easily follow the conversation. To indicate that text has been quoted, email programs typically add a right angle bracket (>) at the beginning of each quoted line (see Figure 18.4). To respond, type your message in the message area, and then click the **Send** button.

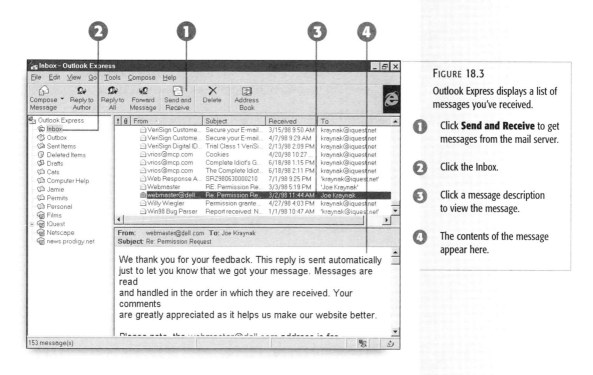

FIGURE 18.3

Outlook Express displays a list of messages you've received.

1. Click **Send and Receive** to get messages from the mail server.

2. Click the Inbox.

3. Click a message description to view the message.

4. The contents of the message appear here.

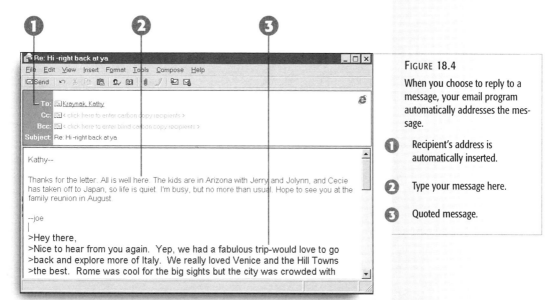

FIGURE 18.4

When you choose to reply to a message, your email program automatically addresses the message.

1. Recipient's address is automatically inserted.

2. Type your message here.

3. Quoted message.

Opening and Saving Attached Files

Email etiquette

Delete as much of the quoted message as possible, leaving only one or two lines to help the recipient follow the thread of the conversation. This makes the message smaller, allows it to reach its destination more quickly, and prevents cluttering the recipient's Inbox.

Email is useful for sending more than simple text messages. You can send images, audio and video clips, documents, and even program files by attaching them to your messages.

When you receive an email message that has a file attached to it, an icon typically appears next to the description of the message to indicate that a file is attached. Double-click the description of the message to open it in its own window. You should now see an icon that represents the attached file. You have two options for working with the file (see Figure 18.5):

- You can save the file to a folder on your hard disk and then open it later in one of your applications. To do so, right-click the icon and select **Save As**.

- You can open the file, assuming it is of a file type that has been associated with an application. To do so, double-click the icon.

FIGURE 18.5

If you receive a message that has an attached file, display the message in its own window.

① Right-click the icon for the attached file.

② Click **Open** to open or play the file in its associated program.

③ Click **Save As** to save the file to your hard disk.

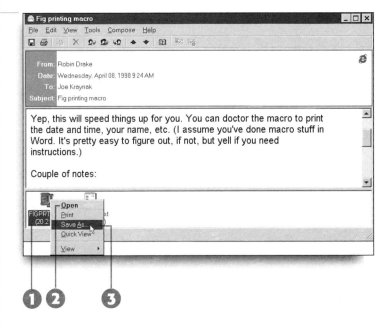

SEE ALSO

➤ *Learn more about Internet security issues and online viruses, page 511*

Composing and Sending Messages

Assuming you know the intended recipient's email address, sending a message is simple. You click the button for composing a new message, type the recipient's address and a brief description of the message, type the message, and click the **Send** button (see Figure 18.6).

Some email programs immediately send the message. Other programs place the messages you send in a temporary Outbox; you must then enter another **Send** command to actually send the messages.

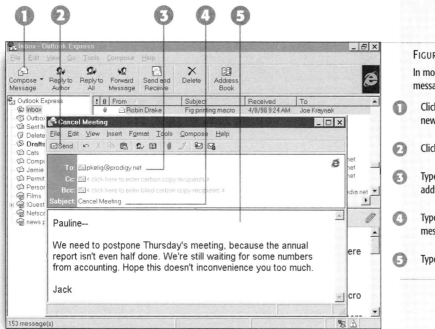

Virus concerns

If you receive a program file from someone you don't know, be careful about running the program; it might contain a virus. If you want to run the program file, be sure to check it first with an antivirus program.

FIGURE 18.6

In most email programs, sending a message is a five-step process.

① Click the button for composing a new message.

② Click the **Send** button.

③ Type the recipient's email address.

④ Type a brief description of the message.

⑤ Type the message.

Formatting Your Message

Most email programs allow you to use special type styles and sizes, add backgrounds, insert pictures, and embellish your messages with other formatting options. You can even add links that

Composing messages offline

To limit your amount of time online, consider composing messages offline (when you're not connected). Disconnect from your ISP and compose the message as you normally do. To send the message, choose **File**, **Send Later**. When you're ready to send the messages, connect to your ISP and click the button for sending and receiving messages.

point to Web pages! The email program lets you create and send the equivalent of a Web page. The only trouble is that you must make sure the recipient's email program is capable of displaying the formats you add; otherwise, the person may receive a message packed with obscure HTML codes.

Both Netscape Messenger and Outlook Express offer a toolbar that contains buttons for the most common enhancements. In Outlook Express (see Figure 18.7), you use the toolbar to make text bold or italic, add bulleted and numbered lists, and insert pictures, horizontal lines, links, and other objects. (If the toolbar does not appear, check the format menu for an HTML option. HTML stands for *Hypertext Markup Language*, the coding system used to format Web pages.)

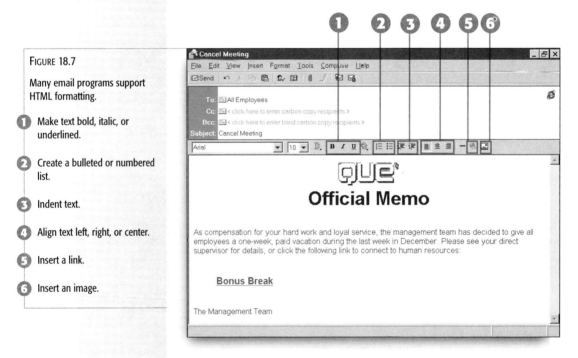

FIGURE 18.7

Many email programs support HTML formatting.

1 Make text bold, italic, or underlined.

2 Create a bulleted or numbered list.

3 Indent text.

4 Align text left, right, or center.

5 Insert a link.

6 Insert an image.

SEE ALSO

➤ *Learn more about HTML formatting options, page 426*

Attaching Files

Outlook Express stationery

Outlook Express has HTML stationery that allows you to send designer email messages. To use the stationery, click the arrow to the right of the **Compose Message** button and click the desired design.

You can send files along with your messages by creating *attachments*. The process is fairly simple, but the steps vary depending on which email program you use. In most email programs, you perform the same steps you take for composing and addressing the message. Then, you click a button for attaching a file (for example, **Attach** or **Insert File**). This displays a dialog box that lets you select the file you want to send (see Figure 18.8). The dialog box looks just like the dialog box you use to open files. Change to the folder that contains the file you want to send and then double-click the file's name.

In some programs, you can attach more than one file. When you are ready to send the message, along with the attachment, click the **Send** button.

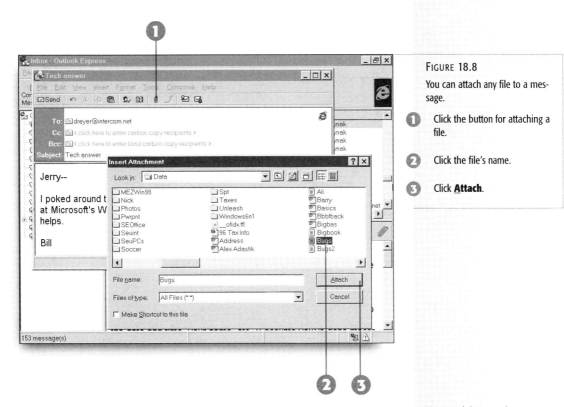

FIGURE 18.8

You can attach any file to a message.

① Click the button for attaching a file.

② Click the file's name.

③ Click **Attach**.

Drag and drop attachments

To quickly attach a file to an outgoing message, drag the file from My Computer into the message area and release the mouse button.

Managing Your Messages

Your email program's Inbox is more like a real mailbox than it seems. If you never took the mail out of your real mailbox, the box would quickly become stuffed with junk mail, greeting cards, bills, magazines, and fliers. In a few days, your mail would be spilling out onto your porch or flying down the street with the next gust.

Your email program's Inbox can likewise become packed with junk mail and messages you no longer need. This useless mail can take up valuable disk space and make it tough to find the messages you do need. Fortunately, your electronic Inbox is a little easier to organize and clean out. Email programs offer several tools for sorting your messages, grouping related messages in folders, and deleting messages that have outlived their usefulness. The following sections show you how to use these tools.

Sorting Messages

If your Inbox is packed with old messages, finding related messages can be nearly impossible. Fortunately, most email programs allow you to sort messages by date, recipient, or subject.

The easiest and fastest way to sort messages is to use the column heading toolbar just above the message list (see Figure 18.9). Click the button for the heading you want your email program to use; for example, to group the messages by sender, click the **From** or **Sender** button. This lists the messages alphabetically according to the names of the people who sent the messages. You can click the button again to reverse the sort order.

Creating New Folders

As you receive more and more messages, they just keep piling up in the Inbox, just as cards, letters, bills, and catalogues pile up on your kitchen table when you're too busy to sort through them. When your kitchen table becomes so cluttered that you can't even eat at the table, you finally pull out some folders and envelopes and start sorting so you can find everything later.

You need to do the same with your email messages. When your Inbox is packed, create a few new folders to store related messages and then move the messages to separate folders. For example, you might have one folder for email notices from your ISP, another for messages from friends, and a third for business-related messages.

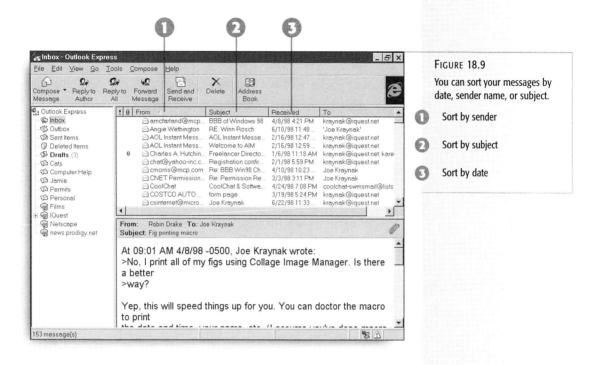

FIGURE 18.9
You can sort your messages by
date, sender name, or subject.

① Sort by sender

② Sort by subject

③ Sort by date

Creating a new folder

1. Enter the command for creating a new folder. In Outlook Express, choose **File**, **Folder**, **New Folder**. In Netscape Messenger, choose **File**, **New Folder**.

2. Type a name for the folder.

3. Choose the folder below which you want the new folder to be placed.

4. Click **OK**.

Moving Messages

After you have a new folder, you can start moving messages to it. Select the messages using the same techniques you use to select files in My Computer or Windows Explorer:

- To select a single message, click its description.

- To select additional messages, Ctrl+click the descriptions of additional messages.

Routing incoming messages to folders

Most email programs offer advanced features that can route incoming mail into separate folders based on the message description or sender's name. In Outlook Express, choose **Tools**, **Inbox Assistant** to set up the router. In Netscape Messenger, choose **Edit**, **Mail Filters**.

- To select a group of neighboring messages, click the description of the first message and Shift+click the description of the last message.

After you've selected the messages you want to move, take one of the following steps to move the messages to the desired folder:

- In Outlook Express, drag the messages over the icon for the desired folder and release the mouse button. (Or, right-click a selected message, click **Move To**, click the folder in which you want the message(s) placed, and click **OK**.)

- In Netscape Messenger, right-click one of the selected messages, point to **File Message**, and click the folder to which you want the messages moved.

Deleting Messages

Although email messages seem small, they can consume a great deal of disk space, especially if they have files attached to them. I recently cleaned up my Inbox and reclaimed more than 100MB of disk space! To prevent email messages from cluttering your disk and to make your Inbox and other email message folders more manageable, you should reorganize the messages you want to keep and delete messages you no longer need.

Before you delete a message, make sure you'll never need to refer to the message or the sender's address ever again. If you want to delete the message but save the sender's address, add the address to your Address Book, as explained in the following section.

Permanently delete messages automatically

You can tell Outlook Express to automatically remove files from the Deleted Items folder whenever you exit: Choose **Tools**, **Options**, click the **General** tab, and turn on **Empty messages from the 'Deleted Items' folder on exit**.

When you're sure you want to delete a message or a group of messages, select the messages and press the Delete key. In most email programs, deleting messages does not remove them entirely from the program. Deleting merely moves the messages to a Deleted Items or Trash folder. To completely purge the messages from your hard disk, change to the Deleted Items or Trash folder, select the messages, and press the Delete key.

When you delete messages from any folder, the email program does not automatically release the disk space occupied by those messages. To reclaim the space, you must *compress* the folder in which those messages were stored. Take one of the following steps:

- In Outlook Express, choose **File**, **Folder**, **Compact All Folders**. (Outlook Express automatically compresses folders when the wasted space in the folder exceeds a specified percentage.)

- In Netscape Messenger, choose **File**, **Compress Folders**.

SEE ALSO

➤ *Learn additional techniques for reclaiming disk space, page 248*

Creating and Using an Address Book

Even if you have a photographic memory and you can rattle off every email address you've ever seen, you don't want to have to retype a person's email address every time you send the person a message. It's much easier to select the address from a list. Nearly all email programs start you out with a default Address Book, so you can immediately start adding the names and email addresses of the people with whom you correspond.

The easiest way to add email addresses to your Address Book is to copy them from the messages you receive. Take one of the following steps to add email addresses to the Address Book in Outlook Express or Netscape Messenger:

- In Outlook Express, double-click the message description to display the message in its own window. Open the **Tools** menu, point to **Add to Address Book**, and click **Sender**. (If the message was sent to additional people, their names appear on the **Add to Address Book** menu, allowing you to add their names to your book.)

- In Netscape Messenger, right-click the message description, point to **Add to Address Book**, and click **Sender**. (If the message was sent to additional people, you can click **All** to add everyone's email address to your Address Book.)

If you don't have an email message from the person whose address you want to add, you can manually enter the address in your Address Book:

- In Outlook Express click the **Address Book** button. In the Address Book, click the **New Contact** button, enter the person's name, email address, and any additional contact information, and click the **Add** button (see Figure 18.10). Click **OK**.

- In Netscape Messenger, open the **Communicator** menu and click **Address Book**. Click the **New Card** button. Enter the person's name, email address, and any additional contact information, and click **OK**.

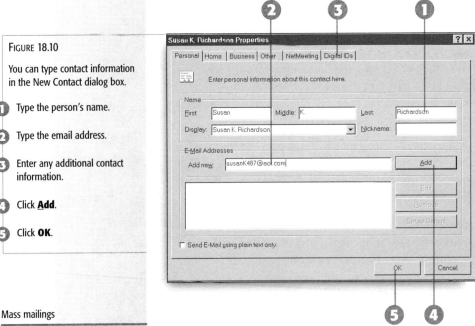

FIGURE 18.10

You can type contact information in the New Contact dialog box.

1 Type the person's name.

2 Type the email address.

3 Enter any additional contact information.

4 Click **Add**.

5 Click **OK**.

Mass mailings

You can use your Address Book to create mailing lists that contain the names of people to whom you frequently send the same email messages. In Outlook Express, click the **New Group** button. In Netscape Messenger, click the **New List** button.

Inserting Addresses from the Address Book

After you have entered a person's name in your Address Book, you can quickly address your messages by inserting addresses instead of typing them.

Addressing a message

1. Click the **Compose Message** or **New Msg** button.

2. Click in the **To** text box.

3. In Outlook Express, click the card icon to the left of the **To** text box. In Messenger, click the **Address** button.

4. Double-click the name of the person to whom you want to send this message (see Figure 18.11).

5. To address the message to additional recipients, double-click their names.

6. Click **OK**.

7. Compose and send the message as you normally do.

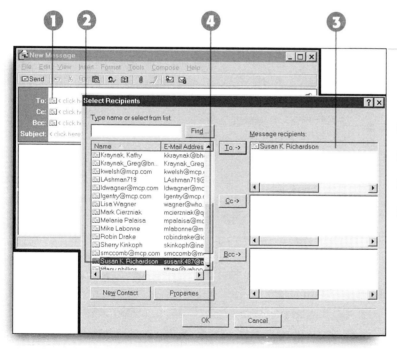

FIGURE 18.11

In Outlook Express, you can add one or more addresses to the recipients list.

① Click the card icon.

② Double-click the person's name.

③ Recipients list

④ Click **OK**.

Finding People on the Internet

The Internet has several electronic directories that you can search for a person's email address or regular mailing address. You can search for people directly from your email program or

In Outlook Express, just start typing

To quickly insert an address into the **To** text box in Outlook Express, start typing the person's name. Outlook Express automatically completes the entry for you, using information from the Address Book.

by using your Web browser to connect to the desired directory. Following is a list of popular directories on the Web:

- Four11 at `four11.com`
- Bigfoot at `bigfoot.com`
- WhoWhere? at `whowhere.com`
- InfoSeek at `infoseek.com`

Find addresses in Outlook Express

1. In the Outlook Express Address Book, open the **Edit** menu and click **Find**. The Find People dialog box appears.
2. Open the **Look in** drop-down list and click the name of the online directory you want to search.
3. In the **Name** text box, type the person's name. You can type the person's full name, last name only, or initial and last name. The more detailed the entry, the more focused the search will be.
4. Click the **Find Now** button. Outlook Express connects to the online directory and displays a list of names and email addresses that match your entry (see Figure 18.12).
5. Click the name of the person you want to add to the Address Book and click the **Add to Address Book** button.

Find addresses in Netscape Messenger

1. In Messenger's Address Book, click the **Directory** button.
2. Open the **Search for items** drop-down list and click the name of the directory you want to search.
3. Open the drop-down list below **Search for items** and choose the field you want to search: Name, Email, Phone Number, Organization, and so on.
4. Click in the rightmost text box and type your search entry. For example, if you chose Name in step 3, type the person's name.
5. Click the **Search** button. Messenger connects to the online directory and displays a list of names and email addresses that match your entry (see Figure 18.13).

SEE ALSO

➤ *Learn how to find information on the Internet, page 419*

Start, Find, People

Use the **Start**, **Find**, **People** command to quickly connect to an online directory.

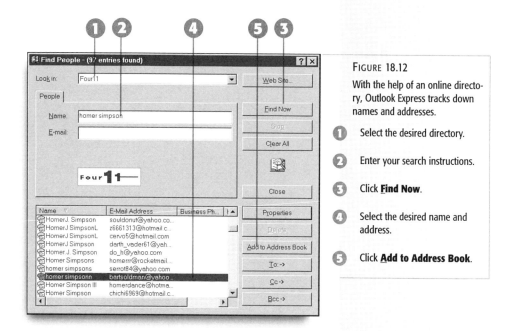

FIGURE 18.12

With the help of an online directory, Outlook Express tracks down names and addresses.

1. Select the desired directory.

2. Enter your search instructions.

3. Click **Find Now**.

4. Select the desired name and address.

5. Click **Add to Address Book**.

6. Click the name of the person you want to add to the Address Book and then click the **Add to Address Book** button.

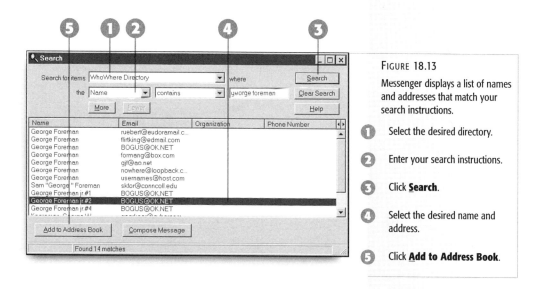

FIGURE 18.13

Messenger displays a list of names and addresses that match your search instructions.

1. Select the desired directory.

2. Enter your search instructions.

3. Click **Search**.

4. Select the desired name and address.

5. Click **Add to Address Book**.

Reading and Posting Newsgroup Messages

Connect to a news server to access newsgroups

Find newsgroups that interest you and subscribe to them

Read and reply publicly to messages posted in newsgroups

Start your own newsgroup discussions

Reply privately to a newsgroup message via email

Usenet

You may often hear the term Usenet in connection with newsgroups. Short for User's Network, Usenet is a group of interconnected computers responsible for managing the exchange of messages posted in most newsgroups.

Setting Up a News Server Account

Newsgroups are electronic forums where people can share knowledge, insights, and concerns. Users can find help, ask and answer questions, and even post graphics and other file types. There are more than 20,000 Internet newsgroups, covering such topics as politics, current events, software, automobiles, pets, body piercing, movies, supermodels, and romance.

To access a newsgroup, you need to use a special program called a *newsreader*. You use the newsreader to connect to an Internet news server, subscribe to your favorite newsgroups, and read messages posted by others. You can then reply to a message that someone posted or start a discussion by posting your own question or comment.

Before you can read and post messages in newsgroups, you must connect to a *news server*. Your Internet service provider should have given you the address of its news server. The address typically looks something like news.internet.com. You must enter this address in your newsreader so it can connect to the news server.

If you ran the Internet Connection Wizard to set up your ISP connection, it prompted you to enter connection settings for your newsgroup account. If you chose not to enter settings, the first time you run your newsreader, it should step you through the setup process. If you chose not to set up an account at first or you need to connect to a different news server, you can enter connection settings by performing the following steps.

Entering news server settings in Outlook Express

1. On the Windows desktop, click the Outlook Express icon.

2. Open the **Tools** menu and click **Accounts**. The Internet Accounts dialog box appears.

3. Click the **Add** button and select **News**. This starts the Internet Connection Wizard, which prompts you to type your name.

4. Type your name as you want it to appear when you post messages to a newsgroup. (This can be your real name or, if you prefer to remain anonymous, a nickname.) Click **Next**.

5. Type your email address so people can reply to the messages you post by sending you email messages. Click **Next**. You are now prompted to type the address of your news server.

6. In the **News (NNTP) Server** text box, type your news server's address as shown in Figure 19.1 (for instance, news.internet.com).

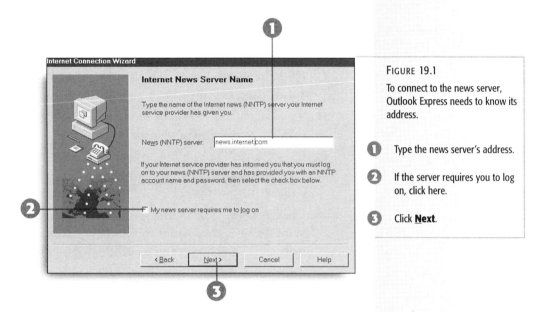

7. If your news server requires you to log on using your username and password, select **My news server requires me to log on**. Click **Next**. (Most ISP news servers do not require users to log on. If you're connecting to a special news server not hosted by your ISP, you may need to enter logon information.)

8. If the server requires you to log on, select one of the following logon settings:

Log On Using if your news server requires you to enter a name and password to connect. Enter the required name and password in the appropriate text boxes.

Log On Using Secure Password Authentication (SPA) if your news server requires you to connect using a digital certification.

Trouble connecting?

If Outlook Express has trouble connecting to the news server, open the **Tools** menu, choose **Accounts**, click the **News** tab, and double-click your news server. Check the information on the **General** tab and, on the **Advanced** tab, check the **Server Timeouts** setting. You usually need to crank up the Timeouts setting to two minutes to keep Outlook Express from disconnecting prematurely.

9. Click **Next**. The wizard prompts you to enter a friendly name for your news server.

10. Type a descriptive name for the server and click **Next**.

11. Click **Connect Using My Phone Line** or **Connect Using My Local Area Network** to specify how you connect to the Internet. Click **Next**.

12. Click **Use an Existing Dial-Up Connection**, and then click the Dial-Up Networking connection you use to connect to the Internet. Click **Next**.

13. Click the **Finish** button. The Internet Accounts dialog box appears, showing the name of the news server you added.

14. To make this your default news server, click its name and click the **Set as Default** button.

15. Click **Close**. The Outlook Express dialog box appears, asking if you want to download a list of newsgroups from the server.

16. Click **Yes**. Outlook Express starts to download the list of available newsgroups from your Internet service provider's news server and displays a dialog box showing the progress.

After downloading the list of available newsgroups, Outlook Express displays a list of their names. See the next section for details on how to proceed.

Entering news server settings in Netscape Collabra

1. Open the **Start** menu, point to **Programs**, **Netscape Communicator**, and click **Netscape Collabra**.

2. Open the **Edit** menu, and click **Preferences**. The Preferences dialog box appears.

3. Click the plus sign next to **Mail & Groups**, to expand the list of options.

4. Click **Groups Server**. This displays options for setting up and configuring the news server (see Figure 19.2).

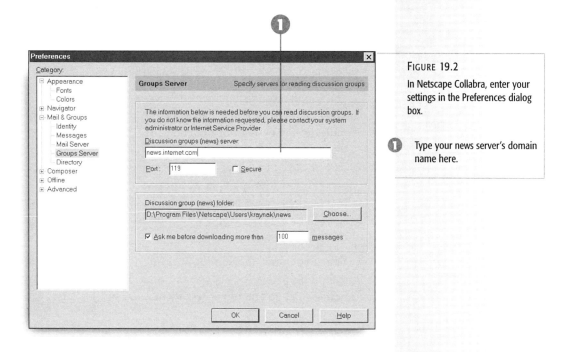

5. Click in the **Discussion groups (news) server** text box, and type the domain name of your service provider's news server.

6. Don't change the entry in the News Directory text box, unless your ISP instructed you to do so. This entry tells Collabra where to store information about the newsgroups you decide to read.

7. Make sure **Ask me before downloading more than 100 messages** has a check mark next to it. This prevents Collabra from cluttering your disk with more message descriptions than your hard drive can handle.

8. Click **OK** to save your changes.

Finding and Subscribing to Newsgroups

When you have a list of more than 20,000 newsgroups, the biggest problem you face is narrowing the list and finding the newsgroups that interest you. Fortunately, your newsreader provides a tool that allows you to search for newsgroups by name.

No automatic delivery

Subscribing to a newsgroup is not like subscribing to a Web site. When you subscribe to a newsgroup, your newsreader does not automatically download newsgroup messages on a specified schedule. Subscribing simply places the newsgroup on a list of newsgroups that interest you.

For example, you can search for newsgroups that deal with gardening by typing "garden." Your newsreader then narrows the list of newsgroups to display only those newsgroups that have "garden," "gardens," or "gardening" in their names.

You can determine a newsgroup's focus by looking at its address. Most addresses are made up of two to three parts. The first part indicates the newsgroup's overall subject area; for example, **rec** is for "recreation," and **alt** stands for "alternative." The second part of the address indicates more specifically what the newsgroup offers. For example, **rec.pets** is about taking care of your pets. If the address has a third part (most do), it focuses even further. For example, **rec.pets.dogs** discusses topics specifically related to dogs.

When you find a newsgroup that interests you, you can *subscribe* to it. This places the newsgroups on a short list of subscribed newsgroups so you can access them more quickly later.

Subscribing with Outlook Express

After you've set up your news server in Outlook Express, you can download a list of newsgroups and subscribe to the ones that catch your eye. To subscribe to newsgroups use the Newsgroups dialog box.

Double-click to subscribe

In the Newsgroups dialog box, you can quickly subscribe or unsubscribe to a newsgroup by double-clicking its name.

Finding and subscribing to newsgroups

1. In the folder list on the left, click the icon for your news server.

2. Click the **Newsgroups** button. This displays a list of all available newsgroups (see Figure 19.3). If this is the first time you clicked the **Newsgroups** button, Outlook Express may take several minutes to download the list.

3. To narrow the list, click in the **Display newsgroups which contain** text box and type a word or term that describes your interest.

4. In the list of available newsgroups, click the newsgroup to which you want to subscribe.

5. Click the **Subscribe** button. A newspaper icon appears next to the newsgroup's name, and the newsgroup appears on the **Subscribed** tab.

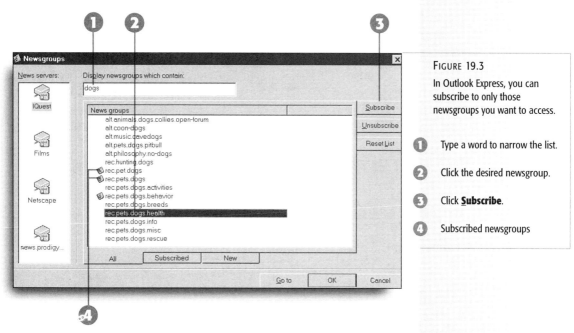

FIGURE **19.3**

In Outlook Express, you can subscribe to only those newsgroups you want to access.

❶ Type a word to narrow the list.

❷ Click the desired newsgroup.

❸ Click **Subscribe**.

❹ Subscribed newsgroups

Subscribing with Netscape Collabra

After you've set up your news server in Collabra, you can use the server to download a complete list of newsgroups. From this list, you can subscribe to selected newsgroups.

Finding and subscribing to newsgroups

1. In Collabra, click the name of your news server.

2. Click the **Subscribe** button. The Subscribe to Discussion Groups dialog box appears. If this is the first time you have chosen to subscribe to discussion groups, Collabra downloads a list of all available groups. This may take several minutes.

3. Click the **Search for a Group** tab.

4. Click in the **Search for** text box and type a word that describes your interest.

5. Click the **Search Now** button.

> **Netscape Communicator 4.5**
>
> In the latest version of Netscape Communicator, which was in development during the writing of this book, email and newsgroups are both handled in Netscape Messenger, eliminating most of the confusion caused by the Messenger/Collabra distinctions.

6. To subscribe to a newsgroup click its name and click the **S̲ubscribe** button, or click the dot in the Subscribe column next to the newsgroup (see Figure 19.4). The dot changes into a check mark, indicating that you have subscribed to the newsgroup.

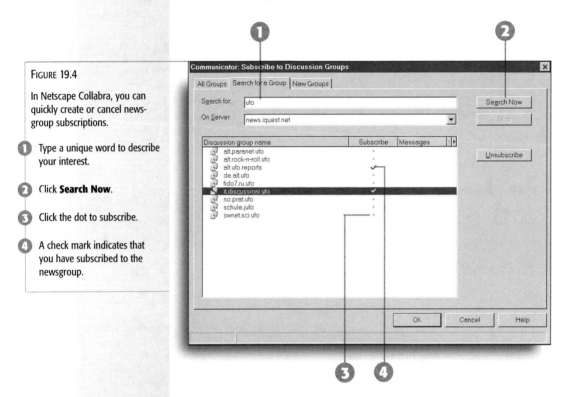

FIGURE 19.4

In Netscape Collabra, you can quickly create or cancel news-group subscriptions.

1 Type a unique word to describe your interest.

2 Click **Search Now**.

3 Click the dot to subscribe.

4 A check mark indicates that you have subscribed to the newsgroup.

Canceling your subscription

To unsubscribe from a newsgroup, open the Message Center and click the plus sign next to your news server. Right-click the newsgroup's name and click **Remove Discussion Group**.

7. Click the **OK** button to return to the Message Center.

In Collabra, you have several newsgroup windows to deal with: the Message Center, the Discussion window, and the Message window. Collabra initially opens the Message Center window, which displays a list of folders with the newsgroups at the bottom. When you double-click a newsgroup in the Message Center, the Discussion window appears, showing a list of messages in the selected newsgroup. If you then double-click a message, the Message window appears. In the latest version of Communicator (version 4.5), this mess has been cleared up, giving you a single Netscape Messenger window to work with.

Below the Netscape N logo in the Message and Discussion window is a green arrow icon. You can click the green arrow to quickly switch to the previous window. In the Message window, click the arrow to go back to the Discussion window. In the Discussion window, click the arrow to return to the Message Center.

Reading Posted Messages

Both Outlook Express and Netscape Collabra display a list of folders followed by an icon for your news server. Assuming you subscribed to newsgroups, the news server icon should have a plus sign next to it. Click the plus sign to view the list of subscribed newsgroups.

Next, double-click the name of a subscribed newsgroup to have your newsreader download and display a list of *headers*, descriptions of the messages posted in the selected newsgroup. Outlook Express displays the header list in the upper-right pane and the contents of the selected message in the lower-right pane. To read a message, you either click its header or double-click the header to display the message in its own window (see Figure 19.5).

If a message has a plus sign next to it, somebody has posted a reply to the message. Click the plus sign to display the reply header(s). You can then click the header to view the contents of the reply. A message and its replies is often called a *thread*. Most newsreaders group messages and their replies so you can follow the discussion.

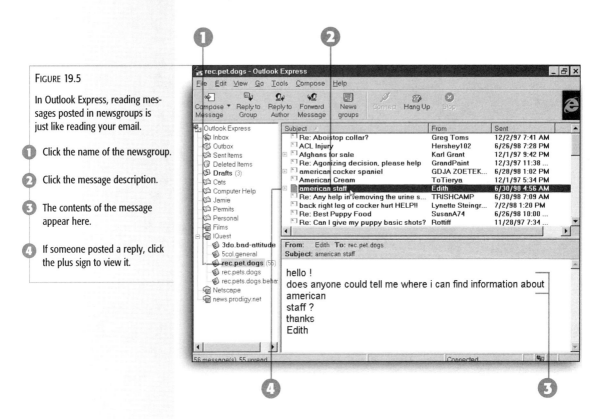

FIGURE 19.5

In Outlook Express, reading messages posted in newsgroups is just like reading your email.

❶ Click the name of the newsgroup.

❷ Click the message description.

❸ The contents of the message appear here.

❹ If someone posted a reply, click the plus sign to view it.

More messages?

By default, Outlook Express downloads the first 300 message headers in the newsgroup. To download the next 300 message headers, open the **Tools** menu and choose **Get Next 300 Headers**.

By default, Collabra doesn't display the message contents in a separate pane. To display the messages in a newsgroup, first click the plus sign next to your news server's name and double-click the desired newsgroup. The Netscape Discussion window appears, displaying a list of messages in the selected newsgroup. Double-click a message to display its contents. Click the **Next** button to display the contents of the next unread message.

Another way to read messages is to divide the Netscape Discussion window into two panes (it may already be divided into two panes). If the window displays a single pane, click the blue triangle in the lower-left corner of the window to display the message contents pane, as shown in Figure 19.6. Whenever you click a message description in the upper pane, the contents of the message appear in the lower pane. You can use the drop-down list just above the message list to select a different subscribed newsgroup or to change to your Inbox folder or another folder.

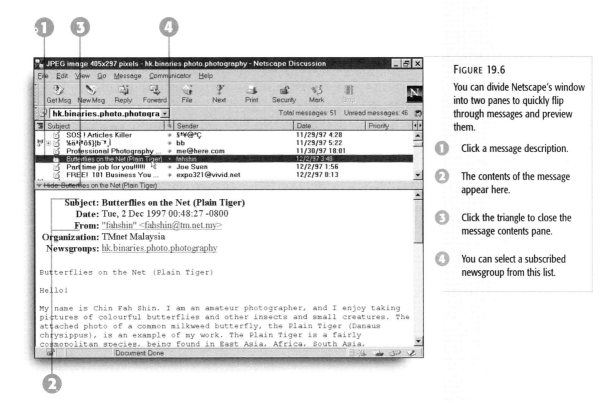

FIGURE 19.6

You can divide Netscape's window into two panes to quickly flip through messages and preview them.

1 Click a message description.

2 The contents of the message appear here.

3 Click the triangle to close the message contents pane.

4 You can select a subscribed newsgroup from this list.

As with Outlook Express, if a message has a plus sign next to it, one or more people have posted replies to the original message. Click the plus sign to display the reply header(s). You can then click the header to view the contents of the reply.

Sorting Messages

If you connect to a newsgroup that contains hundreds of messages, sifting through the list may be time-consuming. To help, you can sort the messages. Click the heading above the column whose entries you want to sort. For example, to sort by name, click the **Sender** column heading. To sort by message description, click the **Subject** heading. You can change the sort order (for instance, from A-Z to Z-A) by clicking again on the column heading.

SEE ALSO

➤ *Learn how to organize and delete messages, page 445*

Finding Specific Messages

Even with some expert sorting, a list of 300 messages can be difficult to navigate. If you know of a specific subject or sender that you want to search for in the message list, you can use your newsreader's search tool to hunt down messages:

- In Netscape Messenger, open the **Edit** menu and select **Search Messages**. Choose the subscribed newsgroup you want to search, enter your search instructions, and click the **Search** button (see Figure 19.7). Messenger displays a list of messages that matched your instructions. Double-click the message to display its contents.

- In Outlook Express, open the **Edit** menu and click **Find Message**. Type a person's name in the **From** text box or type a description of the desired topic in the **Subject** text box. Click the **Find** button. Outlook Express performs the specified search, and highlights the description of the first message it finds that matches your search instructions. Press F3 to skip to the next message that matches your search instructions.

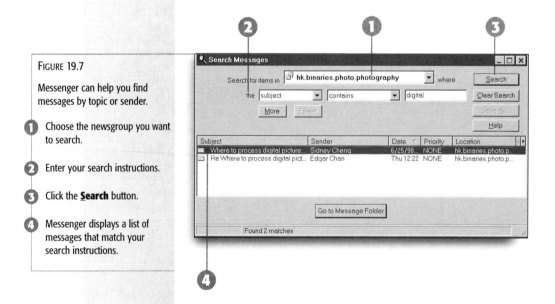

FIGURE 19.7

Messenger can help you find messages by topic or sender.

1 Choose the newsgroup you want to search.

2 Enter your search instructions.

3 Click the **Search** button.

4 Messenger displays a list of messages that match your search instructions.

Posting Messages and Replies

Posting a reply or starting a discussion is as easy as sending an email message. You click a button to post your reply or message, enter a description of the message, type the message itself, and then click the **Post** or **Send** button. However, you do have a few choices on how to post your reply or message:

- Post your reply or message publicly to have it appear in the list of messages so all visitors of the newsgroup can read it.

- Post your reply privately by sending an email message to the person who posted the original message. The person then receives your reply without having to check the newsgroup. (Sometimes, a person specifically requests that you reply via email.)

- Post your reply publicly in the newsgroup and privately via email. This places your message in the newsgroup so all visitors can read it, and it also sends a copy via email to the person who posted the original message.

Posting a Public Reply

When you post a reply to a newsgroup, your message appears in the newsgroup, where anyone can read it. The person to whom you are replying has to check the newsgroup to read your reply.

Posting a reply to a newsgroup

1. Select the message to which you want to respond.

2. In Collabra, click the **Reply** button and click **Reply to Group**. In Outlook Express, click the **Reply to Group** button. A new message window appears, with the newsgroup's address and the subject description filled in for you (see Figure 19.8).

3. Type your message in the message area at the bottom of the window.

4. Click the **Send** or **Post** button. Your newsreader sends your reply as instructed.

> **Newsgroup etiquette**
>
> To avoid getting verbally battered in a newsgroup, follow a few simple rules. Don't insult any person or attack any topic of conversation. Post messages that pertain to the newsgroup and topic of conversation (read the entire conversation before adding your own two cents). Don't advertise in a newsgroup unless the newsgroup is especially designed for advertising. And, don't shout by using all capital letters in your message.

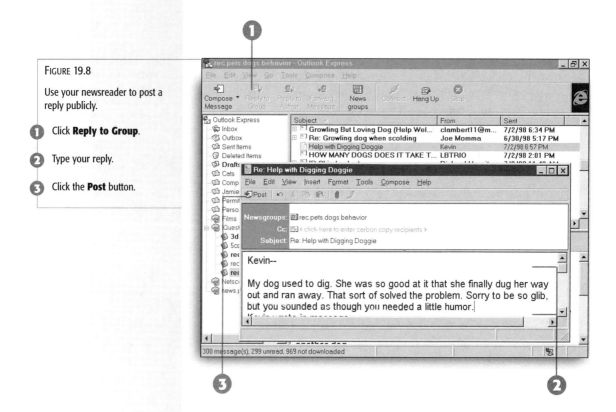

FIGURE 19.8

Use your newsreader to post a reply publicly.

1 Click **Reply to Group**.

2 Type your reply.

3 Click the **Post** button.

Replying Privately Via Email

Many users specifically request that you reply to their messages via email. This saves them the trouble of having to sift through a long list of messages to find your reply, and it keeps your reply confidential. If you reply via email, your reply goes only to the person who posted the original message.

Replying privately

1. Select the message to which you want to respond.

2. In Collabra, click the **Reply** button and click **Reply to Sender**. In Outlook Express, click the **Reply to Author** button. Your newsreader automatically starts the email program and displays a new message window, with the person's email address and the subject description filled in for you.

3. Type your message in the message area at the bottom of the window.

4. Click the **Send** button. Your email program sends your reply to the specified email address.

SEE ALSO

➤ *Learn more about sending email messages, page 443*

Starting Your Own Discussion

Newsgroups are a great place to go to share insights, tell jokes, and obtain help and advice. If you've searched the Web and just can't find a specific answer to your question, try posting the question in an appropriate newsgroup. Whether you need a part for your '67 Chevy, help with a stubborn computer glitch, advice on how to prune roses, or moral support for raising your teenagers, you'll find many knowledgeable people willing to listen and impart some free advice.

Starting a discussion

1. Go to the newsgroup in which you want to post your message. A list of posted messages appears.

2. Click the **New Msg** or **Compose Message** button.

3. Click in the **Subject** text box, and type a brief description of your message.

4. Click in the message area and type your message.

5. Click the **Send** or **Post** button. Your message is posted in the active newsgroup. You can now check the newsgroup on a regular basis, to see if anyone has replied to your message.

Posting follow-ups to the group

If you post a question and receive email replies that answer your question or help you solve a problem, go back to the newsgroup and post a reply to your original message summarizing the answer(s) you received. This lets everyone know they can stop posting replies and informs people of the answer or solution.

Newsgroups on the Web

Another way to find answers to your questions is to search newsgroup archives on the Web. Go to Lycos (**www.lycos.com**), open the **Search** drop-down list, and click **Message Boards**. In the **For** text box, type a few words to describe what you're looking for and click the **Go Get It** button.

Copying Files Across the Internet with FTP

Copy files from FTP servers using your Web browser

Install a real FTP program for faster file transfers

Find and log on to FTP servers

Copy files from your PC to an FTP server

Find files on FTP servers when you know the file's name

Understanding FTP

When the Internet started out, it was little more than a huge file warehouse and electronic postal service. Businesses, universities, and the U.S. government needed a reliable communications network and a convenient system for exchanging files. Email and FTP served those functions well and have continued to function as important Internet features even with the explosive growth and popularity of the Web.

FTP, short for *File Transfer Protocol*, is a set of rules that govern the exchange of files over the Internet. The FTP server acts as a gigantic hard disk complete with multiple folders. Businesses, universities, and other large organizations use FTP servers so that people can share files without having to email them back and forth.

Using an FTP program, or a Web browser that supports FTP file transfers, you can connect to FTP servers and *download* files (copy files from the FTP server to your PC) or *upload* files (copy files from your PC to the FTP server). This chapter shows you how to perform FTP file transfers using your Web browser and how to obtain and use dedicated FTP software to speed up your FTP file transfers.

Downloading Files with Your Web Browser

Anonymous (public) FTP

Some FTP servers are open to the public and others are not. To access a private FTP server, the FTP administrator must assign you a username and password for logging on. You'll learn more about logging on to private FTP servers in this chapter.

You may already have performed some FTP file transfers with your Web browser and never even realized it. Many Web pages include links to files stored on FTP servers. When you click the link, your browser (or a plug-in or ActiveX control) either played the file, or a dialog box popped up asking if you wanted to save the file to your hard disk. You probably gave your okay, chose the drive and folder in which you wanted the file stored, and clicked **Save** to copy the file from the server.

Occasionally you come face to face with an FTP server. You click a link expecting to open a Web page packed with graphics, video, clips, and other media, but instead, you're greeted with something that looks more like a grocery list (see Figure 20.1). In the **Address** or **Go To** text box, instead of the usual http://, the browser displays ftp://, letting you know that you're no longer on the Web.

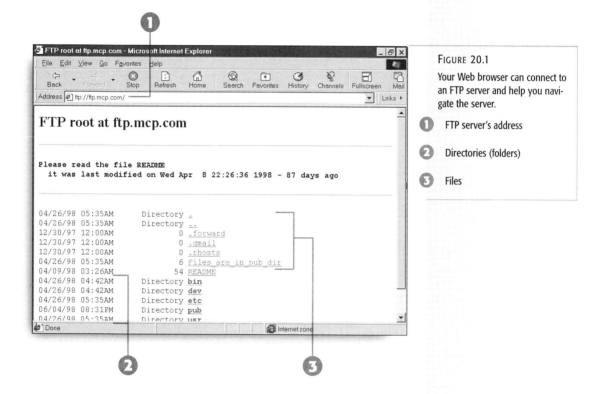

FIGURE 20.1

Your Web browser can connect to an FTP server and help you navigate the server.

1 FTP server's address

2 Directories (folders)

3 Files

If you know the address of a public (anonymous) FTP server you need to access, type its address in the **Address** or **Go To** text box and press Enter. Make sure the address starts with ftp://. Your Web browser will not automatically supply the ftp:// as it supplies the http:// for Web pages.

Navigating an FTP Server

When you log on to an FTP server, notice that the files are grouped in directories or folders, which appear as links in your browser. To open a directory, click the directory name, which acts as a link. To move back up to a higher level in the directory tree, you have the following options:

- Click the browser's **Back** button.
- Click the double dot (..) link.
- If the FTP server has a link called **Up to a Higher Level Directory** (or something similar), click the link. (This link is typically located in the upper-left corner of the viewing area.)

Finding your way to the correct file on an FTP server isn't always easy. You usually have to dig through several layers of directories and subdirectories to find the right file. In addition, FTP servers rarely provide access to *all* directories on the server. If you try to access a directory that's off limits, the server displays a message indicating that access has been denied. You'll have to back up and follow another trail.

Connecting to Public FTP Servers

If a company or organization wants to provide public access to its files, it can set up its FTP server as an *anonymous* FTP server. An anonymous FTP server typically allows users to log on by entering anonymous as the username and entering an email address as the password. For security purposes, anonymous FTP servers provide only download access. You can connect to public directories on the server and download files, but you cannot create new directories or upload files to the server.

Using your browser to connect to public FTP servers is easy. Your browser is set up to enter the standard logon information for you: anonymous (as your username) and your email address as your password. If you have trouble connecting to an anonymous FTP server, obtain the required username and password from the site's administrator and enter it as explained in the following section.

Connecting to Private FTP Servers

For security purposes, companies and organizations rarely provide public access to all directories on their FTP server. They may have sensitive documents or are just not equipped to handle much traffic. In such cases, the FTP administrator sets up the server as a private FTP server. The administrator assigns access privileges to individual users and assigns each user a unique username and password. Your ISP may have given you access to a specific directory on the FTP server for publishing your Web page files or for storing other file types.

If you are given access to a private FTP server, you'll need the following information to log on to the server:

- The FTP server's address (for example, ftp.internet.com).
- Your username for logging on.
- Your password.
- The complete path to the directory you can access. (You may have access to more than one directory.)

When you have the information you need, you can connect to a private FTP server using your Web browser. In the **Address** or **Go To** text box in your browser, type the entry for logging on to the FTP server in the following format:

```
ftp://username:password@ftp.server.com/path/to/directory
```

For example, your entry may look like the following:

```
ftp://bjohnson:34xwetg89@ftp.mcp.com/user/johnson
```

Accessing a private FTP server

1. Run your Web browser.
2. In the **Address**, **Location**, or **Go To** text box, highlight the current entry.
3. Type the address to the FTP server, your logon information, and the path to your directory in the following format:

   ```
   ftp://username:password@ftp.server.com/path/to/directory
   ```
4. Press Enter.

Uploading Files with Your Browser

If you're a telecommuter or your ISP requires you to upload files to an FTP server to publish your Web pages, you may be able to

Sending your email address as password

If you have trouble logging on to an anonymous FTP server in Navigator, choose **Edit, Preferences** and click the **Advanced** category. Make sure **Send Email Address as Anonymous FTP Password** is checked, and then click **OK**.

use your Web browser to upload the files. I say "may be" because some Web browsers cannot handle FTP uploads.

If you're using Netscape Navigator, you'll have no problem. Navigator has had FTP upload support built in to it since version 2.0. Simply connect to the FTP server and change to the directory in which you want the file(s) placed. Then, drag and drop the file(s) from My Computer or Windows Explorer into the page display area in Navigator (see Figure 20.2). You can also use the **File**, **Upload File** command.

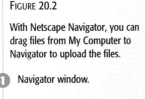

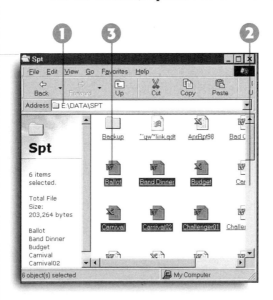

FIGURE 20.2

With Netscape Navigator, you can drag files from My Computer to Navigator to upload the files.

1 Navigator window.

2 My Computer.

3 Drag and drop the files.

Your ability to upload files with Internet Explorer depends on which version of Internet Explorer you're using. Versions 4 and earlier do not support FTP uploads. Microsoft offers an add-on feature that allows you to upload files using an HTML form, but you'll have more success using a dedicated FTP program, as explained later in this chapter. Internet Explorer 5, which was in early beta during the writing of this book, supports drag-and-drop FTP file uploads.

Although an FTP program is easier to use, you can upload files to an FTP server using the Web Publishing Wizard. In My Computer, select the files you want to upload. Right-click one of the selected files, point to **Send To**, and click **Web Publishing Wizard**. (If the wizard isn't on the menu, run Windows setup again to install it.) Follow the wizard's instructions to upload your files.

SEE ALSO

➤ *Learn how to install the Web Publishing Wizard from the Windows CD, page 204*

➤ *Learn more about using the Web Publishing Wizard, page 431*

Working with Compressed Files

Many files you find at FTP sites are *compressed* in some way, so they take up less storage space and travel more quickly over Internet connections. PC files are commonly compressed into a .ZIP format, requiring you to *uncompress* the files using a program such as WinZip or PKZip. Most Mac files are compressed into .SIT or .HQX format, which PC users can avoid. Here's a list of other compressed formats you might encounter:

.Z	Compressed with a UNIX compression program
.z	Compressed with a UNIX pack program
.shar	Archived with UNIX shell archive
.tar	Compressed with UNIX tar
.pit	Compressed with Macintosh Packit
.zoo	Compressed with Zoo210
.arc	Packed with PKARC for DOS
.exe	Self-extracting .ZIP file for a PC
.hqx	Mac BinHex
.sea	Self-extracting .SIT file for the Mac

When downloading files, make sure you get files that can run in Windows. In other words, don't bother downloading a Macintosh .SIT or .SEA file.

Downloading and Installing WinZip

Because most compressed PC files are stored in the ZIP format, download a decompression utility that can extract files from a

ZIP file. The two most popular decompression utilities are PKZip and WinZip. You've probably heard of PKZip because it has been around a long time, but don't waste your time with it; it's a DOS utility that requires you to type complicated commands. Get WinZip.

You can download WinZip using your Web browser. Fire up Internet Explorer or Netscape Navigator and go to www.winzip.com. Click the link for downloading the free evaluation copy and follow the onscreen instructions to download the file to a folder on your hard disk.

The file you download is a self-extracting, self-installing program file. Change to the folder in which you saved the WinZip file and click the file. This initiates the installation routine. Follow the onscreen instructions to install WinZip.

Extracting Files with WinZip

When you install WinZip, the installation routine associates WinZip with ZIP files. This makes it easy to decompress ZIP files. In My Computer or Windows Explorer, click the ZIP file to open it in WinZip. This displays a list of the files contained in the ZIP file. When you use WinZip to extract files, keep the following points in mind:

- If the ZIP file contains files for installing a program, you do not need to extract the files. Simply click the Setup.exe or Install.exe file in the WinZip window. WinZip automatically extracts the necessary files and runs the installation. If you extract the files first, you'll have to delete them after you install the program.

- It's a good idea to extract files to a separate folder, so they don't get mixed up with your other files.

- If you click the WinZip's Extract button before selecting a file, WinZip extracts all the files in the ZIP folder (which is what you usually want to do). If you select a file first, WinZip extracts only the selected file.

Pay for it

WinZip is a shareware (try-before-you-buy) program. If you decide to use it beyond the 30-day trial period, send in the $29; it'll be the best $29 you've ever spent on a program.

Other decompression utilities

Although I highly recommend WinZip, you can find other decompression utilities on the Web. Go to cws.internet.com to check out other programs.

Decompress ZIP Files with WinZip

1. In My Computer, click the icon for the ZIP file.

2. (Optional) To extract selected files, click a file and Ctrl+click any others you want to extract.

3. Click the **Extract** button.

4. Choose the disk and folder in to which you want the extracted file(s) placed (see Figure 20.3).

5. Click the **Extract** button.

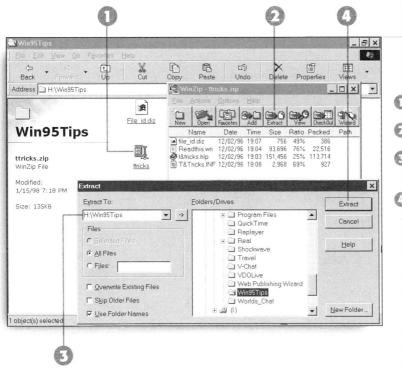

FIGURE 20.3

You can quickly extract files stored in a Zip file.

1. Click the Zip file.

2. Click **Extract**.

3. Choose the destination disk and folder.

4. Click **Extract**.

Compressing Files with WinZip

If you plan on uploading multiple files or large files to an FTP server or sending them via email, consider compressing the files into a single Zip file. (You can also use WinZip to archive old files and reclaim disk space.) With WinZip, you can compress files directly from My Computer or Windows Explorer.

Drag-and-drop compression

To quickly compress files and add them to an existing Zip file, click the Zip file in My Computer to display its contents in the WinZip window. You can then drag and drop files from My Computer into the WinZip window.

Compressing files with WinZip

1. Select the files you want to compress.

2. Right-click one of the selected files and click **Add to Zip**.

3. Click the **New** button.

4. Change to the folder in which you want the new Zip file stored.

5. In the **File Name** text box, type a name for the file, but omit the .ZIP extension (WinZip adds it for you). Click **OK**.

6. Open the **Action** drop-down list and click the desired option: **Add (and Replace) Files** or **Move Files** (to delete the original files after compressing them) as shown in Figure 20.4.

7. Open the **Compression** drop-down list and click the desired compression option: **Maximum** (slowest), **Normal**, **Fast**, **SuperFast**, or **None** (fastest, but what's the point?).

8. Click the **Add** button.

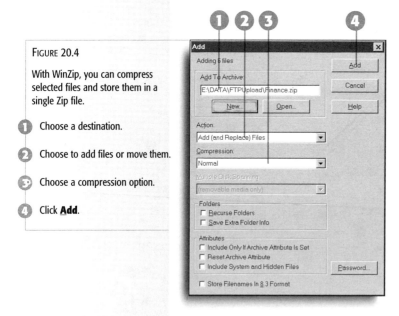

FIGURE 20.4

With WinZip, you can compress selected files and store them in a single Zip file.

1 Choose a destination.

2 Choose to add files or move them.

3 Choose a compression option.

4 Click **Add**.

SEE ALSO

➤ *Learn more about reclaiming disk space, page 248*

➤ *Learn how to send files with email messages, page 444*

Downloading and Installing an FTP Program

For light FTP duty, your Web browser is ideal. It's convenient, and by now you're probably pretty comfortable using it. However, if you need to frequently download or upload files, connect to private FTP servers, or download large files, fire your Web browser and hire on a dedicated, industrial strength FTP program. A dedicated FTP program offers the following advantages:

- *It stores logon information for multiple FTP servers.* To connect to a server, you simply select its name from the server list and click the **Connect** button. The FTP program connects to the specified server, enters your username and password, and changes to your directory.

- *It has a more manageable interface for downloading and uploading files.* One pane displays the disks and folders on your hard disk, and another pane displays the directories and files on the FTP server. You simply copy files from one pane to the other.

- *It's faster.* Web browsers are not designed to handle FTP file transfers as well as dedicated FTP programs.

- *It's more reliable.* Error detection and correction features in FTP programs are better than those in Web browsers.

- *It has a list of servers and necessary information.* A dedicated FTP program has a list of popular public FTP servers and the logon information you need to connect.

- *It can upload files.* If you're using Internet Explorer 4 or earlier as your Web browser, you'll need an FTP program to upload files.

Other FTP programs

Many excellent FTP programs are available as shareware. Check cws.internet.com or www.tucows.com for additional programs. WS_FTP is one of the most popular FTP programs around. It displays the standard two-pane window that makes it easy to copy files from the FTP server to your PC and vice versa.

One of the best FTP programs for PCs is CuteFTP, a shareware program you can download from the Web. Run your Web browser and go to **www.cuteftp.com**. Click the link for downloading CuteFTP and then follow the onscreen instructions to register and download the program. When the download is complete, use My Computer to change to the folder in which you saved the installation file and click the file's name. Follow the installation instructions to complete the installation.

➤ *Learn more about obtaining Internet programs, page 423*

Using Your FTP Program

To use your FTP program, you connect to an FTP server and change directories to locate the files you want. You can then copy files from the server to your PC or from your PC to the server.

To successfully connect to and access files on an FTP server, you must first log on to the server. Most FTP programs have a list of servers that allow anonymous access. To connect to the server, select its name from the list and click the **Connect** button.

Connecting to a server with CuteFTP

  1. Open the **Start** menu, point to **Programs**, **CuteFTP**, and click **CuteFTP**. The CuteFTP window appears, displaying a list of FTP site categories.

  2. Click the category for the desired site. A list of sites in the selected category appears (see Figure 20.5).

  3. Click the name of the FTP site you want to access.

  4. Click the **Connect** button. CuteFTP connects to the site and displays a two-paned window displaying the contents of your hard drive and the contents of the FTP server (see Figure 20.6).

  5. Use CuteFTP to download and upload files, as explained in the following two sections.

  6. When you are done, click the **Disconnect** button.

Index too long?

If you receive a message indicating that the index file is too long, choose to skip the process of downloading the index file.

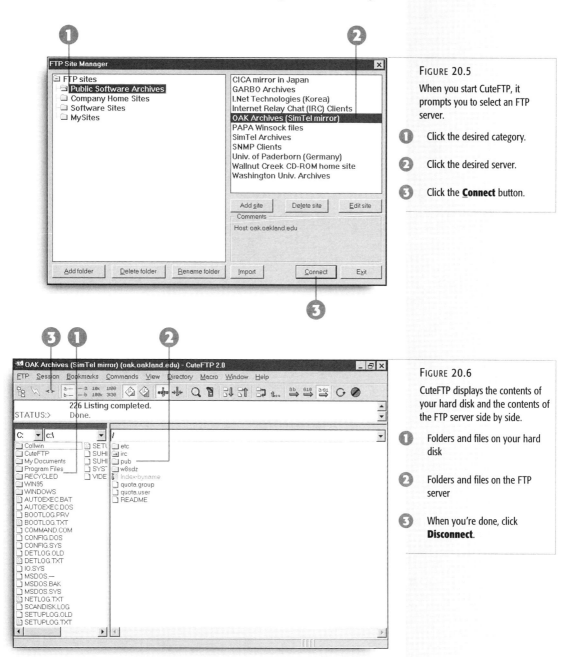

FIGURE 20.5

When you start CuteFTP, it prompts you to select an FTP server.

① Click the desired category.

② Click the desired server.

③ Click the **Connect** button.

FIGURE 20.6

CuteFTP displays the contents of your hard disk and the contents of the FTP server side by side.

① Folders and files on your hard disk

② Folders and files on the FTP server

③ When you're done, click **Disconnect**.

Entering Connection Settings for an FTP Server

To connect to an FTP server that's not on CuteFTP's list, you must add the server's name to the list and enter the required logon settings.

Adding an FTP site in CuteFTP

1. Click the **Site Manager** button 📇 or open CuteFTP's **FTP** menu and click **Site Manager**.

2. Click FTP sites at the top of the folder list and click **Add Folder**.

3. Type a name for your folder (for instance, MyFTP) and click **OK**.

4. Click your new folder in the folder list.

5. Click the **Add Site** button.

6. In the **Site Label** text box, type a descriptive name for the site (see Figure 20.7).

7. In the **Host Address** text box, type the FTP server's address (for instance, ftp.internet.com).

8. If the server requires you to use a special name to log on, click in the **User ID** text box and type your logon name.

9. If the server requires you to log on with a special password, click in the **Password** text box and type your password.

10. To start in a specific directory on the server, click in the **Initial Remote Directory** text box and type a path to the directory (for instance, /pub/user/~jackson).

11. To have CuteFTP start with a specific folder on your hard disk, click the question mark next to **Initial Local Directory**, change to the desired disk and folder, and click **OK**.

12. Enter any other settings as specified by the FTP administrator for this site and then click **OK**.

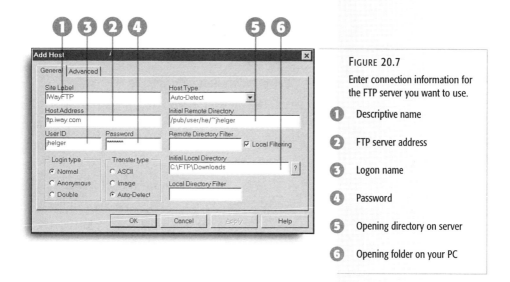

FIGURE 20.7

Enter connection information for the FTP server you want to use.

① Descriptive name

② FTP server address

③ Logon name

④ Password

⑤ Opening directory on server

⑥ Opening folder on your PC

Making New Directories (Folders)

Before you start transferring files between your PC and the FTP server, you should know how to create directories in CuteFTP. Of course, you can create new folders on your hard disk by using My Computer or Windows Explorer, but if you're already connected to the FTP server, it's easier to create folders in CuteFTP. In addition, if you're uploading files to the server, you may want to place your files in a new directory on the server. If you have authorization to create directories on the server, you can create a directory with CuteFTP.

To create a directory, change to the disk and folder below which you want the new directory created. This can be on your PC or on the FTP server. Open the **Commands** menu and click **Make New Dir** or press Ctrl+M. Type a name for the new directory and click **OK**.

Selecting and Downloading Files

Your FTP program is Windows Explorer for the Internet. When you run it and connect to an FTP server, the FTP program displays a two-pane window, displaying the contents of your computer in one pane and the contents of the FTP server in the other. You can transfer files between your PC and the FTP server just by dragging and dropping the files from one pane into the other.

Downloading files with CuteFTP

1. Just above the left pane, open the drive drop-down list and click the desired disk drive on your computer.

2. Double-click the folder in which you want to store the downloaded files.

3. In the directory list for the FTP server, change to the folder that contains the files you want to download.

4. Click the file you want to download and Ctrl+click any additional files.

5. Drag one of the selected files from the FTP Server pane into the pane that displays the open folder on your PC (see Figure 20.8).

6. When prompted to confirm, click **OK**. The status bar displays the progress of the download.

7. When you are done, click the **Disconnect** button.

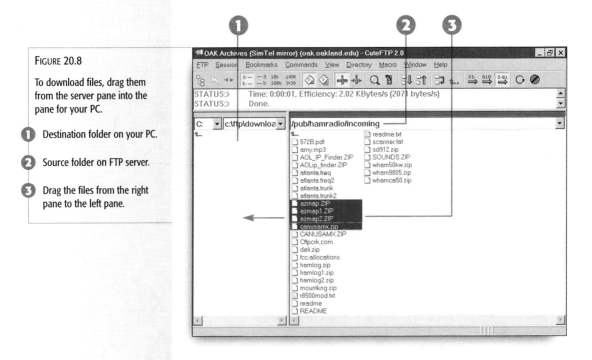

FIGURE 20.8

To download files, drag them from the server pane into the pane for your PC.

1. Destination folder on your PC.

2. Source folder on FTP server.

3. Drag the files from the right pane to the left pane.

Uploading Files to an FTP Server

The steps for uploading files to an FTP server are nearly the same as the steps for downloading files from an FTP server; you just drag from left to right instead of from right to left.

Downloading files with CuteFTP

1. Just above the left pane, open the drive drop-down list and click the disk that contains the files you want to upload.

2. Double-click the folder that contains the files you want to upload.

3. In the directory list for the FTP server, change to the folder into which you want to place the files.

4. Click the file you want to upload and Ctrl+click any additional files.

5. Drag one of the selected files into the pane that displays the open folder on the FTP server and release the mouse button.

6. When prompted to confirm, click **OK**. The status bar displays the progress of the upload.

7. When you are done, click the **Disconnect** button.

Don't forget the toolbar

CuteFTP's toolbar has buttons for the most frequently entered commands. Use the button bar to display the Site Manager, disconnect, sort files, and upload and download files.

Finding Specific Files with Archie

When word gets out that an anonymous FTP server has cool files, every user with a modem and a Internet account tries to connect and grab some free stuff. The administrator then closes the server or restricts access, and you can't get the file you need. The good news is that the files you want are probably stored on other (*mirror*) servers. A mirror server is a duplicate of the original server, although the site may not be updated as frequently as the original server. If you can't get the file at its original location, you can get it at the mirror site.

But how do you find these mirror sites? Many high-traffic sites contain links to take you to mirror sites. If you see a link for a server closer to you, click its link rather than trying to download from the original FTP site. You can also find mirror sites by using a program called Archie, which is a search tool for FTP servers.

Performing an Archie search in your Web browser is easy. You display an Archie Request Form, fill out the form, and submit it. Archie acts as an automated librarian; it finds the files that match your search instructions, and displays a list of servers on which the file is stored.

Searching for files with Archie

1. Run your Web browser.

2. In the **Address** or **Go To** text box, type one of the following addresses:

   ```
   www.ucc.ie/cgi-bin/archie

   cuiwww.unige.ch/archieplexform.html

   www.thegroup.net/AA.html

   archie.rutgers.edu/archie.html

   www.wg.omron.co.jp/AA-eng.html
   ```

3. Press Enter.

4. Enter the name or partial name of the file you're looking for. (If you type a partial name, make sure you enter a setting to search for a substring instead of an exact match.)

5. Enter any other information or settings as desired. For example, most Archie search forms ask if you want the search to be case-sensitive.

6. If you're given a choice, click the **By Host** or **By Date** button to select a sorting preference. **By Host** tells Archie to sort the found files by host name. **By Date** lists newer files first.

7. If you see a **Priority** or **The impact on other users can be** drop-down list, select how pushy you want to be. Not Nice At All tells the Archie server to drop everything to search for your file.

8. If you're given a choice of Archie servers to use, open the drop-down list, and select the Archie server you want to use for this search. A closer server may be faster in off-hours,

whereas a distant server (one located in a time zone where it is evening or early morning) might work better during business hours.

9. If you see a text box that allows you to limit the number of copies of the file you want Archie to find, type a number in the text box. Archie searches can take a long time, so I usually type 30 in this text box.

10. Click the **Start Search** button (or its equivalent). Archie searches can take awhile, so don't expect a list of files to pop up immediately.

The search typically turns up a list of links (see Figure 20.9). You can click a link to start downloading the file with your Web browser, or write down the address of the FTP server (host) and the path to the directory in which the file is stored and download the file using your FTP program. Better yet, print the page so you have a complete list of FTP servers to try; not all servers are going to let you in.

> **Archie etiquette**
>
> Archie servers are busy places. Use Archie only when you absolutely need it, and try to access the Archie server during non-business hours. Let the Archie server process one request before you enter another.

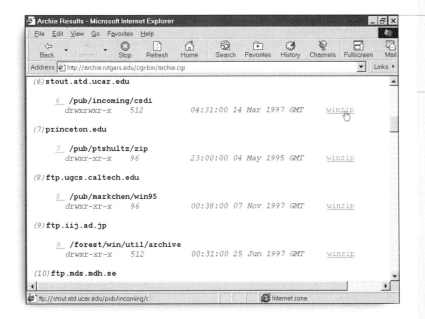

FIGURE 20.9

Archie turns up a list of links that point to files matching your search instructions.

Real-Time Chatting
with Other People

Take a quick tour of the real-time chat

Chat right inside your Web browser

Connect to thousands of chat rooms with IRC chat

Change from one chat room to another

Display information about a person in a chat room

Chat in private

Visit 3D virtual chat rooms

Understanding Internet Chat

The Internet has revolutionized the way we communicate. We correspond with email, post messages in newsgroups, and read magazines on the Web. But that's just the standard fare. The Internet also offers more dynamic and immediate forms of communication through Internet chat.

Internet chat allows you to "talk" with other people on the Internet by typing and sending messages back and forth. You and the other people use an Internet *chat client* to connect to a *chat server* on the Internet. The chat server acts as host, typically offering hundreds of chat rooms (also called *channels*) where people gather to chat. As you type and send messages, your messages appear on the screen of everyone in the chat room. As the other people in the room type and send messages, their messages pop up on your screen (see Figure 21.1).

FIGURE 21.1

You can chat with others on the Internet by typing messages in a chat room.

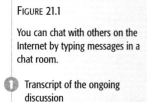

1 Transcript of the ongoing discussion

2 Enter your messages here.

3 List of people in the room

When Internet chat first started, there were few programs and few chat servers to act as hosts. With the increased popularity of the Internet, this has changed. Various companies have come to realize that chat sells and that people are using the Internet not only to search for information, products, and services, but also to find an online community in which they can feel at home. These companies have developed several innovative tools to provide people with alternatives to standard text-only chat. The following list describes some of the more popular chat tools:

- *Internet Relay Chat (IRC).* Internet chat started with IRC. IRC clients, such as mIRC, VisualIRC, or PIRCH, provide a basic interface, like the one shown in Figure 21.1. However, IRC is far from basic, offering a wide range of commands for advanced chatters.

- *Web Form Chat.* In an attempt to bring the simplicity of the Web to the world of chat, developers came up with Web Form Chat. To send a message, you fill out a form and click a button. The Web chat site automatically sends an updated Web page to everyone in the room, showing everybody's recent messages. This type of chat is cumbersome and not very popular.

- *Web Client Chat.* This type of chat is currently the best way to chat on the Web. With a Web browser and the right plug-in or ActiveX control, you can chat right inside the browser window. Many Web chat clients interface with IRC servers, providing you with a smoother interface for performing IRC chat. iChat, described later in this chapter, is one of the most popular Web chat clients.

- *Avatar and Comic Chat.* Avatar and comic chat allow you to play the role of a particular character in a chat room. You can then move the character around in the room, gesture to other chatters, and even bump into people. To use avatar or comic chat, you need a special chat client, such as Microsoft Comic Chat (included with Windows), Microsoft V-Chat, or Worlds Away (in CompuServe).

Chatting on the Web

For any online chat area to be successful, the technology must be easy to use, and the area must draw crowds of people. This is one of the main reasons why America Online is still so popular. AOL chat is easy, and at any time of the day or night, you'll find hordes of people from all over the world chatting in thousands of rooms.

Until recently, Internet chat wasn't easy and it didn't draw the crowds. As you'll see later in this chapter, IRC is not the ideal chat *client* (program). You'll find plenty of people chatting on IRC channels, but trying to navigate the IRC servers and find an active channel that interests you can be nerve-racking. Early Web chat wasn't a viable alternative, offering chatters clunky form-based chat clients, slow plug-ins, and empty chat rooms.

What's Java?

Java is a programming language that makes it possible for Web developers to create programs that run on Web pages. What has made Java so popular is that the same Java program will run on any computer (for instance, a PC or a Macintosh). All the computer needs is a Java-enabled Web browser to interpret the programming code.

New advances in Web chat offer the promise of making Internet chat a practical alternative to chatting on commercial services or via IRC. Web programming tools, including Java and ActiveX, have made Web chat possible. Using these tools, developers can place chat windows right inside the browser window, so chatters don't have to download and install special chat software. The controls in Web-based chat rooms are intuitive and easy to use, and links make it easy to find the rooms that interest you.

With these new tools and the vast numbers of people who already hang out on the Web, Web chat is drawing the crowds required to stitch together an active, growing online community.

SEE ALSO

➤ *Learn how to find, download, and install plug-ins and ActiveX components, page 423*

Finding a Place to Chat

Searching for a place to chat is like searching for a neighborhood to call home. You want a place that's easy to get around in, friendly, populated with a diverse group of people who share similar values, and somewhat active.

Good luck.

There's no utopia on the Web, and I can't point you to the best place for you to hang out. You'll have to poke around a little, see what's out there for yourself, and take the good with the bad. However, I can provide you with a list of some of the more popular (and populated) areas:

- *Yahoo!* (www.yahoo.com) isn't merely a Web search engine. Yahoo! is building its own online community using one of the best Web chat clients on the market—iChat (described in the next section). At Yahoo! you can sign on as a guest and start chatting immediately or register for your own chat identity. On Yahoo!'s home page, click the **Chat** link (below the **Search** text box).

- *Prodigy* (www.prodigy.net) (yes, the commercial online service) isn't an exclusive club like AOL. To bring more people to the chat table, Prodigy has flung open the doors of its chat rooms to the general public. Go to www.prodigy.net, click the **People & Chat** link, and click the **Chat Now!** link to track down a room (see Figure 21.2).

- *Excite* (www.excite.com) is another Web search service that's attempting to build its own community, and it is a great place to check out Web chat. In fact, Excite developed the Web chat client that Prodigy uses and connects you to many of the same rooms. You can find an entrance to Excite's chat rooms at www.excite.com. Click the **Chat Hub** link to display the same window shown in Figure 21.2.

- *Lycos* (chat.lycos.com) is not quite as populated as Yahoo! or Excite, but it offers an excellent Java-based interface that makes it easy to check out other chatters, send private messages, and change rooms (see Figure 21.3). You should definitely check this out and hope it gains popularity. You'll have to set up a (free) account before you can start chatting.

- *Chat Planet* (www.chatplanet.com) is billed as the largest Java-based chat area on the Web, but I have to wonder how they came up with that claim. Chat Planet requires you to follow an excruciatingly long trail of links to find any room, let alone a room with people in it. When you do find someone to chat with, the Java-based chat client is so clunky that you won't want to chat. If you're curious, check it out for yourself.

Go to the source

If you like Yahoo!'s chat areas and the iChat client that Yahoo! uses, go to iChat's home page at www.ichat.com for a long list of iChat's diverse clientele. You'll get to learn about some interesting ways iChat is being used and find some chat communities that aren't quite mainstream.

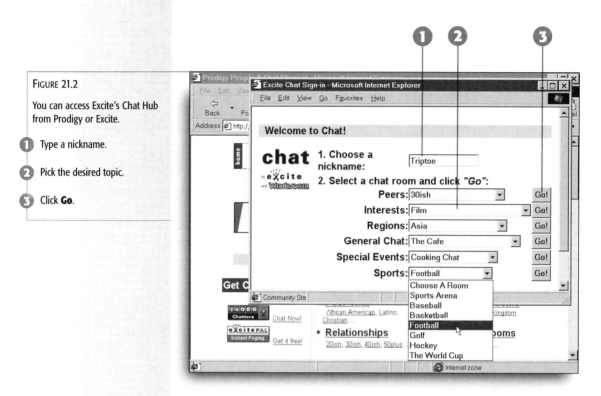

FIGURE 21.2

You can access Excite's Chat Hub from Prodigy or Excite.

1 Type a nickname.

2 Pick the desired topic.

3 Click **Go**.

FIGURE 21.3

Lycos may not be a hot spot for chatters yet, but it has one of the best chat clients of the bunch.

SEE ALSO
➤ *Learn how to find more information about chat on the Web, page 419*

Chatting It Up with iChat

Although chat clients differ, they all provide the same basic interface—a pane displaying the ongoing conversation, a text box for typing your messages, and a list of people in the room. Also, they all feature tools for changing rooms, viewing information about other chatters, sending private messages, creating your own rooms, and changing your identity.

This section shows you one of the more popular chat clients in action, iChat. To follow along, first connect to Yahoo!, enter the chat area, and register, to give yourself a nickname. (For a direct flight to Yahoo! Chat, go to chat.yahoo.com.)

Registering for Yahoo! chat

1. Use your browser to pull up Yahoo!'s Home Page at www.yahoo.com.

2. Click the **Chat** link. This opens a page describing the steps you need to take to set up Yahoo! Chat.

3. Scroll down the page and click the **Get Registered** button. A form appears, prompting you to enter a chat name, password, and other information.

4. Complete the form. Your login name is the name that identifies you to other people in the chat room. Be sure to write down your name and password, so you can sign on later.

5. Click the **Submit This Form** button. Yahoo! processes your form and displays your Yahoo! ID.

6. Click the **Go to Yahoo! Chat** link. In a few moments, the Yahoo! Chat Agreement appears.

7. Read the agreement, especially the chat room rules, and click the **I Accept** or **No way, man!** button. Assuming you clicked **I Accept**, Yahoo! takes you to the Yahoo! Chat page.

8. Under **Select An Area to Begin Chat**, select the desired chat category and click the **Start Chatting** button. Yahoo! places you in a chat room that corresponds with the selected category (see Figure 21.4).

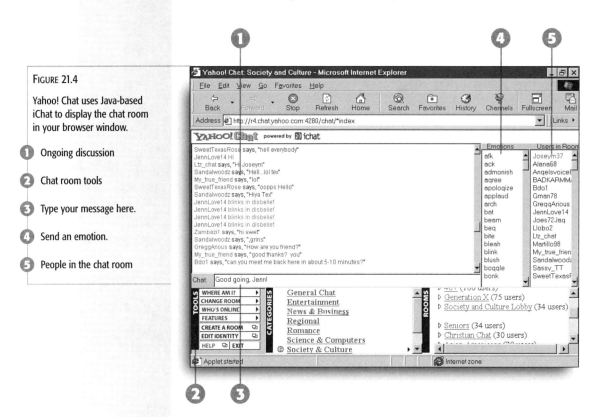

FIGURE 21.4

Yahoo! Chat uses Java-based iChat to display the chat room in your browser window.

1 Ongoing discussion

2 Chat room tools

3 Type your message here.

4 Send an emotion.

5 People in the chat room

After you are in a chat room, start chatting. The ongoing discussion is displayed in the large frame in the upper-left part of the screen. To send a message to the other chatters, click inside the **Chat** text box just below the ongoing discussion, type your message, and press Enter. When you tire of this simple banter, try the following:

- Double-click an emotion in the pane just to the right of the discussion pane. This sends a text description of your gesture.

- Click the name of someone in the room. This displays the Interact with Another User dialog box (see Figure 21.5), which allows you to find out more about the person, send the person a private message or a file, start following the person (if the person changes rooms), or ignore the person (prevent the person's messages from appearing on your screen). "afk" means away from keyboard.

- In the lower-left corner of the window is a list of tools. Click a tool to change to a different chat room, find out who's online (and view information about a person), create your own room (public or private), edit your identity, get help, or exit. (You can edit your identity to provide additional information about yourself; other chatters will then see this information if they choose to view it.)

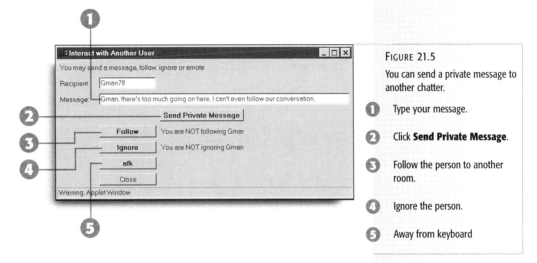

FIGURE 21.5

You can send a private message to another chatter.

1 Type your message.

2 Click **Send Private Message**.

3 Follow the person to another room.

4 Ignore the person.

5 Away from keyboard

Although the chat tools are fairly basic, iChat provides more advanced tools. When you're ready to master a few new moves, check out Table 21.1. To enter any of the commands in Table 21.1, type the command in the **Chat** text box and press Enter.

TABLE 21.1   Advanced iChat commands

Enter	To
`/tell` *username message*	Send a private message to someone without having to use a dialog box.
`/think` *message*	Send a thought, which is formatted sort of like a cartoon bubble. For instance, `/think Where am I?` looks like o O (Where am I?)
`/emote` *message*	Send a message with you as the subject. For example, if your name is Jessie3 and you type `/emote hugs JaneDoll`, the message appears as `Jessie3 hugs JaneDoll`.

continues...

TABLE 21.1   **Continued**

Enter	To
`<color> message`	Display your message in a distinct color. For instance `<red>` displays the message you type in red.
`/goto username`	Follow a person to another room, unless the person turned this feature off.
`/follow username`	Follow a person into whichever room that person goes, assuming the person lets you.
`/stopfollow`	Stop following a person.
`/stopfollow username`	Make a person stop following you.
`/buddy add username`	Place a person on your buddy list. Whenever the person logs on to the chat server, a message appears in the discussion window, letting you know.
`/buddy list`	Display the names you've added to your buddy list.
`/buddy remove username`	Remove someone from your buddy list.
`/buddy onlist`	Find out who has you listed on their buddy list.
`/autogoto no`	Prevent people from going to you.
`/autogoto yes`	Allow people to go to you.
`/autofollow off`	Prevent people from following you.
`/autofollow on`	Allow people to follow you.
`/autofollow ask`	The default setting, displays a message indicating that another person is trying to follow you.
`/allow username`	Lets someone follow you into whichever room you go.
`/disallow username`	Prevent a person from following you.
`/room secure`	Lock a room you created so no one else can enter.
`/room secure add username`	Give a user access to your locked room. Repeat the command to give access to additional users.
`/room secure capacity #`	Set the maximum number of people that can enter a room you created.

Enter	To
`/ignore add username`	Ignore a person.
`/ignore remove username`	Stop ignoring a person.
`/ignore list`	Display a list of people you have chosen to ignore.
`/ignore add movement`	Stop displaying the messages that indicate when people enter and leave the room.
`/ignore remove movement`	Start displaying the messages that indicate when people enter and leave the room.

Chatting with IRC Software

Although Web chat is becoming more popular, you'll find more people chatting with specialized IRC chat clients. Here's a list of some of the better chat programs and information on where you can get them:

- *Microsoft Chat* comes with Windows. To run it, select it from the **Start, Programs, Internet Explorer** menu. Microsoft Chat displays each person as a character in a comic strip, which makes it a bit difficult to follow the conversation (see Figure 21.6). Fortunately, you can turn off the comic strip view to display normal text messages.

- *mIRC* has been one of the most popular shareware IRC clients around because it is so easy to use. It even comes with its own IRC primer to help new users get up to speed in a hurry. You can visit the mIRC home page at `www.geocities.com/SiliconValley/Park/6000/index.html`, where you will find a link for downloading it. (The file is self-extracting, so just click its icon after downloading it.)

- *Visual IRC* is one of the best IRC clients around. It offers a basic chat screen that is easy to navigate and powerful features that you typically find only in an Internet phone program, including voice chat. You can download a free copy of Visual IRC and obtain additional information at `virc.melnibone.org`. (The program is in a compressed format, and you need WinZip to decompress it.)

Microsoft Chat Plain Text Mode

If you're using Microsoft Chat and the cutesy comic strip idea starts getting on your nerves, open the **View** menu and select **Plain Text** or click the **View Text** button in the toolbar. This displays a chat window which is much more efficient for swapping messages. The conversation and member list panes are much larger, and you don't have the comic strip characters crowding the screen.

- *PIRCH* (short for PolarGeek's IRC Hack) is another popular IRC client that offers standard chat features and an interface that's easy to use. You can visit the PIRCH home page at `www.bcpl.lib.md.us/~frappa/pirch.html` where you will find a link for downloading the program. (The file is self-extracting, so just click its icon after downloading it.)

FIGURE 21.6

Microsoft Chat displays the running discussion as a comic strip.

Most of these chat clients use a standard three-paned window, much like the Window used for Yahoo! Chat. Messages are displayed in the large pane in the upper-left part of the screen. A list of chatters appears on the right, and a text box for entering your messages appears at the bottom.

Connecting to a Chat Server

Connection refused?

Don't be surprised if you can't connect to the first server you choose; chat servers can be busy places. If you can't connect to a server, try a different one.

Before you can start chatting, you must connect to a *chat server* (a computer on the Internet specialized for handling IRC). The chat server that you connect to is connected to other chat servers to make a *network* (such as EFnet or Undernet). The chat rooms on a particular network are available to everyone connected to that network, even if they are connected to different servers.

Most IRC clients prompt you to select a server on startup. A dialog box appears, typically offering a list or drop-down list of available servers (see Figure 21.7). You select the desired server from the list, enter your name, email address, and other information, and then click the **OK** or **Connect** button to connect to the server. If the IRC client does not prompt you to choose an IRC server, scan the button bar or the menu system for the required command.

Switch chat servers

If a chat server is on a network that does not provide the types of rooms that interest you, you can disconnect from the chat server and try a chat server on a different network. The program's toolbar or menu system should have a command for disconnecting from the chat server.

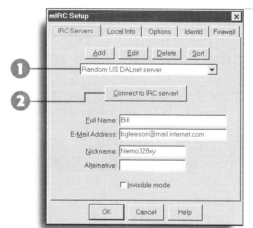

FIGURE 21.7

Most IRC clients prompt you to select a server at startup.

① Pick an IRC server.

② Click **Connect**.

Entering and Leaving Chat Rooms

As soon as you connect to a chat server, your chat program downloads a list of the available chat rooms (sometimes called *channels*) and prompts you to pick one. If the list doesn't pop up on your screen, check the button bar or menu system for the command to display the list of available rooms.

In most cases, the list displays the room name and the number of people in that room, to give you some idea of how popular it is. The list may also include a description of each room, if the person who created the room added a description. Double-click the desired room name or click the name and click the button for entering or joining the room (see Figure 21.8).

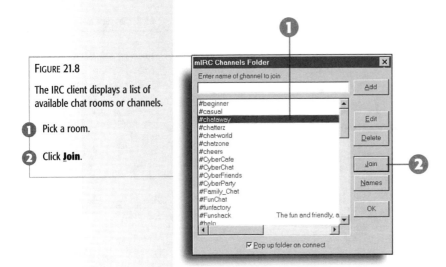

FIGURE 21.8

The IRC client displays a list of available chat rooms or channels.

1 Pick a room.

2 Click **Join**.

If you find that the current discussion doesn't appeal to you, you can leave the chat room. Check the toolbar or menu system for an **Exit Room** or comparable command, or click the chat window's Close (x) button. To enter a different room, enter the command to display the list of available rooms and then select the desired room.

Start Chatting

This is where the fun starts. In a room that's populated with talkative typists, messages scroll by at a frenetic pace. The room may take on a party atmosphere, where two or three people in the room are carrying on their own conversation, completely oblivious to everyone else in the room. Just hang out for a while and watch the comments scroll past.

When you get a feel for the room, look for a text box for sending your own messages. The box is typically below the area where the running discussion is displayed. Type your message and click the **Send** button or press Enter. Your message appears on your screen and on the screens of all the other people in the room (see Figure 21.9).

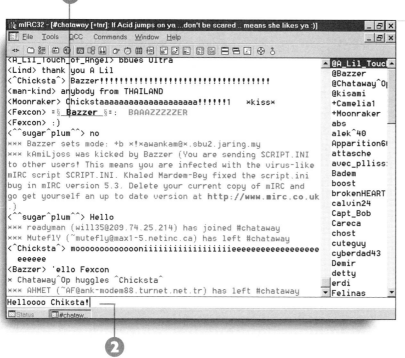

FIGURE 21.9

Start chatting.

1 The running discussion

2 Type your message and press Enter.

The chat window displays a list of people currently in the chat room. In most cases, you can view information the person entered about himself, send the person a private message or a file, or choose to ignore the person. Try right-clicking the person's name to view a context menu with the available options. If that doesn't work, try double-clicking the person's name. In most cases, double-clicking displays a dialog box for sending the person a private message.

Chatting in a Private Room

Although you can send a "private" message to someone by double-clicking the person's name and using the resulting dialog box, the message is not quite private. If someone wants to listen in, they can. For increased privacy, you can hook up with another chatter directly via *DCC*. Short for *Direct Client-to-Client*, DCC allows two chat programs to bypass the IRC server and connect directly. You can then chat, and even exchange files, privately.

Chat in private with DCC

1. To chat directly, click the name of the person with whom you want to chat.

2. Right-click the person's name, point to **DCC**, and click **Chat**.

3. A dialog box appears on the other person's screen, inviting the person to join you.

4. If the person accepts your invitation, a separate chat window appears with just the two of you.

Keeping Track of Your Online Chums

The only trouble with Internet chat is that it's tough to track down friends and relatives to strike up a conversation. Unless you agree to chat in a particular room at a specific time, you may never cross paths again.

Fortunately, developers have come up with some new tools to inform you when your friends and relatives are online. One of the most popular tools is America Online's Instant Messenger. In Instant Messenger, you create a *buddy list*, containing the names and email addresses of your favorite people. When a buddy logs on to the Internet, AOL informs you that the person is online, and you can send the person an instant message

SEE ALSO

➤ *Learn more about America Online, page 367*

Downloading Instant Messenger

To use Instant Messenger, you and your friends and relatives must download and install the program and register with AOL for free (you need not join AOL). This places contact information in AOL's database, so AOL can determine who is online and let you know when someone on your buddy list has logged on.

To get your free copy of Instant Messenger, connect to AOL's home page at www.aol.com and click the **Instant Messenger** link. Click the **Download Now** link. Complete the registration form and click **Submit**. Follow the instructions to download the program.

To install the program, change to the folder in which you downloaded the Setup file, click the file's name, and follow the onscreen installation instructions.

Running Instant Messenger

If you want people to be able to track you down, you must be connected to the Internet, and Instant Messenger must be running. Your name then shows up on the *buddy list* of anyone who added you to his buddy list.

Running Instant Messenger

1. Click the **Start** button, point to **Programs**, **AOL Instant Messenger**, and click **AOL Instant Messenger**.

2. Enter the screen name and password you entered when you registered for Instant Messenger.

3. Click **Save Password** to have Instant Messenger remember your login information.

4. Click the **Sign On** button.

Making a Buddy List

For AOL to notify you when friends and relatives have logged on, you must add their names to your buddy list.

Adding a name to your buddy list

1. Run Instant Messenger and click the **List Setup** tab.

2. Click the folder in which you want to insert the person's name.

3. Click the **Add Buddy** button.

4. Type the person's screen name and press Enter (see Figure 21.10).

Find a screen name

If you know the person's email address, click the **Menu** button and choose **Find a Buddy**, **By Email Address**.

FIGURE 21.10

To have AOL notify you of a person's presence, add the person's name to your buddy list.

1. Click the **List Setup** tab.

2. Click the folder.

3. Click the **Add Buddy** button.

4. Type the person's screen name.

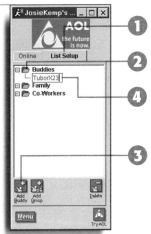

Sending an Instant Message

Whenever someone on your buddy list connects to the Internet, the person's screen name appears on Instant Messenger's Online tab. You can then choose the person's name and send a message.

Contacting a buddy

1. Click the person's screen name.

2. Click the **IM** button (see Figure 21.11).

3. Type your message in the message area and click the **Send** button.

4. The message window displays your messages along with the other person's messages.

Exploring 3D Virtual Chat Rooms

If you're tired of the same old chat, try chatting in 3D with an *avatar chat* program. With avatar chat, you take on the persona of an avatar and mingle with other avatars in 3D space. Avatar chat places great demands on both your navigational skills and typing abilities, but after you get the hang of it, you may never go back to chatting in two dimensions.

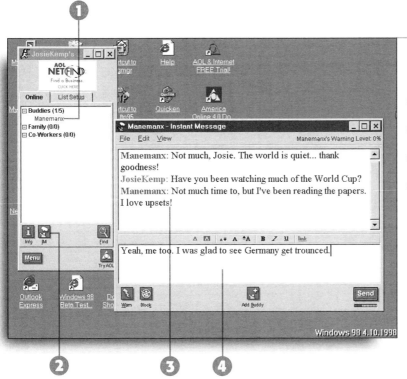

FIGURE 21.11

When a friend is online, you can send the person an instant message.

❶ Click the person's name.

❷ Click **IM**.

❸ Running discussion

❹ Type your message here and press Enter.

Microsoft's V-Chat is one of the best avatar chat programs for new users. V-Chat offers worlds that are easy to navigate and presents cartoon-like worlds that make the chat rooms more playful.

You can download V-Chat at www.microsoft.com/ie/chat/?/ie/chat/. At the V-Chat site, you can also download additional scenes (you need to download a separate scene for each room you want to visit). After installing V-Chat, sign on, assume the identity of your favorite avatar, and start chatting (see Figure 21.12). Here are a few tips to get you started:

- The chat scene is displayed in the large pane at the top of the window; drag the mouse pointer inside the pane to move. To fly, hold down the Ctrl key while dragging up.

- Your avatar is displayed in the lower-right corner of the screen.

- To gesture, click one of the gesture buttons in the toolbar.

- To send a message, click inside the text box below the scene, type your message, and press Enter.

- To choose a different persona, open the **Avatar** menu, and choose **Select Avatar**.

- To view information about a member, right-click the person's name in the Members list, and click **Profile**.

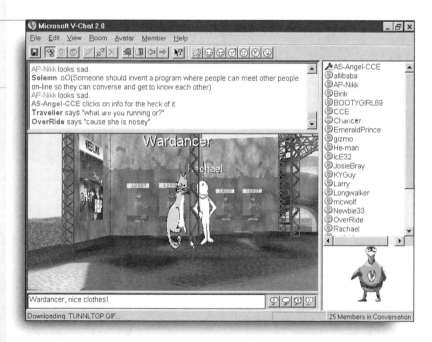

Online Security Issues

Order products on the Internet using secure forms

Protect your system against computer viruses

Enter security settings in Internet Explorer

Censor offensive material on the Internet

Send email messages securely

Understanding the Risks of Going Online

The Internet is no place for the paranoid. Files you download and run could infect your system with a virus. Information you enter on a form could be intercepted and read by a depraved computer hacker desperate for money or thrills. Someone can decide to intercept your email messages and make your private life public. Your kids could wander off to the more seedy side of the Web.

Yes, all that is possible, but if you start worrying about all the things that could possibly go wrong, you'll never experience anything. The trick is to proceed with caution. In this chapter, you'll learn how to enable a few safeguards to protect your data, your system, and your kids on the Internet, so you can experience the Internet completely without worrying too much.

The first step is to understand the risks and determine whether you're doing anything risky on the Internet. The following list describes the major areas you should focus on:

- *Forms.* Most forms that request sensitive data, such as a credit card number, are stored on secure Web servers. The form scrambles the data you send and then the Web server decodes the information it receives. However, you must still make sure you're sending data to a reputable company and that you're using a secure form. This chapter shows you how to confidently send data with forms.

- *Email.* With the millions of email messages travelling through the Internet pipelines, it's unlikely that someone will take the time and trouble to intercept your email messages and read them, but it can happen. If you're sending sensitive information via email, there are ways to keep your messages private.

- *Viruses.* A virus is programming code that acts as a harmless prank or actually destroys data on your computer. Although ActiveX controls and Java applets are potential virus carriers, the most serious risk is posed by program files you download, especially if you run a program that someone sent you via email. You'll learn some virus prevention tactics in this chapter.

- *Offensive material.* For the most part, the Internet is pretty clean; however, it does have a fair share of pornography, racism, violence, and obscenity. If you have kids or a classroom of students, you can block access to this material, as explained in this chapter. However, you'll still need to supervise your underlings.

The Internet poses other security risks that you don't have much control over. For example, if your credit card company doesn't have a secure system, someone could break into the system and get information about you. Of course, people can get a lot of information about you by digging through your trash, listening in on your cellular phone calls, and posing as market researchers, too.

Transmitting Forms Securely

The biggest security risk on the Internet is the result of one of the biggest improvements on the Web: forms. Forms, such as search forms used on Yahoo! and other search sites, let you enter information and receive feedback. They also allow you to order products, register your software, join clubs, and even play interactive games.

The problem with entering any personal information on a form (especially credit card numbers) is that the information is not sent directly to the server that asks for the information. Instead, the information bounces around from one server to another until it finds its destination. At any point in its journey, someone with the proper know-how can read the information. How often this happens, no one really knows, but it *can* happen, and that's the concern.

Most Web browsers, including Internet Explorer and Netscape Navigator have warning messages that pop up whenever you are about to submit information using an insecure form. You can then cancel the operation before sending sensitive information.

If you're just submitting a search phrase, you can cancel the warning and go ahead with the operation.

If you're new to the Internet, keep the warnings on until you feel comfortable entering information on forms. You should also keep the warnings on if you frequently place credit card orders on the Web. However, if the warnings become more of a nuisance than an aid, turn them off. In most browsers, the warning dialog box contains an option for preventing the warning from appearing again. If you turn off the warning messages, there are other ways to tell if you are using a secure form:

- If the Web page address starts with https instead of http, the site is secure.

- In Internet Explorer, look at the right end of the status bar (at the bottom of the window). If there's a padlock icon, the site is secure (see Figure 22.1).

- In Netscape Navigator, look at the lower-left corner of the window for a key icon. A broken key indicates that the site is not secure. A solid key with three teeth indicates a very secure site. A solid key with two teeth indicates that the site is fairly secure.

Entering Security Zone Settings in Internet Explorer

Credit card caution

Anyone can stick a Visa or Mastercard logo on his Web page and pretend to be a legitimate business. Be careful when placing credit card orders. Restrict your purchases to brand name sites until the credit card companies come up with some way to ensure security. If a site looks suspicious, check out the company before you place your order.

As you send data and receive active content on the Web, Internet Explorer supervises your actions and the actions of the remote server, and warns you of any risky activity, including submitting information via insecure forms. You can control these warnings by using Internet Explorer's *security zones*. Each zone has different security settings, allowing you to relax the security settings for sites that you trust and tighten security settings for untrusted or untested sites. Internet Explorer offers the following four security zones:

- *Local Intranet zone* allows your network administrator to set up a list of restricted Internet sites and enter security settings to prevent users throughout your company from accessing risky content.

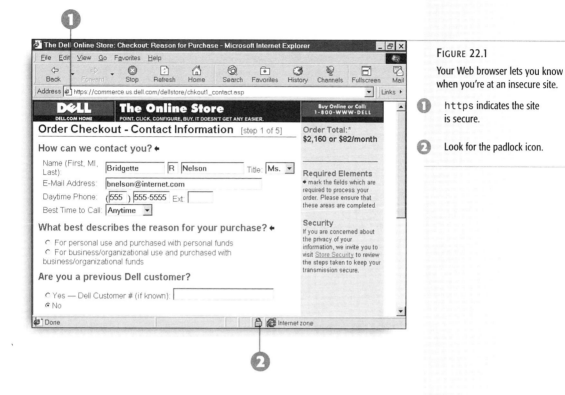

FIGURE 22.1

Your Web browser lets you know when you're at an insecure site.

1 https indicates the site is secure.

2 Look for the padlock icon.

- *Trusted sites zone* allows you to turn off the security warnings for sites you trust. This prevents you from being inundated with warning messages at the sites you visit most frequently.

- *Internet zone* allows you to specify security settings for untested sites. When you wander off to sites you do not frequent, you may want to tighten security.

- *Restricted sites zone* lets you create a list of sites you do not trust and tighten security for those sites. For example, you may want to prevent a particular site from automatically installing and running programs on your computer.

Add sites to a Security Zone

1. In Internet Explorer open the **View** menu and click **Internet Options**. The Internet Options dialog box appears.

2. Click the **Security** tab.

3. Open the **Z̲one** drop-down list and select the zone to which you want to add sites: Local intranet, Trusted sites, or Restricted sites (see Figure 22.2).

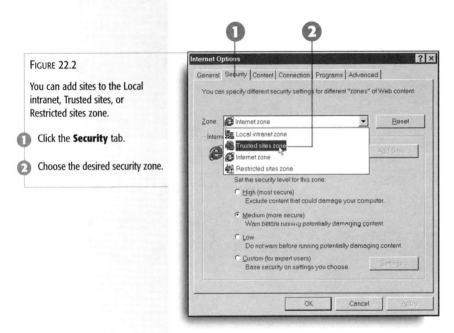

FIGURE 22.2

You can add sites to the Local intranet, Trusted sites, or Restricted sites zone.

1 Click the **Security** tab.

2 Choose the desired security zone.

4. Click the **A̲dd Sites** button. The resulting dialog box shows a list of sites in the selected zone, which should be empty.

5. Click **Require s̲erver verification (https:) for all sites in this zone** to remove the check mark. With this option on, you can't add many sites to the zone.

6. Click in the **A̲dd this Web site to the zone** text box and type the site's address. (You must type http:// at the beginning of the page address.)

7. Click the **A̲dd** button. The site is added to your list (see Figure 22.3).

8. Repeat steps 6 and 7 to place additional sites on the list.

9. Click **OK** to close the zone dialog box and return to the Internet Options dialog box.

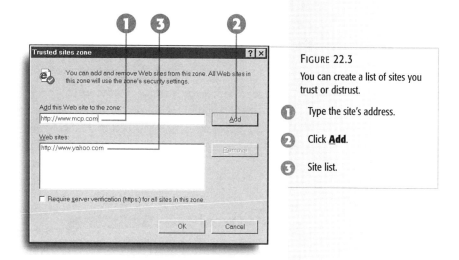

FIGURE 22.3

You can create a list of sites you trust or distrust.

① Type the site's address.

② Click **Add**.

③ Site list.

10. Click the **OK** button to save your list of sites and your security settings.

Changing Security Levels for Zones

In addition to adding sites to each zone, you can tighten or relax security for each zone. To specify a security level for a zone, open the **View** menu, select **Internet Options**, and click the **Security** tab. Open the **Zone** drop-down list, and click the zone whose security level you want to change. Then select the desired level:

- **High** prevents you from submitting any information by way of form, even a search form. If you complete a form, and click the button to submit it, nothing happens. In addition, Internet Explorer won't play Java applets, download ActiveX controls, or transfer any other potentially harmful programs or scripts to your computer. The **High** setting is useful for sites you place in the Restricted sites zone.

- **Medium** turns on prompts, so Internet Explorer displays dialog boxes whenever you attempt to send data or download scripts or other active content. The **Medium** setting is useful for the Internet zone, where you may want to be prompted before doing anything risky.

- **Low** turns off the prompts, allowing you to submit information using a form, and allowing sites to send you active content. The **Low** setting is good for trusted sites, where you are fairly certain that nothing bad is going to happen.

- **Custom** allows you to enter specific security settings. For example, you may want to prevent active content from being automatically downloaded to your computer, but you don't want a dialog box popping up on your screen every time you fill out a form. If you select **Custom**, click the **Settings** button to enter your preferences.

Additional Security Settings

In addition to security zone settings, Internet Explorer offers more general security settings to control the way form data is encrypted and transferred and to prevent other people who have access to your PC from snooping on your Web wanderings. To check these settings or change them, open the **View** menu, click **Internet Options**, and click the **Advanced** tab. The **Security** tab offers the following options:

- **Enable Profile Assistant** allows Internet Explorer to pass any personal information that you enter about yourself to Web sites that request it.

- **PCT 1.0** is a security standard that encrypts any information you enter on a form to protect it from prying eyes. PCT is short for *Private Communications Technology*.

- **SSL 2.0 and 3.0** is another security standard that protects sensitive information from being intercepted and read. SSL is short for *Secure Socket Layer*.

- **Delete Saved Pages When Browser Closed** deletes any cached pages to prevent people from determining what you accessed when you used Internet Explorer.

- **Do Not Save Encrypted Pages to Disk** prevents any encrypted pages from being saved to your disk.

- **Warn If Forms Submit Is Being Redirected** displays a warning if you submit information via a form and the form tries to reroute it through other Internet sites.

- **Warn If Changing Between Secure and Not Secure Mode** tells Internet Explorer to display a warning whenever you move from a secure Web site to an insecure Web site.

- **Check for Certificate Revocation** tells Internet Explorer to check a site's certificate to determine if it has been revoked before trusting the site. (Few sites use site certificates.)

- **Warn About Invalid Site Certificates** displays a warning if there is some evidence that a secure site's certificate has been tampered with.

- **Cookies** tells Internet Explorer to accept or reject cookies. Cookies consist of data that a Web site stores on your computer to help identify you in the future or keep track of products you are ordering online. See "Cookies: A Necessary Evil?," later in this chapter.

In addition to protecting sensitive data, Internet Explorer offers security features to protect your system against threats posed by Java applets (small programs that run inside the browser window). However, many of the most dynamic offerings on the Web use Java. Disabling these features significantly limits your Web browsing experience. You'll find the following options on the **Java VM (Virtual Machine)** tab:

- **Java JIT Compiler Enabled** tells Internet Explorer to automatically compile and run Java applets (small programs embedded on Web pages). (A compiler transforms programming instructions into a language that your computer and operating system can understand.)

- **Java Logging Enabled** tells Internet Explorer to log the activity of any Java applet to help you track down problems and trace any security breaches a Java applet may have caused.

Entering Security Settings in Netscape Navigator

Netscape Navigator (Netscape Communicator's Web browser) stores its security settings in two places. To enter security settings for submitting information securely on the Web, click the **Security** button in the Navigation toolbar. Click **Navigator**. You can then select any of the following options to turn them on or off (see Figure 22.4):

- **Entering an encrypted site.** Displays a warning whenever you view a Web page that complies with the latest security standards. This lets you know for sure that you're about to submit information using a secure form.

- **Leaving an encrypted site.** Displays a warning indicating that you are leaving a secure site. If you fill out a form and the site redirects you to an insecure site, you'll want to know about it.

- **Viewing a page with an encrypted/unencrypted mix.** If part of the page is secure and another part isn't, you may want to avoid submitting information.

- **Sending unencrypted information to a Site.** This is the option that makes the security warning pop up on your screen all the time. If you don't trust yourself, leave it on. Otherwise, turn it off.

- **Enable SSL v2.** Turns on data encryption for Web pages protected with the Secure Sockets Layer (version 2) standard. Keep this on, so when you do enter information on secure Web pages, that information will be encoded.

- **Enable SSL v3.** Turns on data encryption for Web pages protected with the Secure Sockets Layer (version 3) standard. Keep this option on, too. This is the latest security standard from Netscape.

If desired, you can also disable Java and prevent Navigator from downloading and running Java applets automatically. However, Java is a fairly secure Web programming language and is used on many Web pages to display animations, chat windows, financial calculators, stock updates, and much more.

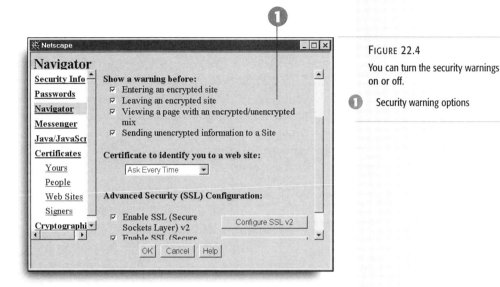

FIGURE 22.4
You can turn the security warnings
on or off.

① Security warning options

If you're worried about programming code running in your
browser window, you can disable Java. Open the **E**dit menu,
choose **P**re**f**erences, and click **Advanced** (at the bottom of the
left column). You can then remove the check mark next to any of
the following options to disable active content:

- **Enable Java.** Removing the check mark prevents Navigator
  from playing Java applets.

- **Enable JavaScript.** Turning this off prevents Navigator
  from playing JavaScripts embedded on Web pages. Although
  JavaScript is less likely to delete or damage files on your system, it can make your system susceptible to online snoops.

- **Enable AutoInstall.** Turning this option off prevents
  Navigator from automatically downloading and installing
  plug-ins, for playing media files that Navigator itself cannot
  play.

- **Cookies.** Cookies are sort of like tokens that a Web page
  hands you when you connect to the page or enter information. For additional details, see "Cookies: A Necessary Evil;"
  later in this chapter.

Protecting Against Computer Viruses

The most dynamic features of the Internet are the most likely to infect your PC with a virus. Programs you download and install from FTP sites could contain destructive code, ActiveX controls could automatically delete files, and even Java (billed as a safe programming language) could potentially destroy data. You could even receive an infected file as an email attachment. How can you prevent viruses from infecting your PC? First, follow a few simple rules:

- Download programs only from reputable and known sites. If you know the company that created the program, go to its Web site or FTP server, and download the file from there instead of from a mirror site that contains a copy of the original file. Most reputable sites regularly scan their systems to detect and eliminate viruses.

- Don't accept copies of a program from another person (for example, via email). Although the program may not have contained a virus when the other person downloaded it, the other person's computer may have a virus that infected the program. Ask the person where he obtained the file, and then download the file from its original location yourself.

- Use your Web browser's security features, as explained in the previous sections. Your Web browser can warn you if you are about to receive a component that could potentially cause damage.

- Run an antivirus program on a regular basis. By identifying and eliminating a virus early, you prevent it from causing additional damage. One of the best antivirus programs on the market is McAfee VirusScan; you can download a trial version at www.nai.com. Symantec also offers an antivirus program Norton Safe on the Web, that works right alongside your Web browser. Go to www.symantec.com for details.

Running an infected program is the most common way you can introduce a virus to your system. However, the Internet poses some additional threats through programmed objects, such as Java applets and ActiveX components. Java is a more secure programming language than ActiveX because it has built-in security features that prevent Java applets from performing destructive acts, such as deleting system files and reformatting your hard drive; however, clever hackers have proven that Java is not completely safe.

ActiveX is less secure because it places the security burden on you and relies on a system of certificates to help you determine if the ActiveX component is safe. There are few built-in security features that prevent the component from performing destructive acts. This makes ActiveX components powerful, but also more vulnerable. Before downloading and installing an ActiveX component, your Web browser will display a dialog box indicating whether the component has been certified or not. If the component has not been certified, it's up to you to cancel the download.

Cookies: A Necessary Evil?

Have you ever noticed that some sites seem to know you? You fill out a search form to look for information about computers, and a computer ad mysteriously pops up at the top of the page. You go to a site you visited last week, and it greets you by your first name. These are *cookies* at work.

Cookies are small bits of computer code that a Web site uploads to your computer. Cookies stay with your Web browser, so the next time you visit the site or visit another area at the site, the Web server can identify you or keep track of items you have ordered.

Most cookies are designed to make your Web browsing experience more productive and enjoyable. However, sites can use cookies to track your Web browsing habits. Although cookies typically do not store your name and email address, they can track you by using your PC's IP address, assigned to you by your service provider. If you are concerned about this, disable cookies:

Not so evil hackers

The term "hacker" has negative connotations, but few hackers are actually evil, destructive individuals. Most are knowledgeable people who enjoy a good challenge and provide a useful service—they test any company's claim that their technology is secure and prod companies to fix the bugs. Hackers typically set out to prove that security features can be cracked. They're not usually interested in stealing or damaging data.

Anonymous Web surfing

To keep from being tracked on the Web, you can use a special service, such as Anonymizer (www.anonymizer.com), which acts as a *proxy server*. The proxy server prevents sites from sending cookies directly to your PC and prohibits sites from logging your activities. However, working through a busy proxy server can significantly slow down your Web browsing.

- In Internet Explorer, choose **V̲iew**, **Internet O̲ptions**, click the **Advanced** tab, scroll down to the **Cookies** options, and click **Disable All Cookie Use**. Click **OK**.

- In Netscape Navigator, choose **E̲dit**, **Pr̲eferences**, click **Advanced**, and click **D̲isable Cookies**. Click **OK**.

To view a list of cookies already on your hard drive, use **Start**, **F̲ind**, **F̲iles or Folders** to search for **cookies**. Before you purge them from your hard disk, keep in mind that some cookies may contain passwords you chose to have a site remember for you. If you delete the cookie and you don't have the password written down somewhere, you won't be able to access the site again.

Censoring the Internet

The Internet is a virtual world, providing access to the best that our society has to offer: literature, music, arts, museums, movies, and medicine. However, like any world, the Internet has its fair share of sites that cater to pornography, racism, violence, and profanity.

Over the years, people have debated the issue of whether the government should control the Internet and prohibit people from transmitting material that some might consider offensive. As society wrestles with this issue, the offensive material remains readily available.

Fortunately, you can do something about it yourself. The following sections show you how to use tools on your PC to block access to offensive sites.

Enabling and Disabling Internet Explorer's Censor

Internet Explorer has a built-in censor, called the Ratings feature, that's good at blocking access to sites (it's almost too good). The problem with the Ratings feature is that it's designed around an ideal system that doesn't exist. Ideally, all Internet content would be tagged with a digital advisory label. The Ratings feature could then check the label and block out potentially offensive material. In reality, few sites are flagged with standard warning labels.

Some sites use them, some don't, and some follow different ratings systems.

For sites with content that is flagged as offensive or inoffensive using the RSAC (Recreation Software Advisory Council) ratings system, the Ratings feature works well. The Ratings feature denies access to all other (unrated) sites. Although you can turn off the feature for blocking access to unrated sites (you'll learn how later), doing so opens the doors to many unrated sites that do contain offensive material.

Be that as it may, the Ratings feature does provide some restrictions that you may find useful. Until you obtain a better censoring utility (as explained later in this chapter), the Ratings feature is better than nothing.

Enabling the Ratings feature

1. Open the **View** menu and click **Internet Options**.
2. Click the **Content** tab.
3. Under Content Advisor, click the **Enable** button. The Create Supervisor Password dialog box appears.
4. Enter your password and click **OK**.
5. In the **Confirm Password** text box, type your password again and click **OK**. The Content Advisor dialog box appears.
6. Click **OK**. You are returned to the Internet Options dialog box.
7. Click **OK** again.

Before you let your kids start wandering the Web unsupervised, make sure the Ratings feature works. Clear the cache and history lists first; the Ratings feature does not prevent access to cached pages. Choose **View**, **Internet Options**, click the **Delete Files** button and click the **Clear History** button.

In the **Address** text box, type www.sex.com and press Enter. You should see the Content Advisor dialog box (see Figure 22.5), displaying a list of reasons why you have been denied access to this site. Click **OK**. If Internet Explorer fails to display this dialog box, close Internet Explorer, run it again, and then try connecting to the site again.

FIGURE 22.5

The Content Advisor tells you why you can't visit this site.

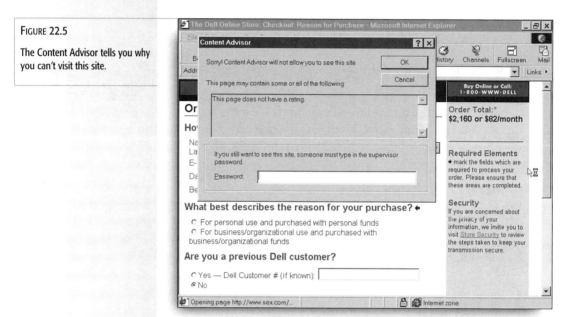

After you have turned on the Ratings feature, you can enter settings to relax the ratings or disable the feature that prevents access to unrated sites. Choose **View**, **Internet Options**, click the **Content** tab, click **Settings**, and enter your password. You can then take the following actions:

- On the **Ratings** tab, click the category of offensive material whose restriction level you want to change: Language, Nudity, Sex, or Violence. Drag the slider below the category list to the right to relax the restrictions or to the left to tighten the restrictions (see Figure 22.6).

- On the **General** tab, choose **Users can see sites that have no rating** to allow access to unrated sites.

- If you don't want the password dialog box popping up when a person tries to access a restricted site, click the **General** tab and turn off **Supervisor can type a password to allow users to view restricted content**.

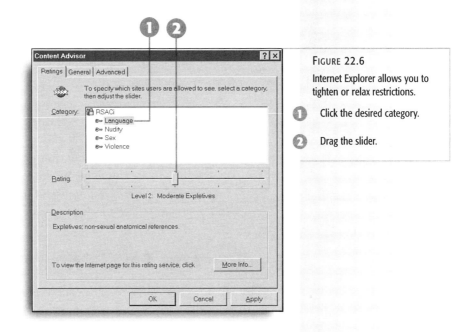

FIGURE 22.6
Internet Explorer allows you to tighten or relax restrictions.

1 Click the desired category.

2 Drag the slider.

Dedicated Internet Censoring Software

Netscape Navigator and most other Web browsers do not have built-in features that you can use to censor the Internet. However, there are several specialized programs that can work along with your browser (and work better than Internet Explorer's Ratings feature) to block access to objectionable Web pages and Internet newsgroups. Following is a list of some of the better censoring programs along with addresses for the Web sites where you can find additional information and download shareware versions of the products:

- *Cyber Patrol* (at www.cyberpatrol.com) is the most popular censoring program. It allows you to set security levels, prevent Internet access during certain hours, and prevent access to specific sites. Passwords allow you to set access levels for different users.

- *CYBERsitter* (at www.solidoak.com) is another fine censoring program. Although a little less strict than Cyber Patrol, CYBERsitter is easier to use and configure. CYBERsitter has a unique filtering system that judges words in context, so it won't block access to inoffensive sites, such as the Anne Sexton home page.

- *Net Nanny* (at www.netnanny.com) is unique in that it can punish the user for typing URLs of offensive sites or for typing any word on the no-no list. If a user types a prohibited word or URL, Net Nanny can shut down the application and record the offense, forcing your student or child to come up with an excuse. However, to make the most of Net Nanny, you're going to have to spend a bit of time configuring it.

Keeping Your Email Private

Email messages are more like postcards than like sealed letters. Anyone with the proper software, know-how, and desire can read your missives as they bounce from server to server to their destination.

To keep your missives private, use an email encryption program. An encryption program scrambles your message when you send it and allows the recipient to decode the message. Here's a quick overview of how it works:

1. You and your friend install the encryption program.

2. You create a set of encryption keys: a private key and a public key.

3. You keep your private key and send your public key to your friend.

4. Before your friend sends you a message, she uses your public key to encrypt the message.

5. When you receive the message, you use your private key to decrypt it.

You can also use an encryption program to digitally sign a message and verify your identity. You attach a digital signature to the message, and your friend can use your public key to verify that you're really the one who sent the message and that it wasn't tampered with along the way.

SEE ALSO

➤ *Learn how to send and receive email messages, page 435*

Sending Messages Securely with S/MIME

Internet Explorer and Netscape Messenger both support S/MIME (short for Secure/Multipurpose Internet Message Extension). With S/MIME, you obtain a digital ID from a certifying authority, such as VeriSign (www.verisign.com), and install it. You can then send your public key to people from whom you want to receive secure email messages.

After installing your digital ID, you must set up your email program to use it:

- In Outlook Express, choose **Tools**, **Accounts**. Click the name of your mail server and click **Properties**. On the **Security** tab, turn on **Use Digital ID,** click the **Digital ID** button, and choose your certificate. When sending a message, click the **Digitally Sign Message** button before clicking **Send**.

- In Netscape Messenger, click the **Security** button, click **Messenger**, and make sure **Encrypt Mail Messages** and **Sign Mail Messages** are both checked.

When you send a digitally signed message, your public key is attached to the message, allowing others to send you encrypted messages. When you receive a digitally signed message from someone, you must add the person's public key to your Address Book, so you can send the person encrypted messages. The procedure varies depending on the email program you're using. Refer to your email program's help system for details.

Other email programs

PGP works best with Outlook Express, Outlook (part of the Microsoft Office suite), and Eudora (a popular email program). You can use PGP with other email programs, although you'll have to encrypt messages using the Clipboard and encrypt file attachments from My Computer.

Pretty Good Privacy

One of the best email encryption programs is PGP (Pretty Good Privacy), which you can pick up free at www.nai.com. Connect to the site, download the file, and click the file to run the installation.

After you install PGP, a wizard leads you through the process of creating your encryption keys. If you're using an email program that's fully compatible with PGP (Outlook, Outlook Express, Eudora), a PGP menu and several buttons are added to your email program to make it easy to encrypt and decrypt messages right from your email program (see Figure 22.7).

FIGURE 22.7

The PGP installation reconfigures your email program.

❶ PGP menu.

❷ Launch PGP keys.

❸ Encrypt message.

❹ Sign message.

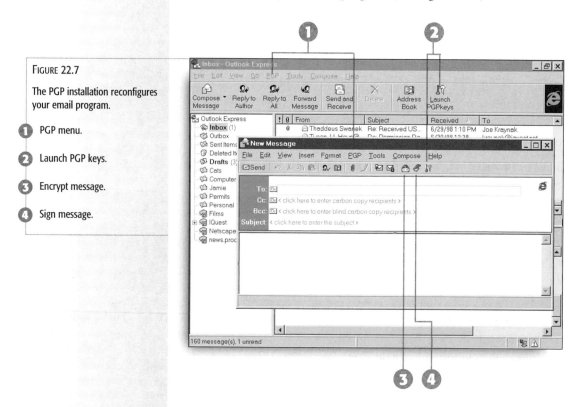

Sending Your Public Key

For someone to send you an encrypted message, the recipient must have your public key. There are three ways you can make your public key available:

- *Paste the key as text into a message.* Click the **Launch PGP Keys** button. Right-click your key and click **Copy**. Create a new message, position the insertion point where you want the key pasted, and press Ctrl+V (see Figure 22.8).

- *Send your key as a file attachment.* Click the **Launch PGP Keys** button. Right-click your key, click **Export**, and save the file to the desired folder. Attach this file to an email message and send it to the person.

- *Post your key on a server.* In your email program, click the **Launch PGP Keys** button. Right-click your key, point to **Send Key to Server**, and click the desired server. If someone needs to send you an encrypted message, can find your key on the server by searching for your email address.

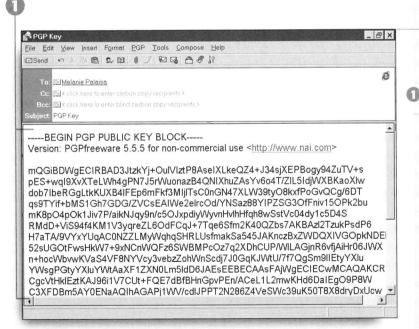

FIGURE 22.8

You can send your key via email as text.

1   Your public key as text.

Adding a Public Key to Your Email Program

For you to send encrypted messages to someone, you must obtain the person's public key and add it to your *keyring* (your list of keys) in PGP. Just as there are three ways to send your public key, there are three ways to obtain someone's public key:

- *Add the key from a message.* Double-click the message to display it in its own window. In the toolbar, click the **Add PGP keys** button (see Figure 22.9).

- *Import the key from a file.* In your email program, display the message that contains the key in its own window. Save the attached PGP key file to your hard disk. Click the **Launch PGP keys** button. Open the **Keys** menu and click **Import**. Change to the folder that contains the file, click its name, and click the **Open** button.

- *Search the key server.* In your email program, click the **Launch PGP Keys** button. Open the **Keys** menu and click **Search**. Choose the server you want to search and enter your search instructions. Click the **Search** button. If the search turns up a match, you'll be asked if you want to add the key to your list of public keys. Click **Yes**.

Sending an Encrypted Message

After you have someone's public key, you can send the person encrypted email messages.

Encrypting a message with PGP

1. Compose your message as you normally do.
2. Click the **Encrypt Message** button (see Figure 22.10).
3. Click the **Send** button.

Decrypting a Message

When you receive an encrypted message, you must decrypt it to read it.

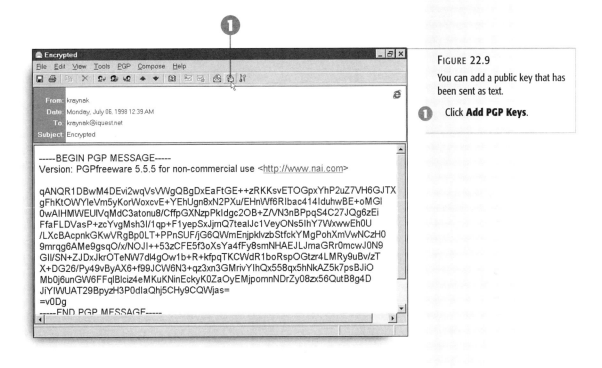

FIGURE 22.9

You can add a public key that has been sent as text.

1 Click **Add PGP Keys**.

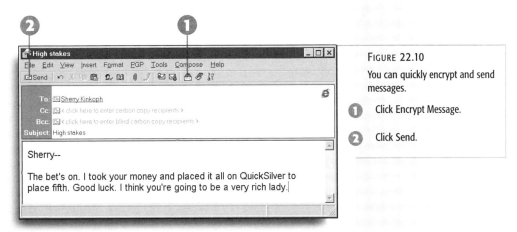

FIGURE 22.10

You can quickly encrypt and send messages.

1 Click Encrypt Message.

2 Click Send.

Decrypting a message

1. Display the message in its own window.

2. Click the **Decrypt PGP Message** button (see Figure 22.11).

3. If prompted for your passphrase, type the passphrase you entered when you created your keys and press **Enter**.

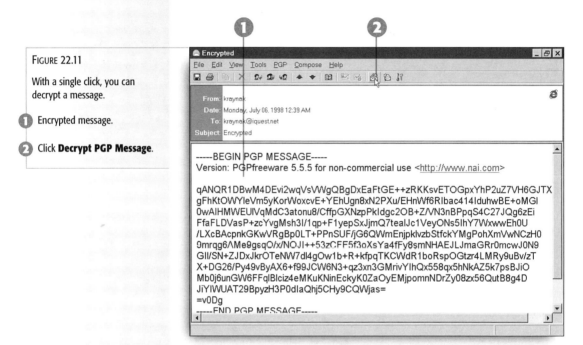

Upgrading Your PC:
Installing New Hardware

Pre-Upgrade Considerations

Decide whether to buy a new PC or upgrade your current PC

Understand common upgrade bottlenecks that limit performance

Choose the best performance upgrade for your system

Check out some intriguing PC toys

Research upgrade products on the Web

Find the best deals on upgrade components

Upgrade Your Old PC or Buy a New PC?

Deciding whether to upgrade your PC or buy a new one can be very easy. If you're happy with your PC's performance, and you just need a faster modem, a bigger hard drive, a little more memory, or a new color printer, there's no question that an upgrade is the way to go.

However, if you have an aging PC and you're looking to boost its overall performance by adding faster RAM, a bigger and faster hard drive, a faster processor, and a video accelerator, the answer isn't so obvious. Upgrades aren't cheap; they're time-consuming, and you always question the return on your investment.

To help you decide whether to upgrade or buy a new PC, the following sections explain some of the major issues.

Why Not Upgrade?

Whenever you consider upgrading your PC, you must ask yourself, "Is it worth it?" For about $2000, you can get a brand spankin' new PC that's primed for the 21st century. How much is it going to cost for the additional RAM, larger hard drive, graphics accelerator, processor upgrade, and all the additional components your old PC needs to bring it up to speed?

To answer this question, make a list of the hardware upgrades you're considering *and* the software you're thinking of purchasing and come up with a total. I recently did this myself when Windows 98 hit the shelves:

5GB hard drive	$300
All-in-one video card	$320
32MB RAM	$150
DVD/CD-ROM drive	$245
150MHz MMX processor	$180
235 watt power supply	$60
Windows 98	$88
Microsoft Office	$479
Total	**$1822**

For about $2500, I could get a new PC with an 8GB hard drive, AGP graphics, 64MB RAM, DVD/CD-ROM drive, 350MHz Pentium II processor, Windows 98, Microsoft Office, plus a new 17-inch monitor, a new keyboard and mouse, USB ports, a stereo sound system, some financial software, and a couple games. In addition, with a new PC, I wouldn't have to perform the upgrades, and all my equipment would come with a warranty from a single company.

You should also ask yourself if your old PC's infrastructure is able to support the desired upgrades. Your old PC may not be equipped to handle a new Pentium II processor, fast SDRAM memory, or an AGP graphics accelerator. In addition, realize that PC components don't run in a vacuum; they work together to determine the overall system speed. For instance, an inadequate amount of slow RAM can severely limit the effects of a fast processor. You may want to reconsider your decision to upgrade if your current PC shows any of the following signs of obsolescence:

- *Slow system bus.* The system bus is the communications network on the motherboard. On 486 PCs, the system bus was restricted to 33MHz. With the introduction of the Pentium processor, the speed was raised to 66MHz. Considering the fact that some 486 and Pentium processors run at speeds in excess of 200MHz, a 33MHz or even a 66MHz system bus is a major bottleneck. Newer PCs use Intel's 440BX or 440LX chipset, which raises the system bus speed limit to 100MHz.

- *Narrow data bus.* A 486 processor uses a 32-bit bus to transfer data to the motherboard. A Pentium uses a 64-bit bus, which can carry twice as much traffic and make up for some of the difference in clock speeds between the processor and the system bus.

- *No L2 cache.* L2 cache is super-fast memory that resides between the processor and the motherboard to reduce the effect of the bottleneck at the system bus. If your system has a small or slow L2 cache (or no L2 cache), adding a faster processor may do little to improve system performance.

- *Slow RAM*. Older PCs are set up to use DRAM memory modules, preventing you from upgrading to the SDRAM standard, which is twice as fast.

- *Old expansion bus*. Most high-end expansion boards plug into 32-bit PCI expansion slots. Older 16-bit ISA slots cannot accommodate the faster PCI expansion boards.

- *Insufficient power supply*. Your old PC may be equipped with a 150-watt power supply that can't supply the juice for many more components. Although the upgrade is cheap (about $30-$60), it adds to the overall cost of your upgrade.

- *No room*. Your system unit may not even have the space for a new component. Are all the expansion slots occupied? Do you have an open drive bay? Is there a free plug on the power supply?

In short, ask yourself if the PC upgrade is going to help your PC lead a *quality* life. If the upgrade acts merely as PC life support, it may be time to pull the plug.

SEE ALSO

➤ *Learn how to shop for a new PC, page 7*

Why Upgrade?

If you purchased a top of the line PC two years ago, it's probably not obsolete. If it has a Pentium processor, a few unoccupied expansion slots, and an open drive bay or two, adding a new processor, additional memory, and a larger hard drive can add two to three years to its productive life.

If you can answer "Yes" to the following three questions, an upgrade is a wise decision:

- *Can my PC handle the upgrade?* Does it have an unoccupied expansion slot for the expansion board I want to install? Does it have an open drive bay for a second hard drive? Is a processor upgrade available for my system?

- *Can I perform all desired upgrades for less than $1000?* If your PC needs only a larger hard drive and more memory, you can upgrade it for about $500, well under the magic $1000 mark. For an extra $100-$200, you can upgrade the processor to give your system an additional boost.

■ *Will the upgrades satisfy me for at least one year?* In the world of PCs, a lot can happen in a year. PC technology will continue to advance at a rapid pace and prices will very likely continue to drop. If you can hold out for a year, you'll find a faster, better-equipped PC for less money than those that are currently on the market.

What About the Year 2000 Bug?

When deciding whether to upgrade, you should also factor in the Year 2000 (or *Y2K* or *Millenium*) "bug." Most PCs can handle years that start with "19" but lose track of years that start with "20." Your PC knows that 11/25/98 is November 25, 1998, but when you enter the date 11/25/01, your PC thinks you're referring to November 25, 1901, not 2001. This can foul up your financial records, databases, and any other programs in which you use dates. Even relatively new PCs (only a year old) may be susceptible.

If possible, contact your PC manufacturer to determine if there is a BIOS update that corrects the problem. (You'll learn more about updating your BIOS in the next chapter.) Although you can attempt to contact the BIOS manufacturer yourself, BIOS manufacturers typically license the BIOS to PC manufacturers and do not support the implementation of the BIOS in specific systems.

Test for the Millenium bug

1. Create a bootable floppy disk. (Format the disk in Windows and choose the option for copying system files to the disk.)

2. Set the time on your computer to four minutes before midnight (23:56:00), and the date to December 31, 1999.

3. Turn off your computer and wait for five minutes.

4. Insert the bootable floppy disk in drive A.

5. Turn on your computer. If your system displays "2000" as the year, your BIOS supports the year 2000.

If your BIOS does not support the year 2000, the fix may be as simple as manually resetting the system clock in the BIOS setup

More Millenium bug information

You can find gobs of information about the Millenium bug on the Web. Search for **y2k**, **millenium bug**, or **year 2000 bug**. Microsoft has several Web pages devoted to the topic. You can also find utilities on the Web for testing your system to determine if it supports the year 2000. If your system has an AMI BIOS, go to www.ami.com. For a Phoenix BIOS, go to www.phoenix.com.

program and allowing a Year-2000-aware operating system (Windows 98) to handle the overall BIOS issues. In other cases, you may have to update the BIOS. On older PCs, this issue may be the one factor that forces you to purchase a new PC rather than upgrade.

SEE ALSO

➤ *Learn how to update your system BIOS, page 571*
➤ *Learn how to manually change the date in the BIOS setup program, page 567*

Prioritizing Your Upgrades

Determining what to upgrade can be as difficult as performing the upgrade itself. Will you see a bigger performance boost by adding RAM or by replacing the processor? Is your system crashing frequently because it has insufficient RAM or an inadequate power supply? You want an upgrade that gives you the best return on your investment, but where do you start?

The following sections help you focus on the three types of upgrades: upgrades for correcting a problem, enhancing performance, or adding a new feature to your PC. Each section provides guidance on how to pick the best upgrades for your system.

Upgrading to Correct a Problem

Upgrade decisions that are based on necessity are fairly obvious. If your CD-ROM drive goes belly-up, you must replace it. If you find yourself deleting files and folders every time you want to install a new program, the fact that you need a new hard drive is painfully clear.

Upgrade decisions based on overall system degradation may not be so obvious. You may notice that your PC is a little slower than usual or that it locks up more frequently. Maybe you insert a new multimedia CD and notice that the opening screen takes forever to appear. Video clips may appear grainy and choppy.

When your PC is having trouble performing its daily chores, it's a pretty good sign that your PC needs an upgrade. But what should you upgrade? Table 23.1 provides some guidance.

TABLE 23.1   **Signs that your PC needs upgrading**

Symptom	Upgrade
Hard disk light on constantly	Add RAM. When Windows doesn't have enough RAM to work with, it uses space on the disk drive as RAM. In addition to slowing down your system, this overworks the drive.
Insufficient memory message	Add RAM. Install larger hard drive.
Frequent crashes	Add RAM. Upgrade power supply. Upgrade graphics card. Upgrade processor.
Slow, jerky video	Add RAM. Upgrade graphics card.
Fuzzy graphics	Upgrade graphics card.
Slow multimedia CDs	Add RAM. Install faster CD player.
Slow Internet connection	Upgrade modem.
Can't play new game	Upgrade processor to MMX or better. Upgrade graphics card.

SEE ALSO

➤ *Learn how to troubleshoot common hardware problems, page 799*

➤ *Learn how to troubleshoot common software problems, page 837*

Upgrading to Boost Performance

PC hardware and software is caught up in a vicious game of one-upmanship. As hardware manufacturers develop technology to enhance the performance of current software, software developers are writing programs that push the limits of the hardware. Three years ago, a system with 16MB RAM and a 500MB hard drive seemed like overkill. That system today would have a difficult time running Windows 98, let alone a 3D game.

To help your PC maintain its speed amidst the growing demands of the latest software, you must add a few performance boosters. Following are the most beneficial performance boosters listed in order from most to least effective:

- *RAM.* Looking for an inexpensive performance boost? Add RAM. Adding 16–32MB or more is the most effective way to increase overall system performance. With additional RAM, Windows takes fewer trips to the slow hard drive to access data. Additional RAM typically gives you more bang for your buck than a processor upgrade.

- *Processor upgrade.* Second only to RAM, a new processor makes everything seem faster, especially when coupled with a RAM upgrade. Moving up from a Classic Pentium to Pentium MMX significantly improves the speed at which your system runs games and graphics designed for MMX. However, a processor's speed represents only its internal speed. If you yoke a 200MHz processor to a 33MHz motherboard, you will see little performance gain.

- *Graphics accelerator.* All those pretty pictures on your screen require a great deal of memory and processing power. A graphics accelerator takes some of the burden off the processor, frees up RAM, and increases the speed at which images are rendered on the screen. If your PC is only two or three years old, it probably has a PCI graphics adapter, which is sufficient for Windows and most standard applications. For games and graphics-heavy applications, a 3D graphics accelerator significantly improves performance.

- *Faster hard drive.* With a faster hard drive, Windows can load programs and open documents more quickly and has rapid access to the disk when using it as virtual memory.

- *Faster modem.* Of course, a faster modem isn't going to increase system performance, but it will make Web pages load much more quickly. If you have a 28.8K modem and you spend much time on the Web, upgrade to a 56K modem, ISDN, a cable modem, or satellite dish.

■ *Faster CD-ROM drive.* If you frequently use your CD-ROM player to play multimedia CDs or games or access clip-art libraries, installing a faster CD-ROM drive is a smart move. However, if you use the drive only to install new software every month or so, don't bother. Your current CD-ROM drive is fine.

SEE ALSO

➤ *Learn how to shop for and install additional RAM, page 577*

➤ *Learn how to shop for and install a new hard drive, page 587*

➤ *Learn how to shop for and install a new processor, page 607*

➤ *Learn how to shop for and install a graphics accelerator, page 641*

➤ *Learn how to shop for and install a new modem, page 674*

Upgrading to Add a New Toy

Upgrading to fix a problem or enhance system performance is like replacing the plumbing in your home. Everything flows a little more smoothly, but who cares? Upgrading to add a new toy to your system is more like installing a hot tub. The upgrade lets you have a little fun with your PC.

I can't tell you which feature upgrades are more valuable than others. What seems new and cool to me may not seem so exciting to you. However, I can provide you with a long list of feature upgrades that you might find compelling:

■ *Digital camera.* Tired of taking snapshots with your 35mm camera and waiting for them to be developed? Then purchase a digital camera. Digital cameras store your photos internally, on floppy disks, or on memory cards, allowing you to download the images to your hard drive and insert them in your documents, on Web pages, or in presentations. You can even send the images via email.

■ *Video camera.* Connect a video camera to your PC for video conferencing and Internet phone calls. Talk face to face with friends, relatives, and complete strangers.

- *Scanner*. Use a full-page scanner to transfer your stacks of paper documents into digitized documents for quick retrieval. Scan documents and use OCR (optical character recognition) software to copy text into your documents. Scan photos to create digital photo albums. Or use a scanner along with a fax modem to fax documents. Better yet, upgrade to an all-in-one printer/scanner/fax/copy machine to save space.

- *Projector*. If you frequently create online presentations and have to convert them to 35mm slides or overhead transparencies, hook a projector to your PC and let your PC display the presentation, complete with audio, video, and animation.

- *Voice-activated computing*. Are you tired of typing? Worried about carpal tunnel syndrome? Then install voice-recognition software and a high-quality microphone. Your PC can then carry out voice commands and take dictation.

- *TV tuner*. To use your PC for home entertainment as well as personal computing, add a TV tuner card and hook your PC up to cable or an antenna. Windows 98 comes with WebTV, which automatically scans for available stations, tunes in, and allows you to download local program listings from the Web. Flip channels with a click of your mouse.

- *Video capture board*. With a video capture board, you can connect your camcorder or a VCR player to your PC, play video clips into your PC, and save your clips as files. You can place the clips on your Web pages, insert them in your presentations, or attach them to your email messages. You can even do a little video editing to create your own custom videos.

- *Game controller*. Although your keyboard and mouse moonlight as game controllers, playing your favorite PC game with your keyboard is no fun. Attach a joystick, gamepad, or other control to your PC for superior control.

- *Big-screen monitor*. That dinky 15-inch monitor that came with your PC is inadequate for the newest desktop publishing programs, games, Web pages, and interactive, multimedia CDs. Add a 19-inch monitor, and you'll feel as though you're sitting in the front row at the movie theater. A big-screen monitor can also help with your business applications, displaying more columns and rows in a spreadsheet and reducing the need to scroll.

- *3D Sound*. If the big-screen monitor isn't enough to make you feel as though you're at the movies, add 3D sound to the mix. The latest sound boards and PC speaker systems can shake your bones.

- *Drawing pad*. Drawing pictures with a mouse is like trying to eat spaghetti with a spoon. Drawing pads let you sketch pictures on the monitor just as if you were drawing them on a sketchpad.

SEE ALSO

➤ *Learn how to choose, install, and use a digital camera, page 757*

➤ *Learn how to choose and install a scanner, page 741*

➤ *Learn how to install a TV-tuner/video capture board, page 714*

Taking Inventory of Your System

Before you upgrade, draw up a list of your system's components. If you never looked at your PC's documentation or the packing slip, dig it out of your filing cabinet and look at it now. You may have several manuals, a document for the system unit itself, hard drive, CD-ROM drive, sound card, modem, video adapter, monitor, and modem. Each manual should have a Specifications list at the front or back. Obtain as much of the following information as possible:

- Processor installed.

- Processor speed.

- Processor upgrade possible.

- RAM installed and maximum capacity.

- Hard drive size and type (IDE or SCSI).

- CD-ROM drive speed.
- Power supply.
- BIOS type.
- Number of PCI slots installed. (You'll learn in the next chapter how to check inside the system unit to determine the number of unoccupied slots.)
- Number of ISA slots installed.
- Modem speed.
- Type of video adapter (VESA, PCI, or AGP) and amount of video memory installed.
- Sound card installed (for example, 16-bit stereo).

You can gather additional information by using the following Windows tools:

- *Windows 98 System Information utility*. Run the System Information utility by choosing **Start, Programs, Accessories, System Tools**. Here, you can obtain information about the amount of memory installed, total and free disk space, and the type of processor.
- *Microsoft Diagnostics*. If you're using an earlier version of Windows, go to the DOS prompt, type msd, and press Enter. Microsoft Diagnostics lists important information about your system, including the amount of memory installed. If you upgraded to Windows 98 from an older version, msd.exe may still be present on your system; if you purchased a brand new PC with Windows 98 on it, you won't have msd.exe.
- *Resource meter*. Install the Resource Meter in Windows 95 or 98, and run it from the **System Tools** menu to determine if your system runs low on memory as you work.

One of the most useful (and stable) utilities for listing and testing hardware components is BCM Diagnostics for Windows 95 (which works pretty well on Windows 98, too). You can download a copy from www.bcmcom.com. Figure 23.1 shows a system summary displayed by BCM Diagnostics.

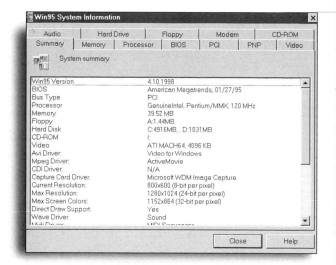

FIGURE 23.1

BCM Diagnostics for Windows takes inventory of your system for you.

SEE ALSO

➤ *Learn how to run and use the Windows 98 system information utility, page 261*

Smart Shopping for Upgrades

When shopping for upgrades, your goal is to find high-quality products at low prices. You want components that are compatible with your current hardware, manufactured by reputable companies, and sold by reputable dealers. You don't want to get stuck with obsolete hardware manufactured by some fly-by-night operation that the dealer is trying to unload at bargain basement prices.

The best place to start shopping for upgrades is through the PC manufacturer or the dealer from whom you purchased your PC. I'm not saying that this is the best place to *buy* upgrade components, but it is the best place to begin. You can pick the dealer's brain to find out which components you need and the types of components that are compatible with your system. You can also get a price to use for comparison purposes.

Another good place to gather information is your local computer retailer, where you take a look at actual products and perhaps even take them for a test drive. Fight the urge to buy until you've done a little more research.

Doing Your Homework

Check your PC's warranty

If your PC is still under warranty, read the warranty statement carefully before purchasing upgrades from an independent dealer. The warranty may state that you must purchase upgrades directly from the PC manufacturer. Some warranties state that you must send the PC to the manufacturer for some upgrades, such as memory or processor upgrades.

The best place to research products is on the Web, where you can find product reviews, dealers, manufactures' Web sites, user testimonials, and additional information. Here's a list of tips for researching upgrade products on the Web:

- Go to ZDNet at www.zdnet.com, click the link for **Product Reviews**, and search for the upgrade product (see Figure 23.2). ZDNet publishes magazines, including *PC Computing*, *PC Magazine*, *FamilyPC*, *Computer Gaming*, and *Computer Shopper*, which all contain comparative reviews of products. Note the date of the review and list any competitive products (especially those that received positive reviews).

FIGURE 23.2

At ZDNet, you can search for product reviews.

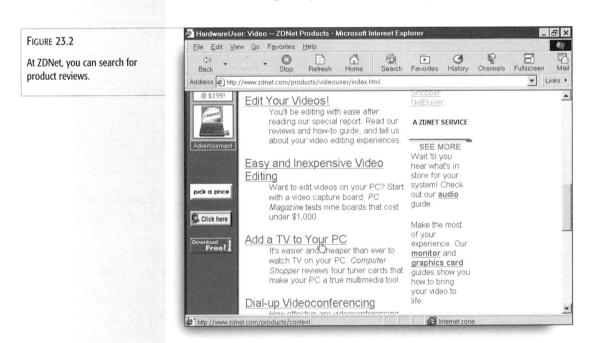

- After reading a few reviews, head to the manufacturer's Web site and locate the product. Find out if the manufacturer has a newer model of the product, so you won't get stuck with an old model that a dealer is trying to unload.

- While you're at the manufacturer's Web site, look for additional links to reviews, and read the reviews. Although manufacturers won't link to negative reviews, the review may mention competing products.

- Check out the manufacturer's technical support resources to find out if the product has any serious, known problems. If there's FAQ (frequently asked questions list), read it. The technical support area also shows that the manufacturer actively supports the products after the sale. This is an important consideration when purchasing products. If no technical support is available, the manufacturer may have little concern for its customers.

- Check out the competition. Just because one product gets more press than another doesn't mean it's better. Research any competing product mentioned in reviews. The manufacturer may also have a chart comparing its product to its major competitor.

- For additional information, use a more general search tool, such as Lycos (`www.lycos.com`) to search for product categories or specific products. This takes a little longer than searching for product reviews in online magazines, but it turns up links to sites you might not otherwise stumble upon.

If you don't have access to the Web, researching specific products is drudge work. Even if you have a big stack of PC magazines, the chances of finding a review on a specific product are slim. If you can locate a manufacturer's phone number, call for additional information about a product, but don't expect them to say anything positive about the competition.

SEE ALSO

➤ *Learn how to access a Web site with your Web browser, page 416*
➤ *Learn how to find specific information on the Web, page 419*

Shopping for Upgrades on the Web

After you've decided on a specific upgrade product, you can start searching for the best price. Again, the Web is the place to find low prices through mail-order companies.

First, check out ZDNet's NetBuyer, an Internet search tool that can help you track down the best deals on the Internet. Go to NetBuyer at www.zdnet.com/netbuyer. Click the **Search** link, click in the **Search** text box, type the product's name, and click **Search Products**. NetBuyer displays a list of links to mail-order companies that sell the product, so you can find the best deal (see Figure 23.3).

FIGURE 23.3

NetBuyer can help you find the best deal.

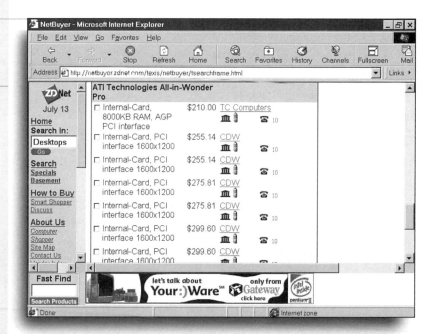

If you don't have Internet access, get a copy of a PC magazine (any PC magazine will do), and flip to the back to search through the ads for mail-order companies. In case you don't have a computer magazine handy, here are a few companies to try:

- *USA Flex* at 800-723-0334 or www.usaflex.com is a good place to shop for printers, graphics cards, CD-ROM drives, scanners, and modems.

- *First Source* at 800-468-9866 or www.firstsource.com is an excellent place to buy memory and processor upgrades. They offer quality products at reasonable prices, and their sales staff can help you figure out what you need for your particular system.

- *Computer Discount Warehouse* at 800-886-4239 or www.cdw.com offers a wide selection of software, multimedia and processor upgrades, monitors, and input devices.

- *Avantec* at 800-898-9494 or www.avantec.com deals in complete systems, motherboards, processors, memory upgrades, and a great selection of upgrade components. The sales staff is knowledgeable and can help you determine if a particular upgrade product is compatible with your system.

Just because these are mail-order companies, don't assume that you're going to get second-rate service. Reputable mail-order companies can ship products via overnight or second-day delivery, their upgrades come with complete instructions from the original manufacturer, the products are high-quality, and most mail-order companies have their own technical support line that you can call for help. They typically offer better service and support than you'll get from a local computer retailer and offer products at much lower prices.

SEE ALSO

➤ *Learn how to order products securely on the Web, page 513*

Buyer beware

When shopping on the Web, shop only from reputable dealers. Anyone with a modem and an ISP account can stick a phony page on the Web. Dealers must register with NetBuyer to be listed, so this ensures that the dealer is legitimate.

General Installation Precautions and Procedures

Put together an upgrade toolkit

Perform upgrades without damaging your system

Upgrade an inadequate power supply

Install an expansion card (printed circuit board)

Check and adjust system settings after an upgrade

Update the system BIOS to correct common problems

Tools of the Trade

You may be surprised at how few tools you need to perform upgrades. In most cases, you can get by with a small Phillips-head screwdriver or a 1/4-inch socket driver. I prefer the socket driver because it's less likely to strip the screw head or slide off a screw and hit another part. (On a Compaq PC, you may need a size 15 Torx screwdriver, which you can pick up at any hardware store.) A pair of tweezers or needle-nose pliers can also come in handy for setting jumpers.

You can purchase a special PC toolkit, which typically includes a screwdriver, socket driver, chip puller (for advanced upgrades), and a pair of tweezers or a three-pronged probe to help you fish out screws from tight places. Although these toolkits include more tools than you need, it's nice to have a set of tools just for your PC (see Figure 24.1).

FIGURE 24.1

A PC toolkit can come in handy.

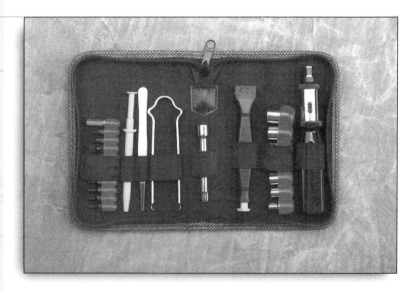

You should also purchase a grounding strap to prevent damaging your system with static electricity. The grounding strap attaches to your wrist and usually to the metal system unit case to discharge any static electricity from your body. That little snap you

hear when you drag your feet across the carpet and then touch
your new upgrade component may not hurt you very much, but
it can destroy a sensitive component.

Safety Precautions

Before you even think about getting inside your system unit, you
should be aware of some safety precautions. Because so many
delicate electrical components reside there, you have to be careful. Follow these standard precautions:

- Back up your hard drives. If you do happen to damage a
  drive during the upgrade, you'll need to restore your programs and data.

- Make sure *all* the parts of your computer are turned off and
  unplugged.

- Before you start, touch a metal part of the system unit to
  discharge any static electricity from your body. Better yet,
  go to an electronics store and buy a grounding strap.

- Avoid dragging your feet across the carpet, especially in arid
  environments. Static electricity is worse in the winter, when
  the air is dry.

- New computer parts usually come in anti-static bags. Before
  handling a part, touch a metal part of the system unit case to
  discharge static electricity.

- Keep parts in their anti-static bags (not on top of the bags)
  until you are ready to use them.

- Never slide parts over your work surface. This can build up
  a static charge in the part.

- If the parts have warranty seals, be careful not to break
  them. Breaking a seal invalidates the warranty.

- Hold parts by their edges and mounting brackets. Avoid
  touching any components or solder on the parts.

- Keep plastic, vinyl, furs, and Styrofoam out of your work
  area.

- When your component arrives, let it adjust to the temperature and humidity of your office before installing it. Any condensation on the new part could damage your system.

- If you drop a stray screw inside the system unit, stick some tape on a pencil and try to fish out the screw; don't use your fingers or a magnet.

- When removing the cover from your system unit, make sure you don't bump any cables loose or pinch them when you replace the cover.

- When working inside the system unit, try not to brush up against circuit boards. If you're rearranging data cables, keep them away from the circuit boards; it's easy to knock a jumper off a board and difficult to find out where to put it back on.

- Before disconnecting anything, draw a picture or note the connections, so you can put everything back together exactly the way it was if the upgrade doesn't work.

Going Inside the System Unit

Read your warranty

If your system is still under manufacturer's warranty, read the warranty carefully before you touch anything. In some cases, opening the system unit case may void a warranty.

You can perform a few upgrades without opening the system unit. For example, to install a scanner or a new monitor, you plug it in to a port on the back of the system unit. For most other upgrades—installing an internal modem, a sound card, SCSI interface, graphics accelerator, additional RAM, a new processor, or a bigger hard drive, you must pop the hood on your system unit and go inside.

The steps for removing the system unit cover vary depending on the unit. Typically, you remove several screws from the back of the system unit (near the edges) and then slide the cover back and up to remove it from the case. Other system units may use thumbscrews or provide a hinged door you can open to go inside.

When removing the cover, keep the following points in mind:

- Remove the right screws. The back of the system unit has screws for securing the power supply and other devices to the case. Remove only the screws that secure the cover; the screws are typically along the outer edge of the system unit.

- Put the screws in an envelope to keep them all together. You don't want them getting mixed up with other screws later.

- Lift the cover slowly, making sure none of its clips snag the cables inside the system unit. A snag can easily sever a wire.

- When replacing the cover, be careful not to pinch a cable between the cover and the case.

When you first go inside, take a look around and identify the places where you'll be working. Use Figure 24.2 as your guide, but realize that disk drives, expansion boards, cables, and other devices may block your view of some of the components.

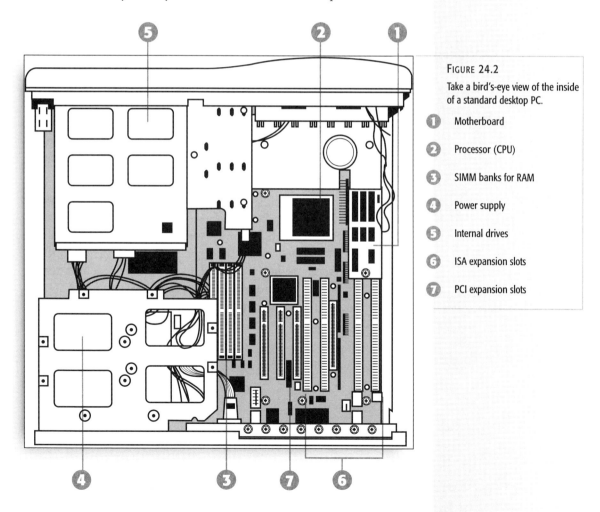

FIGURE **24.2**

Take a bird's-eye view of the inside of a standard desktop PC.

1 Motherboard

2 Processor (CPU)

3 SIMM banks for RAM

4 Power supply

5 Internal drives

6 ISA expansion slots

7 PCI expansion slots

Installing a Printed Circuit Board

Nine out of ten upgrades require you to "install" an expansion board (also called a *card*). An expansion board is a printed circuit board that plugs into an expansion slot on the main printed circuit board (the *motherboard*) inside the system unit. An internal modem is an expansion board. A sound card is an expansion board. In some cases, you might even have to install a card to add a floppy disk drive, CD-ROM drive, or hard drive to your system.

SEE ALSO

➤ *Learn how to install a graphics accelerator card, page 648*

➤ *Learn how to install an internal modem, page 681*

➤ *Learn how to add ports by installing an expansion board, page 787*

Easy Upgrades with Plug and Play

In the past, the most difficult aspect of upgrading a PC was getting all the components to work together and not compete for system resources. When you installed an expansion board, you had to set jumpers to specify settings for the board that would not conflict with settings used by another board. For example, using the wrong jumper settings for a modem could disable the mouse.

To prevent these conflicts, Microsoft, with the cooperation of most hardware manufacturers, developed the Plug and Play (PnP) standard. With Plug and Play, the hardware allows the software (the system BIOS and operating system) to control the board's settings. When you install a device, your system assigns it settings that do not conflict with other devices installed on the system. Windows can then identify the device and lead you through the process of installing the software needed to use it.

For Plug and Play to work properly on your PC, the following four conditions must exist:

- *The BIOS must support Plug and Play.* If your BIOS has a date of 1995 or later, chances are that it supports Plug and Play.

PCs manufactured between 1993 and 1995 may have the required Plug and Play hardware, but lack the BIOS support needed to identify Plug and Play devices. Before upgrading, check your BIOS and update it, if needed, as explained later in this chapter.

- *The motherboard must support Plug and Play.* If your system has a PCI bus, it supports Plug and Play. PCI was designed with Plug and Play in mind. If your system has ISA expansion slots, these usually cooperate with the PCI bus to avoid conflicts. Older systems based on the ISA and Vesa buses typically do not support the Plug and Play standard.

- *The device you're installing must support Plug and Play.* Virtually all PCI expansion boards, including graphics accelerators, modems, and sound cards and most new external devices, including monitor and printers, support Plug and Play. This allows the device to identify itself to the system and request resources not in use by other devices.

- *Your operating system software must support the Plug and Play standard.* Windows 95 and later supports Plug and Play.

SEE ALSO
➤ *Learn how to check your BIOS settings to determine if your system supports Plug and Play, page 567*

Dealing with Non–Plug-and-Play Devices

Some expansion boards on the market do not conform to the rules of Plug and Play. With these types of boards, you must make sure that the new board will not use the same settings as an existing board. Typically, there are three settings you need to consider:

- *IRQ* stands for *interrupt request* and is a number that enables a device to demand attention from the central processing unit. If two devices have the same IRQ, they demand attention at the same time, possibly causing a conflict. One or both devices may not work. IRQ sharing is possible on some systems, provided that your hardware supports it.

- *DMA Channel* is a path to your computer's RAM. Most computers have eight DMA (Direct Memory Access) channels. If two devices have the same DMA channel, usually only one device gains access to RAM. The other device won't work.

- *I/O port address* is a designation that allows a device to take input and generate output at a certain location. As with IRQs and DMAs, if two devices use the same I/O setting, you'll encounter problems.

Try installing the expansion board with the factory settings (don't change anything). If the card doesn't work, then you can try changing the settings, as explained in the documentation. (Change only one setting at a time.) You change these settings on the expansion board by flipping tiny switches or by sliding jumpers over or off of wire posts on the card (see Figure 24.3). Draw a picture of the current switch or jumper settings before you change them.

FIGURE 24.3

To prevent conflicts, you may have to use jumpers on the card.

❶ Slide a jumper off or slide one on to change a setting.

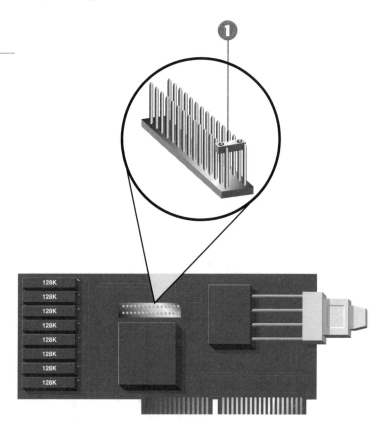

SEE ALSO
➤ *Learn how to track down the cause of a device conflict in Windows, page 802*

Finding an Open Expansion Slot

To install an expansion board, you must first find a compatible, unoccupied expansion slot in the system unit. The expansion slots are near the back of the system unit where most of your external devices are plugged in. Locate a matching expansion slot for the type of board you're installing:

- PCI slots are white and relatively short.
- ISA slots are black and are longer than the PCI slots.
- EISA slots are brown and are as long as ISA slots but a little wider (see Figure 24.4).

Some systems use a *shared* PCI/ISA expansion slot. The shared slots are right next to each other. You can use only one of the two shared expansion slots (either the PCI or ISA), but not both. (Check your PC's documentation.) Typically, you'll use this slot for a PCI board, but if all ISA slots are occupied and you have another ISA expansion board to install, you can use the shared slot for the ISA board.

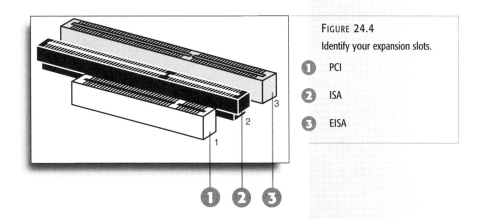

FIGURE **24.4**
Identify your expansion slots.

❶ PCI

❷ ISA

❸ EISA

If the expansion board requires a connection to an external device, such as a scanner, a telephone cable, or speakers, remove the cover plate near the expansion slot you want to use. This is simply a matter of removing one screw and lifting the cover plate (see Figure 24.5).

FIGURE 24.5

Remove the cover plate from the system unit case near the desired expansion slot.

 Remove the cover plate.

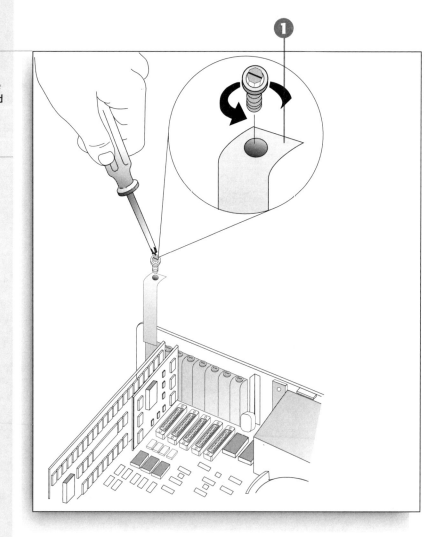

Rocking the Board in Place

To install the expansion board, align the contacts at the bottom of the board with the expansion slot, and then press down on the edge of the card while rocking it *gently* into place (see Figure 24.6). Expect the fit to be snug, but don't push so hard that you crack the board. Make sure the board is seated securely in the socket and that it is not leaning against any other boards (this could cause the board to short circuit). Secure the board in place using the screw you removed from the cover plate. (A good sign that the board is properly seated is that the plate fits snugly over the opening in the back of the system unit.)

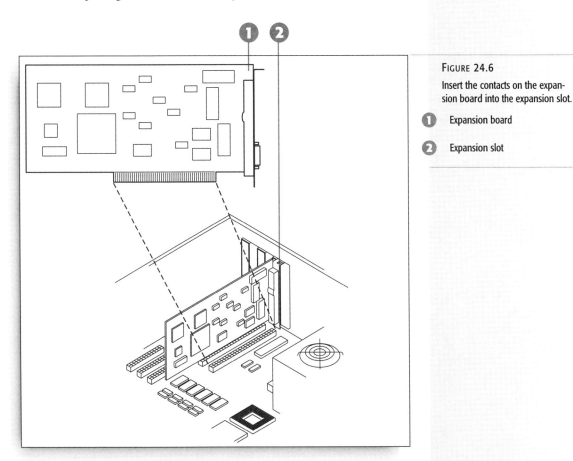

FIGURE 24.6

Insert the contacts on the expansion board into the expansion slot.

1 Expansion board

2 Expansion slot

When you're done, replace the system unit cover, but don't secure it with the screws. If the expansion board does not work, you will have to get inside the system unit again and play with the jumpers.

Installing a Device Driver

After you install an expansion board, you must install its *device driver*, typically from a floppy disk or CD. The driver tells your PC how to work with the expansion board and tells the expansion board how to do its job. Follow the instructions that came with your expansion board to run the setup or installation program. (In many cases, the software includes a diagnostic utility that can determine if the board is installed properly and can help you resolve any conflicts with other devices.)

Windows 95 (and later) comes with a utility called the Add New Hardware Wizard that searches for new components and leads you through the process of installing the device driver. When you turn on your PC after installing a device, Windows detects it and runs the Add New Hardware Wizard. If the wizard does not start automatically, run it from the Control Panel.

Running the Add New Hardware Wizard

1. Exit all running programs. This prevents you from losing any data in case Windows locks up during the process.

2. Click the **Start** button, point to **Settings**, and click **Control Panel**.

3. Click the **Add New Hardware** icon. The Add New Hardware Wizard appears, informing you about what the wizard will do.

4. Follow the onscreen instructions to complete the installation (see Figure 24.7). You may have to insert the Windows CD or a disk that came with the board.

SEE ALSO

➤ *Learn how to find and install updated device drivers in Windows, page 251*

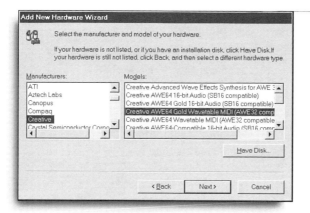

FIGURE 24.7
The Add New Hardware Wizard leads you through the process of installing the device driver.

Checking Your BIOS Settings

The BIOS (Basic Input/Output System), pronounced "BUY-ose," is the built-in set of instructions that tells your PC how to control the disk drives, keyboard, printer port, display adapter, and other components that make up your computer. Think of the BIOS as the little black box inside new cars that keeps everything working in sync.

To enable your PC to exploit the full potential of an upgrade component you install (and, in some cases, to enable your PC to use the device at all), you may need to change the BIOS settings. For example, if you install a new printer that supports bi-directional printing, you may need to change the setting for the printer port to enable its bi-directional printing capabilities.

The procedure for accessing the BIOS settings varies from one system to another. When you start your PC, before Windows starts, you should see a message telling you which key(s) to press to run Setup. Typically, you press F1 or F2. Some PCs hide the keystroke used to access the BIOS setup, because the manufacturer doesn't want users to mess with it. You'll have to refer to the PC's documentation to determine which key to press.

When you press the designated key, the opening BIOS screen appears (see Figure 24.8). Because no mouse is installed, you must use your keyboard to navigate the screen:

- Press the left- or right-arrow key to change from one menu of options to another.

- Use the down- and up-arrow keys to highlight an option you want to check or change.

- Press the plus or minus key to change a value displayed in brackets, for instance to change [Off] to [On].

- Highlight an option preceded by an arrow and press Enter to view its submenu.

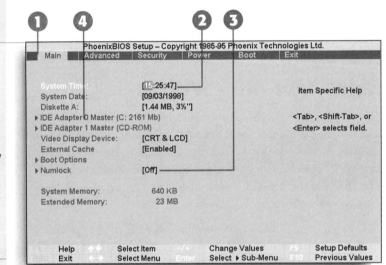

FIGURE 24.8

Use the BIOS Setup screen to enter the required settings.

1 Press the left- or right-arrow key to change menus.

2 Press the up- or down-arrow key to highlight an option.

3 Press + or - to turn an option on or off.

4 Press Enter to view a submenu.

BIOS Precautions

Many people avoid changing any BIOS settings because they fear making some sort of fatal error. However, upgrades may force your hand, or curiosity may inspire you to take a look at what makes your PC tick. By following a few precautions, you can safely check and change settings and even recover if you make a mistake:

- Make a bootable floppy disk and save a copy of the BIOS as a file to the disk, if possible. (Enter the required command in the BIOS setup to save or export your BIOS settings as a file.) If you make a mistake, you can import the original settings.

- Write down each setting before you change it.

- If you don't know what you're changing or why you're changing it, don't change it.

- If you decide to use the password feature, choose a password you will never ever forget and write it down just to be safe.

- If you don't feel comfortable with the changes you've entered, choose the option to exit without saving changes.

BIOS Settings You May Need to Adjust

With most upgrades, you can safely ignore the BIOS. The BIOS typically identifies additional RAM and new drives, and if your BIOS supports Plug and Play, it can even help identify new expansion boards. However, sometimes the BIOS needs you to intervene and enter a few custom settings. The following list explains some of the common adjustments you may need to make:

- *Date and Time*. You can easily change the system date and time from Windows, but you may need to change it in the BIOS (for example, if your BIOS doesn't automatically recognize the date at the turn of the century).

- *Hard drives*. The BIOS typically contains four hard drive entries, which may be labeled C, D, E, F, or IDE Primary Master, IDE Primary Slave, IDE Secondary Master, IDE Secondary Slave. Typically, the BIOS is set to AutoDetect for all drives. However, if you install a new drive and the BIOS doesn't recognize it, you need to enter hard drive settings manually. See Chapter 26, "Installing a New Hard Drive," for details.

- *Floppy drives*. The BIOS typically contains two floppy drive entries, labeled Drive A and Drive B, allowing you to specify the drive type: 3.5-inch 1.44MB, 3.5-inch 720KB, 3.5-inch 2.88MB (on some systems), 5.25-inch 1.2MB, or 5.25-inch 360KB. You may need to change the setting if you replace your floppy disk drive with a different floppy disk drive type.

- *Plug and Play*. Enabling Plug and Play tells the BIOS that the PC is running a Plug and Play operating system

(Windows 95 or later). You might think that Plug and Play would be enabled by default, but if your PC came with Windows 3.1, Plug and Play is disabled. On some systems, Plug and Play works regardless of whether it is disabled or enabled in the BIOS. If you have trouble getting a Plug and Play device to work, enable this setting.

- *Power Management.* Many systems have a built-in power management feature that can automatically shut down the hard drive or monitor when it hasn't been used for the specified amount of time. If you have trouble getting an upgrade to work properly after installation, try disabling power management features in the BIOS.

- *Integrated serial port.* Integrated ports are directly connected to the motherboard instead of being connected through the expansion bus. This typically includes two serial ports and the parallel (printer) port. If both serial ports 1 and 2 are enabled and you want to install a modem that uses serial port 2 (COM2), you may have to disable serial port 2 to free up its resources for your modem.

- *Parallel port mode.* The parallel port isn't just for printers anymore. Many external drives and scanners can also take advantage of high-speed data transfer via the parallel port. If you replace your old printer with a newer model or install an external drive, scanner, or other device that requires high-speed parallel communications, check the Parallel Port Mode setting in your BIOS to ensure that it's set to Bi-Directional, ECP (Extended Capabilities Port), or EPP (Enhanced Parallel Port).

Make your PC start faster

If your PC is set up to check drive A for boot instructions before checking drive C, change the boot option to tell your PC to check drive C first. Also, change the Initialization Timeout setting for any hard drive that is NOT installed to Disabled; this prevents the BIOS from looking for a drive on startup.

The BIOS setup utility contains many more options than those described here. To obtain a brief description of an option, highlight it and press the F1 key.

SEE ALSO

➤ *Learn how to adjust the BIOS settings for a new hard drive, page 598*

PART **IV**

Can Your BIOS Handle the Upgrade?   CHAPTER **24**   571

Can Your BIOS Handle the Upgrade?

Your PC's BIOS was originally designed to handle the hardware available when your PC was manufactured. If your PC is over two years old and you haven't updated the BIOS, the BIOS is probably outdated and may not support the latest hardware. For example, a BIOS that's three years old may not be able to recognize a hard drive over 2GB.

To prevent problems with upgrades, you should make sure you have the most recent BIOS for your system. To find out which BIOS your system uses, and its version number and date, restart your PC, keep a close eye on your monitor, and have a finger ready to press the Pause key. The first text that appears should display the BIOS manufacturer and the version number or date. Press the Pause key. Write down the BIOS manufacturer and the version number or date.

Now, contact the manufacturer of your PC (via phone or the Internet) to find out if an updated BIOS is available for your system. You must obtain answers to the following three questions:

- Is an updated BIOS available?
- What new features does the updated BIOS offer?
- Can you update the BIOS by running a program, or do you have to replace the BIOS chips? (You can update a *flash BIOS* by running an update program.) If you have a Pentium system, it probably uses a flash BIOS. On PCs that use a non-flash BIOS, you may have to replace the BIOS chips.

If the PC manufacture does not offer the BIOS update you need, try the following companies:

Phoenix BIOS: Micro Firmware at www.firmware.com, (405) 321-8333 or Phoenix at www.phoenix.com, (617) 551-4000.

Award BIOS: Unicore at www.unicore.com, 1-800-800-2467.

AMI BIOS: AMI at www.ami.com or Unicore at www.unicore.com, 1-800-800-2467.

Mr BIOS: Unicore at www.unicore.com, 1-800-800-2467.

BIOS no longer supported

PC manufacturers may post BIOS updates to fix bugs in the BIOS, but they rarely provide free updates for new versions of a BIOS. You typically must purchase an upgrade, just as if you were purchasing a new version of a word processor.

You need not update your BIOS with a BIOS from the same manufacturer. For instance, you can replace your AMI BIOS with a Phoenix BIOS or vice versa. However, the BIOS must be compatible with your system. The BIOS distributor will be able to tell you which update you need for your system. Before you call, write down the existing BIOS type and version number.

Before updating your BIOS, save or export the current BIOS settings to a file on a bootable floppy disk. See "BIOS Precautions," earlier in this chapter, for details.

Upgrading a Flash BIOS

Get the right update

Installing the wrong BIOS update is worse than not installing the update and could prevent your system from using any installed devices. Make absolutely sure you're installing the correct BIOS update.

After you obtain the flash BIOS update (either on a floppy disk or by downloading it from your PC manufacturer's Web site), follow the manufacturer's instructions to run the BIOS update program. If the update came as a ZIP or self-extracting ZIP (EXE) file, extract the installation files to your hard drive and then open and read any README files for instructions. If the BIOS came on a floppy disk, follow the manufacturer's installation instructions.

In most cases, you create a bootable floppy disk with the new BIOS on it, and then boot your system from the floppy disk. This runs the BIOS update routine, which leads you through the installation. It may even back up your old BIOS for you.

Swapping BIOS Chips

If the BIOS upgrade requires you to replace chips, you must remove the old BIOS chips from the motherboard and insert the new chips in the sockets. There are a few tricky parts to this upgrade:

- *Finding the old BIOS chips.* Check your PC's documentation to locate the chips or look on the motherboard for chips that match the appearance of your new BIOS chips. Note the orientation of the chips. One corner should be notched to indicate the correct orientation.

- *Extracting the old chips.* Use a chip puller to gently rock the old BIOS chips out of their sockets. A chip puller looks like an oversized pair of tweezers with L-shaped ends. If you don't have a pair of tweezers, you can pry the chips out of their sockets using a small flat-head screwdriver. Pry one end and then the other in tiny increments to unseat the chip.

- *Orienting the new chips.* Make sure you insert the new chips following the same orientation as the chips you removed. One corner of each BIOS chip should be notched to help you align it correctly (see Figure 24.9).

When inserting the BIOS chips into their sockets, gently, but firmly press them into place, being careful not to bend the pins on the chips.

FIGURE 24.9
One end of each BIOS chip is notched to help you align it correctly with the socket.

Can Your Power Supply Keep Up?

Whenever your drive bays and expansion slots start to fill up, check your power supply. It should have a sticker on it displaying the power supply's wattage (maximum power output). If the sticker indicates anything below 200 watts, consider upgrading the power supply.

Power supplies are inexpensive (typically under $60) and can prevent serious problems later. Following is a list of the possible problems that an insufficient power supply can cause:

- *System lock-ups.* It's tempting to blame crashes on software bugs, but if you install a bunch of internal peripherals (expansion boards and internal drives), the crashes and automatic shutdowns can be caused by an overloaded power supply.

- *Keyboard failure.* If your PC displays a startup error indicating that the keyboard has failed, it may not be getting sufficient power. After ruling out common causes, such as cable failures, look to the power supply.

- *Hardware failure.* An overworked power supply can overheat, raising the temperature inside your system unit and causing problems with your internal drives, expansion boards, and even the processor.

- *Power supply failure.* An inadequate power supply can simply burn itself out. Although it usually won't damage any other components, the power failure brings your PC operations to a grinding halt.

When shopping for a power supply, consider its type and physical size. If you have an old system that uses a Baby AT motherboard (typically 8 1/2- by 13-inches), you'll need an AT power supply, which you can usually get for less than $30. Newer systems use an ATX motherboard (12- by 13-inches), requiring an ATX power supply. Also, make sure the fan and the power switch on the new power supply are in the same positions as on the old power supply. Some fans are top mounted, although others look out the back of the system unit. In addition, consider purchasing a power supply that has a ball-bearing cooling fan or a fan that is temperature-regulated, so it will be as quiet as possible. (A good place to shop for power supplies is PowerOn at www.power-on.com or 1-800-983-8889.)

Upgrading the power supply is fairly easy. However, you must make the proper connections to avoid destroying sensitive electrical components on the motherboard.

Upgrading the power supply

1. Shut down your PC and unplug it.

2. Draw a picture of the connections between the power supply and the motherboard. Make note of any colors on the plugs that indicate proper alignment with the sockets.

3. Disconnect the power supply plugs from the motherboard and any internal disk drives or other devices. As you unplug devices, make a checklist of each device you unplug.

4. Remove any screws that mount the power supply to the system unit case.

5. Remove the power switch from your system unit (typically at the front of the case).

6. Slowly lift the power supply from the system unit, ensuring that no cables are still connected.

7. On the back of the new power supply, make sure the voltage switch is set to match the setting on your old power supply (typically 115V or 120V in the United States).

8. Set the new power supply in place and mount it to the system unit case with the screws you removed in step 4.

9. Connect the motherboard plug from the power supply to the power connector(s) on the motherboard. *Make sure you align the plug properly with the connector to prevent damage to the motherboard.* (You may have one large 20-pin plug or two smaller plugs. If connecting two plugs, the black wires on the plugs usually butt up against each other as shown in Figure 24.10.)

10. Connect the other plugs to the disk drives you unplugged in step 3 being careful to align the plugs properly. Use your checklist to ensure that you have replaced the plug on every device.

11. Connect the power supply to the switch on your system unit.

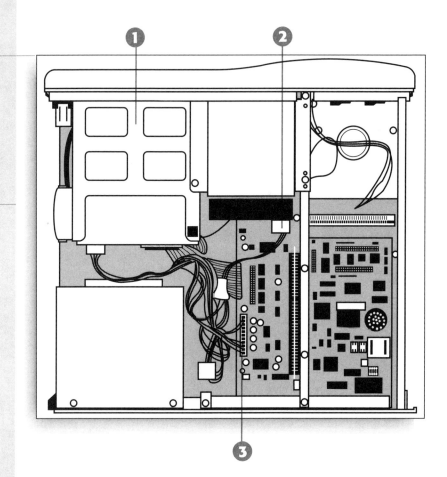

FIGURE 24.10

Plug the power supply into the motherboard and disk drives.

1 Power supply

2 Connection to disk drive

3 Connection to motherboard

Installing Additional RAM (Memory)

Shop for compatible, fast RAM

Remove low-capacity RAM modules

Install high-capacity RAM modules

Make sure your system recognizes the additional RAM

Recycle your old RAM modules

Why Install More RAM?

RAM (*random access memory*) is your PC's temporary storage area, as opposed to disk drives, which act as permanent storage. Your PC uses RAM to store the instructions and data it is actively using, so it can quickly access that information without having to constantly read data from the relatively slow hard drive.

By increasing the amount of RAM installed on your system, you decrease the number of trips your PC makes to the hard drive to fetch data and improve the overall performance of your PC.

If you've been working on a system with 8MB RAM, doubling it to 16MB might seem like a lot, but you should realize that today's programs are memory hogs. Microsoft boasts that Windows can run on 8MB, but if you want to play a fancy computer game, wander the Web, or work with graphics, 8MB is grossly inadequate. Internet Explorer itself requires 12MB, and if you open a Web page with a video clip on it, you can figure in another 4MB. Table 25.1 can help you determine RAM requirements for your system.

TABLE 25.1   RAM requirements

Amount	Usage
8MB	Run Windows. Inadequate for most users.
16MB	Run Windows and another text-based program, such as a word processor. Email, simple CD-ROM titles, limited multitasking.
32MB	Run Windows, multimedia CDs, graphics applications, Web browser. Multitask 3–4 applications.
64MB	Heavy Web browsing, graphics design, presentation software, 3D games. Multitask 4–6 applications.
128MB	High-end, 3D graphics design using CAD programs, heavy database applications, software development. Multitask over 6 applications.

Purchasing Compatible RAM Modules

If you're upgrading RAM on a brand name PC, finding the right RAM modules for your system may be as easy as opening a Web page or calling a mail order company. You specify your PC's make and model, and the Web page or sales person tells you the type of RAM you need (see Figure 25.1). Your PC's documentation should also list the RAM specifications for your system.

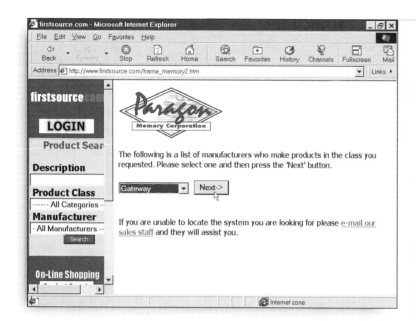

FIGURE 25.1
Mail-order RAM dealers commonly provide forms to help you find the right RAM.

If you have an off-brand PC without documentation, determining the required type of RAM may be nearly impossible. You can gather much of the information you need by looking at the existing RAM modules, but the markings on these modules typically fail to indicate key specifications.

The following sections explain the differences between RAM modules and how to identify them, but if you still cannot determine the type of RAM your system requires, you may have to remove an existing module and take it to a knowledgeable dealer for help.

SIMMs and DIMMs

RAM is packaged on modules, called *SIMMs* (single inline memory modules) or *DIMMs* (dual inline memory modules). The

Proprietary RAM

If your PC uses *proprietary RAM* (specially designed by the manufacturer), you must obtain RAM upgrades from the manufacturer, typically at a greatly inflated price.

module looks like a tiny expansion board and has several oblong DRAM chips soldered to it. SIMMs and DIMMs make it convenient to plug in several DRAM chips at a time.

The most distinguishing characteristic of memory modules is their physical appearance (see Figure 25.2):

- *30-pin SIMMs*. Used in early 486 PCs, 30-pin SIMMs are about 3.5 inches long and have a row of 30 gold or tin contacts at the base. Due to limited capacity and slow data transfer rates, 30-pin SIMMs are all but obsolete.

- *72-pin SIMMs*. Used in later 486 and early Pentium PCs, 72-pin SIMMs are about 4.25 inches long and have two rows of 36 contacts at the base.

- *168-pin DIMMs*. Newer Pentium systems use 168-pin DIMMs, which are available in higher capacities and support faster data transfer rates than 72-pin SIMMs. Unlike SIMMs, which you must install in pairs, you can install a single DIMM.

Determining the type of module that your system uses is fairly easy, after you find the existing RAM modules. Like expansion boards, DIMMs and SIMMs plug into sockets on the motherboard. The sockets are much narrower and shorter than expansion slots and may be at an angle to the motherboard. DIMMs are typically located near the back of the system unit, in close proximity to the expansion slots. SIMMs are typically located near the front. Each SIMM socket has a tiny peg at each end that aligns with a hole in the SIMM. You'll also see a clip on each end that holds the SIMM in place.

DIMM versus SIMM sockets

SIMMs and DIMMs transfer data across a 64-bit bus. A DIMM socket is 64 bits wide, allowing you to upgrade by installing a single DIMM. A SIMM socket is 32 bits wide, so you must install SIMMs in pairs, filling sockets 0 and 1 first and then sockets 2 and 3.

Capacity

The storage capacity of RAM modules varies greatly. An old SIMM may have a capacity as low as 256KB. Installing four SIMMs would provide a total of 1MB. Newer SIMMs can store 4-, 8-, 16-, or even 32MB on a single SIMM. A single DIMM can store as much as 64MB! When evaluating modules of varying capacities, keep the following points in mind:

- Don't exceed the RAM limits imposed by your system. Some older systems may have a maximum capacity of 32MB or 64MB.

- Don't pack the SIMM sockets with low-capacity RAM. For instance, if you want 32MB total RAM, don't fill four sockets with 8MB modules. Use two 16MB modules and leave two sockets free for future expansion.

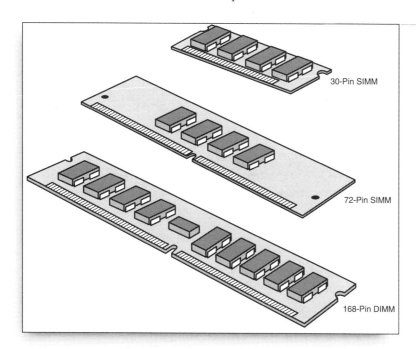

30-Pin SIMM

72-Pin SIMM

168-Pin DIMM

FIGURE 25.2
Identify the type of memory module your PC uses.

DRAM, EDO DRAM, and SDRAM

As you shop for RAM, select the right type of RAM for your system: standard DRAM (dynamic RAM), EDO (extended data out) DRAM, or SDRAM (synchronous dynamic RAM). DRAM and EDO DRAM are packaged on either DIMMs or SIMMs. SDRAM comes only on DIMMs. The memory type is rarely marked on the memory module; you must obtain the information from your system's documentation or from a knowledgeable dealer. You may be able to obtain the information from the BIOS setup screen.

Speed

RAM speed is measured in *nanoseconds* (billionths of a second)—the lower the number, the faster the RAM. It's important that all the RAM modules have a consistent speed rating and that the system supports the speed. If you install 100ns chips in a system that supports a 60ns rating, the chips may fail. Installing 60ns chips in a system that supports 100ns RAM is a waste of money; the system will limit the speed to 100ns.

Fortunately, the speed rating is typically printed on the DRAM chips that are soldered to the SIMM or DIMM. Look for the part number (for example, KM44C4100AK-6). The -6 represents 60ns.

Parity or Non-Parity

Parity-checking is built into some modules to check for data errors. On systems that require parity RAM, you cannot use non-parity RAM. However, systems that use non-parity RAM allow you to use either parity or non-parity.

Parity checking is being phased out because of improvements in RAM modules, so you probably won't find parity RAM on newer systems. There are several ways to determine if your system uses parity or non-parity SIMMs:

- Check the documentation.
- Check your system BIOS settings.
- Check for an odd number of DRAM chips on the SIMM or DIMM. The odd DRAM chip is used for parity checking.
- Check for different sized DRAM chips on the SIMM or DIMM. The off-size chips are used for parity checking.

3.5 Volt or 5 Volt

The voltage rating is one of the most important considerations in choosing RAM. If you install a 3.5-volt RAM module on a 5-volt system, you'll cook the RAM module. Unfortunately, your existing SIMMs or DIMMs may not be marked. Check the documentation or call the manufacturer.

Gold or Tin Contacts

The contacts on SIMMs or DIMMs are made of gold or tin, and you shouldn't mix the two. Over time, the chemical reaction between the two different metals may ruin the contacts. If you're replacing all the modules, purchase modules with gold contacts, which support more reliable data transfers.

Out with the Old RAM, in with the New

If your system has vacant RAM sockets that aren't blocked by a hard drive or other component, installing SIMMs or DIMMs is easy. To install a SIMM, you insert the contacts into the socket at a slight angle and then gently push the top of the SIMM toward the back of the socket until it snaps into place. (Don't force it.) A metal clip on each edge of the socket locks the SIMM in position. To install a DIMM, insert the contacts into the socket and gently press down until the DIMM snaps into place.

However, it's not always that easy. Some manufactures mount a disk drive or other device right above the RAM sockets to make everything fit in the case. You'll need to remove the obstruction to get at the sockets. A screwdriver usually does the trick, but avoid disconnecting any cables in the process. In addition, if all RAM sockets are occupied, you'll have to remove existing low-capacity RAM modules to make room for the new, high-capacity modules.

Replacing SIMM modules

1. Carefully remove any devices that are obstructing the RAM sockets.

2. Push the metal clips on either side of the SIMM socket away from the SIMM until the SIMM pops forward (see Figure 25.3).

3. If the SIMM does not pop forward, continue holding the metal clips open while gently nudging the back of the SIMM.

Maxed out?

If all the RAM sockets are already occupied with high-capacity SIMMs and you need more RAM, you can install a SIMM adapter, which contains additional SIMM sockets. Just make sure the additional RAM doesn't exceed the capacity of your system.

FIGURE 25.3

SIMMs are held in place by small metal clips.

1 Push the clips away from the SIMM.

2 Lift the SIMM from the socket.

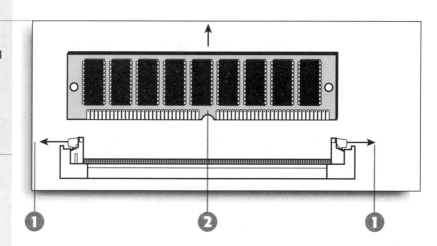

4. When the SIMM is loose, lift it out of the socket and place it in an anti-static bag.

5. Repeat steps 2, 3, and 4 to remove the second SIMM in the pair.

6. Insert the contacts on the new SIMM into one of the empty sockets. Most SIMM sockets are at a slight angle to the motherboard.

7. Gently press the SIMM down and push the top toward the back of the socket until it snaps in place. (Don't force it.)

8. Repeat steps 6 and 7 for the second SIMM.

9. Replace any devices you had to remove to access the RAM slots.

Recycling old RAM

Many companies will reimburse you for old RAM modules, so don't throw them away. Ask the dealer from whom you purchased the new RAM modules if they purchase old memory or know of any companies that do. Sometimes the dealer will send you a box and packing slip to use to send your old memory modules back.

Making Sure the New RAM Is Working

Your system BIOS should identify the new RAM on startup. Turn on your PC, and watch the monitor. It should show the total amount of memory installed. In Windows, Alt+click My Computer to display some general system information, including the amount of physical memory (RAM) installed (see Figure 25.4).

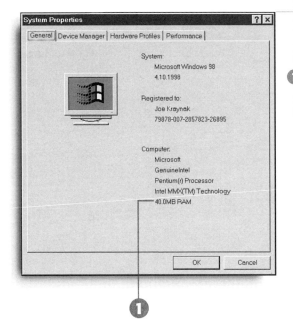

FIGURE 25.4
Alt+click My Computer to display
the amount of installed RAM.

1 Installed RAM

If your system reports less than the total amount of RAM installed, check the following:

- Start your PC and run the BIOS setup program. Without changing any settings, choose the option to exit and save settings. In some cases, this forces the BIOS to update itself and recognize the new RAM.
- Run your BIOS setup program and change the Extended Memory setting to manually enter the correct amount of RAM. If the BIOS setup does not allow you to manually adjust the setting, there is a problem with the RAM itself.
- Turn off your PC and check the RAM module to ensure that it is securely seated in the socket. It can be tough to get the contacts fully inserted in the socket.
- Check the module for cracks or damaged contacts.
- Check the socket for cracks or damaged contacts.
- Make sure the total amount of installed RAM does not exceed the maximum capacity for your system.

- Double-check the type of RAM you installed to ensure that it is compatible with your system. You may have to call the RAM dealer's technical support line to double-check.

Installing a New Hard Drive

Add a second hard drive or replace the main drive

Shop for size and speed

Make sure your PC can support the hard drive you want

Connect two hard drives using a single cable

Enter BIOS settings for the new drive

Format the drive, if necessary

Replace Your Hard Drive or Add a New One?

One of the biggest upgrade dilemmas is whether to replace your old hard drive or leave it in and install a second drive. Following is a list of reasons you should replace your hard drive with a newer model and pitch your old drive:

- If all drive bays are occupied, you have no choice but to replace the old drive.
- If you have only one additional open drive bay, replacing the hard drive leaves one drive bay vacant for an additional drive later.
- Newer hard drives are typically faster. Replacing the drive places your operating system and programs on the faster drive.
- Your new hard drive should have a higher storage capacity. Because virtually every program wants to be installed on drive C, designating your largest hard drive as C makes it much more convenient to install programs later. Also, Windows defaults to using drive C for virtual memory.
- Replacing the hard drive places less strain on the power supply. If you're already pushing the limits of your existing power supply, replace the drive.

There's really only one good reason to leave your existing hard drive in place and tack on a second drive: it's very easy. You mount the drive in an open bay, plug the drive into a cable that connects it with the main drive, connect the power cable, and set a couple jumpers. You don't have to copy files from the old drive to the new drive.

Can Your System Handle a Second Hard Drive?

My recommendation

Set up the new hard drive as the main drive (drive C) and use the old drive as the secondary drive.

Most standard desktop PCs built in the last five years have plenty of room for a second drive. Check inside the system unit to make sure it meets the following requirements:

- *An open drive bay*. You must have a place to mount the new drive. Most systems come with at least five drive bays. Three are usually occupied by the hard drive, floppy disk drive, and CD-ROM drive. If you have an internal ZIP drive or tape backup drive, it occupies the fourth bay. This leaves one bay open for a second hard drive.

- *A free EIDE or SCSI connection*. Most desktop PCs use an EIDE interface for connecting the drives to the mother-board. EIDE supports two cable connections, each of which allows you to connect two EIDE drives (four total). Older systems may use an IDE interface, which supports only one cable connection (two drives, max); if the PC has a hard drive and a CD-ROM drive connected to the IDE interface cable, you must install an IDE interface card and an IDE cable to connect another drive. SCSI, used mainly on network servers supports up to seven devices.

- *A connection to the power supply*. Your power supply must have a free plug for connecting the hard drive. If no plugs are available, you can purchase a Y-connector to connect two devices to a single plug.

Smart Shopping for Hard Drives

When shopping for hard drives, keep two words in mind: "big" and "fast." The following sections explain the key hard drive specifications you need to consider to choose a drive that's big enough, fast enough, and compatible with your PC.

SEE ALSO

➤ *Learn about minimum hard drive requirements for new PCs, page 15*

Drive Types

Translating ads for hard drives is like interpreting caveman paintings. There are too many hard drive acronyms that mean the same thing. The following list helps you understand these cryptic descriptions:

- *IDE.* Short for Intelligent Drive Electronics, IDE is a technology for mass storage devices, such as CD-ROM and hard drives. With IDE, the controller is built into the drive itself. Standard IDE drives are slow and have a maximum storage capacity of 512MB. You'll find standard IDE drives on older (pre-1993) PCs.

- *EIDE.* Short for Enhanced Intelligent Drive Electronics, EIDE is a big step up from IDE, transferring data three to four times faster than standard IDE drives and supporting storage capacities over 8GB. EIDE is the most popular hard drive type on desktop PCs, because of its low cost and high performance. Most desktop PCs have built-in EIDE interfaces that allow you to connect up to four drives.

- *ATA.* Short for AT Attachment, ATA is another name for the IDE or EIDE standard. ATA is the same as IDE, ATA-2 is EIDE, and Ultra ATA (also called Ultra DMA, ATA-33, or DMA-33) is a step up from EIDE.

- *SCSI.* Pronounced "Scuzzy" and short for small computer system interface, SCSI is a parallel data transfer standard that provides superior hard drive performance in some systems. For instance, SCSI drives are commonly used on networks, because they can handle several requests for data at one time. However, a SCSI drive typically costs about $200 more than a comparable EIDE drive and may not perform as well on a standard desktop PC running Windows 95 or 98. In addition, if your PC is not equipped with a SCSI interface, you'll have to install a SCSI adapter card to the tune of about $100.

Your choice usually depends on the type of drive already installed in your PC. If you already have an EIDE drive, it makes little sense to replace it with a SCSI drive.

Size

If you're going through all the trouble to replace an existing drive and transfer files from your old drive, you want the new drive to last a few years. Make sure it has at least double the storage capacity of your existing drive. Don't buy a hard drive with a storage capacity of less than 1GB; I recommend 3GB or larger.

Speed

You would think that you could place ads for several hard drives side-by-side and determine which drive is faster. Unfortunately, comparing the speed of hard drives is much more complicated. Several factors determine a drive's speed:

- *Average seek time*. The time it takes the drive to move the read/write heads to a specific location on the disk. Average seek time is measured in milliseconds and ranges from about 8ms to 13ms. The lower the number, the faster the drive.

- *Transfer rate*. The amount of data the drive can transfer to the system per second. Rates vary greatly depending on the type of hard drive controller your system uses. Standard EIDE controllers range from 11 to 16MBps. Ultra ATA controllers are rated at 33MBps and will soon be replaced by ATA/66 controllers that offer double the transfer rate. SCSI controllers range from 10 to 40MBps. The higher the number, the faster the drive. However, keep in mind that the CPU, RAM, and system bus may limit the drive's performance.

- *Disk rotation speed*. The number of times the disk spins per minute. Speeds range from 3,600 to 7,200 RPM, the higher the number the better. However, the rotation speed is rarely used to compare the performance of different drives.

- *Disk cache*. A disk cache is temporary storage built into the drive. The drive can store frequently accessed data in the cache and then quickly retrieve it without having to return to the disk. Most newer drives come with a 512KB cache or larger.

Compatibility

When you install a new hard drive, you typically connect it to the old drive, so you must make sure that the two drives are compatible. With IDE and EIDE drives, the main drive acts as the *master*, and the second drive acts as the *slave*. SCSI drives are linked to each other in a daisy chain configuration, with all drives acting as equals.

At the most basic level, the two drives must be the same type; you can't connect a SCSI drive to an IDE interface or vice versa. Even within those two categories, there are features that can render two drives incompatible:

- *IDE drive.* When shopping for an IDE drive, tell the dealer the type of drive that's currently installed in your PC, and make sure the new drive will be compatible.

- *SCSI drive.* Several SCSI standards exist, each with its own preferred cable type. When purchasing a SCSI drive, examine the connectors to ensure that you can plug the new drive into the existing SCSI interface.

SEE ALSO
➤ *Learn how to connect external SCSI devices, page 45*
➤ *Learn how to install a SCSI adapter, page 788*

Other Stuff You'll Need

Most new hard drives are packaged as a kit including everything you need to install the drive and transfer data from your old drive to the new drive (see Figure 26.1).

If you purchased the disk by itself in an attempt to save a few bucks, obtain the following items:

- *An IDE or SCSI cable to connect the drive to the drive controller (IDE or SCSI interface).* If your PC has only one hard drive, you can plug the second drive into the open plug on the existing IDE cable.

- *Mounting brackets.* If you're sticking a 3.5-inch hard drive in a 5.25-inch bay, you'll need mounting brackets to adapt the drive to the bay.

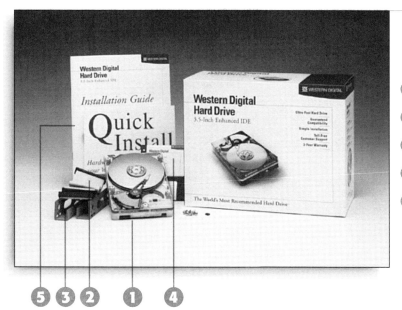

FIGURE 26.1

A typical hard drive kit includes everything you need to install the drive.

1. Hard drive
2. Data cable
3. Mounting brackets
4. Disk utilities
5. Documentation

- *Drive manager software.* EZ-Drive by Micro House (www.microhouse.com) and Ontrack Disk Manager from Ontrack (www.ontrack.com) are both excellent utilities for working around BIOS limitations, safely preparing new drives to store data, and for copying your old drive to your new drive. For about $20, these utilities can preserve your sanity. (Most hard drive upgrade kits include such a utility.)

- *Y-adapter.* If your power supply does not have a free plug, purchase a Y-adapter that allows you to connect two devices to a single power supply plug. Y-adapters are typically not included in the hard drive kit.

Installing a New EIDE Hard Drive

Installing a hard drive isn't quite as easy as hard drive manufacturers like you to think. You'll be setting jumpers on the drive, fumbling with a tangled mess of cables, and possibly rearranging your drives when you realize that there's no way that an 18-inch

IDE to EIDE

In most cases, you will connect your new drive to the existing hard drive controller on the motherboard. If you are upgrading from a standard IDE drive to an EIDE drive, you must install an EIDE controller board in one of your PCs expansion slots.

IDE cable is going to reach your second drive. I'm not trying to discourage you before you start, but you should give yourself one or two hours to complete the task.

Before you install your hard drive, write down the drive's parameters, in case you have to enter BIOS settings manually after the installation. This information should be in the drive's documentation, but sometimes it's missing. The parameters are listed on the sticker attached to the drive. Write down the following information for both the new drive and the old drive:

- Number of cylinders
- Number of heads
- Number of sectors per track
- Drive make and model number
- Drive serial number
- Any additional codes or dates

Master or Slave?

PCs typically have two EIDE connectors on the motherboard—a primary and a secondary IDE interface, each of which supports two drives. An IDE cable connects your existing hard drive to the primary IDE interface and has an additional connector for a second drive. For the drives to work together, you must set jumpers to mark your primary drive (the drive you boot from) as the *master* and the secondary drive as the *slave*. The position of the drive on the data cable does not designate the drive as master or slave; you must set the jumpers.

Most hard drives have three jumper settings to mark the disk as the only disk, the master, or the slave. The jumpers are easy to set; you slide the jumper over the desired set of pins, which are typically marked (see Figure 26.2). If the pins are not clearly marked, refer to the documentation.

Deciding which drive to use as the master and which one should act as the slave may be a little difficult. In most cases, use the new drive (the larger, faster drive) as the master. Set the jumper on your old drive to mark it as the slave. If you are merely

adding another drive, mark the new drive as the slave. If your
old drive is marked as the only drive, set the jumper to mark it as
the master.

At this point, you may wonder what will happen to your new
drive if you make it the slave. Not much. Your system will automatically use the master drive as drive C and boot from it. Your
system will automatically assign your old drive a new letter, and
the files will remain intact.

FIGURE 26.2
Move the jumper to the designated
set of pins to mark the drive as
slave or master.

1 Master

2 Slave

3 Only drive

Installing an EIDE Drive

Installing a hard drive consists of connecting the data and power
cables to the drive and mounting the drive in an open bay. The
only tricky part is connecting the IDE data cable, the flat wide
cable with the red line running along one edge. The red line
must align with pin 1, which should be marked on the drive
(although it may not be). Check the documentation to determine the proper orientation for the connector.

Before you start, turn off your PC and unplug it. During the installation, follow the safety precautions listed in "Safety Precautions," in Chapter 24. Following is a list of additional precautions that pertain only to hard drives:

- Make a Windows Startup disk. Copy Format.exe from the Windows\Command folder to the disk.

- Don't unpack the drive until you're ready to install it.

- Save the packing materials in case you need to return the drive.

- Handle the hard drive only by its edges, being careful not to touch the exposed circuit board at the bottom of the drive.

- Do not drop the drive. Dropping the drive could send the read/write heads crashing against the disks and damaging the surface.

- Never install a drive upside-down. Install it with the label up or to the side.

- When mounting the drive, make sure there is adequate space around the drive for ventilation. Don't lay one drive right on top of another.

Installing an EIDE hard drive

1. To place the new drive where the old drive is mounted, remove the old drive from its bay, but leave it connected. (You can lay the old drive to one side, but don't lay it on top of any other electrical components.)

2. If the drive bay has a cover over it on the front of the system unit, remove the cover, to give yourself additional room to work.

3. If necessary, attach the mounting brackets to the hard drive, and lay the drive inside the open drive bay. Don't mount the drive to the bay yet; you may have to jiggle things around to connect the cables.

4. Match the red stripe on the IDE data cable to pin 1 on the drive's data outlet and plug in the cable (see Figure 26.3).

5. Insert a plug from the power supply into the power outlet on the hard drive.

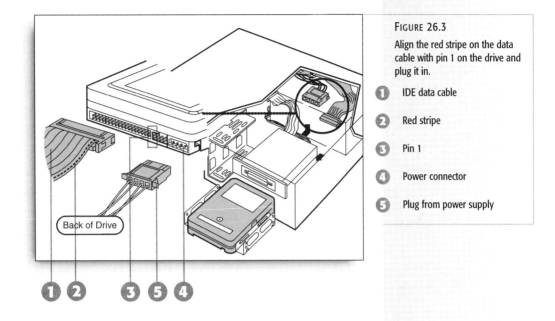

FIGURE 26.3

Align the red stripe on the data cable with pin 1 on the drive and plug it in.

1 IDE data cable

2 Red stripe

3 Pin 1

4 Power connector

5 Plug from power supply

6. Secure the hard drive to the drive bay using the mounting screws.

7. If you removed a drive bay cover in step 2, replace it.

Some hard drive manufacturers specify that you use an IDE cable that's only 18 inches long. This limit can make it difficult to connect two drives. If the cable doesn't reach, try the following solutions:

- Move existing drives to place the two hard drives closer together.

- Try using a different IDE cable. Although the overall length of the cable is limited to 18 inches, the plugs may be staggered differently on another cable, giving you an extra inch or two to work with.

- Use a *slightly* longer cable. In most cases, you should follow the manufacturer's recommendation on cable length, but if the cable doesn't quite reach, you may need to bend the rules.

- Flip the cable. Note the position of the red stripe in relation to the IDE port on the motherboard. (If the cable has no red stripe, look for some other marking to determine the proper orientation of the cable.) Disconnect the cable from the motherboard and plug the opposite end of the cable into the motherboard. Depending on the cable, this may give you the one or two inches you need.

Checking Your System BIOS Settings

Before you turn on your PC, double-check the connections. Check inside to make absolutely sure you haven't left any screws or brackets lying on top of sensitive circuit boards. Leave the cover off the system unit until you're sure the new drive works.

Now, cross your fingers, turn on your PC and press the key for running the BIOS setup. Enter the **Auto Configuration** setting for the new drive, so the BIOS will attempt to enter the required settings for the drive. If **Auto Configuration** is not an option, try entering the following settings manually:

- Number of cylinders
- Number of heads
- Number of sectors per track

Enter any additional settings as specified in the drive's documentation. For example, you may need to enable LBA (Logical Block Addressing) or Translation Mode. If the BIOS recognizes the drive and displays its full capacity, you can partition and format the drive, as explained later in this chapter. If the BIOS does not recognize the drive, you have two options:

- Install a BIOS update that supports the drive you installed. This is the best option, although it costs about $80.
- Run a disk management utility. If your hard drive came with its own utility, use it. Otherwise, you must purchase a separate utility, such as EZ-Drive or Ontrack, described earlier in this chapter.

SEE ALSO

➤ *Learn how to check your system's BIOS settings, page 567*

➤ *Learn how to install a BIOS update, page 571*

Installing a SCSI Drive

If your system has a SCSI interface, you can connect up to seven SCSI devices to it in a *daisy chain* configuration. That is, you connect one device to the SCSI adapter, another device to the first device, and so on. Each device in the chain is assigned a number to indicate its location. The SCSI adapter itself is usually 7, the first hard drive is typically 0, the CD-ROM drive might be 1, and so on, up to 6.

At each end of the chain is a terminator that indicates there are no more devices in the chain. You may have to physically plug a terminator into the open port on the device or flip a switch or set jumpers to enable termination. By default, the SCSI card is terminated. However, if you install both external and internal devices to the SCSI card, it no longer acts as an end of the chain, and you must disable termination for the adapter. (Many newer SCSI cards automatically turn termination on or off as required.)

When installing a SCSI hard drive, you must determine where in the chain you want the drive installed:

- If you have an IDE or EIDE drive installed, you must boot from that drive and use the SCSI drive as a secondary drive; you cannot boot from the SCSI drive. Assign the SCSI drive any number from 0 to 6 that is not already in use.

- If you are replacing an EIDE drive with a SCSI drive, and you want to boot from the SCSI drive, assign it the number 0. (You must also run the BIOS setup and disable the Primary IDE interface.)

- In general, assign low numbers to your hard drives and CD-ROM drive, to give them priority.

When assigning numbers, be careful not to assign the same number to two devices. In addition, if you link a drive to a device that was previously at the end of the SCSI chain, you must turn off termination for that device and turn on termination for the drive.

Installing a SCSI drive

1. Set the jumpers on the drive to specify its SCSI number and turn termination on or off.

2. Reset jumpers on any other devices in the SCSI chain that will be affected by the new hard drive.

3. To place the new drive where the old drive is mounted, remove the old drive from its bay, but leave it connected. (You can lay the old drive to one side, but don't lay it on top of any other electrical components.)

4. If the drive bay has a cover over it on the front of the system unit, remove the cover, to give yourself additional room to work.

5. If necessary, attach the mounting brackets to the hard drive, and lay the drive inside the open drive bay.

6. Plug one end of the SCSI cable into the SCSI IN port on the back of the drive.

7. Plug the opposite end of the SCSI cable into SCSI adapter card or the SCSI OUT port on another SCSI device.

8. Insert a plug from the power supply into the power outlet on the hard drive.

9. Secure the hard drive to the drive bay using the mounting screws.

10. Replace any drive bay covers you removed.

Partitioning and Formatting the Drive

SCSI BIOS?

The SCSI adapter has its own BIOS that manages installed SCSI devices. You shouldn't have to enter any BIOS settings for using your SCSI drive.

Before you can use your drive to store data, you must *partition* the drive and *format* each partition. Partitioning the drive divides the drive into more manageable storage areas. For example, you might divide a 6GB hard drive into three 2GB partitions.

Formatting creates a map on the disk that tells the drive where all the storage areas are located.

If your drive came with its own utility, use it to partition and format the disk. If your drive did not come with such a utility, purchase a standalone utility such as EZ-Drive, DriveCopy, or Ontrack Disk Manager. These programs lead you step by step through the process of partitioning your drive, formatting it, and copying your old drive to your new drive (if desired). They also have built-in safeguards to prevent you from accidentally formatting or partitioning a disk that contains data.

If you don't have one of these utilities and you can't wait, partition and format your new drive using the DOS FDISK and FORMAT commands, as explained in the following sections.

Partitioning a Hard Disk

DOS and Windows 3.1 cannot recognize drives over 528MB, and early releases of Windows 95 cannot recognize drives over 2.1GB, so if you have a larger hard drive, you must partition it into smaller units. Windows 95 OS2 and Windows 98 both include FAT 32 support, which can handle larger partitions; however, the primary partition is limited to 7.8GB. When you partition a drive larger than 512MB in Windows 95 OS2 or Windows 98, FDisk asks if you want to enable large disk support. Choose **Yes**.

You must first create a primary partition to act as the boot drive. You can then create extended partitions to act as additional, *logical* drives:

- Your primary partition appears as drive C.
- If you have a second hard drive installed, it appears as drive D.
- Extended partitions on the first drive appear as E, F, G, and so on.

FDISK and FORMAT can destroy existing data on a disk. When using FDISK and FORMAT, be absolutely sure you are using them only on the new disk. If you run these utilities on your old disk, you will erase all data from the disk. The following steps show you how to partition a new drive that you installed as the master drive.

Partitioning the master drive

If you are using your old drive as the master, *do not* perform these steps. You will destroy data on the disk.

1. Boot your PC using the Windows Startup disk you created earlier in this chapter.

2. At the A:> prompt type `fdisk` and press Enter.

3. If your hard drive is more than 512MB and you are using Windows 95 OS2 or Windows 98, a message appears indicating that you can format drives larger than 2GB as a single drive. If you want to do this, type **Y** and press Enter.

4. From the **FDisk** main menu, choose **1. Create DOS Partition or Logical DOS Drive** and press Enter.

5. From the **Create DOS Partition** menu, select **1. Create Primary DOS Partition** and press **Enter**. FDisk asks if you want to use the maximum available size for a primary partition.

6. Take one of the following steps:

   To create as large a partition as possible, type **Y** (for Yes) and press Enter. Skip to the next section to format the primary partition.

   To create multiple partitions, type **N** (for No) and press Enter. Type the number of megabytes or percentage of disk space to use for the primary partition, and press Enter.

7. If you created multiple partitions in step 6, you must select the active partition. Return to the **FDisk** main menu, select **2. Set Active Partition** and press Enter.

8. Type the number of the partition you want to use as the active partition (the partition for your operating system) and press Enter.

9. Press Esc to return to the **FDisk** main menu.

10. Select **1. Create DOS Partition or Logical DOS Drive** and press Enter.

11. Select **2. Create Extended DOS Partition** and press Enter. FDisk displays the number of megabytes available for an extended partition.

12. Press Enter to accept the default size.

13. Press Esc twice to return to the **FDisk** main menu.

14. Select **1. Create DOS Partition or Logical DOS Drive** and press Enter.

15. Select **3. Create Logical DOS Drive(s) in the extended DOS Partition** and press Enter. FDisk displays the number of megabytes available for the logical drive.

16. Press Enter to use the entire partition as a logical drive.

17. Press Esc twice to exit FDisk.

18. Restart your system. Your PC boots from drive A and displays the A:> prompt. You can now format the new partitions.

If you set up your new drive as the slave, you must create at least one partition on the drive to assign it a drive letter. When partitioning a slave drive, be very careful to partition the slave drive and not the master drive. Run FDisk, select option **5. Change Current Fixed Disk Drive**, press Enter, and choose your slave drive. Otherwise, FDisk assumes you want to partition the master drive. This would erase your existing drive.

After you have selected the slave drive, take the same steps to partition the slave drive as you would to partition the master drive.

Formatting Your New Partitions

Formatting the new partitions is easy, but you must be careful. Formatting a disk that contains data deletes all the data on the disk. Use the FORMAT command only on new partitions. Take one of the following steps to format a new logical drive:

- If you installed your new disk as the master and created a primary partition on it, at the A:> prompt, type format c: /s and press Enter. (The /s switch tells FORMAT to place the system files on drive C.) When the warning appears, indicating that all data will be lost on drive C, type **Y** and press Enter.

- To format any other partitions, don't use the /s switch. For instance, to format drive E, type format e: and press Enter.

Copying Files

If you installed your new drive as the master, you may want to copy all files from the slave to the primary partition on the master drive. The only practical way to do this is to use a special utility, such as EZ-Drive or DriveCopy. These utilities can place an exact duplicate of the old drive on the new drive.

Trying to copy the files using the DOS COPY command or the Windows file management tools is very unreliable and omits system files and hidden files.

The other, much less attractive, option is to reinstall Windows and your programs on the new drive and then copy any data files you want to use from the old drive. After you've installed Windows, you can use My Computer or Windows Explorer to drag and drop folders and files from the old drive to the new drive, or you can restore missing files from your backups.

Common Hard Drive Installation Problems and Fixes

The single biggest problem with upgrades is the limitations of the system BIOS. Upgrade your BIOS before you start, and you'll zip through the installation. Otherwise, you'll need to install a utility to overcome the BIOS limitations.

If you encounter other problems, read through the following list for instructions on how to solve common hard disk upgrade problems:

- *HDD controller failure*. Try rebooting your system. If that doesn't fix the problem, shut down your system, check the cable connections and check the jumper settings for the master and slave drives. Restart your PC and check the BIOS settings.

- *Drive not recognized.* Check the data cable to make sure you've aligned the red stripe on the data cable with pin 1 on the drive. This can also be caused by a BIOS problem.

- *PC displays slightly lower capacity than the capacity of the drive.* The displayed disk size depends on how the BIOS or a utility counts megabytes and gigabytes. A gigabyte is actually 1024MB, but the utility might round it down to 1000. However, if the numbers differ greatly, an old BIOS is usually the cause.

- *PC won't start.* Turn the power off, unplug the system, and check the cable connections and jumper settings. If you installed a SCSI adapter or hard drive controller, make sure it is securely seated in the expansion slot. (This problem can also be caused by BIOS limitations or two incompatible drives.)

- *Can't boot from new hard drive.* Make sure you marked the boot partition as the active partition and that you formatted the drive using format /s. If you forgot to add the /s switch, reformat the drive with format /s.

Installing a Faster Microprocessor

Knowing Your System's Limitations

At first glance, a processor (CPU) upgrade seems like the ideal way to soup up your system. It's like dropping a new engine into your car, right?

Not exactly.

Although the new processor may be a speed demon, the data bus, system bus, memory, and expansion bus may impose restrictions. In addition, the CPU socket on the motherboard may not accommodate the processor you want to install. The following sections explain the most significant CPU upgrade limitations, so you'll know what to expect.

SEE ALSO

➤ *Learn more about system limitations, page 538*

CPU Socket Restrictions

Intel's latest CPU (central processing unit), the Pentium II, doesn't fit into the standard socket 5 or socket 7 CPU connector on earlier motherboards (see Figure 27.1). Instead, the Pentium II plugs into socket 1, an SEC (single edge connector) socket (see Figure 27.2). In short, if you have a system that uses a motherboard designed for the original Pentium or a 486 CPU, you'll have to find your speed fix elsewhere.

FIGURE 27.1

486 and standard Pentium CPUs plug into socket 7 on the motherboard.

Motherboard Speed Limit

Even if you could install a 400MHz processor on a 486 motherboard, the system would have a 32-bit external data bus, half as wide as the Pentium's external bus. The processor would zoom along and then have to wait for the rest of the system to catch up.

To overcome this limitation, some CPU manufacturers, including Cyrix and AMD, developed CPUs that not only increase the speed of the processor, but also have a beefed-up internal cache to reduce the effects of the bottleneck. In addition, these CPUs plug into the standard socket 5 or socket 7 on earlier motherboards.

Finding the Right Processor Upgrade

Although additional RAM is the easiest, and usually best, way to increase the overall speed of your PC, a new processor can give your PC an added boost. For instance, if you have a slow

Pentium processor, say 75MHz, installing a 150Mhz MMX chip can double its speed *and* improve performance for applications that support MMX.

Before you run out and buy a processor upgrade, make sure your system can handle it and that it's the best processor for your system. Although you can't stick a Pentium II processor in your old 486 or standard Pentium system, there are other processor upgrades that can give your system a boost. The following sections explain your options.

SEE ALSO

➤ *Learn how to shop for a processor when purchasing a new PC, page 10*

486 Upgrade Options

Although you'll never bring a 486 PC up to speed with the current Pentium II powerhouses, upgrading the processor can improve performance enough to handle the increased demands of the latest software. The following list describes your 486 CPU upgrade options:

- *Intel 486 OverDrive processor.* Fully compatible with your old 486 processor, the OverDrive processor is faster. For example, you can replace a 486DX-33 with a 486DX-100 processor to triple the processing speed. However, because Intel has stopped manufacturing 486 OverDrive processors, you may have trouble finding one.

- *Evergreen 486-to-586 processor.* Upgrades nearly any 486 CPU to boost performance to near Pentium levels. The Evergreen 586 CPU plugs into a standard 486 CPU socket and can upgrade a 486DX-50 to a 586-100 or a 486-66 to a 586-133. The 586 upgrade includes a 16KB L1 cache, double that of the first 486 CPUs. With this upgrade, you can expect to quadruple the speed of your processor. However, if you already have a 486DX4-100 CPU, the performance increase is insignificant.

- *Kingston TurboChip 133 processor.* Upgrades most 486 systems to bring them up to speed with early Pentium systems. Like

Cyrix and AMD

The Evergreen and Kingston CPU upgrades are based on technology from CPU manufacturers who compete with Intel. The Evergreen CPU is based on the Cyrix 5x86 design. Kingston bases its TurboChip 133 on the AMD-K5 processor. Neither Cyrix nor AMD directly markets their CPUs as upgrades.

the Evergreen 586 processor, the Turbo133 plugs into the standard 486 CPU socket and offers a 16KB L1 cache. With this upgrade, you can expect a 4X performance boost.

Standard Pentium Upgrade Options

Although the first batch of Pentium-based PCs seemed speedy enough, these standard Pentium systems are no match for today's highly graphical applications. For your Pentium system to handle the increased demands of 3D games and graphics, you should replace your Pentium processor with a more advanced MMX processor or better. Check out the following options for upgrading your Pentium processor:

- *Intel Pentium OverDrive Processor with MMX.* The Pentium OverDrive processor is typically twice as fast as the processor you're replacing. It can boost the processing speed from 75MHz to 150MHz or from 90MHz to 180MHz. It also includes a built-in MMX instruction set to increase performance for games and graphics designed for MMX.

- *Evergreen 200MHz processor.* With a 64KB internal cache and a few other internal enhancements, Evergreen's 200MHz MMX processor upgrade outperforms Intel's Pentium OverDrive processors in some tests, and usually for less money. By replacing a 75MHz Pentium with an Evergreen 200MHz processor, you can expect to increase the processing speed to 200MHz.

- *Kingston TurboChip 200 processor.* Kingston's TurboChip 200 processor is based on the AMD-K6 chip and offers a 64KB internal cache. Like the Evergreen 200MHz processor, the TurboChip acts as a replacement for the original Pentium 75MHz (and faster) processors.

Purchasing a Processor Upgrade Kit

Processor upgrade kits typically consist of the processor itself, documentation, and in some cases, a tool for extracting the old processor. You can purchase these kits from a local computer retailer or from a mail order company.

Installation considerations

Although the Evergreen and Kingston processors outperform Pentium OverDrive processors in some tests and are less expensive, Intel Pentium OverDrive processors are typically easier to install. You simply replace the processor. The Evergreen and Kingston processors may require you to set jumpers on the processor and motherboard.

To learn more about Evergreen, Kingston, and Intel processor upgrades and access a list of retailers that sell the upgrade kits, visit the following Web sites:

Intel at www.intel.com

Kingston at www.kingston.com

Evergreen at www.evertech.com

Staying cool

Pentium processors are hot. To keep them cool, they either use passive cooling devices (heat sinks), or active devices–fans. Some fans you have to plug in, but with more advanced designs, the fan draws current from the socket itself.

Swapping Processors

After you've found the right upgrade, installing the new processor is fairly easy, assuming you can locate the old processor on the motherboard and dislodge it. The existing processor should be labeled. Otherwise, refer to the pictures in your PC's documentation. If it's a Pentium chip you're searching for, look for a fan or heat sink (which looks like a set of tiny cooling towers). The fan or heat sink sits right on top of the processor.

Most processors plug into a ZIF (Zero Insertion Force) socket and are very easy to remove. If the socket has a little lever on the side, it's a ZIF socket. Older systems use non-ZIF sockets, which require you to use a chip puller to extract the processor.

Swapping CPUs in a ZIF socket

1. Use a grounding strap or touch a metal part of the system unit before you begin.

2. If the processor has a fan plugged into it, unplug the fan.

3. If the processor has a heat sink on top of it, a clip may secure it to the socket. Use a flat-head screwdriver to gently pry the clip loose from the tabs on the socket (see Figure 27.3).

4. Slide the ZIF lever slightly away from the socket to release it and gently lift up the ZIF lever so it's standing straight up (see Figure 27.4).

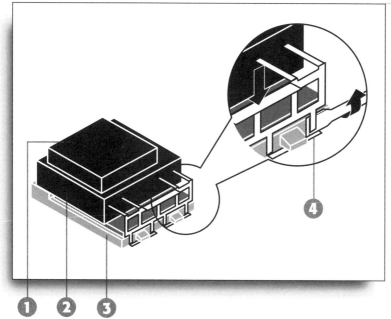

FIGURE 27.3

The heat sink may be clipped to the CPU socket.

1 Heat sink

2 Processor

3 Socket

4 Pry the clip away from the socket.

Grease on the heat sink

The manufacturer may have used thermal grease to attach the heat sink to the processor. This grease conducts electricity, so be careful not to smear it on any circuit boards, pins, or other electrical components.

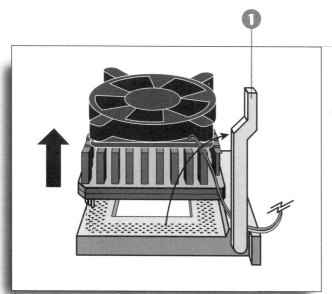

FIGURE 27.4

To release the processor from a ZIF socket, lift the ZIF lever.

1 Lift the ZIF lever.

5. Lift the processor out of the socket and set it aside, pins facing up.

6. Align pin 1 on the CPU with hole 1 in the socket and plug the CPU into the socket. CPU manufacturers typically notch one end of the processor to help you properly align it with the socket (see Figure 27.5).

FIGURE 27.5

Align the pins on the new CPU with the holes in the socket.

1 Notched corner on CPU

2 Missing corner holes on socket

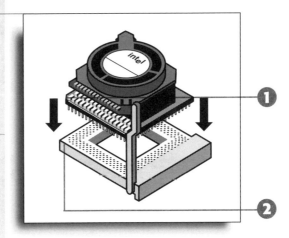

7. Make sure the CPU is firmly seated in the socket, but don't force it. If the CPU has a fan on top of it, DO NOT press down on the fan. Apply pressure to opposite edges of the CPU to press it in place.

8. Lower the ZIF lever that you lifted earlier, to lock the processor in place. The lever should lock in the down position.

9. If the CPU has a fan, attach the cable.

If your motherboard has a non-ZIF socket, use a chip puller to extract the CPU. A chip puller looks like a set of tongs with bent tips. Slide the bent tips between the processor and the socket, squeeze the tongs, and lift gently but firmly to extract the processor. If the processor won't budge, try rocking the processor out of the socket one edge at a time in tiny increments. When installing a CPU in a non-ZIF socket, you must press down on it to securely seat it in the socket, but don't force it. If you have to work at it, the pins may not be properly aligned with the holes in the socket.

Setting Jumpers on the Motherboard

Most motherboards are built to service processors with different clock speeds. For example, the same motherboard may be used for a Pentium 75-, 90-, or 100MHz processor. A jumper on the motherboard tells the motherboard which CPU is installed.

After installing your new processor, you may need to set the jumper to adjust the CPU's clock speed on the motherboard. Check your PC's documentation and the documentation that came with your CPU upgrade kit to determine if you must change the jumper setting. Your PC's documentation should have a picture showing the location of the jumper on your system (see Figure 27.6).

The instructions can be a little misleading. For instance, if you're replacing a 75MHz Pentium processor with a 150MHz OverDrive processor, your PC's documentation may tell you to set the jumper to match the speed of the CPU (150MHz in this case). However, the jumper settings may offer only 75-, 90-, and 100MHz. If the processor documentation does not specify a jumper setting, leave the setting as is. Your system should be able to fully exploit the processor's speed.

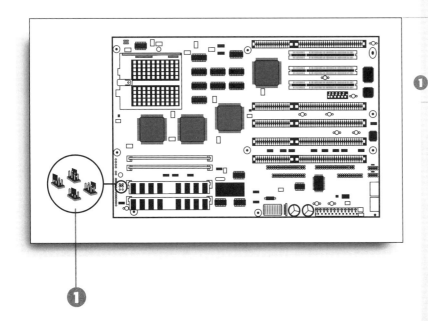

FIGURE 27.6

You may need to set the CPU clock speed on the motherboard.

1   CPU clock speed jumpers

Restarting with Your New CPU

Leave the cover off the system unit until you're sure that the fan and the CPU are working. Remove any stray screws or clips from inside the system unit and then turn on your system. If the CPU has a cooling fan, make sure it's spinning.

Your PC should start as it normally does, but faster. If your PC fails to start, there may be a problem with the installation, or your PC's system BIOS may not recognize the new processor. If your PC doesn't boot properly, check the following:

- If your CPU upgrade kit came with installation software, follow the instructions to run the installation utility. If the CPU came with a diagnostics utility, run it.
- Reboot your system and run the BIOS setup.
- With your PC off, recheck the jumper settings on the motherboard.
- With your PC off, make sure the processor pins are properly aligned with the holes in the socket and that the ZIF lever is locked in the down position.
- If your BIOS is outdated, update it.

SEE ALSO

➤ *Learn how to run the BIOS setup, page 567*

➤ *Learn how to update your BIOS, page 571*

Don't be surprised if the system BIOS does not display the correct speed of your processor. For instance, if you upgrade to a 125MHz processor, your BIOS may indicate that a Pentium 50MHz processor is installed. The BIOS may be unable to display speeds over 100MHz. Run the diagnostic utility that came with the processor to get a more accurate reading. You can also use a shareware utility, such as BCM diagnostics, to check the processor speed.

The Pros and Cons of Overclocking

Overclocking is a trick that spurs the processor into running faster than its rated clock speed. For example, if you have a 125MHz processor, overclocking may force it to run at 166MHz. What makes this possible is the fact that processor manufacturers are slightly conservative when rating the speed of their processors.

Before you decide to overclock your processor, be aware of the risks and limitations involved:

- Overclocking runs the processor at its upper limit and may cause it to overheat. The processor may not fail right away, but over weeks or months of running at top speed, the processor eventually burns itself out. You can install an extra fan or other cooling device to reduce the heat factor.

- If your system is still under warranty, overclocking voids the warranty.

- Overclocking may cause your PC to crash more frequently.

- Overclocking may cause data loss.

- The processor typically runs faster than the rest of your system anyway, so overclocking worsens the bottleneck at the data bus. You may not see much improvement.

In short, you should never, ever overclock your processor.

Having said that, I'll tell you how to overclock your processor. You set the CPU clock speed jumper on the motherboard to a higher setting. For example, if the jumper is currently set to 75MHz, change it to the next higher setting—90MHz. Don't get too greedy; you want to overclock, not overcook. If your system starts acting up, reset the jumper to a lower setting.

Overclocking the system bus

Most motherboards operate at 66MHz, but some motherboards have jumpers for running the board at 75MHz or 83MHz. You can overclock the system bus to make everything work faster. Of course, the benefits and risks of overclocking the system bus are both greater.

Upgrading the L2 Cache

Early 486 CPUs ran at about the same speed as the motherboard—66MHz. As processor speeds have zoomed ahead, the motherboard speed has remained fairly constant at 66MHz or slightly higher. Newer Pentium II motherboards run as fast as 100MHz, but the latest Pentium processors run at four times that speed.

To prevent the CPU from having to wait for data and instructions, PCs use L1 and L2 cache. The L1 cache is a small amount (8–64KB) of super-fast memory built right into the processor. The L2 cache is a much larger amount (128–512KB) of fast memory that sits between the processor and RAM. Both the L1 and L2 act as temporary storage areas for data and instructions that the processor frequently accesses.

If you're upgrading to a CPU that's more than double the speed of the motherboard, you should evaluate the L2 cache as well. An L2 cache of 256KB can boost system performance by 20% or more. Check your PC's documentation to determine the amount of installed L2 cache.

Types of L2 Cache

When evaluating your L2 cache, speed is of primary importance, and the speed is determined by the type of cache:

- *Asynchronous*. Used primarily in 386 and 486 systems, this is the slowest of the three basic cache types. Each time the processor wants to access the cache, it must specify an address and then wait for the requested data or instructions to be delivered.

- *Synchronous*. The least common type of L2 cache (because of cost), synchronous cache works in rhythm with the processor to serve up requested data and instructions and process new requests at the same time. This is the fastest type of L2 cache for systems running on 66MHz motherboards.

- *Pipeline burst*. Used primarily on Pentium systems, pipeline burst cache is relatively inexpensive and provides the same benefits as synchronous cache. Although not as fast as synchronous cache on 66MHz motherboards, pipeline burst cache turns in superior performance on faster motherboards.

Can Your System Handle an L2 Cache Upgrade?

Unfortunately, few systems accept L2 cache upgrades. On Pentium II systems, the L2 cache is packaged as a module right inside the processor. On most other systems, the L2 cache consists of a set of chips soldered to the motherboard.

On some systems, the cache may consist of SIMMs plugged into sockets on the motherboard (similar to standard RAM SIMMs). This type of cache configuration is called COAST (Cache On A Stick). The COAST sockets are typically located near the processor and are much shorter than standard RAM SIMMs. If your motherboard uses COAST, you may be able to install additional cache or upgrade to a faster cache by swapping the COAST modules. However, on systems that have both L2 chips soldered to the board and a COAST socket, you cannot add to the L2 cache by installing a COAST module.

Check your PC's documentation and contact the motherboard manufacturer for details about available L2 cache upgrades and specifications on the type and amount of L2 cache you can install.

Installing L2 Cache

If you've gotten this far without turning back, you should have the L2 cache upgrade in hand as a COAST module. Installing the COAST module is no more complicated than swapping out RAM SIMMs or DIMMs.

Upgrading the L2 cache

1. As with any upgrade, use a grounding strap or touch a metal part of the system unit case to discharge any static electricity.

2. Firmly grasp the edge of the COAST module and lift it out of its socket.

3. Insert the new COAST module into the socket and gently push it down into the socket until it is firmly seated.

After the installation, restart your PC and check the BIOS settings to ensure that your PC has identified the new L2 cache.

Installing a CD-ROM or DVD Drive

Compare CD-ROM and DVD drives

Choose the best drive type for your current and future needs

Replace your CD-ROM drive with a DVD drive

Install a DVD decoder board

Troubleshoot common problems with CD-ROM and DVD drives

CD-ROM or DVD?

Until recently, CD-ROM (*Compact Disk-Read Only Memory*) was the only player on the field. When purchasing a new computer or performing a multimedia upgrade, the choice was simple—did you want the 12X or the 24X model?

A relatively new technology called DVD (*digital video disc* or *digital versatile disk*) has thrown another option into the mix. With DVD, your PC can play full-length movies, blast you with Surround Sound, access huge digital libraries, and still handle everyday business, such as installing a program from a CD.

With that kind of power and versatility, DVD seems like the clear choice. Unfortunately, it's not. Standards battles, incompatibility problems, cost, and lack of quality DVD software, along with the reluctance of PC buyers to embrace yet another new technology, have kept CD-ROM at the top, at least for the time being.

But what about the future? Should you upgrade to DVD now or slap in a 32X CD-ROM drive and hold out until DVD becomes more mainstream? The following sections help you decide.

CD-ROM, Still King of the Hill

Except for a few small programs and utilities that are packaged on floppy disks, CD-ROM (CD-Read Only Memory) discs are the media of choice for most programs and games. With a storage capacity of 650MB–1GB, a single CD-ROM disc is more than capable of storing today's massive office suites, multimedia encyclopedias, and three-dimensional games. Two factors account for the long-lived success of CD-ROM:

- *Reliability*. Except for ever-increasing speeds, CD-ROM standards are stable. Nearly any new CD-ROM drive is capable of playing any CD-ROM disc, new or old.

- *Availability*. Because most PCs have CD-ROM drives, software developers are reluctant to move to DVD. The market for DVD titles hasn't been established. CD-ROM still accounts for the lion's share of software titles.

Considering these two factors, and your budget, a fast CD-ROM drive may be the best upgrade option for your current needs.

DVD, Harbinger of the Future

Given the 1GB storage limit of CD-ROM discs, our insatiable desire for multimedia, and the convergence of computers and home entertainment, CD-ROM is on its way out. Its replacement is DVD, a developing technology that pushes the disc capacity limits to 17GB! DVD provides support for full-screen, full-motion video and superior audio and video quality, making it useful not only for PC applications but also for home entertainment.

DVD is an optical disk storage technology, similar to CD-ROM. In fact, DVD drives look like CD-ROM drives and can play standard PC and audio CDs (see Figure 28.1). Data is written on the disc's surface as a collection of microscopic pits. The drive focuses a laser beam on the spinning disk and reads the change in signals as the beam passes over the smooth and pitted areas. However, DVD adds several twists to the standard optical disk storage scheme:

- *Red laser*. DVD drives use a red light as opposed to the yellow light used in CD-ROM drives. The red light has a shorter wavelength, allowing the drive to focus on smaller pits. With the pits crammed more closely together, the disc can store up to 4.7GB on a single layer on one side of the disc.

- *Two layers*. Unlike a CD, which has only one layer of storage medium, DVD discs use two: an opaque layer on the inside and a semi-transparent layer on the outside. The drive can adjust the laser's power to read data from one layer or the other. This doubles the storage capacity of a single side of the disc to 8.5GB.

- *Two sides*. Unlike CDs, which store data only on one side of the disc (the underside), DVD discs can store data on both sides. A double-sided, 2-layer disc pushes the storage capacity to 17GB. However, most DVD drives require you to flip the disc for side 2.

- *MPEG-2 standard.* Most CDs follow the MPEG-1 video compression standard to cram video data on a disc. This standard supports low-resolution video playback of 30 frames per second. DVD follows the newer, MPEG-2 standard, with a fourfold increase in resolution and a 60-frames-per-second playback rate.

- *Dolby AC-3 Audio.* DVD supports the latest advances in audio technology, AC-3 audio or Surround Sound. With Surround Sound, audio is divided into five separate channels routed to three channels in front and two behind the listener. In addition, a subwoofer is used to play the deep bass signals.

FIGURE 28.1

DVD drives look just like CD-ROM drives and can play standard CDs. Photo courtesy of Creative Technology.

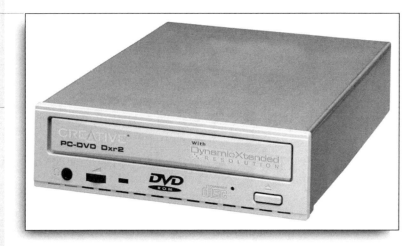

There's no question that DVD-ROM is superior to CD-ROM. The question is whether now is the right time to purchase a DVD drive. DVD standards are still going through a bit of a transitional period and have some glitches that may convince you to hold off for a while:

- *Scarcity of DVD titles.* DVD's main focus is on full-screen, full-motion video, not PC applications. Although many software companies are developing games and multimedia titles for DVD, the selection is still limited. If you're interested in DVD only for playing movies, consider purchasing a DVD player (instead of a DVD-ROM drive), which functions as a VHS replacement.

- *Poor quality of DVD titles.* The first games and applications designed for DVD basically crammed several CDs worth of data onto a single DVD disc. Few titles take advantage of the superior audio and video support that's available with DVD technology.

- *CD-ROM compatibility issues.* Although most DVD drives can read CDs, DVD drives read them slowly (8X or 10X, as compared with 24X for a standard CD-ROM drive). In addition, first generation DVD drives could not read through the green overlay on CD-Rs (CD-Recordable discs). However, newer DVD drives include a second laser (using yellow light, as in CD-ROM drives), to overcome this limitation.

- *Video card compatibility issues.* To achieve high-resolution, full-motion video, DVD needs a video adapter and PCI bus capable of handling the huge amounts of data that need to be pushed through the system and of streaming the audio and video signals to the display adapter and sound card. Most DVD kits work with a limited set of approved graphics adapters.

- *System requirements.* DVD requires a fairly powerful system. If you have a 75MHz Pentium with 8MB RAM, don't expect to be able to upgrade to DVD. In addition, you'll need yet another PCI expansion slot for the DVD decoder card.

- *Price.* DVD drives are three to four times more expensive than CD-ROM drives. If you're on a tight budget and don't plan on watching digital video on your PC, a fast CD-ROM drive might be a better choice.

Many of these issues address limitations in the first generation of DVD drives. Second and third generation DVD drives have overcome most of these limitations and provide improved compatibility with existing CDs.

Smart Shopping for CD-ROM Drives

Reference books on DVD

One of the best applications of DVD is in the reference book market. With DVD, you're no longer limited to using trimmed down encyclopedias on CD or forced to swap discs as you must with a multi-disc collection. Developers can store an entire reference library on a single disc.

In the past, there wasn't much to consider when shopping for a CD-ROM drive; either you settled for the 2X CD-ROM drive or you splurged and went with the 4X model. CD-ROM drive options are no longer that obvious. With advances in removable storage media and devices, you now have a wider selection of drive types from which to choose, including CD-R, and CD-RW drives. In addition, drive speeds have continued to rise, making new buyers wonder just how fast is fast enough. The following sections help guide you through the selection process.

SEE ALSO

➤ *Learn about alternative removable storage devices, page 659*

Speed Versus Cost

A CD-ROM drive's speed is expressed as a transfer rate, the amount of data the drive can pass along per second. The earliest CD-ROM drives had transfer rates of 150KBps. Later drives offered double the speed and came to be known as 2X drives. Since then, speeds have continued the ascent, climbing beyond the popular 24X to 32X levels. And, as is typical in the world of PCs, as the speeds have climbed, the prices of slower models have dropped considerably. You can now purchase an 8X drive for as little as $100.

When shopping for a fast CD-ROM drive, keep in mind that the drive speed is limited to the maximum speed of the disc. Most software developers gear their discs to 4X or 8X CD-ROM drives to make them compatible with a wider user base, so a 32X CD-ROM drive isn't going to produce the performance boost you might expect. However, you should purchase an 8X drive or faster; a slower drive may have trouble reading discs designed for faster drives.

Another point to consider is how you intend to use the drive. If you frequently play multimedia CDs, access reference books on CD, install programs from CD-ROM, or use the CD to record your own multimedia presentations, video clips, or photos, purchase the fastest drive you can afford. If you use the drive to install a couple applications a year, speed isn't all that important.

SEE ALSO
➤ *Learn how to take digital photographs, page 757*

SCSI or IDE?

You can purchase CD-ROM drives that connect to either a SCSI or IDE interface. There's no performance issue here as there is when upgrading a hard drive. CD-ROM drives are relatively slow when compared to hard drives, so you don't have to worry about the drive controller causing a bottleneck.

The major issue is whether your PC can support another internal drive. If your PC has an open drive bay, a free IDE plug, and a power supply connection, an internal IDE CD-ROM drive is the best choice. Most systems support up to four drives, allowing you to install two hard drives, a CD-ROM drive, and a tape backup drive. If your PC has a SCSI adapter, an internal SCSI drive may provide slightly better performance.

If the drive bays are full and your system has no free IDE connector, you have two choices:

- Install a SCSI adapter with an external outlet and connect an external SCSI CD-ROM drive. External SCSI CD-ROM drives perform nearly as fast as internal drives.

- Connect an external CD-ROM drive to the parallel port. However, the parallel port connection provides slow data transfers and can make printing very inconvenient.

SEE ALSO
➤ *Learn more about external drives, page 666*
➤ *Learn how to install a SCSI adapter, page 788*
➤ *Learn how to connect drives to IDE controllers, page 593*

Trays, Caddies, and Disc Changers

CD-ROM drives offer various options for loading CDs. The most popular device is a CD tray. You press a button on the

Disk drive cache

When shopping for speed, look for a drive with a 256KB cache or larger. The drive reads data into the cache, which can then feed the data more smoothly to your PC's audio and video components.

drive, and the tray pops out. You can then lay the CD in the tray and press the button to load it.

Some CD-ROM drives use a removable disc caddy that completely encases the CD. You typically lift the lid on the caddy, load the CD, close the lid, and then insert the caddy into the drive. When you press the eject button, the caddy pops out, and you pull it out of the drive. Although disk caddies provide additional protection for CDs, they're a little less convenient than trays.

If you have a reference library that's stored on several CDs, or you use the same CDs daily, consider purchasing a CD-ROM drive with a disc changer (also called a CD-ROM jukebox). The disc changer is similar to the type used on stereo systems and typically holds from four to six discs. However, CD-ROM drives that use disc changers are more expensive than standard drives and may not support transfer rates comparable to those of standard CD-ROM drives.

CD-R, CD-RW, CD-I, and Other Acronyms

Compatibility issues

Before buying a CD changer, make sure it is compatible with your PC's operating system. If the CD changer was designed for Windows 95, it may not work with Windows 98.

Shopping for any PC product requires a fair share of translation skills. If you don't know your acronyms, you're liable to suffer at the hands of unsupported standards and incompatible equipment. CD-ROM drives have their own stock of acronyms, explained in the following list:

- *CD-R (CD-Recordable)*. Also known as CD-WO (CD-Write Once) and CD-WORM (CD-Write Once, Read Many), CD-R drives not only read CDs, but also record data on blank CDs. CD-R drives are great for creating digitized photo albums, editing video clips, recording music, or creating your own program disks. They're also useful for backups, although the drive cannot write over existing data. If you purchase a CD-R drive, make sure it supports a feature called *multi-session recording*, so you can add to the disc as needed, until it is full. Without multi-session recording, you cannot add to the disc after the first recording session.

- *CD-RW (CD-ReWritable)*. Unlike CD-R drives that can write to a disc only once, CD-RW drives act more like hard drives, writing to the discs several times. One of the major drawbacks of early CD-RW drives is that standard CD-ROM drives cannot read discs created with CD-RW drives. However, a new standard is in the works to enable CD-ROM drives to read CD-RW discs.

- *CD-I (CD-Interactive)*. A CD standard co-developed by Sony and Philips that never quite caught on. A CD-I drive has a built-in processor to improve performance for decompressing video data.

- *CD-ROM XA*. Another, more popular CD-ROM standard developed by Sony, Philips, and Microsoft. CD-ROM XA enables a disk to store several different types of media in a compressed format, including audio, video, and graphics. This standard is compatible with both CD-I drives and standard CD-ROM drives, provided that Microsoft's MSCDEX driver is installed.

CD-ROM Upgrade Kits

If you're replacing your CD-ROM drive, you can get by with purchasing the CD-ROM drive by itself. However, if your PC never had a CD-ROM drive installed on it, consider purchasing an upgrade kit that includes the necessary mounting brackets, cables, and software.

In addition, if your PC is not equipped with a 16-bit sound card or better, now is a great time to install a sound card and speakers. An audio output cable from the CD connects to the sound card inside the system unit, allowing the CD to play audio clips through the sound card. Several companies market multimedia upgrade kits that include both a CD-ROM drive and sound card (see Figure 28.2).

SEE ALSO

➤ *Learn how to install a sound card, page 769*

FIGURE 28.2

CD-ROM kits contain everything you need for the upgrade. Photo courtesy of Creative Technology.

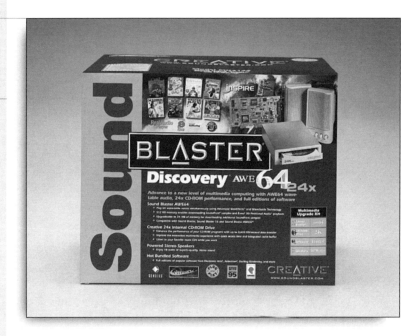

What to Look for in a DVD Drive

You've decided to take the plunge and replace your rickety old CD-ROM drive with a DVD drive, but with all the choices out there, how do you pick the best DVD drive? Choosing a DVD drive isn't merely a matter of weighing speed against cost. You must also consider hardware requirements, compatibility issues, audio and video output quality, the performance of the DVD decoder, and a few other minor issues.

The following sections explain the terminology you need to know before you go shopping and point out the key features you should look for in a DVD drive.

Speed

In the speed category, there is little to compare. DVD drives haven't been around long enough to hit the 32X mark. Most DVD drives are 1X or 2X, but don't confuse a 1X DVD rating with a 1X CD-ROM rating; a 1X CD-ROM drive has a transfer rate of 150KBps, whereas a 1X DVD-ROM drive shovels data at a rate of 1,250KBps! This is roughly equivalent to the rate of an 8X CD-ROM drive.

As for breaking the speed barriers, don't expect much of a performance gain from faster drives. 1X drives are fast enough to feed the DVD decoder the steady stream of data it needs to handle the compressed audio and video signals. A jump to 2X may increase performance between the DVD and the hard drive (for recording), but for standard video playback, a 1X drive is usually sufficient.

DVD Decoder

The DVD decoder card is more crucial than the drive itself in determining video quality and performance. Decoder cards use one of the following two techniques to generate the display:

- *VGA inlay.* Pushes display data through your existing PCI graphics adapter, to provide high-quality video output. However, this approach places a great burden on the PCI bus, which may not be able to handle it. You may have to decrease resolution to get the video clips to even play. Before you buy a decoder based on the VGA inlay approach, make sure it's compatible with your PCI graphics adapter. A faster processor (Pentium 133 or faster) and additional memory also help.

- *Analog overlay.* Takes display input from your VGA adapter and lays its own video output on top of the VGA output. This is a less intrusive approach than VGA inlay, making the decoder card do most of the work. You may have to wrestle with the overlay at first to align it properly on the screen. Video quality is not quite up to par with a board that uses the VGA inlay approach, but analog overlay has less frequent and less serious compatibility issues.

Some DVD schemes handle video and audio decoding through software rather than using a hardware approach. This places greater demands on your system overall, and often results in jerky playback. Don't even think about using a software-based decoder if you're playing video on less than a Pentium II 200+MHz PC with AGP graphics. Even then, you may be disappointed with the quality.

SEE ALSO

➤ *Learn how to choose and install a graphics accelerator card, page 643*

Software Support

DVD upgrade kits comewith the software you need to fully exploit the best DVD features. Make sure the software is manageable and includes the controls you need to adjust the display brightness, contrast, and color. You don't want to have to make these adjustments using Windows Display Properties.

In addition, because DVD stores video on a disc rather than a tape (as does VHS), DVD allows you to quickly switch to your favorite scenes in a movie and play them back. However, without a control that's intuitive and responsive, you won't be able to make the most of this feature.

CD-ROM Compatibility

DVD titles included?

A good rule of thumb when shopping for hardware is to never let bundled software drive your purchase decision. You want the highest quality DVD drive you can afford—worry about getting movies later.

Although CD-ROM compatibility was a major issue with early DVD-ROM drives, developers have worked out most of the bugs. When shopping for a DVD drive, make sure it features a CD-ROM data transfer rate of at least 8X and that it can read CD-R and CD-RW disks.

Audio Output

Dolby AC-3 Audio is supported in virtually all DVD decoders, and system requirements generally call for standard 16-bit stereo, so compatibility issues for audio output are minimal. To take full advantage of DVD audio output capabilities, however, you must add a Dolby AC-3 or ProLogic compatible receiver, four high-quality speakers, and a subwoofer. If audio quality isn't a big issue for you, DVD supports special software that can make a standard two-speaker system produce the illusion of Surround Sound.

SEE ALSO

➤ *Learn how to upgrade your PC's audio system, page 769*

Hardware Requirements

You might think that you'd need a supercomputer to handle all the data processing required by DVD. However, the hardware requirements are fairly modest:

- Pentium 133MHz or faster CPU.

- 16MB of RAM.

- 2MB hard disk space.

- 16-bit stereo sound card.

- VGA display card.

- Microsoft Windows 95 with OSR2 or Windows 98.

- Unoccupied PCI expansion slot that supports *bus mastering*. Bus mastering allows the DVD decoder to stream data to the sound card and graphics adapter without having to pass through the CPU.

- Open drive bay for internal DVD drive.

DVD Upgrade Kits

The easiest way to upgrade to DVD is to purchase an upgrade kit that comes complete with the DVD drive, decoder, cables, and installation software. Most kits also come bundled with several DVD titles, so you can start playing with your new toy right away (see Figure 28.3).

Installing a CD-ROM or DVD-ROM Drive

Assuming you have a full-size desktop PC or larger, a free drive bay, an available plug from the power supply, and the required cables, installing a CD-ROM or DVD drive is a snap. The following sections introduce you to some pre-installation considerations and then provide step-by-step instructions on how to install a CD-ROM drive or DVD-ROM drive and decoder card.

FIGURE 28.3

DVD upgrade kits include all the equipment and software in one package.

1 DVD drive

2 DVD decoder

3 Audio cable

4 CD audio cable

5 External VGA loop cable

6 IDE data cable

7 External audio loop cable

8 DVD software and titles

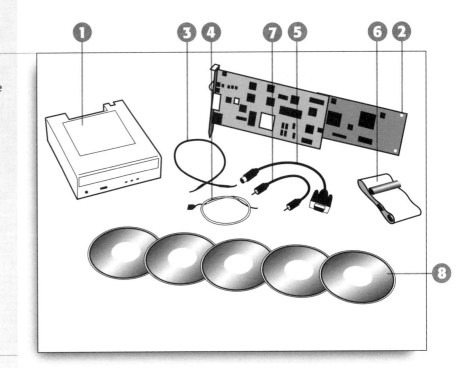

Setting Up the IDE Master and Slave

If your PC is equipped with an IDE controller for the hard drive(s), as opposed to a SCSI interface card, you will probably want to connect your CD-ROM or DVD-ROM drive to one of the EIDE connectors on the motherboard.

PCs typically have two EIDE connectors—a primary and a secondary IDE interface, each of which supports two drives (four total). An IDE cable connects your main, bootable hard drive to the primary IDE interface and has an additional connector. This connector is typically used for a second hard drive, although you can use it to connect your CD-ROM drive. However, I recommend using another IDE cable to connect your CD-ROM drive to your motherboard's secondary IDE interface. This makes it easier to connect a second hard drive later.

SEE ALSO

➤ *Learn more about the IDE interface, page 593*

If you connect two drives to the same IDE interface with a single cable, you must set jumpers to designate one of the drives as the master and the other as the slave. If you have only one drive attached to the cable, set the jumper to mark the drive as the only drive attached (see Figure 28.4).

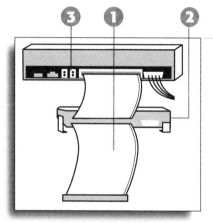

FIGURE 28.4

Set the jumpers on the two drives that share a common IDE cable to mark one as the master and the other as the slave.

① IDE cable.

② Set the hard drive as the master.

③ Set the DVD or CD-ROM drive as the slave.

Setting SCSI Addresses and Termination

If your system has a SCSI adapter, you can connect up to seven SCSI devices to it. Each device in the chain is assigned an address to indicate its location in the chain. The SCSI adapter itself is usually 7. Numbers 0–6 are assigned to the other SCSI devices. Before installing a SCSI drive, set the jumpers or switches on the device to assign it a number that's not already in use.

At each end of the chain is a terminator that indicates there are no more devices in the chain. If the drive is at the end of the SCSI chain, set its jumpers to turn on termination. If the drive is somewhere in the middle of the chain, turn off termination. By default, the SCSI card is terminated. However, if you install both external and internal devices to the SCSI card, it no longer acts as an end of the chain, and you must disable termination for the adapter. (Many newer SCSI cards and some devices automatically turn termination on or off as required.)

Installing a CD-ROM Drive

After you have entered the required settings to mark the drive as the master or slave or set the address for a SCSI drive, you are ready to install the drive.

Installing a CD-ROM drive

1. Turn off the power to your PC and any devices connected to it.

2. Open the system unit and touch a metal part of the case to discharge any static electricity.

3. On the front of the system unit, remove the cover plate from the drive bay into which you are installing the drive.

4. If the CD-ROM drive requires mounting brackets (or rails) to attach the drive to the bay, attach the mounting brackets to the sides of the drive.

5. If you are installing an IDE drive, match the red stripe on the IDE data cable to pin 1 on the drive's data outlet and plug in the cable.

   If you are installing a SCSI drive, use the SCSI cable to connect the drive to another SCSI device or to the connector on the SCSI adapter.

6. Insert a plug from the power supply into the power outlet on the hard drive.

7. Secure the drive to the drive bay using the mounting screws.

8. Connect the audio output cable from the CD-ROM drive to the audio input connector on the sound card. The audio input connector typically consists of four pins near the top center of the sound card (inside the system unit).

Installing a DVD Drive

Installing a DVD drive is a bit more complicated than installing a CD-ROM drive. You must install both the DVD decoder card and the drive itself. If the decoder uses analog overlay, you may need to move your monitor's video cable over to the decoder card and connect the video port and connect your display adapter to the decoder card with a special cable (typically

SCSI DVD?

You may have a hard time tracking down a SCSI DVD drive. Although the technology supports SCSI, manufacturers have invested more in developing DVD drives for the less expensive IDE interface.

No room?

If the data and power cables are wadded up inside the system unit, you may have better luck threading the cables through the drive bay and out the front of the system unit, for easier access to the outlets on the drive. You can then slide the drive into the bay after making the connections.

included in the upgrade kit). In addition, you'll probably need to tinker with the DVD and decoder settings to make the drive, display adapter, sound card, and decoder all work together.

Installing the DVD-ROM drive

1. Turn off the power to your PC and any devices connected to it and unplug your system unit.

2. Open the system unit and touch a metal part of the case to discharge any static electricity.

3. On the front of the system unit, remove the cover plate from the drive bay into which you are installing the drive.

4. If the DVD drive requires mounting brackets (or rails) to attach the drive to the bay, attach the mounting brackets to the sides of the drive.

5. If you are installing an IDE drive, match the red stripe on the IDE data cable to pin 1 on the drive's data outlet and plug in the cable.

   If you are installing a SCSI drive, use the SCSI cable to connect the drive to another SCSI device or to the connector on the SCSI adapter.

6. Insert a plug from the power supply into the power outlet on the DVD drive.

7. Secure the drive to the drive bay using the mounting screws.

8. Restart your PC.

9. In Windows, click My Computer to make sure your system recognizes the new drive. A new drive icon should appear for the DVD drive. If the drive is not shown, troubleshoot the drive installation before installing the decoder card.

Installing the DVD decoder card

1. Locate an open PCI expansion slot inside the system unit. Most decoder cards are full-length cards, so you may need to move an existing, shorter PCI card to a different slot to give the full-length card the space it needs.

2. Remove the screw that secures the PCI expansion slot's cover plate to the back of the system unit, and lift out the cover plate.

3. Insert the DVD decoder card into the PCI expansion slot and use both hands to press the top of the board down until the contacts are firmly seated in the expansion slot.

4. Screw in the screw you removed in step 2 to secure the decoder card in place.

5. If necessary, connect the decoder card to your sound board using the cable included with your DVD kit (see Figure 28.5). (You may need to attach the cable externally or internally; refer to the documentation.)

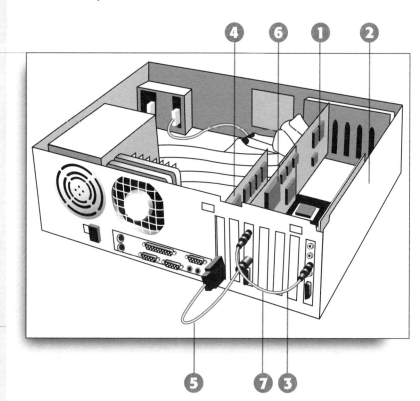

FIGURE 28.5

With some kits, you must connect the decoder card to the sound card externally.

1 Decoder

2 Sound card

3 Audio loop cable

4 Display adapter

5 Pass-through cable

6 Decoder card

7 The monitor plugs in here

6. If necessary, disconnect the monitor cable from the display adapter and connect the display adapter to the Video In port on the decoder card using the special pass-through cable included with your kit (refer to Figure 28.5).

7. Plug the monitor cable into the Video Out port on the decoder card.

SEE ALSO

➤ *Learn basic installation procedures for expansion boards, page 560*

Installing Device Drivers and Other Software

Whenever you install a new CD-ROM or DVD drive, you must install a device driver to tell Windows how to use the device. Shut down Windows and restart it. When Windows starts, a dialog box appears, indicating that Windows found a new device and is installing the required software to use it. Windows typically performs the installation without asking for your help. If Windows fails to detect the new hardware, open the Control Panel and run the Add New Hardware Wizard.

In addition, most DVD drives come with their own setup utilities. Run the setup program that came with your drive kit to install any special drivers or to install controls for the drive and decoder card.

Installation problems?

If Windows doesn't recognize the new drive or cannot use the decoder card, you may have to do a bit of troubleshooting. See Chapter 39, "Troubleshooting Hardware Problems," to help track down the problem.

Upgrading Your Display Adapter and Monitor

Improve system performance with a graphics accelerator

Choose a graphics accelerator that your system can handle

Understand the benefits of AGP

Give your computer a facelift with a new monitor

Configure your display in Windows

What Is a Graphics Accelerator?

A graphics accelerator is a display adapter on steroids. Every PC has a display adapter that tells the monitor how to arrange and color the tiny dots that make up the images on the screen. In the early days of PCs, when most programs were text-based, generating displays took little expertise. The CPU processed the necessary instructions and passed them along to the display adapter, which then translated the instructions and rendered the image on the screen. Standard display adapters could handle the job just fine.

With the explosion of computer graphics, multimedia, and 3D games and the movement to make PCs an integral part of the home entertainment system, standard display adapters just can't handle the complex calculations and instructions required to render images, especially 3D, moving images. That's where graphics accelerators come in.

A graphics accelerator has its own built-in processor and memory (typically 2–8MB). Whenever your programs need to generate an image on the screen, they pass the instructions on to the graphics accelerator rather than to the CPU. This increases system performance in two important ways:

- Because the graphics accelerator specializes in interpreting the instructions for generating images, it's much faster and more efficient than the CPU. Without a graphics accelerator, you'll notice that computer games are slow, program windows take a long time to appear, and scrolling through documents (especially those with embedded graphics) is jerky.
- The graphics accelerator takes some of the processing load off the CPU. While the graphics accelerator is busy generating images on the screen, the CPU can perform other tasks, such as interpreting program instructions and performing calculations.

2D Graphics Accelerators

Windows, with its graphical user interface, ushered in the era of 2D graphics accelerators. In fact, 2D graphics accelerators are commonly called *Windows accelerators*. With all the windows, dialog boxes, menus, and icons that your system needed to display, the CPU needed some help.

With a 2D graphics accelerator and Windows GDI (Graphical Device Interface), programs no longer had to rely on the CPU to generate windows and other graphical objects. The program could send the instructions to the GDI, which would then pass along a request to the graphics accelerator to render an object of the specified size, dimensions, and appearance in a predetermined position on the screen.

3D Graphics Accelerators

Although 2D graphics accelerators can still boost system performance for Windows and standard business applications, such as word processors and spreadsheets, they cannot handle the demands of 3D media, games, and virtual reality. When that third dimension, *depth*, is added to the formula, the 2D graphics accelerator falls flat.

3D graphics accelerators accommodate the third dimension by adding textures, shading, lighting, and *Z-buffering* to create the illusion of three dimensions on a two-dimensional screen. These features require additional processing power and a card that's designed to work with the latest 3D imaging standards.

Smart Shopping for Graphics Accelerators

As you flip through PC magazines and catalogues and wander the aisles of your local computer store, the variety of 3D graphics accelerators and the long list of terms used to describe them may generate more questions than answers: Should you purchase a PCI or AGP adapter? Is 4MB of RAM enough? What's the difference between OpenGL and Direct3D? What's MPEG-2? And do you really need a built-in TV tuner?

Multiple monitors in Windows 98

Windows 98 includes support for multiple monitors, allowing you to run a different program on each monitor and increase your overall work area. To use multiple monitors, your PC must have a PCI or AGP card for each monitor. Check the Windows help system for details.

Z-buffering

In 3D scenes, one object may hide another object that's behind it. Z-buffering keeps information about all objects in memory, so as you move through a scene and your perspective changes, the object can immediately be rendered on screen.

The following sections answer these questions and provide the information you need to make a well-educated purchasing decision.

SEE ALSO

➤ *Learn how to install a TV-tuner, page 691*

Compatibility: VLB, PCI, or AGP?

Before you can do any serious shopping for a graphics accelerator, you must determine the type of bus used for your video card:

- *VLB*. Short for VESA (Video Electronics Standards Association) Local Bus, VLB is common on 486 PCs manufactured in 1993 and 1994. Although VLB was a significant improvement at the time, you won't find any 3D graphics accelerators that plug into VLB slots. To take advantage of 3D acceleration, you would have to gut your system and replace the motherboard or, better yet, purchase a new PC.

- *PCI*. Short for Peripheral Component Interconnect, PCI is prevalent in Pentium-based PCs. As a 64-bit bus offering 133MBps throughput, the PCI bus has the capacity to handle the flow of data required for 3D graphics. In 1997 and 1998, most graphics accelerators on the market required a PCI expansion slot.

- *AGP*. With the introduction of the Pentium II and a corresponding overhaul of the motherboard, AGP (short for Accelerated Graphics Port) has become the display interface of choice for video cards. AGP offers double the throughput of PCI and adds a direct channel to main memory . If you frequently play 3D games or work with 3D design applications and your system has an AGP card, consider upgrading the system RAM to at *least* 64MB.

SEE ALSO

➤ *Learn more about expansion slots, page 29*

➤ *Learn the basics about display adapters and monitors, page 20*

The Least You Should Get

Although the third dimension introduces an entirely new set of standards and features to consider, you must also consider basic features, such as resolution and refresh rates. Any card you purchase should offer at least the following:

- *1280X1040 resolution*. To display a decent picture on a 21-inch monitor, this is the lowest resolution you should settle for. If you're still using a 15-inch monitor, you should consider upgrading your monitor to a 19- or 21-inch model.

- *24-bit true-color depth*. This refers to the number of bits used to determine the color of each dot on the screen. With 24 bits, the card can display 16 million colors.

- *72Hz refresh rate*. This is the rate at which the display is repainted. Any slower, and screen flicker could become a problem. Also, make sure your monitor supports this refresh rate. For 19-inch or larger monitors, look for a higher refresh rate.

- *24-bit Z-buffer*. This refers to the number of bits used to determine the positions of the vertices of the triangles used to render geometrical shapes in the background.

- *Gouraud shading*. Most games and design applications use Gouraud shading to blend the colors of the triangles used to render shapes. This gives the objects a smoother appearance. *Flat shading* makes the lines between objects appear more defined, giving scenes a surrealistic appearance.

Pentium MMX or Pentium II

If you have an older, classic Pentium system and you're thinking of upgrading to a 3D graphics accelerator, upgrade your processor to a Pentium MMX to improve graphics performance.

Graphics Memory

As explained previously, graphics accelerators have their own built-in RAM. If you're on a strict budget, 4MB is enough RAM to handle the resolution and color depth needed for most games and applications—8MB is preferred. If you do purchase a card that comes with 4MB RAM, make sure it leaves open the option to add another 4MB later.

A more important consideration is the speed of the RAM. Avoid cheap cards that use standard, single-ported DRAM, EDO

DRAM, or SDRAM and look for higher quality cards that use VRAM or WRAM. VRAM and WRAM are dual-ported, enabling the video circuit and the processor to access memory at the same time.

SEE ALSO

➤ *Learn how to upgrade your PC's main memory, page 577*

The War of the Standards

For 3D games and software to communicate with 3D hardware, both must support the same API (application programming interface). The API provides programmers with the set of tools they need to put together compatible programs. The trouble is that a few companies are still battling over which API should be used. Here's a list of the top API contenders:

- *Direct3D*. Because Direct3D is built into Windows and is the standard most software developers follow, make sure the card you buy features Direct3D support.

- *OpenGL*. Developed by Silicon Graphics, primarily for its advanced design applications, OpenGL is making some progress toward being incorporated in Windows.

- *3Dfx Voodoo*. This is a proprietary standard for serious computer game players. In short, if you want to play a game that's written for Voodoo, the card must be specifically designed for it. Early Voodoo cards supported only Voodoo, but newer cards (Voodoo2 and later) also include Direct3D support.

FPS: Frames Per Second

To display motion picture video, the graphics adapter flips through a series of frames to produce the illusion of movement. Television in the United States is standardized to 30fps (frames per second) to ensure smooth movement, so don't settle for less in your graphics accelerator. If you're looking for even smoother playback for digital video, look for a card with a 60fps rating.

Most graphics accelerators can output 30fps, but if you're shopping for a graphics accelerator that features video capture, make sure the video capture feature supports 30fps, as well.

MPEG Video Support

MPEG (short for Moving Pictures Expert Group) is a set of standards for audio and video compression and multimedia file formats. MPEG compresses video by storing only the changes from one frame to the next. This omits some detail from each frame, but not enough for the human eye to discern.

MPEG-1 supports low-resolution video (362X250 dpi), which is why most video clips on the Web play inside a window the size of a postage stamp, and 30fps. MPEG-2 raises the bar to 1200X720 dpi and 60fps, providing better-than-TV quality video, and supports CD-quality audio.

For optimum performance, the graphics accelerator should provide hardware support for MPEG-2. That is, the card itself should have the capability of handling the MPEG-2 decompression tasks. Some accelerators provide only software-based support.

All-in-One Video Cards

Before you hand over your hard-earned dollars for 3D graphics accelerator, you should at least consider all-in-one video cards, such as the All-in-Wonder Pro. These cards pack several tools in a single card to free up some PCI expansion slots for other equipment. Here's a list of what most all-in-one cards provide:

- 3D graphics acceleration built into the card.
- Video capture, so you can play video taped recordings into the card, store them on disk, and edit them.
- TV tuner for tuning into TV stations via a cable connection or TV antenna.
- TV-output so you can connect the card to a cable-ready TV set for big-screen output.

- MPEG-2 support to handle MPEG video compression. At the time this book was being written, no all-in-one cards were capable of replacing a dedicated DVD MPEG decoder card, but you should start to see all-in-one video cards with MPEG decoder chips in late 1998 and early 1999.

SEE ALSO

➤ *Learn more about TV tuners and video capture boards, page 691*

Installing a Graphics Accelerator Card

The actual physical installation of a graphics accelerator card is no more difficult than any expansion card installation. You open your system unit case, find an open expansion slot, and plug the thing in. However, there are a few unique considerations and a couple variables you need to deal with to ensure a smooth upgrade. The following sections lead your through the process and provide step-by-step instructions.

SEE ALSO

➤ *Learn basic techniques for installing expansion boards, page 560*

Setting Up a Standard Display Driver in Windows

Because you're working with your display, your only means of seeing what your computer is doing, you have to be a little careful when installing any new video card. If you install your card and Windows cannot identify it, Windows may lock up on start-up or display a blank screen, giving you no way to install the card's device driver. Before you install your card, choose a standard Windows display driver that works with any video card.

Choosing a standard video driver

1. Right-click the Windows desktop and click **Properties**.
2. Click the **Settings** tab.
3. Click the **Advanced** button.
4. Click the **Adapter** tab.
5. Click the **Change** button. The Update Device Driver Wizard appears.

6. Click **Next**.

7. Click **Display a List of All the Drivers in a Specific Location** and click **Next**.

8. Click **Show All Hardware**.

9. Scroll to the top of the **Manufacturers** list and click **(Standard Display Types)**.

10. In the **Models** list, click the option for the standard VGA adapter (see Figure 29.1) and click **Next**.

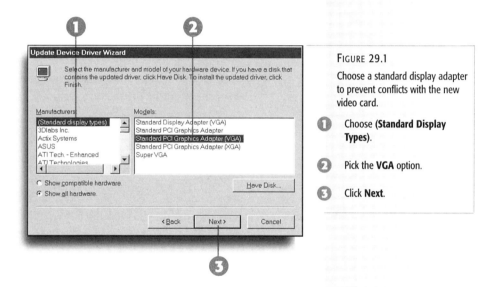

FIGURE 29.1

Choose a standard display adapter to prevent conflicts with the new video card.

① Choose **(Standard Display Types)**.

② Pick the **VGA** option.

③ Click **Next**.

11. If prompted to confirm the selection, click **Yes**.

12. Click **Next**.

13. Click **Finish**.

14. When prompted to restart your PC, click **Yes**.

Windows shuts down and restarts using the standard VGA driver. Your screen may look a little blocky and fuzzy at this point, but you'll at least be able to see what you're doing. Shut down Windows and proceed to the next section to install the card.

Installing the Card

Blank screen on startup

If your screen is blank or Windows locked up on startup, restart your PC. Right after you hear it beep, press the F8 key, and then choose the option for starting Windows in Safe Mode. Perform the same steps you took for installing a standard VGA driver, but this time click the **Have Disk** button and install the driver that came with your card.

As I mentioned earlier, installing the card itself is a snap. However, there's one minor variation on the theme: the pass-through cable. If you have an all-in-one video card, you won't have to mess with the additional cable, 3D acceleration is built right into the board. Most accelerators, however, work with your existing video card, requiring you to install a pass-through cable. You plug one end of the cable into the port on your existing video card and plug the other end into the Video In port on the graphics accelerator. You then connect your monitor to the Video Out port on the graphics accelerator.

Installing a graphics accelerator

1. Disconnect the video cable from your existing video card, and set the monitor on a stable surface.

2. Open your system unit case and touch a metal part of the case to discharge any static electricity.

3. If you are installing an all-in-one video card, remove the existing card.

   If you are installing a graphics accelerator that works along with your existing video card, remove the cover plate near the open expansion slot you want to use.

4. Insert the contacts on the card into the expansion slot and make sure the edge is aligned properly with the expansion slot. Using two hands, firmly press down on the top edge of the board until the board is firmly seated in the expansion slot. (Don't force it.)

5. Secure the mounting plate to the system unit case, using the screw you removed in step 2.

6. If you are installing a graphics accelerator, connect the pass-through cable from your video card's external port to the Video In port on the accelerator card (see Figure 29.2).

7. Replace the cover on the system unit.

8. Plug your monitor into the Video Out port on the new card or the Video Out port on the graphics accelerator.

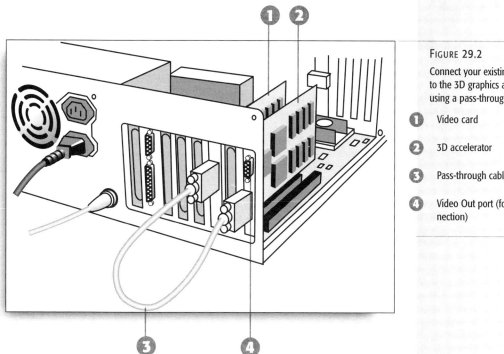

FIGURE 29.2

Connect your existing video card to the 3D graphics accelerator using a pass-through cable.

1 Video card

2 3D accelerator

3 Pass-through cable

4 Video Out port (for monitor connection)

Installing the Display Driver

The card is installed, but Windows is set up to load a standard VGA driver, so the next step is to install the driver that came with the card. Start your PC. On startup, Windows should recognize that a new device is installed and run the Add New Hardware Wizard to lead you through the process of installing the device driver.

Insert the installation CD or floppy disk that came with the card into the CD-ROM or floppy drive, and follow the Wizard's instructions. The wizard searches the installation disk or CD for the best driver and installs it for you. You'll have to restart your computer after the installation.

SEE ALSO

➤ *Learn how to enter display settings and preferences in Windows, page 221*

Smart Shopping for Monitors

Most users upgrade everything on their system but the monitor. They add a 3D graphics accelerator, swap the hard drive and processor, and move up to DVD to keep up with the latest technology, but they seem content staring at the same old 15-inch monitor that came with the system.

If you're moving up to DVD or adding a 3D graphics accelerator to your PC, you're serious about graphics. You plan on using your PC for graphics design, to play the latest computer games, or to integrate your PC with your home entertainment system. Whatever the case, your improved graphics system is going to produce very unimpressive results on a standard 15-inch monitor. You need something bigger and sharper. But how big is big enough? And how can you determine the image quality by reading an ad? The following sections provide the answers, showing you what to look for in a new monitor.

SEE ALSO

➤ *Learn how to upgrade to DVD, page 621*

CRT or Flat-Panel Display?

You've seen CRTs. They're the monitors that look like TV sets, with their protuberant backsides and curved glass fronts. Due to their proven reliability, speed, display quality, and relative low prices, CRTs remain the monitor of choice for most users. However, CRTs do have a few flaws: larger monitors hog space, guzzle power, and throw off massive amounts of heat. In an era when computer gadgets are downsizing, nobody really wants a monitor the size of a sofa, but for the price and quality, you can't beat a CRT.

However, if you're tired of using your desk as a doll house for your monitor, get a *flat-panel* display, also called a *TFT (thin film transistor) display*. These sleek LCD (liquid crystal display) monitors are like the displays used on notebook PCs and are less than half as deep and half as heavy as standard CRT-based monitors. You can push a flat-panel monitor to the back of your desk and still have plenty of room to lay papers and books (see Figure 29.3). In addition, flat-panel displays consume much less power

Look at it

You wouldn't buy a TV set without first looking at the quality of the picture, so don't buy a monitor until you've seen it in action and compared it with other monitors in the same class. Although standards provide a good way to double-check your gut feeling about a monitor, don't let standards alone drive your purchase decision.

and emit very little heat. So what's the catch? The following list explains the major drawbacks of flat-panel displays:

- *Price*. Expect to pay $300–$400 more for a comparably equipped flat-panel display.

- *Reliability*. Flat-panel displays use thousands of transistors to illuminate the dots that make up the display. When a transistor bites the dust, you lose a dot.

- *Digital/Analog conversions*. Video cards convert digital signals to analog signals to drive the monitor. Flat-panel displays are digital, so they must convert the analog signals back into digital signals. Newer flat panel displays are designed to overcome this problem, but they require cooperation from the video card.

- *Full-motion video*. Although flat-panel displays can handle video, some displays don't support the refresh rates required to display moving pictures. This may result in a ghost effect.

- *Standards issues*. As with any new technology, LCD standards are in transition and in conflict. Until they're resolved, and a standard LCD graphics port is built into new PCs, you'll probably need to purchase a special video card along with your new LCD for optimum performance and display quality.

My advice is to hold off on the flat-panel display until the industry gets its act together. If you just can't wait, do your homework. Take a look at several flat-panel displays and compare them to comparable CRTs.

Size Versus Price

Size is one of the most important (and obvious) considerations, especially if you purchase a flat-panel display and push it to the back of your desk, farther away from yourself. As with TVs, size is measured diagonally. When comparing sizes, be sure to compare the actual viewing area, not the tube size. The viewing area can differ by as much as a half inch on monitors of the same size; for example, one 21-inch monitor may have a viewing area of 19 1/2 inches whereas another has a viewing area of 20 inches.

FIGURE 29.3

A flat-panel monitor can free up a lot of real estate on your desk.

In general, bigger is better. However, when balancing size against price, you may need to consider your minimum display needs:

- *15-inch monitors appeal only to the pocketbook*. For gaming, graphics design, and general comfort for your tired eyes, 15-inch doesn't even make the list.

- *17-inch monitors offer an excellent balance between size and price.* They handle the resolutions and colors required by the latest games and graphics software and provide a little extra room for page layout and wide spreadsheets.

- *19-inch monitors take the display (and the price) to the next level.* For serious game playing and graphics design, heavy-duty multitasking, and wide spreadsheets, 19 inches is the minimum requirement.

- *21-inch monitors cross the price barrier of most budgets and appeal to the professional graphics designer or programmer.* However, if you plan on using your PC as an extra TV set, that extra two inches can make a big difference.

The All Important Dot Pitch Consideration

As you move up the screen size scale, you must also consider *dot pitch*. Dot pitch is the distance between the dots that make up the display. The closer together the dots, the sharper the image. Table 29.1 lists the maximum dot pitch for the monitors described in the previous list. The smaller the number, the better.

TABLE 29.1   **Maximum dot pitch for different sized monitors**

Monitor Size	Maximum Dot Pitch
15-inch	.28mm
17-inch	.26mm
19-inch	.21mm
21-inch	.21mm

Resolution

For high-quality displays, monitors must be able to display enough dots (*pixels*) on the screen to render a smooth image and enough colors to support the images, videos, and 3D texturing you want to display.

Resolution, measured in dpi (dots per inch) is the most important consideration and is directly linked to the screen size. Larger screens require a higher dpi setting to display a clear image that fits the screen. Table 29.2 lists the optimum resolutions based on the size of the monitor.

TABLE 29.2   **Optimum display resolutions**

Monitor size	Optimum resolution (dpi)
15-inch	800X600
17-inch	1024X768
19-inch	1280X1024
21-inch	1600X1200

In addition to resolution, you should consider the number of colors the monitor supports. The number of colors is commonly referred to as color depth and is expressed as the number of bits used to define the color of each pixel. So, for example, 24-bit color indicates that the monitor can display up to 16.7M colors (2^{24}).

For most applications and even for playing video clips on the Web, you could set your monitor to display 256 colors and never miss the reduction in quality. However, a higher number of colors enables more realistic rendering of shadows and objects in 3D applications and games. Make sure your monitor supports 24-bit color, although you may want to crank down this setting when you're working with standard applications.

Refresh Rate: The Flicker Factor

This one's easy. You want a monitor with a refresh rate of 75–100Hz; 75Hz for 15- to 17-inch monitors, 85–100Hz for larger monitors. Slower refresh rates cause the display to flicker, which is annoying and hard on your eyes.

Video card RAM

The amount of RAM required on a video card is directly determined by the resolution and color depth. For example, an 800X600 image displayed at 24-bit color would require about 1.5MB. Make sure your display card can keep up.

Accessible Controls

Some manufacturers apparently don't want you to adjust the display. They stick the brightness, contrast, and vertical and horizontal controls on the back of the monitor. Worse yet, some manufacturers place the controls inside the monitor, so you need a special plastic screwdriver to make any adjustments. Make sure the monitor you purchase positions the controls on the front of the monitor. Of course, if you have young children, you may want the controls less accessible.

Connecting Your New Monitor

You don't need instructions to explain how to unplug your monitor from the video port and plug in a new monitor. However, before you disconnect anything, make sure Windows is set up to use a standard monitor. By doing this, you ensure that Windows will be able to generate a display on your new monitor when you restart.

Upgrading your monitor

1. Right-click the Windows desktop and click **Properties**.

2. Click the **Settings** tab.

3. Click the **Advanced** button.

4. Click the **Monitor** tab.

5. Click the **Change** button. The Update Device Driver Wizard appears.

6. Click **Next**.

7. Click **Display a list of all the drivers in a specific location** and click **Next**.

8. Click **Show all hardware**.

9. Scroll to the top of the **Manufacturers** list and click **(Standard Monitor Types)**.

10. In the **Models** list, click the Standard VGA 640x480 (see Figure 29.4) and click **Next**.

11. If prompted to confirm the selection, click **Yes**.

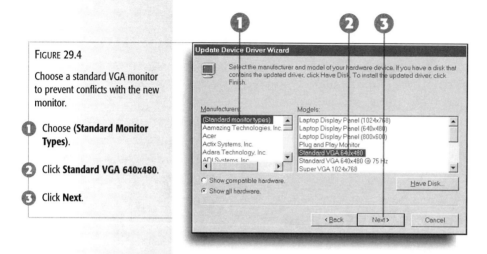

FIGURE 29.4

Choose a standard VGA monitor to prevent conflicts with the new monitor.

1 Choose (**Standard Monitor Types**).

2 Click **Standard VGA 640x480**.

3 Click **Next**.

Windows doesn't recognize the monitor

If Windows does not identify the new monitor and prompt you to install the driver, right-click the desktop and click **Properties**. Perform the same steps you took to change the monitor to Standard VGA, but click the **Have Disk** button and install the driver from the floppy disk or CD that came with the monitor.

12. Click **Next**.

13. Click **Finish**.

14. When prompted to restart your PC, click **Yes**. Windows shuts down and restarts using the driver for the standard VGA monitor.

15. Shut down Windows, disconnect your old monitor, and connect the new monitor.

16. Turn on your monitor and then turn on the system unit. Windows boots and displays a dialog box indicating that it has found a new device.

17. Follow the onscreen instructions to install the device driver that came with your monitor (on a floppy disk or CD).

SEE ALSO

➤ *Learn how to troubleshoot video problems, page 819*

Installing a Portable Disk Drive

Expand storage space without replacing your hard drive

Use swappable hard disks

Share a drive between two PCs

Back up to a portable disk

Quickly transfer large amounts of data between two PCs

Smart Shopping for Portable Storage Devices

The 3.5-inch floppy disk drive is all but dead. With hard drives exceeding 10GB and individual graphics files over 1MB, using a 1.44MB floppy disk to store documents or back up files isn't even a consideration. The only reason you haven't surgically removed the drive long ago is that every once in awhile you must install a driver or small utility from a floppy disk.

Because standard floppy disk drives have become so inadequate, many companies have rushed in to address the need for alternative portable storage devices—devices that use removable disks or cartridges. The good news is that these companies have developed some innovative products that can store gobs of data on a single disk. The following list describes the most common types of removable storage devices:

- *High-capacity floppy disks.* Special floppy disk drives can handle 2.88MB disks instead of the standard 1.44MB disks.

- *LS-120 and Zip disks.* Similar to floppy disks, these high-capacity floppy disks, an LS-120 can store up to 120MB on a single disk and can use standard 1.44MB floppy disks. Iomega Zip disks can store 100MB per disk but cannot read standard floppy disks.

- *Removable hard disks.* These hard disks are encased in plastic or metal cartridges, which you can insert and eject from the drive (see Figure 30.1). With capacities of 1–2GB and high-speed data transfer these drives function as additional hard drives and fast backup drives.

- *CD-R and CD-RW discs.* Recordable CDs are becoming more popular as removable storage media, allowing you to store up to 600MB on a single disc and access the files from a standard CD-ROM drive.

- *Tape backup drives.* High-capacity tape drives are excellent for backing up disks but lack the speed to make them useful for anything else.

The bad news is that the industry has still not agreed upon a standard, high-capacity replacement for floppy disk drives. In addition, there are so many products out there, it's difficult to figure out just what you need. The following sections help you choose a portable storage solution that's best for you.

FIGURE 30.1
The Iomega Jaz 2GB drive uses removable hard disks. (Photo courtesy of Iomega Corporation.)

SEE ALSO

➤ *Learn more about CD-RW drives, page 628*

➤ *Learn how to upgrade your hard drive, page 587*

Assessing Your Storage Needs

For what purpose are you going to use the drive? To back up your system? To share data with colleagues? To store presentations, video, or digitized photographs? To give your system more storage space?

Nobody seemed to be asking these questions when Iomega's Zip drive first came out. Customers flocked to the stores to hop on the Zip drive bandwagon, and PC manufactures started including them with their systems. Customers seemed to think that the 100MB disks would be great for backing up their systems. Few users considered the fact that these systems also came with 8GB hard drives, and they'd need a hefty stack of Zip disks for backups. A Zip drive offers the perfect solution for those who need to take work on the road or tote around a graphics-heavy business presentation to show to potential customers, but it's no backup drive.

The point here is that you must assess your needs and get a drive that serves the intended purpose. The following list provides some guidance:

- *Backing up your hard drive.* Get a high-capacity tape backup drive. Although slow, nothing can match the storage capacity and low cost of a good tape backup drive (see Figure 30.2). CD-RW drives also offer a practical, inexpensive solution that's somewhat more reliable.

- *Adding hard drive storage.* Don't fool around—upgrade your hard drive. Portable drives can't hold a candle to the speed and capacity of a real hard drive, and they're much more expensive. However, if you're determined to go portable and you need to do it with an external drive, install a SCSI drive. Drives that connect to the parallel port are slow.

- *Sharing data with colleagues.* Get together with your colleagues and pick a drive. One-upping your colleagues is playing the same game the manufacturers play and you achieve the same results: nobody can share anything.

- *Sharing data between two PCs.* Consider an external drive that connects to the parallel port. You can then disconnect the drive from one system and use it on another. This is a great solution taking work on the road if you have a notebook PC or transporting data between your home and office.

- *Storing presentations, photos, and video.* A Zip drive or similar type of drive is an excellent choice, but consider using a CD-R or CD-RW drive instead. Not only do you get a new CD-ROM drive, but you can make your own discs that run on any PC that has a standard CD-ROM drive. In addition, CDs rarely go bad.

- *Distributing data.* A CD-R drive is excellent for distributing data on CD. CDs are inexpensive and typically provide all the storage you need.

Multiple users

Fast, high-capacity removable hard disks can help alleviate some of the problems with PCs that are shared by several users. With 2–4GB removable disks, each user can store his or her own data and programs on a separate disk, reducing clutter on the main drive.

SEE ALSO

➤ *Learn how to transfer files between two PCs without using disks, page 306*

Capacity: The Primary Consideration

Don't let your budget decide the maximum storage capacity of a portable storage device. You will regret it. When I purchased my PC, it had a 700MB hard drive and a 100MB tape backup drive. I figured that using three or four tapes to back up a full drive wouldn't be so bad. I used the tape drive maybe five times before deciding to take my risks with not backing up.

When purchasing a drive, make sure it can handle at least your current needs, and then tack on a little extra for future needs. Again, you must consider the drive's intended purpose:

- *Backups.* Get a drive that can store the entire contents of a full hard drive on a single disk or tape. Backup utilities can compress the data, so the backup drive's capacity should be at least half of the hard drive capacity. If your hard drive is partitioned into smaller, logical drives, the backup drive should be able to store as much data on a single disk or tape as the *largest* partition can store.

Floppy disk drive replacement

If you're replacing your floppy disk drive with an LS-120 drive, you'll need to update your BIOS to boot from the LS-120 drive. If you have an older BIOS, it may not have a setting for LS-120 drives, in which case, you must update the BIOS.

- *Increasing storage*. If your hard drive is packed, you can move data or programs to portable disks. When you need to use the data or programs, just pop in the disk. Don't settle for less than 1GB per disk. This allows you to store several programs and a good chunk of data on a single disk, so you don't have to keep swapping disks.

- *Sharing data*. How large are the files you typically share? An LS-120 disk can store 120MB per disk and a Zip drive can store 100MB, which is usually sufficient.

- *PC-to-PC data transfers*. If you take work on the road, transfer files between the home and office, or swap files between your notebook and desktop PC, how much data do you usually swap? Again, an LS-120 or Zip drive is usually sufficient.

- *Presentations and large data files*. You'll rarely create a presentation that's over 100MB, but if it contains graphics or digital video clips, 100MB a single disk may be insufficient. Consider use a CD-R or CD-RW drive, instead. For higher larger, high-quality presentations, move up to a DVD-R drive.

SEE ALSO
➤ *Learn what upgrades your BIOS can handle, page 567*
➤ *Learn how to update your BIOS, page 571*

Budget Considerations

Comparing the prices of drives is obvious, but you must also consider the cost of the storage media. To obtain an accurate comparison, figure out the cost of storage per megabyte. Table 30.1 provides some ballpark figures. I threw the "Hard Drive" entry in there for comparison purposes.

TABLE 30.1 **Approximate cost per megabyte of data storage**

Medium	Capacity	Cost	Cost Per Megabyte
CD-R	640MB	$3	.5 cent
Backup tape	3.5GB	$35	1 cent

Medium	Capacity	Cost	Cost Per Megabyte
CD-RW	640MB	$14	2 cents
Hard drive	5GB	$200	5 cents
Jaz disk	1GB	$90	9 cents
LS-120	120MB	$12	10 cents
Zip disk	100MB	$13	13 cents
Floppy disk	1.44MB	50¢	34 cents

Speed

No removable drive can match the speed of an internal hard drive. However, speed issues, like most other issues described in this section, vary depending on the intended purpose of the drive. If you're using the drive to make unattended backups, speed is irrelevant; you're not going to sit around waiting anyway.

Speed for portable drives is linked closely with disk capacity. Floppy disk drive replacements, such as the LS-120 and Zip drives are relatively slow, CD-R drives are faster, and 1GB and 2GB are more in line with hard drive speeds. Drive manufacturers commonly list several speed ratings, including average seek time, data transfer burst rate, and sustained data transfer rate. Table 30.2 lists the approximate sustained data transfer rates for common portable drive types.

TABLE 30.2 **Drive speeds compared**

Drive Type	Sustained Transfer Rate
SCSI hard drive	10–40MBps
EIDE hard drive	11–33MBps
Quest or Jaz drive	8–10MBps
CD drive	150Kbps–4.8MBps
Zip drive	1–1.5MBps
LS-120 drive	300–500KBps

Future Compatibility Issues

The most annoying consequence of the computer industry's failure to agree upon a set of standards for removable storage devices is that every couple years, some new, revolutionary removable storage device comes out, making your current device obsolete. Not only do you have to replace your device, you then have to figure out some way to transfer your archived data to the new media. This means you must connect both drives to your system.

The only solution is to stick with an established storage technology and a company and product that have a good track record. When it's time to upgrade, check with the company to determine if they manufacture a device that is backward compatible with your current storage media.

Internal or External Drive?

Most of the drives described in this chapter offer internal and external models. Your choice depends on your answer to two questions: Does your system unit have an unoccupied drive bay? Do you need the drive for only one PC?

If you answer yes to both questions, and you don't plan on using the free drive bay for another drive, purchase the internal model. Internal drives are generally faster and more convenient and don't require any more space on your desk.

If you answer no to either of those questions, purchase an external drive. Most external drives plug into either the parallel port or a SCSI adapter:

- *SCSI.* If your PC has an open expansion slot, add a SCSI adapter card and buy a SCSI drive. The SCSI adapter provides a much faster connection and doesn't cause conflicts with your printer. However, this adds another $100 to your purchase.

- *Parallel.* If you need to use the drive on two or more PCs, you're on a strict budget, and you don't need a super-fast connection, get a drive that connects to the parallel port.

The parallel port connection is especially useful for sharing the drive with a notebook PC, on which a SCSI upgrade is not an option.

SEE ALSO

➤ *Learn how to install a SCSI hard drive, page 599*

➤ *Learn how to install a SCSI adapter, page 788*

Popular Removable Storage Devices

With standards up in the air and given the wide selection of removable storage devices, if I were to recommend a particular device, it would probably be obsolete by the time you read this. However, I can point you to the market leaders, and to some of the products that have the best reputations:

- *Iomega*. Iomega Zip drives are so popular that people have started calling any disk over 1.44MB a Zip disk. Iomega's Jaz drives (removable hard disk drives) are one of the best high-end removable hard disk drives on the market. And the Ditto drive is an excellent option for backing up large hard drives. Contact Iomega at www.iomega.com or 800-697-8833.

- *SyQuest*. Iomega's primary competition raised the limits for removable storage media. Its Quest drive, which stores over 4GB per cartridge offers double the capacity of Iomega's Jaz 2GB drive. Its EZ-Flyer stores up to 230MB on a single cartridge. Contact SyQuest at www.syquest.com or 510-226-4000.

- *Summatec*. Although Jaz and Quest drives offer high speeds and removability, Summatec's Mobile Drive offers the same at higher speeds. Summatec offers Mobile Drive as an EIDE device, so it connects to your system as a standard hard drive. The only difference is that you can eject the hard disk. Check out Summatec's product line at www.summatec.com or call 1-800-971-7713.

- *Imation*. Imation made its mark with the LS-120 drive. Developed by 3Com, the LS-120 is attractive as a floppy disk drive replacement. It can use both LS-120 disks

Another SCSI advantage

If you use SCSI drives, you can link several devices to a single port. If you upgrade to a removable storage device that is not backward compatible with your old removable disks, you can connect both drives to the SCSI port. You can even transfer your old archives to the new media.

(for storing up to 120MB) and 3.5-inch 1.44MB floppy disks. For more information about the LS-120 contact Imation at www.imation.com or call 888-466-3456 (see Figure 30.3).

FIGURE 30.3

A 120MB SuperDisk disk can store as much as 83 1.44MB floppy disks.

- *Sony*. Although better known for its consumer electronics products, Sony's computer products offer the same quality. Sony's offers the Spressa CD-R drives, DAT tape backup drives, and magnetic optical (MO) drives, which combine laser and magnetic technologies. For details about Sony's line of storage products, visit its storage page on the Web at www.ita.sel.sony.com/products/storage.

- *Avatar*. For notebook PCs, the Avatar Shark 250 is an excellent choice for backups and for transferring files between a notebook and desktop PC (get the parallel port model for this). You can check out Avatar's products at www.goavatar.com or call 888-462-8282.

- *Hewlett-Packard*. Hewlett-Packard is not only trying to place an HP printer on every desk, but also a recordable CD drive. Its HP SureStore is a CD-RW drive, which is excellent for backups and distributing data on CDs. You can record up
to 1,000 times on a single CD-RW disc. You can check out Hewlett-Packard's products at www.hp.com/go/cdr or call 800-810-0134.

Magnetic optical drives

Magnetic optical (MO) drives are a cross between hard drives and CDs. They read magnetic charges from the disks as do hard drives. However, when writing to the disk, a laser first passes over the medium to heat and soften it before the magnetic charge is applied. When the medium cools, it locks in the polarity of the medium. This gives MO disks a longer storage life than standard magnetic disks.

Installing Your New Drive

The installation procedure for your new drive depends on the type of drive you purchase. For instance, connecting a drive to a parallel port is more like plugging in a printer than installing a hard drive. The following sections explain the various installation procedures and highlight specific installation issues for the various drive types.

Plugging In a Parallel Port Drive

If you purchase a drive that connects to the parallel port, your installation is a snap. The drive typically comes with its own parallel cable and a pass-through device that allows you to connect your printer to the same port.

Installing a parallel port drive

1. With the PC's power off, unplug your printer from the parallel port.

FIGURE 30.4

A parallel port pass-through device allows you to connect your drive and printer to a single parallel port.

2. Plug the pass-through device into the parallel printer port (see Figure 30.4).

3. Plug the cable from the drive and your printer cable into the pass-through device.

4. Start your PC.

5. Install the software that came with the drive.

SCSI Drive Considerations

Installing a SCSI drive is almost as easy as plugging an external drive into the parallel port. However, because most PCs don't include a SCSI adapter and because SCSI allows you to connect several devices in a daisy-chain configuration, the installation can be a little more involved than connecting a cable. The following list explains some of the issues you may face along with references to sections that include more information about SCSI upgrades:

- If your PC does not have a SCSI adapter, you must install the SCSI adapter first.

- If you just installed the SCSI adapter for this drive, and no other devices are connected to the adapter, use a SCSI cable to connect the drive directly to the SCSI adapter's internal or external port. Make sure SCSI termination is on for the drive.

- If other devices are already connected to the SCSI adapter, use a SCSI cable to connect the drive to an existing SCSI device. Make sure SCSI termination is on for the drive, and turn off termination for the device to which you connected the drive. Also, check the address on the SCSI drive to ensure that no other SCSI device is using that address.

The actual step-by-step procedure is the same for installing any SCSI drive.

➤ *Learn how to set SCSI addresses and termination, page 635*

➤ *Learn how to install a SCSI drive, page 599*

➤ *Learn how to install a SCSI adapter, page 788*

Replacing Your Floppy Disk Drive

Replacing your floppy disk drive is a simple matter of removing your old floppy disk drive and inserting the new drive in its place. Mount the new drive right inside the bay vacated by the old floppy disk drive and use the same power supply and data cables that you disconnected from your old floppy disk drive.

Installing a Tape Backup Drive

A PC's motherboard typically has three outlets for connecting drives: a primary IDE, secondary IDE, and floppy disk drive controller. You can connect two hard drives to each IDE controller, but the floppy disk drive controller allows you to connect three drives. You plug one of the open connectors into the data port on the drive and connect the drive to the power supply.

Installing a tape backup drive

  1. Shut down your PC, unplug it, and remove the system unit cover.

SCSI/parallel port adapter

If you have no room inside your PC for a SCSI adapter, you can purchase a plug-in SCSI adapter for the parallel port. This type of pass-through device allows you to print and use your SCSI devices at the same time. However, the parallel port will severely limit the data transfer rate for your SCSI devices. Check for adapters at www.adaptec.com.

2. Touch a metal part of the case to discharge any static electricity.

3. Set any jumpers on the drive to match your PC's configuration. Check your system's documentation for the proper settings.

4. Pry off the cover plate for the drive bay you want to use from the front of the system unit.

5. Connect the data cable from the floppy disk drive controller to the data port on the back of the tape drive. Make sure the red line on the data cable aligns with pin 1 on the drive.

6. Plug a free connector from the power supply into the 4-pin power outlet on the back of the drive.

7. Slide the drive into the bay and secure it with the screws that came with the drive.

SEE ALSO

➤ *Learn how to back up files in windows, page 341*

Installing the Device Driver

The procedure for installing the device driver varies depending on the drive. If the drive came with its own installation instructions and setup utility, run the setup utility that came with the disk.

If the drive did not come with its own setup utility, when you restart Windows, it should identify the new drive and install the required device driver. If Windows does not install the driver, open the Control Panel, click **Add New Hardware**, and follow the Add New Hardware Wizard's instructions to install the correct driver.

SEE ALSO

➤ *Learn how to install a device driver in Windows, page 566*

Modems and Satellite Connections

Determine the best way to speed up your Internet connection

Compare modem speeds and costs

Check out DSL and cable modems

Weigh the advantages and disadvantages of a satellite connection

Install an internal or external modem

Install a modem driver in Windows

Crank up your Internet connection with DirecPC

Smart Shopping for a Fast Connection

For your PC to access the Internet or establish a connection with a remote computer or network, it needs a device that can receive and send signals. For many years, standard modems have served this purpose. However, with the increased popularity of the Web and the ever-increasing demands of media files, standard modems are fast becoming obsolete.

If you spend much time on the Internet, you want the fastest connection possible. But how do you strike a balance between performance and cost? The following sections help you decide.

Chugging Along with Standard Modems

Short for MODulator DEModulator, a modem converts incoming analog signals traveling through phone lines into digital signals that the PC can process. To send a signal, a modem converts the digital signal from your PC into an analog signal that can be transmitted over phone lines.

Modems transfer data at different speeds, commonly measured in *bits per second (bps)*. The higher the number, the faster the modem can transfer data. Common rates include 28,800bps, 33,600bps, and 56,800bps. Because these modem speed numbers are becoming so long, manufacturers have started to abbreviate them. You'll commonly see speeds listed as 33.6Kbps. When they start dropping the bps and list something like 56K, you know it's really fast. Although you pay more for a higher transfer rate, you save time and decrease your phone bill by purchasing a faster modem.

Some ads claim that the modem is *downward-compatible* (or *backward-compatible*). This means that if you connect the 56Kbps modem with a slower modem (say 28.8Kbps), the two modems can still communicate. Most modems are downward-compatible even if the ad doesn't say so.

The bottom line is that if you're buying a standard modem, you should look for a 56Kbps modem. But before you run out and buy one, you should know a few things:

Souped up dual-line modems

For some time, computer buffs have speeded up their Internet connections by hooking up two modems to their PCs. Now, some modem manufacturers have gotten into the game, offering dual-line modems. Diamond Multimedia offers a modem called Shotgun that links two 56K modems to support transfer rates of up to 112Kbps. Of course, you'll need two phone lines and two ISP accounts or an ISP that supports dual analog connections (such as Netcom at www. netcom.com). For details, check out www.diamondmm.com.

- *56K limits.* 56K pushes the limits of phone line communications. The phone company limits connection speeds to 53K, although there is some talk of raising the speed limit. You will rarely see data transfers at 56Kbps. Expect a maximum speed of about 40–45Kbps, and that's only when your modem is receiving data. A 56K modem still sends data at 28.8–33.6Kbps due to other limitations, such as line noise. Also, make sure your online service supports 56K connections.

- *x2 and 56Kflex and V.90.* x2 and 56KFlex are competing 56K standards. x2 was developed by U.S. Robotics (now 3COM), and 56KFlex was developed by Hayes, Lucent Technologies, Rockwell, and others. These proprietary standards were developed before ITU (the International Telecommunication Union) defined the standard for 56K modems as V.90. Before buying a 56K modem, find out which standard your online service supports. A 56KFlex modem can't connect at 56K to a 56K x2 modem.

- *ITU.* ITU is the international standard for 56K modems. If given the option of buying an x2, 56KFlex, or ITU, get the ITU. Because many modem manufacturers were making 56K modems following either the x2 or Flex standard before the ITU standard was finalized, you can upgrade most x2 and 56KFlex modems to the ITU standard by running special software. Contact your modem manufacturer or visit its Web site to obtain the required update. To help you translate the various ITU standards you see in ads, Table 31.1 lists the standards and the corresponding modem speeds.

Standard modems offer three benefits: the modem itself is inexpensive and easy to install, the modem plugs into a standard phone jack, and online services offer modem connections at bargain rates. However, for speedy Internet connections, consider the options described in the following sections.

TABLE 31.1   **ITU modem standards translated into speeds**

ITU Standard	Modem Speed
V.32	4800–9600bps
V.32bis	14.4Kbps
V.34	28.8Kbps
V.42bis	36.6Kbps
V.90	56Kbps

Speeding Up Your Connections with ISDN

Unlike standard modems that must perform analog-to-digital conversions, ISDN deals only with digital signals, supporting much higher data transfer rates: 128Kbps, more than twice as fast as 56K modems. ISDN modems use two separate 64Kbps channels, called *B channels,* that work together to achieve the 128Kbps transfer rates. This two-channel approach also allows you to talk on the phone while surfing the Web at 64Kbps; when you hang up, your modem can use both channels for PC communications. A third, slower channel (channel D) is used by the phone company to identify callers and do basic line checking.

Although ISDN may sound like the ideal solution for home and small-business use, add up the costs before your decide. You can expect to pay about $150–$300 for the ISDN adapter and $150–$200 for the phone company's installation fee (total=$300–$500). In addition, expect monthly charges from both the phone company *and* your Internet service provider. Phone companies typically charge about $30–$50 per month, and most ISPs charge $20–$30 *per channel* (for a total of $60–$110 per month).

Shop for the ISDN service before you shop for an IDSN modem or adapter and ask your phone company for recommendations. The performance of your ISDN connection relies on how well your ISDN adapter works with your phone company's connection. Many phone companies have a package deal that includes an ISDN. You must also choose the type of adapter you want:

Pre-fielding check

Before signing up for ISDN service, ask the phone company to perform a pre-fielding check to determine if the wiring in your home or office supports an ISDN connection. You may need to have your phone lines replaced.

- *External adapter.* External ISDN adapters (sometimes called *ISDN modems*) grab the digital signals from your phone company and stuff them through the serial port. If you have an older PC, the serial port may follow the 16550 UART (Universal Asynchronous Receiver-Transmitter) standard, which supports speeds only up to 115Kbps (10% slower than the top modem speed). To determine if your COM port supports UART 16650 or later, open the Control Panel, and click the Modems icon. Click the **Diagnostics** tab, click the COM port you want to check, and click **More Info**. You may need to install a high-speed COM port or, better yet, install an ISDN adapter card instead.

- *Adapter card.* An ISDN adapter card plugs into your PC's expansion slot, so it does not have the potential bottleneck you might experience with an ISDN modem.

- *Router.* A router allows you to connect several PCs to a single ISDN line. If you have a medium-size network, a router provides the perfect solution for multiple connections to an ISDN line. With smaller networks, there are other solutions, including external adapters that have two or more serial ports. You can also use a modem sharing program.

SEE ALSO

➤ *Learn how to use a modem sharing program, page 315*

After you've made the big decision on the general type of ISDN adapter you want to purchase, look for the following features to narrow the field:

- *Analog support.* If you use a modem on your notebook PC to dial into your desktop PC when you're on the road, make sure the modem supports 33–56Kbps modem connections. Look for adapters that have at least two analog ports, so you have one port for a phone line and another for a fax machine or other device.

- *NT1.* Short for Network Terminator, NT1 terminates the connection coming in from the phone company's ISDN center. If NT1 is not built-in to the ISDN modem, you must add it by attaching a box. Ads may list NT1 as a built-in *U-loop*.

- *Two serial ports*. If you purchase an external ISDN adapter, consider purchasing an adapter that has two serial ports. This allows you to share the device with another PC without having to set up a network connection. If you already have a network in place, this isn't a consideration.

- *Smart connection*. Some ISDN adapters are smarter than others and can switch to single- or dual-channel mode as needed. The Eicon Technology Diva adapter, for instance, can keep the ISDN connection live using the D channel to connect at 9,600bps. When you start cruising the Web and downloading files, it activates one or both high-speed channels. Because some ISPs base connect time charges on B-channel usage, this can cut down on your connect time charges.

- *Support for phone services*. Not all modems support caller ID, voice mail, and other phone services you might use.

- *BRI or PRI*. BRI is the standard 2-B channel service for individual use. PRI offers 23 B channels and is useful for small offices.

The New Kid on the Block: DSL Modems

Short for *digital subscriber line*, DSL promises to put a big dent in the ISDN market and challenge cable companies. Using standard phone lines, DSL can achieve data transfer rates of up to 1.5Mbps (9Mbps if you're within two miles of an ADSL connection center). DSL achieves these rates over standard, analog phone lines by using frequencies not used by voice signals. The only drawback is that DSL is a relatively new product (although the technology has been around awhile) and may not be available in your area or supported by your ISP.

As for costs, expect DSL to be slightly more expensive than ISDN, at least for the time being. The price of the modem itself could run as high as $900, although prices will surely drop over time to about $500. Monthly service charges from the phone company should be roughly equivalent to ISDN charges: about $50–$60 per month.

Because there is no single DSL standard, don't purchase a modem without first checking with your phone company. Most DSL providers market their service as a package deal and include a DSL modem that works with the service.

The Pros and Cons of Cable Modems

Like cable television connections, a cable Internet connection allows high-speed data transfers to your PC, allowing you to cruise the Internet at the same speed you can flip channels. In addition to speed, cable modems are relatively inexpensive (starting at about $200) and are easy to install. You can expect to pay about $60 per month for cable Internet access, which makes it competitive with ISDN service. However, cable modems do have a few drawbacks:

- *Availability*. Your cable company may not offer Internet cable service.

- *Variable connection speeds*. Cable service is set up to serve a pool of users. The more users that are connected to one service station, the slower the connection. Although cable companies commonly advertise 8Mbps data transfer rates, the rate you'll experience will likely be around 1–2Mbps.

- *Upload problems*. Cable was developed to bring signals into homes, not carry them out. However, cable companies are developing two-way systems to eliminate this limitation. If your cable service handles only incoming signals, you'll need to install a standard modem, too.

When shopping for a cable connection, the primary consideration is how the cable service handles return signals. Most services use either *telephone-return* or *RF-return*. With RF-return, the cable modem transmits signals along the cable. With telephone-return, the modem sends signals along a standard modem connection. Before you purchase a modem, check with the cable service to determine the type of return system it uses. Also, make sure the modem supports the communications standard that your service uses; this is typically MCNS (Multimedia Cable Network Service).

High-Speed Satellite Connections

If you're tired of waiting for the standards battles to cool off and the cable and phone companies to lay new cables in your neighborhood, move up to a satellite connection, such as DirecPC from Hughes Network Systems (www.direcpc.com or 1-800-347-3272).

DirecPC offers transfer rates of up to 400Kbps—three times faster than ISDN and seven times faster than 56K modems. And all you need to connect is the kit from Hughes Network Systems. As with all systems, however, DirecPC has its own shortcomings:

- *The kit is expensive.* $300 for the satellite dish and adapter.
- *The service is expensive.* $50 activation fee. Monthly rates vary: $30 per month for 25 hours, $50 per month for 100 hours, or $130 per month for 200 hours. Extra hours are billed at $2 per hour. (If you already have an ISP, rates are slightly lower.)
- *Clear line of site to satellite required.* If your house is nestled in a quaint wooded area or is surrounded by high-rises, you may have trouble aiming the satellite dish at the communications satellite.
- *Complicated installation.* You can hire out the installation for $100–$200. Otherwise, you'll have to mount the dish to the side of your house (or the roof), run BNC cable from the dish to your PC, and figure out how to point the dish at a satellite floating somewhere near the equator. And after you get all that working properly, you have to install a modem.
- *Modem required.* Because satellites send signals to your PC, you'll still need a modem and separate service provider to request data from the server and upload files. In short, you'll have to pay your regular ISP *and* Hughes.
- *Fair weather friend.* Satellite communications are susceptible to rain, lightning, and snow storms. In addition, satellites sometimes wobble out of orbit and interrupt the transmissions, meaning you must readjust the dish to point it at a

different satellite. For the most part, however, satellite communications are pretty reliable.

Despite these drawbacks, after you get your PC satellite dish up and running, you'll never want to go back to your 56K or ISDN connection again. Web pages pop right up on your screen without delay and large media files that used to take 15 minutes to download arrive in two minutes.

Installing an External Modem or ISDN Adapter

Installing an external modem or ISDN adapter is nearly as easy as plugging in a printer, although you must make the extra phone line connections. Before you start, make sure you have the appropriate modem cable and adapters for connecting the serial ports. In most cases, you use a 9-pin-to-25-pin serial cable. The 9-pin connector plugs into the 9-pin serial port on the back of your PC, and the 25-pin connector plugs into the 25-pin serial port on the modem. Some PCs have both a 9-pin and 25-pin port. If the 9-pin port is occupied (for instance, by a mouse), you can purchase a 9-pin-to-25-pin adapter to connect the cable to the 25-pin serial port on your PC. Also, make sure you have the proper male or female connectors; for example, if you have a 9-pin male adapter on your PC, the 9-pin cable connector must be female.

Connecting an external modem or ISDN adapter

1. Plug the serial cable into the 25-pin port on the modem or ISDN adapter. Figure 31.1 shows a typical 25-pin port on an ISDN adapter.

2. Plug the other end of the serial cable into the 9-pin or 25-pin serial port on your PC.

3. To connect a standard modem, plug the phone cord into the RJ-11 Line In jack on the modem and the other end into the wall jack for your phone. For ISDN, use RJ-45 connectors to connect the modem to the ISDN wall jack.

FIGURE 31.1

A typical external ISDN adapter.

1 Jacks for connecting a phone or fax machine

2 ISDN jack

3 25-pin data port

4 Power outlet

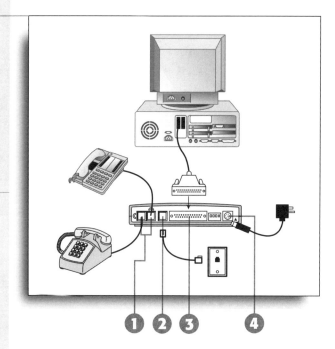

Surge suppresser

To protect your system from power surges, purchase a surge suppresser that has RJ-11 or RJ-45 jacks. Connect one cable from the wall jack to one of the jacks on the surge suppresser and run a second cable from the other jack on the surge suppresser up to your modem.

4. To share the phone line with a phone or fax machine, plug the phone or fax machine into the Phone jack on the modem, using a standard phone cable (with RJ-11 connectors).

5. Connect the power cable to the modem and plug the cable into a power outlet.

Installing an Internal Modem or ISDN Adapter

To install an internal modem or ISDN adapter, you must flip the hood on your system unit and insert the expansion card into one of your PC's expansion slots.

Unlike external modems that require a connection to the serial port, internal modems connect directly through the expansion bus, so you don't need a serial cable or power cable. If you're setting up a standard (analog) modem, use a phone cord (with

RJ-11 connectors) to connect the Line In or Telco jack on the modem with the phone jack on the wall. If you're setting up an ISDN adapter, use an ISDN cable (with RJ-45 jacks) to connect the ISDN-U port or NT-1 port with the ISDN wall jack.

To share the phone line with a phone or fax machine, plug another RJ-11 phone cord to the phone jack on the modem or adapter and into the jack on the phone or fax machine.

SEE ALSO

➤ *Learn how to install an expansion board, page 560*

Setting Up a Standard Modem in Windows

After you physically install the modem, you must install the modem driver and enter settings to tell Windows how to use the modem. The procedure is fairly straightforward, assuming everything goes according to plan, but Windows is notorious for installing the wrong modem driver.

When you start your PC after installing the modem, Windows should detect the modem and install a modem driver. Although Windows may install the wrong driver, go ahead and let Windows pick the modem for you. This ensures that Windows assigns a COM (communications) port for the modem that does not conflict with another COM port. You can then install the correct modem driver.

Changing modem drivers

1. Open the Windows Control Panel and click the Modems icon.

2. If the correct modem is listed, click **Close** or **Cancel** and stop here. If the wrong modem is listed, click its name and click the **Remove** button (see Figure 31.2).

3. Click the **Add** button. The Install New Modem dialog box appears.

4. Click **Next**. Windows scans your COM ports for a modem and picks the wrong modem again.

5. Click the **Change** button.

FIGURE 31.2

Use the Modems Properties dialog box to determine which modem is installed.

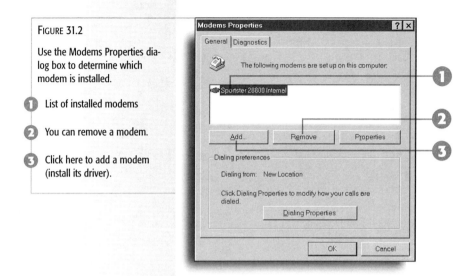

1 List of installed modems

2 You can remove a modem.

3 Click here to add a modem (install its driver).

6. Insert the disk that came with your modem and click the **Have Disk** button.

7. Click the **Browse** button and choose the drive and folder in which the modem driver file is stored. Click **OK**.

8. In the Install from Disk dialog box, click **OK**.

9. In the **Manufacturers** list, click the name of the modem manufacturer (see Figure 31.3).

FIGURE 31.3

Pick the modem manufacturer and model.

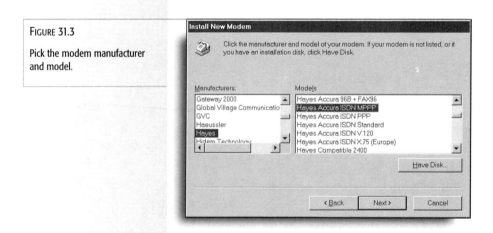

10. In the **Models** list, click the modem's name. Click **OK**.

11. Click **Next**. Windows indicates that it found the modem.

12. Click **Finish**.

SEE ALSO

➤ *Learn how to install a device driver, page 566*

Setting Up Your ISDN Adapter in Windows

After physically installing your ISDN adapter, you must install the device driver that came with it. Make sure your ISDN adapter is turned on and turn on your PC. Windows should identify the adapter and lead you through the process of installing the required device driver. If Windows fails to identify the device, run the Add New Hardware Wizard.

After the device driver is installed, run the setup program that came with your ISDN modem and enter the required connection settings. The procedure for entering the required settings varies from program to program, but all programs request the following information (supplied by your phone company):

- *Phone company*. In many cases, you select the phone company and enter your area code; the ISDN setup program enters the required connection settings for you. However, you should check the settings to be sure.

- *Switch type*. This entry specifies the software that the phone company uses for ISDN connections.

- *SPID*. Short for Service Profile IDentifier, the SPID identifies the type of ISDN service you're using. In most cases, this is a 14-digit number. The first ten digits typically match the DN (Directory Number) or phone number, and the last four digits specify the service type. You must enter a SPID and DN number for each 64-bit channel.

- *DN number*. Short for Directory Number, this is the phone number you must dial to connect to the ISDN service. In most cases, this is a 7-digit phone number, and the setup program may insert it automatically based on the SPID. Whatever the case, make sure you enter the number exactly as specified by your phone company.

After entering the required connection settings, you should enter preferences to control any additional features the ISDN adapter supports. For example, if the adapter supports smart switching between single- and dual-channel mode, you may have to turn on this feature.

If the setup program does not run you through the steps for creating a Dial-Up Networking connection to connect to your ISP, you'll have to set one up yourself. This can be a fairly complicated procedure, especially if you're using a protocol that requires you to dial a separate number for each channel. Refer to the ISDN adapter's documentation and work closely with your ISP.

SEE ALSO
➤ *Learn how to run the Add New Hardware Wizard, page 566*

➤ *Learn how to set up a Dial-Up Networking connection, page 396*

Installing a Cable Modem

The steps required for installing a cable modem are the same for installing any expansion board. After installing the card, use a standard BNC cable to connect the modem to the cable outlet installed by your cable company—this is just like connecting your TV set to the cable service.

When you turn on your PC and start Windows, it should identify the cable modem and lead you through the process of installing the required device driver. Be sure to install the driver that came with your cable modem; Windows may have its own driver, but it's probably outdated. If Windows fails to identify the device, run the Add New Hardware Wizard.

The connection to the cable service is less like a modem connection and more like a network connection. With a two-way cable connection, there is no Dial-Up Networking connection, no phone number to call. You install the required network protocol and use a network password to log on to the service.

However, you don't need to deal with entering the settings, because the cable guy is going to come to your house at the scheduled time (or one or two days later), test your current cable to ensure the incoming signal is of sufficient strength, and set up the connection for you.

SEE ALSO

➤ *Learn how to install an expansion board, page 560*

➤ *Learn how to run the Add New Hardware Wizard, page 566*

➤ *Learn how to enter basic network settings, page 291*

Installing DirecPC

Unlike other connection types, whose physical installation is fairly easy, installing DirecPC's satellite dish is the type of challenge that inspires material for sitcoms. Unless you have an area on the ground that has a clear site to the southern sky, you'll be lugging the satellite dish up to the roof and trying to figure out a good spot to drill a hole through your house.

The best solution is to hire a licensed, insured professional (typically for $100–$200). If that sounds like a lot of money, consider the disadvantages of doing it yourself:

- Unless you have a clear line of site between your home and the southern sky (no trees or buildings in the way), you'll probably be toting the satellite dish up a ladder.

- You'll need a compass and an angle finder to determine the general location of the satellite. And, you must know how to accurately read the angle finder and compass.

- You must run coaxial (BNC) cable from the satellite dish to your PC. You have two choices here: measure the distance and order a custom cable or purchase bulk cable and create your own custom length. Do you have a set of cable cutters? Coaxial cable strippers? A crimping tool?

- Pointing the dish directly at a satellite is tough. The satellite dish comes with its own program that displays the signal strength as you position the dish, but you need a helper to watch the screen and yell to you from inside.

- If you point the satellite properly and your PC doesn't pick up the signal, you'll need to test the BNC cable for continuity. If you don't have the test equipment, you'll be facing another $50–$80 for a continuity tester.

- Of course, there are other more obvious considerations, such as the possibility that you'll fry yourself on a power line, fall off the ladder, slip on the roof, drill through a power line or water pipe inside your house, or rip a couple shingles off your roof. Are those risks worth $100?

If you decide to go it alone, I strongly recommend that you purchase a DSS signal meter (for $50–$100). You take the signal meter up on the roof with you, connect it to the PC satellite dish, and then move the dish until it produces a signal of sufficient strength. You can then fine-tune the dish to get the strongest signal possible.

Although the installation procedure is much too involved to handle in a short section about DirecPC, the following steps provide an overview to show you what's involved.

Installing DirecPC

1. Install the DirecPC adapter card in an open ISA or PCI expansion slot, depending on the type of card and expansion slot you have.

2. Before you even think about installing the satellite dish, run the DirecPC setup program from the CD and enter billing information to set up an account.

3. Enter the requested settings for connecting to your current ISP via modem.

4. Pick the state and city in which you live, so the program can display settings to point the satellite dish in the general direction of the satellite (see Figure 31.4).

5. Using a compass and angle finder, find a place to mount the satellite dish that has a clear line of site to the satellite.

Azimuth and elevation

The two main adjustments you need to make when pointing the dish are azimuth and elevation. To adjust the azimuth, you rotate the dish from side to side. To adjust elevation, you pivot the dish up and down.

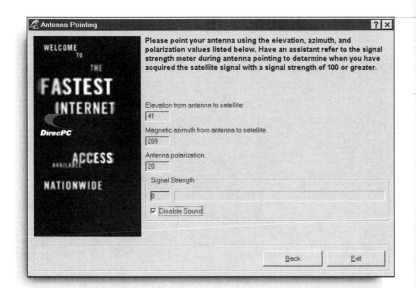

FIGURE 31.4

DirecPC indicates the approximate settings required to point the satellite dish at the satellite.

6. Mount the satellite dish and use the aluminum grounding wire to properly ground the dish.

7. Use a compass and angle finder to point the satellite dish in the general direction of the satellite.

8. If you have a DSS signal meter, connect it to the back of the satellite dish and adjust the dish to receive the strongest possible signal. If you don't have a DSS signal meter, skip this step.

9. Run coaxial cable from the satellite dish, through your home or office, and to your PC. Connect it to the DirecPC adapter card.

10. Assuming the satellite dish is pointed directly at the satellite, your screen should show that the satellite signal is sufficiently strong. If the signal is not strong enough, readjust the satellite until you receive a strong signal.

After the satellite dish is properly aligned, using DirecPC is a snap. Click the DirecPC Navigator icon on the Windows desktop. DirecPC establishes a connection with the satellite. You can then click the button for running your Web browser (shown in Figure 31.5).

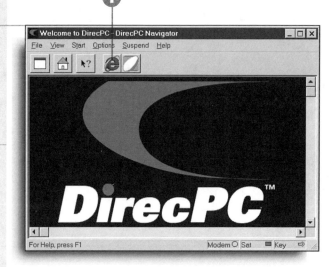

FIGURE 31.5

DirecPC Navigator establishes the satellite connection and lets you run your Web browser.

1 Click the button for your Web browser.

Installing a TV Tuner/Video Capture Board

Understand the differences between video capture devices

Set up your system for videoconferencing

Record video clips with a VCR or camcorder and save them as files

Tune in to TV stations with a TV tuner card

Use WebTV to flip channels on your PC

What's in It for You?

The hot new topic in the computer industry is *convergence*, the melding of PC, TV, audio, video, telephone, and other consumer electronics devices into a single technology. The idea behind convergence is to link the processing power of the PC with the input and output quality of video recording devices and entertainment systems.

This chapter focuses on the convergence of the PC with TV, video, and telephone. With the devices described in this chapter, you will be able to do some pretty cool stuff with your PC:

- Connect a video camera to your PC and talk face to face with people via modem.

- Record video clips and save them as files, so you can include them on your Web pages or attach them to email messages.

- Edit your own video tapes and record the edited clips to another tape or a CD or DVD disc. This is great for condensing months of family videos to a single hour of the best clips. If you have a CD-R or DVD-R, you can record the video clips to a disc for easy, inexpensive distribution.

- Use a TV tuner to attach your PC to your cable TV service or an antenna and watch TV shows on your PC. You can display shows full-screen or in a window (so you can watch TV at work).

- Output video to a standard TV screen instead of your dinky 15-inch monitor.

SEE ALSO

➤ *Learn about CD-R drives, page 628*

➤ *Learn more about DVD, page 623*

➤ *Learn about 3D graphics accelerators, page 641*

Smart Shopping for Video Capture Devices

You'll find more options for video capture hardware than for any other hardware category (modems run a close second). You can use anything from cheap parallel port adapters that capture low-resolution shots at 15 frames per second (fps) to professional, dedicated video capture boards that capture better-than-TV-quality video at up to 60fps.

If you need to capture a 20 second video clip to plop down on your Web page, you don't need a $500 video capture board to do it. Likewise, if you're planning on editing your family's home videos, a $99 QuickClip parallel port adapter isn't going to get you there. Before you purchase a video capture device, ask yourself what you plan on doing with the device and narrow the field. Table 32.1 provides some guidance, listing popular video capture devices from low end to high end.

TABLE 32.1 **Video capture options from low end to high end**

Intended Purpose	Cost	Video Capture Device
Video snapshots	$100	Snappy adapter captures any scene from a VCR, TV, or camcorder as a high-resolution still image.
Bargain motion video	$100	QuickClip allows you to record small, low-quality video clips from a VHS player or camcorder through a USB or parallel port. No expansion card needed.
Video conferencing	$150–$200	QuickCam, FlexCam and similar products consist of a small video camera that mounts on your monitor or desk and plugs into a USB or parallel port. High-end videoconferencing kits include a modem that supports video streaming.

continues...

TABLE 32.1 Continued

Intended Purpose	Cost	Video Capture Device
Moderate video recording	$200–$300	A plain-vanilla video capture board can handle the video while your sound card records the audio. However, the synchronization of video and audio may be a little off.
High-end video editing	$250–up	A high-quality video capture board that includes its own audio input, MPEG hardware support, and analog output for recording to tape is all you need for professional video recording and editing.
All-in-one boards	$300–$500	Why add three boards when one will do? All-in-one boards feature 3D graphics acceleration, video input, and TV tuner capabilities.

SEE ALSO

➤ *Learn how to use all-in-one video cards, page 647*

Budget Video

Your expansion bus is overpopulated, you just maxed out your credit card on the latest upgrade, you don't need full screen video, but you do want to capture some clips for your Web pages and email messages. The solution: use a parallel port video capture adapter. For less than $100, these adapters can capture high-resolution still images or short video clips at 15fps that run in a small frame on the screen.

Although these devices are simple, shopping for the right adapter can be complicated. For example, you might think that the $99 Snappy adapter, which has video input jacks for connecting to a camcorder, could record moving video. In fact, it captures a still image from a video tape and stores it as a high-resolution graphic. To record video, you need a more advanced adapter, such as QuickClip (also $99) that can capture video clips at up to 17fps. Following is a list of features to check for when purchasing a video capture adapter:

All-in-one

If your video recording needs are modest, go with an all-in-one video adapter, such as ATI's All-in-Wonder Pro. For about $300, you get a 3D graphics accelerator, TV tuner, and video capture board that plugs into a single PCI or AGP slot. You can then purchase a desktop digital camera or use your camcorder for input and purchase videoconferencing and video editing software separately, as needed.

- *Motion video*. Make sure the adapter can record at a rate no lower than 15fps.

- *Resolution*. No lower than 320X240. This is half the size of a standard 640X480 display. Any smaller and the clip will look as though it's playing on the back of a postage stamp.

- *Color*. Who wants grayscale?

- *Video playback*. If you want to record edited video clips onto another tape, make sure the device can play back video at 15fps or faster.

- *S-video input*. S-video divides the video signal into two parts: one for color and one for brightness. The S-video ports match up with those found on high-end VCRs and camcorders and produce higher quality video. Low-end units use a single, composite port.

- *Parallel pass-through port*. Without a pass-through device, you must disconnect your printer whenever you want to record video.

- *AC or keyboard power*. Some adapters come with an internal battery, which can be a bit of a hassle to replace. Other devices use their own AC power adapter or grab power from the keyboard or mouse port (you'll need to install a keyboard pass-through device).

- *Graphics formats*. For still images, the device should support TIFF, JPEG, and BMP—the more formats the better. The popular GIF format is rarely used because its 256-color limit is insufficient for most applications.

- *MPEG or AVI video*. For video, MPEG and AVI are the preferred formats. Lower-end devices support AVI, which are larger files. Look for devices that have built-in hardware support for MPEG compression rather than performing the compression via software.

- *TWAIN support*. Most word processing and desktop publishing programs allow you to import images into your documents using a TWAIN compatible device (typically a scanner). Make sure the device is TWAIN-compatible.

- *Software included*. You'll want some programs for touching up the captured images or editing the recorded video clips. The device should include a standard graphics editor. A morphing tool can also be a lot of fun.

Following is a list of the more popular video capture adapters for parallel and USB ports along with Web site addresses where you can learn more about each product:

- *Snappy*. If you only need to capture still images from video, Snappy is a steal at $100. Snappy Deluxe includes a good collection of software for touching up digital photos and morphing. Go to www.play.com for product information.

- *Zipshot*. Another frame-grabber device (like Snappy), Zipshot produces still images of slightly lower quality than Snappy. However, Zipshot offers some support for motion video at 8fps, has built-in parallel pass-through, runs off power from the keyboard port, and comes with a good collection of imaging software, including email support. For details, visit www.arcsoft.com.

- *QuickClip*. Although not as adept at capturing high-resolution still images, QuickClip supports video recording (moving pictures) for the same price as Snappy and for less than Zipshot. For information about QuickClip, visit www.connectix.com.

- *Video Sphinx Pro*. A couple rungs up the ladder from Snappy and QuickClip, Video Sphinx Pro has an on-board MPEG-1 encoder, making it superior for storing captured video clips in compact MPEG-1 files. Video Sphinx Pro supports audio and S-video input and includes advanced synch support to ensure that the sound and video match up; however, at $350, Video Sphinx Pro doesn't really fit in the budget video category. For that price, you can purchase an all-in-one card that includes 4MB video memory, 3D acceleration, and throws in a free TV tuner. For more information, visit www.futuretel.aa.psiweb.com (see Figure 32.1).

FIGURE 32.1
Video Sphinx Pro is a compact device that plugs into the parallel port on your PC.

- *Dazzle.* Not quite up to par with Video Sphinx Pro, Dazzle features an on-board MPEG-1 encoder, S-video and composite input ports, and parallel port pass-through. However, its lack of on-board audio support is a drawback. For details, visit www.dazzlemultimedia.com.

Dedicated Video-Conferencing Cameras

With faster modems and the availability of affordable, high-quality video cameras, video-conferencing over network and Internet connections is becoming more and more popular. You can now talk to people all over the world, face to face without paying long-distance charges, assuming, of course, that you and the other person have the proper hardware.

AVI-to-MPEG conversion

If you have an adapter that does not have built-in MPEG support, you can use a software utility to convert AVI files into compressed MPEG files. For a trial version of XingMPEG decoder, go to www.xing.com.

Do you need a digital video camera?

If you have a camcorder, you can hook it up to just about any video capture board and use it for videoconferencing. However, if you're looking for something smaller that you can leave on your desk, a digital camera is a good investment.

To videoconference successfully, the most important component is a high-speed Internet connection. If your system has a 28.8Kbps modem and a half-duplex sound card, audio and video signals will crawl through the lines like mud. Here's the supporting cast you'll need for serious videoconferencing:

- *V.80 Modem.* You need a video enabled V.80 modem (33.6K or 56K) or ISDN adapter. (V.80 is a modem standard for videoconferencing.) The modem should support both H.323 and H.324 standards. Both of these ITU standards set the rules for digital video transfer. These standards are intended to ensure that two people using different videoconferencing hardware can successfully connect. H.323 governs videoconferencing over the Internet and network connections. H.324 governs videoconferencing via POTS (plain old telephone system) using an analog modem, and has generated the latest wave of consumer-based videoconferencing products.

- *Full-duplex sound card.* A full-duplex sound card can process audio input and output at the same time, providing for smooth transitions while you and the other person talk. A half duplex sound card can do only one thing at a time: input audio or output audio. If you try to carry on a normal conversation (without long pauses), half duplex will drive you up a wall.

- *Speakers and microphone.* The sound card generates the audio output through the speakers and receives input from a microphone. Consider purchasing a headset or a microphone that clips onto your lapel to place the microphone closer to your mouth. Otherwise, the microphone is going to pick up a lot of background noise.

- *Powerful PC.* Most videoconferencing kits recommend 150MHz or 166MHz systems, because the processor is in charge of handling the compression.

When shopping for a videoconferencing kit, first consider the limitations of your system. If you have a 56Kbps modem or slower, shopping for a camera that spits out 30fps makes little sense; the modem will choke at that rate. With that in mind, here are the most important features to consider when shopping for a videoconferencing kit:

- *Resolution.* Expect maximum resolutions of 620X240. Having to shove all that video data down the telephone pipeline is a feat.

- *Frames per second.* Opt for a videoconferencing package that offers 15fps or higher. Some systems attain smooth video with less than 15fps, but if the number drops below 10fps, proceed with caution. (Depending on your modem, you may be lucky to see 5fps.)

- *Lighting adjustments.* Most videoconferencing cameras allow you to adjust the lighting and focus using software controls. Lower-end products may provide no controls, forcing you to manually adjust the lighting in your office.

- *Videoconferencing software.* For videoconferencing over the Internet or across network connections, Microsoft's NetMeeting and White Pine Software's CU-SeeMe lead the pack. For modem-to-modem video conferencing, most videoconferencing kits include third-party software from VDOnet or Smith Micro Software. Intel has released its own videoconferencing software, called Video Phone, which is available only on new videoconferencing-enabled PCs (you can't just go out and purchase a copy).

Following is a list of the more popular videoconferencing cameras and kits, along with a brief description of each:

- *BigPicture.* 3Com has one of the more interesting marketing schemes of the bunch, offering two BigPicture kits for $300. This marketing scheme reveals something important about the H.324 standard—modem-to-modem videoconferencing works best when both parties are using the same hardware. BigPicture consists of a Philips color camera with built-in microphone and a PCI video capture board, which performs much better than the parallel port adapters used in other kits. For information, visit www.3com.com.

- *SupraVideo*. Diamond Multimedia's entry into the videoconferencing market, SupraVideo ranks right up there with 3Com's BigPicture for quality and ease of setup. Like BigPicture, SupraVideo includes a PCI card and camera and the required videoconferencing software. For details, visit www.diamondmm.com.

- *QuickCam VC*. Connectix has bundled its popular QuickCam desktop video cameral with its VideoPhone software to create this videoconferencing kit. QuickCam VC supports both the H.323 and H.324 standards for Internet and modem-to-modem videoconferencing. For details, go to www.connectix.com. You'll need a full-duplex sound card and a 28.8Kbps modem (for Internet use) or V.80 modem for modem-to-modem connections.

- *EggCam*. Panasonic's EggCam gets its name from the egg-shaped digital camera included in the kit. EggCam's primary focus is video email. It includes a self-executing video player that you can attach to outgoing email messages. It also includes a copy of CU-SeeMe, one of the best Internet videoconferencing programs around. You can try to find information about the product at www.panasonic.com, but Panasonic's Web site can confound the most expert Web surfer.

Video Capture Boards

Video email

Video email is becoming more and more popular with the introduction of email programs that support HTML (such as Outlook Express and Netscape Messenger). You can slap a video clip right inside the message to add voice and video to your greetings…as if our inboxes aren't already packed.

The video capture devices discussed up to this point are low-end specialty devices designed for the budget-conscious consumer. If you're looking for a higher-end, general-purpose device, purchase a video capture board. A high-quality video capture board not only receives input from desktop digital cameras and standard camcorders and VCRs, but also provides analog output for recording to tape. These cards typically feature audio input and output as well, making them perfect for recording, editing, and playing back video clips.

Dedicated video capture boards plug into the expansion bus and specialize in capturing analog video and audio signals into a compressed, digital format. These cards can range from $300 to over $2000. When shopping for a video capture board, look for the following features:

- *S-video input and output.* S-video splits the video signal into two parts: color and brightness to create high-quality recordings. An S-video connector looks like a PS/2 keyboard or mouse plug and contains several pins. Composite video connectors look like speaker connectors.

- *Audio input.* Better video capture cards have an audio input jack for recording audio along with video. If you must record audio through a separate sound card, the audio and video is more susceptible to recording out of sync.

- *Analog-to-digital converter (ADC).* To process analog signals from a TV, VCR, or camcorder and store them in digital format for distributing on the Web or storing on CDs or other digital storage media, the card should have an analog-to-digital converter (ADC). Some video editing systems, such as Pinnacle's Studio 200 are excellent for editing video tapes and transferring the edited clips to another tape, but without ADC, your future options are limited.

- *Digital video compression hardware.* The key component in any video capture board is MPEG compression. Without compression, you can expect a 1-minute, high-resolution video clip captured at 30fps to come in at 1GB. That's way too much data for your PC to process and for your hard drive to store. MPEG compression can compress video up to 200-to-1, making files more manageable. High-end video capture boards for professional editing support Motion JPEG, a low-level compression scheme (20:1 ratio) that keeps each frame intact for later editing.

- *PCI or AGP bus connection.* For high-powered video capture, a parallel or USB port adapter can't handle the job. Make sure the board plugs into a PCI or AGP expansion slot and that your PC has an unoccupied slot.

- *Compatibility.* Make sure the capture board is compatible not only with your expansion slots but also with the video equipment you're using. For example, if you're going to use an 8mm camcorder or a VHS player, make sure the capture board supports input from the device.

For $500 to $1000, you can purchase a high-quality video capture board that includes the cables and software required to transform your PC into a video editor. Following is a list of video capture kits you should check out when you go shopping:

- *Pinnacle Systems miroVideo.* An excellent choice for quality and convenience, miroVideo consists of a PCI card and a breakout box that contains the audio and video input and output jacks. The breakout box plugs into a port on the PCI card, so you don't have to reach around the back of your PC to connect devices. miroVideo captures at up to 30fps and includes jacks for both video input and output and audio input and output. For more information about miroVideo and other video capture products from Pinnacle, visit www.pinnaclesys.com.

- *Data Translation Broadway.* Broadway is one of the easiest video-capture and editing systems to use. Designed for digital video and VCR recording, Broadway Beginner provides a PCI video capture board with MPEG compression and user-friendly software for editing clips. The professional edition supports video streaming for real-time Web broadcasts. The only drawback is that Broadway does not include audio capture capabilities; you capture audio through your sound card. For details, visit www.datatranslation.com.

- *Matrox Rainbow Runner Studio.* One of the more popular video capture boards, Rainbow Runner is actually an add-on board (daughterboard) for the Matrox Mistique video adapter. Together and combined with a TV tuner add-on, the boards actually qualify as an all-in-one video card. Rainbow Runner supports both Motion JPEG and MPEG video compression and includes software for controlling resolution and frame rates. For details, visit www.matrox.com.

- *Fast Multimedia AV Master.* Fast Multimedia markets professional-grade video capture hardware, including AV Master.

A bit pricey at just under $1000, AV Master captures at resolutions up to 640X480 and 30fps. However, a SCSI hard drive is required for fast data transfers to disk. Find out more at www.fastmultimedia.com.

SEE ALSO

➤ *Learn more about FireWire, page 785*

Setting Up Your Audio-Video Equipment

Installing a video capture board is like installing any expansion board. You'll also have to install the device driver for the board. After you've installed the board, you can focus on connecting your video input and output devices.

SEE ALSO

➤ *Learn basic installation procedures and tips for circuit boards, page 560*

➤ *Learn how to install the device driver for the circuit board, page 566*

The audio and video connections vary depending on the video capture card, the cables that were included with it, and the audio-visual equipment you need to connect:

- Most video capture boards have a single A/V Input jack for audio and video input. You'll need a *four-headed input adapter* to make the necessary connections. This adapter contains a single plug for the A/V Input jack on your video capture card and four cables for connecting to the camera: one for left audio, one for right audio, one for S-video, and one for Composite video. You use either the S-video or Composite video connector depending on the camera (see Figure 32.2). (S-video produces higher quality recordings.)

- If your video capture card has an A/V output port, you can connect the card to a VCR to record to tape or a TV set that has RCA jacks. To make the connections, you need an adapter that plugs into the A/V output port on the video capture board and has the proper connectors for the S-video In or Composite In jacks on your VCR or TV set. If the card does not support audio output, you must connect it to the Line In jack on your sound card (see Figure 32.3).

All digital

Recording to VHS tapes is becoming obsolete. The latest video capture and editing equipment is pure DV (digital video). Using the same technology used in digital camcorders, DV capture devices record video and audio signals on hard disks, CDs, or DVDs. Many of the newer DV recorders support FireWire connections for faster, more reliable input.

FIGURE 32.2

Use the proper cables to connect the video player to the A/V In port on your video capture card.

1 Video player

2 A/V In port on video capture board

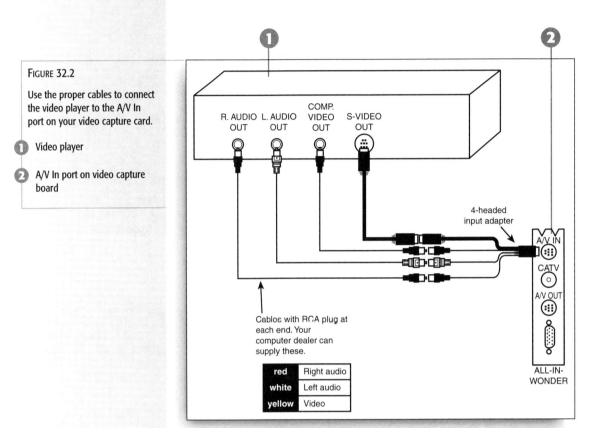

- If you're setting up for videoconferencing, you may need to replace you modem with a V.80 modem. Connect your camera to the Video In port on the video capture card or to the parallel or USB port. If the camera has a built-in microphone, you may need to plug it into the Line In jack on your sound card.

SEE ALSO

➤ *Learn to install an internal modem, page 682*

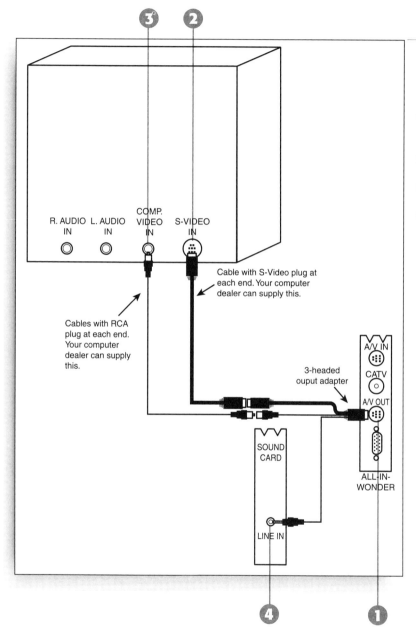

Cable with S-Video plug at
each end. Your computer
dealer can supply this.

Cables with RCA
plug at each end.
Your computer
dealer can supply
this.

A/V IN

CATV

A/V OUT

ALL-IN-
WONDER

3-headed
ouput adapter

SOUND
CARD

LINE IN

FIGURE 32.3

Some video capture cards allow
you to output recorded clips to a
TV set or VCR.

1 A/V Out port on video capture
card

2 S-video in on TV or VCR

3 Composite Video In on TV or VCR

4 Audio output to Line In jack on
sound card

Using Your Video Capture Device

After you've installed the video capture board and made the necessary cable connections, you can start to use your equipment to videoconference, capture video clips from tape, record video using a camcorder or digital desktop camera, and transfer your recorded video clips to tapes or CDs.

The following sections introduce you to the world of digitized audio by showing you the possibilities. However, the actual steps vary depending on your audio-video equipment and on the videoconferencing and video capture software you use.

Videoconferencing

There are three ways to videoconference—over the Internet, over a network connection, or by way of a modem-to-modem connection:

- To conference over the Internet, you log on to a central server, which displays a list of people you can call. You select the person from the directory or enter the person's logon name or email address. With your videoconferencing setup, you can talk to the other person and send live video. If the other person has a digital camera, you can see the person. Otherwise, you receive only audio.

- Videoconferencing over network lines is similar to videoconferencing over the Internet. You can even use the same videoconferencing software, such as Microsoft NetMeeting. The two main differences are that the connection is much faster and you place your call by typing the person's network logon name or the name of the person's computer. (See the step-by-step instructions following this list.)

- Modem-to-modem videoconferencing is a more private affair. You use your modem and videoconferencing software to dial another person's modem directly. Assuming the other person's modem answers the phone (and both systems use compatible software), you can talk face to face.

To get a feel for what's involved in videoconferencing, read through the following step-by-step instructions for using NetMeeting to call someone on the Internet. Because NetMeeting is included with Internet Explorer, you may want to perform the steps to get some hands-on experience.

Setting up NetMeeting

1. Click the **Start** button, point to **Programs**, **Internet Explorer**, and click **Microsoft NetMeeting**.

2. Click **Next**.

3. Open the directory server list and choose the server that the people you want to call will be using. (If you're not sure, leave the current selection.) Click **Next**. NetMeeting prompts you to enter information about yourself.

4. Type the requested information. The **First Name**, **Last Name**, and **Email Address** entries are required. Click **Next**.

5. Click the option that best describes how you intend to use NetMeeting: personal, business, or adults-only use. Click **Next**. NetMeeting prompts you to specify your connection type.

6. Choose your modem speed or ISDN (if you are using an ISDN modem), or, if you are using NetMeeting on a network, choose **Local Area Network**. Click **Next**. NetMeeting prompts you to choose the video capture device you want to use (see Figure 32.4).

What's an ILS?

An ILS is a telephone directory for NetMeeting. You can open the ILS to view a list of people who are connected to a specific ILS server. To call the person, you select his or her name from the list. Without the ILS, you have to enter his or her email address to call the person.

FIGURE 32.4
NetMeeting prompts you to choose the video capture device.

7. Assuming you have only one video capture device installed, click **Next**. NetMeeting connects to the server and displays a list of people currently connected. You can now place a call. NetMeeting displays a message telling you to close any programs that record or play audio.

8. Close any programs, as needed, and click **Next**. The Audio Tuning Wizard appears.

9. Click the **Test** button to make sure your sound card and speakers are working. NetMeeting sounds a beep. If the beep is too loud or too soft, drag the **Volume** slider to adjust the volume. Click **Next**. The wizard displays a bar showing the recording volume.

10. Speak into your microphone while watching the bar. The bar should expand to the right as you speak. If the bar does not extend past the halfway port mark, use the **Record Volume** slider to increase the volume. Click **Next**. The wizard indicates that you have successfully set up NetMeeting.

11. Click **Finish**.

Placing a videoconference call

1. Click the Directory icon in NetMeeting's Navigation bar.

2. Open the **Server** drop-down list, and select the ILS you want to use to find people. NetMeeting logs on to the server, and displays a list of all the people on the server (see Figure 32.5). If a red asterisk appears in the left column, the person is already participating in a call. Additional icons indicate whether the person is using an audio or video connection.

3. To filter the list, you can choose an option from the **Category** drop-down list. For example, you can choose to view a list of only those people who are not participating in a call.

4. Scroll down the list, and then double-click the person's name or right-click the person's name and select **Call**.

5. When you place a call, a dialog box pops up on the screen of the person you called, and their computer "rings." If the person you called wants to talk with you, she clicks the **Accept** button, and you can start talking (see Figure 32.6).

FIGURE 32.6
After you are connected, you can start talking.

6. To adjust the display, choose **Tools**, **Options,** click the **Video** tab, and enter your preferences (see Figure 32.7).

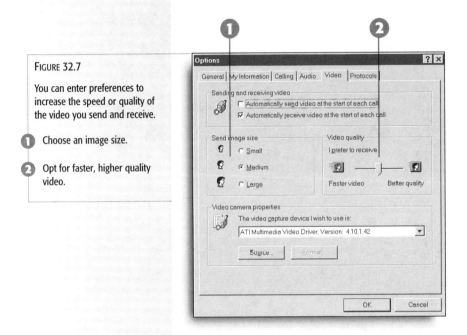

FIGURE 32.7

You can enter preferences to increase the speed or quality of the video you send and receive.

❶ Choose an image size.

❷ Opt for faster, higher quality video.

7. Click the **Source** button to adjust the image brightness and color. Enter your preferences for brightness, contrast, color, and tint (see Figure 32.8).

8. When you finish talking, click the **Hang Up** button in the toolbar.

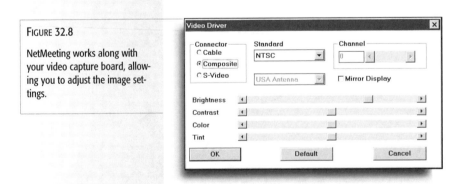

FIGURE 32.8

NetMeeting works along with your video capture board, allowing you to adjust the image settings.

Recording Video Clips

Video capture boards perform two main functions: They transform analog video (from tape or directly from a camcorder) into digital video and they output digital video to analog devices, such as VCRs, camcorders, and TVs. You can take advantage of these capabilities to perform the following real world tasks:

- Include digital video clips on your Web pages and in email messages.
- Use video clips in your electronic presentations, created with tools such as PowerPoint.
- Edit your own video tapes to remove some of the less interesting material, and save the highlights to a new tape.
- Transform your home movies from bulky video tapes to CDs or DVDs.

Although you can spend a great deal of time editing and touching up video clips, the actual capture process is fairly easy. Before you start capturing video from tape, take a few preliminary steps:

- Rewind the tape and zero out the counter on your player.
- Fast-forward to the section you want to record and write down the number on the counter so you can quickly go to that segment later.
- Fast-forward through the segment and write down the number on the counter to indicate where it ends.
- Adjust brightness, contrast, color and other settings in your video capture program before you start recording (see Figure 32.9).

Capturing video from tape

1. Run your video capture program.
2. Fast-forward your video tape to just before the beginning of the segment you want to record.
3. Hit the Play button on your VCR or camcorder and when you reach the segment you want to tape, press Pause.

FIGURE 32.9

Adjust the display settings for
your capture program before you
start recording.

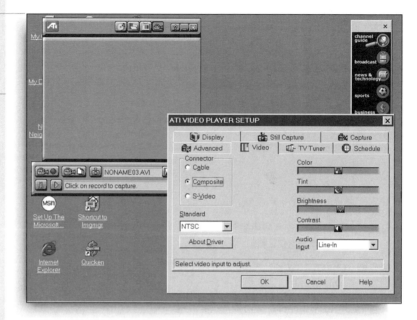

4. In your video capture program, click the button to start
    recording. The program typically displays a dialog box with
    a button for initiating the recording process.

5. On your VCR or camcorder, press the Play or Pause button
    and click the button in the video capture program to initiate
    recording (see Figure 32.10). (Getting the timing right on
    this is tricky.)

FIGURE 32.10

Start playing your video tape and
click the Record button.

6. At the end of the clip, click the video capture program's **Stop** button and press the Stop button on your VCR or camcorder.

7. Save the clip and name it.

Outputting Digitized Clips to Tape

To record a series of clips, first make sure you have your recording device and media in place. Connect the VCR or camcorder to the A/V out port on the video capture card and load a tape in the VCR.

Most video capture programs store each clip as a separate file. To transfer these clips to tape, create a list of the files you want to record in the order in which you want them recorded (see Figure 32.11). When you're ready to record, press the Record button on your VCR and click your video program's **Play** button.

Huge files

Video files are huge. To avoid bogging down your hard drive with these large files, consider purchasing a removable hard drive or CD-RW drive. Zip drives are especially useful for storing small amounts of video data.

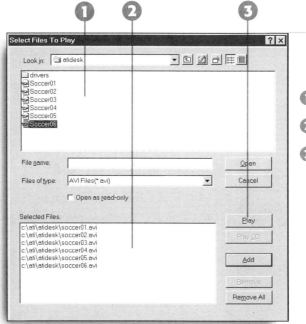

FIGURE 32.11

Create a list of the clips you want to record.

❶ Available video clips

❷ List of clips that will play

❸ When you're ready to record, click **Play**.

Watching TV on Your PC

TV tuners are inexpensive devices that people rarely purchase as separate cards. It just doesn't make sense to fill a valuable expansion slot on your PC with a card that lets you watch TV. However, a TV tuner feature on an all-in-one video card is a valuable (or at least fun) addition. With a TV tuner, you can pull TV stations into your PC via cable or satellite and watch CNN during your lunch break.

To use your TV tuner, first connect its CATV port to a cable connection or amplified TV antenna, just as you would connect a TV set.

Installing WebTV

Although your TV tuner probably came with its own program for flipping stations, Windows 98 includes WebTV, an excellent program for flipping channels and controlling the TV window. WebTV also allows you to download programming information from the Web, placing a TV guide right on your screen, where you'll never misplace it.

WebTV is not installed during a typical Windows 98 installation. Use the Add/Remove Programs utility in the Windows Control Panel to install WebTV.

SEE ALSO

➤ *Learn how to install WebTV, page 204*

Flipping Channels with WebTV

After WebTV is installed, click the Launch WebTV icon in the Quick Launch toolbar to run it. WebTV runs through the standard introductory screens to welcome you to WebTV and explain some of its features. At the end of the introduction, WebTV prompts you to scan for channels. Click the **Scan** button. WebTV flips through the available stations and adds the numbers for any stations that provide signals of sufficient strength (see Figure 32.12).

To preview a channel, click its number. WebTV displays the program in a small box in the upper-right corner of the screen. To display the channel in its own window, click <u>W</u>**atch**.

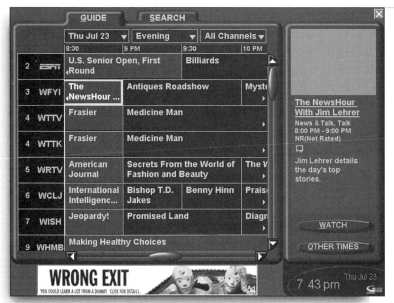

FIGURE 32.12

WebTV displays an electronic channel changer.

① Click a channel to preview the program.

② The program preview area.

③ Click **Watch** to display the program in its own window.

④ Windows can download a TV guide.

Replacing or Adding an Input Device

Consider alternatives to the standard keyboard and mouse

Find comfort and power in a new keyboard

Doodle with a pen-based input device

Shop for a top-notch game controller

Make your PC follow verbal commands and take dictation

Why Upgrade Your Keyboard or Mouse?

When you upgrade your PC, you typically consider every component but the one you use most—the input device. You're more concerned with beefing up disk space and memory, souping up your processor, and trying to extract the highest quality output from your monitor and printer. Your old keyboard and mouse are so familiar that they go almost unnoticed.

However, when you're measuring overall productivity, your efficiency matters as much as your PC's, perhaps even more. If you keep overshooting icons with your mouse or continually moving your hand from the mouse and keyboard and back, the seconds you waste decrease your productivity. In addition, those repetitive movements are unhealthy, leading to carpal tunnel syndrome and general discomfort.

Over the years, the computer industry hasn't given us much to choose from: wavy keyboards, a few extra shortcut keys, second-rate voice recognition software, and quirky touchpads that took us three steps back on the road to progress.

Fortunately, manufacturers have come up with some more innovative input devices designed both for efficiency and comfort. Improvements in voice-activated systems, better ergonomic designs, and self-calibrating devices promise to make computing a little more comfortable and efficient. This chapter introduces you to some of the better input devices and tells you which ones to avoid.

The Comfort and Power of a New Keyboard

Sit down in front of your keyboard and rest your fingers on the home keys as you normally do. Now, try to notice all the adjustments *you* have to make to accommodate the keyboard:

- Your forearms probably reach in at a 35- to 45- degree angle instead of being perpendicular to your torso (as they should be), and your wrists bend back to make your fingers align with the keys.

- Your forearms rotate 90 degrees to make your fingers parallel to the horizontal (flat) keyboard.

- Your wrists bend up slightly to reach from the desk to the keys.

The experts tell you to adjust your chair so that your hands float over the keys, but have you ever tried to do that? With your chair up that high, your knees bump the desk, and you have to hang your head down to look at the monitor. Besides, a chair adjustment helps only with the problem of your wrists bending *up*. It does nothing for the problem of having to reach inward and bend your wrists to the sides.

The best ergonomic keyboards adjust to your position. I have a Lexmark keyboard that separates into two separate halves; I place each half even with my shoulders, so I don't have to reach in toward the keyboard. I can also tilt each side up so I don't need to rotate my wrists. Standard split keyboards, such as the SmartBoard (see Figure 33.1) fan the keys on an angle to reduce wrist strain. (Lexmark no longer manufactures keyboards. To learn more about the SmartBoard, check out www.darwinkeyboards.com.)

FIGURE 33.1
A split keyboard reduces the strain on your wrists.

In addition to comfort, a keyboard should help you work efficiently, requiring you to press as few keys as possible to enter common commands. Most newer keyboards, for example, have a Windows key that you can press to perform common tasks, such as opening the Windows **Start** menu, run Windows Explorer, and find files (see Table 33.1).

TABLE 33.1   **Windows key shortcuts**

Press	To
Windows+Tab	Cycle through buttons on the taskbar
Windows+F	Search for files
Ctrl+Windows+F	Find a computer on your network
Windows+F1	Display help
Windows+R	Display the Run dialog box
Windows	Open the **Start** menu
Windows+Break	Display the System Properties dialog box
Windows+E	Open Windows Explorer
Windows+D	Minimize or restore all windows

When buying a new keyboard, follow two simple rules: never buy a keyboard without first typing something on it and don't overlook the obvious. You should like the click and feel of the keys, and the keyboard should be roomy enough for your fingers. Don't buy a space-saving device just to open up a couple inches on your desk.

If money is no object, check out DataHand Professional II (www.datahand.com). For a mere $1000, this "keyboard" consists of two sections contoured to the shape of your hands and mounted to a desk that sits in your lap. Because your fingers are always over the home keys, you don't have to deal with typos caused by having your fingers over the wrong keys.

SEE ALSO

➤ *Learn how to connect a keyboard to your PC, page 50*

Go wireless with infrared?

I'm not a big fan of infrared devices in their current state. They're pretty quirky and if your desk is as cluttered as mine, you have plenty of objects to break the "direct line of sight" required to make them work. If you must go wireless, get a device that's controlled by radio frequency signals; these devices do not require a direct line of sight.

Building a Better Mouse

I have worked with just about every pointing device on the market, and I stand by my old two-button mouse. Touchpads are overly sensitive to the natural moisture and heat of your fingers, trackballs make it tough to drag objects accurately, and pen-based pointers are just too difficult to keep lifting and setting back down.

However, if you're tired of picking hairballs out of your mouse or your desk is too small (or too cluttered) for rolling around a mouse, consider a more stationary device, such as a trackball or touchpad:

- On some newer trackballs, the buttons are in more convenient locations, making it easier to drag. Look for a trackball that has buttons at the sides or front rather than under the palm of your hand. Logitech (www.logitech.com) manufactures a wide selection of innovative designs (see Figure 33.2).

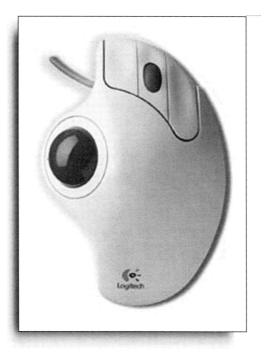

FIGURE 33.2
Logitech makes a wide selection of innovative trackballs. (Photo courtesy of Logitech.)

■ Touchpads have no place on a keyboard, where flailing fingers are apt to accidentally tap the pad and send the mouse pointer scurrying across the screen. However, when set off from the keyboard, they're much more useful. Make sure the touchpad offers pressure-sensitive dragging, so you can drag with one hand instead of having to hold down a button with the other hand. Cirque (www.cirque.com) is one of the leading manufacturers of quality touchpads (see Figure 33.3).

FIGURE 33.3

Touchpads save space on your desktop and let your fingers do the walking.

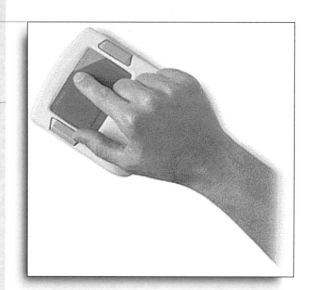

New, improved mouse pads

If you think a mouse pad is just a cutesy decoration for your desktop, check out the 3M Precise Mounting Surface, a textured mouse pad that cuts down on the distance you need to drag the mouse and provides for more precise mouse pointer movement. For more information, go to www.mmm.com.

If you're just looking for an improved mouse, try the Microsoft IntelliMouse. This mouse has a wheel between the left and right buttons that allows you to scroll without using a scrollbar:

■ Rotate the wheel forward to scroll up or backward to scroll down.

■ To pan up or down, click and hold the wheel while moving the mouse pointer in the direction of the text that you want to bring into view.

- To autoscroll up or down, click the wheel, and then move the mouse pointer up (to scroll up) or down (to scroll down). Autoscrolling remains on until you click the button again.

- To zoom in or out, hold down the Ctrl key while rotating the wheel. Rotate forward to zoom in or back to zoom out.

SEE ALSO

➤ *Learn how to connect a mouse to your PC, page 48*

Point, Draw, and Write with Pens and Pads

For some tasks, such as drawing and editing, nothing provides the precise control of a simple pen or pencil. Pen-based devices typically consist of a pressure- or light-sensitive pad and a pen. You can use the pen and pad as a touchpad to perform basic mouse movements, such as pointing, clicking, and dragging. In addition, you can use the pen to draw, sign faxes, and write comments on documents. Some devices even include handwriting recognition software to transform your handwritten notes into typed text.

If you're interested in pen-based pointers, your first stop should be Cross Pen Computing Group at www.cross-pcg.com. Here, you'll find information about the iPen and iPen Pro. Both devices include a pad and pen, but the iPen Pro includes additional features for annotating and signing documents.

Joysticks and Other Game Controllers

When you're fighting bad guys and trying to negotiate air space with enraged aliens, you need a control stick that responds to your every move. You'll find plenty to choose from—everything from the standard joystick to virtual reality goggles and gloves.

When shopping for game controllers, your choice depends more on the games you want to play than on the actual controller. For any type of game that requires flight, joysticks are still the controller of choice. Just make sure you purchase a digital joystick. Older, analog joysticks require regular recalibration and don't respond as precisely to your moves.

For more specialized game play, check out the following devices:

- *Driving wheels.* If driving the NASCAR circuit, transform your PC into a virtual racing car with the ThrustMaster NASCAR Pro Racing Wheel, complete with steering wheel and pedals (see Figure 33.4). For more information, go to www.thrustmaster.com.

FIGURE 33.4

Thrustmaster features a wide selection of game controllers, like the NASCAR Pro Racing Wheel shown here. (Courtesy of ThrustMaster, INC.© & ™ 1997. All rights reserved NASCAR™ is a Licensed Trademark of NASCAR Racing League USA.)

- *Flight controllers.* For the best flight controllers, check out Thrustmaster and Saitek (www.saitekusa.com). Saitek's X36 Ultimate Flight Controller includes both an ergonomic joystick and throttle, each with plenty of buttons and adjustments to help you configure the controller for comfort and responsiveness.

■ *Play stations*. If you're a serious gamer and willing to shell out $800 for a thrill, take a look at Rock-N-Ride. Rock-N-Ride is a cockpit complete with seat and monitor stand that tilts up to 55 degrees as you move the joystick. Rock-N-Ride comes with its own air compressor that tilts you and your equipment as you move the joystick to give you a real feel for the game. For details, go to www.rocknride.com.

■ *Virtual visors*. If you've strapped on a virtual reality visor at the local arcade (and liked it), you'll be happy to hear that you can purchase one of these game visors for your home. One of the best is the Philips Scuba Virtual Immersion Visor (www.scubafx.com). Scuba connects to most multimedia devices, including DVD players, VCRs, dedicated game machines, and PCs that have NTSC (TV) output (see Figure 33.5).

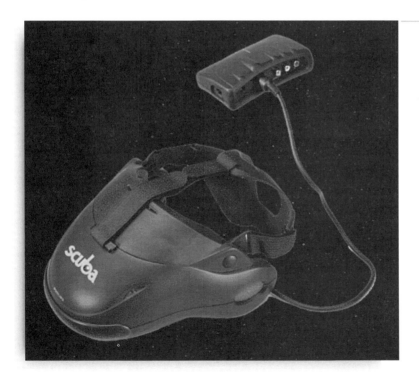

FIGURE 33.5

Philips Scuba Virtual Immersion Visor lets you strap on the game controller.

Connecting a Game Controller

Although some game controllers come with their own expansion card, most plug into the MIDI/game port on your PC or sound card. If you have more than one controller, consider purchasing a controller switch. The switch plugs into the game port on your PC and has a box with multiple game ports. To switch from one controller to another, you press the trigger on the device you want to use. Check out the Joystick Switchbox from CH Products (www.chproducts.com). If you have only two controllers, purchase a Y-cable.

CH also markets a two-game-port expansion card that allows you to adjust the speed of the port to match the speed of your controller. If your PC's game port is too slow to handle the latest games, you really should consider upgrading your game port.

SEE ALSO
➤ *Learn how to upgrade your game port, page 783*

Calibrating Your Joystick in Windows

Installing a joystick is fairly easy. You plug it into the game port and use the Add New Hardware Wizard to install the joystick driver. However, making your joystick behave requires calibration. (If you have a digital joystick, it calibrates itself.)

Calibrating your joystick

1. Click **Start**, **Settings**, **Control Panel**.

2. Click the **Game Controllers** icon.

3. Click the joystick you want to calibrate and click the **Properties** button.

4. Click the **Calibrate** button.

5. Move the joystick and click its buttons as instructed. Click **Next** after performing each step in the calibration (see Figure 33.6).

6. When you are done, Windows displays a message indicating that the calibration has been successfully completed. Click **Finish**.

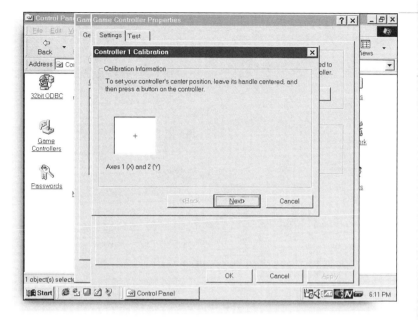

FIGURE 33.6

Follow the onscreen instructions to calibrate your joystick.

7. Click **OK** to return to the **Game Controllers** dialog box.

8. Click **OK** to save your changes.

Voice-Activating Your PC for Commands and Dictation

You've probably seen the commercial with the "You talk, it types" slogan. The commercial leaves me with one question: What is it typing? Voice recognition systems are notorious for misinterpreting what you say. They can handle voice commands, such as "Save File," pretty well, but they're not all that precise when it comes to taking dictation. In addition, you may have to spend long hours training the system to recognize your speech.

Be that as it may, voice recognition software is better than it used to be and is worth a second look if the standard input devices are forcing you to visit the local hand clinic.

If you're thinking of moving up to voice-activated computing or a combination of mouse, keyboard, and microphone input, first check the hardware requirements. Speech-recognition requires a fairly powerful PC. Following is a list of requirements for IBM ViaVoice:

- Intel Pentium 166MHz MMX with 256KB L2 cache.
- 32MB RAM for dictation. 48MB if you're dictating a Word for Windows document.
- 180MB free hard disk space.
- 2X or faster CD-ROM drive.
- 16-bit sound card.

When shopping for speech recognition software, don't skimp. Go with the leaders in voice recognition:

- *IBM ViaVoice*. ViaVoice is the most popular speech recognition software, offering support for both voice commands and dictation. Of the two products listed here, ViaVoice is better at handling dictation, but is a little more difficult to use and train and does not handle voice commands as well as Dragon Systems Naturally-Speaking. ViaVoice includes a head-mounted microphone. For details, visit www.software.ibm.com/is/voicetype.

- *Dragon Systems Naturally-Speaking*. One of the easiest speech recognition programs to set up and use, Naturally-Speaking provides a smooth transition from typing to dictating. Although its recognition of specific words is a little less precise than ViaVoice, it is much better at handling voice commands. To find out more about Naturally-Speaking, visit www.dragonsystems.com.

Get a high-quality microphone

For voice recognition, you should have the best microphone you can afford, preferably a headset device that places the microphone near your mouth and is less likely to pick up background sounds.

Setting up the hardware for speech recognition is very easy—you plug a microphone into the MIC jack on your sound card. Training the software to recognize your voice and enter appropriate commands can be quite difficult and time-consuming.

Installing a New Printer

Choose the right printer for the right job

Consider the cost of consumables—paper and ink

Save space with an all-in-one printer/scanner/copier/fax machine

Choose a printing companion for your notebook PC

Connect your printer and install its driver

Smart Shopping for Printers

You can make a costly mistake by not considering all your options when purchasing a new printer. You might think that you don't really need color output and that you won't use a built-in scanner. Three months later, you find yourself shopping for a fast color printer or looking for a separate scanner and wondering where you're going to plug it in.

With so many different types of printers from different manufacturers offering a wide range of features, it's tough to filter through all the specs to find what you need. Table 34.1 provides a quick overview of the features you should look for. The rest of the sections in this chapter provide additional details.

TABLE 34.1 **Printer buyer's checklist**

Feature	What You Should Consider
Laser	Fast, high-quality output, and inexpensive, but if you need inexpensive color output, an inkjet printer is better.
Inkjet	Somewhat slow, but can handle monochrome and color at reasonable costs. Print quality rivals that of a laser printer.
Color	Highly recommended, but if you're sure you won't need color output, laser printers produce superior black-and-white printouts at high speeds. If you're buying an inkjet printer, don't even consider a black-and-white model.
Quality	600dpi (dots per inch) or higher. If you need photo-quality output, go with 1200dpi.
Speed	For monochrome, 4–8 ppm (pages per minute) or faster, for color, 2–4 ppm. Otherwise, you'll be twiddling your thumbs waiting for the printer to spit out the last page.
Memory	With insufficient memory, a printer may not be able to print a complex page with high-resolution graphics. Make sure the printer comes with sufficient memory for the type of printing you do.
Price	$500 for a good, color inkjet or high-quality black-and-white laser. If you want a combination fax, copier, scanner, inkjet printer, expect to pay $1000. Color laser printers start at about $3000.

Feature	What You Should Consider
Consumables	Expect to pay 3–10 cents per page to print. How much do the print cartridges cost and how many pages can each one print? Do you need to print on special paper? A cheap printer that uses large quantities of expensive consumables may cost much more in the long run.
Paper capacity	At least 100 sheets of standard printer paper. Some high-end printers may be able to handle an entire 500-page ream or more.
Envelope Feed	Paper tray should have an easy way to feed business envelopes into the printer.
Fax	(Recommended, unless you have a dedicated fax machine.) 300dpi, 14.4Kbps transmission, auto-redial, speed dial numbers, page memory to store received faxes if the printer runs out of paper.
Scanner	(Recommended unless you already have a scanner.) TWAIN-compatible color flatbed scanner that can handle 8 1/2- by 11-inch pages and scans at 600dpi or better. 24-bit color, 8-bit grayscale. TWAIN allows you to quickly import scanned images into your documents in most advanced Windows applications.
Copier	(Optional, but a nice feature.) 600X300dpi, multiple copies.

Color or Monochrome?

The first question you should ask yourself before you go shopping for a printer is whether you need color printouts. If you're printing exclusively in black-and-white and grayscale, the only choice is a laser printer. Starting at about $200, monochrome laser printers produce exceptional printouts at high speeds for a few cents a page.

When you add color to the mix, the price of laser printers sky-rockets out of the hundreds range and into the thousands. You can expect to pay $3000–$9000 for a high-quality color laser printer, placing them out of the price range for most home users. For more affordable color, an inkjet printer is the best choice. Although there are other options for high-quality color output, such as thermal dye transfer printers, they cost as much or more than color laser printers and have additional drawbacks.

Buyer beware

Don't buy a printer until you've checked out the latest models from the manufacturer. Many retail stores try to unload older models that don't include the latest features. For example, when I was recently shopping for an all-in-one printer, Hewlett-Packard had a model with an automatic sheet feeder for the copy machine. However, in every retail store I checked, I could find only the older model that supported manual feed.

Laser Printers

For printing black-and-white text and grayscale graphics, nothing beats a laser printer. Laser printers are affordable (starting at $200), fast, and produce higher quality printouts than a comparably priced inkjet printer. Laser printers fall into four categories based on the expected workload:

- *Personal laser.* Typically used in the home or small office, a personal laser printer costs $200–$500, has a paper tray that can handle 50–200 sheets of paper, and prints at about 4–6ppm.

- *Business laser.* For $350–$1000, business lasers boost the paper tray capacity to 200–250 sheets and increase the printing speed to 8–10ppm.

- *Network laser.* If you have a network, consider sharing a more expensive, network laser printer. For smaller networks (5–20 PCs) a $1000–$3000 network laser printer can handle 1000–1500 sheets of paper and print at 12–20ppm. At the high end, a $3000–$20,000 printer can handle 2,000 sheets or more and print at 25–40ppm.

- *Laser/copier.* For heavy network use, an all-in-one laser/copier might be the best choice. Pricey, at about $30,000, these printer/copier combos can handle 2000 sheets or more, print at 25–40ppm, and act as high-end copy machines—collating, stapling, and binding both copies and printouts. Most of these high-end machines can also handle two-sided printouts.

Inkjet Printers

Inkjet printers are the printers of choice for homes and small businesses. For about $300, you can purchase a 600dpi inkjet printer that prints in both grayscale and color on standard paper. For sharper output, you move up to a higher grade of paper. When shopping for an inkjet printer, focus on the following issues:

- *Quality.* The printer should support 600dpi printing.

- *Speed.* Inkjet printers max out at about 4–6ppm for black-and-white print. For high-quality color printouts, speeds vary widely; you can expect some pages to take one or two minutes to print.

- *Separate black and color cartridges.* Some older inkjet printers mix the three primary colors to produce black, which ends up looking green or brown. This approach also uses up your expensive, color ink more quickly. Look for inkjet printers that use a separate cartridge for black ink. These are commonly called four-color printers or CMYK (Cyan, Magenta, Yellow, and blacK).

- *Ink consumption.* Ink cartridges are expensive, and some printers are better at conserving precious resources than others. For example, one printer may use a dollar's worth of ink printing a high-resolution, full-page graphic, whereas another uses 20-cent's worth. Read reviews before you buy; you won't find this information in ads.

Thermal Dye and Wax Transfer Printers

Thermal dye and thermal wax transfer printers produce the highest quality output for both black-and-white and color printing. Instead of ink or toner cartridges, these printers use cubes of solid ink that they melt and then apply to the paper. This gives the print a glossy, embossed effect and produces rich color output. However, these printers have several disadvantages:

- *Expensive.* The price of a good thermal printer ranks right up there with the price of color laser printers. You can expect to pay $2000–$17000 for a good thermal wax transfer printer.

- *Slow.* Because the printer must melt the ink before applying it, it may take several minutes for the printer to start up and be ready for printing. After the ink is in liquid form, however, the printer can keep up with a standard laser or inkjet printer.

- *Loud.* During the initial startup, the printer melts the ink blocks and performs a self-cleaning ritual that can be fairly loud.

Get print samples

Never judge a printer by its dpi rating. Some printers with high dpi ratings produce fuzzy images and type. The only way to compare print quality is to compare actual printouts on standard inkjet printer paper. When comparing, print some small text (6- or 7-point). Smaller text reveals problems better than large text. If possible, print a normal document. Many printers on display are set up to print samples designed to show off the best features of the printer and hide its worst features.

Because the startup operation is so slow and loud, many manufacturers recommend that you leave the printer on at all times.

Portable Printers

Thermal printers

For more information about thermal printers, check out the Web site of the leading manufacturer: Tektronix at www.tek.com. Tektronix provides free black ink for all its thermal printers.

If you need to do a little printing on the road, consider purchasing a portable printer. Portable printers typically weigh 3–5 pounds and use paper trays that have a limited capacity (typically about 10–20) pages. You may even need to feed individual pages through the printer by hand.

One of the best portable printers on the market is the portable Canon BJC (BubbleJet Color) printer. The BJC weighs in at 2 pounds, can print in resolutions up to 720–360dpi, and supports connections by way of the parallel or infrared port. In addition, you can purchase a cartridge that adds scanner capabilities to the printer.

SEE ALSO

➤ *Learn how to use infrared devices with your notebook PC, page 279*

All-in-One: Printer/Scanner/Fax/Copier

Printer manufacturers have finally considered the needs of the home office user and have come out with some innovative all-in-one machines (also called *multifunction printers*) that can handle printing, faxing, scanning, and moderate copy jobs. For $600–$1000, you can purchase an inkjet printer that manages all your paper needs and occupies just a little more space than a standard printer. When shopping for an all-in-one printer, here's what you should look for:

- *Quality*. Few all-in-one printers can handle both text and graphics equally well. If you print mostly text, make sure the printer is optimized for text quality. If you're printing graphics or scanned images, look for optimal graphics output.

- *Speed*. With all-in-one devices, you must consider two speeds: printing and scanning. Both speeds should be no slower than 3ppm. These two speeds taken together determine the speed of the copier.

- *Resolution*. Resolution and output quality go hand-in-hand. For printer resolution, don't settle for less than the standard 600X600dpi. Scanner resolution is a little more difficult to judge. Look for resolutions of 300X300dpi, 256 levels of gray, and 24-bit color.

- *Software*. All-in-one machines have more than just a printer driver. Many come with fax software, scanning software, an OCR (optical character recognition) program, and fax document management tools. Check the software that's included.

- *Controls*. Easy-to-use front panel controls are a must. You need to be able to quickly switch between the printer, fax, copy, and scan functions without going through a complicated ritual (see Figure 34.1).

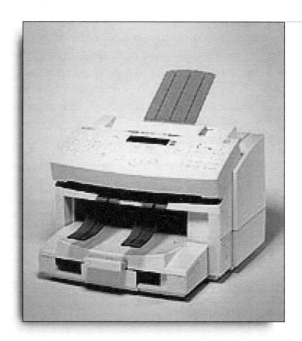

FIGURE 34.1

Look for a multifunction printer that has easily accessible controls.

Bidirectional Printers

Most newer printers are bidirectional, allowing them to print faster, assuming your PC has a bidirectional printer port and you use a bidirectional (IEEE 1284) cable. If your PC doesn't have a bidirectional printer port, you can add one with an ISA or PCI expansion card.

Before you install a bidirectional printer, check your PC's documentation to determine if it has an enhanced parallel port: EPP (Enhanced Parallel Port) or ECP (Enhanced Capabilities Port). You should also check your PC's BIOS setup to ensure that bidirectional communications is enabled for the port.

SEE ALSO

➤ *Learn how to check your PC's BIOS settings, page 567*

Considering the Cost of Consumables

The price of a printer is nothing compared to the cost of supplies (*consumables*) over the life of the printer. Before you choose a printer, compare the cost of consumables. For a standard inkjet printer, you can expect to pay 3–4 cents per page for black-and-white and 8–20 cents per page for color, and that's just for the ink. Although you can pick up inexpensive inkjet paper for about a penny a page, you'll need paper with a glossy finish for the quality stuff. This fancy paper can cost anywhere from 10 cents to two dollars a page.

Laser printers are much more economical. Although the price of toner cartridges may give you a sticker shock, they last much longer than inkjet cartridges and end up costing you 2–3 cents per page. In addition, laser printers can produce high-quality printouts on cheap paper. You can go with the penny a page paper stock to produce razor-sharp text.

Connecting Your New Printer

A printer requires two cable connections: one to a power source and the other to the system unit. The connection to the system unit varies depending on whether the printer you're connecting has a parallel or USB connection. In either case, you shut down your PC and printer, disconnect the current printer, and plug in the new printer.

A popular option is to connect two printers to a single PC. For example, you might want to use an inexpensive laser printer to produce high-quality black-and-white printouts and use a color inkjet printer for any color printouts. With such a configuration, you can save enough on consumables to afford the cost of the second printer.

To connect two printers to a single port, purchase a parallel port switch. A simple switch has three connectors: one that plugs into the parallel port on the system unit and a port for each printer. You typically switch from one port to the other using a special utility included with the port or by manually flipping a switch on the adapter. For more information about parallel port switches, check out Belkin's Web site at www.belkin.com.

SEE ALSO

➢ *Learn how to connect a printer to your PC, page 59*

➢ *Learn how to maintain your printer, page 85*

➢ *Learn how to enter printer settings in Windows, page 234*

Installing a Printer Driver

After installing the printer, you must enter settings in Windows to tell Windows which port the printer is connected to and to install a printer driver. The printer driver provides instructions that tell Windows how to communicate with the printer. Most printers come with their own printer driver on a set of floppy disks or a CD. For those printers that do not have their own driver, Windows has a wide selection of drivers from which to choose. Don't use a Windows driver unless you have to; the driver that comes with the printer typically makes better use of the printer's features.

Sharing printers between two PCs

Even more common than sharing two printers on one PC is sharing one printer with two PCs. Belkin has several printer adapters available for connecting 2, 4, and even 8 PCs to a single printer without having to set up a network.

Installing a device driver for your printer

1. Click the **Start** button, point to **Settings**, and click **Printers**.

2. My Computer opens and displays the Printers folder. Click the **Add Printer** icon. Windows starts the Add Printer Wizard, which informs you of what it is about to do.

3. Click **Next**. If you are connected to a network, the wizard asks if you want to install a local or network printer.

4. Click **Local Printer** or **Network Printer** and click **Next**. The wizard displays a list of manufacturers and printers.

5. If your printer came with its own driver, click **Have Disk** (see Figure 34.2). If the printer did not come with its own driver, skip to step 7.

FIGURE 34.2

If your printer came with its own driver, click **Have Disk**.

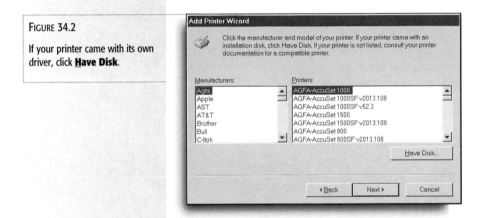

6. Insert the printer installation disk in your computer's CD-ROM or floppy drive, select the drive letter from the drop-down list, and click **OK**.

7. In the **Manufacturers** list, click the name of the printer's manufacturer (see Figure 34.3). The **Printers** list displays the models produced by the selected manufacturer.

8. Click the printer model that matches your printer. If no model in the list is an exact match, pick the closest model name and number. Click **Next**. The wizard prompts you to specify the port to which the printer is connected.

9. Choose **LPT1** if you connected the printer to the parallel port. Choose one of the COM ports if the printer is connected to a serial port. Click **Next**. You are now prompted to type a name for the printer.

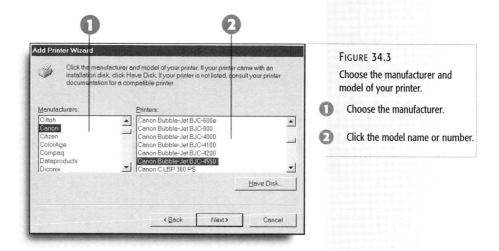

FIGURE 34.3

Choose the manufacturer and model of your printer.

1 Choose the manufacturer.

2 Click the model name or number.

10. Type the name as you want it to appear in the Printers folder.

11. To use this printer as the default for printing from all your Windows programs, click **Yes** near the bottom of the dialog box. Click **Next**.

12. The wizard asks if you would like to print a test page. Click **Yes** or **No**. Then click **Finish**.

13. If the driver for the selected printer has not been installed, Windows prompts you to insert the Windows 98 CD-ROM disc or installation disk. Insert the CD-ROM disc or installation disk and click **OK**.

14. Windows copies the printer driver and any additional files from the CD-ROM disc or floppy disk to the hard disk drive.

SEE ALSO

➤ *Learn how to share a printer on a network, page 313*

➤ *Learn how to manage print jobs in Windows, page 242*

Adding Scanner Capabilities

Choose a high-quality scanner that is within your budget

Understand TWAIN compatibility

Connect your scanner to a SCSI or parallel port

Scan images right into your documents

Turn your PC into a fax machine with a scanner and fax modem

Dealing with Photographs and Paper Documents

Although much has been said about the inevitability of a paperless society, the fact is that paper documents are here to stay. You still receive contracts, business cards, bills, service agreements, and other paper documents that you must save and organize. In addition, you probably have photos, drawings, pictures, and other two-dimensional hardcopy to deal with. To manage these stacks of pages and hardcopy and pull them into your electronic documents, use a scanner.

With a scanner and the right software, you open a two-way street between your PC and the world of paper, allowing you to use your PC to manage the paper side of life:

- Scan photos, drawings, maps, and other graphics and insert them into your documents.

- Transform typed documents into text files to insert in documents you create with your word processing and desktop publishing applications.

- Scan a paper document and use your fax modem to transmit the document to a standard fax machine.

- Use your scanner and printer together as a copy machine.

- Archive your paper documents for quick retrieval. Store all your bills, receipts, service agreements, tax forms, and other personal documents in separate folders on disk to create a manageable database.

- Scan photographs to create a digital photo album and (optionally) print the album.

- Store business cards to keep track of contacts.

- Scan want ads that pertain to your area of expertise, so you know where to look for a job when you need one.

The list could go on, but you get the point: If you want to pull something off a 2D surface and use it in your documents, you need a scanner.

Smart Shopping for Scanners

The first step in choosing a scanner is to assess your scanning needs. If you're scanning images only to place them on Web pages or other electronic documents, a 1200dpi scanner is overkill—Web page graphics are rarely over 100dpi. However, if you're planning on turning your box of photographs into a family photo album, you'll need a scanner that supports higher resolutions and more colors. Use Table 35.1 to assess your scanning needs and narrow the field.

TABLE 35.1   **Assess your scanning needs**

Job Description	Minimum Requirements
Professional graphics	Flatbed scanner capable of scanning at 1200X1200dpi, 36-bit color, and support for oversized pages.
Home or business graphics	Flatbed or sheet-fed scanner capable of scanning at 300X600dpi, 30-bit color.
Web page publishing	Sheet-fed or hand-held scanner capable or scanning at 300X300dpi, 24-bit color.
Text documents only	Flatbed or sheet-fed scanner capable of scanning at 300X300dpi, monochrome.

After you have assessed your general scanning requirements, read through the following sections for additional details on what to look for in a scanner.

Hand-Held, Flatbed, or Sheet-Feed?

About five years ago, hand-held scanners were the rage. If you had a hundred bucks and a lifetime to get accustomed to using one, you could scan small pictures and bits of text into your PC. Now, you would be hard-pressed to find a hand-held scanner. They're just too small and too difficult to use. If someone offers you a good deal on a hand-held scanner, it's not a good deal.

That narrows the field to flatbed and sheet-feed scanners. This is a pretty easy choice, too. If you can clear enough space on

Color or grayscale?

With 300x600dpi, 30-bit color scanners available for under $80, the choice between color and grayscale scanning is no longer an issue. If you do come across a grayscale scanner, just realize that you can have color for a few bucks more.

your desk and you don't need to take the scanner on the road, get a flatbed scanner (see Figure 35.1). Flatbed scanners are more versatile, because they allow you to scan from books and magazines without cutting out the pages. With a flatbed scanner, you can even scan 3D objects.

Sheet-feed scanners are a little more affordable and much more compact (see Figure 35.2). You can easily fit a sheet-feed scanner into a briefcase or your notebook PC's carrying case and take it on the road. However, the limitations of what you can feed through the scanner make sheet-feed scanners a poor choice for most homes and offices.

FIGURE 35.1

A flatbed scanner is the most flexible of all scanners.

FIGURE 35.2

A sheet-feed scanner is compact and portable.

When shopping for a flatbed scanner, you should be aware of the available options:

- If you need to scan 35mm slides or transparencies, make sure the flatbed scanner offers a special tray or template for loading slides. This removes the glass from between the originals and the scanning head to reduce glare and increase the quality of the scan.

- Most flatbed scanners let you load only one page at a time, which isn't conducive to scanning in large amounts of text. If you need to scan entire documents, make sure the scanner has a document feeder (typically sold separately).

TWAIN Compatibility

Short for *Technology (or Toolkit) Without An Interesting Name*, TWAIN support is an absolute must for any scanner. Most new desktop publishing, word-processing, graphics, and fax software features TWAIN support, which allows you to scan on-the-fly (without having to switch to a separate scan program). You enter the command to insert a scanned object and then enter the command to start scanning. The object appears right inside your document. See "Scanning Images into Your Documents," later in this chapter to see the magic of TWAIN compatibility.

Scan Resolution

Resolution and color depth are the two yardsticks used to measure a scanner's quality. The resolution is expressed in dpi (dots per inch)—the higher the number, the sharper the image. Manufacturers typically advertise two resolutions: *optical* and *interpolated*. The optical resolution is the physical number of dots per inch the scanner can pick up. To make an image appear smoother, the scanner uses graphic tricks to fill in the gaps between dots. This gives the scanner its interpolated resolution rating. Use the following list to choose a scanner with the optical and interpolated resolution you need:

- For picking up fine details in photographs or other images and for scanning small text (under 10 points), look for optical resolutions of 600dpi or higher.

Specialized scanners

Some scanners are specially designed for scanning 35mm slides, business cards, or small photographs. For example, the CardScan Plus can scan business cards and transform them into an electronic Rolodex on a PalmPilot (a hand-held computer).

- If you're looking to scan small images and then increase their size, you can go with a lower optical resolution and a higher interpolated resolution. As you increase the size of the image, the dots fill in the gaps so the image doesn't look too blocky.

- For general use, 300–600dpi optical resolution with 2400dpi interpolated resolution is sufficient.

- For scanning photographs, don't settle for less than 600dpi optical resolution. Any lower and your scan won't look anything like the photograph.

- For high-resolution scans and for scanning small photographs and 35mm slides, look for a scanner that offers optical resolutions of 1200–2700dpi. Because 35mm slides are so small, the scanner must use higher resolutions to pick up the fine detail.

Color Depth

Color depth is expressed in bits—typically 24-bit, 30-bit, and 36-bit, and generally coincides with the number of colors the scanner supports. For instance a 24-bit color scanner can pick up over 16 million different colors. 30- and 36-bit color scanners can detect billions of colors.

Comparing color depths is a little complicated because of the various ways scanners achieve their color depth ratings. Two factors contribute to color depth: the CCD (charge-coupled device) or scan head and the ADC (analog-to-digital converter). The CCD controls the actual number of colors the scanner can pick up. A typical 24-bit scanner uses a 24-bit CCD and an 8-bit ADC to achieve 24-bit color depths. A "higher-quality" scanner may still use a 24-bit CCD but couple it with a 10-bit ADC and claim a 30-bit color depth. Although the CCD isn't picking up any more colors, the ADC supposedly does a better job of interpreting those colors and may make color images look slightly better. However, a good 24-bit color scanner may produce better images than a 30-bit color scanner.

The bottom line: Don't let the color depth ratings fool you, and don't settle for less than 24-bit color. Look at some sample scans

or read the hardware reviews to determine which scanner produces the best output for the desired price range.

Speed

Scanner speeds are expressed in ppm (pages per minute), just like
printer speeds, and vary depending on the resolution of the scan.
With a parallel port scanner, you can expect a rate of 2–3ppm at
300–600dpi. Faster, SCSI scanners can scan at up to 6ppm.

SCSI, Parallel, or USB?

Scanners typically connect to a SCSI, parallel, or USB port. To
choose which is best, balance convenience against speed. The
most convenient (and portable) option is a parallel port scanner.
Most parallel port scanners include a pass-through device that
allows you to connect both your printer and scanner to a single
port. You won't be able to scan and print at the same time, but
with a pass-through device, you won't have to disconnect your
printer when you want to scan.

If your PC already has a SCSI adapter, a SCSI scanner is the
perfect choice, because SCSI ports support faster data transfer
rates. If you're purchasing a high-resolution scanner, SCSI may
be the only choice. The parallel port is not designed to handle
the data flow from a high-resolution scanner. Most high-end
scanners ship with a SCSI connector.

With the introduction of USB, USB scanners are becoming
more readily available. USB ports support data transfer rates of
up to 12Mbps, which is faster than most scanners can transfer
data, and, like SCSI adapters, a USB port allows you to chain
several devices to a single port. However, because USB scanners
are relatively new, you can expect to pay quite a bit more for
them than for standard parallel port scanners.

Software Included

Purchasing a scanner is as much a software decision as a hardware decision. Sure, you want a high-quality scanner, but if you
get it home and you can't touch up your photos or scan in your

old typed documents, what's the point? The scanner should come with top-of-the-line software for performing the following tasks:

- *TWAIN driver*. This allows the scanner to work along with applications that have TWAIN support.

- *Photo editing*. Although the scanner should do a pretty good job of adjusting the brightness, contrast, and color, you'll want to touch up your photos and other images for the highest quality. One of the best photo editing programs popularly packaged with scanners is Adobe PhotoShop.

- *Optical character recognition (OCR)*. To scan typed or printed documents and transform them into digital text for a word processor or desktop publishing program, you need a good OCR program. Quality varies greatly in this category. The two best OCR programs popularly bundled with scanners are TextBridge and OmniPage. However, don't get your hopes up when it comes to OCR—even the best OCR software is very limited.

- *Document Management*. When you're scanning paper documents to file them electronically, a document management utility is a great tool to have. Visioneer PaperPort is about the best document management software you can get (although it's a little weak in some other areas, such as OCR). It displays a list of folders on the left, thumbnail sketches of scanned documents and images on the right, and a toolbar with buttons for each application that supports scanning. You can quickly open a scanned object by dragging it over the button for the application in which you want it placed (see Figure 35.3).

Connecting Your Scanner

The process of connecting your scanner to the system unit varies depending on the type of scanner you have. Installing a parallel port scanner is as easy as plugging in a printer. However, each type of scanner has its own connection issues, as explained in the following sections.

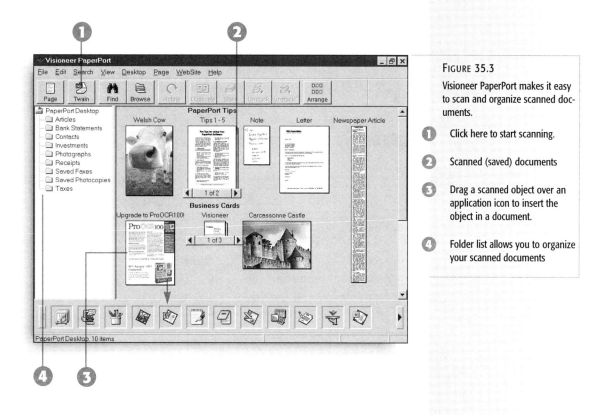

FIGURE 35.3

Visioneer PaperPort makes it easy to scan and organize scanned documents.

1 Click here to start scanning.

2 Scanned (saved) documents

3 Drag a scanned object over an application icon to insert the object in a document.

4 Folder list allows you to organize your scanned documents

Before you install any device (except a USB device), shut down your PC and turn off the power.

Installing a Parallel Port Scanner

If you have a parallel port scanner, it should come with a built-in parallel pass-through port or a separate adapter. Unplug your printer, plug the pass-through adapter into the parallel port on the system unit, and then plug your printer into the adapter (or the pass-through port on the scanner). Plug the scanner into a power outlet on your surge suppresser or UPS.

Keep in mind that the pass-through adapter is only there for convenience. Don't try to print and scan at the same time. You may have to fiddle with the parallel port settings in the BIOS if you have trouble printing or scanning after connecting the scanner. Although pass-through devices are fairly reliable, your PC may not have a bi-directional port or may not be set up to use it. In addition, you may have trouble if you have a Zip drive or other external storage device connected to the parallel port.

SEE ALSO

➤ *Learn how to change the parallel port setting in the BIOS setup, page 567*

Installing a SCSI Scanner

If you just purchased a SCSI scanner, and your PC does not have a SCSI adapter, you must first install a SCSI adapter. After the SCSI adapter is installed, plug your scanner into the external SCSI port, just as if you were connecting a printer.

If you plug your SCSI scanner into another SCSI device, check the address and termination settings on all SCSI devices in the chain and change them as needed to prevent any conflicts. After you connect the scanner to the SCSI port, plug the scanner's power cord into a power outlet on your surge suppresser or UPS.

SEE ALSO

➤ *Learn how to install a SCSI adapter, page 788*

➤ *Learn how to set address and termination settings for SCSI devices, page 635*

Installing a USB Scanner

If you have a USB port and scanner, your job's easy. Plug the scanner into the USB port on the system unit or hub or any other USB device that has an open port. Because the USB cable doubles as a power cable, the USB scanner should require only the USB connection.

SEE ALSO

➤ *Learn how to upgrade to USB, page 788*

➤ *Learn how to connect USB devices, page 44*

Installing the Scanner Driver

As with all hardware installations, after you've connected the scanner, you must install the driver that tells Windows how to use it. In most cases, when you start Windows, it identifies the scanner and leads you through the process of installing the driver. If Windows fails to identify the scanner on startup, open the Control Panel, run the Add New Hardware Wizard, and follow the onscreen instructions.

SEE ALSO

➤ *Learn how to install hardware drivers, page 566*

Using Your Scanner

Now for the fun part—scanning photos, pictures, documents, and snippets from your life. The following sections provide a brief overview of the common tasks you can perform with your scanner and the proper software. Of course the steps vary depending on the type of scanner you have and your software.

Scanning Images

You can scan an image using your scanning software and save the image or scan it directly into a document. If you have a flatbed scanner, first position the image face down on the glass as specified in the scanner's documentation. Click the button to initiate the scanning operation. This typically calls up a dialog box that allows you to enter color settings, specify the resolution, and mark the area you want to scan (see Figure 35.4).

If the dialog box has a button for previewing the image, click the button, so you can mark the area you want to scan. Don't be shocked if the preview looks bad; the preview area typically shows a low-resolution version of the image. Enter your preferences and click the **Scan** button to start scanning.

If you have an application that features TWAIN support, you can scan an image directly into a document. For example, in Microsoft Word (with Photo Editor installed), position the insertion point were you want the image inserted and choose **Insert**, **Picture**, **From Scanner** (see Figure 35.5). Photo Editor starts and then runs your scanning program. Scan the image as you normally would. The image appears in Photo Editor. Touch up the image as desired and then choose **File**, **E**x**it and Return to** *DocumentName*. The image is placed at the insertion point.

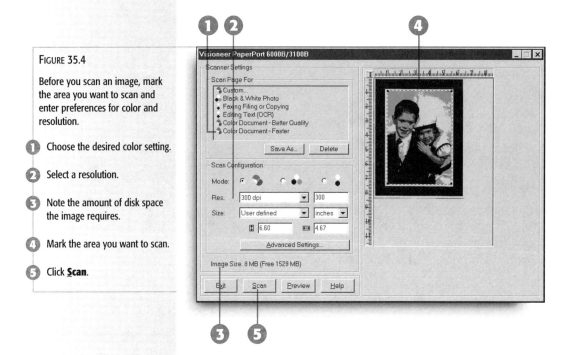

FIGURE 35.4

Before you scan an image, mark the area you want to scan and enter preferences for color and resolution.

1 Choose the desired color setting.

2 Select a resolution.

3 Note the amount of disk space the image requires.

4 Mark the area you want to scan.

5 Click **Scan**.

FIGURE 35.5

You can scan images directly into your documents.

No **From Scanner** option?

Microsoft Photo Editor is included with Microsoft Office 97 Professional Edition (not the Small Business Edition). It is not installed during a typical installation. You must run the Office Setup program again to install Photo Editor.

SEE ALSO

➤ *Learn how to work with graphics in a document, page 154*

Scanning Tips

When you first start playing with your scanner, the inclination is to crank up the resolution and color settings for the best possible scan. Don't. You'll end up packing your hard drive with 50–100MB files that are *too* good. Table 35.2 lists various resolutions and file sizes to help you gauge your scans.

TABLE 35.2   Increasing resolution increases file size

Image size	Color depth	Resolution	File size
4×6 inch	24-bit	72dpi	360KB
4×6 inch	24-bit	300dpi	6.5MB
4×6 inch	24-bit	600dpi	26MB
8×10 inch	24-bit	600dpi	85MB

For high-quality, manageable scans, follow these guidelines:

- *Don't overscan.* If you're printing at 300dpi, scanning at 600dpi is a waste of time and disk space. In general, scan at 300dpi for outputting to most inkjet printers and 100dpi for Web pages and other electronic documents. Save the 1200dpi for high-end laser output or photo-quality output.

- *Don't underscan.* To scan large images (say 8×10 inches), scan at higher resolutions. If you're scanning small images (say 2 1/2X3 inches) and you plan on enlarging the image, scan at the maximum resolution so you don't lose details when you enlarge the image.

- *Crop.* The larger the area you crop, the larger the file. Mark only the area you need to show before initiating the scan.

- *Use the right file type.* BMP and TIFF are uncompressed file formats that produce the highest quality output. To save disk space, save scanned images in JPEG or GIF format. JPEG is referred to as a "lossy" format, because it drops details from the image to achieve high compression ratios. JPEG graphics are commonly used on Web pages and sent via email, because they consume less space and travel faster across Internet connections.

Importing Text from Paper into Your Documents

With OCR software, you can scan text and save it as a text file, so you can insert the text into a word processing or desktop publishing document. The steps for scanning text pages are similar to those for scanning images. The only difference is that when you perform the scan, you must choose the option for scanning text or using the OCR utility.

During the scanning operation, the OCR software converts the graphic representations of the characters into editable text. As you can see from Figure 35.6, the OCR software may not be able to recognize some characters. In most cases, you must go back through the document and do a little clean-up work. Don't expect anything close to 100% accuracy from even the best OCR software. Results vary greatly depending on the quality of the original document, the font size, the scanner, and the OCR software.

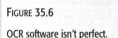

FIGURE 35.6

OCR software isn't perfect.

Scanning and Faxing Documents

A standard fax machine is little more than a combination scanner, printer, and modem rolled into a compact unit. With your PC, a fax modem, a scanner, and a printer, you have a fax machine, although it's a little less compact. Because fax documents are transmitted as graphics, you don't need to use OCR. You scan the document at a low resolution (typically 200dpi for faxing) and then attach the image to your outgoing fax using your fax program.

Visioneer PaperPort makes it easy to send a fax. At the bottom of the PaperPort desktop is a button for your fax program. Drag the icon for your scanned document over the button for your fax program and release the mouse button. This transforms the scanned document into a faxable image. You can then address the fax and add a cover page, as desired.

Some fax programs, such as WinFax Pro, feature their own OCR support. You address your fax as you normally do and then enter the command to scan in any attachments.

Using a Digital Camera

Stop paying and waiting to have your film developed

Choose the right digital camera for your needs and budget

Avoid getting stuck with a feature-starved digital camera

Place photos on your Web pages

Send digital photos via email

Make your own photo album

The Dawning of the Digital Rage

Digital cameras are not practical. For fifty bucks, you can get a 35mm camera at Wal-Mart that's capable of taking better snapshots than a $700 digital camera. For another eighty bucks, you can get a 600×600dpi, 24-bit color scanner that produces better digitized images.

So, why are so many people running out and buying digital cameras? I can think of several reasons:

- They're fun. Take a digital camera with an LCD viewfinder to a party, and you'll be the center of attention...or at least your camera will be.
- They provide immediate gratification. With a digital camera, you don't even have to wait for one-hour service. You plug the camera in to your PC, download the images, and print as many copies as you like.
- They're private. You can take a picture of your kid in his birthday suit without fearing a visit from the FBI.
- They let you create digital photo albums that you can write to CDs or DVDs for easy storage and management.
- They make it easy to post pictures on Web pages and send photos via email.

In addition, digital cameras are a technology that people can relate to. A digital camera looks just like a standard 35mm camera (see Figure 36.1) and has many of the same features and buttons. To take a picture, you point and shoot.

How's it work?

Imagine a very portable, compact, 3D scanner that looks like a 35mm camera—that's a digital camera. Like a scanner, a digital camera is built around a CCD (charge-coupled device). When you snap a picture, the shudder opens and bombards the CCD with light. The CCD converts the light into electrical impulses, which are then applied to a magnetic storage medium, such as a disk or PC card.

Smart Shopping for Digital Cameras

You can pick up a digital camera for under $100, but after the first few pictures, you'll realize why it was so cheap. Hundred dollar digital cameras produce low-resolution photographs, have no flash, store only a couple pictures, and can take forever to process a single snapshot.

But with all the digital cameras on the market, how can you compare cameras and prices? The following sections explain the most critical features of digital cameras and help you choose the right camera for your budget.

SEE ALSO

➤ *Learn about scanners, page 741*

➤ *Learn how to capture still images from video, page 693*

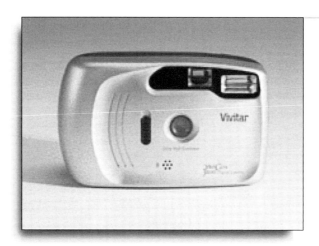

FIGURE 36.1

The ViviCam 3100 digital camera looks and acts like a standard 35mm camera. (Photo courtesy of Vivitar Digital Imaging.)

The Wide Open Price Range

Good digital cameras don't come cheap. At the low end, you can expect to pay $200 for the bare-boned basics. At the high end, you might need to consider taking out a second mortgage. In between those two extremes are some more realistic numbers:

- *$250–$400.* 640×480dpi, 24-bit color images, 16–20 photo storage capacity, 30–50 photos per charge, no LCD display, no flash.

- *$500–$700.* 640×480dpi, 24-bit color images, 20–40 photo storage capacity with removable memory cards, 50–100 photos per charge, LCD display, flash, connectors for outputting to TV.

- *$800–$1000.* 640×480dpi, 24-bit color images, zoom lens, 40–50 photo storage capacity with removable memory cards, 100–300 photos per charge, LCD display, flash, connectors for outputting to TV.

If all this talk of 640×480dpi, 24-bit color, LCD, and memory cards seems a little much, the following sections explain these features in greater detail.

Resolution

The most important consideration when purchasing a digital camera is resolution—the higher the resolution the better the image. Don't settle for less than 640×480, which is optimal for 3×5-inch printouts. For larger printouts (5×7-inch), look for resolutions of 1024×768 or higher. Lower resolutions are acceptable only for email and Web pages.

You should also determine if the camera uses a CCD or a low-cost, power-saving CMOS (Complementary Metal Oxide Semiconductor) sensor. Although CMOS sensors make the camera less expensive and increase the number of photos you can shoot on a single charge, they're not as light-sensitive as CCDs. A camera that uses a CMOS sensor may support the same resolutions as a camera using a standard CCD, but the image quality is lower.

Colors

Most digital cameras support at least 24-bit color (over 16 million colors), but you should check the color depth just to make sure. High-end cameras support 30- or 36-bit color, but if you're printing photos on a color inkjet printer or displaying them onscreen, 24-bit color is sufficient. In addition, the increased color depth increases the size of the files, reducing the number of photos the camera can store.

Storage Capacity

When you take pictures with a regular camera, you can pop rolls of film in and out as needed. Your digital camera should provide the same convenience or at least enough built-in memory to store 40 high-resolution photos. When considering storage, you have the following options:

- *Built-in storage*. If you decide to purchase a camera that does not allow you to swap cards or disks, make sure the camera has at least 4MB of built-in memory. Otherwise, you'll be running home near the middle of the party to download your pictures.

- *Swappable memory cards*. Most cameras use high-speed 1MB or 2MB PC cards. When a card is full, you pop it out and pop in a new one. After you download the images from the card to your PC, you can then erase the card and use it again. The trouble with standard swappable cards is that they're expensive: about $50 per megabyte. Look for cameras that use CompactFlash memory cards that cost about $10 per megabyte.

- *Standard floppy disks*. A few cameras, such as Sony's Digital Mavica store images on standard 3 1/2-inch floppy disks. At less than 50 cents per megabyte, floppy disks present the most economical storage solution. However, floppy disks limit you to 1.44MB per disk and lag behind PC cards in performance.

Focus

Focus options for digital cameras coincide with focus options available with standard 35mm cameras. For general snapshots, look for cameras that feature autofocus or zone focus. With zone focus cameras, you flip a switch to specify the distance your subject is from the camera (for example, 2–4 feet or infinity). High-end cameras offer manual focus and may offer manual aperture settings.

Give some serious consideration to digital cameras that have a zoom lens option. If you need a close-up shot and you're thinking you can just take the picture from 4 feet away and then use your imaging software to blow it up, think again. Whenever you enlarge a digital image, it becomes blocky and distorted. With a zoom lens, you can take a close-up photograph of just what you want and not have to worry about cropping and enlarging the image later.

Saving space with digital compression

When considering storage, you should also think about compression, the capability of the camera to compress files and store more photos per megabyte of storage. Make sure the camera can store photos as JPEG files and that it allows you to choose the compression level. As digital camera technology advances, look for cameras that offer improved compression techniques, such as Wavelet compression.

Built-in Flash

Contrary to what some digital camera manufacturers seem to think, a built-in flash is not an optional feature. However, there are a few options to consider when comparing cameras that have a built-in flash:

- *Automatic*. The camera automatically senses the amount of light and turns on the flash when it's needed.

- *Always on*. Also called *fill* or *fill-in*, this mode is used for backlit scenes. The flash remains on until you turn it off.

- *Off*. For manual control of lighting (for example, when you're taking a close-up shot), you can turn off the flash so the camera doesn't automatically turn it on.

- *Red-eye correction*. Red-eye correction reduces the red-eye effect commonly seen in flash photos.

Battery Life

Several factors determine the number of pictures a digital camera can take with a new set of batteries. If the camera uses a flash or has an LCD viewer, battery life dips considerably. For example, many digital cameras can take up to 100 pictures with the LCD on or nearly 300 pictures with the LCD off. With that in mind, look for the following features to help conserve battery power:

- If LCD is included, make sure you can turn it off and use a standard view finder.

- Make sure you can turn off the flash. Even autoflash may use additional power.

- Look for cameras that have A/C adapters. Although you won't want to plug in the camera when you're taking pictures, the adapter can help conserve power when you're downloading images to your PC.

- Automatic power off when not in use. It's tough to remember to turn off your camera when you're taking photos. Make sure the camera can power itself down after ten seconds or less of inactivity.

Interfacing with PC and TV

Nine out of ten digital cameras come with a serial cable attachment for transferring images from the camera to a PC. Some cameras also come with cables for attaching the camera to a TV or VCR, so you can view your photos on TV and record them on tape.

Additional Features

Although the stock features are the most important, you should be aware of some of the modern conveniences some cameras offer. If you spend $700 on a camera and later realize that a countdown feature would have been nice, trying to unload that camera a month later when prices have dropped may be impossible. Before you make your final decision, check out the following options:

- *LCD viewfinder*. An LCD viewfinder can help you frame a picture. However, LCDs use up a lot of battery power. If you purchase a camera with an LCD, make sure you can turn it off and that the camera has a standard "porthole" you can look through.

- *Automatic timer*. If you want to be in the picture, get a camera with a countdown timer that can automatically snap the picture for you.

- *Photo delete*. Most cameras automatically delete images from the internal storage or PC card after you download the images to your PC. However, if you mess up a picture, it's nice to be able to delete it before you snap the next shot to free up storage space on the card.

- *TWAIN driver*. Virtually all scanners have Twain drivers, which allow you to scan images directly into documents, but few digital cameras offer TWAIN support. Although TWAIN support is not essential, it can come in handy, especially if you decide to use imaging software other than the stock programs that come bundled with the camera.

- *Voice annotations.* The ViviCam 3100 and a few other digital cameras allow you to capture short audio clips along with your photographs. If you're using the camera primarily for personal photographs, voice annotations can be a big plus.

Taking Pictures

Because digital cameras are modeled off of standard 35mm cameras, snapping a picture is easy. You just point and shoot. However, before you snap too many pictures, you should check the camera settings.

Most digital cameras have two buttons: one for changing modes (such as flash, image quality, timer, and audio) and another for changing the mode settings. You change to the desired mode (for instance, Flash) and then press the other button to change the setting (for instance, Auto Flash or Flash On). Check the following settings before taking a picture:

- *Resolution.* To fit more pictures in storage, crank down the resolution setting. For higher-quality pictures, choose a higher setting.

- *Flash.* In most cases, leave the flash setting at Auto. If you're taking all your pictures outside, turn off the flash. For back-lit scenes, turn on the flash, if this option is available on your camera.

- *Audio.* If your camera supports audio input, turn on Audio, if desired. Keep in mind that audio recordings consume quite a bit of storage space.

Copying Pictures to Your PC

Check the remaining storage

As you snap pictures, keep track of the amount of storage remaining. Most cameras have a small LCD display (not to be confused with the LCD viewfinder) that shows the number of pictures you've taken and the available storage.

Digital cameras come with their own software that transfers the image files from the camera to your PC. In addition, the camera should include a cable for connecting to one of the ports on your PC (typically the serial port, although USB connections are likely to become more popular). Some digital cameras require a PC card reader.

To transfer the images, connect the cable to your camera and to the specified port. Run the photo transfer utility and enter the command to retrieve the images. The program retrieves the images from the camera and displays them onscreen (see Figure 36.2). The program then deletes the images from the PC card or other storage area or gives you the option to have the images deleted.

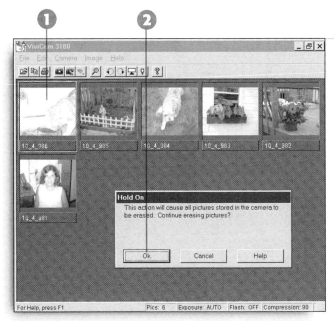

FIGURE 36.2

The photo transfer utility grabs the photos from the camera and displays them onscreen.

1 Images retrieved from camera

2 After retrieving images, you have the option of deleting them from the camera.

Most photo transfer utilities double as photo editing tools. After you retrieve the images from your camera, you can adjust the brightness, color, and contrast of an image, crop it, flip it, resize it, and perform other digital imaging gymnastics.

For more control over your images, try a photo management utility, such as PhotoRecall (see Figure 36.3). With PhotoRecall, you can create virtual photo albums and flip the pages right onscreen. To pick up a free 30-day demonstration copy of PhotoRecall, go to www.ga-imaging.com.

FIGURE 36.3

PhotoRecall allows you to create
virtual photo albums.

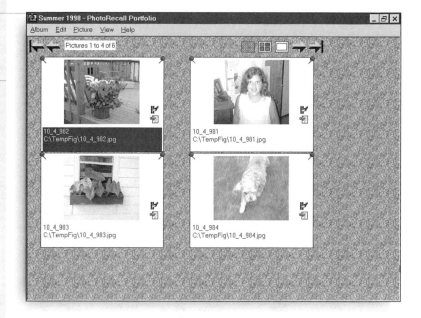

Inserting Digital Images in Email and Web Pages

One of the best features of digital cameras is that they create graphic files that you can immediately use on Web pages and in email messages. You don't have to scan the picture after taking it, because it's already in a digital format.

To place a picture on your Web page, insert it as you would insert any graphic. In addition, if your email program supports HTML, you can insert images right inside the message area when composing an email message (see Figure 36.4).

SEE ALSO

➤ *Learn how to create your own Web page, page 424*

➤ *Learn how to create and send email messages, page 435*

➤ *Learn how to work with graphics, page 422*

➤ *Learn how to format your email message, page 443*

Kodak's PhotoNet

To make the most of your digitized photos, check out Kodak's PhotoNet online at `kodak.photonet.com`. This service allows you to post photos, so your friends and relatives can check them out and order their own prints or special items, such as T-shirts or mugs. In addition, you can email photos directly from the service. Kodak is also working with AOL on a similar service called "You've Got Pictures" for AOL members.

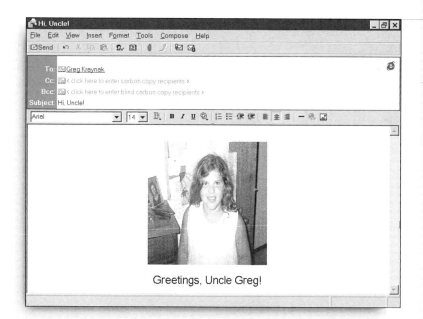

FIGURE 36.4

You can insert digital photos right inside your email messages.

Upgrading Your Audio System

Determine if your PC can handle the desired audio upgrade

Buy a sound card that can keep up with the latest games and multimedia

Choose a speaker system that can keep up with your sound card

Install your new sound card

Hook up your speakers, subwoofer, and microphone

Adjust audio output in Windows

Cranking Up the Volume with Audio Upgrades

Do the sounds from your DVD player rattle the rafters? Do your PC games shake your bones and make your skin crawl with their eerie realism? Do your neighbors complain when you crank up the volume on your PC? If not, then your PC audio system probably needs a tune-up. The 16-bit stereo sound card and 5-watt speakers that came with your system may be unable to handle the advanced sound technology built into the latest digital movies and games.

To give your PC the equivalent of an audio makeover, you need to install a new sound card and a high-quality speaker system. Sound expensive? Well, it could be. If you're adding a top-of-the-line sound card and the five speakers and subwoofer required for Surround Sound, you may be looking at a steep bill. However, there are a few less expensive (and less complicated) options that provide virtual 3D sound, which is almost as good as the real thing.

The following sections explore the options and guide you through the complexities of audio equipment, standards, and connections.

Audio Central: The Sound Card

Although every PC has a built-in speaker to play the beeps and burps your computer emits on startup, the tiny speaker is no match for even the cheapest stereo output. A sound card improves the audio capabilities of your PC by offering the following components and features (see Figure 37.1):

- *Digital-to-analog converter*. Converts digital signals from CDs and from your PC into analog audio signals that a speaker system can play.

- *Analog-to-digital converter*. Converts audio input into digital signals that your PC can process and record. (Audio input includes voices spoken into a microphone and input from another audio player, such as a CD player or TV cable.)

- *Audio processing chip or digital signal processor (DSP).* Combines, mixes, and redirects the signals for recording and playback. Think of the DSP as the sound generator, the major controller on the sound card.

- *Analog input ports.* Allow you to connect input (recording) devices, including a microphone, CD player, DVD player, and MIDI instruments.

- *Analog output ports.* Provide connections for analog audio output devices—mainly speakers.

- *Optional amplifier.* Some sound cards include a built-in amplifier to increase audio output for systems that have no external amplifier. However, you'll get cleaner audio output by amplifying the sounds externally.

FIGURE 37.1

A sound card is an expansion board that adds audio capability to your PC. (Photo courtesy of Creative Labs.)

A few years ago, sound cards seemed to have reached a plateau with Sound Blaster-compatible, 16-bit stereo sound cards and audio-capable CD players. However, with the emergence and increased popularity of 3D audio, the need for full-duplex audio in videoconferencing applications, and improvements in audio recording technologies, picking a sound card is no longer such an easy task.

PCI or ISA Card

Whenever you're given a choice of installing a PCI or ISA expansion card, your decision typically hinges on whether your PC has an open PCI expansion slot. Because the PCI bus is much more advanced than the ISA bus, PCI cards are usually the better choice. In the real world, however, you don't have an unlimited number of PCI expansion slots—you need to prioritize, and the sound card may be a close call.

To make the call, keep in mind that a standard 16-bit stereo sound card that plugs into an ISA slot can handle CD-quality audio. If you don't have a DVD drive or play advanced PC video games, it makes little sense to occupy a valuable PCI slot with an advanced sound card. However, if you do have a DVD drive or want to fully experience an advanced computer game, a PCI sound card is the only way to go. As opposed to the ISA bus, which can handle a maximum of 8Mbps, the PCI bus can transfer up to 132Mbps, giving a PCI sound card the capability to manage the increased traffic of multiple audio streams.

PCI sound cards have the additional advantage of offloading some of the storage and processing load to system RAM and the CPU. Some ISA cards, although older and less advanced, are more expensive than PCI cards, because the ISA cards require built-in RAM or ROM.

Wave Audio

All sound cards support wave audio, a digital reproduction of analog sounds. With wave audio, you can plug your audio CD player into the sound card and play audio CDs. Wave audio also enables your system to play WAV files commonly included with Windows and Windows applications. To find WAV files on your PC, choose **Start**, **Find**, **Files and Folders** and search your entire system for ***.wav**. To play a file, click its name.

However, Wave audio is impractical for most applications. To create a WAV file, the sound card plots points along the incoming analog sound wave to create a digital representation of the sound wave. Because thousands of points are required to digitally describe an analog sound wave, WAV files can become extremely large. To reduce the size of audio files, most sound cards support MIDI recording and playback, as described in the next section.

MIDI: From Synthesizer to Real-World Sounds

Short for *Musical Instrument Digital Interface*, MIDI links real-world sounds to digital signals to help reduce audio file sizes while at the same time allowing for the recording and playback of realistic sounds. Two types of MIDI are available:

- *FM MIDI.* Frequency modulated MIDI uses a complex translation system to simulate the sounds of real instruments. Instruments recorded using an FM synthesizer have a distinct digital sound; they don't sound like real instruments. Sound cards that support FM MIDI are rare.

- *Wavetable MIDI.* Stores real-world sounds on the card (or on disk or system memory) and assigns those sounds to digital signals to produce realistic recordings and playback.

When shopping for a sound card, focus on two aspects of MIDI: the number of devices or "voices" the sound card can play at one time and the MIDI wave set (the number of real-world sounds the card comes with):

- *Multiple instruments.* For more realistic playback, MIDI must be able to play several instruments or "voices" at the same time. For example, a Sound Blaster AWE64 can play 64 instruments at one time.

- *MIDI wave set.* The more real-world sounds the card stores, the more realistic the MIDI audio playback sounds. In most cases, the size of the wave set is measured in megabytes: 2MB, 4MB, and 8MB sets are common.

- *Location of MIDI wave set.* Where the sound card stores the MIDI wave set is important. Some sound cards store the wave set in built-in ROM, but most PCI cards use system RAM, which allows for a greater expansion of the wave set. Which system is better? Storing the wave set in ROM avoids having to clutter system RAM with more data, but increases the price of the card and limits the size of the wave set. In other words, it's a toss-up.

3D Audio

DLS support

One of the latest MIDI standards is DLS (Downloadable Sounds), which allows games and other software to add MIDI sounds to the MIDI wave set. This dynamic approach to keeping the wave set up-to-date is a definite plus; look for sound cards that offer DLS support.

For years, developers have been researching ways to make audio systems sound more realistic, more three-dimensional. One approach consisted of fitting a dummy head with microphones to record sound as a "person" would hear it. This system, called *binaural audio* worked fairly well, although optimum quality was achieved through headphones.

Digital recording and processing has given rise to more sophisticated systems. The following list explains some of the more popular 3D systems and the standards you should look for when purchasing a new sound card:

- *DirectSound 3D.* Part of Microsoft's DirectX initiative, DirectSound 3D is the most popular standard for *positional 3D audio.* With positional 3D audio, the sound card can actually separate and direct audio signals to different speakers to create the illusion of 3D sound. When shopping for a sound card, make sure it supports DirectSound 3D or the 3Dxp extension.

- *AC-3.* Developed by Dolby to enhance the audio playback in home entertainment systems, the AC-3 specification is based on the 5.1 speaker configuration. The 5.1 speaker configuration consists of five speakers and a subwoofer. AC-3 intelligently directs audio signals to the five speakers and subwoofer positioned around the room, to produce Surround Sound.

- *Environmental Audio.* A relatively new standard developed by Creative Labs, Environmental Audio is similar to AC-3, in that it directs audio signals to various speakers positioned around the room. To make the most of Environmental Audio, you need a special speaker system, consisting of four speakers and a subwoofer. Because Creative Labs is the leader in PC audio, look for Environmental Audio to be supported in most new video games.

Full-Duplex

You typically use a sound card to play *or* record audio, but you rarely use the sound card to do both at the same time…except when you're engaged in an Internet phone call or video-conference. Because Internet phone calls and videoconferencing were not available when the first sound cards hit the market, few early sound cards (referred to as *half-duplex* sound cards) could handle recording and playback at the same time.

Trying to carry on a conversation over the Internet with a half-duplex sound card is an exercise in futility. You must talk and then wait until the other person's reply is *completely* finished playing on your system before you can say something else. If you happen to talk when the other person's voice is playing, the signals slam into one another and sound like a jumbled mess. It's sort of like trying to converse with walkie-talkies.

With a full-duplex sound card, Internet phone conversations proceed relatively smoothly. You can both talk and interrupt each other, just as you do in a normal conversation but the interruptions are caused by the natural flow of human conversation rather than the limitations of your audio equipment. In short, when shopping for a sound card, make sure you get a *full-duplex* sound card.

Speakers

If you plug a cheap set of speakers into your sound card and are disappointed by the audio output, don't blame the sound card. For decent audio output, you'll need 5–10-watt per channel output. For games and presentations, look for 20–40-watt per channel output plus a subwoofer to handle the deep bass sounds. For general use, a 2-speaker-plus-subwoofer system is sufficient (see Figure 37.2).

If you purchased a 3D sound card for game play or DVD, get a 3D speaker system to match. Check the sound card manufacturer's recommendations to determine the type of speaker system that works best with the card. For high-quality, Dolby Surround Sound, you need a 5.1 speaker system, consisting of five speakers

Happy with your old sound card?

If you're satisfied with your old sound card, but it is half-duplex, check with the manufacturer to determine if a full-duplex device driver is available for your sound card. Creative Labs has drivers for its old Sound Blaster 16, 32, AWE32, and AWE64 cards that can add full-duplex capabilities to the card. Go to **www.soundblaster.com/ wwwnew/tech/faqs/** and click the link for full-duplex information.

plus a subwoofer. Creative Labs' Environmental Sound requires a four-speaker-plus-subwoofer configuration.

Multi-speaker systems create the effect of 3D sound by blasting audio signals at you from various points in the room. These systems typically consist of four or five speakers (called *satellites*) plus a subwoofer. In a 5.1 configuration (typically used for Dolby Surround Sound), you place four satellites in the far corners of a room, one satellite in front of you, and the subwoofer on the floor in front of you. The satellite that sits in front of you carries the voices, the other four satellites carry the music and background sounds, and the subwoofer carries the bone-shaking bass.

FIGURE 37.2

A pair of high-quality speakers along with a subwoofer can handle most audio needs. (Photo courtesy of Creative Labs.)

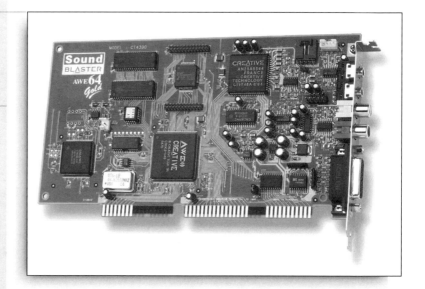

Connecting your stereo system

You can connect the audio out jack on your sound card to the Line In jack on your stereo system and use its amplifier to crank up the sound. However, be careful when using standard, unshielded speakers around your computer equipment. Standard speakers produce a strong electrical field that could damage data.

Microphone

Most PC microphones are not professional grade microphones, but they're capable of keeping up with the low-quality microphone input of most sound cards. When shopping for a microphone, the most important consideration is how well the microphone blocks out background noise. The best microphones are head-mounted units that place the microphone right next to your mouth. Microphones that clip onto your tie or collar are also fairly good at blocking out background noise.

Avoid microphones that are built in to a keyboard or trackball or that sit on your desk. As you type, bump the desk, and move papers, the microphone picks up the vibrations. This can cause significant line noise and interfere with communications, especially if you're using sensitive speech recognition software.

Installing Your Sound Card

Installing a sound card is fairly easy, assuming you don't run into any conflicts with other installed devices. If you're installing a PCI sound card on a Plug and Play system, you shouldn't have any problems. ISA sound cards are notorious for causing conflicts. If you're installing an ISA card, expect a little troubleshooting after the installation.

Installing a sound card

1. If you are replacing an existing sound card, remove its driver. Alt+click My Computer and click the **Device Manager** tab.

2. Click the plus sign next to **Sound, video, and game controllers**.

3. Click the entry for your existing sound card and click **Remove** (see Figure 37.3).

4. Click **OK** to remove the device driver.

5. Exit all Windows applications, shut down Windows, and turn off your PC. Unplug your PC.

6. Take the cover off the system unit and touch a metal part of the case to discharge any static electricity.

7. If your PC has an existing sound card, remove any cables attached to the sound card, including external cables that connect to speakers and internal cables that connect to a CD or DVD player.

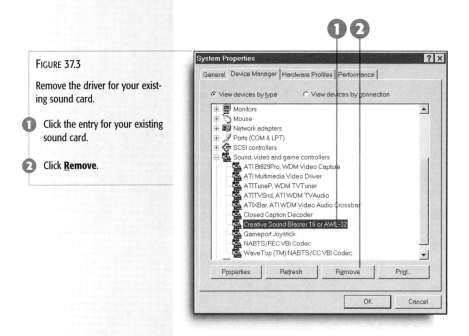

FIGURE 37.3

Remove the driver for your existing sound card.

1 Click the entry for your existing sound card.

2 Click **Remove**.

8. Remove the existing sound card from its expansion slot. If you're removing an ISA sound card and installing a PCI sound card, remove the cover plate near the PCI slot you want to use and move it to the opening left by the ISA sound card you just removed.

9. Insert the contacts on the sound card into the expansion slot and press down firmly but gently on the top of the card until it is securely seated in the slot.

10. Plug the internal cable from the CD or DVD player into the audio input connector on the sound card (see Figure 37.4).

11. Replace the system unit cover.

12. Reconnect the speakers and microphone you disconnected in step 7, or connect your new speakers and microphone.

13. Restart your system and follow the onscreen instructions to install the device driver for your sound card.

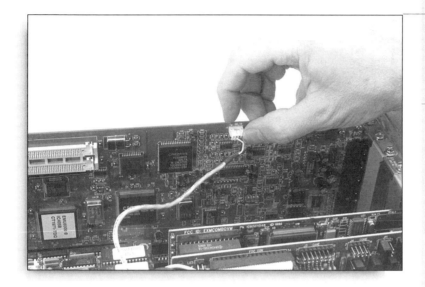

FIGURE 37.4

Connect the internal audio cable from the CD or DVD drive to the audio input connector on the sound card.

SEE ALSO

➤ *Learn how to connect speakers and a subwoofer to your sound card, page 52*

➤ *Learn how to install a device driver for your sound card, page 566*

➤ *Learn how to troubleshoot hardware conflicts, page 802*

➤ *Learn how to troubleshoot audio problems, page 814*

Adjusting the Audio Output in Windows

When you start playing audio clips in Windows, you'll find that there are more volume controls than you really want to deal with. You may find a volume control on your sound card, in the program that's playing the sounds, and in Windows itself. To experience the full range of audio output, you may need to adjust more than one control.

Adjusting volume in Windows

  1. Right-click the **Volume** icon in the system tray and click **Open Volume Controls.**

Avoid using the sound card's amplifier

If your sound card has two audio output jacks (one for amplified audio and the other for unamplified output), connect your speakers to the unamplified output jack and use your external amplifier to increase the volume. The sound card's built-in amplifier may introduce noise and distortion.

2. Open the **Options** menu and click **Properties**.

3. Place a check mark next to all the volume controls in the list except **PC Speaker**, and click **OK**.

4. Make sure all **Mute** check boxes are NOT checked. These **Mute** options are often turned on for no apparent reason without prompting you for confirmation.

5. Drag the volume sliders up or down to set the desired volume and balance for the various input and output devices (see Figure 37.5).

6. Click the **Close** (x) button.

FIGURE 37.5

Check the volume and balance settings in Windows.

1 Turn off **Mute all**.

2 Drag the Volume slider up or down to increase or decrease volume.

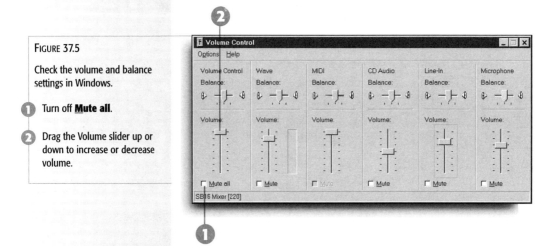

Adding Ports for Connecting Additional External Devices

Understand the benefits and shortcomings of the various port types

Take inventory of the available ports on your system

Determine when you need to upgrade an existing port

Expand your system with a SCSI or USB adapter

Check port settings in Windows

Understanding Ports

The easiest way to upgrade your system is to plug an external device into a port on the back of the system unit. With external devices, you don't have to open the system unit, fiddle with expansion boards or jumpers, or worry about zapping the motherboard.

Most system units come with two serial ports (which is usually one too many) and one parallel port (which is never enough). Of course, you can purchase pass-through devices and switches for connecting multiple devices to a single port, but these adapters rarely provide the ideal solution.

To make your PC more expandable from the outside, consider installing additional ports. The following sections describe the ports you can add to your PC and the pros and cons of each type of port. Later in this chapter, you'll learn how to obtain and install the ports you need.

Serial Ports

Newer PCs typically come with two 9-pin serial ports or one 9-pin and one 25-pin serial port. Serial ports were commonly used for connecting a mouse or external modem, but are now more commonly used for downloading images from digital cameras.

Compared to other ports (parallel, SCSI, USB, and so on), serial ports are slow. Older serial ports max out at about 115Kbps. Newer ports can transfer data at about 300Kbps. This is a snail's pace compared to parallel ports, which offer data rates of about 2Mbps.

Because serial ports are so slow, few upgrade devices are designed to connect to the serial port. One serial port is usually enough for most users. The only time you may want to install a serial port is if you decide to install an external ISDN modem and need to replace your old serial port with a faster serial port to support the 128Kbps data transfer rate of your ISDN modem.

SEE ALSO

➤ *Learn how to connect a modem to the serial port, page 681*

➤ *Learn how to download pictures from a digital camera to your PC via the serial port, page 764*

SCSI Ports

SCSI adapters are typically used on network servers to connect several hard drives to a single expansion card. However, they have gained a larger following from the popularity of external, removable hard drives, such as the Iomega Jaz drive. Offering transfer rates of 5–80MBps, external SCSI drives can outperform internal IDE drives and zoom past any disk drive connected to the relatively slow parallel port. There are several reasons to consider installing a SCSI adapter:

- If your internal drive bays are all occupied and you need a fast hard drive, install a SCSI adapter and an external SCSI hard drive.

- Plugging a scanner, Zip drive, and printer into a single parallel port is asking for trouble. With a SCSI adapter, you can easily chain together several SCSI devices, use all three devices at the same time, and not have to worry about conflicts or performance issues.

- With a SCSI adapter, you can chain together 7–15 devices (depending on the controller type). This leaves room for adding another hard drive, backup drive, scanner, and other SCSI device later (see Figure 38.1).

SEE ALSO

➤ *Learn how to connect SCSI devices, page 45*

Game Ports

Most sound cards have a MIDI/game port that allows you to connect a MIDI musical instrument or plug in a game controller. Some home PCs come with an additional built-in game port for connecting another game controller. One game port is typically sufficient; however, to play two-player games or if you have two or connect different types of game controllers to a single port, you may want to add game ports:

Cheap SCSI

If you need to install a SCSI device and you don't have the room for a SCSI adapter, purchase a SCSI-to-parallel adapter and connect the SCSI device to the parallel port. (Check Belkin at www.belkin.com.) Linking a fast SCSI device to a slow parallel port is somewhat pointless, but if you purchase an external SCSI hard drive and find out that you have no room for a SCSI card, the adapter may be the only option.

FIGURE 38.1

With a SCSI adapter, you can chain several devices to a single port.

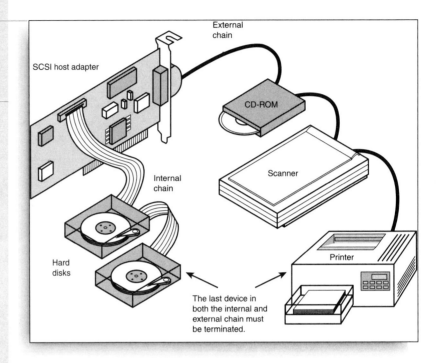

- For two-player games, install an expansion board with two game ports. Try Game Card 3 from CH Products at www.chproducts.com.

- To attach two or more controllers to a single port, purchase a multi-game controller connection box. The box is a more practical solution than installing another expansion board, keeping your expansion slots open for additional upgrades. You plug the box into the existing game port and then plug your game controllers into the game ports on the box. To switch from one controller to the other, you press a button on the controller you want to use. CH Products (www.chproducts.com) is also a great place to pick up a joystick switchbox.

SEE ALSO

➤ *Learn how to connect and calibrate a joystick or other game controller, page 723*

USB Ports

If you've been struggling over the past year or so to make your scanner, printer, and Zip drive stop fighting over control of the one parallel port on your PC, you know that a new port design is long overdue. Enter USB, the Universal Serial Bus. With USB, you can connect your scanner to the USB port, plug a USB printer into the scanner, plug a video camera into your printer, and keep stringing together devices in this way or via USB hubs, until you reach the magic number of 127 total external devices!

With the external expandability that USB offers, you'll never again have to unplug your scanner to get your printer to work and fiddle around with device conflicts when your Zip drive and scanner don't get along. USB offers several advantages over existing ports:

- *Hot swapping*. You can connect and disconnect devices without turning the power off or shutting down Windows.

- *Low power supply*. For devices that don't require much power, such as the keyboard, mouse, and some digital cameras and scanners, no power cord is required. The USB connection supplies enough power to run the device.

- *No addressing*. With SCSI connections, you must assign an address to each device in the SCSI chain. USB handles the addressing automatically.

- *Auto termination*. With SCSI connections, you must turn on termination for the last device in the chain. USB devices provide auto-termination, so you don't have to flip any switches after plugging in the device.

SEE ALSO

➤ *Learn how to connect USB devices to a USB port, page 44*

FireWire

Although USB has received a lot of press, FireWire (also referred to as IEEE 1394) is poised to become the port of choice for high bandwidth devices, such as video cameras, hard drives,

VCRs, TVs, DVD drives, networks, and perhaps even Internet connections. Offering transfer rates of 100-, 200-, and 400Mbps, FireWire is capable of handling the most demanding external devices.

During the writing of this book, few new PCs featured FireWire support. As a technology designed mainly for consumer electronics, it is just starting to gain acceptance in the PC world. FireWire is used mainly for high-end video capture and professional digital video recording and is much more popular on Macintosh computers. You probably won't see FireWire become very popular until Microsoft builds more support for it into the next version of Windows.

Infrared Ports

Infrared ports are used primarily on notebook PCs and on home PCs that double as entertainment centers. Infrared ports allow peripherals to communicate with your PC via light rather than by transferring data over cables. Infrared ports are most useful on notebook PCs for establishing wireless connections to printers and networks.

You'll rarely find an infrared port on a desktop PC. However if you need to connect your notebook PC to your desktop PC to share files and resources, you may want to install an infrared port on your desktop PC rather than mess around with network cards and cables. In addition, if you purchased infrared devices for your notebook PC and want to use them on the desktop PC, you'll need to install an infrared port on your desktop PC.

SEE ALSO

➤ *Learn how to connect and use infrared devices in Windows, page 279*

PC Card (PCMCIA) Ports

In making notebook PCs lightweight and compact, manufacturers left no room for adding hard drives and expansion cards. Instead, notebook PCs use external slots into which you insert PC cards. PC cards allow you to swap devices, including modems, networking cards, and memory, into and out of your notebook PC, so you can use only the device you need.

So why don't desktop PCs use PC cards? The main reason is convenience. On desktop PCs, we want all our equipment permanently connected. We don't want to trade a modem for a network adapter or swap RAM for disk space—we want everything available whenever we need to use it. This is why USB and FireWire hold out so much promise for desktop PC users; they offer permanent connections that allow us to tack on additional equipment at will—no swapping required.

However, if you like the idea of swappable PC cards, you can add PC card slots to your desktop PC. You'll learn how to add a PC card drive later in this chapter.

SEE ALSO

➤ *Learn how to safely insert and remove PC cards in Windows, page 270*

Installing Additional Ports

Installing ports is typically motivated by necessity rather than a desire to improve system performance. While upgrading, you run out of ports and have to figure out some way to connect the equipment you want to use.

Although you can use Y-cables, adapters, and pass-through devices as a cheap, temporary fix, you eventually must consider a more permanent solution: installing a multiple-port, SCSI, or USB adapter.

SEE ALSO

➤ *Learn general procedures for upgrading your PC, page 555*

Developing an Upgrade Strategy

Whenever you upgrade your PC, especially when adding ports, you should consider the future. Today, you want to add a scanner, but what about a month from now? Will you want to upgrade your audio system? Add a game controller? Install an external drive?

Without foresight, today's upgrade decision can severely limit tomorrow's possibilities. For example, if you choose an inexpensive parallel port scanner today and decide you want to add an external, parallel port drive to your PC later, you're going to encounter a major bottleneck at the parallel port.

You would do better to purchase a SCSI or USB adapter right away and base your future upgrade decisions on these more expandable ports. For example, if you're purchasing an external drive, you can purchase a SCSI adapter for the drive and give yourself the option of adding a SCSI scanner, DVD drive, and internal hard drive later. By taking this approach, you keep your parallel port free for your printer and give yourself virtually unlimited upgrade options for the future.

Installing Ports and Adapters

Ports are connected to expansion cards, so the steps you take to install a port are the same steps for installing an expansion card. If you are installing a parallel or serial port, you may need to connect cables from the ports to connectors on the expansion card and then secure the port to the system unit case with its mounting bracket (see Figure 38.2).

FIGURE 38.2

Parallel and serial ports may connect to the expansion board via cable.

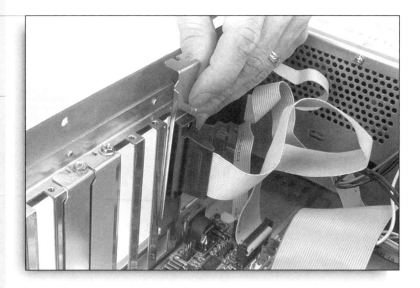

After installing the port, restart your PC. Windows should identify the port and lead you through the process of installing the device driver for it. You may need to adjust port settings, if the new port conflicts with existing ports.

SEE ALSO

➤ *Learn basic procedures for installing expansion boards, page 560*

➤ *Learn how to adjust port settings, page 794*

SCSI Compatibility Issues

When purchasing a SCSI adapter, you should be aware of the various SCSI standards. Table 38.1 lists the available SCSI standards.

TABLE 38.1   **SCSI standards**

Standard	Description
SCSI-1	8-bit bus, data transfer rates of 4MBps, supports up to 7 devices. Useful for relatively slow devices, such as standard CD-ROM drives, hard drives, and scanners.
SCSI-2	8-bit data bus, data transfer rates of 4MBps, and supports up to 15 devices. Useful for high-performance hard drives, 8X or faster CD-ROM drives, removable hard disk drives (such as Jaz drives).
Wide SCSI	16-bit data bus, data transfer rates of 8MBps, uses 68-pin connector.
Fast SCSI	8-bit data bus, data transfer rates of 10MBps.
Fast Wide SCSI	16-bit data bus, data transfer rates of 20MBps.
Ultra SCSI	8-bit data bus, data transfer rates of 20MBps.
SCSI-3 (or Ultra Wide SCSI)	16-bit data bus, data transfer rates of 40MBps.
Ultra2 SCSI	8-bit data bus, data transfer rates of 40MBps.
Wide Ultra2 SCSI	16-bit data bus, data transfer rates of 80MBps.

With the differences in SCSI standards and variations in connectors, be careful when purchasing SCSI devices and cables to ensure compatibility. To identify the required SCSI connectors for your devices, refer to Figure 38.3. For a wide selection of SCSI adapters, devices, and cables try SCSI STUFF at www.scsistuff.com.

FIGURE 38.3

When shopping for SCSI cables, make sure you get the right connectors.

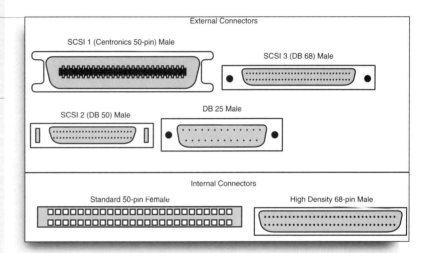

SEE ALSO

➤ *Learn how to install a SCSI hard drive, page 599*

➤ *Learn how to assign addresses and turn termination on or off for devices, page 635*

Upgrading to USB (Unlimited Options)

Most new PCs come with two USB ports connected to a single controller, so you can connect a total of 127 devices (not 127 devices per USB port, but 127 devices per USB controller). If you have an older PC, don't run out and buy a new PC just yet. A company called ADS Technologies (www.adstech.com) markets several products for making your current PC USB-ready:

- *A PCI expansion board with two USB ports* (see Figure 38.4).

- *A four-port USB hub.* A hub is a box that allows you to connect several devices to a single port. You plug the hub into a

USB port on your PC and connect up to four USB devices to the hub. Some USB devices, such as keyboards or printers function as hubs.

■ *A two-port USB PC card for notebook PCs.* You insert the USB PC card into your notebook's PC card slot. You can then plug USB devices into the ports on the card.

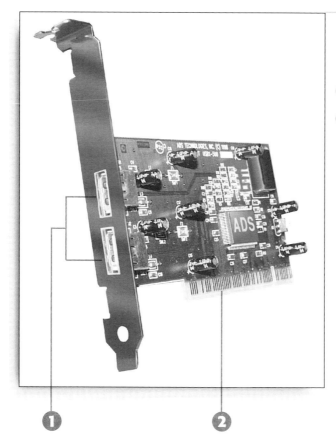

FIGURE 38.4

ADS Technologies manufactures PCI-to-USB expansion boards and other USB products.

① Two USB ports

② Contacts for plugging into PCI expansion slot

Another place to check out available USB adapters, cables, and devices is USB STUFF at www.usbstuff.com. At USB STUFF, you'll find not only the standard adapters and hubs but other innovative adapters, connectors, and devices that can help free up your existing parallel and serial ports:

- *USB-to-parallel port adapter*. Allows you to plug a standard parallel port printer into a USB port. Improves printing performance while opening your parallel printer port for an external drive or scanner.

- *USB-to-serial port adapter*. Add serial ports to your PC through the USB port, without having to worry about introducing COM port conflicts. USB adapters may provide several ports for connecting both serial and parallel port devices. The fast data transfer rate of the USB port makes it perfect for connecting high-speed ISDN modems externally.

- *USB-to-infrared remote*. Adds infrared capabilities to your PC through the USB port. Includes a remote control for pointing and clicking at a distance.

- *USB keyboards, mice, joysticks, and more*. If you purchased a system with USB ports and can't find any devices to connect to those ports, USB STUFF is the place to start searching.

SEE ALSO

➤ *Learn how to install a USB scanner, page 750*

Finding the Right FireWire Adapter

Unless you need to do some heavy-duty video recording and editing, FireWire currently is not the most practical upgrade. FireWire devices are not very available right now.

However, if you do need to record and edit video or are just trying to plan ahead, check out Adaptec's SCSI/FireWire-to-PCI adapter. Called HotConnect Ultra 8945, this card allows you to connect up to 15 SCSI devices and 62 FireWire (IEEE 1394) devices to a single adapter. With a fast SCSI hard drive and a video player that has an IEEE 1394 connector, you have the ultimate system for recording video clips. For more information, go to www.adaptec.com.

Adding a PC Card Drive to a Desktop PC

Most PC card drives for desktop PCs are designed to read cards from digital cameras. You plug the card reader into your PC's parallel port and then quickly download the images to your PC. Some PC card drives can handle standard PC cards as well as cards designed for digital cameras. These drives allow you to quickly swap devices, such as network cards, modems, and even joysticks, providing more flexible and dynamic ways to upgrade your PC.

If you would rather install the PC card drive internally, you have a couple options:

- If you have an unoccupied drive bay that has an opening to the outside of the system unit, consider purchasing an internal PC card drive. Most internal drives come with an ISA expansion card. You connect the drive to the card using a data cable. This leaves your PCI slots open for more high-end devices.

- If you don't have an open drive bay, you can purchase PC card drives that are built-in to the ISA card. However, having to eject the PC cards from the back of the system unit isn't the best option for swapping cards. This configuration is practical only if you are using PC cards that you plan on keeping in the drive for long periods, such as a network or modem card.

Because PC cards are not very popular for desktop PCs, you won't see many PC card drives around. However, you can find high-quality PC card drives on the Web at www.envoydata.com and www.anmax.com.

Finding an Infrared Adapter for Your Desktop PC

Unlike a typical port, which pokes out the back of the system unit and provides a direct cable connection to a particular device, an infrared port requires a direct line of site to the infrared device. Manufacturers have developed a couple ways to achieve the required direct line of site:

- *Wrap-around cable*. The infrared expansion card plugs into an expansion slot as usual. The expansion card comes with its own receiver on a 1–2-foot long cable. You plug the receiver into the expansion card and point the receiver at the infrared device you want to use.

- *Infrared drive.* Instead of having the infrared port poke out the back of the system unit, it mounts in an open drive bay, so it looks out the front of the system unit. If you have an unoccupied drive bay, this configuration is the most convenient and flexible. Most Pentium systems and all Pentium II systems have an IrDA connector on the motherboard, so you need not add an expansion board.

Before purchasing an Infrared drive, make sure your motherboard has the required IrDA connector and that your BIOS supports IrDA communications. For information about infrared drives, including installation instructions, go to www.baybeamer.com. For a less expensive alternative that doesn't require opening your system unit, try Belkin's Red-Eye or Puma Technologies' TranXit, an infrared receiver that plugs into your PC's serial port. To learn more about Red-Eye or TranXit, visit www.belkin.com or www.pumatech.com.

If you have a parallel printer, you can transform it into an infrared printer by attaching an infrared adapter. A good place to shop for infrared adapters, cables, and equipment is Computergate at www.computergate.com. Adaptec also has a healthy selection of infrared options (www.adaptec.com)

Checking Your Port Settings

Whenever you install a port, you can expect to encounter conflicts. Windows may display a warning, or the new port (or one of your old ports) may stop functioning. If you install a port and encounter problems using the port or another port on your PC, check the port settings in Windows.

Checking port settings in Windows

1. Alt+click **My Computer**.
2. Click the **Device Manager** tab.

3. Click the plus sign next to **Ports** (see Figure 38.5). If there is a yellow or red caution symbol next to a port's name, the port is using settings that conflict with another device.

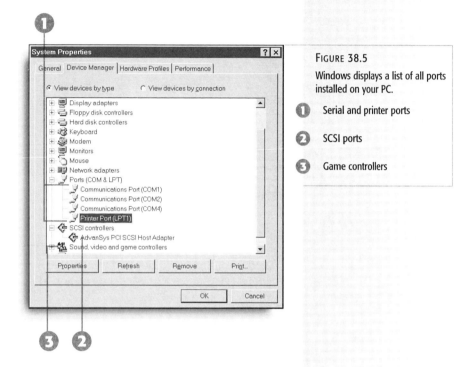

FIGURE 38.5

Windows displays a list of all ports installed on your PC.

1 Serial and printer ports

2 SCSI ports

3 Game controllers

4. To check a port's settings, double-click its name to display the port's Properties dialog box.

5. Click the **Resources** tab. Windows displays the IRQ (Interrupt Request) and I/O (Input/Output) range for the port (see Figure 38.6).

By checking a port's settings, you can often troubleshoot conflicts with other devices. If two ports use the same interrupt (IRQ) setting, Windows will flag the conflict. You can easily resolve the problem by setting the IRQ jumpers on one of the devices to change its setting or changing the port's setting in the BIOS setup.

FIGURE 38.6

Windows displays the interrupt and resources currently assigned to the device.

1 Input/Output range

2 Interrupt (IRQ)

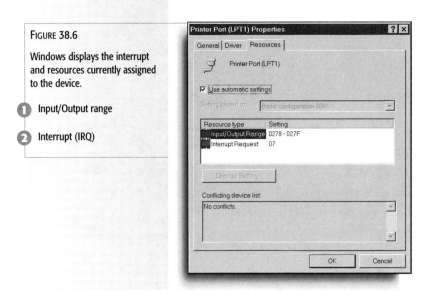

However, if a resource conflict exists, Windows may overlook the conflict and indicate that all devices are working properly. Tracking down and resolving such conflicts can be difficult.

SEE ALSO

➤ *Learn how to track down and resolve hardware conflicts, page 802*

Troubleshooting Your PC

Troubleshooting Hardware Problems

Track down hardware conflicts in Windows

Get your modem to dial out and establish a connection

Solve audio problems

Eliminate problems with your display adapter and monitor

Track down and resolve printing problems

Identify and correct Internet connection problems

General Troubleshooting Tactics

With a little patience, you can solve most hardware problems on your PC. You just have to know how to go about it—what to do and what not to do. The overall approach is twofold: You need to trace the problem to its cause, and not make the problem worse than it already is.

When you run into a hardware problem that doesn't have an obvious solution, the best course of action is inaction; that is, don't do anything until you've given the problem some thought. Then, start looking for clues:

- *Are there any onscreen messages?* Look at the monitor for any messages that indicate a problem. Although onscreen messages are usually very general, they provide a starting point.

- *Is everything plugged in and turned on?* If a part of your computer is dead—no lights, no sound, no action—it probably isn't connected or isn't turned on. If everything is turned on, turn everything off and check the connections. Don't assume that just because something looks connected it is; wiggle the plugs.

- *When did the problem start?* Think back to what you did before the problem arose. Did you install a new program? Did you enter a command? Did you add a new device? When my Windows couldn't format my floppy disk drive, I realized that the problem started after I installed a new hard drive. I had knocked the floppy disk drive cable loose; it was connected just well enough for Windows to read data off disks but not tight enough for Windows to format disks.

- *Did anything else stop working?* Sometimes it's easier to track down a problem if two devices stop working at the same time. A quick look at the settings used for each device typically reveals the conflict immediately.

Although your PC or the device you installed may be causing the problem, most hardware problems are caused by software problems. A setting in the BIOS or in Windows is usually the cause of the problem.

Using the Windows Troubleshooters

Windows 98 comes with several troubleshooters that can help you determine the causes of common problems. Following is a list of these troubleshooters:

Dial-Up Networking Troubleshooter

DirectX Troubleshooter

Direct Cable Connection Troubleshooter

Display Troubleshooter

DriveSpace 3 Troubleshooter

Hardware Conflict Troubleshooter

Memory Troubleshooter

The Microsoft Network Troubleshooter

Modem Troubleshooter

MS-DOS Programs Troubleshooter

Networking Troubleshooter

PC Card Troubleshooter

Print Troubleshooter

Sound Troubleshooter

Startup and Shutdown Troubleshooter

Troubleshooters help by displaying a series of questions that lead you through checks and corrections.

Running a Windows Troubleshooter

1. Click the **Start** button and choose **Help**. The Windows Help window appears with the <u>**Contents**</u> tab in front.

2. In the <u>**Contents**</u> list, click **Troubleshooting**.

3. Click **Troubleshooting** and then click **Windows 98 Troubleshooters**. This displays a list of available troubleshooters.

4. Click the troubleshooter you want to use. The troubleshooter starts or a button or link for running the troubleshooter appears in the right pane. If necessary, click the button or link for running the troubleshooter. The right pane displays a list of problems and questions.

Is it a virus?

It's tempting to blame strange happenings on viruses, but over 90% of the problems most users report as viruses are caused by human error, program bugs, or wrong settings in Windows.

5. Click the desired problem or question and follow the troubleshooter's instructions (see Figure 39.1).

FIGURE 39.1

The Windows Troubleshooters can help you track down common problems.

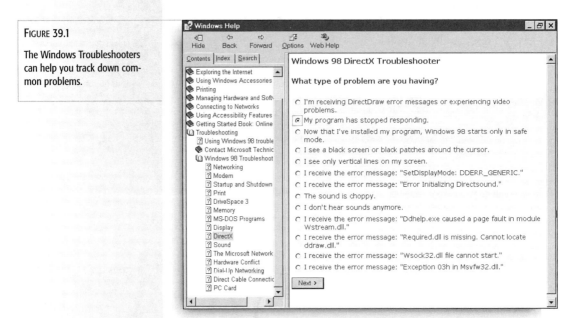

Tracking Down Hardware Conflicts

If you install a new device, and it doesn't work or causes another device to stop working, chances are that the two devices are trying to use the same resources. Typically, there are three settings you need to look at:

- *IRQ* stands for *interrupt request* and is a number that enables a device to demand attention from the central processing unit. Although PCI expansion cards can share IRQs, built-in printer ports, serial ports, and legacy (non–Plug and Play) ISA cards cannot. If two such devices try to use the same IRQ, one or both devices may not work, may not work well, or may cause intermittent problems.

- *DMA Channel* is a path to your computer's RAM. Most computers have eight DMA (Direct Memory Access) channels. If two devices are set up to use the same DMA channel, usually only one device gains access to RAM and the other doesn't work. Fortunately, very few devices (floppy disk drives, tape drives, sound cards, and some CD-ROM drives) use DMA channels.

- *I/O port address* is a designation that allows a device to input and output information at a certain location. As with IRQs and DMAs, if two devices use the same I/O setting, problems occur. I/O addresses are particularly susceptible to conflicts. And, because there are so many I/O addresses, because they overlap, and because Windows rarely indicates conflicts in I/O addresses, the conflicts are tough to track down.

Checking the Settings for a Device

Although you can rarely fix a device conflict in Windows, you can use Windows to determine which devices are conflicting.

Finding conflicting devices

1. Alt+click **My Computer**.
2. Click the **Device Manager** tab.
3. If a device is conflicting with another device and Windows knows it, Windows displays a yellow or red caution symbol next to the name of the device.

   If no device is marked, click the plus sign next to the category under which the problem device is listed (for example, Modem or Mouse).
4. Double-click the name of the device marked with the red or yellow caution symbol or the device that is not working.
5. Click the **Resources** tab. Windows displays the IRQ (Interrupt Request) and I/O (Input/Output) range for the port (see Figure 39.2).
6. Write down the settings and click **OK**.
7. Follow steps 3–5 to determine if any other devices are using the same settings. (Keep in mind that PCI cards can safely share the same IRQ setting.) Note any settings that conflict or overlap.

Using special utilities

Although you can track down hardware conflicts on your own, special programs, such as Norton Utilities and Nuts & Bolts can help you track down stubborn conflicts and help you resolve them.

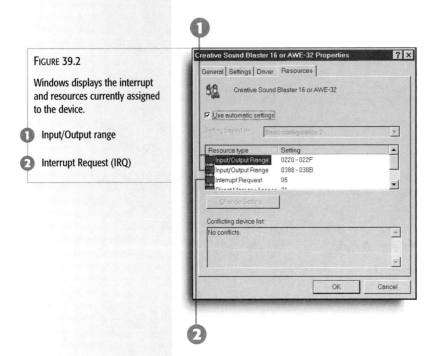

FIGURE 39.2

Windows displays the interrupt and resources currently assigned to the device.

1 Input/Output range

2 Interrupt Request (IRQ)

In Windows 98, you can use the System Information Utility to help track down conflicts and gather additional clues. Choose **Start**, **Programs**, **Accessories**, **System Tools**, **System Information**. Click the plus sign next to **Hardware Resources**. Click the name of the resource you want to check (see Figure 39.3).

Simple Fixes

Disable a device

If you suspect that two devices are conflicting, but are unsure, try disabling one of the devices. In Device Manager, double-click the name of one of the conflicting devices, click **Disable in This Profile**, and click **OK**. If you disable the device and the other device works okay, you have found the conflict and can take steps to resolve it.

In some cases, fixing the problem may be very easy. If a device is listed twice, remove one of the entries for the device (click its name in Device Manager and click the **Remove** button).

You may also be able to eliminate a conflict by reinstalling the driver for a device. If the device has a red or yellow caution symbol next to it, click the name of the device, click **Remove**, and restart Windows. Windows should detect the device and lead you through the process of reinstalling the driver.

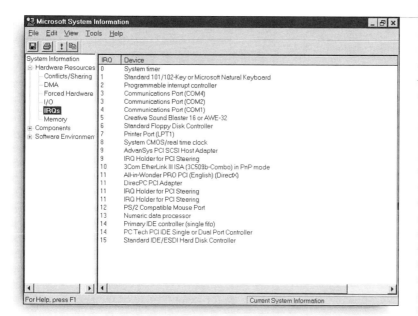

A Little More Difficult: Resolving IRQ Conflicts

Although IRQ conflicts are notorious for causing problems, Windows does a fairly good job of identifying IRQ conflicts and marking the conflicting devices in Device Manager. For additional help, Table 39.1 lists the 16 IRQs along with the devices that typically try to use them.

TABLE 39.1   Standard IRQ assignments

IRQ	Typically Used By
0	System timer
1	Keyboard
2	Programmable Interrupt Controller
3	COM 2 and COM 4
4	COM 1
5	Sound card (common area for conflicts)
6	Floppy disk drive

continues…

TABLE 39.1   **Continued**

IRQ	Typically Used By
7	Printer port
8	CMOS clock
9	Network card, SCSI adapter, PCI card
10	Network card, SCSI adapter, PCI card
11	Network card, SCSI adapter, PCI card
12	PS/2 mouse
13	Numerical control
14	Primary IDE
15	Standard IDE

Although tracking down the conflict is relatively easy, resolving the conflict can be a challenge depending on how the IRQ for the device is set. The following list explains common ways to change the IRQ settings for devices. Before changing a setting, always write down the current setting and the new setting:

- Older ISA adapters (typically sound cards, modems, and network cards) use jumpers on the card to set the IRQ. Check the documentation that came with the device to determine the available IRQ settings. Make sure you change the setting to an IRQ that is not being used by another device.

- Your PC's BIOS may automatically assign an IRQ to the PCI expansion slots. If a PCI card is trying to use the same IRQ setting that an older ISA card is using, enter the BIOS setup and manually assign an IRQ to the PCI slot. Again, make sure you assign an IRQ that is not being used by another device.

- If you are having trouble with a serial or printer port, try changing the IRQ setting for the port that's experiencing problems in the BIOS setup.

Tougher Problems: Tracking I/O Address Conflicts

Tracking down and resolving IRQ conflicts is child's play when compared to detecting and resolving conflicts with I/O addresses. The list of I/O addresses is lengthy and ranges often overlap, causing conflicts that even Windows does not detect. Table 39.2 provides a list of I/O address ranges along with descriptions of devices that commonly operate in these ranges. However, it can take quite a bit of detective work to track down conflicts.

Two PCI cards, one IRQ

If Windows displays two (or three) PCI devices using the same IRQ, don't panic. Windows uses a technique called IRQ steering to allow the PCI cards to share an IRQ without conflicting.

TABLE 39.2 **I/O addresses and areas of concern**

I/O Address Range	Typically Used By
000–00F	Direct memory access controller.
020–021	Programmable interrupt controller.
040–043	System timer.
060–064	PS/2 keyboard, mouse, PC speaker.
070–08F	System CMOS clock and other system resources.
130–14Fh, 140–15Fh	SCSI adapters.
200–207	Gameport/joystick.
220–22Fh	Sound cards and SCSI adapters.
240–24Fh	Sound cards and network cards.
260–26Fh, 270–27Fh	Sound cards and network cards. Some network cards may conflict with system devices, including parallel port, when set to use these addresses.
280–28Fh	Sound cards and network cards.
300–30Fh	Network cards and MIDI port on some sound cards.
320–32Fh, 330–33Fh	Network cards, MIDI port on sound cards, some SCSI adapters. This is a common area for conflicts.
340–34Fh	SCSI adapters, network cards, and other devices. Another common area for conflicts.
360–36Fh, 370–37Fh	First parallel port, secondary IDE controller, network card, tape drive accelerator. Another common area for conflicts.

continues…

TABLE 39.2 Continued

I/O Address Range	Typically Used By
3B0–3BBh, 3C0–3DFh	VGA adapters.
3E8–3EFh	COM3. Rare conflicts.
3F0–3F7h	Shared without problems between floppy disk drive controller and primary controller's slave driver. However, if other devices attempt to use this I/O address range, problems occur.

If you have any PCI cards installed, you may notice that the I/O addresses listed in the System Information Utility go far beyond the "300" numbers listed here. PCI cards use their own, internal I/O addresses to access resources.

Getting Your Modem to Work

If you have a Plug and Play modem or a PCMCIA modem (on a notebook computer), you can plug in the modem, and when you start Windows, Windows detects, configures, and installs it automatically without a problem.

With modems that are not Plug and Play compatible, installation can be quite difficult, especially if you have several other devices installed in your computer—additional serial ports, pointing devices, sound cards, and so on. It is not uncommon for a modem installation to fail or for the modem to work but disable one of your other devices. To track down device conflicts, run the Windows Modem Troubleshooter, as mentioned earlier.

Modem Cannot Detect Dial Tone

You can turn dial tone detection off, but before you do that, check your phone line. If you use the same phone line for voice calls from your home or office, make sure the phone is not currently being used. Also check the phone line from your modem to the phone jack to make sure it has not been disconnected. If you have an external modem, turn it off, wait a few seconds, and turn it back on. If the modem still doesn't work, try turning off dial tone detection.

Turning off Dial Tone Detection

1. Open the Windows Control Panel and click the Modems icon.

2. Make sure your modem is selected and click the **Properties** button.

3. Click the **Connection** tab and remove the check mark from the **Wait for Dial Tone Before Dialing** check box. Click **OK**.

4. Click **OK** again to save your settings.

Modem Dials Wrong Number

If you need to dial a 9 to get an outside line or dial a 1 and another number to place a long distance call, check your modem's dialing properties.

Checking your modem's Dialing Properties

1. Open the Windows Control Panel and click the Modems icon.

2. In the Modems Properties dialog box, click the **Dialing Properties** button.

3. In the **Area Code** text box, make sure the area code for your current location is correct.

4. If you need to dial the area code to reach a particular number within the same area code, click the **Area Code Rules** button, choose **Always Dial the Area Code**, and click **OK**.

5. If you need to dial an extra number to access an outside line, type that number in the **For Local Calls** text box.

6. In most cases, the **For Long Distance Calls** text box should be blank. If you typed a 1 in this text box, thinking that you have to dial 1 before a long-distance number, clear the 1 from this box. Type a number only if your phone system requires you to dial one number for outside, local calls and a different number for outside long-distance calls. Click **OK**.

7. When you return to the Modems Properties dialog box, click **OK** to save your changes.

Modem Hangs Up Prematurely

If the line you are calling is busy, Windows might immediately hang up without informing you that the line is busy. If your modem's speaker is turned on, you should hear the busy signal. Try the call again later.

If Windows keeps aborting the call, check to make sure that the phone number you entered is correct. Windows may be trying to dial a number that doesn't exist.

Dial-Up Networking Cannot Establish Connection

Click the icon for your Dial-Up Networking connection, enter your username and password, and click **Connect**. Watch the Connecting To dialog box for clues. If your modem dials the correct number for your service provider and tries to establish a connection, and the service provider accepts your username and password but then disconnects you, Dial-Up Networking might be set up to use a server type that does not match your service provider's server. Check your Dial-Up Networking settings.

Checking the Dial-Up Networking settings

1. Open My Computer and click the Dial-Up Networking icon.

2. Right-click the icon for your service provider and choose **Properties**.

3. Click the **Server Types** tab.

4. Open the **Type of Dial-Up Server** drop-down list and choose the server type specified by your Internet service provider (usually PPP).

5. Under **Allowed Network Protocols**, make sure **TCP/IP** is the only protocol selected, and then click the **TCP/IP Settings** button. (Enabling protocols other than TCP/IP may cause connection problems with some ISPs.)

6. Most service providers assign you an IP address that identifies your computer on the Internet. Make sure **Server assigned IP address** is selected, unless your service provider assigned you a permanent IP address.

7. Most service providers specify a Domain Name Server address. If your service provider specified an address, choose **Specify na_me server addresses** and type the address in the **Primary _D_NS** text box (see Figure 39.4). If your ISP has a secondary DNS, type its address in the **Secondary D_N_S** text box.

8. While you're at it, make sure **Log On to Network** (on the **Server Types** tab) is turned off. If this option is selected, Windows looks for a Windows network before logging on, which can cause delays or aborted calls. Click **OK**.

9. When you return to the Dial-Up Networking properties dialog box for this connection, click **OK** to save the new settings.

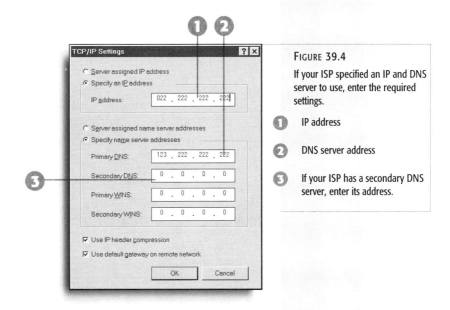

FIGURE 39.4

If your ISP specified an IP and DNS server to use, enter the required settings.

❶ IP address

❷ DNS server address

❸ If your ISP has a secondary DNS server, enter its address.

If this does not fix the problem, open the Windows Control Panel again and click the Network icon. In the list of network components, double-click the TCP/IP entry that is linked to your modem. Click the **DNS Configuration** tab, make sure **Enable DNS** is off. Then save your changes and try the call again. If you still have problems, contact your ISP's technical support department.

Disconnected When Using Modem

Several factors might be at work here. If you use the same phone line for voice calls and you or someone else picks up a phone that's on the same line, you might be automatically disconnected. In addition, if you have a weak phone line connection, an old phone line, or a connection with a lot of noise, the connection might not be clear enough to transfer data.

In addition, if you have call waiting, any incoming calls automatically disconnect the modem. You should disable call waiting whenever you dial into your online service or Internet service provider.

Disabling Call Waiting

1. Open the Windows Control Panel and click the Modems icon.

2. Make sure your modem is selected and click the **Properties** button.

3. Click the **Dialing Properties** button.

4. Choose **To Disable Call Waiting, Dial** and choose or type the number you must dial to disable the call waiting feature. This number is usually *70. Click **OK**.

5. When you return to the Modems Properties dialog box, click **OK** to save your changes.

Slow Internet Connection

When you are pulling up Web pages that contain large graphics and audio and video clips, expect your Internet connection to slow to a crawl. These files are large and take a long time to travel over the phone lines. You should also expect your connection to your service provider to be slower than the maximum speed of your modem. Remember that because of phone line noise and other hardware limitations, data transfers via modem are not perfect.

To check the speed of your connection, establish your connection, and then right-click the Dial-Up Networking icon (in the system tray on the right end of the taskbar) and choose **Status**. Take a look at the Connected To dialog box. It displays the speed of the connection (in bytes per second) between your computer and the service provider. If you have a 28.8Kbps modem, a perfect connection would list 28,800bps. If you are connected at 24,000bps or higher, consider this a good connection. If it's any slower, you should disconnect, reconnect, and check the speed again. Sometimes you'll get lucky and end up with a cleaner connection simply by reconnecting.

However, having a clean connection does not ensure that you will be cruising the Internet at warp speed. Several factors determine the speed at which you can download files, including the speed of the server you are connected to, how busy the server is, how busy the Internet is, and the size of the files you are downloading. If you want speed, try connecting during off hours, such as late at night and early in the morning.

If the connection itself is slow (you have a 28.8Kbps modem that's connecting at 16,000bps), you can often increase the speed of your connection by specifying a speed that is greater than your modem's maximum speed. Open the Windows Control Panel, click the **Modems** icon, and click the **Properties** button. Choose a higher speed from the **Maximum Speed** drop-down list and click **OK**.

Other factors that can slow down your Internet connection include the following:

- *Slow Internet service provider*. Not all Internet service providers can provide high-quality service. If the service provider is new and has many new users, the service you receive may suffer.

- *Defective phone lines*. Check not only the phone line from your modem to the phone jack but also the phone line from the jack to your connection box (typically on the outside of the house). A loose wire can result in a weak connection.

Troubleshooting Audio Problems

If you just installed a sound card, and it doesn't work, or if you installed another device and your sound card stopped working, tracking down the problem can be tough. The solution can range from something as simple as cranking up the volume to something as complex as fooling around with switches on the card. First, look for simple solutions:

- Are your speakers plugged in to the right jack—the output jack? (It's easy to plug the speakers into the microphone jack or the input jack by mistake.)

- If you have amplified speakers, are they plugged into the power supply and turned on?

- Is the volume cranked up? (Most sound cards have a volume control like on a radio.)

- Is the sound cranked up in Windows? Right-click the Volume icon in the system tray (on the right end of the taskbar) and choose **Open Volume Controls**. Make sure the **Speaker** and **Wave** volume controls are at their maximum settings and that the **Mute** options are NOT selected.

- Are you running a program that plays sounds and that is compatible with your sound card? Is sound turned on (and turned up) in the program?

- Did you install the drivers? The sound card should come with one or more disks containing the sound card drivers. You must run the installation program to set up your computer to use the sound card.

Is the sound card in conflict with another device? Use the Sound Troubleshooter, as mentioned earlier in this chapter, to identify the conflict.

No Conflict, No Sound

If you worked through the previous section and your sound card still does not emit a sound, check your sound card's properties in Windows.

Checking your sound card's properties

1. Open the Windows Control Panel and click the Multimedia icon.

2. On the **Audio** tab, under **Playback**, open the **Preferred Device** drop-down list and choose your sound card.

3. Click the **Advanced** tab.

4. Click the plus sign (+) next to **Audio Devices**, and then right-click your sound card and choose **Properties**.

5. Make sure **U**se audio features on this device is selected (see Figure 39.5). Click **OK**.

6. When you return to the Multimedia Properties dialog box, click **OK** to save your changes.

FIGURE 39.5
Make sure Windows is set up to use your sound card's audio features.

If the problem persists, the WAV or CD audio device might not be installed. Click the Multimedia icon in the Control Panel, click the **Advanced** tab, and click the plus sign (+) next to **Media Control Devices**. CD Audio Device and WAV Audio Device should be listed there. If they are in the list, right-click each device, choose **Properties**, and make sure **U**se This Media Control Device is selected. If these devices are not in the list, use the Add New Hardware Wizard to install them.

Microphone Doesn't Work

Make sure that your microphone is plugged in to the MIC jack on the sound card and that the microphone switch (if it has one) is turned on. Then check the recording volume in Windows.

Checking the microphone volume

1. Right-click the Volume icon in the system tray (on the right end of the taskbar) and choose **Open Volume Controls**.

2. Drag the **Microphone** slider all the way up. (If the Microphone volume control is not displayed, open the **Options** menu, choose **Properties**, place a check mark in the **Microphone** check box, and click **OK**.)

3. Click the Speaker window's **Close (x)** button.

The tough part of tracking down recording problems is determining whether the cause is related to recording or playback. If you still have problems playing back recorded sounds, use the program you are trying to record in to open a WAV file in the Windows\Media folder and play it. If the sound does not play, the problem is probably related to sound output, not sound input.

Stereo Sound Card, Mono Output

Check your speakers. With many desktop speakers, one speaker is connected to the other by a plug-in cable. The cable might have become disconnected. Also, if each speaker has a separate volume control, make sure both controls are turned up. Likewise, if the speakers have a balance control, make sure it is in the center position. You should also check your output and speaker settings in Windows.

Checking speaker settings

1. Open the Windows Control Panel and click the Multimedia icon.

2. On the **Audio** tab, under Playback, click the **Advanced Properties** button.

3. On the **Speakers** tab, open the drop-down list and choose the type of speakers you are using (for example, Desktop Stereo Speakers). Click **OK**.

4. When you return to the Multimedia Properties dialog box, click the button with the speaker icon on it under **Playback**. This displays the volume controls.

5. Under **Speaker**, drag the **Balance** slider to the center position. Click the Speaker window's **Close (x)** button.

6. When you return to the Multimedia Properties dialog box, click **OK** to save your settings.

Correcting Mouse Problems

If you can't bring the mouse pointer into view, turn off your computer and check the mouse cable and plug. Make sure the cable is in good condition (no cracks or exposed wires) and that it is plugged in to the mouse port (not the keyboard port). Check the plug to make sure that the pins are not bent or pushed in. You can repair pins in a plug by using a pair of tweezers and a gentle touch. Reconnect the mouse and restart your computer.

If the mouse cable and plug are in good condition, but you still cannot see the mouse pointer or the mouse locks up Windows when you move it, restart your computer, and press F8 when you hear the first beep. Choose the option to start Windows in Safe mode. Windows loads a standard mouse driver, so you can use your mouse to install an updated mouse driver.

Jumpy Mouse Pointer

Your mouse is dirty. Turn it over and check to see if there's a piece of paper, a dustball, or a hair restricting the movement of the mouse ball. Remove the obstruction.

SEE ALSO
➤ *Learn how to give your mouse a thorough cleaning, page 82*

Mouse Stopped Working After Installing Modem

If your mouse plugs into a serial (COM) port, it may be trying to use the same COM port as the modem. Normally a serial mouse uses COM1, and the modem uses COM2. If your mouse and modem don't seem to get along, they're probably trying to use the same COM port. Leave the mouse port setting as is, and try changing the setting for the modem (try COM2 or COM4). For internal modems, you have to flip some switches on the modem itself and change the COM port setting in the communications program.

The modem might also be using IRQ or I/O address settings that conflict with the mouse. See "Tracking Down Hardware Conflicts," earlier in this chapter, for details.

Mouse Pointer Moves Too Fast or Too Slow

You can easily adjust the speed at which the mouse pointer travels across the screen and the speed at which you must click twice to execute a double-click. In the Windows Control Panel, click the Mouse icon. Use the resulting dialog box to enter the desired settings for controlling the mouse (see Figure 39.6).

FIGURE 39.6

Enter settings to control the movement of the mouse pointer.

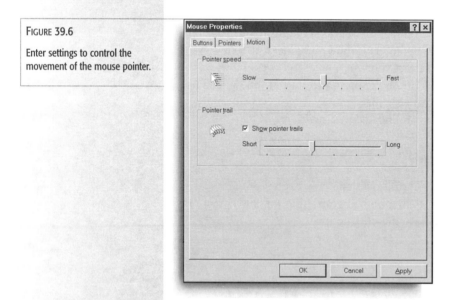

Correcting Display Problems

If your screen is completely blank, first check for obvious causes:

- Is the monitor connected to the system unit and turned on?
- The Windows power saving feature automatically shuts down the monitor and hard disk drive after a certain period of inactivity. If you did not shut down the computer, move the mouse and press a key (the Shift key is a safe key to press), and then wait to see if the computer comes out of Standby mode.
- If the monitor is still blank, press Ctrl+Alt+Delete to see if you can restart Windows.
- If your system is locked up, press the Reset button on the system unit.

If the screen is blank, restart the computer, wait for it to beep, and immediately press F8. Select the command for starting Windows in Safe mode. Windows starts and loads a standard video driver. You can then install the correct video driver.

Installing a new video driver

1. Right-click a blank area of the desktop and choose **Properties**.
2. In the Display Properties dialog box, click the **Settings** tab.
3. Click the **Advanced** button.
4. Click the **Adapter** tab and make sure Windows is set up to use the correct display adapter. If the display adapter is incorrect or missing, click the **Change** button and use the Upgrade Device Driver Wizard to choose the correct adapter.
5. When you return to the Properties dialog box, click the **Monitor** tab and make sure Windows is set up to use the correct monitor driver. If the wrong monitor is displayed, click the **Change** button and use the Upgrade Device Driver Wizard to choose the correct driver.
6. Click **OK**, and then restart your computer.

Fuzzy or Blocky Graphics

Your display resolution or colors are set too low. Try increasing the resolution and color settings.

Adjusting the display properties

1. Right-click a blank area of the Windows desktop and choose **Properties**.

2. Click the **Settings** tab.

3. Open the **Colors** drop-down list and choose a setting of **256 Colors** or higher.

4. Under **Screen Area**, drag the slider to the right to set the screen area at **800-by-600** or higher.

5. Click **OK** and restart Windows if required.

System Locks Up for No Reason

Make sure Windows is using the correct display driver. You might have to obtain a new video driver from the monitor or video card manufacturer or from the computer manufacturer. If Windows is using the correct display driver, try decreasing hardware acceleration.

Decrease hardware acceleration

1. Open the Windows Control Panel and click the Display icon.

2. Click the **Settings** tab and click the **Advanced** button.

3. Click the **Performance** tab.

4. Drag the **Hardware acceleration** slider to the left one notch to decrease the setting (see Figure 39.7).

5. Click **OK** to return to the Display Properties dialog box, and then click **OK** to save your settings. You might have to restart Windows.

If you still have the same problem, repeat the steps to decrease the **Hardware acceleration** setting another notch.

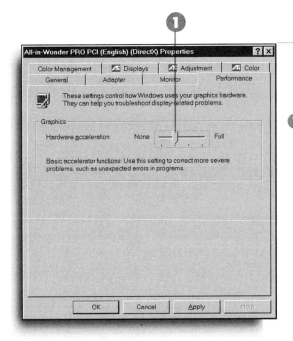

FIGURE 39.7

Your display adapter may be running a little faster than your system can handle.

❶ Drag the **Hardware acceleration** slider to the left.

Flickering Screen

Turn off your computer and check your monitor cables. If the power cable or the cable that connects the monitor to the system unit is loose, it might cause the screen to flicker. You should also check the display adapter card inside the system unit to make sure it has not jiggled loose from the expansion slot.

If the connections are secure, check the display's refresh rate. Right-click the desktop and click **Properties**. Click the **Settings** tab and click the **Advanced** button. Select the next higher refresh rate. (The control for setting the refresh rate varies depending on the monitor and display adapter and may not be available on some systems.)

If you continue to have problems, try decreasing the **Hardware acceleration** setting for the monitor, as explained in the previous section.

Refresh rate caution

Do not choose a refresh rate that is higher than your monitor's maximum refresh rate. Doing so could damage the monitor. If you hear a high-pitched beep from your monitor, the refresh rate setting may be too high. Lower it immediately.

New Game Won't Play

Many newer programs, especially Windows games, require DirectX support. In Windows 98, use Windows Update to make sure you have the latest version of DirectX.

SEE ALSO

➤ *Learn how to update Windows using Windows Update, page 251*

Troubleshooting CD-ROM Problems

If you just installed a CD-ROM drive and no letter for the drive appears in My Computer, turn off your computer and check the cables that connect your CD-ROM drive to the motherboard or expansion board inside your computer. Also check the cable from the power supply to the CD-ROM drive to ensure that the connections are secure. You might have jiggled a cable loose when you replaced the system unit cover.

If the cables are properly connected, Windows might be set up to use the wrong driver for your CD-ROM drive, or the driver might be corrupted. Try reinstalling the driver.

Reinstalling the CD-ROM driver

1. Open the Windows Control Panel and click the System icon.

2. In the System Properties dialog box, click the **Device Manager** tab.

3. Click the plus sign (+) next to **CD-ROM**.

4. Click the name of the CD-ROM driver to select it, and then click the **Remove** button. Click **OK** to remove the driver.

5. When you return to the System Properties dialog box, click **OK**, and then restart Windows.

6. Follow the onscreen instructions to install the CD-ROM driver.

Cannot Read Disc

If you are having problems with a single disc, the problem is probably the disc and not the drive. Make sure the printing on the disc is facing up; CD-ROM drives read from the bottom (unpainted side) of the disc. If the disc was positioned in the drive properly, check the bottom of the disc for dust, dirt, and scratches. If the disc is dusty, wipe it off with a lint-free cloth, using a motion from the center to the outside edges. If the disc has something sticky on it, spray the disc with window cleaner and wipe it thoroughly, again going from the center to the outside edges.

If you are having problems with more than one disc, the reading mechanism in the CD-ROM drive might be dirty. Purchase a CD-ROM drive cleaning kit and use it to clean the reading mechanism. These kits typically contain a CD with some cleaning solution. You squirt the cleaning solution on the disc, insert it in the drive, and remove it when it stops spinning.

Audio CD Won't Play

In most cases, the CD-ROM drive is not at fault. The sound in Windows is just turned way down. Right-click the Volume icon in the Windows taskbar and choose **Open Volume Controls**. Make sure the **Speaker**, **CD Player**, and **Wave** volumes are maxed. Also, make sure the **Mute** check boxes are *not* checked. (If these controls are not displayed, open the **Options** menu, choose **Properties**, and turn on the controls.)

If those adjustments do not correct the problem, check the volume control on your CD-ROM drive and on your sound card. (If the sound card has a volume control, it is on the back of the sound card where you plug in the speakers.) Also, make sure your speakers are plugged securely into the OUT jack on your sound card and that the speakers are plugged in and turned on.

The volume control on the CD-ROM drive typically controls only the headphone output, not the speaker output from your sound card. You can check your CD-ROM drive by plugging in a set of headphones and trying to play audio through the headphones. If you can hear audio through the headphones, you know that the problem is in either the sound card or the connection between the CD-ROM drive and the sound card.

If the audio does not play through the sound card, check the cable that connects the CD-ROM drive to the sound card. This cable typically has four wires connected to a small plug that you connect to the sound card *inside* your computer. Make sure the cable is in good condition and is securely connected.

CDs Don't Automatically Play

Multimedia, music CDs

Some newer music CDs contain interactive, multimedia presentations. You insert the disc expecting to hear music, and up pops a presentation complete with music, graphics, animation, and video. If you just want to hear the music, run CD Player (**Start**, **Programs**, **Accessories**, **Multimedia**, **CD Player**.)

Not all CDs have AutoPlay built into them. Many CDs act like floppy or hard disks: You must first enter a command or click an icon for the CD (in My Computer or Windows Explorer) to run the program or the installation utility. Then again, maybe AutoPlay has been disabled on your computer.

Enabling AutoPlay

1. Open the Windows Control Panel and click the System icon.
2. Click the **Device Manager** tab.
3. Click the plus sign (+) next to **CD-ROM**, and then double-click the icon for your CD-ROM drive. This displays the CD-ROM drive's properties.
4. Click the **Settings** tab and make sure there is a check mark in the **Auto insert notification** check box (see Figure 39.8). Click **OK**.
5. When you return to the System Properties dialog box, click **OK** to save your changes. You must then restart your computer.

Can't Access CD-ROM Drive from DOS

When you install Windows 98, it automatically disables your CD-ROM driver in DOS to prevent conflicts between the DOS and Windows CD-ROM drivers. When you restart in MS-DOS mode, the required driver is not loaded. Therefore, when you try to change to the CD-ROM drive at the DOS prompt, you receive the Invalid Drive Specification error message.

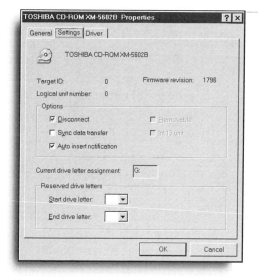

FIGURE 39.8
To enable AutoPlay, turn on **Auto insert notification**.

To use your CD-ROM drive from the DOS prompt, use your Windows Startup disk to restart your PC. When Windows displays the startup options, choose to start with CD-ROM drive support.

Tracking Down Printer Problems

Printers are the biggest troublemakers connected to any PC, because there are so many areas where things can go wrong. When the printer refuses to print, first check for obvious causes:

- Are the printer cables secure?
- Is the power on?
- Does the printer have paper?
- Is the printer online?

After you have ruled out the obvious causes, proceed to the following sections for instructions on how to approach more specific issues.

No Printout or Partial Printout

Check the paper rack on the printer to make sure it is seated properly and that the paper feed levers are in the proper position for the type of paper that's loaded. If everything checks out, but the printer still refuses to print, check the following:

- Turn the printer off, wait a minute, and turn it back on. This clears the printer's memory and can return it to normal. (If your printer doesn't have an on/off switch, unplug it and then plug it back in.)

- In My Computer, right-click drive **C** and click **Properties**. Make sure your hard disk has at least 10MB of free space. If you have less than that, run Cleanup Disk or the Windows Maintenance Wizard to free some space.

- Check to see if printing has been paused. Choose **Start**, **Settings**, **Printers**, and then right-click the printer icon. If **Pause Printing** has a check mark next to it, choose **Pause Printing** to remove the check mark.

- Check the printer setup in Windows. Choose **Start**, **Settings**, **Printers**, and then right-click the printer icon and choose **Properties**. Make sure the printer is set to the correct port (usually LPT1).

- Check the printer timeout settings. Choose **Start, Settings, Printers**, and then right-click the printer icon and choose **Properties**. Click the **Details** tab and increase the **Timeout settings** by 15 seconds each. The **Timeout settings** tell Windows how long to wait before giving up (see Figure 39.9).

- Check to see if your printer is set up as the default printer. Choose **Start**, **Settings**, **Printers**, and then right-click the printer icon and choose **Set As Default**.

- Make sure the correct printer is selected. Choose **Start**, **Settings**, **Printers**, and then right-click the printer icon and choose **Properties**. Make sure the correct printer driver is being used. If the wrong printer or driver is listed, click the **New Driver** button and choose the correct manufacturer and model.

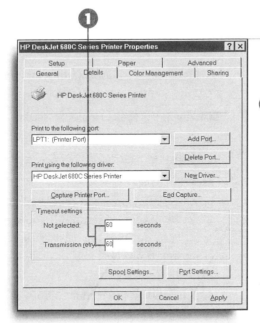

If several pages of a document printed, but not the whole thing, check the print settings in the program from which you are trying to print. Open the **File** menu and choose **Print**. Under **Page Range**, make sure you selected the setting for printing **All pages** (the entire document).

If a portion of a page printed and it is a page with complex graphics and several fonts, it's possible that your printer has insufficient memory to print the document. You should install additional memory in your printer. For the time being, try to use smaller, less-complex graphics and fewer fonts. You might also try printing in a lower resolution. When printing the document, click the **Properties** or **Options** button in the Print dialog box and choose **Draft Output** or a lower resolution.

Rough Edges on Print

If you just installed a new print cartridge in an inkjet printer, use the utility that came with the printer to align the cartridge. There is a little play in the cartridge holder that might cause the

Print the document once

When you run into printing problems, it is tempting to keep trying to print the document. That keeps sending the document to the print queue; when you finally do coax your printer into printing, you will get several copies of the document.

color and black ink cartridges to move out of alignment when you change cartridges. You might also try using a better grade of paper.

The graphics resolution setting in Windows can also cause graphics to print poorly. Check the quality setting for graphics.

Checking the graphics resolution setting

1. Click the **Start** button, point to **Settings**, and click **Printers**.

2. Right-click the icon for your printer and choose **Properties**.

3. Check the options in the Properties dialog box for a graphics or resolution setting. If you are using a Windows printer driver instead of the driver that came with your printer, the setting is on the **Graphics** tab. Choose the setting for the highest quality.

4. Click **OK** to save your settings.

Paper Feed Woes

Persistent paper feed problems

If your printer consistently has paper feed problems, contact the manufacturer. Don't do anything drastic like taking steel wool or sandpaper to the rollers; you'll void the warranty and make the problem even worse.

Check the paper feed tray. Make sure the tray is seated properly; it's easy to knock it loose when you're loading or unloading paper. Make sure the feed levers are in the correct position. If you have a lever pushed in to print envelopes and you are trying to print on standard paper, the paper won't feed properly.

In some cases, the rollers on the paper feed mechanism collect paper dust that makes the rollers slippery. Wipe the rollers off as best you can with a clean cloth (no cleaning solution, but you can use water). (You might find it nearly impossible to get to the entire surface of the rollers; don't force them, just clean what you can.)

Streaky Ink

Your ink cartridge might be on its way out, or it might be dirty. If your printer has been sitting for some time, ink might have dried on the print head. Many printers come with a special utility designed to purge dried ink. Check the printer documentation to determine how to use this utility.

Do not try to clean the cartridge with a paper towel or any kind of solution unless the manufacturer recommends it. Touching any of the contacts that connect the print cartridge to the printer could ruin the cartridge.

On a related note, it is tempting to refill cartridges to save money. If you have ever tried to refill an inkjet cartridge, you probably already realize that refilling cartridges is more mess than it's worth. If the mess is not enough to dissuade you, keep in mind that any damage to the printer caused by refilled cartridges usually voids the printer's warranty.

Error Printing to LPT1

This message usually pops up when you try to print a document right after you turn on the printer. It usually means that the printer wasn't ready right when Windows wanted to use it. To fix the problem, increase the timeout setting for the printer. Choose **Start**, **Settings**, **Printers**. Right-click the icon for your printer and click **Properties**. Click the **Details** tab and increase the timeout setting to 60 seconds.

If you still receive the error message, your computer might have a problem printing in Enhanced Metafile (EMF) format. Display the printer's properties dialog box again, click the **Details** tab, and click the **Spool Settings** button. Open the **Spool Data Format** drop-down list, choose **RAW**, and click **OK**. Click **OK** to save your changes.

Slow Printer

Printing is one of the slowest operations a computer performs, especially if you are printing high-resolution color graphics. However, there are a few things you can try to speed up printing:

- Make sure you have plenty of space on your hard drive for Windows to temporarily store printed documents as it prints them.
- Close or don't use other programs while you are printing.

- Add memory to your printer to allow it to store larger chunks of printing instructions.

- Install an updated printer driver.

- Use only printer fonts and TrueType fonts in your documents. Printer fonts are fastest because they are built into the printer. TrueType fonts are the fastest soft fonts.

- Lower the graphics resolution or print in draft mode when you do not need high-quality printouts.

Blank Sheet of Paper Inserted

If your printer spits out a blank sheet of paper at the end of the document, check the end or your document to determine if it ends with a page break mark (typically a dotted horizontal line). If you have several blank paragraphs at the end of the document, they might have caused the program to insert a page break. Delete the extraneous paragraph marks.

If the problem persists no matter which document you print, you might have Windows set up to print a separator page between documents. Separator pages are commonly used on network printers to prevent multiple users' documents from becoming mixed up. When you choose to print a document in one of your programs, check the printer options to determine if the program is set up to print a separator page.

Troubleshooting Web Problems

If you wander the Web for 10 minutes and don't receive an error message, you can consider yourself very fortunate. Given all the possible problem areas (your Web browser and modem, your ISP connection, the remote Web server, and even the Web page you're trying to load), it's amazing that Web browsing proceeds as smoothly as it does. However, you should be aware of the possible problems, as described in the following sections.

Browser Can't Find Page

Usually, this means that somebody moved or deleted the Web page you're trying to pull up. Try chopping the end off the right side of the page address and entering the shortened URL into the **Address** text box. For instance, if you initially typed www.yahoo.com/Entertainment/Movies/, try typing www.yahoo.com/Entertainment or just www.yahoo.com. You can then use links to move to the specific page you want.

If you still have trouble connecting to the page, and you have been entering abbreviated Web server addresses (for example, yahoo, instead of www.yahoo.com), try typing the entire address.

403 Forbidden **and Other 400 Codes**

The hostile 400 messages typically mean that you tried to connect to a Web server where you're not welcome or one that does not recognize your request. Perhaps the server does not allow public access, or maybe you are trying to connect to a site that requires you to pay a subscription price. Whatever the case, you can't do anything to side-step this message so just back up and try another page.

Can't Find DNS Server

DNS (short for Domain Name Server) is a system that matches the domain name you type (for example, www.yahoo.com) with its IP (Internet Protocol) number (for example, 129.98.170.98). In plain English, this means that the Domain Name Server finds Web sites.

If you type a page address and the DNS can't find a matching number for the address, your Web browser displays a dialog box telling you so. Check the following:

- Did you type the address correctly? One tiny typo (an uppercase letter that should be lowercase, a slash mark that points the wrong way, or even a misplaced period) can give you the DNS error message. Retype the address and press Enter.

- Are you connected to the Internet? If your connection was terminated (or you didn't connect in the first place), your Web browser can't find the page because Internet Explorer isn't even connected to the Internet. Establish your Internet connection and try again.

- If you received the error after clicking a link, the URL behind the link may have a typo. Rest the mouse pointer on the problem link and look at the address in the status bar. If you see an obvious typo, retype the address in the **Address** text box, and press **Enter**.

- If you're connected to the Internet, but you keep getting this error message no matter which Web page you try to load, maybe your service provider's DNS server is down or you have the wrong address for it. Try disconnecting and then reconnecting.

If the problem persists, contact your service provider to find out the correct address for the DNS server. To change the DNS server's address, right-click the Dial-Up Networking icon for your ISP and choose **Properties**. Click the **Server Types** tab and click the **TCP/IP Settings** button. Enter the DNS server's address in the **Primary DNS** text box. If your ISP has a secondary DNS server, enter its address in the **Secondary DNS** text box.

Web Page Takes Forever to Load

If a page takes an inordinate amount of time to download, the Web site might be too busy to handle your request. In such a case, after about one minute, your Web browser will give up trying to connect to the site and will display an error message indicating that the site is too busy. These traffic jams are common. Wait about five minutes, and then try connecting to the site again.

Tracking Down Network Problems

Setting up a network is like installing a modem—it can be tough to set up, but after it's working, it's relatively trouble-free.

However, making all the network computers work together in the first place can be quite a chore. The following sections focus on the most common network problems.

SEE ALSO

➤ Learn how to set up a simple peer-to-peer network, page 291

Can't Access the Network

Make sure you have installed the cables properly. Focus on the following cable issues:

- If you are using a twisted-pair cable (similar to a phone cable) to connect only two computers, make sure the cable is a cross-over cable. If it is a standard twisted-pair cable, the cable will not work.

- If you are using standard twisted-pair cables to connect more than two computers, you must use a cable to connect each computer to a central hub.

- If you are using coaxial cables, each network card must have a T-connector. If the computer is connected to only one other computer, the open end of the T-connector must be capped with a 50ohm RG58/AU terminator (not an RG59 terminator commonly sold for TV use).

If the cabling is okay, check the network card on your computer to make sure it is not conflicting with other devices. To track down device conflicts, run the Windows Network Troubleshooter, as mentioned earlier in this chapter.

If the network card is okay, click the Network icon in the Windows Control Panel and check the list of components to determine if the proper network protocols are installed. All computers on the network must be set up to use the same protocols. Remove any unnecessary network protocols from the list. For example, if each computer on the network has the NetBEUI protocol installed and bound to the network adapter, the computers should be able to establish a connection.

Check the Network properties on each computer to make sure that each computer has the same workgroup name. To check a computer's identity, in the Control Panel, click the Network icon and then click the **Identity** tab. Each computer should have the same Workgroup name.

Problems with a Direct Cable Connection

Assuming you are using the correct type of cable, that the cables are connected to the proper ports, and that you installed and configured Direct Cable Connection properly, three common problems can prevent the successful connection:

- If you are currently connected to the Internet, disconnect. Dial-Up Networking commonly causes problems with Direct Cable Connection.

- The port on one or both of your computers is conflicting with another device connected to your computer.

- One of the installed network components is causing a problem.

First, check for conflicts between your COM and LPT ports, as explained earlier in this chapter. If your ports have no conflicts, the problem may be caused by the IPX/SPX network protocol. Remove the IPX/SPX-Compatible protocol.

Removing a network protocol

1. Open the Windows Control Panel and click the Network icon.

2. Click the **IPX/SPX-Compatible Protocol** entry and click the **Remove** button. Repeat this step for all IPX/SPX-Compatible Protocol entries.

3. Make sure NetBEUI is in the list of network protocols. If it is not listed, click the **Add** button to add it. Then click **OK**.

If you still have a problem establishing the connection, try the following corrections:

- Network Neighborhood must be on the Windows desktop. If it is not present, use the options on the **Windows Setup** tab in the Add/Remove Programs dialog box to install it.

- Open the Windows Control Panel, click the Network icon, click the **Identification** tab, and make sure the workgroup name is the same on both computers.

- If you are connecting the two computers with a parallel cable, check your computer's setup program to make sure that the parallel port is set up as EPP (Enhanced Parallel Port) or ECP (Extended Capabilities Port). You typically run a computer's startup program by pressing a special key (usually F1 or F2) right after you turn on the computer's power and before Windows starts. Check the parallel port settings on both computers and try to match them.

Only One Computer in the Network Neighborhood

Network Neighborhood displays only those computers that are in the same workgroup. To see other computers, your computer and the other computers you want to access must all use the same workgroup name. In addition, each computer on the network must have a different computer name. To check the computer and workgroup names, open the Windows Control Panel, click the Network icon, and click the **Identification** tab.

Can't Use Drives or Printers on Network Computer

Before you can share disks, folders, files, or printers on your computer with other computers on the network, you must install File and Printer Sharing and mark drives, folders, and printers as shared.

SEE ALSO

➤ *Learn to install File and Printer Sharing, page 302*

➤ *Learn to mark resources as shared, page 307*

CHAPTER 40

Troubleshooting Software Problems

How to tell whether software or hardware is causing the problem

Isolate and identify software problems

Deal with buggy software until you find a more permanent solution

Find answers in the README file

Locate and install a software patch to fix the problem

Dealing with Software Problems

Your program just crashed. You can't open a menu or type. Your mouse pointer disappeared. The image on your screen may even be distorted or missing some key buttons and icons.

In most cases, a crash is a minor problem. Unfortunately, tracking down the cause is tough. Sometimes a new device, such as a mouse or modem, can cause a system-wide problem. In other cases, you might be running two or more programs that interfere with one another. In still other cases, your system might not be locked up at all; the program might be performing a complex task that does not allow you to perform another task, cancel the operation, or even close the program.

So, what can you do about it?

You need to do two things—regain control of your system and keep the program from locking up your system again. The following sections show you what to do.

Regaining Control of Your System

Your immediate concern is to regain control of your system so you can save any files you've been working on. Try the following possible techniques to make Windows respond:

- Wait a couple minutes for the program to complete whatever task it might be in the process of performing.

- If Windows is still locked up, press Ctrl+Alt+Delete. A list of currently running programs appears. Click the program that has (not responding) next to its name, and then click the **End Task** button. If prompted to confirm, click **End Task**. This usually closes the problem program and returns control to Windows (see Figure 40.1).

- If pressing Ctrl+Alt+Delete does not work, try to save any work you've done in your other programs and exit them (to prevent losing documents or changes), and then press Ctrl+Alt+Delete again and try to close the problem program.

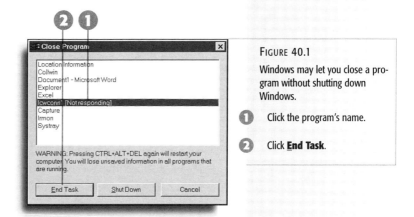

- If your system is still locked up, press Ctrl+Alt+Delete, and then click the **Shut Down** button or press Ctrl+Alt+Delete again. This restarts Windows. (If even that doesn't work, press the Reset button on your computer.)

In some cases, especially if you have to shut down Windows to correct the problem, Windows might place temporary files on your hard disk drive that cause your system to lock up in the future. After restarting from a lockup, you should always run ScanDisk to remove these files. Windows typically runs ScanDisk automatically when you start your computer after an improper shutdown.

Quick Fixes and Workarounds

When you're trying to get some work done in a hurry, you don't have time to troubleshoot software problems and find permanent solutions. For now, try the following quick fixes and workarounds until you have time to find a more permanent solution:

- *Reinstall the program.* In the Windows Control Panel, run Add/Remove Programs and remove the program. Reinstall the program. Reinstalling a program may fix a problem with one of the program's files.

Persistent crashes

If your computer continues to lock up regularly no matter which programs you are running, you should suspect a problem with your mouse driver, video driver, sound card, or modem. See Chapter 39, "Troubleshooting Hardware Problems," for details.

- *Run the program by itself.* Exit all other programs and run this program by itself. If the program is crashing because of a conflict with another program, this will prevent crashes until you can identify the conflict.

- *Exit any programs that are running in the background.* Most programs that run in the background display an icon in the system tray (see Figure 40.2). Right-click the icon and choose the option for exiting the program. Antivirus programs commonly conflict with other applications.

- *Turn off the Active Desktop.* Some programs, especially games, may have trouble running with the Active Desktop enabled. To disable the Active Desktop, right-click the desktop and click **Properties**. Click the **Web** tab, remove the check mark next to **View My Active Desktop as a Web Page**, and click **OK**.

- *Turn off any screen savers.* If you use a screen saver, turn it off. To turn off a Windows screen saver, right-click the desktop and click **Properties**. Click the **Screen Saver** tab and choose **(None)** from the **Screen Saver** drop-down list.

- *Disable power management utilities.* Turn off the Windows power-saving options.

SEE ALSO

➤ *Learn to adjust the power saving settings, page 224*

Resolving Software Problems

When your system crashes, the program rarely displays a dialog box telling you what went wrong. If the program displays any message at all, it's usually a cryptic message that no average user could possibly decipher. Because of this, tracking down the cause of a system crash can be nearly impossible.

To help, the following sections point out some of the major causes of system crashes and software problems, show you where to find additional troubleshooting information, and show you how to obtain and install a *patch* that's designed to fix a known problem with a program.

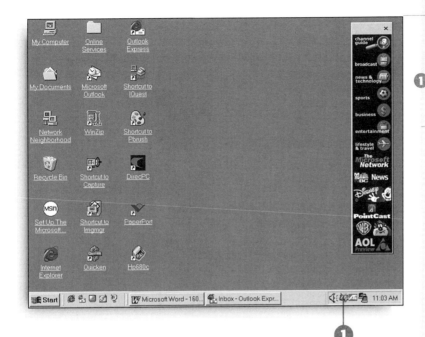

FIGURE 40.2

Programs that run in the background may cause problems.

1 System tray displays icons for programs running in the background

How Much Memory Is Available?

When your system locks up, it's tempting to blame Windows or point your finger at a particular program, but the problem may be that your PC doesn't have the memory required to run the program. Before you do anything else, check the amount of memory installed on your system.

Determining the amount of memory installed on Your PC

1. Alt+click the My Computer icon. The amount of physical memory (in the form of RAM chips) appears near the bottom of the dialog box. Your computer should have at least 16MB of RAM. If your computer has less, consider installing additional memory in the form of memory modules.

2. Click the **Performance** tab. This tab also displays the amount of physical memory installed. The amount of memory (RAM or random access memory) is displayed near the top of the dialog box.

3. Click the **Virtual Memory** button. The value in the **Hard Disk** text box, although gray, indicates the amount of free space available for Windows to use as virtual memory (see Figure 40.3).

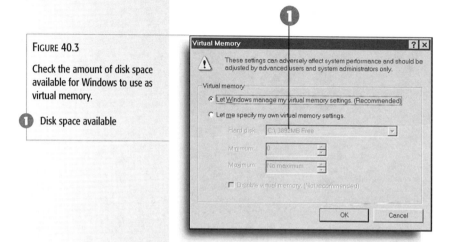

FIGURE 40.3

Check the amount of disk space available for Windows to use as virtual memory.

1 Disk space available

4. Add the two numbers to determine the total amount of available memory. (Even if your system has plenty of disk space to use as virtual memory, some programs may have trouble running with less than 16MB of bona-fide RAM.)

Your PC should have at least 30MB disk space set aside for virtual memory. If any less is available, remove some files from your hard drive.

SEE ALSO

➤ *Learn how to clear files from your hard drive, page 248*

Checking Your System Resources

Windows has some built-in limitations. Although Windows can create its own (virtual) memory by using free disk space, it sets aside limited blocks of memory (called *resources*) for tasks such as displaying data and dialog boxes.

Windows reserves memory for the following three resources: System (to keep track of running programs), User (to manage dialog boxes), and the GDI (to handle graphics). You can have plenty of free memory available, but if these reserved areas start to fill up, you might encounter the same problems as if your system were low on memory.

To monitor your system resources in Windows, use the Resource Meter. (If Resource Meter is not on this menu, you must install it using Windows Setup.)

Monitoring system resources

1. Click the **Start** button, point to **Programs**, **Accessories**, and then **System Tools**, and click **Resource Meter**.

2. The Resource Meter dialog box indicates that it, too, will consume system resources. Click **OK**.

3. The Resource Meter icon appears in the system tray on the right end of the taskbar. Right-click it and choose **Details**. The Resource meter displays bar graphs showing the available System, User, and GDI resources (see Figure 40.4).

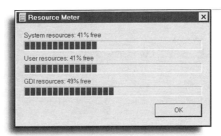

FIGURE 40.4

The Resource Meter can show you when system resources are running low.

If you see that your system resources are running low in any category, close all your programs and exit Windows. This clears any wayward data and program instructions from memory so Windows can start from fresh. To determine how well this fix works, run Resource Meter again after you restart to check the amount of resources you reclaimed in Windows.

Finding Answers in the README File

Memory leaks

Some programs, especially Web browsers, have bugs that cause *memory leaks*. When you exit a program, the program is supposed to turn control of resources back over to Windows. If a program has a bug, it might retain control of the resources or it might continue to use more and more resources as it is running—until your system completely locks up.

If your system has plenty of memory and free resources and you encounter problems in only one program, chances are that the program has a bug, a design flaw, or programming error. Tracking down the cause of such a problem on your own is nearly impossible. You must rely on the information supplied by the program developer.

Fortunately, most programs include a README file that lists problems that the developer is aware of and possible solutions to the problems. The README file is typically stored in the folder in which you installed the program or in one of the folders on the program's installation disk or CD-ROM.

Use My Computer (or **Start**, **Find**, **Files or Folders**) to track down the README file. README files are typically stored as DOC or TXT documents. To open the document in Notepad or WordPad, click the file's name (see Figure 40.5).

FIGURE 40.5

The README file may have information about known problems and workarounds.

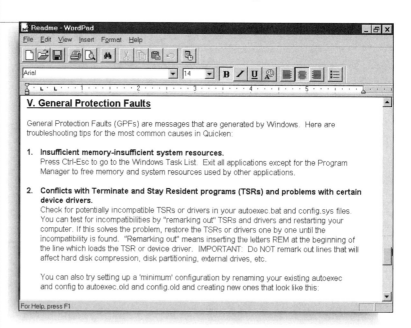

Preventing Programs from Running in the Background

When you install programs, they may set up utilities that automatically run on startup and stay running in the background. These programs are commonly called TSRs (Terminate and Stay Resident). In some cases, a TSR program displays an icon in the system tray, so you can manually exit the program. In other cases, you may never know the program is running.

If you suspect that a particular TSR program is causing a problem, you can prevent Windows from loading it on startup using the System Configuration Utility. You may need to disable TSR programs one at a time to determine which one is causing the conflict. This can be a long, tedious process.

Preventing TSR programs from starting

1. Click **Start**, **Programs**, **Accessories**, **System Tools**, **System Information**. The System Information window appears.

2. Open the **T**ools menu and click **System Configuration Utility**.

3. Click the **Startup** tab.

4. Click the check box next to each program you want Windows to skip on startup (remove the check mark) (see Figure 40.6).

5. Click **OK**.

6. Exit all programs and restart Windows.

After you have resolved the problem, use the System Configuration Utility to enable any TSRs that are not causing problems to load at startup.

Installing a Patch: A Permanent Solution

In a rush to beat the competition to market, software developers frequently release programs that have bugs. A month or two later, after receiving complaints from customers, the developer often releases a *fix* or *patch*, a utility that corrects one or more problems with the original program.

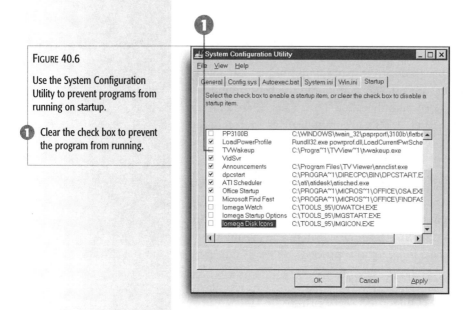

❶

FIGURE 40.6

Use the System Configuration Utility to prevent programs from running on startup.

❶ Clear the check box to prevent the program from running.

Don't expect to receive a letter in the mail informing you that your program is defective. And certainly don't expect to receive a disk that contains the fix. In most cases, you must go to the developer's Web site and download the patch (copy it to your hard drive). The patch typically comes as an executable program file. Simply click its icon in My Computer to run the patch.

SEE ALSO

➤ *Learn how to find technical assistance on the Internet, page 851*

➤ *Learn how to download files from Web sites, page 472*

Troubleshooting Windows Error Messages

If you're lucky, Windows displays an error message when Windows or one of your applications crashes. Although cryptic, these error messages can point you to the cause of a problem and help you resolve it...assuming you decipher the error message. The following sections list the most common error messages in Windows 95 and 98 and translate the error messages into plain English.

When you receive an error message, write it down. Most error messages provide a general indication of the problem along with specific information about the location of the problem (for instance, a memory address). This specific information can help you locate the answer you need using the manufacturer's online technical support or help a well-informed technical support person provide specific instructions on how to fix the problem.

General Protection Fault

The mother of all error messages, a GPF (General Protection Fault) results when an application tries to use RAM that Windows has assigned to another application or device. In most cases, you can quickly recover from a GPF by closing down the offending application and restarting it. However, if the problem persists, check the following:

Bugs and fixes

For the latest information about Windows bugs and fixes (official and unofficial), check out the WinFiles.com Bugs and Fixes page at **www.winfiles. com/bugs/**.

- *Available system resources.* When system resources dip, an application may become more aggressive in trying to use resources allocated to other applications. Try running fewer programs, installing additional RAM, and clearing space on your hard disk.
- *Device drivers.* A device driver can cause GPFs. Make sure you are using the latest drivers for your hardware components.
- *Program bugs.* Contact technical support for the application that's causing the problem and determine if a fix is available.

Invalid Page Fault

A page fault occurs when a program requests data that is not stored in RAM or virtual memory. In most cases, page faults do not cause errors. Your PC retrieves the requested data from disk and places it in RAM, where the program can access it. However, if your PC cannot locate the requested data anywhere, an invalid page fault occurs. Invalid page faults are commonly caused by corrupted memory (RAM or virtual memory). Check the following:

- *Low RAM.* The amount of physical memory (in the form of RAM) chips is insufficient. If your PC has 32MB or less of RAM, install additional RAM.

- *Low disk space.* The hard disk that Windows uses for virtual memory is running low on disk space. Clear files off the disk to reclaim space.

- *Corrupted virtual memory.* One of your programs may have corrupted the data stored in virtual memory making it inaccessible. Try shutting down and restarting Windows. If the problem persists or occurs with all applications, your system may be running low on memory and disk space.

- *Data sharing errors.* You may encounter an invalid page fault if one application is trying to access data being used or modified by another application. Shut down one of the conflicting applications.

Insufficient Memory

Insufficient memory messages commonly pop up when you try to run more applications than your system has memory to store or try to open several large documents. In some cases, you can clear memory by exiting all applications and restarting Windows. If the problem persists, there are only two practical and permanent solutions:

- *Clear disk space.* If your system has at least 32MB RAM, it should be able to run most applications and moderate multitasking, assuming Windows has enough hard disk space to use as virtual memory. Clear files off your hard disk.

- *Install more physical RAM.* 32MB is the bare minimum. 64MB is sufficient for most users.

SEE ALSO
➤ *Learn to clear files off your hard disk, page 248*
➤ *Learn how to install more physical RAM, page 577*

Parity Errors

There are two types of RAM—parity and non-parity. Parity SIMMs include extra chips dedicated to checking for memory errors. Whenever data is stored in RAM, the parity chips quickly check the data to ensure that it hasn't been corrupted in transit. If it detects a problem, the parity check generates an error message and prevents the potentially corrupted data from being saved to disk.

If your PC uses parity-checking RAM, a parity error message usually indicates a physical problem with the RAM chips. When a parity error occurs, write down the memory address that's displayed and save the address for future reference. If your system continues to encounter parity errors at this memory address, you may need to systematically remove and reinstall individual SIMMs to determine which SIMM has the defective chip.

Fatal Exception Error

The Fatal Exception Error message typically appears on a blue screen and indicates a serious compatibility problem. If the problem occurs on startup, you may need to restart Windows in Safe mode just to track down the problem: start Windows, press F8 at the first beep, and choose the option for starting in Safe mode. If the problem occurs when you attempt to run a program or use a particular device, Windows may shut down the program or make the device inaccessible.

Fortunately, Fatal Exception Error messages start popping up as soon as you install a new device or application, providing a clear indication of what's causing the problem. To regain control of your system, uninstall the application or the driver for your new hardware. Contact the manufacturer's technical support department for specific instructions on how to work around the conflict.

The parity debate

Due to the improved reliability of SIMMs and the lower cost of non-parity SIMMs, most manufacturers make non-parity SIMMs. Although this reduces the cost of memory and the overall cost of new PCs, when a non-parity SIMM goes bad, it's tough to track down the problem.

Mmsystem.dll or *Rundll32* Error Message

`Mmsystem.dll` and `Rundll32` may often generate a General Protection Fault (GPF) error message if the System.ini file is corrupted or is missing the line "drivers=mmsystem.dll." To fix the problem, run any text editor (such as Notepad) and open System.ini (from the C:\Windows folder).

Scroll down to the [boot] section. If the drivers=mmsystem.dll is not listed, move the insertion point to the end of a line in the [boot] section, press Enter, type `drivers=mmsystem.dll`, and save the System.ini file. Restart Windows.

Spool32 **Error Message**

The Spool32 error message relates to background printing. To eliminate spooling problems, try changing the spool settings for your printer. Click the **Start** button, point to **Settings**, and click **Printers**. Right-click the icon for your printer and click **Properties**. On the **Details** tab, click the **Spool Settings** button. Open the **Spool Data Format** drop-down list and click **RAW**. Save your settings and try printing again.

Finding Help on the Internet

Check out your computer manufacturer's tech support Web page

Find technical support and bug fixes for software

Find help in computer magazines on the Web

Find answers to your questions in newsgroups

Finding Tech Support on the Web

Nearly every computer hardware and software company has its own Web site, where you can purchase products directly and find technical support for products you own. If your printer is not feeding paper properly, you're having trouble installing your sound card, you keep receiving cryptic error messages in your favorite program, or you have some other computer-related problem, you can usually find the solution on the Internet.

In addition, computer and software companies often upgrade their software and post updates and fixes on their Web sites for downloading. If you are having problems with a device, such as a printer or modem, you should check the manufacturer's Web site for updated drivers. If you run into problems with a program, check the software company's Web site for a *patch*, a program file that you install to correct the problem.

Table 41.1 provides Web page addresses of popular software and hardware manufacturers to help you in your search.

TABLE 41.1   Computer hardware and software Web sites

Company	Web Page Address
Acer	www.acer.com
Borland	www.borland.com
Broderbund	www.broderbund.com
Brother	www.brother.com
Canon	www.ccsi.canon.com
Compaq	www.compaq.com
Corel	www.corel.com
Creative Labs	www.soundblaster.com
Dell	www.dell.com
Epson	www.epson.com
Fujitsu	www.fujitsu.com

Company	Web Page Address
Gateway	www.gw2k.com
Hayes	www.hayes.com
Hewlett-Packard	www.hp.com
Hitachi	www.hitachipc.com
IBM	www.ibm.com
Intel	www.intel.com
Iomega	www.iomega.com
Lotus	www.lotus.com
Micron Electronics	www.micronpc.com
Microsoft	www.microsoft.com
Motorola	www.mot.com/MIMS/ISPD/support.html
NEC	www.nec.com
Packard Bell	www.packardbell.com
Panasonic	www.panasonic.com
Sony	www.sony.com
Toshiba	www.toshiba.com
3COM (U.S. Robotics)	www.3com.com

Most of the home pages listed have a link for connecting to the support page. If a page does not have a link to the support page, use its search tool to locate the page. You might also see a link labeled FAQ (frequently asked questions), Common Questions, or Top Issues. This link can take you to a page that lists the most common problems other users are having and answers from the company (see Figure 41.1).

If the manufacturer you're looking for is not listed in the previous table, don't give up. Connect to your favorite Web search page and search for the manufacturer by name or search for the problem you're having.

Check the manual

Although manufacturers like to keep the tech support phone number a secret, they want you to know their Web page address, so you can check out their other products. The Web site's technical support areas also cut down on calls to tech support.

FIGURE 41.1

Check out the FAQ or Top Issues link for answers to common questions.

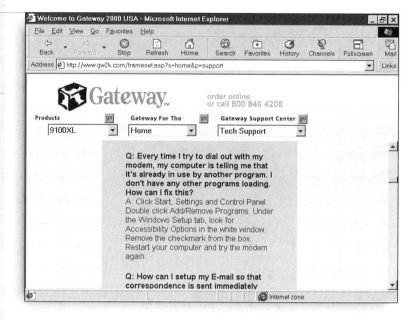

Obtaining Windows Help and Updates Online

Although the Windows Help system is packed with instructions for performing most tasks and troubleshooting the most common problems, it doesn't contain the most up-to-date information. To keep you informed, Microsoft provides access to Support Online, its help system on the Web.

Using Windows support online

1. Click the **Start** button and click **Help.** The Windows Help window appears.

2. Click the **Web Help** button.

3. Scroll down the pane on the right and click the **Support Online** link. Internet Explorer runs and opens the Support Online search form (see Figure 41.2).

4. Open the **My search is about** drop-down list and click the name of the Microsoft product for which you need help.

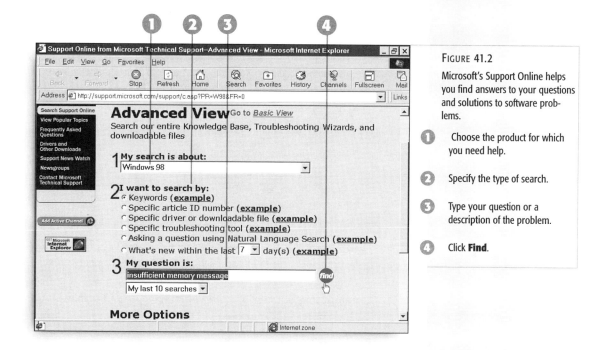

FIGURE 41.2

Microsoft's Support Online helps you find answers to your questions and solutions to software problems.

❶   Choose the product for which you need help.

❷   Specify the type of search.

❸   Type your question or a description of the problem.

❹   Click **Find**.

5. Under **I want to search by**, choose the type of search you want to perform.

6. In the **My question is** text box, type your question or type a word or phrase that describes the problem.

7. Click the **Find** button. The search tool displays a list of links for any articles it has turned up.

8. Click the link for the desired article.

In addition to offering updated information, Microsoft's Web site offers the latest drivers for your hardware and patches for Windows.

SEE ALSO

➤ *Learn how to update Windows, see page 251*

Finding Help in Online Magazines

If the manufacturer's Web site doesn't answer your question, the Web provides access to several computer magazines that may have the answer you're looking for. Following is a list of some excellent resources:

- *ZDNet* at www.zdnet.com is the home of several quality computer magazines, including *PC Computing*, *Windows Sources*, and *ComputerLife*. You will find articles on general computing, hardware and software reviews, tips, and answers to specific questions (see Figure 41.3).

- *c|net* at www.cnet.com is a great place if you need technical support for Internet problems. It's also a great place to check out gaming information and obtain shareware programs. Although you won't find as much information about general computing issues as you will at ZDNet, the information on this site is very useful.

- *Windows Magazine* at www.winmag.com is an excellent place to find answers to your Windows questions, learn about the latest improvements, and check out software reviews.

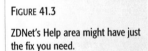

FIGURE 41.3

ZDNet's Help area might have just the fix you need.

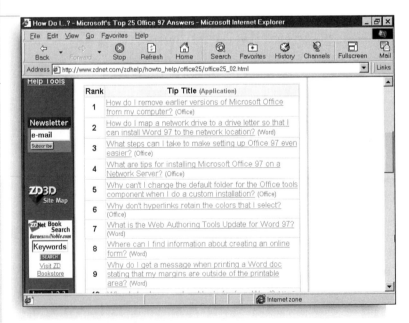

Seeking Help from Your Peers in Newsgroups

If you explored newsgroups in Chapter 19, "Reading and Posting Newsgroup Messages," you know that there are a lot of knowledgeable people out there willing to impart their wisdom for free. If you can't find an answer to your problem anywhere else, try posting your question in a newsgroup.

Before posting your question, you may want to check newsgroup archives to see if the problem you're having has already been addressed in a newsgroup. Some Web search sites, including Lycos, allow you to search through newsgroup archives. In addition to helping you find solutions to problems, these archives provide a little moral support, showing that you're not the only one experiencing this particular problem.

Search Lycos newsgroup archives

1. Use your Web browser to open the Lycos search page at www.lycos.com.

2. Type a description of the problem you're having.

3. Open the drop-down list, choose **Discussion Groups,** and then click the **Go Get It** button. Lycos displays a list of links to messages posted in newsgroups.

4. Scroll down the list and click a link that looks as if it deals with the problem you're having. Lycos displays the message.

5. Click the **View Thread** link just above the message to display a list of replies (see Figure 41.4).

6. Click the link for the reply you want to view.

Searching newsgroup archives for answers can be a tedious process and turn up long lists of links that have nothing to do with the problem you're having; however, in many cases, you'll find just the answer you are looking for.

If you still can't find the answer, use your newsreader program to find and subscribe to newsgroups for the manufacturer, program, or device that you are having problems with. Before posting your message, check to see whether the newsgroup has a FAQ posting and read through it. (It's considered impolite to post a question that has already been answered in the FAQ.) If you can't find the answer in the FAQ, post your question and a detailed description of the problem. You might also request that people reply via email. Be sure to thank people for their help.

FIGURE 41.4

Lycos can help you find news-group postings on the Web.

1 Click the **View Thread** link to display a list of replies.

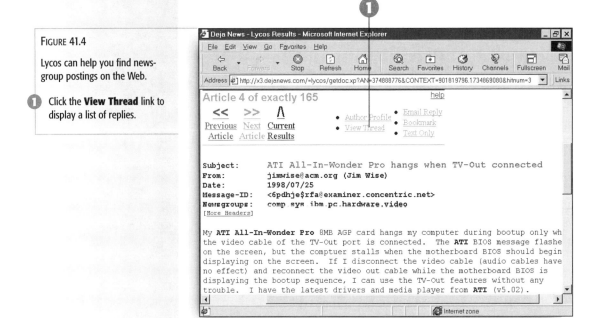

Preparing Your PC for Use by the Disabled

Find specialized input and output devices for your PC

Check out software that can make your PC easier to use

Install the Windows Accessibility features

Adjust the keyboard settings for special applications

Use your keyboard to move the mouse pointer

Specialized Input and Output Devices

PCs are the most adaptable machines you'll encounter. You can enter commands and data using a keyboard, mouse, joystick, microphone, scanner, and any other device that can convert your actions into a digital form that the PC can process. Output devices offer the same flexibility. Although monitors and printers are the most commonly used output devices, PCs can also produce spoken output and print in Braille with the right equipment and software.

The only challenge is to find the appropriate device and software for your needs. The first step is to determine what's available. The following list describes some of the more innovative and useful input and output devices:

- *Screen enlargers*. For users with visual impairments, a screen enlarger zooms in on a selected area of the screen to make it more visible. This is especially useful for typing text.

- *Screen reviewer utilities*. Another tool for users with severe visual impairments, a screen reviewer utility translates the information generated for the display into alternative media, such as synthesized speech or a refreshable Braille display.

- *Speech synthesizers*. Although most sound cards can generate synthesized speech, a dedicated speech synthesizer can usually do a better job of it. With a speech synthesizer, you can customize your applications to provide spoken feedback in addition to the standard video feedback.

- *Speech recognition*. With speech recognition software and a high-quality microphone, you can enter commands and data by talking, rather than by clicking and typing. Two of the best speech recognition programs are IBM ViaVoice (www.ibm.com) and Dragon Naturally-Speaking (www.dragonsys.com). Dragon Dictate is one of the more popular programs for entering voice commands, but it recognizes *discrete* speech (rather than *continuous* speech), making it less useful for dictation.

- *Switch controls*. A single-switch control typically consists of an onscreen scanner that highlights commands or keys.

When the desired command or key is highlighted, the user activates the switch to select it. Any movement can activate the switch. Dual switch controls provide additional options for entering commands using either or both switches.

- *Sip-and-puff controls.* For users whose physical movements are severely limited, sip-and-puff devices provide a means for entering commands and using an onscreen keyboard to type data.

- *Onscreen keyboards.* For users who cannot type on ordinary keyboards, onscreen keyboards allow users to point and click with a mouse or use sip-and-puff switches and other alternative devices.

- *Oversized keyboards.* Oversized keyboards, such as the popular *IntelliKeys* keyboard provide larger keys and alternative mouse control. The keyboard works on a bar code system, allowing you to use custom keyboard overlays to change the functions of the keys for different needs. (For more information, check out IntelliTools at www.intellitools.com.)

- *Chord keyboards.* With a chord keyboard, you press two or three keys to type a single letter. Using key combinations, a chord keyboard allows you to type and enter commands with one hand.

- *Word prediction software.* To cut down on the number of keystrokes required for each word, consider using a word prediction program, such as Co:Writer. As you start to type a word, Co:Writer finishes the word for you based on what you typed, the context of the word, and on what Co:Writer has recorded concerning your writing habits. Some standard word processing programs include a feature that allows you to create your own shorthand entries (for instance, the AutoText feature in Word). (You can learn more about Co:Writer at www.donjohnston.com.)

- *Joystick-to-mouse converters.* A joystick-to-mouse converter lets you use a joystick or other type of game controller to move the mouse pointer. You can even use head-mounted VR devices designed for games to improve interaction with the Windows interface.

- *Digitizing tablets.* Digitizing tablets provide precise control of mouse pointer movements and alternative ways to input data. A related technology, the light pen, allows you to point, click, and drag onscreen.

- *Eye and head motion trackers.* Eye and head motion trackers provide alternative ways to move the mouse pointer around on the screen. To move the mouse pointer, you shift your head or eyes in the desired direction. One of the most popular head motion trackers is HeadMouse from Origin Instruments (www.orin.com).

- *Foot controllers.* Foot controllers or switches allow you to move the mouse pointer and enter commands by moving your feet rather than your hands. Most foot controllers require a MIDI interface and may act more as foot controls for musical instruments, but the idea is the same. Switches and controls inside the device generate signals that tell the mouse pointer how to move.

In addition to devices designed for those with disabilities, consider some of the ergonomic furniture and equipment that's available. Wrist supports, adjustable split keyboards, ergonomic trackballs, touchpads, and other "standard" input and output devices provide additional alternatives that can make it easier to use your PC. Many of the most innovative and useful input and output devices consist of home-engineered adaptations of standard input and output devices.

Manufacturers, Dealers, and Other Resources

Shareware

For some helpful shareware utilities, check out www.at-center.com. Here, you'll find an onscreen keyboard, shorthand program (for assigning abbreviations to commonly used words and phrases), and a program that can read the contents of the Windows Clipboard to you.

Although many companies manufacture and market alternative input and output devices, finding these companies can be a chore. To help, the following resource list provides contact information for manufacturers and retailers along with information about organizations where you can obtain additional information:

- *IntelliTools, Inc.* For the widest variety of alternative input devices, IntelliTools is the place to go. Here, you will find alternative keyboards, single-switch input devices, specialty cables, software, and other innovative products for enhancing input.

     IntelliTools
     Telephone: 800 899-6687
     Web: www.intellitools.com

- *Origin Instruments Corporation.* For an alternative pointing device, Origin's HeadMouse may be the perfect solution. With the HeadMouse, a small receiver rests on top of the monitor or system unit and detects the movement of a tiny, disposable target placed on the user's forehead. HeadMouse works along with SofType, an onscreen keyboard.

     Origin Instruments Corporation
     854 Greenview Drive
     Grand Prairie, TX 75050
     Telephone: 972 606-8740
     Web: www.orin.com

- *Don Johnston, Incorporated.* An excellent resource for students with reading and writing disabilities and physical disabilities. Don Johnston is a great place to shop for alternative input devices and software designed to make data input more efficient. Ask about Ke:nx (pronounced "connects"), a system that allows you to input commands and data using single switch.

     Don Johnston, Inc.
     1000 N. Rand Rd, Bldg 115
     P.O. Box 639
     Wauconda, IL 60084-0639
     Telephone: 800 999-4660
     Web: www.donjohnston.com

- *HumanWare.* For the blind or visually impaired, HumanWare provides a wide selection of Braille terminals, refreshable displays, notetakers, and embossers, along with speech synthesizers and video enlargers.

HumanWare
6245 King Road
Loomis, CA 95650
Telephone: 800 722-3393
Web: www.humanware.com

- *Optelec U.S.A., Inc.* Manufactures LP-Windows, a screen enlarger for Windows, designed to help users with visual impairments focus on specific areas of the screen.

    Optelec U.S.A.
    P.O. Box 729
    6 Lyberty Way
    Westford, MA 01886
    Telephone: 800 828-1056
    Web: www.optelec.com

- *Trace Research and Development.* For a comprehensive list of products designed to make computers more accessible to people with disabilities, contact Trace. Trace publishes a book called the Trace ResourceBook, which provides descriptions and photographs of about 2,000 products.

    Trace R&D Center
    University of Wisconsin
    S-151 Waisman Center
    1500 Highland Avenue
    Madison, WI 53705-2280
    Web: tracecenter.org

- *ABLEDATA.* A non-profit service that provides an up-to-date database of products and services for the disabled.

    ABLEDATA
    8455 Colesville Road
    Suite 935
    Silver Spring, MD 20910
    Telephone: 800 227-0216
    Web: www.abledata.com

- *ABLE.NET.* A non-profit organization dedicated to establishing a network of students, professionals, and people with disabilities to foster a dynamic exchange of ideas.

    ABLE.NET
    5850 Hardy Avenue Suite 112
    San Diego, CA 92182-5313

Telephone: 619 594-4220 Fax: 619 594-4208
Web: `ablenet.sdsu.edu`

■ *Microsoft.* Windows 98 has several built-in accessibility features, described in this chapter. In addition, Microsoft's
Accessibility Web page provides lists of Windows-
compatible devices and links to other resources. Check
out the page at `www.microsoft.com/enable/`.

Using the Windows Accessibility Features

Windows comes with a few of its own accessibility features for
customizing the display, using your keyboard to move the mouse
pointer, and transforming audio signals into visual messages.
The following sections describe these tools and show you how to
use some standard Windows features to make your PC more
accessible.

Before you start, make sure all the Accessibility features are
installed. Open the Control Panel, click **Add/Remove
Programs**, and click the **Windows Setup** tab. Click the check
box next to **Accessibility**, so it appears white with a check mark
in it. Click **OK** and follow the onscreen instructions to complete
the installation.

SEE ALSO

➤ *Learn how to add and remove Windows components, page 204*

Using Standard Windows Features to Improve Accessibility

Although they may not be considered bona-fide accessibility features, Windows has several standard features you can use to
make your computer more accessible to users with impaired
vision, hearing, or manual dexterity:

■ *Display settings.* Right-click the desktop and click
Properties. Enter preferences for using larger fonts or
icons; change the screen colors for better contrast; and

decrease the screen area (on the **Settings** tab) to make everything bigger.

- *Mouse settings.* In the Control Panel, click the Mouse icon. Choose a large mouse pointer or change the speed of the mouse to make it easier to control. Turning on single-click access in My Computer can also be a big help.

- *Keyboard settings.* In the Control Panel, click the Keyboard icon. Adjust the **Repeat Delay** and **Repeat Rate** as desired. In most cases, you will want to drag the sliders all the way to the left to essentially disable repeating keys.

- *WinPopup.* If you're on a network, you can use WinPopup to type messages rather than talking on the phone. For typing messages across modem connections, use NetMeeting or Microsoft Chat.

SEE ALSO

➤ *Learn how to change the display settings, page 221*

➤ *Learn how to adjust the mouse settings, page 228*

➤ *Learn how to adjust the keyboard settings, page 230*

➤ *Learn how to send messages across the network, page 318*

Running the Accessibility Wizard

To quickly set up the Windows accessibility features on your PC, run the Accessibility Wizard. The wizard leads you step-by-step through the process of choosing the accessibility features you want to use.

Using the Accessibility Wizard

1. Click the **Start** button, point to **P**rograms, **Accessories**, **Accessibility**, and click **Accessibility Wizard**.

2. Follow the wizard's instructions to enter your preferences (see Figure A.1).

If you use the Accessibility Wizard, you can skip the remaining sections. However, if you decide to change the accessibility settings later, refer to the following sections for details.

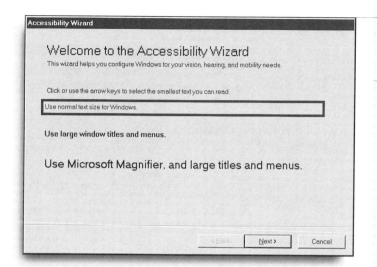

FIGURE A.1
The Accessibility Wizard leads you through the setup.

Installing Alternate Input Devices

Windows supports multiple pointing devices, so you can leave your mouse connected to the PS/2 port and plug an alternative pointing device or input device into your PC's serial port. However, if you install another pointing device on the serial port, enable the SerialKeys feature, so Windows will know to look for the device.

Enabling SerialKeys

1. In the Windows Control Panel, click the Accessibility Options icon.

2. Click the **General** tab.

3. Click **Support SerialKey Devices**.

4. Click the **Settings** button.

5. Choose the serial (COM) port to which the device is connected and choose the maximum speed of the device.

6. Click **OK** to return to the Accessibility Properties dialog box and click **OK** to save your settings.

SEE ALSO

➤ *Learn more about the serial port, page 782*

➤ *Learn how to troubleshoot problems with devices connected to the serial port, page 802*

Zooming In on Portions of the Screen

Although you can increase the overall size of the Windows desktop, you may want to keep the desktop the normal size and zoom in on only those areas you're interested in. To enlarge an area of the screen, use the Windows Magnifier.

Zoom in with the Magnifier

1. Click the **Start** button, point to **Programs**, **Accessories**, **Accessibility**, and click **Magnifier**. A pane opens at the top of the desktop showing the magnified area (see Figure A.2).

2. In the Magnifier dialog box, use the **Magnification Level** spin box to enter the desired magnification level.

3. Choose the desired options to specify what you want the magnifier to follow: the keyboard, mouse, or text editing.

4. You can choose to invert colors in the magnifier window or display it in high-contrast mode.

5. Click **OK** to save your settings.

FIGURE A.2

The Magnifier zooms in on the currently active area of the screen.

1. Enter the desired magnification level.

2. Specify the desired area of focus.

3. Specify the appearance of the magnified area.

4. Magnified area

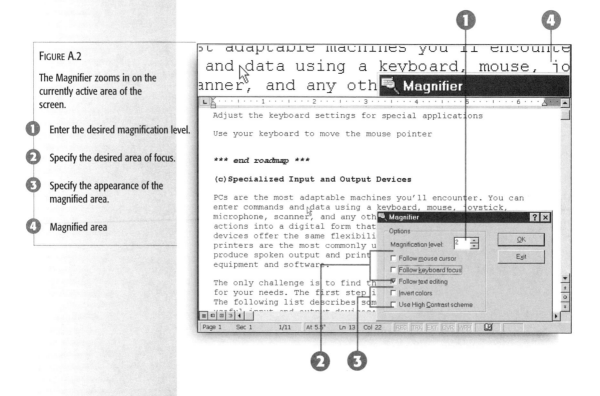

Using a High-Contrast Display

If you have trouble viewing the Windows desktop, icons, and other objects that comprise the Windows interface, consider using a high-contrast, black-on-white or white-on-black display.

Using a high-contrast display

1. In the Windows Control Panel, click the Accessibility Options icon.

2. Click the **Display** tab.

3. Click **Use High Contrast** to place a check in its box.

4. Click the **Settings** button.

5. If desired, turn on **Use Shortcut**, so you will be able to toggle the high-contrast display on and off by pressing the designated keystroke.

6. Under **High Contrast Color Scheme**, choose the desired color combination for high-contrast display: **White on Black** or **Black on White**.

7. Click **OK** to return to the Accessibility Properties dialog box and click **OK** to save your settings. Figure A.3 shows the Windows desktop with a black-on-white high-contrast display.

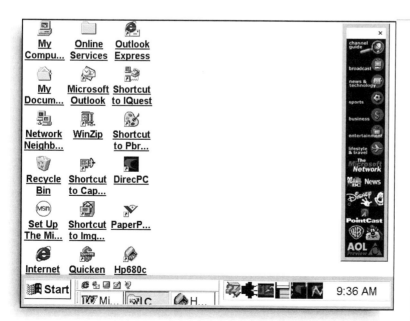

FIGURE A.3

The Windows desktop in black-on-white.

Using the Keyboard to Move the Mouse

Although the mouse is an excellent pointing device, it requires you to slide it some distance to move the mouse pointer. Windows has a feature called MouseKeys that allows you to use the arrow keys on the numeric keyboard to move the mouse pointer.

Turning on MouseKeys

1. In the Windows Control Panel, click the Accessibility Options icon.

2. Click the **Mouse** tab.

3. Click **Use MouseKeys**.

4. Click the **Settings** button.

5. Enter the desired preferences for controlling the speed and behavior of the mouse pointer and click **OK**.

6. Click **OK** to save your changes.

Making Sounds Visible

Windows provides important audio cues as you perform tasks. For example, if you try to type in an area that does not accept typed input, Windows may sound a beep to let you know that you can't do what you're attempting to do. If you cannot hear the sounds, turn on Sound Sentry and Show Sounds to have Windows notify you visually, instead.

Turn on visual notifications

1. In the Windows Control Panel, click the Accessibility Options icon.

2. Click the **Sound** tab.

3. Click **Use SoundSentry** to turn it on.

4. Click the **Settings** button and enter your preferences to specify how you want Windows to display the visual notification. (For example, you can have Windows flash the title bar or the entire window.) Click **OK**.

5. To have Windows display a caption explaining why the window or bar is flashing, turn on **Use S<u>h</u>owSounds**.

6. Click **OK** to save your settings.

Entering Special Keyboard Settings

Although the keyboard is one of the greatest tools for inputting data, it can be a little tough to control. To help, Windows offers the following tools to make your keyboard behave:

- *StickyKeys* makes the Ctrl, Alt, or Shift keys stay "pressed" when you press and release the key. This makes it easier to press two keys at the same time, such as Ctrl+B or Shift+Enter.

- *FilterKeys* makes your keyboard less sensitive to inadvertent key presses and long key presses. With FilterKeys on, Windows ignores a glancing key press and increases the key repeat delay.

- *ToggleKeys* plays a sound when you press a toggle key, such as NumLock or CapsLock.

To turn on any of these keyboard accessibility features, open the Control Panel and click the Accessibility Options icon. Enter the desired settings on the **Keyboard** tab.

Index

buying